Applied Microsoft Power BI

Bring your data to life!

Fourth Edition

Teo Lachev

Prologika Press

Applied Microsoft Power BI
Bring your data to life!
Fourth Edition

Published by:
Prologika Press
info@prologika.com
http://prologika.com

Copyright © 2019 Teo Lachev
Made in USA

All rights reserved. No part of this book may be reproduced, stored, or transmitted in any form or by any means, without the prior written permission of the publisher. Requests for permission should be sent to info@prologika.com.

Trademark names may appear in this publication. Rather than use a trademark symbol with every occurrence of a trademarked name, the names are used strictly in an editorial manner, with no intention of trademark infringement. The author has made all endeavors to adhere to trademark conventions for all companies and products that appear in this book, however, he does not guarantee the accuracy of this information.

The author has made every effort during the writing of this book to ensure accuracy of the material. However, this book only expresses the author's views and opinions. The information contained in this book is provided without warranty, either express or implied. The author, resellers or distributors, shall not be held liable for any damages caused or alleged to be caused either directly or indirectly by this book.

ISBN 13	978-0-9766353-9-0
ISBN 10	0-9766353-9-9

Author:	Teo Lachev
Editor:	Edward Price
Cover Designer:	Zamir Creations

The manuscript of this book was prepared using Microsoft Word. Screenshots were captured using TechSmith SnagIt.

contents

1 Introducing Power BI 1

1.1 What is Microsoft Power BI? 1
Understanding Business Intelligence 1 • Introducing the Power BI Products 3 • How Did We Get Here? 5 • Power BI and Microsoft Data Platform 10 • Power BI Editions and Pricing 13

1.2 Understanding the Power BI Capabilities 15
Understanding Power BI Desktop 16 • Understanding Power BI Pro 18 • Understanding Power BI Premium 22 • Understanding Power BI Mobile 23 • Understanding Power BI Embedded 25 Understanding Power BI Report Server 26

1.3 Understanding the Power BI Service Architecture 27
The Web Front End (WFE) Cluster 27 • The Back End Cluster 28 • Data on Your Terms 29

1.4 Power BI and You 30
Power BI for Business Users 30 • Power BI for Data Analysts 32 • Power BI for Pros 34 Power BI for Developers 36

1.5 Summary 37

PART 1 POWER BI FOR BUSINESS USERS 38

2 The Power BI Service 39

2.1 Choosing a Business Intelligence Strategy 39
When to Choose Organizational BI 39 • When to Choose Self-service BI 41

2.2 Getting Started with Power BI Service 43
Signing Up for Power BI 43 • Understanding the Power BI Portal 45 Understanding Application Menus 48

2.3 Understanding Power BI Content Items 50
Understanding Datasets 50 • Understanding Reports 53 • Understanding Dashboards 55

2.4 Connecting to Data 57
Using Service Apps 57 • Importing Local Files 59 • Using Live Connections 61

2.5 Summary 62

3 Creating Reports 63

3.1 Understanding Reports 63
Understanding Reading View 64 • Understanding Editing View 69 • Understanding Power BI Visualizations 73 • Understanding Custom Visuals 80 • Understanding Subscriptions 81

3.2 Working with Power BI Reports 83
Creating Your First Report 83 • Getting Quick Insights 87 • Subscribing to Reports 89

3.3 Working with Excel Reports 90
Connecting to Excel Reports 91 • Analyzing Data in Excel 93 Comparing Excel Reporting Options 94

3.4 Summary 95

4 Creating Dashboards 96

- 4.1 Understanding Dashboards 96
  Understanding Dashboard Tiles 96 • Sharing Dashboards 102
- 4.2 Adding Dashboard Content 105
  Adding Content from Power BI Reports 105 • Adding Content from Q&A 107 • Adding Content from Predictive Insights 108 • Adding Content from Power BI Report Server 109
- 4.3 Working with Dashboards 111
  Creating and Modifying Tiles 111 • Creating and Modifying Tiles 112
  Using Natural Queries 112
- 4.4 Summary 113

5 Power BI Mobile 114

- 5.1 Introducing Mobile Apps 114
  Introducing the iOS Application 114 • Introducing the Android Application 116
  Introducing the Windows Application 116
- 5.2 Viewing Content 117
  Getting Started with Power BI Mobile 117 • Viewing Dashboards 119 • Viewing Reports 121
- 5.3 Sharing and Collaboration 124
  Posting Comments 124 • Sharing Content 125 • Annotating Visuals 126
- 5.4 Summary 127

PART 2 POWER BI FOR DATA ANALYSTS 128

6 Data Modeling Fundamentals 129

- 6.1 Understanding Data Models 129
  Understanding Schemas 130 • Introducing Relationships 132
  Understanding Data Connectivity 135
- 6.2 Understanding Power BI Desktop 139
  Installing Power BI Desktop 139 • Understanding Design Environment 140
  Understanding Navigation 141
- 6.3 Importing Data 148
  Understanding Data Import Steps 148 • Importing from Databases 152
  Importing Excel Files 156 • Importing Text Files 157 • Importing from Analysis Services 158
  Importing from the Web 160 • Entering Static Data 161
- 6.4 Advanced Storage Configurations 162
  Understanding Composite Models 162 • Understanding Aggregations 165
- 6.5 Summary 168

7 Transforming Data 169

- 7.1 Understanding the Power Query Editor 169
  Understanding the Power Query Environment 169 • Understanding Queries 174
  Understanding Data Preview 176 • Shaping and Cleansing Data 177 • Applying Basic Transformations 178 • Working with Custom Columns 180 • Loading Transformed Data 182
- 7.3 Using Advanced Power Query Features 182
  Combining Datasets 183 • Using Functions 185 • Generating Date Tables 188
  Working with Query Parameters 189

- 7.4 Staging Data with Dataflows 192
  Understanding the Common Data Model 192 • Understanding Common Data Service for Apps 193 • Understanding Dataflows 194 • Working with Dataflows 197
- 7.5 Summary 201

8 Refining the Model 202

- 8.1 Understanding Tables and Columns 203
  Understanding the Data View 203 • Exploring Data 204 • Understanding Column Data Types 206 • Understanding Column Operations 209 • Working with Tables and Columns 210
- 8.2 Managing Schema and Data Changes 212
  Managing Data Sources 212 • Managing Data Refresh 214 • Refreshing Data Incrementally 216
- 8.3 Relating Tables 219
  Relationship Rules and Limitations 220 • Auto-detecting Relationships 223 • Creating Relationships Manually 225 • Understanding the Relationships View 227 • Working with Relationships 230
- 8.4 Refining Metadata 232
  Working with Hierarchies 232•Working with Field Properties 234•Configuring Date Tables 235
- 8.5 Summary 236

9 Implementing Calculations 237

- 9.1 Understanding Data Analysis Expressions 237
  Understanding Calculated Columns 238 • Understanding Measures 239 • Understanding DAX Syntax 241 • Understanding DAX Functions 243
- 9.2 Implementing Calculated Columns 248
  Creating Basic Calculated Columns 248 • Creating Advanced Calculated Columns 250
- 9.3 Implementing Measures 251
  Implementing Implicit Measures 252 • Implementing Quick Measures 254 Implementing Explicit Measures 255
- 9.4 Implementing Advanced Relationships 258
  Implementing Role-Playing Relationships 258 • Implementing Parent-Child Relationships 259 Implementing Many-to-Many Relationships 261
- 9.5 Implementing Data Security 262
  Understanding Data Security 262 • Implementing Basic Data Security 265 • Implementing Dynamic Data Security 266 • Externalizing Security Policies 268
- 9.6 Summary 270

10 Analyzing Data 271

- 10.1 Performing Basic Analytics 271
  Getting Started with Report Development 271 • Working with Charts 273 • Working with Cards 273 • Working with Table and Matrix Visuals 274 • Working with Maps 275 Working with Slicers 275 • Working with Filters 277
- 10.2 Getting More Insights 278
  Drilling Down and Across Tables 278 • Drilling Through Data 280 • Configuring Tooltips 281 Grouping and Binning 283 • Applying Conditional Formatting 285 • Working with Links 287 Working with Images 288
- 10.3 Data Storytelling 289
  Asking Natural Questions 290 • Integrating with Windows Cortana 291 • Narrating Data 294

Sharing Insights with Bookmarks 295

10.4 Integrating with PowerApps 298
Understanding PowerApps 298 • Implementing Report Writeback 299

10.5 Summary 302

11 Predictive Analytics 303

11.1 Using Built-in Predictive Features 303
Explaining Increase and Decrease 303 • Implementing Time Series Forecasting 304
Clustering Data 305

11.2 Using R and Python 306
Using R 307 • Using Python 310

11.3 Integrating with Azure Machine Learning 312
Understanding Azure Machine Learning 312 • Creating Predictive Models 313
Integrating Machine Learning with Power BI 316

11.4 Summary 319

PART 3 POWER BI FOR PROS 320

12 Enabling Team BI 321

12.1 Power BI Management Fundamentals 321
Managing User Access 322 • Understanding Office 365 Groups 325 • Using the Power BI Admin Portal 326 • Understanding Tenant Settings 329 • Auditing User Activity 331

12.2 Collaborating with Workspaces 332
Understanding Workspaces 332 • Managing Workspaces 335 • Working with Workspaces 336

12.3 Distributing Content 339
Understanding Organizational Apps 340 • Comparing Sharing Options 342 • Working with Organizational Apps 344 • haring with External Users 344

12.4 Centralizing Data Management 346
Understanding the On-premises Data Gateway 346 • Getting Started with the On-Premises Data Gateway 347 • Using the On-Premises Data Gateway 349

12.5 Summary 350

13 Power BI Premium 351

13.1 Understanding Power BI Premium 351
Understanding Premium Performance 352 • Understanding Premium Workspaces 354

13.2 Managing Power BI Premium 355
Managing Security 355 • Managing Capacities 356 • Assigning Workspaces to Capacities 358

13.3 Understanding Power BI Report Server 359
Understanding Reporting Roadmap 360 • Getting Started with Power BI Report Server 362
Understanding Integration with Power BI 363 • Managing Power BI Reports 364

13.4 Summary 367

14 Organizational BI 368

14.1 Implementing Classic BI Solutions 369
Understanding Microsoft BISM 369 • Understanding Setup Requirements 373
Using Analysis Services in Power BI Service 376

14.2 Integrating Paginated Reports 377
Understanding Paginated Reports 378 • Working with Paginated Reports 379

14.3 Implementing Real-time BI Solutions 380
Using the Streaming API 380 • Using Azure Stream Analytics 383

14.4 Summary 387

PART 4 POWER BI FOR DEVELOPERS 388

15 Programming Fundamentals 389

15.1 Understanding Power BI APIs 389
Understanding Object Definitions 390 • Understanding Operations 391

15.2 Understanding OAuth Authentication 394
Understanding Authentication Flows 395 • Understanding Application Registration 397

15.3 Working with Power BI APIs 402
Implementing Authentication 402 • Invoking the Power BI APIs 403

15.4 Working with PowerShell 405
Understanding Power BI Cmdlets 405 • Automating Tasks with PowerShell 405

15.5 Summary 407

16 Power BI Embedded 408

16.1 Understanding Power BI Embedded 408
Getting Started with Power BI Embedded 408 • Configuring Workspaces 411

16.2 Understanding Embedded Features 412
Embedding Tiles 413 • Embedding Dashboards 416 • Embedding Q&A 417
Embedding Reports 418

16.3 Report-enabling Intranet Applications 423
Understanding the Sample Application 423 • Authenticating Users 424
Embedding Reports 427

16.4 Report-enabling Internet Applications 428
Understanding the Sample Application 429 • Authenticating Users 430
Implementing Data Security 431

16.5 Summary 432

17 Creating Custom Visuals 433

17.1 Understanding Custom Visuals 433
What is a Custom Visual? 433 • Understanding the IVisual Interface 435

17.2 Custom Visual Programming 435
Introducing TypeScript 436 • Introducing D3.js 437 • Understanding Developer Tools 438

17.3 Implementing Custom Visuals 443
Understanding the Sparkline Visual 443 • Implementing the IVisual Interface 444
Implementing Capabilities 447

17.4 Deploying Custom Visuals 449
Packaging Custom Visuals 449 • Using Custom Visuals 451

17.5 Summary 451

Glossary of Terms 453 • Index 456

preface

To me, Power BI is the most exciting milestone in the Microsoft BI journey since circa 2005, when Microsoft got serious about BI. Power BI changes the way you gain insights from data; it brings you a cloud-hosted, business intelligence and analytics platform that democratizes and opens BI to everyone. It does so under a simple promise: "five seconds to sign up, five minutes to wow!"

Power BI has plenty to offer to all types of users who're interested in data analytics. If you are an information worker, who doesn't have the time and patience to learn data modeling, Power BI lets you connect to many popular cloud services (Microsoft releases new ones every week!) and get insights from prepackaged dashboards and reports. If you consider yourself a data analyst, you can implement sophisticated self-service models whose features are on a par with organizational models built by BI pros.

Speaking of BI pros, Power BI doesn't leave us out. We can architect hybrid organizational solutions that don't require moving data to the cloud. And besides classic solutions for descriptive analytics, we can implement innovative Power BI-centric solutions for real-time and predictive analytics. If you're a developer, you'll love the Power BI open architecture because you can integrate custom applications with Power BI and visualize data your way by extending its visualization capabilities.

From a management standpoint, Power BI is a huge shift in the right direction for Microsoft and for Microsoft BI practitioners. Not so long ago, Microsoft BI revolved exclusively around Excel on the desktop and SharePoint Server for team BI. This strategy proved to be problematic because of its cost, maintenance, and adoption challenges. Power BI overcomes these challenges. Because it has no dependencies to other products, it removes adoption barriers. Power BI gets better every week, and this should allow us to stay at the forefront of the BI market. As a Power BI user, you're always on the latest and greatest version. And Power BI has the best business model: most of it it's free!

I worked closely with Microsoft's product groups to provide an authoritative (yet independent) view of this technology and to help you understand where and how to use it. Over more than a decade in BI, I've gathered plenty of real-life experience in solving data challenges and helping clients make sense of data. I decided to write this book to share with you this knowledge, and to help you use the technology appropriately and efficiently. As its name suggests, the main objective of this book it so to teach you the practical skills to take the most of Power BI from whatever angle you'd like to approach it.

Trying to cover a product that changes every week is like trying to hit a moving target! However, I believe that the product's fundamentals won't change and once you grasp them, you can easily add on knowledge as Power BI evolves over time. Because I had to draw a line somewhere, *Applied Microsoft Power BI (Fourth Edition)* covers features that were released or were in public preview by December 2018.

Although this book is designed as a comprehensive guide to Power BI, it's likely that you might have questions or comments. As with my previous books, I'm committed to help my readers with book-related questions and welcome all feedback on the book discussion forums on my company's web site (http://bit.ly/powerbibook). Consider also following my blog at http://prologika.com/blog and subscribing to my newsletter at http://prologika.com to stay on the Power BI latest.

Bring your data to life today with Power BI!

Teo Lachev
Atlanta, GA

acknowledgements

Welcome to the fourth revision of my Power BI book! As Power BI evolves, I've been refreshing the book every year for the past four years to keep it up with the ever-changing world of Power BI and the Microsoft Data Platform. Writing a book about a cloud platform, which adds features monthly, is like trying to hit a moving target. On the upside, I can claim that this book has no bugs. After all, if something doesn't work now, it used to work before, right? On the downside, I had to change the manuscript every time a new feature popped up. Fortunately, I had people who supported me.

This book (my tenth) would not have been a reality without the help of many people to whom I'm thankful. As always, I'd like to first thank my family for their ongoing support.

The main personas in the book, as imagined by my daughter Maya, and son Martin.

As a Microsoft Most Valuable Professional (MVP), Gold Partner, and Power BI Red Carpet Partner, I've been privileged to enjoy close relationships with the Microsoft product groups. It's great to see them working together! Special thanks to the Power BI, Analysis Services, and Reporting Services teams.

Finally, thank *you* for purchasing this book!

about the book

The book doesn't assume any prior experience with data analytics. It's designed as an easy-to-follow guide for navigating the personal-team-organizational BI continuum with Power BI and shows you how the technology can benefit the four types of users: information workers, data analysts, pros, and developers. It starts by introducing you to the Microsoft Data Platform and to Power BI. You need to know that each chapter builds upon the previous ones, to introduce new concepts and to practice them with step-by-step exercises. Therefore, I'd recommend do the exercises in the order they appear in the book.

Part 1, *Power BI for Information Workers*, teaches regular users interested in basic data analytics how to analyze simple datasets without modeling and how to analyze data from popular cloud services with predefined dashboards and reports. Chapter 2, *The Power BI Service*, lays out the foundation of personal BI, and teaches you how to connect to your data. In Chapter 3, *Creating Reports*, information workers will learn how to create their own reports. Chapter 4, *Creating Dashboards*, shows you how to quickly assemble dashboards to convey important metrics. Chapter 5, *Power BI Mobile*, discusses the Power BI native mobile applications that allow you to view and annotate BI content on the go.

Part 2, *Power BI for Data Analysts*, educates power users how to create self-service data models with Power BI Desktop. Chapter 6, *Data Modeling Fundamentals*, lays out the ground work to understand self-service data modeling and shows you how to import data from virtually everywhere. Because source data is almost never clean, Chapter 7, *Transforming Data*, shows you how you can leverage the unique Power Query component of Power BI Desktop to transform and shape the data. Chapter 8, *Refining the Model*, shows you how to make your self-service model more intuitive and how to join data from different data sources. In Chapter 9, *Implementing Calculations*, you'll further extend the model with useful business calculations. Chapter 10, *Analyzing Data*, shares more tips and tricks to get insights from your models. And Chapter 11, *Predictive Analytics*, shows different ways to apply machine learning techniques.

Part 3, *Power BI for Pros*, teaches IT pros how to set up a secured environment for sharing and collaboration, and it teaches BI pros how to implement Power BI-centric solutions. Chapter 12, *Enabling Team BI*, shows you how to use Power BI workspaces and apps to promote sharing and collaboration, where multiple coworkers work on the same BI artifacts, and how to centralize access to on-premises data. Chapter 13, *Power BI Premium*, shows how you can achieve consistent performance and reduce licensing cost with Power BI Premium and how to implement on-premises report portals to centralize report management and distribution. Written for BI pros, Chapter 14, *Organizational BI*, walks you through the steps to implement descriptive, predictive, and real-time solutions with Power BI.

Part 4, *Power BI for Developers*, shows developers how to integrate and extend Power BI. Chapter 15, *Programming Fundamentals*, introduces you to the Power BI REST APIs and teaches you how to use OAuth to authenticate custom applications with Power BI. In Chapter 16, *Power BI Embedded*, you'll learn how to report-enable custom apps with embedded dashboards and reports. In Chapter 17, *Creating Custom Visuals*, you'll learn how to extend the Power BI visualization capabilities by creating custom visuals to present effectively any data.

source code

Applied Microsoft Power BI covers the entire spectrum of Power BI features for meeting the data analytics needs of information workers, data analysts, pros, and developers. This requires installing and configuring various software products and technologies. **Table 1** lists the software that you need for all the exercises in the book, but you might need other components, as I'll explain throughout the book.

Table 1   The software requirements for practices and code samples in the book

Software	Setup	Purpose	Chapters
Power BI Desktop	Required	Implementing self-service data models	6, 7, 8, 9, 10, 11
Visual Studio 2015 (or higher) Community Edition	Required	Power BI programming	15, 16, 17
Power BI Mobile native apps (iOS, Android, or Windows depending on your mobile device)	Recommended	Practicing Power BI mobile capabilities	5
SQL Server Database Engine Developer, Standard, or Enterprise 2012 or later with the AdventureWorksDW database	Recommended	Importing and processing data	6
Analysis Services Tabular Developer, Business Intelligence, or Enterprise 2012 or later edition	Recommended	Live connectivity to Tabular	2, 14
Analysis Services Multidimensional Developer, Standard, Business Intelligence, or Enterprise 2012 or later edition	Optional	Live connectivity to Multidimensional	6
Power BI Report Server Developer or Enterprise	Optional	Importing from SSRS and integrating Power BI with Power BI Report Server	4, 6, 13

Although the list is long, don't despair! As you can see, most of the software is not required. In addition, the book provides the source data as text files and it has alternative steps to complete the exercises if you don't install some of the software, such as SQL Server or Analysis Services.

You can download the book source code from the book page at http://bit.ly/powerbibook. After downloading the zip file, extract it to any folder on your hard drive. Once this is done, you'll see a folder for each chapter that contains the source code for that chapter. The source code in each folder includes the changes you need to make in the exercises in the corresponding chapter, plus any supporting files required for the exercises. For example, the Adventure Works.pbix file in the Ch06 folder includes the changes that you'll make during the Chapter 6 practices and includes additional files for importing data. Save your files under different names or in different folders to avoid overwriting the files that are included in the source code.

 NOTE The data source settings of the sample Power BI Desktop models in this book have connection strings to databases and text files. If you decide to test the provided samples and refresh the data, you must update some data sources to reflect your specific setup. To do so, open the Power BI Desktop model, and then click the Edit Queries button in the ribbon's Home tab. Select the query that fails to refresh in the Queries pane, and then double-click the Source step in the Applied Steps section (Query Settings pane). Change the server name or file location as needed.

PREFACE   xi

(Optional) Installing the Adventure Works databases

Some of the code samples import data from the AdventureWorksDW database. This is a Microsoft-provided database that simulates a data warehouse. I recommend you install it because importing form a relational database is a common requirement. You can install the database on an on-prem SQL Server (local or shared) or Azure SQL Database. Again, you don't have to do this (installing a SQL Server alone can be challenging) because I provide the necessary data extracts.

NOTE Microsoft ships Adventure Works databases with each version of SQL Server. More recent versions of the databases have incremental changes and they might have different data. Although the book exercises were tested with the AdventureWorksDW2012 database, you can use a later version if you want. Depending on the database version you install, you might find that reports might show somewhat different data.

Follow these steps to download the AdventureWorksDW2012 database:

1. Open your browser and navigate to https://github.com/Microsoft/sql-server-samples/releases/tag/adventureworks2012.
2. Click the adventure-works-2012-dw-data-file.mdf file to download the file.
3. Open SQL Server Management Studio (SSMS) and connect to your SQL Server database instance. Attach the file. If you're not sure how to attach a database file, read the instructions at https://docs.microsoft.com/en-us/sql/relational-databases/databases/attach-a-database.

(Optional) Installing the Adventure Works Analysis Services models

In chapters 2 and 14, you connect to the Adventure Works Tabular model, and Chapter 6 has an exercise for importing data from Analysis Services Multidimensional. If you want to do these exercises, install the Analysis Services models as follows:

1. Navigate to https://github.com/Microsoft/sql-server-samples/releases/tag/adventureworks-analysis-services.
2. Download the adventure-works-tabular-model-1200-full-database-backup.zip file and unzip it.
3. In SSMS, connect to your instance of Analysis Services Tabular and restore a new database from the file.
4. On the same page, download the adventure-works-multidimensional-model-full-database-backup.zip file and unzip it.
5. In SSMS, connect to your instance of Analysis Services Multidimensional and restore a new database from the *abf file in the appropriate file folder depending on the edition (Standard or Enterprise) of your Analysis Services Multidimensional instance.
6. In SQL Server Management Studio, connect to your Analysis Services instance. (Multidimensional and Tabular must be installed on separate instances.)
7. Expand the Databases folder. You should see the Analysis Services database listed.

Reporting errors

Please submit bug reports to the book discussion list on http://bit.ly/powerbibook. Confirmed bugs and inaccuracies will be published to the book errata document. A link to the errata document is provided in the book web page. The book includes links to web resources for further study. Due to the transient nature of the Internet, some links might be no longer valid or might be broken. Searching for the document title is usually enough to recover the new link.

Your purchase of APPLIED MICROSOFT POWER BI includes free access to an online forum sponsored by the author, where you can make comments about the book, ask technical questions, and receive help from the author and the community. The author is not committed to a specific amount of participation or successful resolution of the question and his participation remains voluntary. You can subscribe to the forum from the author's personal website http://bit.ly/powerbibook.

Chapter 1

Introducing Power BI

1.1 What is Microsoft Power BI? 1
1.2 Understanding the Power BI Capabilities 15
1.3 Understanding the Power BI Service Architecture 27
1.4 Power BI and You 30
1.5 Summary 37

Without supporting data, you are just another person with an opinion. But data is useless if you can't derive knowledge from it. And, this is where Microsoft data analytics and Power BI can help! Power BI changes the way you gain insights from data; it brings you a cloud-hosted, business intelligence and analytics platform that democratizes and opens BI to everyone. Power BI makes data analytics pervasive and accessible to all users under a simple promise: "five seconds to sign up, five minutes to wow!"

This guide discusses the capabilities of Power BI, and this chapter introduces its innovative features. I'll start by explaining how Power BI fits into the Microsoft Data Platform and when to use it. You'll learn what Power BI can do for different types of users, including business users, data analysts, professionals, and developers. I'll also take you on a tour of the Power BI features and its toolset.

1.1 What is Microsoft Power BI?

Before I show you what Power BI is, I'll explain business intelligence (BI). You'll probably be surprised to learn that even BI professionals disagree about its definition. In fact, Forester Research offers two definitions (see https://en.wikipedia.org/wiki/Business_intelligence).

DEFINITION Broadly defined, BI is a set of methodologies, processes, architectures, and technologies that transform raw data into meaningful and useful information that's used to enable more effective strategic, tactical, and operational insights and decision-making. A narrower definition of BI might refer to just the top layers of the BI architectural stack, such as reporting, analytics, and dashboards.

Regardless of which definition you follow, Power BI can help you with your data analytics needs.

1.1.1 Understanding Business Intelligence

The definition above is a good starting point. but to understand BI better, you need to understand its flavors. First, I'll categorize who's producing the BI artifacts, and then I'll show you the different types of analytical tasks that these producers perform.

Self-service, team, and organizational BI
I'll classify BI by its main users and produced artifacts and divide it into self-service, team, and organizational BI.

- Self-service BI (or personal BI) – Self-service BI enables data analysts to offload effort from IT pros. For example, Maya is a business user and she wants to analyze CRM data from Salesforce. Maya can connect Power BI to Salesforce and get prepackaged dashboards and reports without building a data model. In the more advanced scenario, Power BI empowers analysts to build data models for self-service data exploration and reporting. Suppose that Martin from the sales department wants to analyze some sales data that's stored in a Microsoft Access database or in an Excel workbook. With a few clicks, Martin can combine data from various data sources into a data model (like the one shown in **Figure 1.1**), build reports, and gain valuable insights. In other words, Power BI makes data analytics more pervasive because it enables more employees to perform BI tasks.

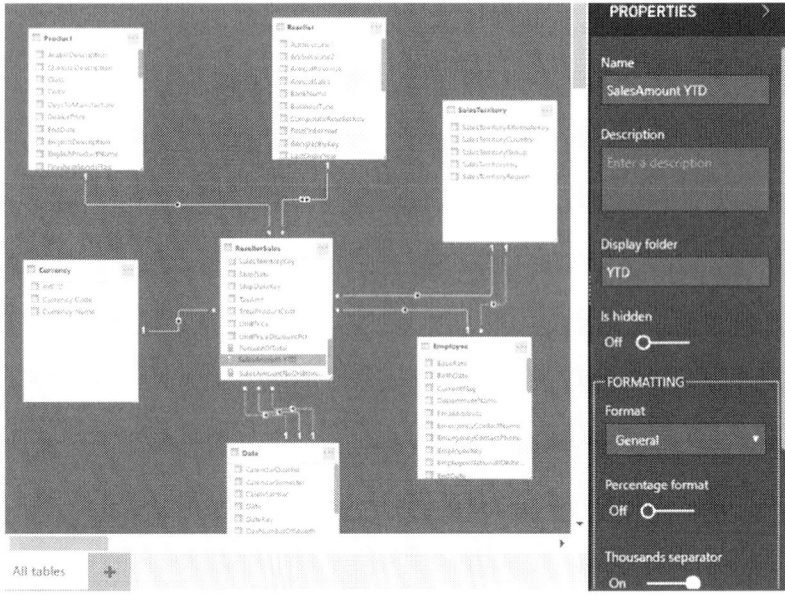

Figure 1.1 Power BI allows analysts to build data models whose features are on par with professional models implemented by BI pros.

- Team BI – Business users can share the reports and dashboards they've implemented with other team members without requiring them to install modeling or reporting tools. Suppose that Martin would like to share his sales model with his coworker, Maya. Once Martin has uploaded the model to Power BI, Maya can go online and view the reports and dashboards Martin has shared with her. She can even create her own reports and dashboards that connect to Martin's model.
- Organizational BI (or corporate BI) – BI professionals who implement organizational BI solutions, such as semantic models or real-time business intelligence, will find that they can use Power BI as a presentation layer. For example, as a BI pro, Elena has developed a Multidimensional or Tabular model layered on top of the company's data warehouse that is hosted on her company's network. Elena can install connectivity software on an on-premises computer so that Power BI can connect to her model. This allows business users to create instant reports and dashboards in Power BI by leveraging the existing infrastructure investment without moving data to the cloud! Or, if management asks for a real-time dashboard, Elena can write some code to push data to Power BI so that the dashboard updates itself as new data streams in.

 NOTE To learn more about Analysis Services, I covered implementing Analysis Services Multidimensional models in my book "Applied Microsoft Analysis Services 2005" and Tabular models in "Applied Microsoft SQL Server 2012 Analysis Services: Tabular Modeling".

Descriptive, predictive and prescriptive analytics
The main goal of BI is to get actionable insights that lead to smarter decisions and better business outcomes. Another way to classify BI is from a time perspective. Then we can identify three types of data analytics (descriptive, predictive, and prescriptive).

Descriptive analytics is retrospective. It focuses on what has happened in the past to understand the company's performance. This type of analytics is the most common and well understood. Coupled with a good data exploration tool, such as Power BI or Microsoft Excel, descriptive analytics helps you discover import trends and understand the factors that influenced these trends. You do descriptive analytics when you slice and dice data. For example, a business analyst can create a Power BI report to discover sale trends by year. Descriptive analytics can answer questions, such as "Who are my top 10 customers?", "What is the company's sales by year, quarter, month, and so on?", or "How does the company's profit compare against the predefined goal by business unit, product, time, and other subject areas?"

Predictive analytics is concerned with what will happen in the future. It uses machine learning algorithms to determine probable future outcomes and discover patterns that might not be easily discernible based on historical data. These hidden patterns can't be discovered with traditional data exploration since data relationships might be too complex, or because there's too much data for a human to analyze. Typical predictive tasks include forecasting, customer profiling, and basket analysis. Machine learning can answer questions, such as, "What are the forecasted sales numbers for the next few months?", "What other products is a customer likely to buy along with the product he or she already chose?", and, "What type of customer (described in terms of gender, age group, income, and so on) is likely to buy a given product?" Power BI includes several predictive features. Quick Insights applies machine learning algorithms to find hidden patterns, such as that the revenue for a product is steadily decreasing. You can use the Power BI clustering algorithms to quickly find groups of similar data points in a subset of data. You can add time-series forecasting to a line chart to predict sales for future periods. Thanks to the huge investments that Microsoft has made in open source software, a data analyst can use R or Python scripts for data cleansing, statistical analysis, data mining, and visualizing data. Power BI can integrate with Azure Machine Learning experiments. For example, an analyst can build a predictive experiment with the Azure Machine Learning service and then visualize the results in Power BI. Or, if a BI pro has implemented a predictive model in R or Python and deployed to SQL Server, the analyst can simply query SQL Server to obtain the predictions.

Finally, *prescriptive analytics* goes beyond predictive analytics to not only attempt to predict the future but also recommend the best course of action and the implications of each decision option. Typical prescriptive tasks are optimization, simulation, and goal seek. While tools for descriptive and predictive needs have matured, prescriptive analytics is a newcomer and currently is in the realm of startup companies. The good news is that you can get prepackaged advanced analytics and prescriptive solutions with Cortana Analytics Suite, such as solutions for product recommendations and customer churn. The Microsoft Cortana Analytics Suite is a fully managed big data and advanced analytics suite that enables you to transform your data into intelligent action. The suite includes various cloud-based services, such as Azure Machine Learning for predictive analytics, Stream Analytics for real-time BI, and Power BI for dashboards and reporting. I'll show you some of these capabilities, including the Cortana digital assistant in Chapter 10, Azure Machine Learning in Chapter 11, and Stream Analytics in Chapter 14.

1.1.2 Introducing the Power BI Products

Now that you understand BI better, let's discuss what Power BI is. Power BI is a set of products and services that enable you to connect to your data, visualize it, and share insights with other users. Next, I'll introduce you to the Power BI product offerings.

What's behind the Power BI name?
At a high level, Power BI consists of several products (listed in the order they appear in the Products menu on the powerbi.com home page):

- Power BI Desktop – A freely available Windows desktop application that allows analysts to design self-service data models and for creating interactive reports connected to these models or to external data sources. For readers familiar with Power Pivot for Excel, Power BI Desktop offers similar self-service BI features in a standalone application (outside Excel) that updates every month.
- Power BI Pro – Power BI Pro is one of the licensing options of Power BI Service (the other two are Power BI Free and Power BI Premium). Power BI Service is a *cloud-based* business analytics service (powerbi.com) that allows you to host your data, reports, and dashboards online and share them with your coworkers. Because Power BI is hosted in the cloud and managed by Microsoft, your organization doesn't have to purchase, install, and maintain an on-premises infrastructure.
- Power BI Premium – Targeting large organizations, Power BI Premium offers a dedicated capacity environment, giving your organization more consistent performance without requiring you to purchase per-user licenses. Suppose you want to share reports with more than 500 users within your organizations and most of these users require read-only access. Instead of licensing each user, you can reduce cost by purchasing a Power BI Premium plan that doesn't require licenses for viewers and gives you predictable performance. Power BI Premium also adds features that are not available in Power BI Pro, such as larger dataset sizes and incremental data refresh.
- Power BI Mobile – A set of freely available mobile applications for iOS, Android, and Windows that allow users to use mobile devices, such as tablets and smartphones, to get data insights on the go. For example, a mobile user can view and interact with reports and dashboards deployed to Power BI.
- Power BI Embedded – Power BI Embedded is a collective name for a subset of the Power BI APIs for embedding content. Integrated with Power BI Service, Power BI Embedded lets developers embed interactive Power BI reports in custom apps for internal or external users. For example, Teo has developed a web application for external customers. Instead of redirecting to powerbi.com, Teo can use Power BI Embedded to let customers view interactive Power BI reports embedded in his app.
- Power BI Report Server – Evolving from Microsoft SQL Server Reporting Services (SSRS), Power BI Report Server allows you to deploy Power BI data models and reports to an on-premises server. This gives you a choice for deployment and sharing: cloud and/or on-premises. And the choice doesn't have to be exclusive. For example, you might decide to deploy some reports to Power BI to leverage all features it has to offer, such as natural queries, quick insights, and integration with Excel, while deploying the rest of the reports to a Power BI Report Server portal.

 DEFINITION Microsoft Power BI is a data analytics platform for self-service, team, and organizational BI that consists of several products. Although Power BI can access other Office 365 services, such as OneDrive and SharePoint, Power BI doesn't require an Office 365 subscription and it has no dependencies to Office 365. However, if your organization has Office 365 E5 plan, you'll find that Power BI Pro is included in it.

Product usage scenarios

The Power BI product line has grown over time and a novice Power BI user might find it difficult to understand where each product fits in. **Figure 1.2** should help you visualize the purpose of each product at a high level.

1. Power BI Desktop – The Power BI journey typically starts with Power BI Desktop. You can use Power BI Desktop to mash up data from various data sources and create a self-service data model. Or, you can use Power BI Desktop to connect directly to a data source, such as a semantic model, and start analyzing data immediately without importing data and do any modeling.
2. Power BI Report Server – One option to share your Power BI artifacts is to deploy them to on-premises Power BI Report Server. This is a good option if your organization needs an on-premises report portal that

hosts not only Power BI reports but also operational SSRS reports and Excel reports, without requiring all Power BI features.

3. Power BI Service – Another sharing option is to deploy to the cloud Power BI Service (powerbi.com). Power BI Service has three licensing options:
   - Power BI Free – Any user can use Power BI service for personal data analytics for free!
   - Power BI Pro – Requiring per-user licensing, Power BI Pro gives you most of the Power BI Service features, including sharing BI content.
   - Power BI Premium – To avoid licensing per user for many users who will only view reports, a larger organization might decide to purchase a Power BI Premium plan. Besides cost savings, Power BI Premium is appealing from a performance standpoint as it offers a dedicated environment just for your organization and adds even more features.

4. Power BI Mobile – Although Power BI reports can render in any modern browser, your mobile workforce can install the Power BI Mobile apps on their mobile devices so that Power BI reports are optimized for the display capabilities of the device.

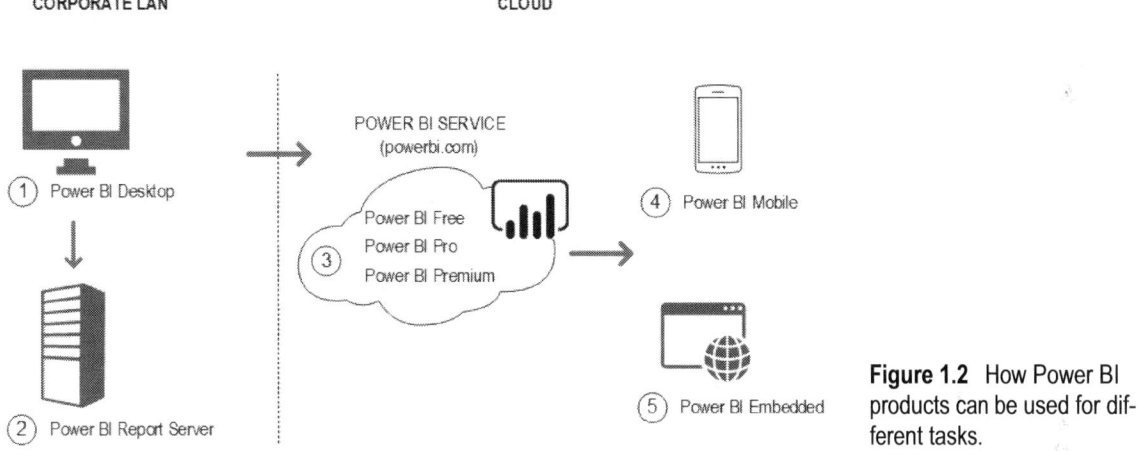

Figure 1.2 How Power BI products can be used for different tasks.

5. Power BI Embedded – A developer can integrate a custom web app with Power BI Embedded to embed Power BI reports, so they render inside the app.

As you could imagine, Power BI is a versatile platform that enables different groups of users to implement a wide range of BI solutions depending on the task at hand.

1.1.3 How Did We Get Here?

Before I delve into the Power BI capabilities, let's step back for a moment and review what events led to its existence. **Figure 1.3** shows the major milestones in the Power BI journey.

Power Pivot
Realizing the growing importance of self-service BI, in 2010 Microsoft introduced a new technology for personal and team BI called PowerPivot (renamed to Power Pivot in 2013 because of Power BI rebranding). Power Pivot was initially implemented as a freely available add-in to Excel 2010 that had to be manually downloaded and installed. Office 2013 delivered deeper integration with Power Pivot, including distributing it with Excel 2013 and allowing users to import data directly into the Power Pivot data model.

INTRODUCING POWER BI

NOTE I covered Excel and Power Pivot data modelling in my book "Applied Microsoft SQL Server 2012 Analysis Services: Tabular Modeling". If you prefer using Excel for self-service BI, the book should give you the necessary foundation to understand Power Pivot and learn how to use it to implement self-service data models and how to integrate them with SharePoint Server.

The Power Pivot innovative engine, called xVelocity (initially named VertiPaq), transcended the limitations of the Excel native pivot reports. It allows users to load multiple datasets and import more than one million rows (the maximum number of rows that can fit in an Excel spreadsheet). xVelocity compresses the data efficiently and stores it in the computer's main memory.

DEFINITION xVelocity is a columnar data engine that compresses and stores data in memory. Originally introduced in Power Pivot, the xVelocity data engine has a very important role in Microsoft BI. xVelocity is now included in other Microsoft offerings, including SQL Server columnstore indexes, Tabular models in Analysis Services, Power BI Desktop, and Power BI.

For example, using Power Pivot, a business user can import data from a variety of data sources, relate the data, and create a data model. Then the user can create pivot reports or Power View reports to gain insights from the data model.

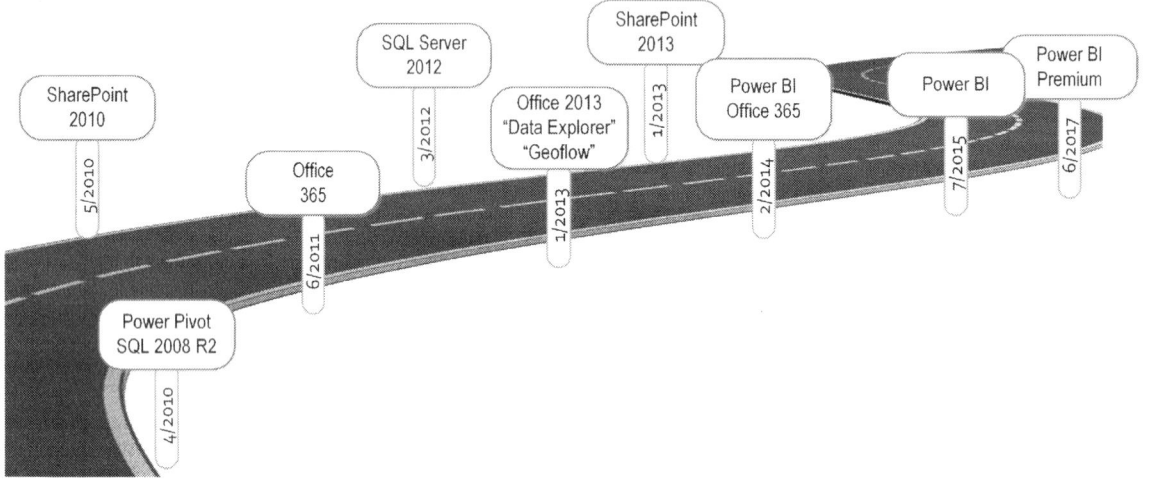

Figure 1.3 Important milestones related to Power BI.

SQL Server
Originally developed as a relational database management system (RDBMS), Microsoft SQL Server is now a multi-product offering. In the context of organizational BI, SQL Server includes Analysis Services, which has traditionally allowed BI professionals to implement multidimensional cubes. SQL Server 2012 introduced another path for implementing organizational models called Tabular. Think of Analysis Services Tabular as Power Pivot on steroids. Just like Power Pivot, Tabular allows you to create in-memory data models but it also adds security and performance features to allow BI pros to scale these models and implement data security that is more granular.

SQL Server includes also Reporting Services, which has been traditionally used to implement paper-oriented standard reports (also referred to as paginated reports). However, SQL Server 2012 introduced a SharePoint 2010-integrated reporting tool, named Power View, for authoring ad hoc interactive reports. Power View targets business users without requiring query knowledge and report authoring experience. Suppose that Martin has uploaded his Power Pivot model to SharePoint Server. Now Maya (or anyone else who has access to the model) can quickly build a great-looking tabular or chart report in a few minutes to visualize the data from the Power Pivot model. Or, Maya can use Power View to explore data in a Multidimensional or Tabular organizational model. Microsoft used some of the Power View features to deliver the same interactive experience to Power BI reports.

In Office 2013, Microsoft integrated Power View with Excel 2013 to allow business users to create interactive reports from Power Pivot models and organizational Tabular models. And Excel 2016 extended Power View to connect to multidimensional cubes. However, Microsoft probably won't enhance Power View in Excel anymore (it's disabled by default in Excel 2016) to encourage users to transition to Power BI Desktop, which is now the Microsoft premium data exploration tool.

SharePoint Server

Up to the release of Power BI, Microsoft BI has been intertwined with SharePoint. SharePoint Server is a Microsoft on-premises product for document storage and collaboration. In SharePoint Server 2010, Microsoft added new services, collectively referred to as Power Pivot for SharePoint, which allowed users to deploy Power Pivot data models to SharePoint and then share reports that connect to these data models. For example, a business user can upload the Excel file containing a data model and reports to SharePoint. Authorized users can view the embedded reports and create their own reports.

SharePoint Server 2013 brought better integration with Power Pivot and support for data models and reports created in Excel 2013. When integrated with SQL Server 2012, SharePoint Server 2013 offers other compelling BI features, including deploying and managing SQL Server Reporting Services (SSRS) reports, team BI powered by Power Pivot for SharePoint, and PerformancePoint Services dashboards.

Later, Microsoft realized that SharePoint presents adoption barriers for the fast-paced world of BI. Therefore, Microsoft deemphasized the role of SharePoint as a BI platform in SharePoint Server 2016 in favor of Power BI in the cloud and Power BI Report Server on premises. SharePoint Server can still be integrated with Power Pivot and Reporting Services but it's no longer a strategic on-premises BI platform.

Microsoft Excel

While prior to Power BI, SharePoint Server was the Microsoft premium server-based platform for BI, Microsoft Excel was their premium BI tool on the desktop. Besides Power Pivot and Power View, which I already introduced, Microsoft added other BI-related add-ins to extend the Excel data analytics features. To help end users perform predictive tasks in Excel, Microsoft released a Data Mining add-in for Microsoft Excel 2007, which is also available with newer Excel versions. For example, using this add-in, an analyst can perform a market basket analysis, such as to find which products customers tend to buy together.

 NOTE In 2014, Microsoft introduced a cloud-based Azure Machine Learning Service (http://azure.microsoft.com/en-us/services/machine-learning) to allow users to create predictive models in the cloud, such as a model that predicts the customer churn probability. SQL Server 2016 added integration with R and SQL Server 2017 added integration with Python. Azure Machine Learning and R supersede the Data Mining add-in for self-service predictive analytics and Analysis Services data mining for organizational predictive analytics. It's unlikely that we'll see future Microsoft investments in these two technologies.

In January 2013, Microsoft introduced a freely available Data Explorer add-in for Excel, which was later renamed to Power Query. Power Query is now included in Excel 2016 and Power BI Desktop. Unique in the self-service BI tools market, Power Query allows business users to transform and cleanse data before it's imported. For example, Martin can use Power Query to replace wrong values in the source data or to un-pivot a crosstab report. In Excel, Power Query is an optional path for importing data. If data doesn't require transformation, a business user can directly import the data using the Excel or Power Pivot data import capabilities. However, Power BI always uses Power Query when you import data so that its data transformation capabilities are there if you need them. For example, **Figure 1.4** shows that I have applied several steps to cleanse and shape the data in Power Query. In 2018, Power BI added dataflows for self-service data staging to a data lake store and they are also powered by Power Query.

Another data analytics add-in that deserves attention is Power Map. Originally named Geoflow, Power Map is another freely available Excel add-in that's specifically designed for geospatial reporting. Power

Map is included by default in Excel 2016. Using Power Map, a business user can create interactive 3D maps from Excel tables or Power Pivot data models. Power Map is not included in Power BI but you can get some of its capabilities in Power BI when you import the GlobeMap custom visual.

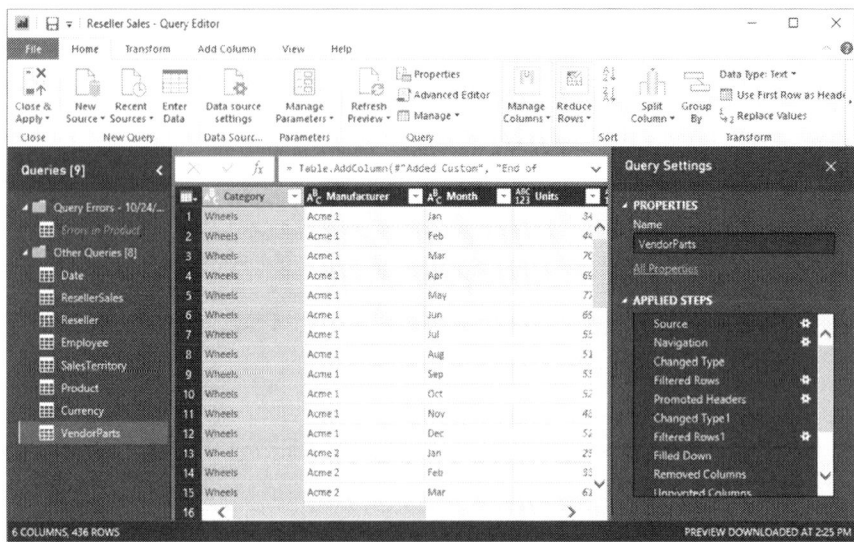

Figure 1.4 A data analyst can use Power Query to shape and transform data.

Power BI for Office 365

Unless you live under a rock, you know that one of the most prominent IT trends nowadays is toward cloud computing. Chances are that your organization is already using the Microsoft Azure Services Platform - a Microsoft cloud offering for hosting and scaling applications and databases through Microsoft datacenters. Microsoft Azure gives you the ability to focus on your business and to outsource infrastructure maintenance to Microsoft.

In 2011, Microsoft unveiled its Office 365 cloud service to allow organizations to subscribe to and use a variety of Microsoft products online, including Microsoft Exchange and SharePoint. For example, at Prologika we use Office 365 for email, a subscription-based (click-to-run) version of Microsoft Office, OneDrive for Business, Skype for Business, Dynamics Online and other products. From a BI standpoint, Office 365 allows business users to deploy Excel workbooks and Power Pivot data models to the cloud. Then they can view the embedded reports online, create new reports, and share BI artifacts.

In early 2014, Microsoft further extended SharePoint for Office 365 with additional BI features, including natural queries (Q&A), searching and discovering organizational datasets, and mobile support for Power View reports. Together with the "power" desktop add-ins (Power Pivot, Power View, Power Query, and Power Map), the service was marketed and sold under the name "Power BI for Office 365". While the desktop add-ins were freely available, Power BI for Office 365 required a subscription. Microsoft sold Power BI for Office 365 independently or as an add-on to Office 365 business plans.

Because of its dependency to SharePoint and Office, Power BI for Office 365 didn't gain wide adoption. One year after unveiling the new Power BI platform, Microsoft discontinued Power BI for Office 365. Power BI for Office 365 shouldn't be confused with the new Power BI platform, which was completely re-architected for agile and modern BI.

Power BI

Finally, the winding road brings us to Power BI, which is the subject of this book. In July 2015, after several months of public preview, Microsoft officially launched a standalone version of the cloud Power BI Service that had no dependencies on Office 365, SharePoint and Microsoft Office. What caused this change? The short answer is removing adoption barriers for both Microsoft and consumers. For Microsoft it became clear that to be competitive in today's fast-paced marketplace, its BI offerings can't depend on other product groups and release cycles. Waiting for new product releases on two and three-year cadences couldn't introduce the new features Microsoft needed to compete effectively with "pure" BI vendors (competitors who focus only on BI tools) who have entered the BI market in the past few years.

After more than a decade working with different BI technologies and many customers, I do believe that Microsoft BI is the best and most comprehensive BI platform on the market! But it's not perfect. One ongoing challenge is coordinating BI features across product groups. Take for example SharePoint, which Microsoft promoted as a platform for sharing BI artifacts. Major effort underwent to extend SharePoint with SSRS in SharePoint integration mode, PerformancePoint, Power Pivot, and so on. But these products are owned by different product groups and apparently coordination has been problematic. For example, after years of promises for mobile rendering, Power View in SharePoint Server still requires Microsoft Silverlight for rendering, thus barring access from non-Windows devices.

Seeking a stronger motivation for customers to upgrade, Excel added the "power" add-ins and was promoted as the Microsoft premium BI tool on the desktop. However, the Excel dependency turned out to be a double-edged sword. While there could be a billion Excel users worldwide, adding a new feature must be thoroughly tested to ensure that there are no backward compatibility issues or breaking changes, and that takes a lot of time. Case in point: we had to wait almost three years until Excel 2016 to connect Power View reports to multidimensional cubes (only Tabular was supported before), although Analysis Services Multidimensional has much broader adoption than Tabular.

For consumers, rolling out a Microsoft BI solution has been problematic. Microsoft BI has been traditionally criticized for its deployment complexity and steep price tag. Although SharePoint Server offers much more than just data analytics, having a SharePoint server integrated with SQL Server has been a cost-prohibitive proposition for smaller organizations. As many of you would probably agree, SharePoint Server adds complexity and troubleshooting it isn't for the faint of heart. Power BI for Office 365 alleviated some of these concerns by shifting maintenance to become Microsoft's responsibility, but many customers still find its "everything but the kitchen sink" approach too overwhelming and cost-prohibitive if all they want is the ability to deploy and share BI artifacts.

Going back to the desktop, Excel wasn't originally designed as a BI tool, leaving the end user with the impression that BI was something Microsoft bolted on top of Excel. For example, navigating add-ins and learning how to navigate the cornucopia of features has been too much to ask from novice business users.

How does the new Power BI address these challenges?
Power BI embraces the following design tenets to address the previous pain points:

- Simplicity – Power BI was designed for BI from the ground up. As you'll see, Microsoft streamlined and simplified the user interface to ensure that your experience is intuitive, and you aren't distracted by other non-BI features and menus.
- No dependencies to SharePoint and Office – Because it doesn't depend on SharePoint and Excel, Power BI can evolve independently. This doesn't mean that business users are now asked to forgo Excel. To the contrary, if you like Excel and prefer to create data models in Excel, you'll find that you can still deploy them to Power BI.
- Frequent updates – Microsoft delivers weekly updates for Power BI Service and monthly updates for Power BI Desktop. This should allow Microsoft to stay at the forefront of the BI market. For example, Microsoft delivered more than 1,500 new features and enhancements since Power BI became generally available in July 2015, as you can witness at http://aka.ms/pbifeatures!
- Always up to date – Because of its service-based nature, as a Power BI subscriber you're always on the latest and greatest version. In addition, because Power BI is a cloud service, you can get started with Power BI Pro or Premium in a minute as you don't have to provision servers and software.

- Great value proposition – As you'll see in "Power BI Editions and Pricing" (later in this chapter), Power BI has the best business model: most of it is free! Power BI Desktop and Power BI Mobile are free. Following a freemium model, Power BI is free for personal use and has subscription options that you could pay for if you need to share with other users. Cost was the biggest hindrance of Power BI, and it's now been turned around completely. You can't beat free!

1.1.4 Power BI and the Microsoft Data Platform

No tool is a kingdom of its own and no tool should work in isolation. If you're tasked to evaluate BI tools, consider that one of the Power BI strengths is that it's an integral part of a much broader Microsoft Data Platform that started in early 2004 with the powerful promise to bring "BI to the masses." Microsoft subsequently extended the message to "BI to the masses, by the masses" to emphasize its commitment to democratize. Indeed, a few years after Microsoft got into the BI space, the BI landscape changed dramatically. Once a domain of cost-prohibitive and highly specialized tools, BI is now within the reach of every user and organization!

Figure 1.5 The Microsoft Data Platform provides services and tools that address various data analytics and management needs on premises and in the cloud.

Understanding the Microsoft Data Platform
Figure 1.5 illustrates the most prominent services of the Microsoft Data Platform (and new cloud services are added almost every month!)

 DEFINITION The Microsoft Data Platform is a multi-service offering that addresses the data capturing, transformation, and analytics needs to create modern BI solutions. It's powered by Microsoft SQL Server on premises and Microsoft Azure in the cloud.

Table 1.1 summarizes the various services of the Microsoft Data Platform and their purposes.

Table 1.1 The Microsoft Data Platform consists of many products and services, with the most prominent described below.

Category	Service	Audience	Purpose
Capture and manage	Relational	IT	Capture relational data in SQL Server, Analytics Platform System, Azure SQL Database, Azure SQL Data Warehouse, and others.
	Non-relational	IT	Capture Big Data in Azure HDInsight Service and Microsoft HDInsight Server.
	NoSQL	IT	Capture NoSQL data in cloud structures, such as Azure Table Storage, Cosmo DB, and others.
	Streaming	IT	Allow capturing of data streams from Internet of Things (IoT) with Azure StreamInsight.
	Internal and External	IT/Business	Referring to cloud on your terms, allow connecting to both internal and external data, such as connecting Power BI to online services (Google Analytics, Salesforce, Dynamics CRM, and many others).
Transform and analyze	Orchestration	IT/Business	Create data orchestration workflows with SQL Server Integration Services (SSIS), Azure Data Factory, Power Query, Power BI Desktop, and Data Quality Services (DQS).
	Information management	IT/Business	Allow IT to establish rules for information management and data governance using SharePoint, Azure Data Catalog, and Office 365, as well as manage master data using SQL Server Master Data Services.
	Complex event processing	IT	Process data streams using SQL Server StreamInsight on premise and Azure Stream Analytics Service in the cloud.
	Modelling	IT/Business	Transform data in semantic structures with Analysis Services Multidimensional, Tabular, Power Pivot, and Power BI.
	Machine learning	IT/Business	Create data mining models in SQL Server Analysis Services, Excel data mining add-in, and Azure Machine Learning Service.
	Cognitive services	IT/Business	Build intelligent algorithms into apps, websites, and bots so that they see, hear, speak, and understand your user needs.
Visualize and decide	Applications	IT/Business	Analyze data with desktop applications, including Excel, Power BI Desktop, SSRS Designer, Report Builder, Power View, Power Map.
	Reports	IT/Business	Create operational and ad hoc reports with Power BI, SSRS, and Excel.
	Dashboards	IT/Business	Implement and share dashboards with Power BI and SSRS.
	Mobile	IT/Business	View reports and dashboards on mobile devices with Power BI Mobile.
	PowerApps	IT/Business	Implement low code/no code data-driven apps.
	Flow	IT/Business	Build data-driven workflows.

About Cortana Intelligence Suite

While I'm on the subject of the Microsoft Data Platform, you should know that Microsoft has a much broader vision for building intelligent applications, collectively known as Cortana Intelligence Suite (see **Figure 1.6**). Cortana Intelligence Suite was built on years of Microsoft's research in perceptual intelligence, including speech recognition, natural user interaction, and predictive analytics. The key benefit is Cortana Intelligence will let you roll out prepackaged analytics solutions, reducing time to market and project costs over do-it-all-yourself approaches. For example, there will be prepackaged solutions for Sales and Marketing (customer acquisition, cross-sell, upsell, loyalty programs, and marketing mix optimization), Finance and Risk (fraud detection and credit risk management), Customer Relationships Management (lifetime customer value, personalized offers, and product recommendation), and Operations and Workspace (operational efficiency, smart buildings, predictive maintenance, and supply chain).

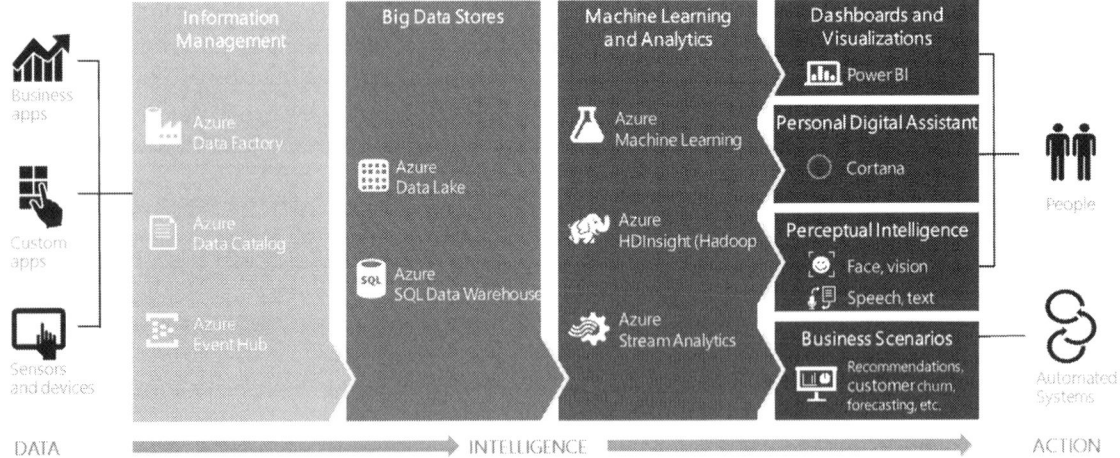

Figure 1.6 Cortana Intelligence Suite is a set of tools and services for building intelligence applications.

Cortana Intelligence Suite provides services to bring data in so that you can analyze it. For example, you can use Azure Data Factory (a cloud ETL service) so that you can pull data from any source (both relational and non-relational data sources), in an automated and scheduled way, while performing the necessary data cleansing and transformations. As I mentioned, Event Hubs ingests data streams. The incoming data can be persisted in Big Data storage services, such as Data Lake and SQL Data Warehouse.

You can then use a wide range of analytics services from Azure Machine Learning and Stream Analytics to analyze the data that is stored in Big Data storage. This means you can create analytics services and models that are specific to your business needs, such as real time-demand forecasting. The resulting analytics services and models that you create by taking these steps, can then be surfaced as interactive dashboards and visualizations powered by Power BI.

These same analytics services and models can also be integrated with various applications (web, mobile, or rich-client applications), as well as via integrations with Cortana Personal Digital Assistant (demonstrated in Chapter 10). This way, end users can naturally interact with them via speech. For example, end users can be notified proactively by Cortana if the analytics model finds a new data anomaly, or whatever deserves the attention of the business users. For more information about Cortana Analytics Suite, visit http://www.microsoft.com/en-us/server-cloud/cortana-analytics-suite/overview.aspx.

About Microsoft Power Platform
Yet another way to appreciate the potential of Power BI for addressing your business needs is to consider it in the context of the Microsoft Power Platform (https://dynamics.microsoft.com/microsoft-power-platform/), which consists of three products:
- Power BI – The subject of this book.
- PowerApps – An Office 365 offering that helps business users build no-code/low-code apps. Every organization has business automation needs which traditionally have been solved by developers writing custom code. However, just like Power BI democratizes BI, PowerApps empowers business users to create their own apps. Further, Power BI can integrate with PowerApps to redefine the meaning of reports. I demonstrate how you can leverage this integration to change the data behind a Power BI report (report writeback) in Chapter 10.

- Flow – Besides apps, automating business processes typically requires a workflow. Microsoft Flow (another Office 365 app) lets you implement no-code/low-code workflows that react to conditions. For example, my company uses Flow (another Office 365 app) to monitor leads posted to Dynamics Online and generate automatic replies.

 TIP You can monitor the Microsoft Business Applications Release Notes (https://docs.microsoft.com/business-applications-release-notes) to view the near-future roadmap of the Microsoft Power Platform and other applications, such as Microsoft Dynamics and Azure Analysis Services.

The role of Power BI in the Microsoft Data Platform

Microsoft has put a lot of effort to make Power BI a one-stop destination for your data analytics needs. Power BI plays an important role in the Microsoft Data Platform by providing services for getting, transforming and visualizing your data. As far as data acquisition goes, it can connect to cloud and on-premises data sources so that you can import and relate data irrespective of its origin.

Capturing data is one thing but making dirty data suitable for analysis is quite another. However, you can use the data transformation capabilities of Power BI Desktop (or Power Query in Excel) to cleanse and enrich your data. For example, someone might give you an Excel crosstab report. If you import the data as it is, you'll quickly find that you won't be able to relate it to the other tables in your data model. However, with a few clicks, you can un-pivot your data and remove unwanted rows. Moreover, the transformation steps are recorded so that you can repeat the same transformations later if you're given an updated file.

The main purpose and strength of Power BI is visualizing data in reports and dashboards without requiring any special skills. You can explore and understand your data by having fun with it. To summarize insights from these reports, you can then compile a dashboard. Or, you can build the dashboard by asking natural questions. **Figure 1.7** shows a sample dashboard assembled from existing reports.

Figure 1.7 Power BI lets you assemble dashboards from existing reports or by asking natural questions.

1.1.5 Power BI Service Editions and Pricing

Power BI editions and pricing are explained at https://powerbi.microsoft.com/pricing. As it stands, Power BI Service is available in three editions: Free, Power BI Pro, and Power BI Premium.

NOTE These editions apply to the cloud Power BI Service (powerbi.com) only. Power BI Desktop and Power BI Mobile are freely available. Power BI Embedded has its own licensing options and can be acquired by purchasing a Power BI Premium plan or Azure Power BI Embedded plan. Power BI Report Server can be licensed under Power BI Premium or with a SQL Server Enterprise Edition with Software Assurance license.

Understanding the Free edition

The Power BI Free edition is a free offering which include most of the Power BI Service features, but it's licensed for personal use. "Personal" means that a Power BI Free user can't share BI artifacts deployed to the cloud with other users. Specifically, here are the most significant features that are not available in Power BI Free:

- Dashboard sharing – A Power BI free user can't share dashboards with other users.
- Workspaces – A Power BI Free user can't create workspaces or be a member of a workspace.
- Apps – A Power BI Free user can't create an app (Power BI apps are a mechanism to distribute prepackaged external or internal content).
- Subscriptions – Power BI supports report subscriptions so that reports are delivered via email to subscribed users when the data changes. Power BI Free users can't create subscriptions.
- Connect to published datasets – This feature allows users to connect Excel or Power BI Desktop to datasets published to Power BI and create pivot reports. This is conceptually like connecting directly to an Analysis Services semantic model.

NOTE Microsoft views Power BI Free as an experimental edition for testing Power BI features without requiring a formal approval or on-boarding process. Any user can sign up for Power BI Free using a work email and can keep on using it without time restrictions. Any form of sharing or collaboration requires a paid SKU (Power BI Pro or Power BI Premium).

Understanding the Power BI Pro edition

This paid edition of Power BI Service has a sticker price of $9.99 per user per month but Microsoft offers discounts so check with your Microsoft reseller. Also, if your organization uses Office 365, you'll find that Power BI Pro is included in the E5 business plan. Power BI Pro offers all the features of Power BI Free, plus sharing and collaboration, and data integration with dataflows.

NOTE Not sure if the Power BI Pro edition is right for you? You can evaluate it for free for 60 days. To start the trial period, log in the Power BI portal, click the Settings menu in the top right corner, and then click "Manage Personal Storage". Then click the "Try Pro for free" link.

Understanding the Power BI Premium edition

Think of Power BI Premium as an add-on to Power BI Pro. It requires your organization to commit to a monthly plan. A Power BI Premium plan gives you preconfigured hardware (called a node) that is isolated from other organizations. You can purchase additional nodes to scale out your workload. A Power BI Premium plan has a fixed monthly cost irrespective of how many Power BI Free users you distribute content to. However, every user who will contribute content or change existing content requires a separate Power BI Pro license. Microsoft provides a nice online calculator at https://powerbi.microsoft.com/calculator/ to help you estimate your workload of contributors (Pro users), frequent users, and occasional users. Once you plug in the numbers, the online calculator recommends a Power BI Premium plan. For example, given 1,000 total users (200 Pro users, 350 frequent users, and 450 occasional users), the calculator recommends one node on P1 plan costing 6,993 per month ($1,998/month for the 200 Pro users and $4,995 per month for the 1 P1 node). This is $3,007 less compared to Power BI Pro per-user licensing!

NOTE From a cost perspective alone, it's obvious that the break-even point between Power BI Pro and Power BI Premium is about 500 users. Above that number, Power BI Premium saves money.

From a feature standpoint and compared to Power BI Pro, Power BI Premium adds larger datasets (currently up to 10 GB), higher dataset refresh rates (Power BI Pro is limited to a maximum of 8 refreshes per day), incremental dataset refresh, more flexible dataflows, and deploying SSRS paginated (RDL) reports. Microsoft has promised more Power BI Premium-specific features in the future, such as even larger dataset sizes, pin to memory, read-only replicas, and geo distribution.

Comparing editions and features

Table 1.2 summarizes features so you can compare editions side by side.

Table 1.2 Comparing Power BI editions and features.

Feature	Power BI Free	Power BI Pro	Power BI Premium
Connect to all data sources	Yes	Yes	Yes
Create self-service data models	Yes	Yes	Yes
Publish to web (anonymous access)	No	Yes	Yes
Dashboard and report sharing	No	Yes (can't share to Power BI Free)	Yes (can share to Power BI Free)
Workspaces	No	Yes	Yes
Organizational apps	No	Yes (can't distribute to Power BI Free)	Yes (can distribute to Power BI Free)
Subscriptions	No	Yes (can't distribute to Power BI Free)	Yes (can distribute to Power BI Free)
Connect Excel and Power BI Desktop to published datasets	No	Yes	Yes
Maximum dataset size	1GB	1GB	10GB
Maximum workspace storage quota	1GB	10GB	100TB (across the entire capacity)
Incremental refresh	No	No	Yes
Dataset refresh frequency	8/day	8/day	48/day
Isolation with dedicated capacity	No	No	Yes
Data staging with dataflows	No	Serial ingestion, no incremental refresh, no linked entities	Parallel ingestion, incremental refresh, linked entities, calculation engine
Deploying SSRS paginated reports	No	No	Yes

1.2 Understanding the Power BI Capabilities

Now that I've introduced you to Power BI and the Microsoft Data Platform, let's take a closer look at the Power BI capabilities. I'll discuss them in the context of each of the Power BI products. As I mentioned in section 1.1, Power BI is an umbrella name that unifies several products: Power BI Desktop, Power BI Pro, Power BI Premium, Power BI Mobile, Power BI Report Server, and Power BI Embedded. Don't worry if you don't immediately understand some of these technologies or if you find this section too technical. I'll clarify them throughout the rest of this chapter and the book.

1.2.1 Understanding Power BI Desktop

Business analysts meet self-service BI needs by creating data models, such as to relate data from multiple data sources and then implement business calculations. With Power BI, the design tool for implementing such models is Power BI Desktop. Power BI Desktop is a freely available Windows app for implementing self-service data models and reports. You can download it for free from https://powerbi.microsoft.com/desktop or from the Downloads menu in the Power BI portal (powerbi.com) after you log in. Windows 10 users can also install Power BI Desktop from Microsoft Store.

Understanding Power BI Desktop features

Before Power BI, data analysts could implement data models in Excel. This option is still available, and you can upload your Excel data models to Power BI. However, to overcome the challenges associated with Excel data modeling (see section 1.1.3), Microsoft introduced Power BI Desktop.

If you are familiar with Excel self-service BI, think of Power BI Desktop as the unification of Power Pivot, Power Query, and Power View. Previously available as Excel add-ins, these tools now converge in a single tool. No more guessing which add-in to use and where to find it! At a high level, the data modelling experience in Power BI Desktop now encompasses the following steps (see **Figure 1.8**).

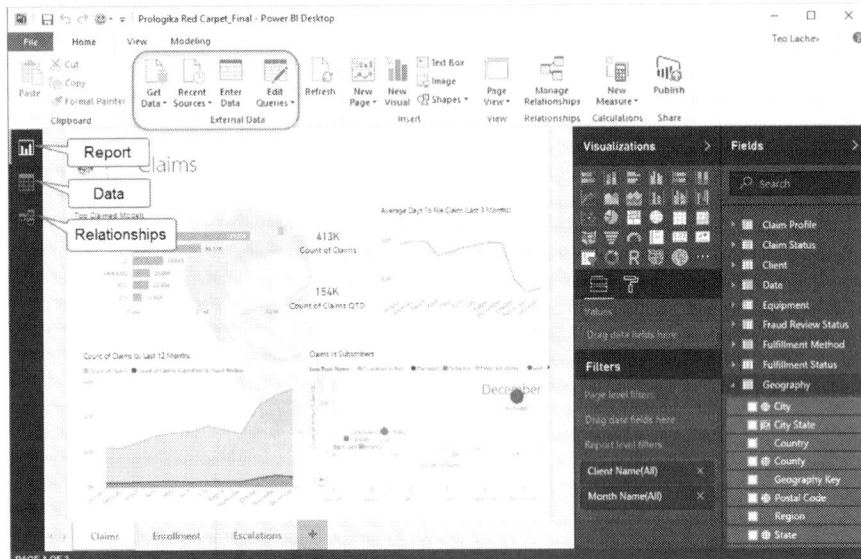

Figure 1.8 Power BI Desktop unifies the capabilities of Power Pivot, Power Query, and Power View.

1. Former Power Query – Use the Get Data button in the ribbon to connect to and transform the data. This process is like using Excel Power Query. When you import a dataset, Power BI Desktop creates a table and loads the data. The data is stored in a highly compressed format and loaded in memory to allow you to slice and dice the data without sacrificing performance. However, unlike Excel, Power BI Desktop allows you to connect directly to a limited number of fast databases, such as Analysis Services and Azure SQL Data Warehouse, where it doesn't make sense to import the data.
2. Former Power Pivot – View and make changes to the data model using the Data and Relationships tabs in the left navigation bar. This is like Power Pivot in Excel.
3. Former Power View – Create interactive reports using the Report tab on the left, as you can do using Power View in Excel (version 2013 or higher).

NOTE Some data sources, such as Analysis Services, support live connectivity. Once you connect to a live data source, you can jump directly to the Report tab and start creating reports. There are no queries to edit and models to design. In this case, Power BI Desktop acts as a presentation layer that's directly connected to the data source.

Comparing design environments

Because there are many Power Pivot models out there, Power BI allows data analysts to deploy Excel files with embedded data models to Power BI Service and view the included pivot reports and Power View reports online. Analysts can now choose which modeling tool to use:

- Microsoft Excel – Use this option if you prefer to work with Excel and you're familiar with the data modelling features delivered by Excel Power Pivot and Power Query.
- Power BI Desktop – Use this free option if you prefer a simplified tool that's specifically designed for data analytics and that's updated more frequently than Excel.

Table 1.3 compares these two tools side by side to help you choose a design environment. Let's go quickly through the list. While Excel supports at least three ways to import data, many users might struggle in understanding how they compare. By contrast, Power BI Desktop has only one data import option, which is the equivalent of Power Query in Excel. Similarly, Excel has various menus in different places that relate to data modelling. By contrast, if you use Power BI Desktop to import data, your data modelling experience is much more simplified.

Table 1.3   This table compares the data modeling capabilities of Microsoft Excel and Power BI Desktop.

Feature	Excel	Power BI Desktop
Data import	Excel native import, Power Pivot, Power Query	Power Query
Data transformation	Power Query	Power Query
Modeling	Power Pivot	Data and Relationships tabs
Reporting	Excel pivot reports, Power View, Power Map	Power BI reports (enhanced Power View reports)
Machine learning	Commercial and free add-ins, such as for integration with Azure Machine Learning	Built-in features, such as time series forecasting, clustering, Quick Insights, natural queries
Integration with R and Python	No	Yes
Update frequency	Office releases or more often with Office 365 click-to-run	Monthly
Server deployment	SharePoint, Power BI Service, and Power BI Report Server	Power BI Service and Power BI Report Server
Power BI deployment	Import data or connect to the Excel file	Deployed as Power BI Desktop (pbix) file
Convert models	Can't import Power BI Desktop models	Can import Excel data model
Upgrade to Tabular	Yes	Yes (Azure Analysis Services only)
Object model for automation	Yes	No
Cost	Excel license	Free

Excel allows you to create pivot, Power View (now deprecated), and Power Map reports from Power Pivot data models. At this point, Power BI Desktop supports interactive Power BI reports (think of Power View reports on steroids) and some of the Power Map features (available as a GlobeMap custom visual), although it regularly adds more visualizations and features. Power BI Desktop includes features for machine learning and supports integration with the open source R and Python languages for data preparation, statistical analysis, machine learning and data visualization.

INTRODUCING POWER BI

The Excel update frequency depends on how it's installed. If you install it from a setup disk (MSI installation), you need to wait for the next version to get new features. Office 365 includes subscription-based Microsoft Office (click-to-run installation) which delivers new features as they get available. If you take the Power BI Desktop path, you'll need to download and install updates as they become available. Power BI Desktop is updated monthly so you're always on the latest!

As far as deployment goes, you can deploy Excel Power Pivot models to SharePoint, Power BI Report Server, or Power BI. Power BI Desktop models (files with extension *.pbix) can be deployed to Power BI and Power BI Report Server. Behind the scenes, both Excel and Power BI Desktop use the in-memory xVelocity engine to compress and store imported data.

Power BI Desktop supports importing Power Pivot models from Excel to allow you to migrate models from Excel to Power BI Desktop. Excel doesn't support importing Power BI Desktop models yet, so you can't convert your Power BI Desktop files to Excel data models. A BI pro can migrate Excel data models to Analysis Services Tabular models when professional features, such as scalability and source control, are desirable. It's also possible to upgrade Power BI Desktop models to Azure Analysis Services Tabular.

 NOTE Power BI Desktop resonates well with business users and most data analysts prefer it over Excel Power Pivot. I recommend Power BI Desktop because it's designed from ground up for business intelligence and has more data analytics features.

1.2.2 Understanding Power BI Pro

At the heart of Power BI cloud-based business analytics service is the *Power BI Service* (powebi.com). Although not exactly technical accurate, this is what most people refer to when they say "Power BI". You use the service every time you utilize any of the powerbi.com features, such as connecting to online services, deploying and refreshing data models, viewing reports and dashboards, sharing content, or using Q&A (the natural language search feature). Recall that Power BI Services has three SKUs: Power BI Free, Power BI Pro, and Power BI Premium. Since Power BI Free doesn't let users share content, most organizations start with Power BI Pro. Next, I'll introduce you to some of Power BI Pro most prominent features.

Connect to any data source
The BI journey starts with connecting to data that could be a single file or multiple data sources. Power BI allows you to connect to virtually any accessible data source, either hosted on the cloud or in your company's data center. Your self-service project can start small. If all you need is to analyze a single file, such as an Excel workbook, you might not need a data model. Instead, you can connect Power BI to your file, import its data, and start analyzing data immediately. However, if your data acquisition needs are more involved, such as when you relate data from multiple sources, you can use Power BI Desktop to build a data model whose capabilities can be on par with professional data models and cubes!

Some data sources, such as Analysis Services models, support live connections. Because data isn't imported, live connections allow reports and dashboards to always be up to date. In the case when you need to import data, you can specify how often the data will be refreshed to keep it synchronized with changes in the original data source. For example, Martin might have decided to import data from the corporate data warehouse and deploy the model to Power BI. To keep the published model up to date, Martin can schedule the data model to refresh daily.

Service apps
Continuing on data connectivity, chances are that your organization uses popular cloud services, such as Salesforce, Marketo, Dynamics CRM, Google Analytics, Zendesk, and others. Power BI apps (also known as content packs) for online services allow business users to connect to such services and analyze their data without technical setup and data modeling. Apps include a curated collection of dashboards and reports that continuously update with the latest data from these services. With a few clicks, you can connect

to one of the supported online services and start analyzing data using prepackaged reports and dashboards. If the provided content isn't enough, you can create your own reports and dashboards. **Figure 1.9** shows a prepackaged dashboard for analyzing website traffic. This dashboard is included in the Power BI Google Analytics app.

Dashboards and reports
Collected data is meaningless without useful reports. Insightful dashboards and reports is what Power BI Service is all about. To offer a more engaging experience and let users have fun with data while exploring it, Power BI reports are interactive. For example, the report in **Figure 1.10** demonstrates one of these interactive features. In this case, the user selected Linda in the Bar Chart on the right. This action filtered the Column Chart on the left so that the user can see Linda's contribution to the overall sales. This feature is called cross highlighting.

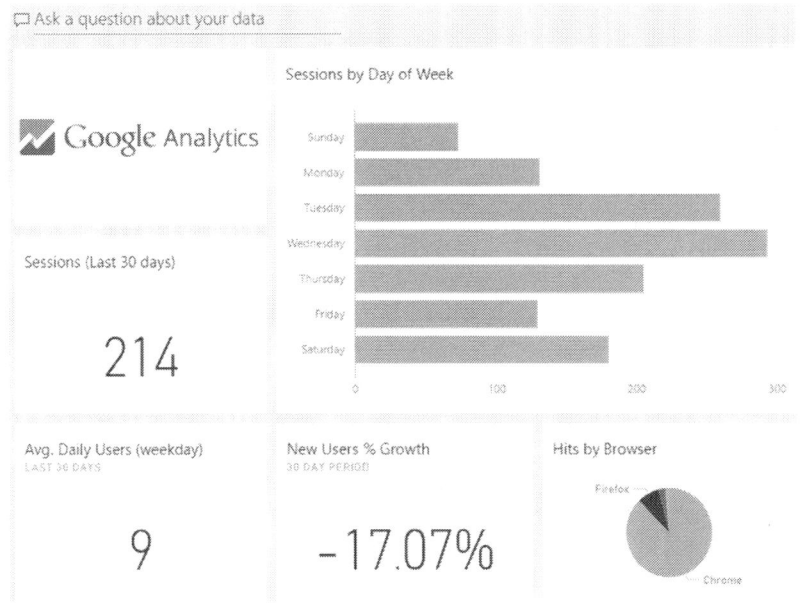

Figure 1.9 Apps allow you to connect to online services and analyze data using prepackaged reports and dashboards.

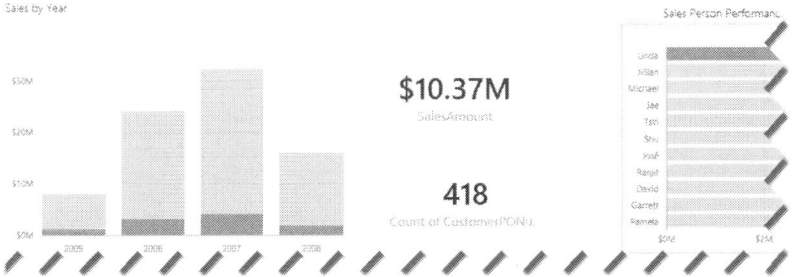

Figure 1.10 Interactive reports allow users to explore data in different ways.

Natural queries (Q&A)
Based on my experience, the feature that excites the users the most is Power BI natural queries or Q&A. End users are often overwhelmed when asked to create ad hoc reports from a data model. They don't know which fields to use and where to find them. The unfortunate "solution" by IT is to create new reports to answer new questions. This might result in a ton of reports that are replaced by new reports and are never used again. However, Power BI allows users to ask natural questions, such as "this year's sales by district in descending order by this year's sales" (see **Figure 1.11**).

INTRODUCING POWER BI 19

Not only can Power BI interpret natural questions, but it also chooses the best visualization! While in this case Q&A has decided to use a Bar Chart, it might have chosen a map if the question was phrased in a different way. And, you can always change the visualization manually if the Power BI selection isn't adequate, such as to switch from a column chart to a treemap.

 NOTE As of the time of writing this book, Q&A is supported only when data is imported into Power BI, such as when you create a Power BI Desktop model that sources data, and then upload the model to Power BI Service. Q&A is also available when Power BI connects live to an Analysis Services Tabular model but not with other data sources that support direct connections. Q&A is currently in English only (Spanish language support is in preview).

Figure 1.11 Q&A allows users to explore data by asking natural questions.

Sharing and collaboration
Once you've created informative reports and dashboards, you might want to share them with your coworkers. Power BI supports several sharing options but recall that all of them require Power BI Pro or Premium subscriptions. To start, you can share dashboards as read-only with your coworkers. Or you can use Power BI Pro workspaces to allow groups of people to have access to the same workspace content and collaborate on it. For example, if Maya works in sales, she can create a Sales Department workspace and grant her coworkers access to the workspace. Then all content added to the Sales Department workspace will be shared among the group members.

Yet a third way to share content is to create an organizational app. Like an online app that you can use to analyze data from popular online services, you can use a Power BI app to share content from a workspace across teams or even with everyone from your organization. Users can discover and open organizational apps from the Power BI AppSource page (see **Figure 1.12**). In this case, the user sees that someone has published a Reseller Sales app. The user can connect to the pack and access its content as read-only.

Alerts and subscriptions
Do you want to be notified when your data changes beyond certain levels? Of course, you do! You can set up as many alerts as you want in both Power BI Service and Power BI Mobile. You can set rules to be alerted when single number tiles in your dashboard exceed limits that you set. With data-driven alerts, you can gain insights and act wherever you're located.

Would you like Power BI to email you your favorite report when its data changes? Just view the report in Power BI Service and subscribe to a report page of interest. Power BI will regularly send a screenshot of that report page directly to your mail inbox and a link to the actual report.

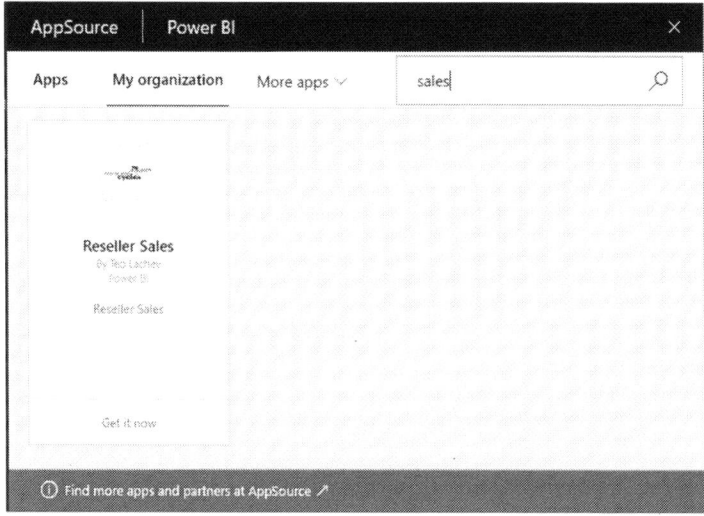

Figure 1.12 Users within your organization can use the Power BI AppSource to discover published external (online services) or internal (organizational) apps.

Data staging and preparation

Data quality and integration is a big issue for many organizations. Although you can use Power Query that is included in Power BI Desktop to shape and transform data before it becomes available for reporting, some scenarios might require additional data staging and preparation. Suppose that your organization uses a cloud-based customer relationship management (CRM) system, such as Salesforce or Microsoft Dynamics Online. Since CRM data is so important to your company, many data analysts import this data and create personal data models. When doing so, they apply the same data transformations. They might also run into long data refresh times to synchronize data extracts with changes to the CRM system.

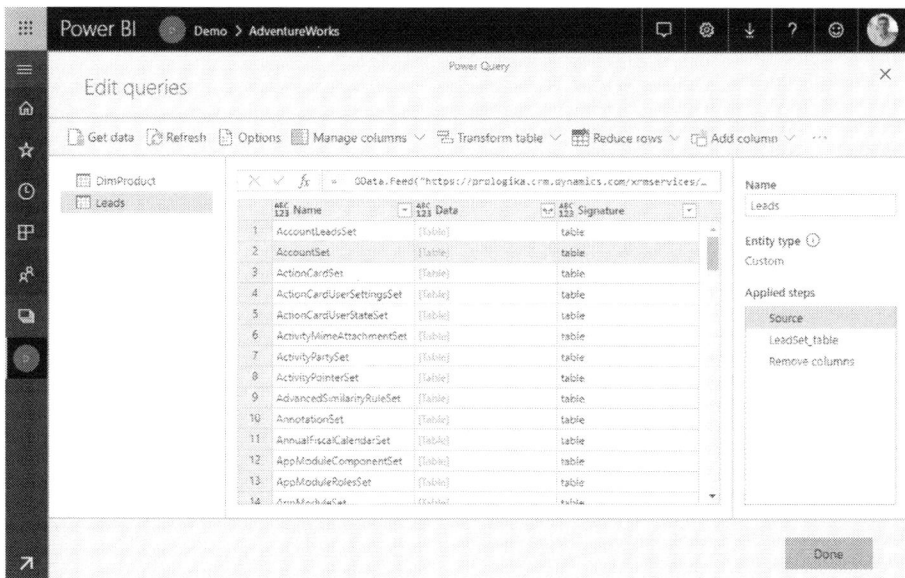

Figure 1.13 Using a dataflow to stage data from Microsoft Dynamics Online.

INTRODUCING POWER BI

Instead of duplicating data transformation steps, a better approach might be to stage the CRM data using Power BI dataflows. Think of a dataflow as "Power Query in the cloud". For example, **Figure 1.13** shows how I used a dataflow to connect to Microsoft Dynamics Online and select which entity I'd like to stage. Once the dataflow is created, I can schedule it to extract and save the data periodically. Then, data analysts can use Power BI Desktop to connect to the staged data and import it in their models.

Another good scenario for using a dataflow is to prepare a collection of certified datasets. For example, a data steward could be responsible for curating data and for maintaining a list of certified entities, such as Product and Organization, that data analysts can import.

1.2.3 Understanding Power BI Premium

I previously explained that Power BI Premium extends the Power BI Pro capabilities by providing a dedicated environment with more features and ability to reduce licensing cost by not requiring licenses for uses who only require access to view reports. Let's take a quick look at some of the most prominent Power BI Premium features.

Understanding shared and dedicated capacities
Like how a Windows folder or network share is used to stored logically related files, a Power BI workspace is a container of logically related Power BI artifacts. A workspace is in a shared capacity when its workloads run on computational resources shared by other customers. Power BI Free and Power BI Pro workspaces always run in a shared capacity. However, in Power BI Premium, a Power BI Pro user with special capacity admin permissions can move a workspace to a premium capacity. Premium capacity is a dedicated hardware provisioned just for your organization.

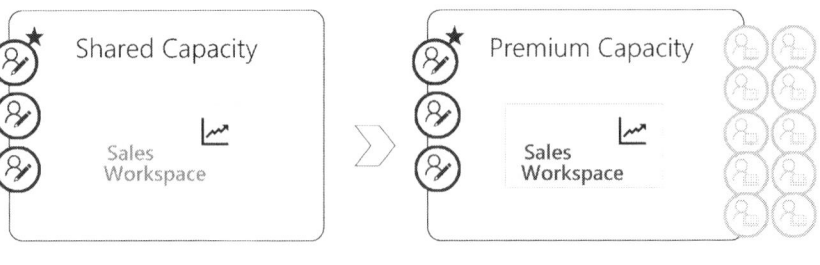

Figure 1.14 The Capacity Admin can move workspaces in and out of dedicated capacity.

In **Figure 1.14**, the Sales workspace was initially created in a shared capacity. Its report performance could be affected by workloads from other Power BI customers. To avoid this, the admin might decide to move it to a premium capacity. Now the workspace is isolated, and its performance is not affected by other organizations that use Power BI. However, it's still dependent on the activity of other premium workspaces in *your* organization and the resourced constraints of the Power BI Premium plan that it's associated with.

The interesting detail is that the admin can move a workspace in and out of the premium capacity at any point of time. For example, increased seasonal workloads may prompt the admin to move some workspaces to a premium capacity for a certain duration and then move them back to shared capacity when the workloads are reduced. You control which workspaces are in what capacity.

Understanding content distribution
Glancing again at **Figure 1.14**, we can see that when the Sales workspace was in a shared capacity, only Power BI Pro members can access its content. Power BI Free users would need to upgrade to Power BI Pro to gain access as members. However, when the workspace is moved to a premium capacity, its content can

be shared to Power BI Free users in two ways: dashboard sharing and apps. This is how Power BI Premium helps large organizations reduce Power BI licensing cost and distribute content to many users when only read-only access is enough.

Understanding premium features
Power BI Premium includes all Power BI Pro capabilities and adds the more features. At this point, here are the most prominent premium features:

- Large datasets – Power BI Premium increases the maximum dataset size up to 10 GB and the workspace quota across the entire capacity up to 100 TB.
- Incremental refresh – Large datasets can be refreshed incrementally, such as to refresh only sales transactions for the past 10 days.
- More frequent refreshes – Datasets can be scheduled for refresh up to 48 times per day.
- More flexible dataflows – Dataflows can reference entities staged by other dataflows in the same or different workspaces. Entities within a dataflow are refreshed in parallel to speed up the overall refresh time. Finally, Power BI Premium allows organizations to bring their own storage for storing dataflow entities. This enables interesting integration scenarios. For example, other applications can act upon the data, such by applying machine learning algorithms, before the data is ingested in dataflows.

1.2.4 Understanding Power BI Mobile

Power BI Mobile is a set of native mobile applications for iOS, Windows and Android devices. You can access the download links from https://powerbi.microsoft.com/mobile. Why do you need these applications? After all, thanks to Power BI HTML5 rendering, you can view Power BI reports and dashboards in your favorite Internet browser. However, the native applications offer features that go beyond just rendering. Although there are some implementation differences, this section covers some of the most compelling features (Chapter 4 has more details).

Optimized viewing
Mobile devices have limited display capabilities. The Power BI mobile apps adjust the layout of dashboards and reports, so they display better on mobile devices. For example, by default viewing a dashboard in a phone in portrait mode will position each dashboard tile after another. Rotating the phone to landscape will show the dashboard as it appears in Power BI Service (**Figure 1.15**). You can further tune the mobile layout by making changes to dashboards and reports in a special Phone View layout mode.

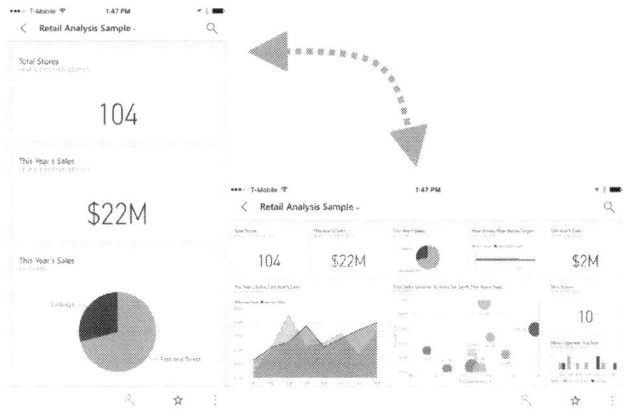

Figure 1.15 Power BI Mobile adjusts the dashboard layout when you rotate your phone from portrait to landscape.

Favorite dashboard tiles
Suppose that, while viewing dashboard tiles on your iPad, you want to put your favorite tiles in one place. You can just tap a tile to mark it as a favorite. These tiles appear in a separate "Favorites" folder. The dashboard tiles displayed on your device are live snapshots of your data. To interact with a tile, just tap it!

Alerts
Instead of going to powerbi.com to set up an alert on a dashboard tile, you can set up alerts directly in your mobile app. For example, **Figure 1.16** shows that I've enabled an iPhone data alert to be notified when this year's sales exceed $23 million. When the condition is met, I'll get a notification and email.

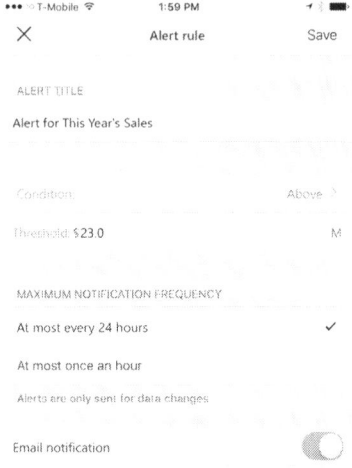

Figure 1.16 Alerts notify you about important data changes, such as when sales exceed a certain threshold.

Annotations and discussions
Annotations allow you to add lines, text, and stamps to dashboard tiles (see **Figure 1.17**). For example, you could use annotations to ask the person responsible to sign that the report is correct. Then you can mail a screen snapshot to recipients, such as to your manager.

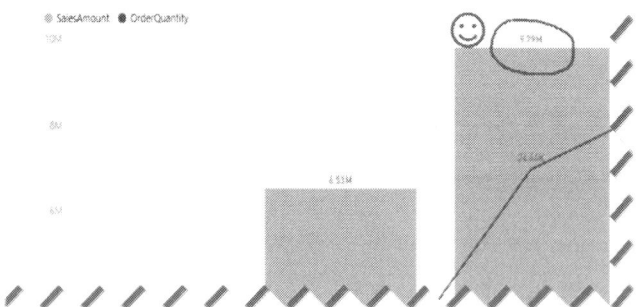

Figure 1.17 Annotations allow you to add comments to tiles and then send screenshots to your coworkers.

Besides annotations, users can start a conversation at a dashboard, report, or even visual level. Think of a conversation as a discussion list. Users can type comments and reply to comments entered by other users.

Sharing
Like Power BI simple sharing, you can use mobile device to share a dashboard by inviting coworkers to access the dashboard. Dashboards shared by mail are read-only, meaning that the people you share with can only view the dashboard without making changes.

1.2.5 Understanding Power BI Embedded

Almost every app requires some reporting capabilities. Traditionally, developers would either use third-party widgets or embed Reporting Services reports using the Microsoft ReportViewer control. The first approach requires a lot of custom code. The latter limits your users to static (canned) reports. What if you want to deliver the Power BI interactive experience with your apps? Microsoft didn't have a good answer in the past. Enter Power BI Embedded!

Introducing Power BI Embedded features
Power BI Embedded allows developers and Independent Software Vendors (ISV) to add interactive Power BI reports in their custom apps for internal or external users. Because Power BI Embedded uses the same APIs as Power BI Service, it has feature parity with Power BI Service. Suppose Teo has developed an ASP.NET MVP app for external customers. The app authenticates users any way it wants, such as by using Forms Authentication. Teo has created some nice reports in Power BI Desktop that connect directly to an Analysis Services semantic model or to data imported in Power BI Desktop.

With a few lines of code, Teo can embed these reports in his app (see **Figure 1.18**). If the app connects to a multi-tenant database (customers share the same database), the app can pass the user identity to Power BI Embedded, which in turn can pass it to the model. Then, row-level security (RLS) filters can limit access to data.

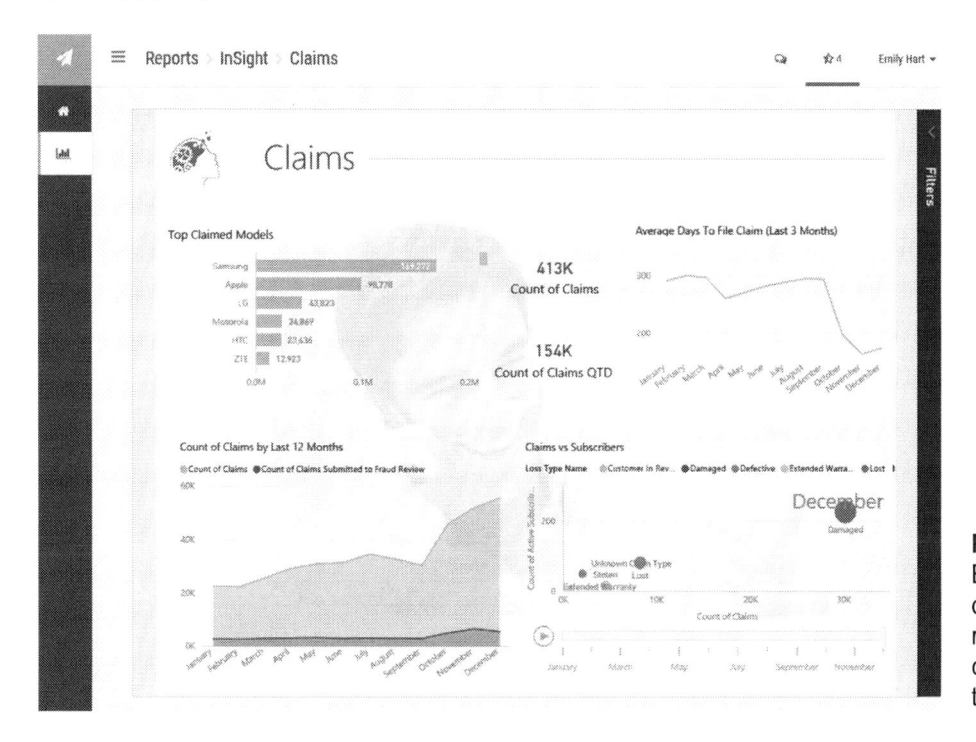

Figure 1.18 Power BI Embedded allows developers to embed Power BI reports in custom applications for internal or external users.

Power BI Embedded is extensible. Teo can use its JavaScript APIs to programmatically manipulate the client-side object model. For example, he can replace the Filters pane with a customized user interface to filter data. Or, can navigate the user programmatically to a specific report page.

INTRODUCING POWER BI

About Power BI Embedded licensing

Per-user, per-month licensing is not cost effective for delivering reports to many users. Like Power BI Premium, Power BI Embedded utilizes capacity-based pricing. Power BI Embedded can be acquired by purchasing a Power BI Premium P plans or EM plans. The Power BI Premium P plans give you access to both embedded and service deployments. The EM plans are mostly for embedded deployments.

Power BI Embedded can also be acquired outside Power BI Premium by purchasing an Azure Power BI Embedded plan (https://azure.microsoft.com/pricing/details/power-bi-embedded/). More information about these plans can be found at https://azure.microsoft.com/pricing/details/power-bi-embedded/. I'll also provide more details when I discuss Power BI Embedded in Chapters 13 and 16.

1.2.6 Understanding Power BI Report Server

Many organizations have investments in on-premises reporting with Microsoft SQL Server Reporting Services (SSRS). Starting with SQL Server 2017, SSRS doesn't ship with SQL Server anymore but can be downloaded separately from the Microsoft Download Center as two SKUs:

- Microsoft SQL Server Reporting Services – This is the SSRS SKU you are familiar with that continues to be licensed under SQL Server. It allows you to deploy operational (RDL) reports and SSRS mobile reports but it doesn't support Power BI reports and Excel reports.
- Power BI Report Server – This SKU associates with the strong Power BI brand. It's still SSRS but in addition to operational and mobile reports, it also supports Power BI reports and Excel reports (the latter requires integration with Microsoft Office Online Server). With Power BI Report Server, you have full flexibility to decide what portions of the data and reports you want to keep on-premises and what portions should reside in the cloud.

NOTE Besides splitting SSRS into two products, decoupling SSRS from SQL Server allows Microsoft to deliver new features faster and be more competitive in the fast-changing BI world. Also, while there is nothing stopping you from deploying Power BI Desktop files and Excel files to SSRS, reports won't render online, and the user will be asked to download and open the file locally. So, when I said that Power BI Report Server supports Power BI and Excel reports I meant that these reports render online, and that their management is integrated in the report portal.

Introducing Power BI Report Server features

As of this time, Power BI Report Server is limited to basic integration with Power BI reports, but Microsoft is actively working to deliver more features every two months or so. You can deploy Power BI Desktop files to the server and then view them online (see **Figure 1.19**). Report interactivity is supported. Power BI reports share the same security model as other items deployed to the report catalog. Power BI reports deployed to Power BI Report Server can also be viewed in Power BI mobile apps.

Understanding Power BI Report Server licensing

Power BI Report Server can be acquired in two ways:

- Power BI Premium P Plan – A P plan licenses the same number of on-premises cores as the number of v-cores licensed for cloud usage. Suppose your organization has purchased the Power BI Premium P1 plan. This plan licenses 8 v-cores of a premium capacity in Power BI Service. When you install Power BI Report Server on premises, it will be licensed for 8 cores, giving you a total of 16 licensed cores!
- SQL Server Enterprise with Software Assurance license – Not interested in the cloud yet? You can cover Power BI Report Server under the SQL Server Enterprise licensing model, just as you license SSRS Enterprise Edition.

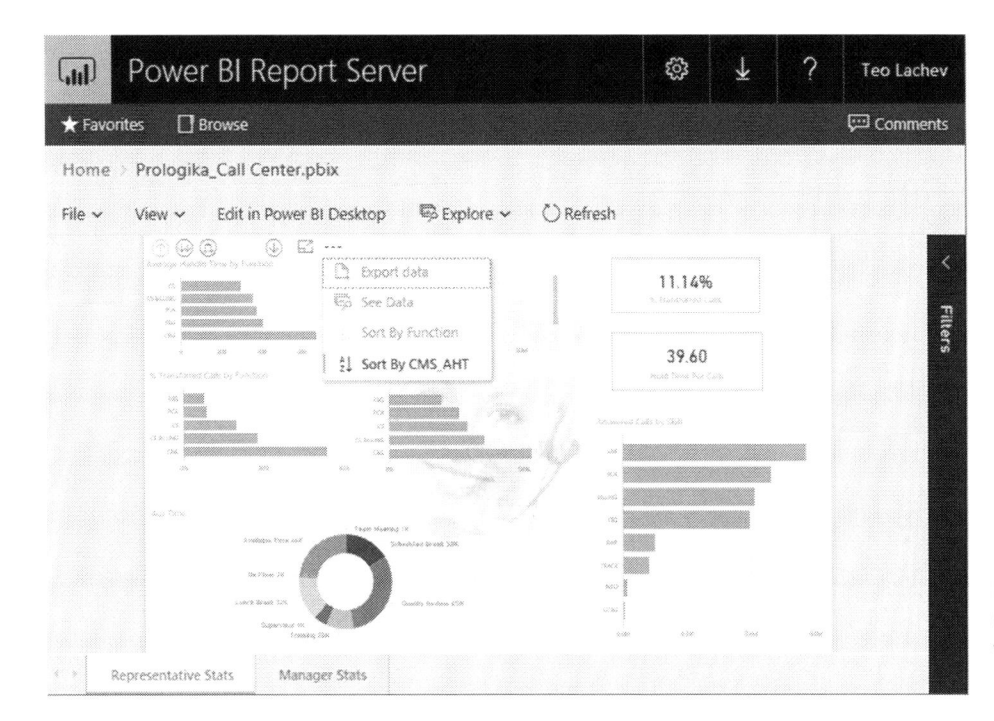

Figure 1.19 Power BI reports render online when deployed to Power BI report server.

> **NOTE** Like Power BI, Power BI Report Server requires Power BI Pro licenses for content creators. For example, if you have 5 report developers that will deploy reports to Power BI Report Server, you would need 5 Power BI Pro licenses (recall that each Power BI license is $9.99 per user, per month). Licensing content creators is honor-based as currently there is no mechanism to ensure that the user is licensed on deploying content to the Power BI Report Server.

1.3   Understanding the Power BI Service Architecture

Microsoft has put a significant effort into building Power BI Service that consists of various Azure services that handle data storage, security, load balancing, disaster recovery, logging, tracing, and so on. Although it's all implemented and managed by Microsoft (that's why we like the cloud) and it's completely transparent for you, the following sections give you a high-level overview of these services to help you understand their value and Microsoft's decision to make Power BI a cloud service.

The Power BI Service is hosted on Microsoft Azure cloud platform and it's deployed in various data centers around the world. **Figure 1.20** shows a summarized view of the overall technical architecture that consists of two clusters: a Web Front End (WFE) cluster and a Back End cluster.

1.3.1   The Web Front End (WFE) Cluster

The WFE cluster manages connectivity and authentication. Power BI relies on Azure Active Directory (AAD) to manage account authentication and management. Power BI uses the Azure Traffic Manager (ATM) to direct user traffic to the nearest datacenter. Which data center is used is determined by the DNS record of the client attempting to connect. The DNS Service can communicate with the Azure Traffic Manager to find the nearest datacenter with a Power BI deployment.

INTRODUCING POWER BI

> **TIP** To find where your data is stored, log in to Power BI and click the Help (?) menu in the top-right corner, and then click "About Power BI". Power BI shows a prompt that includes the Power BI version and the data center.

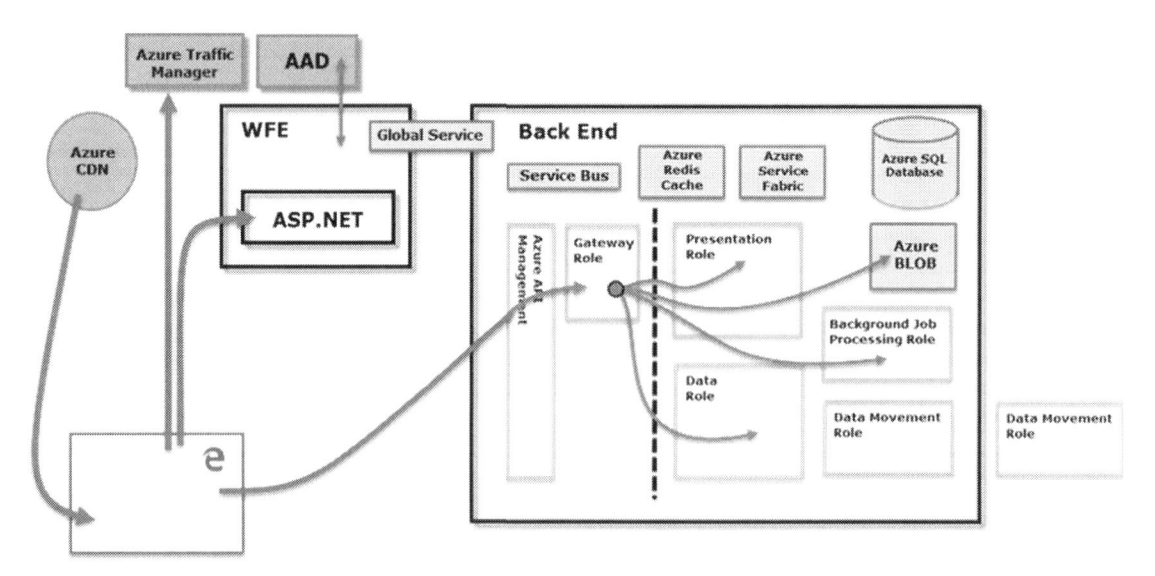

Figure 1.20 Power BI is powered by Microsoft Azure clusters.

Power BI uses the Azure Content Delivery Network (CDN) to deliver the necessary static content and files to end users based on their geographical locale. The WFE cluster nearest to the user manages the user login and authentication, and provides an access token to the user once authentication is successful. The ASP.NET component within the WFE cluster parses the request to determine which organization the user belongs to, and then consults the Power BI Global Service.

The Global Service is implemented as a single Azure Table that is shared among all worldwide WFE and Back End clusters. This service maps users and customer organizations to the datacenter that hosts their Power BI tenant. The WFE specifies to the browser which Back End cluster houses the organization's tenant. Once a user is authenticated, subsequent client interactions occur with the Back End cluster directly and the WFE cluster is not used.

1.3.2 The Back End Cluster

The Back End cluster manages all actions the user does in Power BI Service, including visualizations, dashboards, datasets, reports, data storage, data connections, data refresh, and others. The Gateway Role acts as a gateway between user requests and the Power BI service. As you can see in the diagram, only the Gateway Role and Azure API Management (APIM) services are accessible from the public Internet.

When an authenticated user connects to the Power BI Service, the connection and any request by the client is accepted and managed by the Gateway Role, which then interacts on the user's behalf with the rest of the Power BI Service. For example, when a client attempts to view a dashboard, the Gateway Role accepts that request, and then sends a request to the Presentation Role to retrieve the data needed by the browser to render the dashboard.

Where is data stored?
As far as data storage in the cloud goes, Power BI uses two primary repositories for storing and managing data. Data that is uploaded from users or generated by dataflows is stored in Azure BLOB storage, but all the metadata definitions (dashboards, reports, recent data sources, workspaces, organizational information, tenant information) are stored in Azure SQL Database.

The working horse of the Power BI service is Microsoft Analysis Services in Tabular mode, which has been architected to fulfill the role of a highly scalable data engine where many servers (nodes) participate in a multi-tenant, load-balanced farm. For example, when you import some data into Power BI, the actual data is stored in Azure BLOB storage, but an in-memory Tabular database is created to service queries.

Analysis Services Tabular enhancements
For BI pros who are familiar with Tabular, new components have been implemented so that Tabular is up to its new role. These components enable various cloud operations including tracing, logging, service-to-service operations, reporting loads and others. For example, Tabular has been enhanced to support the following features required by Power BI:

- Custom authentication – Because the traditional Windows NTLM authentication isn't appropriate in the cloud world, certificate-based authentication and custom security were added.
- Resource governance per database – Because databases from different customers (tenants) are hosted on the same server, Tabular ensures that any one database doesn't use all the resources.
- Diskless mode – For performance reasons, the data files aren't initially extracted to disk.
- Faster commit operations – This feature is used to isolate databases from each other. When committing data, the server-level lock is now only taken for a fraction of the time, although database-level commit locks are still taken, and queries can still block commits and vice versa.
- Additional Dynamic Management Views (DMVs) – For better status discovery and load balancing.
- Data refresh – From the on-premises data using a gateway.
- Additional features – Microsoft adds features first to Tabular in Power BI and later to Azure Analysis Services and SSAS. At this point, the following Analysis Services features are only available in Power BI: incremental refresh, composite models and aggregations.

1.3.3 Data on Your Terms

The increasing number of security exploits in the recent years have made many organizations cautious about protecting their data and skeptical about the cloud. You might be curious to know what is uploaded to the Power BI service and how you can reduce your risk for unauthorized access to your data. In addition, you control where your data is stored. Although Power BI is a cloud service, this doesn't necessarily mean that your data must be uploaded to Power BI.

Live connections
In a nutshell, you have two options to access your data. If the data source supports live connectivity, you can choose to leave the data where it is and only create reports and dashboards that connect live to your data. Currently, a subset of the supported data sources supports live connectivity, but that number is growing! Among them are Analysis Services, SQL Server (on premises and on Azure), Oracle, Azure SQL Data Warehouse, and Hadoop Spark.

For example, if Elena has implemented an Analysis Services model and deployed to a server in her organization's data center, Maya can create reports and dashboards in Power BI Service by directly connecting to the model. In this case, the data remains on premises; only the report and dashboard definitions are hosted in Power BI. When Maya runs a report, the report generates a query and sends the query to the model. Then, the model returns the query results to Power BI. Finally, Power BI generates the report and sends the output to the user's web browser. Power BI always uses the Secure Sockets Layer (SSL) protocol to encrypt the traffic between the Internet browser and the Power BI Service so that sensitive data is protected.

> **NOTE** Although in this case the data remains on premises, aggregated data needed on reports and dashboards still travel from your data center to Power BI Service. This could be an issue for software vendors who have service level agreements prohibiting data movement. You can address such concerns by referring the customer to the Power BI Security document (http://bit.ly/1SkEzTP) and the accompanying Power BI Security whitepaper. Or, you can wait for the next version of Reporting Services that will support deploying Power BI Desktop models to your on-premises report server.

Importing data

The second option is to import and store the data in Power BI. For example, Martin might want to build a data model to analyze data from multiple data sources. Martin can use Power BI Desktop to import the data and analyze it locally. To share reports and allow other users to create reports, Martin decides to deploy the model to Power BI. In this case, the model and the imported data are uploaded to Power BI, where they're securely stored.

To synchronize data changes, Martin can schedule a data refresh. Martin doesn't need to worry about security because data transfer between Power BI and on-premises data sources is secured through Azure Service Bus. Azure Service Bus creates a secure channel between Power BI Service and your computer. Because the secure connection happens over HTTPS, there's no need to open a port in your company's firewall.

> **TIP** If you want to avoid moving data to the cloud, one solution you can consider is implementing an Analysis Services model layered on top of your data source. Not only does this approach keep the data local, but it also offers other important benefits, such as the ability to handle larger datasets (millions of rows), a single version of the truth by centralizing business calculations, row-level security, and others. Finally, if you want to avoid the cloud whatsoever, don't forget that you can deploy Power BI reports to an on-premises Power BI Report Server.

1.4 Power BI and You

Now that I've introduced you to Power BI and its building blocks, let's see what Power BI means for you. As you'll see, Power BI has plenty to offer to anyone interested in data analytics, irrespective of whether you're a content producer or consumer, as shown in **Figure 1.21**. By the way, the book content follows the same organization so that you can quickly find the relevant information depending on what type of user you are. For example, if you're a business user, the first part of the book is for you and it has four chapters (chapters 2-5) for the first four features shown in the "For business users" section in the diagram.

1.4.1 Power BI for Business Users

To clarify the term, a business user is someone in your organization who is mostly interested in consuming BI artifacts, such as reports and dashboards. This group of users typically includes executives, managers, business strategists, and regular information workers. To get better and faster insights, some business users often become basic content producers, such as when they create reports to analyze simple datasets or data from online services.

For example, Maya is a manager in the Adventure Works Sales & Marketing department. She doesn't have skills to create sophisticated data models and business calculations. However, she's interested in monitoring the Adventure Works sales by using reports and dashboards produced by other users. She's also a BI content producer because she must create reports for analyzing data in Excel spreadsheets, website traffic, and customer relationship management (CRM) data.

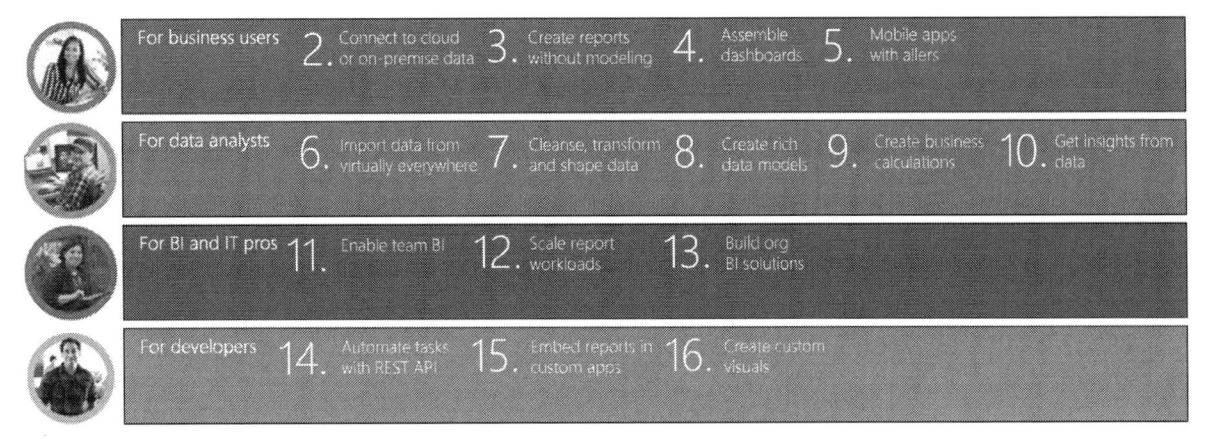

Figure 1.21 Power BI supports the BI needs of business users, analysts, pros, and developers.

Connect to your data without creating models
Thanks to the Power BI apps, Maya can connect to popular cloud services, such as Google Analytics and Dynamics CRM, and get instant dashboards. She can also benefit from prepackaged datasets, reports, and dashboards, created jointly by Software as a Service (SaaS) partners and Microsoft. Power BI refers to these connectors with the prepackaged artifacts collectively as *service apps*.

For example, the Dynamics CRM service app provides an easy access to analyze data from the cloud-hosted version of Dynamics CRM. This app uses the Dynamics CRM OData feed to generate a model that contains the most important entities, such as Accounts, Activities, Opportunities, Products, Leads, and others. Pre-built dashboards and reports, such as the one shown in **Figure 1.22**, provide immediate insights and can be further customized.

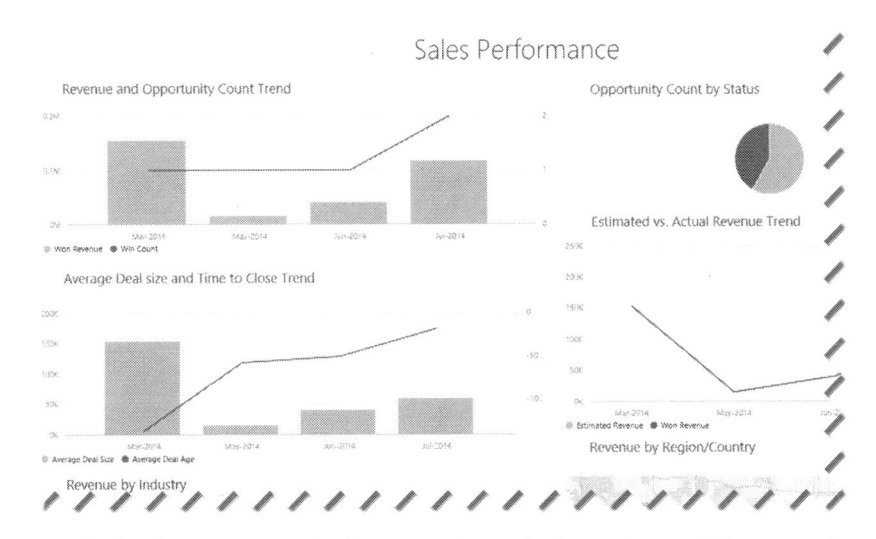

Figure 1.22 The Dynamics CRM app includes prepackaged reports and dashboards.

Similarly, if Maya uses Salesforce as a CRM platform, Power BI has a service app to allow Maya to connect to Salesforce in a minute. Power BI apps support data refresh, such as to allow Maya to refresh the CRM data daily.

INTRODUCING POWER BI

Create reports

Power BI can also help Maya analyze simple datasets without data modeling. For example, if Maya receives an Excel file with some sales data, she can import the data into Power BI and create ad hoc reports with a few mouse clicks. The experience is not much different than creating Excel pivot reports.

Create and share dashboards

Maya can easily assemble dashboards from her reports and from reports shared with her by her colleagues. She can also easily share her dashboards with coworkers. For example, Maya can navigate to the Power BI portal, select a dashboard, and then click the Share button next to the dashboard name (see **Figure 1.23**).

Go mobile

Some business users, especially managers, executives, and sales people, would need access to BI reports on the go. These users would benefit from the Power BI Mobile native applications for iPad, iPhone, Android, and Windows. As I explained in section 1.2.4, Power BI Mobile allows users to not only to view Power BI reports and dashboards, but to also receive alerts about important data changes, as well to share and annotate dashboards.

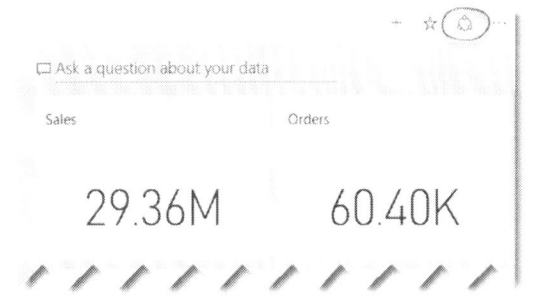

Figure 1.23 Business users can easily share dashboards with coworkers using the Power BI portal or Power BI Mobile.

For example, while Maya travels on business trips, she needs access to her reports and dashboards. Thanks to the cloud-based nature of Power BI, she can access them anywhere she has an Internet connection. Depending on what type of mobile device she uses, she can also install a Power BI app, so she can benefit from additional useful features, such as favorites, annotations, and content sharing.

1.4.2 Power BI for Data Analysts

A data analyst or BI analyst is a power user who has the skills and desire to create self-service data models. A data analyst typically prefers to work directly with the raw data, such as to relate corporate sales data coming from the corporate data warehouse with external data, such as economic data, demographics data, weather data, or any other data purchased from a third-party provider.

For example, Martin is a BI analyst with Adventure Works. Martin has experience in analyzing data with Excel and Microsoft Access. To offload effort from IT, Martin wants to create his own data model by combining data from multiple data sources.

Import and mash up data from virtually everywhere

As I mentioned previously, to create data models, Martin can use Microsoft Excel and/or Power BI Desktop, which combines the best of Power Query, Power Pivot, and Power View in a single and simplified design environment. If he has prior Power Pivot experience, Martin will find Power BI Desktop easier to use and he might decide to switch to it to stay on top of the latest Power BI features. Irrespective of the design environment chosen, Martin can use either Excel or Power BI Desktop to connect to any accessible data source, such as a relational database, file, cloud-based services, SharePoint lists, Exchange servers, and many more.

Figure 1.24 shows the supported data sources in Power BI Desktop. Microsoft regularly adds new data sources and developers can create custom data sources using the Power BI Data Connector SDK.

Cleanse, transform, and shape data
Data is rarely cleaned. A unique feature of Power BI Desktop is cleansing and transforming data. Inheriting these features from Power Query, Power BI Desktop allows a data analyst to apply popular transformation tasks that save tremendous data cleansing effort, such as replacing values, un-pivoting data, combining datasets and columns, and many more tasks.

For example, Martin may need to import an Excel financial report that was given to him in a crosstab format where data is pivoted by months on columns. Martin realizes that if he imports the data as it is, he won't be able to relate it to a date table that he has in the model. However, with a couple of mouse clicks, Martin can use a Power BI Desktop query to un-pivot months from columns to rows. And once Martin gets a new file, the query will apply the same transformations so that Martin doesn't have to go through the steps again.

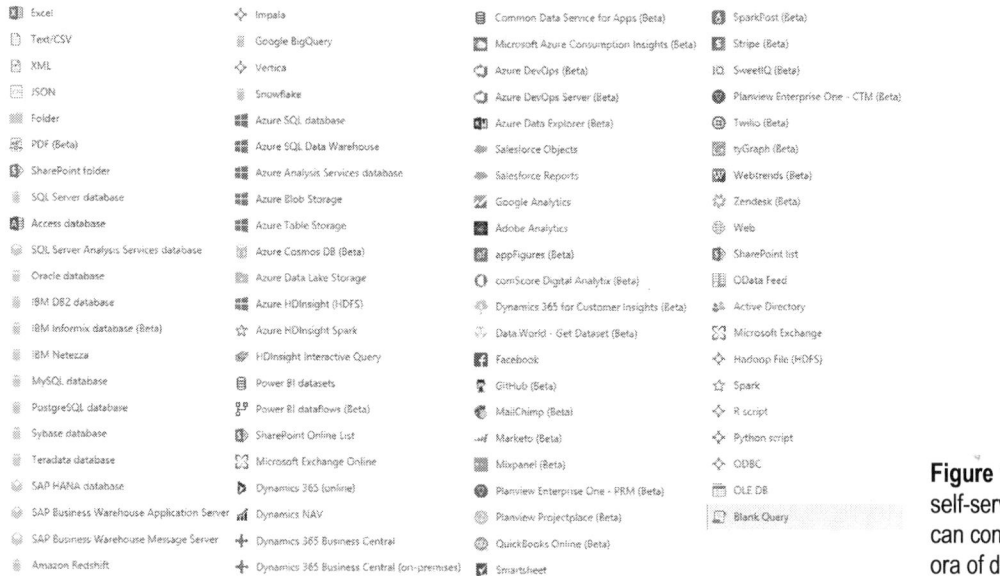

Figure 1.24 Power BI self-service data models can connect to a plethora of data sources.

Implement self-service data models
Once the data is imported, Martin can relate the datasets to analyze the data from different angles by relating multiple datasets (see **Figure 1.1** again). No matter which source the data came from, Martin can use Power BI Desktop (or Excel) to relate tables and create data models whose features are on par with professional models. When doing so, Martin can also create a composite model spanning imported tables and tables with live connections.

For example, if some tables in an ERP system are frequently updated, Martin could decide to access the sales transactions via a live connection so that he always sees the latest data, while the rest of the data is imported. Further, Power BI supports flexible relationships with one-to-many and many-to-many cardinality, so Martin can model complex requirements, such as analyzing financial balances of joint bank accounts.

Create business calculations
Martin can also implement sophisticated business calculations, such as time calculations, weighted averages, variances, period growth, and so on. To do so, Martin will use the Data Analysis Expression (DAX) language and Excel-like formulas. To help you get started with common business calculations, Power BI includes *quick measures*: prepackaged DAX expressions. For example, the formula shown in **Figure 1.25**

calculates the year-to-date (YTD) sales amount. As you can see, Power BI Desktop supports IntelliSense and color coding to help you with the formula syntax. IntelliSense offers suggestions as you type.

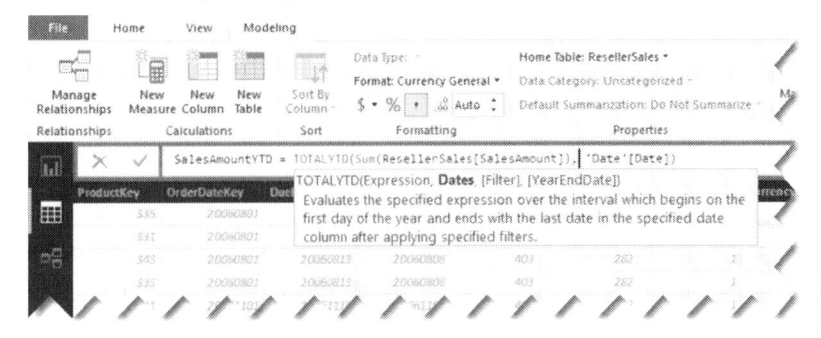

Figure 1.25 Business calculations are implemented in DAX.

Get insights

Once the model is created, the analyst can visualize and explore the data with interactive reports. If you come from using Excel Power Pivot and would like to give Power BI Desktop a try, you'll find that not only does it simplify the design experience, but it also supports new visualizations, including Funnel and Combo Charts, Treemap, Filled Map, and Gauge visualizations, as shown in **Figure 1.26**. And when the Microsoft-provided visualizations aren't enough, Martin can use a custom visual contributed by Microsoft and the Power BI community. To do this, Martin uses the Power BI Desktop "Import from store" feature to navigate to the Microsoft Store (https://appsource.microsoft.com). Then Martin picks a visual and start visualizing data in awesome ways!

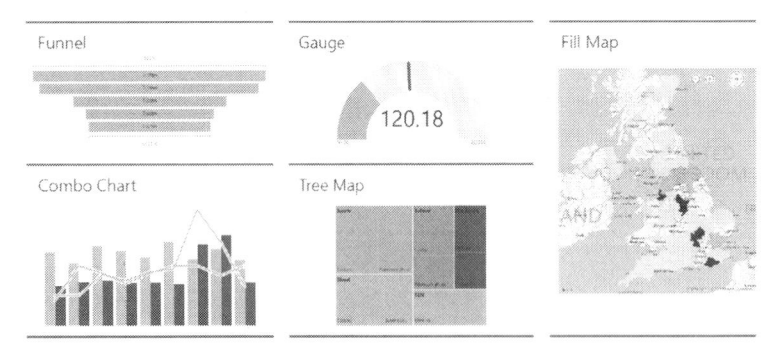

Figure 1.26 Power BI Desktop adds new visualizations.

Once Martin is done with the report in Power BI Desktop, he can publish the model and reports to Power BI, so that he can share insights with other users. If they have permissions, his coworkers can view reports, gain more insights with natural query (Q&A) questions, and create dashboards. Martin can also schedule a data refresh to keep the imported data up to date.

1.4.3 Power BI for Pros

BI pros and IT pros have much to gain from Power BI. BI pros are typically tasked to create the backend infrastructure required to support organizational BI initiatives, such as data marts, data warehouses, cubes, ETL packages, operational reports, and dashboards. IT pros are also concerned with setting up and maintaining the necessary environment that facilitates self-service and organizational BI, such as providing access to data, managing security, data governance, and other services.

In a department or smaller organization, a single person typically fulfills both BI and IT pro tasks. For example, Elena has developed an Analysis Services model on top of the corporate data warehouse. She needs to ensure that business users can gain insights from the model without compromising security.

Enable team BI
Once she provided connectivity to the on-premises model, Elena must establish a trustworthy environment needed to facilitate content sharing and collaboration. To do so, she can use Power BI workspaces. As a first step, Elena would set up groups and add members to these groups. Then Elena can create workspaces for the organizational units interested in analyzing the SSAS model. For example, if the Sales department needs access to the organizational model, Elena can set up a Sales Department group. Next, she can create a Sales Department workspace and grant the group access to it. Finally, she can deploy to the workspace her sales-related dashboards and reports that connect to the model.

If Elena needs to distribute BI artifacts to a wider audience, such as the entire organization, she can create an app and publish it. Then her coworkers can search, discover, and use the app read-only.

Scale report workloads
No one likes to wait for a report to finish. If Elena works for a larger organization, she can scale report workloads by purchasing a Power BI Premium plan. She then decides which workspaces can benefit from a dedicated capacity and promote them to premium workspaces. Not only Power BI Premium delivers consistent performance but also it allows the organization to save on the Power BI licensing cost. Elena can now share out content in premium workspaces to "viewers" by sharing specific dashboards or distributing contents with apps.

Implementing BI solutions
Based on my experience, most organizations could benefit from what I refer to as a classic BI architecture that includes a data warehouse and semantic model (Analysis Services Multidimensional or Tabular mode) layered on top of the data warehouse. I'll discuss the benefits of this architecture in Part 3 of this book. If you already have or are planning such a solution, you can use Power BI as a presentation layer. This works because Power BI can connect to the on-premises Analysis Services, as shown in **Figure 1.27**.

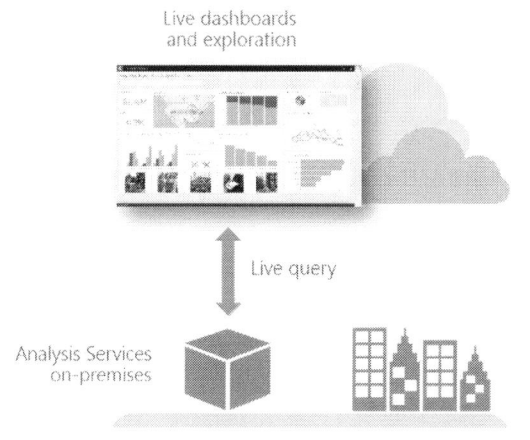

Figure 1.27 Power BI can directly connect to on-premises databases, such as Analysis Services semantic models.

So that Power BI can connect to on-premises SSAS models, Elena needs to download and install a component called a gateway to an on-premises computer that can connect to the semantic model. The gateway allows Elena to centralize management and access to on-premises data sources. Then Elena can implement reports and dashboards that connect live to Analysis Services and deploy them to Power BI. When users open a report, the report will generate a query and send it to the on-premises model via the gateway. Now you have a hybrid solution where data stays on premises but reports are hosted in Power BI.

If you're concerned about the performance of this architecture, you should know that Power BI only sends queries to the on-premises data source so there isn't much overhead on the trip from Power BI to the source. Typically, BI reports and dashboards summarize data. Therefore, the size of the datasets that travel back to Power BI probably won't be very large either. Of course, the speed of the connection between Power BI and the data center where the model resides will affect the duration of the round trip.

Another increasingly popular scenario that Power BI can help you implement is real-time BI. You've probably heard about Internet of Things (IoT) which refers to an environment of many connected devices, such as barcode readers, sensors, or cell phones, that transfer data over a network without requiring human-to-human or human-to-computer interaction. If your organization is looking for a real-time platform, you should seriously consider Power BI. Its streamed datasets allow an application to stream directly to Power BI with a few lines of code. If you need to implement Complex Event Processing (CEP) solutions, Microsoft Azure Stream Analytics lets you monitor event streams in real time and push results to a Power BI dashboard.

Finally, BI pros can implement predictive data analytics solutions that integrate with Power BI. For example, Elena can use the Azure Machine Learning Service to implement a data mining model that predicts the customer probability to purchase a product. Then she can easily set up a REST API web service, which Power BI can integrate with to display results. If all these BI pro features sound interesting, I'll walk you through these scenarios in detail in Part 3 of this book.

1.4.4 Power BI for Developers

Power BI has plenty to offer to developers as well because it's built on an open and extensible architecture. In the context of data analytics, developers are primarily interested in incorporating BI features in their applications or in providing access to data to support integration scenarios. For example, Teo is a developer with Adventure Works. Teo might be interested in embedding Power BI dashboards and reports in a web application that will be used by external customers. Power BI supports several extensibility options, including apps, real-time dashboards, custom visuals, and embedded reporting.

Automate management tasks
Power BI has a set of REST APIs to allow developers to programmatically manage certain Power BI resources, such as enumerating datasets, creating new datasets, and adding and removing rows to a dataset table. This allows developers to push data to Power BI, such as to create real-time dashboards. In fact, this is how Azure Stream Analytics integrates with Power BI. When new data is streamed, Azure Stream Analytics pushes the data to Power BI to update real-time dashboards.

The process for creating such applications is straightforward. First, you need to register your app. Then you write OAuth2 security code to authenticate your application with Power BI. Then you'd write code to manipulate the Power BI objects using REST APIs. For example, here's a sample method invocation for adding one row to a table:

```
POST https://api.powerbi.com/beta/myorg/datasets/2C0CCF12-A369-4985-A643-0995C249D5B9/Tables/Product/Rows HTTP/1.1
Authorization: Bearer {AAD Token}
Content-Type: application/json
{    "rows":
    [{
        "ProductID":1,
        "Name":"Adjustable Race",
        "Category":"Components",
        "IsCompete":true,
        "ManufacturedOn":"07/30/2014"}
    ]}
```

Microsoft supports a Power BI Developer Center website (https://powerbi.microsoft.com/developers) where you can read the REST API documentation and try the REST APIs.

Embed reports in custom applications
Many of you would like to embed beautiful Power BI dashboards and reports in custom applications. For example, your company might have a web portal to allow external customers to log in and access reports and dashboards. Up until Power BI, Microsoft hasn't had a good solution to support this scenario.

For internal applications where users are already using Power BI, developers can call the Power BI REST APIs to embed dashboard tiles and reports. As I mentioned, external applications can benefit from Power BI Embedded. And, because embedded reports preserve interactive features, users can enjoy the same engaging experience, including report filtering, interactive sorting, and highlighting. I cover these integration scenarios in Chapter 16.

Implement custom visuals
Microsoft has published the required interfaces to allow developers to implement and publish custom visuals using any of the JavaScript-based visualization frameworks, such as D3.js, WebGL, Canvas, or SVG. Do you need visualizations that Power BI doesn't support to display data more effectively? With some coding wizardry, you can implement your own! You can use whatever tool you prefer to code the custom visual (visuals are coded in TypeScript), such as Microsoft Visual Code or Visual Studio. When the custom visual is ready, you can publish it to Microsoft AppSource at https://appsource.microsoft.com where Power BI users can search for it and download it.

Power BI is an extensible platform and there are other options for building Power BI solutions outside the scope this book, including:

- Integrate Power BI with Microsoft Flow and PowerApps – For example, in Chapter 10, I'll show you how you can integrate Power BI with PowerApps to change the data behind a report.
- Implement custom data connectors – You can extend the Power BI data capabilities by implementing custom data connectors in M language (the programming language of Power Query). To learn more, see the M Extensions GitHub repo at https://github.com/Microsoft/DataConnectors/blob/master/docs/m-extensions.md.
- Implement service apps – I've already discussed how Power BI online services apps can help you connect to popular online services, such as Dynamics CRM or Google Analytics. You can implement new apps to facilitate access to data and to provide prepackaged content. You can contact Microsoft and sign up for the Microsoft partner program which coordinates this initiative.

1.5 Summary

This chapter has been a whirlwind tour of the innovative Power BI cloud data analytics service and its features. By now, you should view Power BI as a flexible platform that meets a variety of BI requirements. An important part of the Microsoft Data Platform, Power BI is a collective name of several products: Power BI, Power BI Desktop, Power BI Premium, Power BI Mobile, Power BI Embedded, and Power BI Report Server. You've learned about the major reasons that led to the release of Power BI. You've also taken a close look at the Power BI architecture and its components, as well as its editions and pricing model.

Next, this chapter discussed how Power BI can help different types of users with their data analytics needs. It allows business users to connect to their data and gain quick insights. It empowers data analysts to create sophisticated data models. It enables IT and BI pros to implement hybrid solutions that span on-premises data models and reports deployed to the cloud. Finally, its extensible and open architecture lets developers enhance the Power BI data capabilities and integrate Power BI with custom applications.

Having laid the foundation of Power BI, you're ready to continue the journey. Next, you'll witness the value that Power BI can deliver to business users.

PART I

Power BI for Business Users

If you're new to Power BI, welcome! This part of the book provides the essential fundamentals to help you get started with Power BI. It specifically targets business users: people who use Excel as part of their job, such as information workers, executives, financial managers, business managers, people man-agers, HR managers, and marketing managers. But it'll also benefit anyone new to Power BI. Remember from Chapter 1 that Power BI consists of six products. This part of the book teaches business users how to use two of them: Power BI Service and Power BI Mobile.

First, you'll learn how to sign up and navigate the Power BI portal. You'll also learn how to use service apps to get immediate insights from popular online services. Because business users are often tasked to analyze simple datasets, this chapter will teach you how to import data from files without explicit data modelling.

Next, you'll learn how to use Power BI Service to create reports and dashboards and uncover valuable insights from your data. As you'll soon see, Power BI doesn't assume you have any query knowledge or reporting skills. With a few clicks, you'll be able to create ad hoc interactive reports! Then you'll create dashboards from existing visualizations or by asking natural questions.

If you frequently find yourself on the go, I'll show you how you can use Power BI Mobile to access your reports and dashboards on the go if you have Internet connectivity. Besides mobile rendering, Power BI Mobile offers interesting features to help you stay on top of your business, including data alerts, favorites, and annotations.

As with the rest of the book, step-by-step instructions will guide you through the tour. Most features that I'll show you in this part of the book are available in the free edition of Power BI, so you can start practicing immediately. The features that require Power BI Pro will be explicitly stated.

Chapter 2

The Power BI Service

2.1 Choosing a Business Intelligence Strategy 39
2.2 Getting Started with Power BI Service 43
2.3 Understanding Power BI Content Items 50
2.4 Connecting to Data 57
2.5 Summary 62

In the previous chapter, I explained that Power BI aims to democratize data analytics and make it available to any user…BI for the masses! As a business user, you can use Power BI to get instant insights from your data irrespective if it's located on premises or in the cloud. Although no clear boundaries exist, I define a business user as someone who would be mostly interested in consuming BI artifacts, such as reports and dashboards. However, when requirements call for it, business users could also produce content, such as to visualize data stored in Excel or text files. Moreover, their basic data analytics requirements can be met without explicit modeling.

This chapter lays out the foundation of self-service data analytics with Power BI. First, I'll help you understand when self-service BI is a good choice. Then I'll get you started with Power BI by showing you how to sign up and navigate the Power BI portal. Next, I'll show you how to use service apps to connect to a cloud service and quickly gain insights from prepackaged reports and dashboards. If you find yourself frequently analyzing data in Excel files, I'll teach you how to do so without any data modeling.

2.1 Choosing a Business Intelligence Strategy

Remember that self-service BI enables business users (information workers, like business managers or marketing managers, and power users) to offload effort from IT pros so they don't stay in line waiting for someone to enable BI for them. And, team BI allows the same users to share their reports with other team members without requiring them to install modeling or reporting tools. Before we go deeper in personal and team BI, let's take a moment to compare it with organizational BI. This will help you view self-service BI not as a competing technology but as a completing technology to organizational BI. In other words, self-service BI and organizational BI are both necessary for most businesses, and they complement each other.

2.1.1 When to Choose Organizational BI

Organizational BI defines a set of technologies and processes for implementing an end-to-end BI solution where the implementation effort is shifted to IT professionals (as opposed to information workers and people who use Power BI Desktop or Excel as part of their job).

Classic organizational BI architecture
The main objective of organizational BI is to provide accurate and trusted analysis and reporting. **Figure 2.1** shows a classic organizational BI solution.

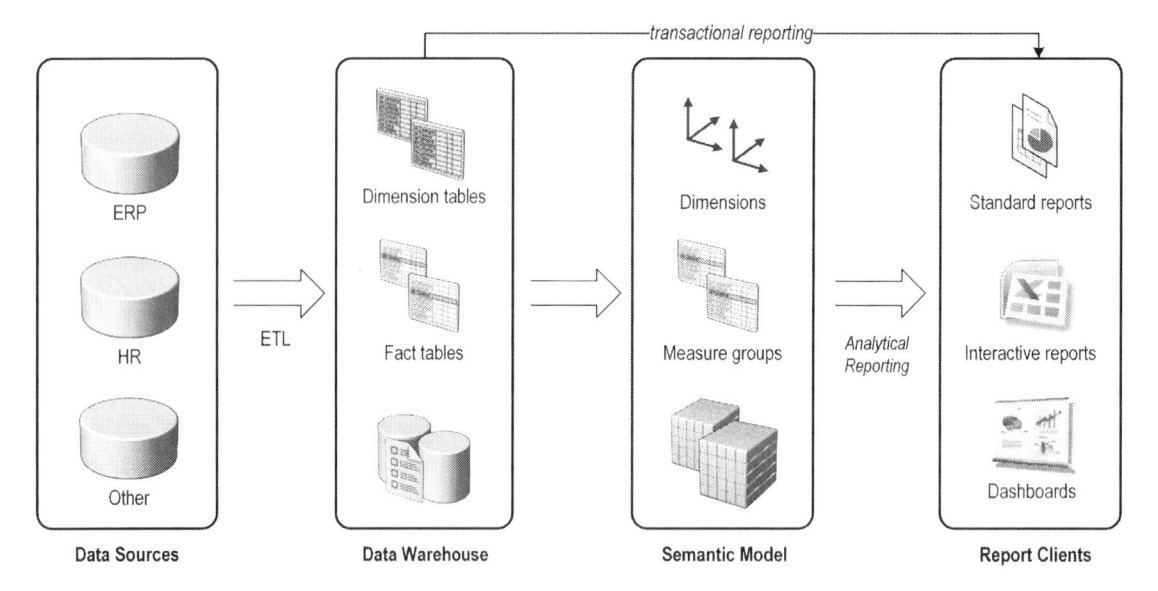

Figure 2.1 Organizational BI typically includes ETL processes, data warehousing, and a semantic layer.

In a typical corporate environment, data is scattered in a variety of data sources, and consolidating it presents a major challenge. Extraction, transformation, and loading (ETL) processes extract data from the original data sources, clean it, and then load the trusted data in a data warehouse or data mart. The data warehouse organizes data in a set of dimensions and fact tables. When designing the data warehouse, BI pros strive to reduce the number of tables to make the schema more intuitive and facilitate reporting processes. For example, an operational database might be highly normalized and have Product, Subcategory, and Category tables. However, when designing a data warehouse, the modeler might decide to have a single Product table that includes columns from the Subcategory and Category tables. So instead of three tables, the data warehouse now has only one table, and end users don't need to join multiple tables.

While end users could run transactional reports directly from the data warehouse, many organizations also implement a semantic model in the form of one or more Analysis Services Multidimensional cubes or Tabular models for analytical reporting. As an information worker, you can use Power BI Desktop, Excel, or another tool to connect to the semantic model and author your own reports so that you don't have to wait for IT to create them for you. And IT pros can create a set of standard operational reports and dashboards from the semantic model.

NOTE Everyone is talking about self-service BI, and there are hundreds of vendors out there offering tools to enable business users to take BI into their own hands. However, my experience shows that the best self-service BI is empowering users to analyze data from trusted semantic models sanctioned and owned by IT. If the architecture shown in **Figure 2.1** is in place, a business user can focus on the primary task, which is analyzing data, without being preoccupied with the data logistics (importing data, shaping data, modeling data). This will require more upfront effort, but the investment will pay for itself in time.

Understanding organizational BI challenges
Although it's well-defined and established, when implementing organizational BI, your company might face a few challenges, including the following:
- Upfront planning and implementation effort – Depending on the data integration effort required, implementing an organizational BI solution might not be a simple task. Business users and IT pros must work together to derive requirements. Most of the implementation effort goes into data logistics processes to clean, verify, and load data. For example, Elena from the IT department is

tasked to implement an organizational BI solution. First, she needs to meet with business users to obtain the necessary business knowledge and gather requirements (business requirements might be hard to come by). Then she must identify where the data resides and how to extract, clean, and transform the data. Next, Elena must implement ETL processes, models, and reports. Quality Assurance must test the solution. And IT pros must configure the hardware and software, as well as deploy and maintain the solution. Security and large data volumes bring additional challenges.

- Highly specialized skillset – Organizational BI requires specialized talent, such as someone experienced in ETL, Analysis Services, and data warehousing. System engineers and developers must work together to plan the security, which sometimes might be more complicated than the actual BI solution.

- Less flexibility – Organization BI might not be flexible enough to react quickly to new or changing business requirements. For example, Maya from the Marketing department might be tasked to analyze CRM data that isn't in the data warehouse. Maya might need to wait for a few months before the data is imported and validated.

The good news is that self-service BI can complement organizational BI quite well to address these challenges. Given the above example, while waiting for the pros to enhance the organization BI solution, Maya can use Power BI to analyze CRM data or Excel files. She already has the domain knowledge. Moreover, she doesn't need to know modeling concepts. At the beginning, she might need some guidance from IT, such as how to get access to the data and understand how the data is stored. She also needs to take *responsibility* that her analysis is correct and can be trusted. But isn't self-service BI better than waiting?

> **REAL WORLD** Influenced by the propaganda by vendors and consultants, my experience shows that many organizations get overly excited about the perceived quick gains with self-service BI. Everyone wants a shortcut! Unfortunately, many underestimate the data complexity and integration. After pushing the tool to its limits for some time, they realize the challenges related to data quality and the extent of the transformation required before the data is ready for analysis. Although I mentioned that upfront planning and implementation is a negative for organizational BI, it's often a must and it needs to be done by a pro with a professional toolset. If your data doesn't require much transformation and it doesn't exceed a few million rows (if you decide to import the data), then go ahead with self-service BI. However, if you need to integrate data from multiple source systems, then a self-service BI would probably be a stretch. Don't say I didn't warn you!

2.1.2 When to Choose Self-service BI

Self-service BI empowers business users to take analytics into their own hands with guidance from their IT department. For companies that don't have organizational BI or can't afford it, self-service BI presents an opportunity for building customized ad hoc solutions to gain data insights outside the capabilities of organizational BI solutions and line-of-business applications. On the other hand, organizations that have invested in organizational BI might find that self-service BI opens additional options for valuable data exploration and analysis.

> **REAL WORLD** I led a self-service BI training class for a large company that has invested heavily in organizational BI. They had a data warehouse and OLAP cubes. Only a subset of data in the data warehouse was loaded in the cubes. Their business analysts were looking for a tool that would let them join and analyze data from the cubes and data warehouse. In another case, an educational institution had to analyze expense report data that wasn't stored in a data warehouse. Such scenarios can benefit greatly from self-service BI.

Self-service BI benefits
When done right, self-service BI offers important benefits. First, it makes BI pervasive and accessible to practically everyone! Anyone can gain insights if they have access to and understand the data. Users can import data from virtually any data source, ranging from flat files to cloud applications. Then they can

mash it up and gain insights. Once data is imported, the users can build their own reports. For example, Maya understands Excel, but she doesn't know SQL or relational databases. Fortunately, Power BI doesn't require any technical skills. Maya could import her Excel file and build instant reports.

Besides democratizing BI, the agility of self-service BI can complement organizational BI well, such as to promote ideation and divergent thinking. For example, as a BI analyst, Martin might want to test a hypothesis that customer feedback on social media, such as Facebook and Twitter, affects the company's bottom line. Even though such data isn't collected and stored in the data warehouse, Martin can import data from social media sites, relate it to the sales data in the data warehouse and validate his idea.

Finally, analysts can use self-service BI tools, such as Power BI Desktop and Power Pivot, to create prototypes of the data models they envision. This can help BI pros to understand their requirements.

Self-service BI cautions
Self-service BI isn't new. After all, business users have been using tools like Microsoft Excel and Microsoft Access for isolated data analysis for quite a while (Excel has been around since 1985 and Access since 1992). Here are some considerations you should keep in mind about self-service BI:

- What kind of user are you? – Are you a data analyst (power user) who has the time, desire, and patience to learn a new technology? If you consider yourself a data analyst, then you should be able to accomplish a lot by creating data models with Power BI Desktop and Excel Power Pivot. If you're new to BI or you lack data analyst skills, then you can still gain a lot from Power BI, and this part of the book shows you how.
- Data access – How will you access data? What subset of data do you need? Data quality issues can quickly turn away any user, so you must work with your IT to get started. A role of IT is to ensure access to clean and trusted data. Analysts can use Power BI Desktop or Excel Power Query for simple data transformations and corrections, but these aren't meant as ETL tools.
- IT involvement – Self-service BI might be good, but managed self-service BI (self-service BI under the supervision of IT pros) is even better and sometimes a must. Therefore, the IT group must budget time and resources to help end users when needed, such as to give users access to data, to help with data integrity and more complex business calculations, and to troubleshoot issues when things go wrong. They also must monitor the utilization of the self-service rollout.
- With great power comes great responsibility – If you make wrong conclusions, damage can be easily contained. But if your entire department or even organization uses wrong reports, you have a serious problem! You must take the responsibility and time to verify that your model and calculations can be trusted. Data governance supervised by IT is important. For example, IT can set up a governance committee that meets on a regular basis to review new self-data models and reports, and "certify" them for wider distribution.
- "Spreadmarts" – I left the most important consideration for the CIO for last. If your IT department has spent a lot of effort to avoid decentralized and isolated analysis, should you allow the corporate data to be constantly copied and duplicated?

TIP Although every organization is different, I recommend an 80/20 split between organizational BI and self-service BI. This means that 80% of the effort and budget should be spent in organizational BI, such as a data warehouse, improving data quality, centralized semantic models, trusted reports, dashboards, Big Data initiatives, master data management, and so on. The remaining 20% would be focused on agile and managed self-service BI.

Now that you understand how organizational BI and self-service BI compares and completes each other, let's dive into the Power BI self-service BI capabilities which benefit business users like you.

2.2 Getting Started with Power BI Service

In Chapter 1, I introduced you to Power BI and its products. Recall that the main component of Power BI is its cloud-hosted Power BI Service (powerbi.com) that enables team BI by letting you share your data and reports with your coworkers. If you're a novice user, this section lays out the necessary startup steps, including signing up for Power BI and understanding its web interface. As you'll soon find out, because Power BI was designed with business users and data analytics in mind, it won't take long to learn it!

2.2.1 Signing Up for Power BI

The Power BI motto is, "5 seconds to sign up, 5 minutes to wow!" Because Power BI is a cloud-based offering, there's nothing for you to install and set up. But if you haven't signed up for Power BI yet, let's put this promise to the test. But first, read the following steps.

> **NOTE** A possible danger awaits the first user who signs up from a company with multiple locations. Power BI will ask you about your location to determine the data center where the Power BI will store data. The issue is that currently is not possible to change that data center unless you ask Power BI Support to remove all Power BI content and start over again. Power BI Premium could mitigate this issue because it lets IT create capacities in different data centers but not Power BI Pro. If you don't want your data and reports to travel across states and event continents (not to mention data privacy regulations), you must involve IT to choose the right location.

Five seconds to sign up
Follow these steps to sign up for the Power BI Service:

1. Open your browser, navigate to http://powerbi.com, and then click "Sign up free" button in the top right corner or "Start Free" button (see **Figure 2.2**).

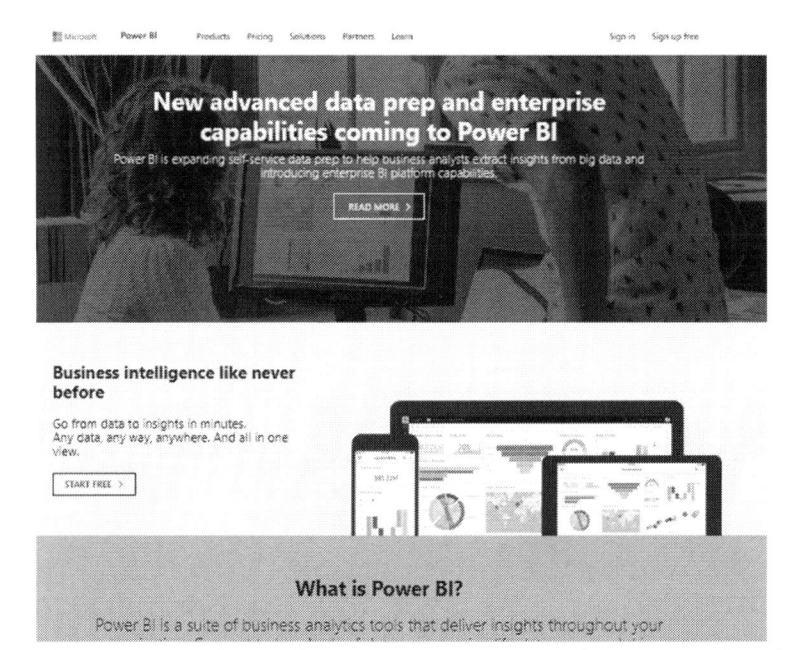

Figure 2.2 This is the landing Power BI web page.

2. The next page asks you how you want to start with Power BI: download Power BI Desktop so that you can start your BI journey on the desktop or sign up for Power BI so that you can use the Power BI Service. I'll

discuss Power BI Desktop in Part 2 of this book so let's ignore this option for now. Click the "Try free" button to sign up for Power BI Service.

3. In the Get Started page, enter your work email address. Notice that the email address must be your work email. At this time, you can't use a common email, such as @hotmail.com, @outlook.com, or @gmail.com. This might be an issue if you plan to use Power BI for your personal use. As a workaround, consider registering a domain, such as a domain for your family (some Internet providers give away free domains).

> **NOTE** The reason why personal email addresses are not allowed for signing up to Power BI is because of the General Data Protection Regulation (GDPR), which imposes a set of regulations on data protection and privacy for individuals.

4. If your organization already uses Office 365, Power BI will detect this and ask you to sign in using your Office 365 account. If you don't use Office 365, Power BI will ask you to confirm the email you entered and then to check your inbox for a confirmation email.

5. Once you receive your email conformation with the subject "Time to complete Microsoft Power BI signup", click the "Complete Microsoft Power BI Signup" link in the email. Clicking on the link will take you to a page to create your account (see **Figure 2.3**).

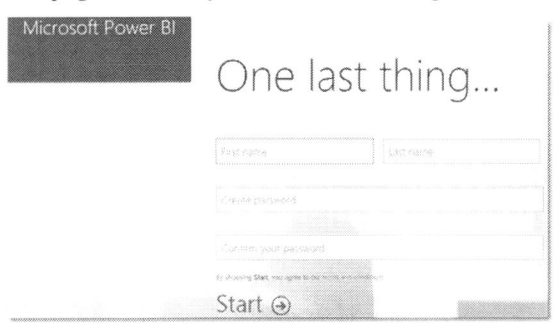

Figure 2.3 Use this page to create a Power BI account to gain access to Power BI Service.

6. You need to provide a name and a password, and then click Start.

This completes the process which Microsoft refers to as the "Information Worker (IW) Sign Up" flow. As I said, this signup flow is geared for an organization that doesn't have an Office 365 tenant.

The main page
After you complete the signup process, the next time you go to powerbi.com, click the Sign In button in the top-right corner of the main page (see **Figure 2.2** again). The main page includes the following menus:

- Products – Provides submenus to learn about each Power BI product.
- Pricing – Explains the Power BI licensing options. Recall that Power BI Service has Power BI Free, Power BI Pro, and Power BI Premium pricing levels.
- Solutions – Explains how Power BI addresses various data analytics needs.
- Partners – Includes links to the Partner Showcase (where Microsoft partners, such as Prologika, demonstrate their Power BI-based solutions) and to pages to find a partner to help you if you need training or implementation assistance.
- Learn – Includes links to the product documentation, the community forums where you can ask questions, a page to provide feedback to Microsoft, and Power BI blog (I recommend you subscribe to it).

What happens during signup?
You might be curious why you're asked to provide a password given that you sign up with your work email. Behind the scenes, Power BI stores the user credentials in Azure Active Directory (Azure AD). If

your organization doesn't have an Office 365 subscription, the Information Worker flow creates a tenant for the domain you used to sign up. For example, if I sign up as teo@prologika.com and my company doesn't have an Office 365 subscription, a prologika.onmicrosoft.com tenant will be created in Azure AD and that tenant won't be managed by anyone at my company. If the domain in the email address matches the tenant, Power BI will add your coworkers to the same tenant when they sign up.

> **NOTE** What is a Power BI tenant? A tenant is a dedicated instance of the Azure Active Directory that an organization receives and owns when it signs up for a Microsoft cloud service such as Azure, Microsoft Intune, Power BI, or Office 365. A tenant houses the users in a company and the information about them - their passwords, user profile data, permissions, and so on. It also contains groups, applications, and other information pertaining to an organization and its security. For more information about tenants, see "What is an Azure AD tenant" at http://bit.ly/1FTFObb.

If your organization decides one day to have better integration with Microsoft Azure, such as to have a single sign-on (SSO), it can synchronize or federate the corporate Active Directory with Azure, but this isn't required. To unify the corporate and cloud directories, the company IT administrator can then take over the unmanaged tenant. I provide more details about managing the Power BI tenant in Chapter 12, but for now remember that you won't be able to upgrade to Power BI Pro if your tenant is unmanaged.

2.2.2 Understanding the Power BI Portal

I hope it took you five seconds or less to sign up with Power BI. (Or at least hopefully it feels quick.) After completing these signup steps, you'll have access to the free edition of Power BI. Let's take a moment to get familiar with the Power BI portal where you'll spend most of your time when analyzing data.

> **NOTE** Currently, the Power BI portal isn't customizable. For example, you can't rearrange or remove menus, and you can't brand the portal. If these features are important to your organization, your IT department has options. One of them is to use Power BI Embedded to embed Power BI Reports in a custom web portal. Another is to sign up for SharePoint Online and then embed Power BI dashboards and reports inside SharePoint. SharePoint supports a comprehensive set of branding and UI customization features, and you can embed Power BI content on SharePoint pages.

Welcome to Power BI page
Upon signup, Power BI discovers that you don't have any BI artifacts yet. Therefore, it navigates you to the "Welcome to Power BI" page, which is shown in **Figure 2.4**.

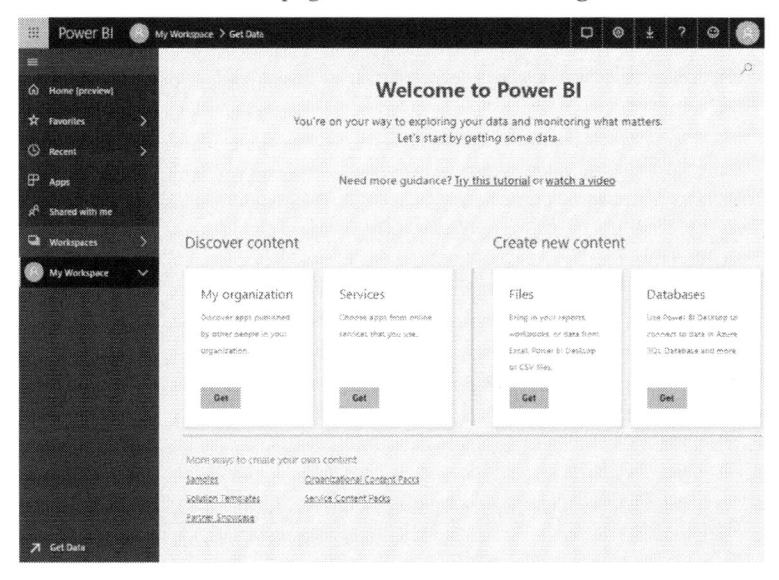

Figure 2.4 The "Welcome to Power BI" page allows you to connect to data and install samples.

Before analyzing data, you need to first connect to wherever it resides. Therefore, the "Welcome to Power BI" page prompts you to start your data journey by connecting to your data. The My Organization tile under the "Discover content" section allows you to browse and use organizational apps (discussed in Chapter 12), if someone within your organization has already published BI content as apps. The Services tile allows you to use Microsoft-provided service apps to connect to popular online services, such as Google Analytics, Salesforce, Microsoft Dynamics CRM, and many more.

The Files tile under the "Create new content" section lets you import data from Excel, Power BI Desktop, and CSV files. And the Databases tile allows you to connect to four popular data sources that support live connections: Azure SQL Database, Azure SQL Data Warehouse, SQL Server Analysis Services and Spark on Azure HDInsight.

NOTE As you'll quickly discover, a popular option that's missing in the Databases tile is connecting to an on-premises database, such as SQL Server or Oracle. Currently, this scenario requires you create a data model using Power BI Desktop or Excel before you can import data from on-premises databases. Power BI Desktop also supports connecting directly to some data sources, such as SQL Server. Then you can upload the model to Power BI. Because it's a more advanced scenario, I'll postpone discussing Power BI Desktop until Chapter 6.

1. To get some content you can explore in Power BI and quickly get an idea about its reporting capabilities, click the Samples link.
2. In the Samples page, click the "Retail Analysis Sample" tile. As the popup informs you, the Retail Analysis Sample is a sample dashboard provided by Microsoft to demonstrate some of the Power BI capabilities. Click the Connect button. Are you concerned that samples might clutter the portal? Don't worry; it's easy to delete the sample later. To do this, you can just delete the Retail Analysis Sample dataset which will delete the dependent reports.

The Power BI portal

After installing the Retail Analysis Sample, Power BI navigates you to the "Retail Analysis Sample" dashboard and shows a popup that your dataset is ready. Dismiss the popup. Let's explore the portal. It has the following main sections (see the numbered areas in **Figure 2.5**):

Figure 2.5 The Power BI portal home page

46 CHAPTER 2

Marked with the number 1 is the Navigation Pane, which organizes the content deployed to Power BI. You can show/hide the navigation pane by toggling the "Hide the navigation pane" button (the three stacked lines).

Power BI Home

Currently in preview, the Home menu navigates to the Power BI Home page. Unless you mark a dashboard as featured by clicking the "Set as featured" menu, Power BI Home is your default landing page every time you sign in to Power BI. Like a typical web app, Power BI Home is meant to help find relevant content. It has the following features:

- Global search – You can search for content by typing a keyword. For example, typing "sales" will find all workspaces, reports and dashboards that you have access to and that have this word in their names.
- Key metrics – If you have marked dashboards as favorites, you'll see the first six visuals from each of the first two favorite dashboards. Clicking the metric navigates you the dashboard. Currently, Power BI selects the metrics and you can't overwrite this behavior or choose specific metrics.
- Favorites – This section shows tiles for each favorite dashboard.
- Recents – This section tracks the most recent content you visited
- Shared with me – This section shows tiles for reports, dashboards, and organizational apps that someone has shared with you.
- Learn how to use Power BI – Lastly, at the bottom, there is a special section with shortcuts to learning resources to jumpstart your Power BI journey.

Favorites and Recent menus

Moving down the navigation pane, the next two menus are Favorites and Recent. While you can have one featured dashboard, you can have several favorite dashboards and reports that you can access from the Favorites menu. And the Recent link shows a list of the last 20 reports and dashboards that you've visited recently.

Apps and "Shared with me" menus

Recall from Chapter 1 that apps are for consuming prepackaged content from online services or from Power BI workspaces. You can click the Apps button to see what service or organizational apps you have accessed to. If someone has shared specific dashboards and reports with you, they can be accessed from the "Shared with me" menu.

Workspaces

In Power BI, workspaces can be used to organize and secure content. For example, a Sales workspace can let members of the Sales department create and collaborate on BI content. If you have Power BI Pro subscription, you can access all workspaces you are a member of by clicking the Workspaces menu. Think of My Workspace as your private desk. By default, all BI content you publish to Power BI is deployed to My Workspace. Unless you share content with other users, no one else can see what's in your workspace.

To see the actual published content in a workspace (My Workspace or another workspace you are a member of), simply click on the workspace name or expand it. For example, to see what's inside My Workspace, expand the down arrow next to it or click My Workspace in the navigation pane. If you expand the workspace, you'll see sections for Dashboards, Reports, Workbooks, Datasets and Dataflows (Power BI Pro only) in the navigation pane.

Workspace content page

If you click the workspace, you'll be navigated to another page where the workspace content is organized in several tabs, as shown in **Figure 2.6**. As your workspace gets busier, you'd probably favor the tabbed interface because it allows you to search for items by name.

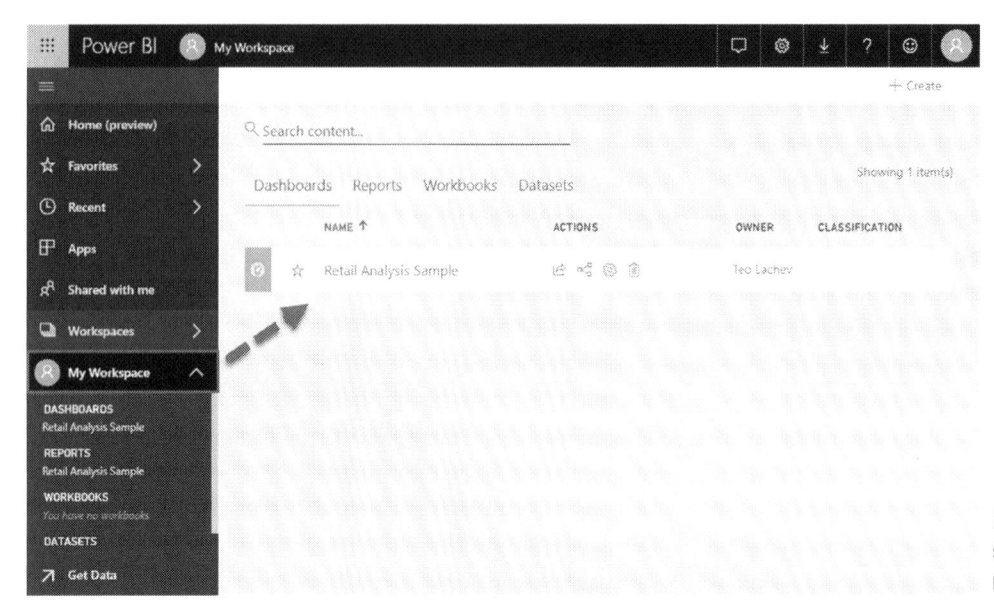

Figure 2.6 The workspace content is organized in several tabs.

The Dashboards tab includes the dashboards that you've developed or that someone shared with you. Similarly, the Reports section contains all reports that are available to you. The Workbooks session brings you to Excel files that you've connected to (yes, Power BI allows you to bring in existing Excel reports). The Datasets section shows all the datasets that you've created or that someone shared with you. Lastly, the Dataflows tab (Power BI Pro only) lists dataflows defined in this workspace (recall from Chapter 1 that you can see dataflows for data staging and preparation).

If you have a lot of items and you still find it difficult to locate something, use the "Search content" field to search within the content in the corresponding tab. Besides simply clicking the item to open it, you can perform additional tasks from the Actions column, such as to share a dashboard, delete a dashboard, and access the dashboard settings.

Get Data
Going down the navigation pane, the Get Data button at the bottom brings you to the Get Data page. Like the "Welcome to Power BI" page, the Get Data page allows you to connect to your cloud and on-premises data.

2.2.3 Understanding Application Menus

Glancing back at **Figure 2.5**, there are additional menus that are worth exploring.

Navigation menus
Starting from the top left, you have the following navigation menus (denoted with numbers 2, 3, and 4):
1. Office 365 application launcher – If you have an Office 365 subscription, this menu allows you to access the Office 365 applications you are licensed to use. Doesn't Microsoft encourage you to use Office 365?
2. Power BI – No matter where you are in the portal, this menu takes you to Power BI Home or your featured dashboard.
3. Navigation breadcrumb – Displays the navigation path to the displayed content.

Application Toolbar

On the top right and denoted with the number 5 on **Figure 2.5**, is the application toolbar. Let's explain the available menus starting from the left:

- Enter Full Screen Mode menu (available for dashboards and reports) – Shows the active content in full screen and removes the Power BI UI (also called "chrome"). Once you're in Full Screen mode, you have options to resize the content to fit to screen and to exit this mode (or press Esc). Another way to open a dashboard in a full screen mode is to append the chromeless=1 parameter to the dashboard URL, such as:

https://app.powerbi.com/groups/me/dashboards/3065afc5-63a5-4cab-bcd3-0160b3c5f741?chromeless=1

- Notifications menu – Power BI publishes important events, such as when someone shares a dashboard with you or when you get a data alert, to the Power BI Notification Center.
- Settings menu – This menu expands to several submenus. Click "Manage Personal Storage" to check how much storage space you've used (recall that the Power BI Free and Power BI Pro editions have different storage limits) or to start a Power BI Pro 60-day trial. Previously, content packs were used to distribute content to a wider audience, but they are now superseded by apps (more details in Chapter 12). If you have Power BI Pro, the "Create content pack" submenu allows you to create an organizational content pack, while "View content pack" allows you to access published content packs. If you are a Power BI administrator, you can use the Admin Portal to monitor usage and manage tenant-wide settings, such as if users can publish content to web for anonymous access. The "Manage gateways" menu allows you to view and manage gateways that are set up to let Power BI access on-premises data. Use the Settings submenu to view and change some Power BI Service settings, such as if the Q&A box is available for a given dashboard, or to view your subscriptions. The "Manage embed codes" menu is to obtain the embedded iframe code for content you shared to the web.

TIP Not sure what Power BI edition you have? Click the Settings menu, and then click "Manage Personal Storage". At the top of the next page, notice the message next to your name. If it says "Free User", you have the Power BI free edition. If it says "Pro User", then you have Power BI Pro subscription.

- Download menu – This menu allows you to download useful Power BI components, including Power BI Desktop (for analysts wanting to create self-service data models), data gateways (to connect to on-premises data sources), Power BI for Mobile (a set of native Power BI apps for your mobile devices), Power BI publisher for Excel (an Excel add-in to connect to your Power BI data and to create and publish pivot reports), and Analyze in Excel updates (to download updates for the Power BI Analyze in Excel feature).
- Help and Support menu – Includes several links to useful resources, such as product documentation, the community site, and developer resources.
- Feedback menu – Rate your experience with Power BI on a scale from 1 to 10, submit an idea (new Power BI features are ranked based on the number of votes each idea gets), and submit an issue to community discussion lists.

Dashboard and report specific menus

Lastly, when you view a report or dashboard, you'll see another menu bar on top of the content. In **Figure 2.5**, I selected the Reseller Sales Sample dashboard and the following areas are available:

1. Natural question box (Q&A) – When you select a dashboard and the dashboard uses a dataset that supports natural queries, you can use this box (denoted with the number 6 in **Figure 2.5**) to enter the natural query. For example, you can ask it how many units were shipped in February last year.

2. Context menu (denoted with number 7) – It displays different options depending on the item selected. In the case of dashboard, it gives you access to dashboard-related tasks, such as to add a tile, type comments, view related content that the dashboard depends on, mark the dashboard a favorite, subscribe to the dashboard to get a snapshot via email periodically, share a dashboard with your coworkers, and switch between web and mobile views. And the ellipsis menu (…) lets you perform additional tasks, such as to print the dashboard or go to the dashboard settings.

2.3   Understanding Power BI Content Items

The key to understanding how Power BI works is to understand its three main content items: datasets, reports, and dashboards. These elements are interdependent, and you must understand how they relate to each other. For example, you can't have a report or dashboard without creating one or more datasets. **Figure 2.7** should help you understand these dependencies.

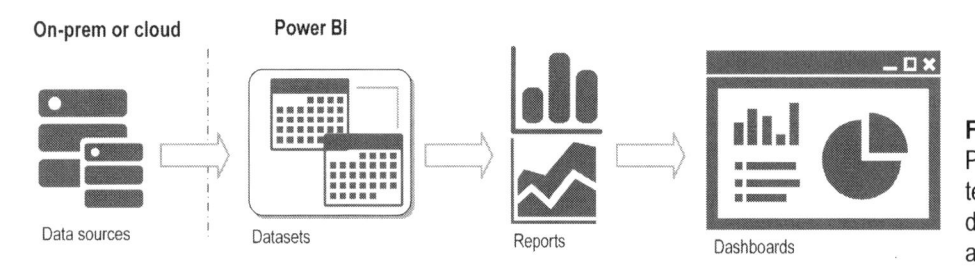

Figure 2.7 The Power BI main content items are datasets, reports, and dashboards.

2.3.1   Understanding Datasets

Think of a dataset as a blueprint or a definition of the data that you analyze. For example, if you want to analyze some data stored in an Excel spreadsheet, the corresponding dataset represents the data in the Excel spreadsheet. Or, if you import data from a database table, the dataset will represent that table. Notice that a dataset can have more than one table.

For example, if Martin uses Power BI Desktop or Excel to create a data model, the model might have multiple tables (potentially from different data sources). When Martin uploads the model to Power BI, his entire model will be shown as a single dataset, but when he explores it (he can click the Create Report icon next to the dataset under the Datasets tab to create a new report), he'll see that the Fields pane shows multiple tables. You'll encounter another case of a dataset with multiple tables when you connect to an Analysis Services semantic model.

Understanding cloud and on-prem data sources
Data sources with useful data for analysis are everywhere (see **Figure 2.8**). As far as the data source location goes, we can identify two main types of data sources:

- Cloud (SaaS) services – These data sources are hosted in the cloud and available as online services. Examples of Microsoft cloud data sources that Power BI supports include OneDrive, Dynamics CRM, Azure SQL Database, Azure SQL Data Warehouse, and Spark on Azure HDInsight. Power BI can also access many popular cloud data sources from other vendors, such as Salesforce, Google Analytics, Marketo, and many others (the list is growing every month!).
- On-premises data sources – This category encompasses all other data sources that are internal to your organization, such as databases, cubes, Excel, and other files. For Power BI to access on-premises data sources, it needs a special connectivity software called a *gateway*.

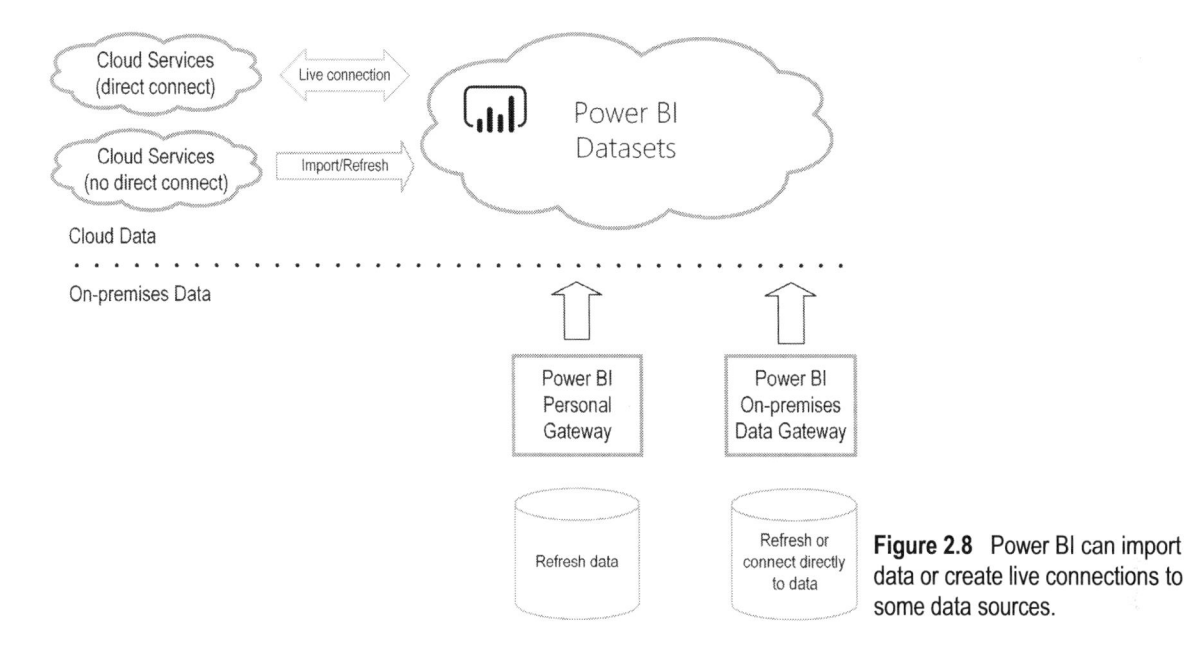

Figure 2.8 Power BI can import data or create live connections to some data sources.

> **DEFINITION** A Power BI gateway is connectivity software that is installed on premises to enable Power BI to access data in your corporate network. While Power BI can connect to online data sources, it can't tunnel directly into your corporate network unless it goes through a gateway.

Depending on the capabilities and location of the data source, data can be a) imported in a Power BI dataset or b) left in the original data source without importing it, but it can be accessed directly via a live connection. If the data source supports it, direct connectivity is appropriate when you have fast data sources. In this case, when you generate a report, Power BI creates a query using the syntax of the data source and sends the query directly to the data source. So, the Power BI dataset has only the definition of the data but not the actual data. Not all data sources support direct connections. Examples of cloud data sources that support direct connections include Azure SQL Database, Azure SQL Data Warehouse, Spark on Azure HDInsight, and Azure Analysis Services. And on-premises data sources that support direct queries include SQL Server, Analysis Services, SAP, Oracle, and Teradata. The list of directly accessible data sources is growing in time.

Because only a limited set of data sources supports direct connectivity, in most cases you'll be *importing* data irrespective of whether you access cloud and on-premises data sources. When you import data, the Power BI dataset has the definition of the data *and* the actual data. In Chapter 1, I showed you how when you import data, Microsoft deploys the dataset to scalable and highly-performant Azure backend services. Therefore, when you create reports from imported datasets, performance is good and predictable. But the moment the data is imported, it becomes outdated because changes in the original data source aren't synchronized with the Power BI datasets. Which brings me to the subject of refreshing data.

Refreshing data
Deriving insights from outdated data in imported datasets is rarely useful. Fortunately, Power BI supports automatic data refresh from many data sources. Refreshing data from cloud services is easy because most vendors already have connectivity APIs that allow Power BI to get to the data. In fact, chances are that if you use an app to access a cloud data source, it'll enable automatic data refresh by default. For example, the Google Analytics dataset refreshes by default every hour without any manual configuration.

TIP OneDrive and SharePoint Online are special locations for storing Excel, Power BI Desktop, and CSV files because Power BI automatically synchronizes changes to these files once every hour.

On-premises data sources are more problematic because Power BI needs to connect to your corporate network, which isn't accessible from outside. Therefore, if you import corporate data, you or IT will need to install a gateway to let Power BI connect to the original data source. For personal use, you can install the gateway in personal mode to refresh imported data without waiting for IT help. For enterprise deployments, IT can centralize data access by setting up the gateway on a dedicated server (discussed in Chapter 12). Besides refreshing data, this installation mode supports direct connections to data sources that supports this connectivity option.

Table 2.1 summarizes the refresh options for popular data sources.

Table 2.1 This table summarizes data refresh options when data is imported from cloud and on-premises data sources.

Location	Data Source	Refresh Type	Frequency
Cloud (Gateway not required)	Most cloud data sources, including Dynamics Online, Salesforce, Marketo, Zendesk, and many others.	Automatic	Once a day
	Excel, CSV, and Power BI Desktop files uploaded to OneDrive, OneDrive for Business, or SharePoint Online	Automatic	Once every hour
On premises (via gateway)	Supported data sources (see https://powerbi.microsoft.com/en-us/documentation/powerbi-refresh-data/)	Scheduled or manual	As configured by you up to 8/day or unlimited with Power BI Premium
	Excel 2013 (or later) Power Pivot data models with Power Query data connections or Power BI Desktop data models	Scheduled or manual	As configured by you up to 8/day or unlimited with Power BI Premium
	Local Excel files via Get Data in Power BI Service	Not supported	

Understanding dataset actions
Once the dataset is created, it appears under the Datasets tab in the workspace content. For example, when you installed the Retail Analysis Sample, Power BI added a dataset with the same name. You can perform several tasks from the Datasets tab (see **Figure 2.9**). Some of these tasks are also available when you click the ellipsis (…) menu next to the dataset name in the navigation pane.

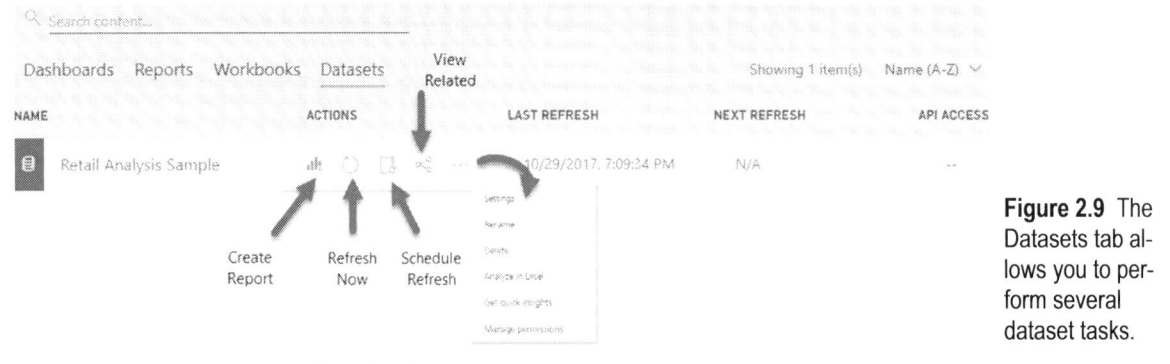

Figure 2.9 The Datasets tab allows you to perform several dataset tasks.

Create Report lets you visualize the data by creating a new report (the subject of the next section). Refresh Now initiates an immediate refresh while Schedule Refresh allows you to schedule the refresh task (refreshing applies to datasets with imported data). Use the View Related icon to find which reports and dashboards use the dataset. More Options (…) opens the following tasks:

- Settings – allows you to see how the dataset is configured for refresh, to enable integration with Windows Cortana, and to enter featured Q&A questions.
- Rename – renames the dataset. Don't worry if you have existing reports connected to the dataset when you rename it because changing the dataset name won't break dependent reports and dashboards.
- Delete – removes the dataset. If you delete a dataset, Power BI will automatically remove dependent reports and dashboard tiles that connect to that dataset, so be very careful.
- Analyze in Excel – Lets Excel users connect Excel on the desktop to this dataset and create pivot reports.
- Security (not shown) – Applicable only to datasets configured for row-level security, this task allows you to configure role members.
- Get Quick Insights – As I mentioned in Chapter 1, Quick Insights runs machine algorithms and auto-generates useful reports that might help you to understand the root cause of data fluctuations.
- Manage permissions – When you share a specific dashboard or report, recipients are given access to the underlying dataset. Use this menu to see who can view the data in this dataset
- Download *.pbix – For datasets created with Power BI Desktop, downloads the dataset as a Power BI Desktop (*.pbix) file.

There are additional properties next to the dataset. The Last Refresh and Next Refresh columns show the dates when the dataset was last refreshed and will be refreshed next respectively. The API Access property is for developers. For example, Power BI supports streaming datasets to allow developers to implement real-time dashboards (discussed in Chapter 14) and such a dataset will be denoted as streaming in the API Access column.

2.3.2 Understanding Reports

Let's define a Power BI report as an interactive view for quick data exploration. Unlike other reporting tools that you might be familiar with and that require report authoring and database querying skills, Power BI reports are designed for business users in mind and they don't assume any technical skills. Reports are the main way to analyze data in Power BI. Reports are found under the Reports section in the left navigation pane (see **Figure 2.10**).

Figure 2.10 The Reports tab lists the reports in the workspace and lets you perform report-related actions.

Understanding report actions
Going through the list of available actions, the first icon allows you to share this report with someone else. The Excel icon lets you analyze the report data in Excel pivot reports by connecting Excel to the report dataset. The light bulb icon is for generating and viewing Quick Insights from the report data. The View Related icon shows the dashboards that use content from the selected reports and the dataset the report depends on. The Settings action lets you manage the following report properties:

- Report name – Renaming the report doesn't break dependent dashboards.
- Persistent filters – By default, when users change report slicers and filters, Power BI "remembers" the user-specified settings unless you turn on the "Don't allow end user to save filters on this report" slider.
- Visual options – By default, every report visual has a header to let the interactive user perform certain tasks, such as exporting the visual data. You can turn on the "Hide the visual header in reading view" slider to hide the header for every visual on the report when the report is open in Reading View.
- Export data – By default, the interactive user can export either the summarized or detail data behind a report visual unless this is prohibited by the Power BI administrator. This list controls what options are available to the user. For example, if you allow only the summarized data behind a chart showing sales by year, the user will be able the export only the aggregate data and not the sales transactions.

Lastly, the Delete action removes the report from the workspace. Deleting a report removes any dashboard tiles that came from the report but keeps the underlying dataset the report was connected to.

Viewing reports
Clicking the report name in the Reports tab opens the report for viewing. For example, if you click the Retail Analysis Sample report, Power BI will open it in a reading mode (called Reading View) that supports interactive features, such as filtering, but it doesn't allow you to change the report layout. If you have permissions, you can change the report layout by clicking the Edit Report menu on the top of the report (see **Figure 2.11**). I'll go through the menus and features of both modes in the next chapter.

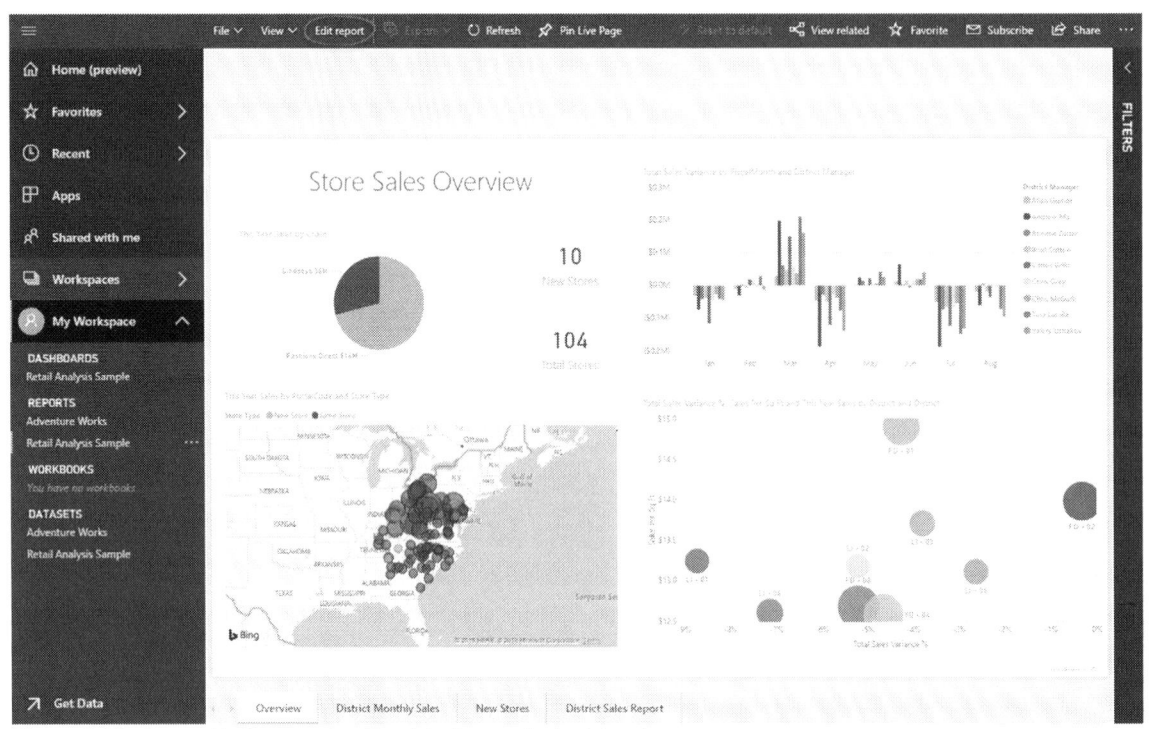

Figure 2.11 A report helps you visualize data from a single dataset.

Creating reports
Reports can be created in several ways:
- Creating reports from scratch – Once you have a dataset, you can create a new report by exploring the dataset (the Create Report action in the dataset context menu). Then you can save the report.
- Importing reports – If you import a Power BI Desktop file and the file includes a report, Power BI will import the report and add it to the Reports tab. If you import Excel Power Pivot data models, only Power View reports are imported (Excel pivot and chart reports aren't imported).

> **NOTE** Power BI Service can also connect to Excel files and show pivot table reports and chart reports contained in Excel files. The Excel workbooks you connected to will appear under the Workbooks tab in the workspace content page. I'll postpone discussing Excel reports to the next chapter. For now, when I talk about reports I'll mean the type of reports you can create in the Power BI portal.

- Distributing reports – If you use Power BI organizational apps, the reports included in the app are available to you when you install the app.

How reports relate to datasets
Currently, a Power BI report can only connect to and source data from a single dataset only. Suppose you have two datasets: Internet Sales and Reseller Sales. You can't have a report that combines data from these two datasets. Although this might sound like a limitation, you have options:

1. Create a dashboard – If all you want is to show data from multiple datasets as separate visualizations on a single page, you can just create a dashboard.
2. Implement a self-service model – Remember that a dataset can include multiple tables. So, if you need a consolidated report that combines multiple subject areas, you can build a self-service data model using Power BI Desktop or Excel. This works because when published to Power BI, the model will be exposed as a single dataset with multiple tables.
3. Connect to an organizational model – To promote a single version of the truth, a BI pro can implement an organizational data model using Analysis Services. Then you can just connect to the model; there's nothing to build or import. Finally, if all you want is to show data from multiple datasets as separate visualizations on a single page, you can just create a dashboard.

For the purposes of this chapter, this is all you need to know about reports. You'll revisit them in more detail in the next chapter.

2.3.3 Understanding Dashboards

For a lack of a better definition, a dashboard is a summarized one-page view with strategic metrics related to the data you're analyzing. Dashboards convey important metrics so that management can get a high-level view of the business. To support root cause analysis, dashboards typically allow users to drill from summary sections (called tiles in Power BI) down to more detailed reports. Why do you need dashboards if you have dashboard-like reports? There are several good reasons to consider dashboards:

- Combine data from multiple reports and thus from multiple datasets – For example, you might have a report with some sales data and another report with inventory data. A dashboard can combine (but not filter or join) visuals from these two reports. That's why dashboards are available only in Power BI Service and not available in Power BI Desktop, which is limited to a single report per file.

- Expose only certain elements from reports – You might have created a report with many pages, but you want another user to focus only on the most import sections. You can create a dashboard that shows the relevant visuals or entire pages. Remember though that dashboards are not a security mechanism as the user can always click a tile, drill down to the underlying report, and see all the pages.
- Dashboard-specific features – Some Power BI features, such as data alerts and streaming tiles, are only available at a dashboard level.

Understanding dashboard actions
Dashboards are listed under the Dashboards section in the workspace content page (see again **Figure 2.6**). The first icon to the right of the dashboard name is for sharing the dashboard with someone else (besides this sharing option, Power BI supports other sharing options to distribute content to a larger audience). The View Related action shows you the reports that the dashboard depends on.

The Settings action allows you to rename the dashboard, turn off Q&A, turn on a feature called "tile flow" to automatically align dashboard tiles to the top left corner of the canvas (instead of the default layout to freely position tiles on the dashboard), and change the dashboard classification (classifications are discussed in Chapter 12). And the Delete icon removes the dashboard from the workspace content. Deleting a dashboard doesn't affect the dependent datasets and reports.

Creating dashboards
A dashboard consists of rectangular areas called *tiles*. Dashboard tiles can be created in several ways:
- From existing reports – If you have an existing report, you can pin one or more of its visualizations to a dashboard or even an entire report page! For example, the Retail Analysis Sample dashboard was created by pinning visualizations from the report with the same name. It's important to understand that you can pin visualizations from multiple reports into the same dashboard. This allows the dashboard to display a consolidated view that spans multiple reports and thus multiple datasets.
- By using Q&A – Another way to create a dashboard is to type in a question in the natural question box (see **Figure 2.5** again). This allows you to pin the resulting visualization without creating a report. For example, you can type a question like "sales by country" if you have a dataset with sales and geography entities. If Power BI understands your question, it will show you the most appropriate visualization.
- By using Quick Insights – This powerful predictive feature examines your dataset for hidden trends and produces a set of visualizations. You can pin a Quick Insights visualization to a dashboard.
- From Excel – If you connect to an Excel file, you can pin any Excel range as an image to a dashboard. Or, if you use Analyze in Excel, you can pin the pivot report as an image.
- From Power BI Report Server reports – If your organization uses Power BI Report Server and has enabled Power BI integration, you can pin image-producing report items (charts, gauges, maps) to dashboards as images.
- From other dashboards – Dashboards can be shared via mail or distributed with apps. You can add tile to your dashboard from another dashboard you have access to.

Drilling through content
To allow users to see more details below the dashboards, users can drill into dashboard tiles. What happens when you drill through depends on how the tile was created. For example, if it was created by pinning a report visualization, you'll be navigated to the corresponding report page. Or, if it was created through Q&A, you'll be navigated to the page that has the visualization and the natural question that was asked. Or, if it was pinned from an Excel or SSRS report, you'd be navigated to the source report.

1. In the Power BI portal, click the Retail Analysis Sample dashboard in the Dashboard tab.
2. Click the "This Year Sales, Last Year Sales" surface Area Chart. Notice that Power BI navigates to the "District Monthly Sales" tab of the Retail Analysis Sample report.

That's all about dashboards for now. You'll learn much more in Chapter 4. Now let's get back to the topic of data and practice the different connectivity options.

2.4 Connecting to Data

As a first step in the data exploration journey, you need to connect to your data. Let's practice what we've learned about datasets. Because this part of the book targets business users, we'll practice three data connectivity scenarios that don't require creating data models in Power BI Desktop. It might be useful to refer to **Figure 2.4** or click the Get Data button to see these options. First, you'll see how you can use a Power BI service app to analyze Google Analytics data. Next, I'll show you how you can import an Excel file. Finally, I'll show you how to connect live to an organizational Analysis Services semantic model.

2.4.1 Using Service Apps

Power BI comes with pre-defined service apps (previously known as service content packs) that allow business users to connect to popular online services. Suppose that Maya wants to analyze the Adventure Works website traffic. Fortunately, Power BI includes a Google Analytics app to get her started with minimum effort. On the downside, Maya will be limited to whatever data the app's author has decided to import which could be just a small subset of the available data.

> **TIP** If you need more data than what's included in the app, consider creating a data model using Excel or Power BI Desktop that connects to the online service to access all the data. For example, your organization might have added custom fields or tables to Salesforce that you need for analysis. Besides data modeling knowledge, this approach requires that you understand the entities and how they relate to each other. So, I suggest you first determine if the app has the data you need.

To perform this exercise, you'll need a Google Analytics account and you must add a tracking code to the website you want to analyze. Google supports free Google Analytics accounts. For more information about the setup, refer to http://www.google.com/analytics. If setting up Google Analytics is too much trouble, you can use similar steps to connect to any other online service that you use in your organization, if it has a Power BI app. To see the list of the available connectors, click the Get Data link in the navigation bar, and then click the Get button in the Services tile. Alternatively, you can click Apps in the navigation bar, click Get Apps, and then select the Apps tab in the AppSource page.

Connecting to Google Analytics
If Maya has already done the required Google Analytics setup, connecting to her Google Analytics account takes a few simple steps:

1. To avoid cookie issues with cached accounts, I suggest you use private browsing. If you use Internet Explorer (IE), open it and then press Ctrl-Shift-P to start a private session that ignores cookies. (Or right-click IE on the start bar and click "Start InPrivate Browsing".) If you use Google Chrome, open it and press Ctrl-Shift-N to start an incognito session. (Or right-click it on the start bar and click "New incognito window".)
2. Go to powerbi.com and sign in with your Power BI account. In the Power BI portal, click the Get Data link in the navigation pane.
3. In the Get Data page, click the Get button in the Services tile whose message reads "Choose content packs from online services that you use".

4. In the Services page, search for "Google Analytics", and then click the Google Analytics app. In the popup that follows, click Connect.

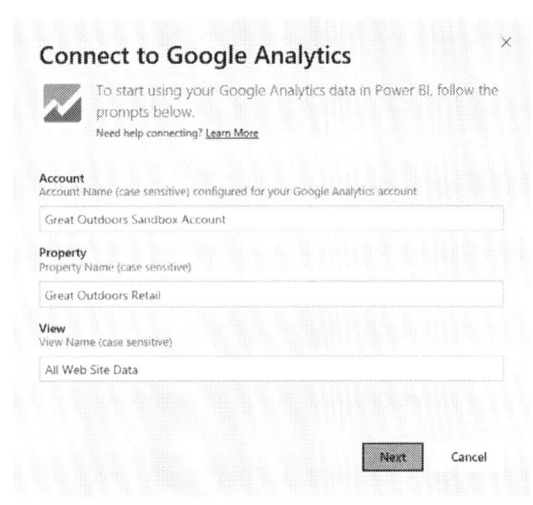

Figure 2.12 As a part of using the Google Analytics app, you need to specify the account details.

5. In the "Connect to Google Analytics" window, specify the Google Analytics details, including account, property, and view. You can get these details by logging into Google Analytics and navigating to the Administration section (Property Settings page). In my case, I'm using a fictitious company provided by Google for testing purposes (see **Figure 2.12**). Click Next.
6. When asked to choose an authentication method, the only option you should see is OAuth. Click Next.
7. In the Google confirmation page that follows, click the Allow button to let Power BI connect to Google Analytics. When asked to authenticate, enter your Google account credentials (typically your Gmail account credentials).
8. Return to the Power BI portal. If all is well, Power BI should display a popup informing you that it's importing your content.

Understanding changes

Like the Retail Analysis Sample, the Google Analytics content pack installs the following content in Power BI:

- A Google Analytics dataset – A dataset that connects to the Google Analytics data.
- A Google Analytics report – This report has multiple pages to let you analyze site traffic, system usage, total users, page performance, and top requested pages.
- A Google Analytics dashboard – A dashboard with pinned visualizations from the Google Analytics report.

That's it! After a few clicks and no explicit modeling, you now have prepackaged reports and dashboards to analyze your website data! If the included visualizations aren't enough, you can explore the Google Analytics dataset and create your own reports.

> **TIP** With the exception of the Microsoft Dynamics service app, whose Power BI Desktop file is available at http://bit.ly/dynamicsp-biapps, the app source code is not available. Consequently, while you can create your own reports, you can't change the dataset included in the app. Again, if you find the service apps limiting, consider importing data in Power BI Desktop.

As I previously mentioned, service apps usually schedule an automatic data refresh to keep your data up to date. To verify:

1. In the navigation pane, click My Workspace and then click the Datasets tab. Notice that the Last Refresh column shows you the time when the dataset was last refreshed.

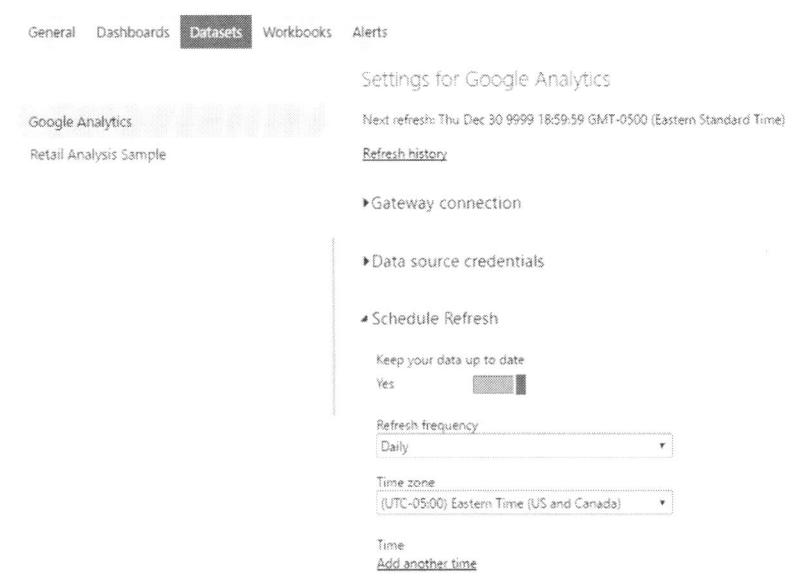

Figure 2.13 The content pack configures automatic daily refresh to synchronize the imported data with the latest changes in the data source.

2. Click the Schedule Refresh action to open the dataset settings page. Notice the app is scheduled for a daily refresh (see **Figure 2.13**).

> **NOTE** As you can imagine, thousands of unattended data refreshes scheduled by many users can be expensive in a multi-tenant environment, such as Power BI. Therefore, Power BI Free and Pro limit you to up to 8 dataset refreshes per day and it doesn't guarantee that the refresh will start exactly at the scheduled time. Power BI queues and distributes the refresh jobs using internal rules. Power BI Premium edition increases the refresh rate to 48 dataset refreshes per day.

3. Expand the "Gateway connection" section. It shows that the service app connects directly to Google Analytics. That's because both Power BI and Google Analytics are cloud services and no gateway is needed.

2.4.2 Importing Local Files

Another option to get data is to upload a file. Suppose that Maya wants to analyze some sales data given to her as an Excel file or text file. Thanks to the Power BI Get Data feature, Maya can import the Excel file in Power BI and analyze it without creating a model.

Importing Excel data

In this exercise, you will create a dataset by importing an Excel file. You'll analyze the dataset in the next chapter. Start by familiarizing yourself with the raw data in the Excel workbook.

1. Open the Internet Sales.xlsx workbook in Excel. You can find this file in the \Source\ch02 folder of the source code.
2. If Sheet1 isn't selected, click Sheet1 to make it active. Notice that it contains some sales data. Specifically, each row represents the product sales for a given date, as shown in **Figure 2.14**. Also, notice that the Excel data is formatted as a table so that Power BI knows where the data is located.

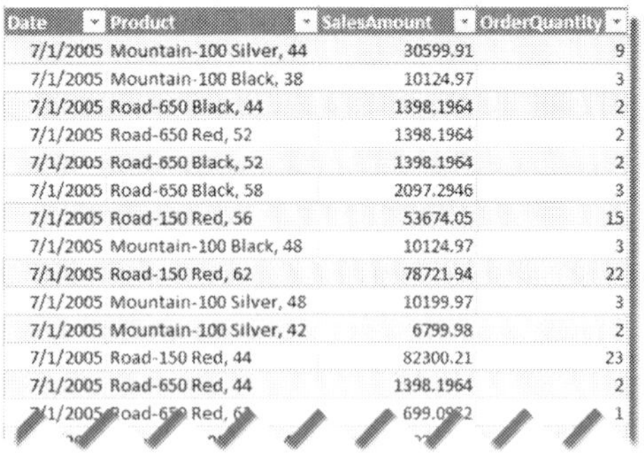

Figure 2.14 The first sheet contains Internet sales data where each row represents the product sales amount and order quantity for a specific date and product.

> **TIP** The Excel file can have multiple sheets with data, and you can import them as separate tables. Currently, Power BI Service (powerbi.com) doesn't include modelling capabilities, such as relating tables or creating business calculations (you need Power BI Desktop to do so). In addition, Power BI requires that the Excel data is formatted as a table. You can format tabular Excel data as a table by clicking any cell with data and pressing Ctrl-T. Excel will automatically detect the tabular section. After you confirm, Excel will format the data as a table. Formatting the Excel data as a table before importing it is a Power BI Service limitation and it's not needed with Power BI Desktop.

3. Close Excel.
4. Next, you'll import the data from the Internet Sales.xlsx file in Power BI. In Power BI, click Get Data.
5. In the Files tile, click the Get button. If you are in the workspace content page, another way to add content is to click the plus (+) sign in the upper-right corner of this page.
6. In the Files page, click "Local File" because you'll be importing from a local Excel file. Navigate to the source code \Source\ch2 folder, and then double-click the Internet Sales file.
7. In the Local File page, click the Import button to import the file (let's postpone connecting to Excel files until the next chapter).
8. Power BI imports the data from the Excel file into the Power BI Service. Once the task completes, you'll see a notification that your dataset is ready. If you click View Dataset, you'll be able to create a report from the dataset but let's not do this now.

Understanding changes

Let's see where the content went:

1. In the navigation pane, click My Workspace (you can also expand My Workspace in the navigation pane).
2. In the workspace content page, click the Datasets tab. A new dataset Internet Sales has been added to the lists of datasets. The asterisk next to the database name denotes that this is a new dataset.
3. Click the Reports tab and notice that there isn't a new report. However, if the Excel had Power View reports, Power BI would import them and add them to the Reports tab.
4. Click the Dashboard tab and notice that there is a new dashboard with the same name as the Excel file (Internet Sales.xlsx). Click the dashboard to open it. Notice that it has a single tile "Internet Sales.xlsx".
5. Click the "Internet Sales.xlsx" tile.
6. Notice that this action opens an empty report (see **Figure 2.15**) to let you explore the data on your own. The Fields pane shows a single table (Internet Sales) whose fields correspond to the columns in the original Excel table. From here, you can just select which fields you want to see on the report. You can choose a visualization from the Visualizations pane to explore the data in different ways, such as a chart or a table.

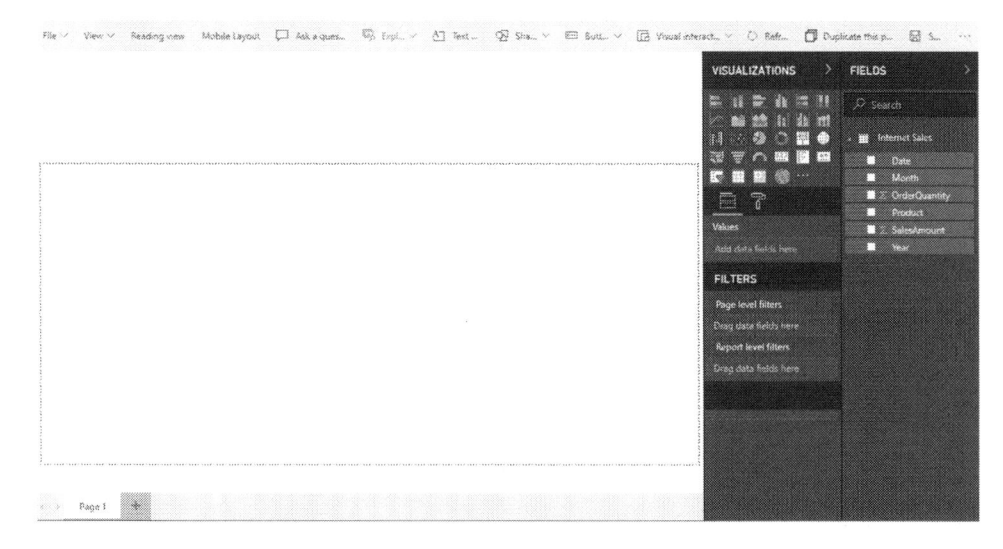

Figure 2.15 Exploring a dataset creates a new report.

> **TIP** As I mentioned previously, Power BI can't refresh local Excel files imported with Get Data in Power BI Portal. Suppose that Maya receives an updated Excel file on a regular basis. Without the ability to schedule an automatic refresh, she needs to delete the old dataset (which will delete the dependent reports and dashboard tiles), reimport the data, and recreate the reports. As you can imagine, this can get tedious. A better option would be to save the Excel file to OneDrive, OneDrive for Business, or SharePoint Online. Power BI refreshes files saved to OneDrive every hour and whenever it detects that the file is updated.

2.4.3 Using Live Connections

Suppose that Adventure Works has implemented an organizational Analysis Services semantic model on top of the corporate data warehouse. In the next exercise, you'll see how easy it is for Maya to connect to the model and analyze its data.

Understanding prerequisites

As I explained in the "Understanding Datasets" section, Power BI requires special connectivity software, called *On-premises Data Gateway*, to be installed on an on-premises computer so that Power BI Service can connect to an on-premises Analysis Services. This step needs to be performed by IT because it requires admin rights to Analysis Services. I provide step-by-step setup instructions to install and configure the gateway in Chapter 12 of this book. You can't install the gateway in personal mode on your laptop because in this mode the gateway doesn't support live connections.

Besides setting up the gateway, to perform this exercise, you'll need help from IT to install the sample Adventure Works database and Tabular model (as per the instructions in the book front matter) and to grant you access to the Adventure Works Tabular model.

Connecting to on-premises Analysis Services

Once the gateway is set up, connecting to the Adventure Works Tabular model is easy.

1. In the Power BI portal, click Get Data.
2. In the Get Data page, click the Get button in the Databases pane that reads "Connect to live data in Azure SQL Database and more."

THE POWER BI SERVICE

3. In the Databases & More page (see **Figure 2.16**), click the SQL Server Analysis Services tile. In the popup that follows, click Connect. If you don't have a Power BI Pro subscription, this is when you'll be prompted to start a free trial.

Figure 2.16 Use the SQL Server Analysis Services tile to create a live connection to an on-premises SSAS model.

4. In the SQL Server Analysis Services page that follows, you should see all the Analysis Services databases that are registered with the gateway. Please check with your IT department which one you should use. Once you know the name, click it to select it.
5. Power BI verifies connectivity. If something goes wrong, you'll see an error message. Otherwise, you should see a list of the models and perspectives that you have access to. Select the "Adventure Works Tabular Model SQL 2012 – Model" item and click Connect. This action adds a new dataset to the Datasets tab of the workspace content page.
6. Click the Create Report action to explore the dataset. The Fields lists will show all the entities defined in the SSAS model. From here, you can create an interactive report by selecting specific fields from the Fields pane. This isn't much different from creating Excel reports that are connected to an organizational data model.
7. Click File ⇨ Save and save the report as *Adventure Works SSAS*.

2.5 Summary

Self-service BI broadens the reach of BI and enables business users to create their own solutions for data analysis and reporting. By now you should view self-service BI not as a competing technology but as a completing technology to organizational BI.

Power BI is a cloud service for data analytics and you interact with it using the Power BI portal. The portal allows you to create datasets that connect to your data. You can either import data or you can connect live to data sources that support live connections. Once you have a dataset, you can explore it to create new reports. And once you have reports, you can pin their visualizations to dashboards.

As a business user, you don't have to create data models to meet simple data analytics needs. This chapter walked you through a practice that demonstrated how you can perform basic data connectivity tasks, including using a service app to connect to an online service (Google Analytics), importing an Excel file, and connecting live to an on-premises Analysis Services model. The next chapter will show you how you can analyze your data by creating insightful reports!

Chapter 3

Creating Reports

3.1 Understanding Reports 63
3.2 Working with Power BI Reports 83
3.3 Working with Excel Reports 90
3.4 Summary 95

In the previous chapter, I showed you how Power BI Service allows business users to connect to data without explicit modeling. The next logical step is to visualize the data so that you can derive knowledge from it. Fortunately, Power BI lets you create meaningful reports with just a few mouse clicks. A data analyst would typically use Power BI Desktop for report authoring. However, a regular business user might prefer to create reports directly in the Power BI Portal and that's the scenario discussed in this chapter.

I'll start this chapter by explaining the building blocks of Power BI reports. Then I'll walk you through the steps to explore Power BI datasets and to create reports with interactive visualizations directly inside Power BI Service (powerbi.com). Because Excel is such an important tool, I'll show you three ways to integrate Power BI with Excel: importing data from Excel files, connecting to existing Excel workbooks, and creating your own pivot reports connected to Power BI datasets. You can also pin Reporting Services reports to dashboards, but I'll postpone this integration scenario to the next chapter. Because this chapter builds on the previous one, make sure you've completed the exercises in the previous chapter to install the Retail Analysis Sample and to import the Internet Sales dataset from the Excel file.

3.1 Understanding Reports

In the previous chapter, I introduced you to Power BI reports. I defined a Power BI report as an interactive visual representation of a dataset. Power BI also supports Excel and SSRS reports. Let's revisit the three report types that you can have in Power BI Service:

- Power BI native reports – This report type delivers a highly visual and interactive report that has its roots in Power View. This is the report type I'll mean when I refer to Power BI reports. For example, the Retail Analysis Sample report is an example of a Power BI report. You can use Power BI Service, Power BI Desktop, and to some extent Excel Power View (deprecated) to create these reports.

- Excel reports – Power BI allows you to connect to Excel 2013 (or later) files and view the included table, pivot and Power View reports. For example, you might have invested significant effort into creating Power Pivot models and reports. Or, a financial analyst might prefer to share an Excel spreadsheet with results from some complex formulas. You don't want to migrate these Excel reports to Power BI Desktop, but you'd like users to view them as they are, and even interact with them! To get this to work, you can just connect Power BI to your Excel files. However, you still must use Excel Desktop to create or modify the reports and data model (if the Excel file has a Power Pivot model).

- Reporting Services reports – SSRS is Microsoft's most customizable reporting tool for creating standard (paginated) reports. If your organization has Power BI Report Server and it's configured for Power BI integration, you can pin report items to Power BI dashboards. For example, a report developer might have implemented a sophisticated map with multiple layers. Now Maya wants to add this map to her dashboard. Maya can open the report and pin the map image as a dashboard tile. When Maya clicks the map, she's navigated to the SSRS report, but Maya needs to be on the corporate network for this to happen. Power BI Premium brings the integration with SSRS even further by allowing IT to publish paginated reports directly to Power BI Service so that business users like you can view them inside the Power BI Portal.

Most of this chapter will be focused on Power BI native reports but I'll also show you how Power BI integrates with Excel reports. And chapter 13 shows the Power BI admin how to deploy SSRS reports.

3.1.1 Understanding Reading View

Power BI Service supports two report viewing modes. Reading View allows you to explore the report and interact with it, without worrying that you'll break something. Editing View lets you make changes to the report layout, such as to add or remove a field.

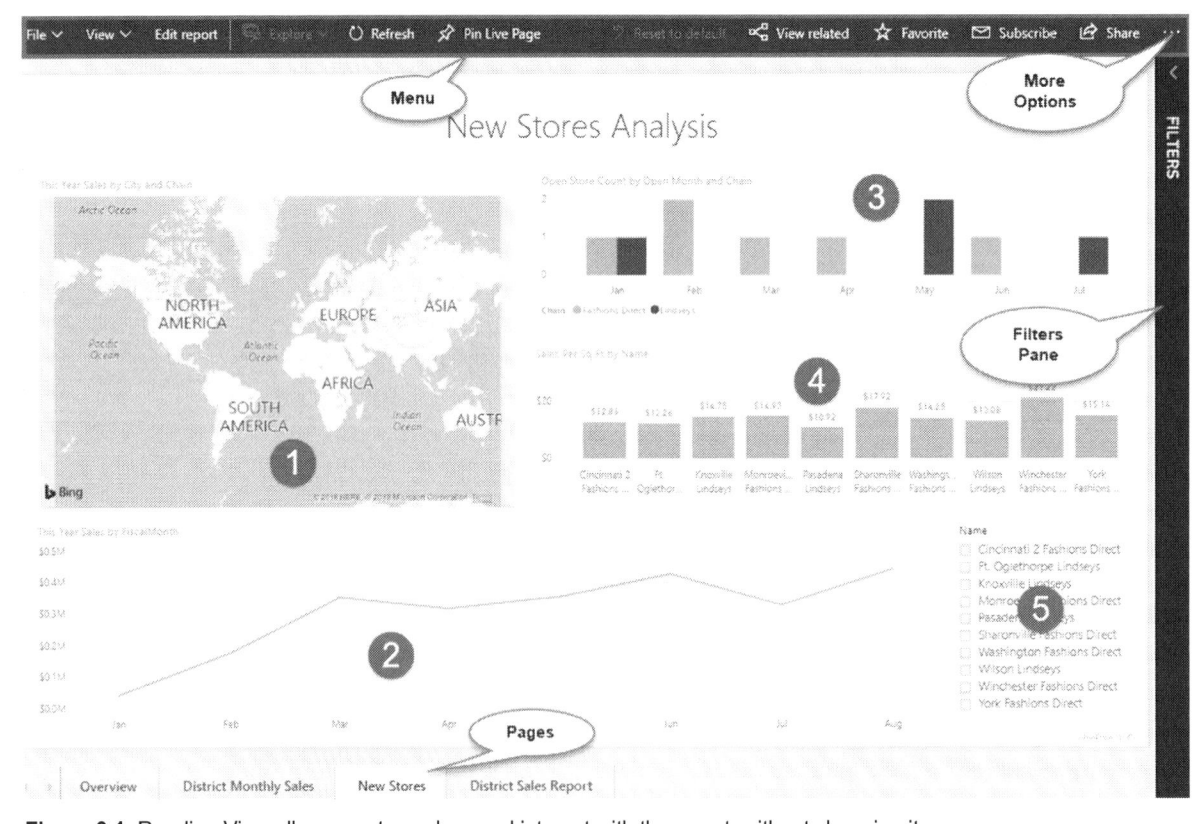

Figure 3.1 Reading View allows you to analyze and interact with the report, without changing it.

Opening a report in Reading View
Power BI defaults to Reading View when you open a report. This happens when you click the report name in the Reports tab or when you click a dashboard tile to open the underlying report.

64   CHAPTER 3

1. In the Power BI portal, click My Workspace. In the workspace content page, click the Reports tab and then click the Retail Analysis Sample report to open it in Reading View.
2. On the bottom-left area of the report, notice that this report has four pages. A report page is conceptually like a slide in a PowerPoint presentation – it gives you a different view of the data story. So, if you run out of space on the first page, you can add more pages, but you must be in Edit Report mode. Click the "New Stores" page to activate it. Notice that the page has five visualizations (see **Figure 3.1**), including a map, line chart, two column charts and a slicer (for filtering data on the report).

Understanding the File menu

Expanding the File menu gives you access to the following features:

- Save as – Creates a new report with a different name in the current workspace.
- Print – Prints the current report page. Printing doesn't expand visualizations to show all the data. In other words, what you see on the screen is what you get when you print the page.
- Publish to web – If the "Publish to web" feature is enabled by the Power BI administrator in the Admin Portal (it is by default) and you're a Power BI Pro user, this feature allows you to publish the report for anonymous access. You'll be given a link that you can send to someone and an embed code (iframe) that you can use to embed the report on a web page, such as in a blog. To find later which reports you've published to the web, go to the Settings menu (the upper-right gear button in the portal), and then click Embed Codes. Be very careful with this feature as you might expose sensitive data to anyone on the Internet!
- Export to PowerPoint – Export the report as a PowerPoint presentation. Each report page becomes a slide and all visualizations are exported as static images.
- Download report – Exports the report and underlying dataset as a Power BI Desktop file. Currently, this feature works only for reports connected to datasets published from Power BI Desktop. Therefore, it's disabled for the Retail Analysis Sample report which you obtained from one of the Power BI samples (the developer has implemented the sample as an Excel Power Pivot model). This menu will also be disabled for the report that you'll later create from the Internet Sales dataset because you created this dataset directly in Power BI Service. As this feature stands, its primary goal is to recover reports and data if the Power BI Desktop file ever gets lost. You can download existing, new, and changed reports, and the underlying datasets can contain imported data or connect directly to the data source.

> **TIP** Instead of relying on users to export reports they've created directly in Power BI Service to Power BI Desktop as a disaster recovery procedure, a better option might be to use Power BI Desktop to connect to the published dataset (Get Data ⇨ Power BI datasets) and then create the reports. Since you always start with Power BI Desktop, you always have its file in case someone deletes the published reports.

Understanding the View menu

The View menu is for adjusting the report size. The "Fit to page" option scales the report content to best fit the page. "Fit to width" resizes the report to the width of the page. And "Actual size" displays content at full size. For now, let's skip the "Edit report" menu which switches you to Editing View to edit the report.

> **TIP** While I'm on the subject of report sizing, both Power BI Service and Power BI Desktop support predefined and custom page sizes. In Power BI Service, while editing the report, you can use the Visualizations pane (Format tab) to specify a page layout for the selected report page, such as 16:9, 4:3, Cortana, Letter, or a custom size. For example, the District Sales Report page in the Retail Analysis Sample report has Cortana layout which is optimized to be rendered by Windows Cortana. Power BI Desktop supports also specifying a mobile view which optimizes the layout for viewing in a Power BI mobile app.

You can use the View menu to enable the Selection Pane so that you toggle the visibility of report elements. In edit mode, this could be useful to temporarily hide visualizations on a busy report page while you are working on a new visual. If the report has bookmarks (discussed in Chapter 10), you can also enable the Bookmarks pane so that you can tell your data story by navigating to specific bookmarks.

Understanding the Explore menu
This menu is enabled when you click a report visual. Some Power BI visualizations, such as charts, allow you to drill down the data. For example, you might have a column chart that has Country and City fields added to the Axis area. The chart initially shows data by country. If you select the chart and click Explore ⇨ Show Data (or right click a bar and click Show Data), you can see the actual data behind the chart (as if you flip the chart to a Table visualization). Similarly, when you toggle Explore ⇨ See Records (or right click a bar and click See Records) and then click a chart bar, you see the actual data behind that bar only. This is also called drilling through data. The rest of the exploration menus fulfill the same role as the interactive features for data exploration when you hover on the chart.

Understanding the Refresh menu
Clicking the Refresh menu refreshes the data on the report. The report always queries the underlying dataset when you view it. The report Refresh menu could be useful if the underlying dataset was refreshed or has a live connection and you want to get the latest data without closing and reopening the report.

Understanding the Pin Live Page menu
You can quickly assemble a dashboard from existing report visualizations. You can also pin entire report pages to a dashboard. This could be useful when the report page is already designed as a dashboard. You can pin the entire page instead of pinning individual visualizations. Although this might sound redundant, promoting a report to a dashboard gives you access to dashboard features, such as Q&A.

Another scenario for pinning report pages is when you want to filter dashboards tiles because dashboards don't have filtering features (the Filter pane is not available). To accomplish this, you can create a report page that has the visualizations you need, add a slicer, and then pin the entire page.

Understanding the "View related" and Favorite menus
Like dashboards and datasets, "View related" shows the related items to this report, including the dashboards that have visualizations pinned from this report and the dataset that the report is connected to. The "Related content" page shows the last time the underlying dataset was refreshed for datasets with imported data.

You can favor/unfavor a report by clicking the Favorite menu. This adds the report to the Favorite section in the navigation pane and to the Power BI Home page (the first menu in the navigation page).

Understanding the Subscribe menu
I've already explained the purpose of the View Related menu. Besides viewing a report interactively (on demand), Power BI lets you subscribe to it. The Subscribe menu is only available in Reading View. It brings you to a window where you can indicate which report pages you want to subscribe to and to manage subscriptions you've created. Once you set up a subscription, Power BI will detect data changes in the underlying report dataset and send you an email with screenshots of the subscribed pages. Subscribed report delivery is a Power BI Pro feature. If a Power BI Free user clicks the Subscribe menu, the user will be informed that this feature is not available unless the user upgrades.

Interacting with visualizations
Although the name might mislead you, Reading View allows you to interact with the report and filter data.

1. Expand the Filters pane on the right of the report. Notice that the report author has added a Store Type filter that filters only new stores. Note also that you can change the filter, such as to show all store types.

2. In the fourth visualization ("Sales Per Sq Ft by Name") on the New Stores page, click the first column "Cincinnati 2 Fashions Direct" (you can hover on the column bar and a tooltip pops up to show the full name). Notice that the other visualizations change to show data only for the selected store. This feature is called *cross filtering* (or *interactive highlighting*), and it's another way to filter data on the report. Cross filtering is automatic, and you don't need to do anything special to enable it. Click the bar again or an empty area in the same chart to show all the data.

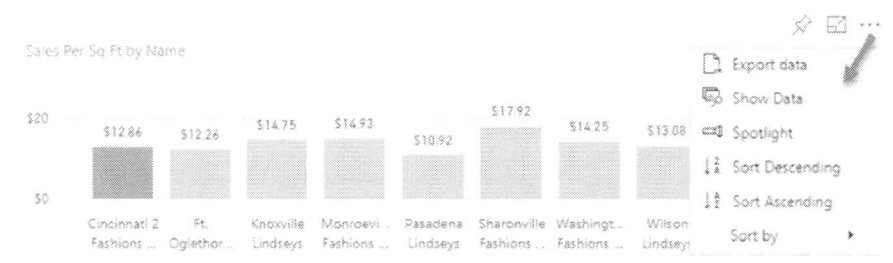

Figure 3.2 You can see how the visualization is sorted and you can change or remove the sort.

3. Hover on the same visualization and notice that Power BI shows an ellipsis menu "More options" in the top-right corner (see **Figure 3.2**).
4. Notice that you can sort by fields added to the chart. Expand "Sort by" and click Name to sort the chart by the store name in a descending order. If you change the sort, an orange bar will appear to the left of the sorted field.

To wrap up the "More options" menu, the Show Data option lets you see the data that the chart is bound to without exporting (same as Explore main menu ⇨ Show Data). Used with bookmarking, the Spotlight option allows you to draw attention to a visual while it fades the other visuals on the page when you tell your data story. I'll discuss "Export data" in the next section.

5. On the left of the "…" menu, there is another "Focus mode" button that lets you pop out the visualization in focus mode in case you want to examine the visual data in more detail. Try it out.
6. Notice the pin button to the left of the "Focus mode" button. It lets you pin the visualization to a dashboard.

Exporting data

You can export the data behind a visualization in a Comma-Separated Values (CSV) or Excel format. What you can export is control by the Power BI administrator and report author.

1. Click Export Data in the More Options menu. In the "Export data" window (see **Figure 3.3**), notice that by default Power BI will export the summarized data as it's aggregated on the chart. The "Underlying data" option lets you export the underlying (detail) data that Power BI retrieve from the table to produce the summarized results.

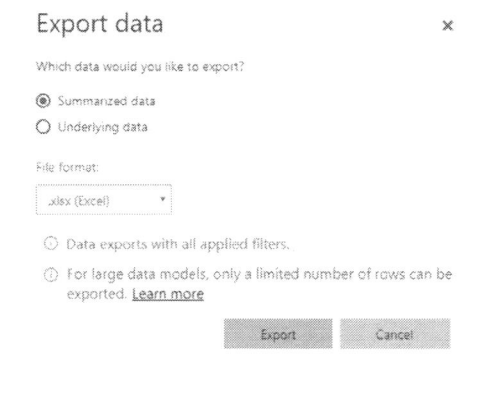

Figure 3.3 You can export the visualization data in Excel or CSV format.

CREATING REPORTS

2. Click the Export button and export the chart data as an Excel file. If the report has any filters applied, the exported data will be filtered accordingly.

> **TIP** Currently, Power BI caps See Records (drillthrough) to 1,000 rows and exporting data to 10,000 rows. There is nothing you can do to change these limits. One workaround is to use the Analyze in Excel feature and drill through a cell in a pivot report. In this case, there is no limit on the number of rows returned.

Drilling down

Drilling down is a popular data analytics feature that lets you explore data in more detail. For example, the default chart might show sales by country but then you might want to drill down to cities. If the chart had multiple fields or a hierarchy added to the Axis zone (the "Sales per Sq Ft" chart doesn't), you'll also see Explore Data indicators (shown by the red circles at the top of **Figure 3.4**) that fulfill the same role as the corresponding options in the Explore main menu.

Because, by default, Power BI initiates cross filtering when you click a chart element, the indicators allow you to switch to a drill mode. For example, you can click the down arrow indicator (in the top-right corner) to switch to a drill mode, and then click a bar to drill through and see the underlying data. To drill up, just click the up arrow indicator in the top-left corner. Or, you can simply right-click a bar and initiate the same actions from the context menu. If you find the indicators confusing, you can simply right-click a data point, such as a column in a column chart, and click Drill Down.

Figure 3.4 You can drill down the next level if the visualization is designed for this feature.

1. If you want to test the data exploration options, select the Overview report page (the Overview tab at the bottom of the report), and then click the scatter chart to select it. Although you can't tell unless you switch to report edit mode, this chart is configured for drilling through from District to Store.
2. Hover over the scatter chart and click the double-arrow indicator to go to the next level (the next field the chart has in the Axis area). This is the same as Show Next Level in the Explore main menu and it will show the data by Store as though the District field isn't in the Axis area. By contrast, clicking the "Expand all down" button (the third one from the group on the left), would drill down all data points to the next level but it'll preserve the parent grouping, such as to show data by Store grouped by District.

> **TIP** Some visualizations, such as column and scatter charts allow you to add multiple fields to specific areas when you configure the chart, such as in the Axis area. So, to configure a chart for drilldown, you need to open the report in Editing View and just add more fields to the Axis area of the chart. These fields define the levels that you drill down to. Power BI Desktop allows the modeler to create hierarchies to define useful navigational paths. If hierarchies are defined, you can just drag the hierarchy to the chart axis.

3. Power BI has more interactive features. Hover on top of any data point in a chart. Notice that a tooltip pops up to let you know the data series name and the exact measure value. By default, the tooltip shows only the fields added to the chart. However, you can switch to Editing View and add more fields to the visualization's Tooltips area if you want to see these fields appear in the tooltip.

3.1.2 Understanding Editing View

If you have report editing rights, you can make changes to the report layout. You have editing rights when you're the original report author or when the report is available in a workspace you're a member of and you have rights to edit the content. You have editing rights to all content in My Workspace. You can switch to Editing View by clicking the Edit Report menu.

> **NOTE** Edit mode allows you to make report layout changes only, as you can do in Power BI Desktop. However, it lacks modeling capabilities, such as adding tables, renaming fields, relationships, or calculations. Among all the Power BI products, modeling features are available in Power BI Desktop only. In addition, although creating and editing reports directly in Power BI Service might be convenient for business users, it might not be a best practice. For example, deleting a dataset would delete all related reports and there is no way to restore them. A better, although more advanced option, might be to create reports in Power BI Desktop that connect to published datasets using the Power BI Datasets data source.

Understanding menu changes
One of the first things you'll notice when you switch to Editing View is that the report menu changes (see **Figure 3.5**). Let's go quickly through the changes. The File menu adds a Save submenu to let you save changes to the report. The View menu adds Show Gridlines, Snap to Grid, Lock Objects menus, and options to enable Selection, Bookmark, and Sync Slicers panes. When you enable "Show Gridlines", Power BI adds a grid to help you position items on the report canvas. If "Snap to Grid" is enabled, the items will snap to the grid so that you can easily align them. And when "Lock Objects" is enabled, you can't make layout changes, such as when you're learning Power BI and you want to avoid making inadvertent changes to an existing report. Let's postpone discussing the various panes that can be enabled from the View menu. Moving to the right, the "Reading view" menu brings you back to opening the report as read-only.

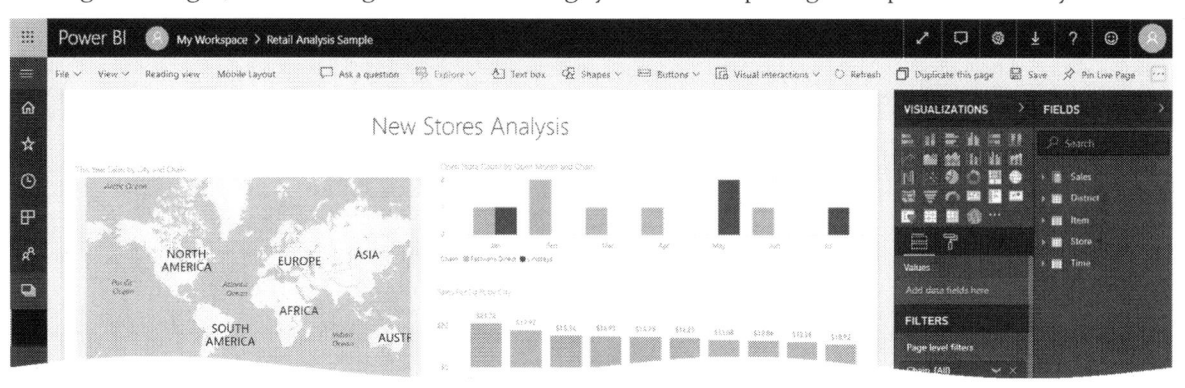

Figure 3.5 The Editing View menu adds more menus to make changes to the report layout.

The "Ask a question" menu is for exploring data using natural questions (Q&A). That's right! You can ask a question, such as "show me sales by store" and Power BI will try to interpret it and add a visual to show the results. Editing View also has menus for editing features. Use the Text Box menu to add text boxes to the report which could be useful for report or section titles, or for any text you want on the report. The Text Box menu opens a comprehensive text editor that allows you to add static text, format it, and implement hyperlinks, such as to navigate the user to another report or a web page.

The Shapes menu allows you to add rectangle, oval, line, triangle, and arrow shapes to the report for decorative or illustrative purposes. Currently, you can't add images, such as a company logo. You can use Power BI Desktop to add images. The Buttons menu adds predefined button shapes, such as to let the user navigate to a bookmark (a bookmark could be another report page or a preconfigured view of an existing page) or to invoke Q&A and allow interactive users to explore the report data using natural queries.

The Visual Interactions menu allows you to customize the behavior of the page's interactive features. You can select a visual that would act as the source and then set the interactivity level for the other visualizations on the same page. For example, you can use this feature to disable interactive highlighting to selected visualizations. To see this feature in action, watch the "Power BI Desktop November 2015 Update" video at https://youtu.be/ErHvpkyQjSg.

The Duplicate Page menu creates a copy of the current report page. This could be useful if you want to add a new page to the report that has similar visualizations as an existing page, but you want to show different data. The Save menu is a shortcut that does the same thing as the File ⇨ Save menu.

Understanding the Visualizations pane

The next thing you'll notice is that Editing View adds two panes on the right of the report: Visualizations and Fields. Use the Visualizations pane to configure the active visualization, such as to switch from one chart type to another.

> **NOTE** When you make changes to the Visualizations pane, they are applied to the currently selected (active) visualization. An active visualization has a border around it with resize handles. You need to click a visualization to activate it.

1. If it's not already active, click the "New Stores Analysis" page to select it.
2. Click the "Sales Per Sq Ft by Name" visualization to activate it. **Figure 3.6** shows the Visualizations pane. The Filters section occupies the bottom part of the Visualizations pane, but the screenshot shows it adjacent to the Visualizations pane to accommodate space constraints.

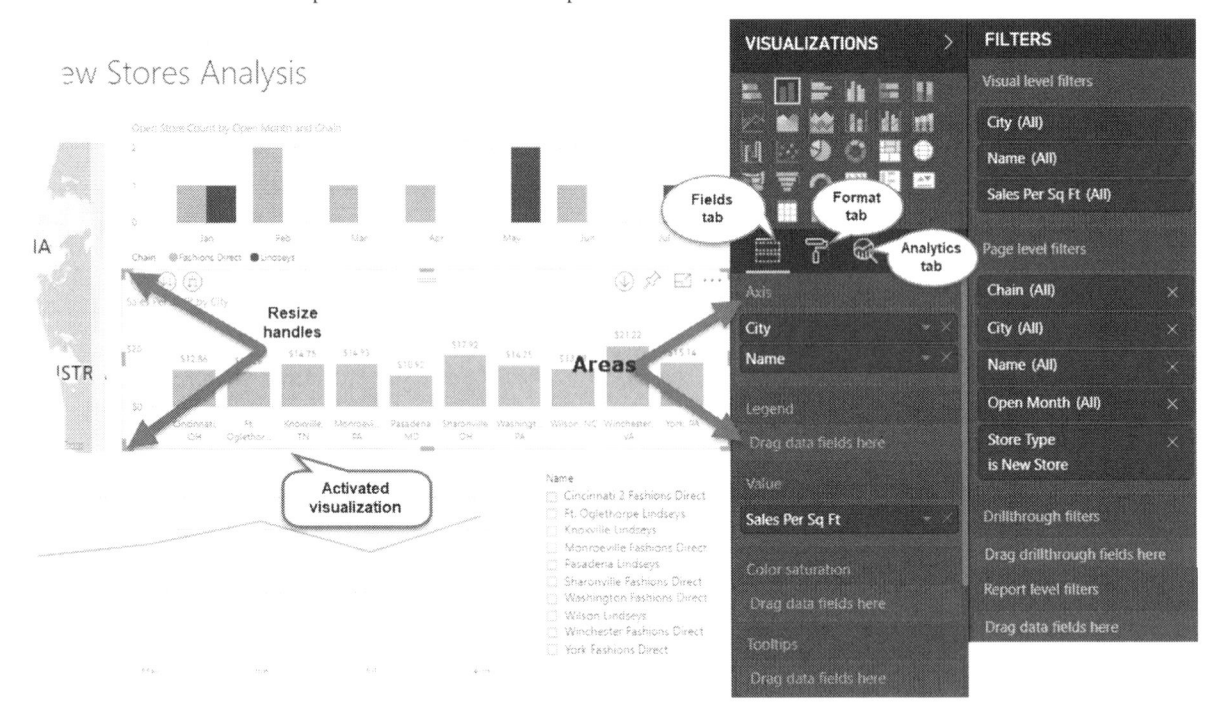

Figure 3.6 The Visualizations pane allows you to switch visualizations and to make changes to the active visualization.

The Visualizations pane consists of several sections. The top section shows the Power BI visualization types, which I'll discuss in more detail in the next section "Understanding Power BI Visualizations". The ellipsis button below the visualizations allows you to import custom visuals from a file or from Microsoft

AppSource, or to delete a custom visual you added by mistake. So, when the Power BI-provided visualizations are not enough for your data presentation needs, check AppSource. Chances are that you'll find a custom visual that can fill in the gap!

The Fields tab consists of areas (also called cards) that you can use to configure the active visualization, similarly to how you would use the zones of the Excel Fields List when you configure a pivot report. For example, this visualization has the Name field of the Store table added to the Axis area and the "Sales Per Sq Ft" field from the Sales table added to the Value area.

> **TIP** You can find which table a field comes from by hovering on the field name. You'll see a tooltip pop up that shows the table and field names, such as 'Store'[Name]. This is the same naming convention that a data analyst would use to create custom calculations in a data model using Data Analysis Expressions (DAX).

The Filters section of the Fields tab is for filtering data on the report. Use the "Visual level filters" section to filter the data in the active visualization. By default, you can filter any field that's used in the visualization, but you can also add other fields. For example, the "Visual level filters" has the Name and "Sales per Sq Ft" fields because they are used on the chart. The (All) suffix next to the field tells you that these two fields are not filtered (the chart shows all stores irrespective of their sales).

Use the "Page Level Filters" section to apply filters to all visualizations on the active page. For example, all four visualizations on this page are filtered to show data for new stores (Store Type is "New Store"). The "Drillthrough Filters" is for defining a drillthrough target page, such as in the case where you want to start with a summary view but allow the user to drill to another page to see the details. Finally, filters in the "Report Level Filters" section are applied globally to all visualizations on the report even if they are on different pages.

The Format tab of the Visualizations pane is for applying format settings to the active visualization. Different visualizations support different format settings. For example, column charts support custom colors per category (for tips and tricks for color formatting see https://powerbi.microsoft.com/en-us/documentation/powerbi-service-tips-and-tricks-for-color-formatting), data labels, title, axis labels, and other settings. As Power BI evolves, it adds more options to give you more control over customizing the visual appearance.

Finally, the Analytics tab is for adding features to the visualization to augment its analytics capabilities. For example, Maya plots revenue as a single-line chart. Now she wants to forecast revenue for future periods. She can do this by adding a Forecast line (discussed in more detail in Chapter 11). The analytics features vary among visualization types. For example, table and matrices don't currently support analytics features, a bar chart supports a constant line, while a linear chart supports constant, min, max, average, median, percentile, and forecast lines.

> **NOTE** Do you need more control over Power BI visuals, such more customization? Remember from Chapter 1 that Microsoft committed to a monthly release cadence, so you might not have to wait long to get a frequently requested feature. But to prioritize your wish, I encourage you to submit your idea or vote for an existing feature at https://ideas.powerbi.com. If you don't want to wait, a web developer in your organization with JavaScript experience can create custom visuals and the last chapter shows how this can be done.

Understanding filter conditions
Revisiting the Filters area on the Fields tab of the Visualization pane, currently Power BI supports three filter modes (**Figure 3.7**):
- Basic filtering – Presents a list of distinct values from the filtered field. The number to the right of the value tells you how many times this value appears in the dataset. You can specify which values you want to include in the filter by checking them. This creates an OR filter, such as Product

is "AWC Logo Cap" or "Bike Wash – Dissolver". To exclude items, check "Select All" and then uncheck the values you don't need.

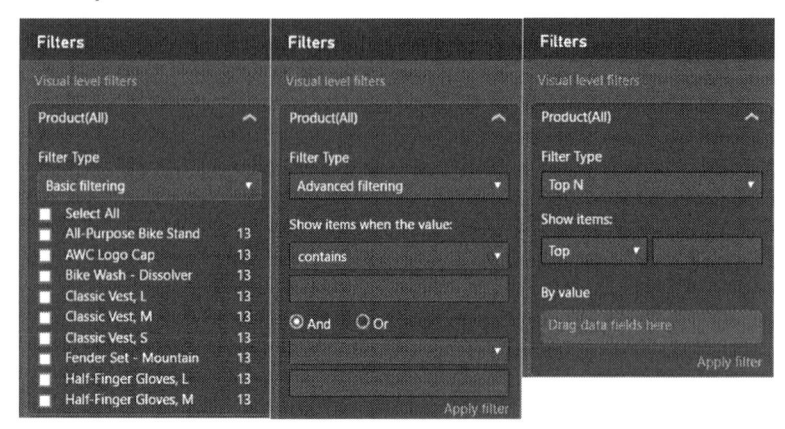

Figure 3.7 Power BI supports three filtering types: Basic, Advanced, and Top N.

- Advanced filtering – Allows you to specify more advanced filtering conditions, such as "contains", "starts with", "is not". In addition, you can add an AND or OR condition, such to specify a filter Product contains "bikes" OR Product contains "accessories".
- Top N filtering – Filters the top N or bottom N values of the field. You can also drag a data field to the "By value" area and specify an aggregation function. For example, you can drag SalesAmount and specify Top N 10 to return the top 10 products that sold the most.

NOTE Currently in preview is a new filter experience that brings more flexibility to report filters, such as to lock and hide filters. I'll postpone demonstrating it to Chapter 10.

Understanding the Fields pane

Positioned to the right of the Visualizations pane is the Fields pane. The Fields pane shows the tables in your dataset. When implementing the Retail Analysis Sample, the author implemented a self-service data model by importing several tables. By examining the Fields pane, you can see these tables and their fields (see **Figure 3.8**). For example, the Fields pane shows Sales, District, Item, and Store tables. The Store table is expanded, and you see some of its fields, such as Average Selling Area Size, Chain, City, and so on. If you have trouble finding a field in a busy Field pane, you can search for it by entering its name (or a part of it) in the Search box.

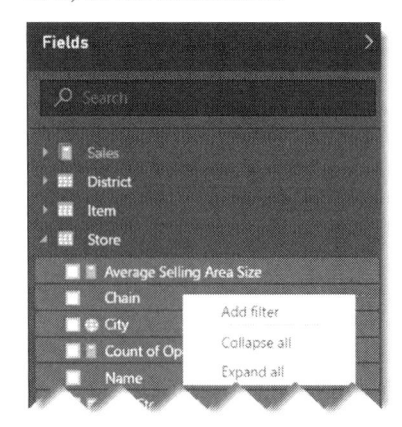

Figure 3.8 The Fields pane shows the dataset tables and fields and allows you to search the model metadata.

72   CHAPTER 3

Power BI gives you clues about the field content. For example, if the field is prefixed with a calculator icon ▣, such as the "Average Selling Area Size" field, it's a calculated field that uses a formula. Fields prefixed with a globe icon ▣ are geography-related fields, such as City, that can be visualized on a map. If the field is checked, it's used in the selected visualization. If the name of the table has an orange color, one or more of its fields are used in the selected visualization. For example, if the "Sales by Sq Ft by Name" chart is selected on the New Stores report page, the Sales and Store tables are orange because they each have at least one field used in the selected visualization.

Each field has an ellipsis menu to the right of the field that allows you to add the field as a filter. If you have selected a visualization, the field will be added as a visual-level filter. For example, if you select a chart on the report and add the City field as a filter, you can filter the chart data by city, such as to show data for Atlanta only. If no visualization is selected, the field will be added as a page-level filter. For example, if you add the City field as a filter but you haven't selected a specific visualization, it'll get added to the "Page level filters" area and you can filter all the visualizations on the page by this field. The "Collapse All" option collapses all the fields so you can see only the table names in the Fields list. And "Expand All" expands all tables so that you can see their fields.

Working with fields

Fields are the building blocks of reports because they define what data is shown. In the process of creating a report, you add fields from the Fields pane to the report. There are several ways to do this:

- Drag a field on the report – If you drag the field to an empty area on the report canvas, you'll create a new visualization that uses that field. If you drag it to an existing visualization, Power BI will add it to one of the areas of the Visualizations pane.
- Check the field's checkbox – It accomplishes the same result as dragging a field. If a visualization is selected on the report, Power BI decides which area on the Fields tab to add the field to.
- Drag a field to a visualization – Instead of relying on Power BI to infer what you want to do with the field, you can drag and drop a field into a specific area of the Fields tab in the Visualizations pane. For example, if you want a chart with a data series using the "Sales per Sq Ft" field, you can drag this field to the Value area of the Fields tab in the Visualizations pane (see again **Figure 3.6**).

> **NOTE** Power BI always attempts to determine the right default. For example, if you drag the City field to an empty area, it'll create a map because City is a geospatial field. If you drag a field to an existing visualization, Power BI will attempt to guess how to use it best. For example, assuming you want to aggregate a numeric field, it'll add it to the Value area.

Similarly, to remove a field, you can uncheck its checkbox in the Fields pane. Or, you can drag the field away from the Visualizations pane to the Fields pane. If the field ends up in the wrong area of the Visualizations pane, you can drag it away from it and drop it in the correct area.

> **TIP** Besides dragging a field to an empty area, you can create a new visualization by just clicking the desired visualization type in the Visualizations pane. This adds an empty visualization to the report area. Then, you can drag and drop the required fields onto the visualization or to specific areas in the Fields tab to bind it to data.

3.1.3 Understanding Power BI Visualizations

You use visualizations to help you analyze your data in the most intuitive way. Power BI supports various common visualizations and their number has been growing in time. And because Power BI supports custom visuals, you'll be hard pressed not to find a suitable way to present your data. But let's start with the Power BI-provided visualizations.

> **TIP** Need visualization best practices? I recommend the "Information Dashboard Design" book by the visualization expert Stephen Few, whose work inspired Power View and Power BI visualizations. To sum it up in one sentence: keep it simple!

Column and Bar charts

Power BI includes the most common charts, including Column Chart, Bar Chart, and other variants, such as Clustered Column Chart, Clustered Bar Chart, 100% Stacked Bar Chart, 100% Stacked Column Chart, and Ribbon charts. **Figure 3.9** shows the most common ones: column chart and bar chart. The difference between column and bar charts is that the Bar Chart displays a series as a set of horizontal bars. In fact, the Bar Chart is the only chart type that displays data horizontally by inverting the axes, so the x-axis shows the chart values and the y-axis shows the category values.

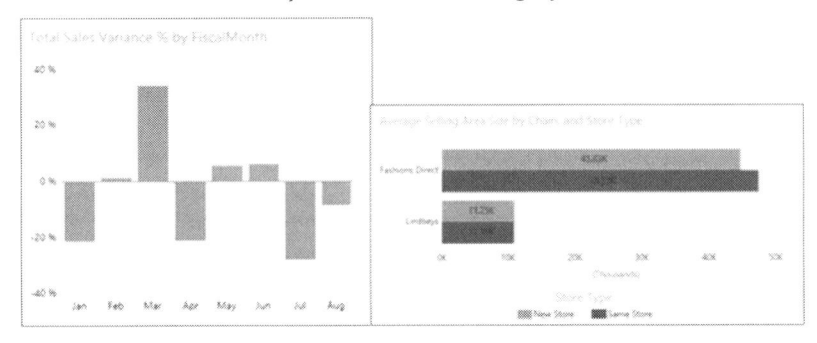

Figure 3.9 Column and bar charts display data points as bars.

Line charts

Line charts are best suited to display linear data. Power BI supports basic line charts and area charts, as shown in **Figure 3.10**. Like a Line Chart, an Area Chart displays a series as a set of points connected by a line with the exception that all the area below the line is filled in. The Line Chart and Area Chart are commonly used to represent data that occurs over a continuous period. Currently, a single line chart is the only chart type that supports forecasting.

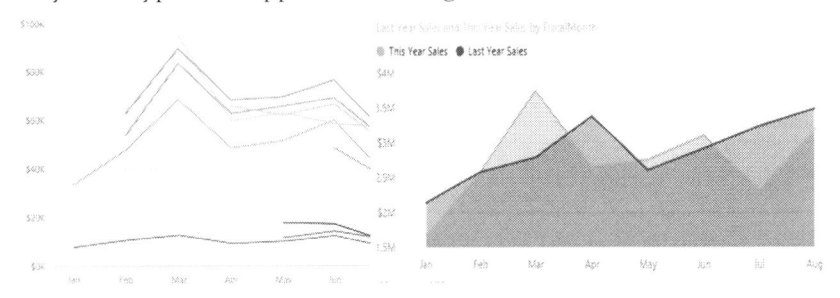

Figure 3.10 Power BI supports line charts and area charts.

Combination Chart

The Combination (combo) Chart combines a Column Chart and a Line Chart. This chart type is useful when you want to display measures on different axes, such as sales on the left Y-axis and order quantity on the right Y-axis. In such cases, displaying measures on the same axis would probably be meaningless if their units are different. Instead, you should use a Combination Chart and plot one of the measures as a Column Chart and the other as a Line Chart, as shown in **Figure 3.11**.

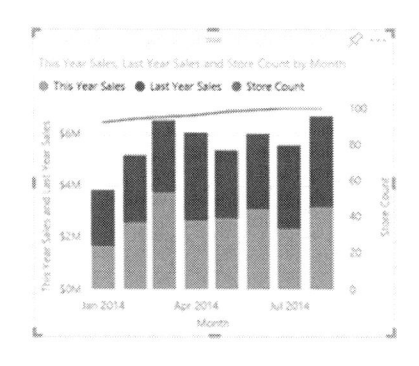

Figure 3.11 A Combo Chart allows you to plot measures on different axes. In this example, the This Year Sales and Last Year Sales measures are plotted on the left Y-axis while Store Count is plotted on the right Y-axis.

Scatter Chart
The Scatter Chart (**Figure 3.12**) is useful when you want to analyze correlation between two variables. Suppose that you want to find a correlation between units sold and revenue. You can use a scatter chart to show Units along the y-axis and Revenue along the x-axis. The resulting chart helps you understand if the two variables are related and, if so how. For example, you can determine if these two measures have a linear relationship; when units increase, revenue increases as well.

A unique feature of the scatter chart is that it can include a Play Axis. You can add any field to the Play Axis, you would typically add a date-related field, such as Month. When you "play" the chart, it animates and bubbles move!

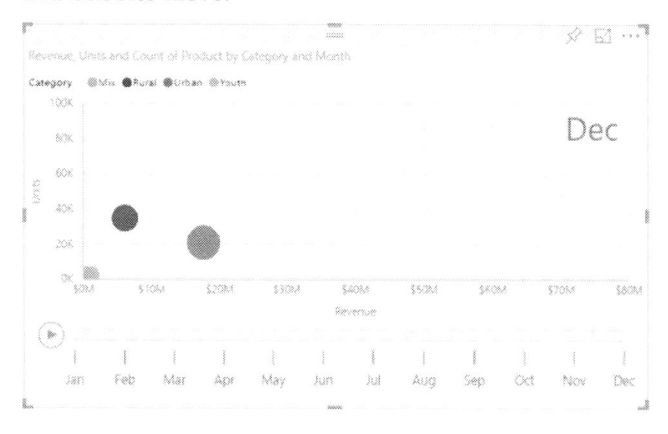

Figure 3.12 Use a Scatter Chart to analyze correlation between two variables.

Shape charts
Shape charts are commonly used to display values as percentages of a whole. Categories are represented by individual segments of the shape. The size of the segment is determined by its contribution. This makes a shape chart useful for proportional comparison between category values. Shape charts have no axes. Shape chart variations include Pie, Doughnut, and Funnel charts, as shown in **Figure 3.13**. All shape charts display each group as a slice on the chart. The Funnel Chart order categories from largest to smallest.

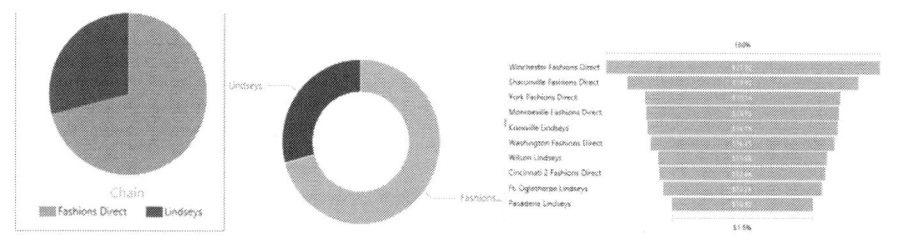

Figure 3.13 Pie, Doughnut, and Funnel charts can be used to display values as percentages of a whole.

CREATING REPORTS

Treemap and Waterfall charts

A treemap is a hierarchical view of data. It breaks an area into rectangles representing branches of a tree. Consider the Treemap Chart when you have to display large amounts of hierarchical data that doesn't fit in column or bar charts, such as the popularity of product features. Power BI allows you to specify custom colors for the minimum and maximum values. For example, the chart shown in **Figure 3.14** uses a red color for show stores with less sales and a green color to show stores with the most sales.

Consider a waterfall chart to show a running total as values are added or subtracted, such as to see how profit is impacted by positive and negative revenue reported over time.

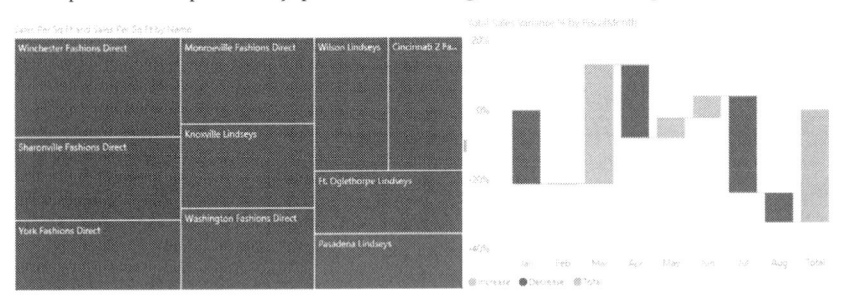

Figure 3.14 Consider Treemap to display large amounts of hierarchical data and Waterfall chart to show a running total as values are added or subtracted.

Table and Matrix visualizations

Use the Table and Matrix visualizations to display text data as tabular or crosstab reports. The Table visualization (left screenshot in **Figure 3.15**) displays text data in a tabular format, such as the store name and sales as separate columns.

Figure 3.15 Use Table and Matrix visualizations for tabular and crosstab text reports.

The Matrix visualization (right screenshot in **Figure 3.15**) allows you to pivot data by one or more columns added to the Columns area of the Visualization pane, to create crosstab reports. Both visualizations support interactive sorting by clicking a column header, such as to sort stores in an ascending order by name. Matrix supports drilling down from one level to another.

Both visualizations support pre-defined quick styles that you can choose from in the Format tab of the Visualizations pane to beautify their appearance. For example, I chose the Alternating style to alternate the background color of the table rows. These visualizations also support conditional formatting as the Table visual demonstrates. You can access the conditional formatting settings by expanding the drop-down next to the measure in the Values area and clicking "Conditional formatting" and then selecting what will be formatted: background color, font color, or show values as data bars (see **Figure 3.16**).

Then you can let Power BI figure the lowest and highest value for the color range or enter specific numbers. In **Figure 3.16**, I checked the Diverging setting to have a center zone and specified that cells with low values will be colored in Red and cells with higher values will be colored in Blue. You can also expand the "Format by" drop-down and select "Color by rules" to specify more advanced rules, such as to color negative values in red, and their precedence order.

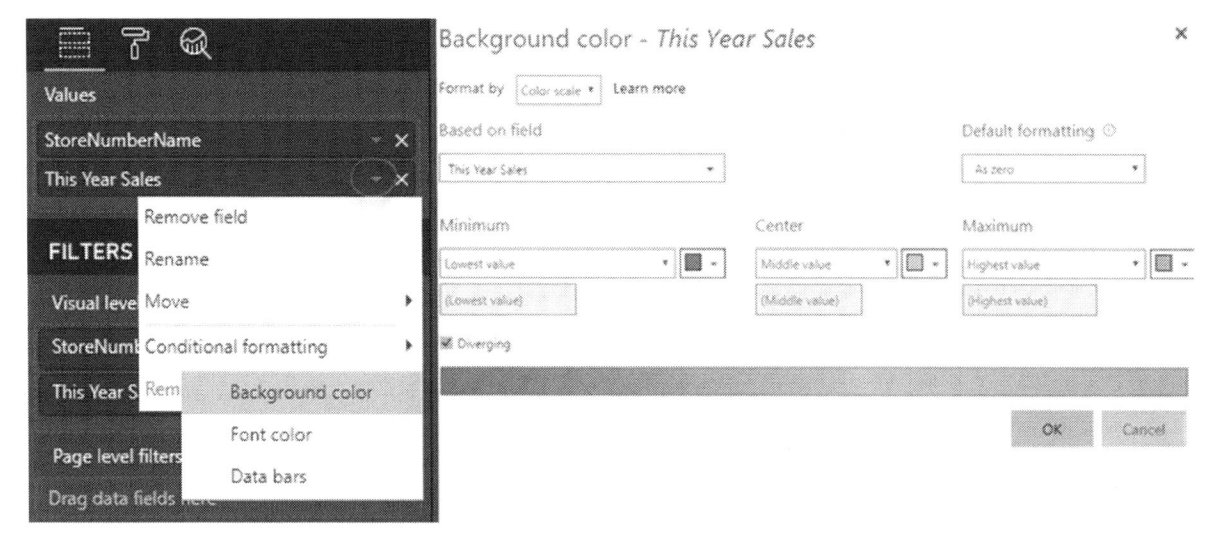

Figure 3.16 Power BI supports basic and rule-based conditional formatting to format Table and Matrix cells.

Map visualizations

Use map visualizations to illustrate geospatial data. Power BI Service includes four map visualizations: Basic Map, Filled Map, ArcGIS, and ShapeMap (currently available as a Power BI Desktop preview feature). **Figure 3.17** shows Basic Map and Filled Map. All maps are license-free and use Microsoft Bing Maps, so you must have an Internet connection to see the maps.

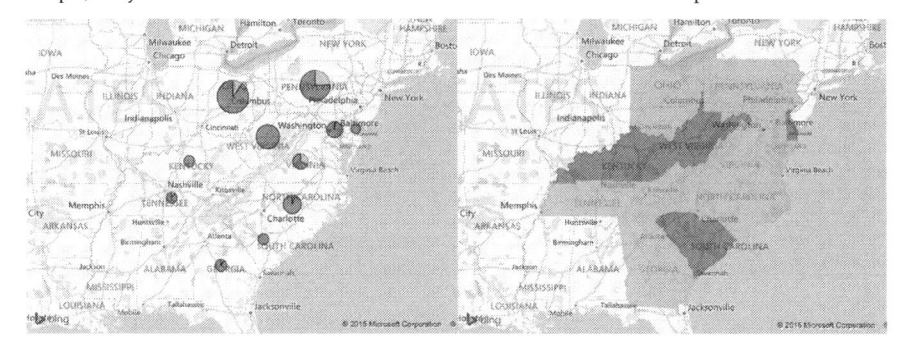

Figure 3.17 Examples of basic maps and filled maps.

You can use a Basic Map (left screenshot in **Figure 3.17**) to display categorical and quantitative information with spatial locations. Adding locations and fields places dots on the map. The larger the value, the bigger the dot. When you add a field to the Legend area of the Visualization pane, the Basic Map shows pie charts on the map, where the segments of the chart correspond to the field's values. For example, each Pie Chart in the Basic Map on the left of **Figure 3.17** breaks the sales by the store type.

As the name suggests, the Filled (choropleth) Map (right screenshot in **Figure 3.17**) fills geospatial areas, such as USA states. This visualization can use shading or patterns to display how a value differs in proportion across a geography or region. You can zoom in and out interactively, by pressing the Ctrl key and using the mouse wheel. Besides being able to plot precise locations (latitude and longitude), they can infer locations using a process called geo-coding, such as to plot addresses.

Like the Filled Map, the Shape Map fills geographic regions. The big difference is that the Shape Map allows you to plug in TopoJSON maps. TopoJSON is an extension of GeoJSON - an open standard format designed for representing simple geographical features based on JavaScript Object Notation (JSON).

CREATING REPORTS

> **TIP** You can use tools, such as Map Shaper (http://mapshaper.org), to convert GeoJSON maps to TopoJSON files. David Eldersveld maintains a collection of useful TopoJSON maps that are ready to use in Power BI at github.com/deldersveld/topojson.

The latest addition to the Power BI mapping arsenal is the ArcGIS map. This map type was contributed by Esri, a leader in the geographic information systems (GIS) mapping industry. Now not only can you plot data points from Power BI, but you can also add reference layers! These layers include demographic layers provided by Esri and public web maps, or those published into Esri's Living Atlas (http://doc.arcgis.com/en/Living-Atlas). For example, the map in **Figure 3.18** plots customers in Georgia as bubbles on top of a layer showing the 2016 USA Average Household Income (the darker the state color, the higher the income). The ArcGIS map also adds useful feature, such as lassoing data points, such as to select quickly a few customers so that you can filter the other page visuals to show data for only these customers and selecting data points in a given radius.

For more information about ArcGIS maps, visit http://doc.arcgis.com/en/maps-for-powerbi. Esri also offers a subscription that offers more ArcGIS features, such as global demographics, satellite imagery, using your own reference layers and ready-to-use data. More details can be found at http://go.esri.com/plus-subscription.

Figure 3.18 This ArcGIS map plots customers in Georgia on top of a layer showing the average household income.

Gauge visualizations

Gauges are typically used on dashboards to display key performance indicators (KPIs), such as to measure actual sales against budget sales. Power BI supports Gauge and KPI visuals for this purpose (**Figure 3.19**) but they work quite differently. To understand this, examine the data shown in the table below the visuals.

CalendarYear	SalesAmount	SalesAmountQuota
2005	$8,065,435	$9,513,000
2006	$24,144,430	$29,009,000
2007	$32,202,669	$38,782,000
2008	$16,038,063	$18,410,000
Total	**$80,450,597**	**$95,714,000**

Figure 3.19 The Gauge and KPI visuals display progress toward a goal.

The Gauge (the left radial gauge on the left) has a circular arc and displays a single value that measures progress toward a goal. The goal, or target value, is represented by the line (pointer). Progress toward that goal is represented by the shaded scale. And the value that represents that progress is shown in bold inside the arc. The Gauge aggregates the source data and shows the totals. It's not designed to visualize the trend of the historical values over time.

By contrast, the KPI visual can be configured to show a trend, such as how the indicator value changes over years. If you add a field to the Trend axis (CalendarYear in this example), it plots an area chart for the historical values. However, the indicator value always shows the last value (in this example, 16 million for year 2008). If you add a field to the "Target goals" area, it shows the indicator value in red if it's less than the target.

Because both visuals show a single scalar value, your users can subscribe for data alerts when these visuals are added to a dashboard. For example, assuming a dashboard tile shows a Gauge visual, Maya can go to the tile properties and create an alert to be notified when the sales exceed 80 million.

Card visualizations

Power BI supports Single Card and Multi Row card visualizations, as shown in **Figure 3.20**.

Figure 3.20 The Single Card on the left displays a single value (total stores) while the Multi Row Card displays managers and their sales.

The Single Card visualization (left screenshot in **Figure 3.20**) displays a single value to draw attention to the value. Like gauges, you can set up data alerts on single cards, such as to receive a notification when the number of stores exceed a given value. If you're looking for another way to visualize tabular data than plain tables, consider the Multi Row Card visualization (right screenshot in **Figure 3.20**). It converts a table to a series of cards that display the data from each row in a card format, like an index card.

Slicer

The Slicer visualization isn't really meant to visualize data but to filter data. Unlike page-level filters, which are found in the Filter pane when the report is displayed in Reading View, the Slicer visualization is added on the report, so users can see what's filtered and interact with the slicer without expanding the Filter pane. Slicer is a versatile visual that supports different configurations depending on the data type of the field bound to the slicer. **Figure 3.21** shows three different slicer configurations.

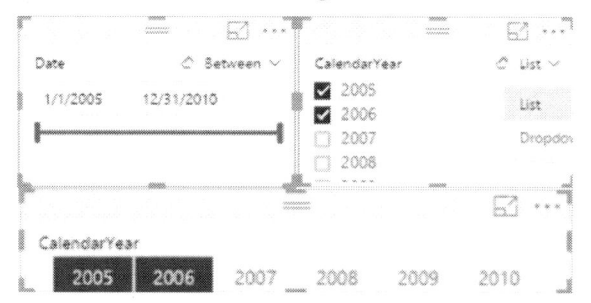

Figure 3.21 Use the Slicer visualization to create a filter that filters all visualizations on the report page.

When you bind the slicer to a field of a Date data type, it becomes a slider (the upper-left configuration). You can either use the sliders to set the dates or pick the date using a calendar. It also supports relative dates expressed as a specified number of last, this, or next periods of time. The configuration on the right shows the slicer in the default vertical configuration where you can check values from a list or pick a single value from a drop-down.

CREATING REPORTS

By default, the slicer is configured for a single selection, but it also supports multi-value selection by holding the Ctrl key and selecting items or by changing the Single Selection property to Off in the Format tab of the Visualizations pane. You can also configure the slicer for a horizontal layout (the bottom slicer). Slicer supports a Search mode, such as to filter a long list of values as you type. To enable the Search mode, bind the slicer to a text field, expand the ellipsis (…) menu in the top-right corner, and then select Search.

By default, the slicer slices only the visuals on the current page. However, in report Editing View, you can enable the View ⇨ "Selection pane" menu and configure the slicer to apply to other pages.

3.1.4 Understanding Custom Visuals

No matter how much Microsoft improves the Power BI visualizations, it might never be enough. When it comes to data presentation, beauty is in the eye of the beholder. However, the Power BI presentation framework is open, and developers can donate custom visuals that you can use with your reports for free!

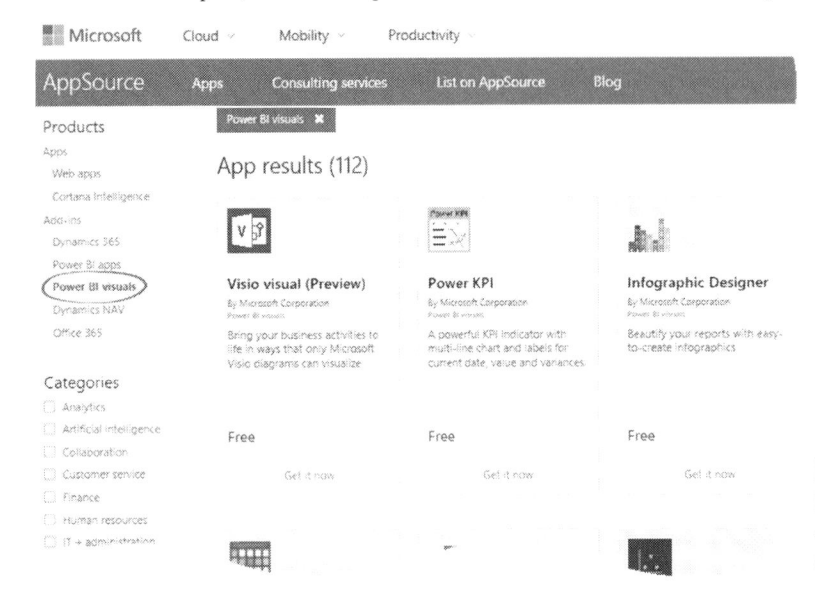

Figure 3.22 In AppSource you can find and download custom visuals contributed by Microsoft and the community.

Understanding AppSource

Custom visuals contributed by the community are available on the Microsoft AppSource site (https://appsource.microsoft.com), as shown in **Figure 3.22**. There you can search and view custom visuals. When you find an interesting visual, click it to see more information about the visual and its author. Custom visuals are contributed by Microsoft and the Power BI community. If you decide to use the visual, click "Get it now" to download the visual and then import it using the ellipsis menu (…) in the Visualizations pane. Visuals are distributed as files with the *.pbiviz extension.

Using custom visuals

Business users can use custom visuals in Power BI Service and data analysts can do the same in Power BI Desktop. To make it even easier for you to add a custom visual, AppSource is integrated with Power BI Service and Power BI Desktop. You can click the ellipsis menu (…) in the Visualizations pane and then click "Import from store" to browse AppSource (only Power BI visuals will show up) and import a visual. Once the visual is imported, it's included in the report and it can be used in that report only. If you decide that you don't need the visual, right-click the visual icon in the Visualizations pane and then click "Delete custom visual".

NOTE Custom visuals are written in JavaScript, which browsers run in a protected sandbox environment that restricts what the script can do. However, the script is executed on every user who renders a report with a custom visual. When it comes to security you should do your homework to verify the visual origin and safety. If you're unsure, consider involving IT to test the visual with anti-virus software and make sure that it doesn't pose any threats. IT can then use the Power BI Admin Portal (Organization Visuals tab) to add the certified visual so that it appears under "My Organization" when you click the "..." menu and select "Import from marketplace". For more information about how you or IT can test the visual, read the "Review custom visuals for security and privacy" document at https://powerbi.microsoft.com/documentation/powerbi-custom-visuals-review-for-security-and-privacy/.

Once you import the visual, you can use it on reports just like any other visual. **Figure 3.23** shows that I imported the Bullet Chart visual and its icon appears at the bottom of the Visualizations pane. Then I added the visual and configured it to show this year sales by store type.

Figure 3.23 The Bullet Chart custom visual is added to the Visualizations pane and can be used on reports.

3.1.5 Understanding Subscriptions

Besides on-demand report delivery where you view a report interactively, Power BI can deliver the report to you once you set up a subscription. A Power BI Pro feature, subscriptions let you automate the process of generating and distributing reports. Subscribed report delivery is convenient because you don't have to go to Power BI Service to view the report online. Instead, Power BI sends the report to you. Subscription require a Power BI Pro license. Every Power BI Pro user can create individual subscriptions to report pages, if that the user has rights to view the report.

Creating subscriptions
Creating a subscription takes a few clicks. Open the report in Reading View and click the Subscribe menu. In the "Subscribe to emails" window, select which report page you want to subscribe to. **Figure 3.24** shows the available options for two reports that connect to different dataset types. Notice that you can you also subscribe other users.

The Retail Analysis Sample report (the screenshot on the left) connects to a dataset with imported data. In this case, you can't specify the subscription frequency. Instead, you'll get an email when the dataset is refreshed, if you haven't gotten an email in the last 24 hours. In other words, the subscription schedule follows the dataset refresh schedule although you get an email at most once a day. The DirectQuery report (the screenshot on the right) connects directly to the data source. In this case, you can specify the mail frequency (Daily or Weekly).

As you know by now, a report can have multiple pages. When you create a subscription, you subscribe to a page in a report. For example, if Maya wants to subscribe to all four pages in the "Retail Analysis Sample" report, she'll have to create four subscriptions. She can do that by clicking "Add another subscription". If the report connects directly to the data source, each subscribed page can have its own frequency for sending mails.

Once you're done configuring your subscriptions, click "Save and close" to save your changes. You'll start receiving emails periodically with screenshots of each page you subscribe to. If you want to temporarily disable a subscription for a given page, turn the slider for that page off. To permanently delete a page subscription, click the trashcan icon next to the page.

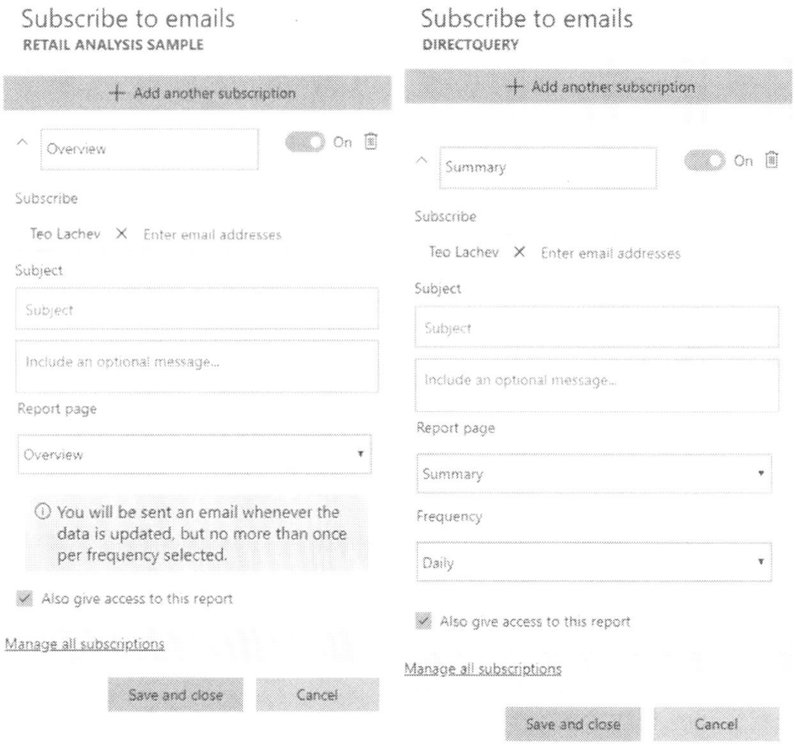

Figure 3.24 When setting up a subscription, specify which page you want to subscribe to and the subscription frequency for DirectQuery reports.

Understanding subscription frequency
The subscription schedule (the frequency you receive emails) depends on how the report dataset connects to the source data. **Table 3.1** summarizes the schedule options.

Table 3.1 Schedule options for report subscriptions.

Dataset	Custom schedule interval	Can detect data changes?	Description
Imported data with scheduled refresh	None	No	Follows the dataset refresh schedule. You can't specify a different schedule. You will get an email every time the scheduled refresh happens, if you haven't gotten an email in the last 24 hours.
DirectQuery	Daily or Weekly	No	Power BI checks the data source every 15 minutes. You'll get an email as soon as the next check happens, if you haven't gotten an email in the last 24 hours (if Daily is selected), or in the last seven days (if Weekly is selected).
Live connection to Analysis Services (on premise/cloud)	None	Yes	Power BI checks the data source every 15 minutes and it's capable of detecting if the data has changed. You'll get an email only if the data has changed if you haven't gotten an email in the last 24 hours.
Connected Excel reports	None	Yes	Power BI checks the data source every hour. You'll get an email only if the data has changed if you haven't gotten an email in the last 24 hours.

Managing your subscriptions
As the number of your subscriptions grows, you might find it difficult to keep track of which reports you've subscribed to. Luckily, Power BI lets you view your subscriptions in one place - the Subscriptions

tab in the Power BI Settings page (**Figure 3.25**). To get there, click the "Manage all subscriptions" link in the "Subscribe to emails" window.

Alternatively, click the Power BI Settings (cog) menu in the upper-right corner of the Power BI portal and then click Settings. You can see the number of pages you subscribed to for each report. Click the Actions icon if you want to make changes to a given report subscription. This brings you to the "Subscribe to emails" window.

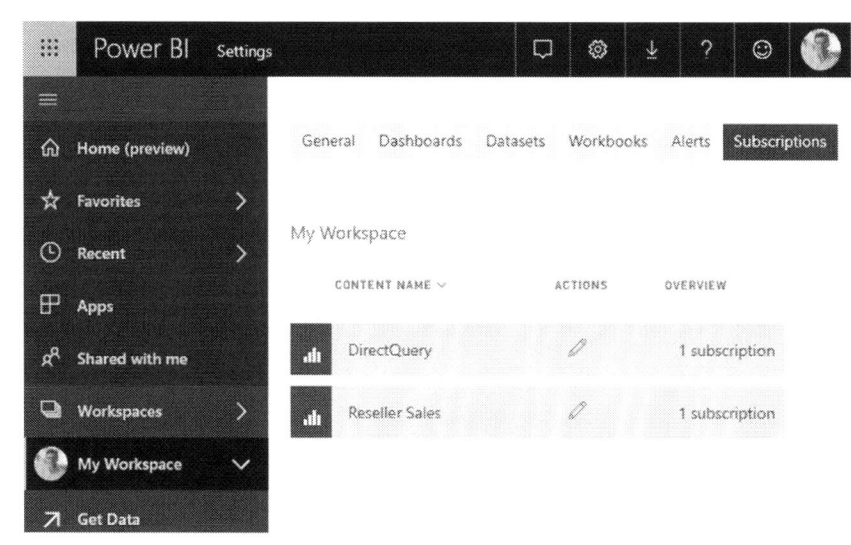

Figure 3.25 Use the Subscriptions tab in the Settings page to view and manage your subscriptions.

Understanding subscription limitations
As of time of writing, Power BI subscriptions have these limitations:

- The only export option is screenshot. You can't receive the page exported to PowerPoint, for example.
- You can specify subscription frequency for reports that connect directly to the data source (DirectQuery connections). For other datasets, subscriptions either follow the dataset refresh schedule (for imported datasets), or Power BI determines when to send emails (for datasets connected to Analysis Services or Excel).
- The Power BI admin can't see or manage subscriptions across the tenant.

3.2 Working with Power BI Reports

Now that you know about visualizations, let's use them on reports. In the first exercise that follows, you'll create a report from scratch. The report will source data from the Internet Sales dataset that you created in Chapter 2. In the second exercise, you'll modify an existing report. You'll also practice working with Excel and Reporting Services reports.

3.2.1 Creating Your First Report

In Chapter 2, you imported the Internet Sales Excel file in Power BI. As a result, Power BI created a dataset with the same name. Let's analyze the sales data by creating the report shown in **Figure 3.26**. This report consists of two pages. The Summary page has six visualizations and the Treemap page (not shown in **Figure 3.26**) uses a Treemap visualization to help you analyze sales by product at a glance. (For an example of a Treemap visualization skip ahead to **Figure 3.28**.)

CREATING REPORTS

Figure 3.26 The Summary page of the Internet Sales Analysis report includes six visualizations.

Getting started with report authoring
One way to create a new report in Power BI is to explore a dataset.

1. In the Power BI portal, expand My Workspace in the navigation pane and then click the Internet Sales dataset. Alternatively, in the navigation pane click My Workspace. In the workspace content page, select the Datasets tab. Click the Create Report icon ( ) next to the Internet Sales dataset to create a new report that is connected to this dataset.
2. Power BI opens a blank report in Editing View. Expand the View menu and turn on Snap to Grid so that you align easier elements on the report canvas.
3. Click the Text Box menu to create a text box for the report title. Type *"Internet Sales Analysis"* and format as needed. Position the text box on top of the report.
4. Note the Fields pane shows only the table "Internet Sales" because the Internet Sales dataset, which you imported from an Excel file, has only one table.
5. Double-click the "Page 1" page to enter edit mode (or right click the tab and click Rename Page) and enter *Summary* to change the page name.
6. Click the Save menu and save the report as *Internet Sales Analysis*. Remind yourself to save the report (you can press Ctrl-S) every now and then so that you don't lose changes.

> **NOTE** Power BI times out your session after a certain period of inactivity to conserve resources in a shared environment. When this happens, and you return to the browser, it'll ask you to refresh the page. If you have unsaved changes, you might lose them when you refresh the page so get in the habit to press Ctrl-S often.

Creating a Bar Chart
Follow these steps to create a bar chart that shows the top selling products.

1. Click an empty space on the report canvas. In the Fields pane, check the SalesAmount field. Power BI defaults to a Column Chart visualization that displays the grand total of the SalesAmount field.
2. In the Fields pane, check the Product field. Power BI adds it to the Axis area of the chart.
3. In the Visualizations pane, click the Stacked Bar Chart icon (first icon) to flip the Column Chart to a Bar Chart. Power BI sorts the bar chart by the product name in an ascending order.
4. Point your mouse cursor to the top-right corner of the chart. Click the ellipsis "..." menu and check that the data is sorted by SalesAmount in a descending order. Compare your results with the "SalesAmount by Product" visualization in the upper left of **Figure 3.26**.
5. (Optional) With bar chart selected, select the Format tab in the Visualizations pane. Switch "Data labels" to On to show data labels on the chart.

> **TIP** Clicked the wrong button or menu? Don't worry, you can undo your last step by pressing Ctrl-Z. To undo multiple steps in a reverse order, press Ctrl-Z repeatedly.

Adding Card visualizations

Let's show the total sales amount and order quantity as separate card visualizations (items 2 and 3 in **Figure 3.26**) to draw attention to them:

1. Click an empty space on the report canvas outside the Bar Chart to deactivate it.

> **TIP** As I explained, another way to create a new visualization is to drag a field to an empty space on the canvas. If the field is numeric, Power BI will create a Column Chart. For text fields, it'll default to a Table. And for geo fields, such as Country, it will default to a Map.

2. In the Field list, check the SalesAmount field. Change the visualization to Card. Position it as needed.
3. Repeat the last two steps to create a new card visualization using the OrderQuantity field.
4. (Optional) Experiment with the card format settings. For example, suppose you want a more descriptive title. In the Format tab of the Visualization pane, switch "Category label" to Off. Switch Title to On. Type in a descriptive title and change its font and alignment settings.

Creating a Combo Chart visualization

The fourth chart in **Figure 3.26** shows how the sales amount and order quantity change over time:

1. To practice another way to create a visual, drag the SalesAmount field and drop it onto an empty area next to the card visualizations to create a Column Chart.
2. Drag the Date field and drop it onto the new chart.
3. Switch the visualization to "Line and Stacked Column Chart". This adds a new Line Values area to the Visualizations pane.
4. Drag the OrderQuantity field and drop it on the Line Values area. Power BI adds a line chart to the visualization and plots its values to a secondary Y-axis. Compare your results with the "SalesAmount and OrderQuantity by Date" visualization (item 4 in **Figure 3.26**).
5. To avoid the sharp dip in the last bar of the chart caused by incomplete sales, apply a visual-level filter to exclude the last date. To do so, with the combo chart selected, expand the Date field in the "Visual level filters" area (Filters section on Fields tab of the Visualizations pane), check "Select All", then scroll all the way down the list, and then uncheck '7/1/2008'.

Creating a Matrix visualization

The fifth visualization (from **Figure 3.26**) represents a crosstab report showing sales by product on rows, and years on columns. Let's build this with the Matrix visualization:

1. Drag the SalesAmount field and drop it onto an empty space on the report canvas to create a new visualization. Change the visualization to Matrix.
2. Check the Product field to add it to the visualization on rows.
3. Drag the Year field and drop it on the Columns zone to see data grouped by years on columns.
4. Resize the visualization as needed. Click any of the column headers to sort the visualization interactively in an ascending or descending order.
5. (Optional) In the Format tab of the Visualizations pane, expand the Style section and then change the matrix style to Minimal. Expand the Grid section and change the "Horiz grid" to Off.
6. (Optional) In the Fields tab of the Visualizations pane, expand the drop-down button next to the SalesAmount field in the Values area. Notice that the SalesAmount is aggregated using the Sum aggregation function but you can choose another aggregation function. In the same drop-down menu, click "Conditional formatting" and experiment with different conditional format settings, such as to color cells with lower values in Red.

TIP Want to see "Sales Amount" instead of SalesAmount in the Matrix? You can rename column captions to show fields with different names on reports. To do so, just double-click the field name in the Fields tab of the Visualizations pane. Or, right-click the field name in the Fields tab and then click Rename.

Creating a Column Chart visualization

The sixth visualization listed shows sales by year:

1. Create a new visualization that uses the SalesAmount field. Power BI should default to Column Chart.
2. In the Fields pane, check the Year field to place it in the Axis area of the Column Chart.
3. Hover on one of the chart columns. Notice that a tooltip pops up to show Year and SalesAmount. Assuming you want to see the order quantity as well, drag OrderQuantity from the Fields pane and drop it to the Tooltips area of the Fields tab in the Visualizations pane.
4. (Optional) Suppose you want to change the color of the column showing the 2008 data. Switch to the Format tab in the Visualizations pane. Expand Data Colors and turn "Show all" to On. Change the color of the 2008 item.
5. (Optional) Suppose you need a trend line on the chart. Switch to the Analytics tab in the Visualizations pane. Expand the Trend Line section and then click Add. Change the format settings of the trend line as needed.
6. (Optional) Change the chart type to Line Chart. Notice that the Analytics tab adds a Forecast section. Add a forecast line to predict sales for future periods.

Filtering the report

Next, you'll implement page-level and visual-level filters. Let's start by creating a page-level Date filter that will allow you to filter all visualizations on the page by date.

1. Click an empty area on the report canvas to make sure that no visualization is activated.
2. Drag the Date field onto the Page Level Filters area. This creates a page-level filter that filters all visualizations on the activated page.
3. Practice different ways to filter. For example, switch to Advanced Filtering mode and filter out dates after June 30th, 2008, as shown on the left screenshot in **Figure 3.27**.

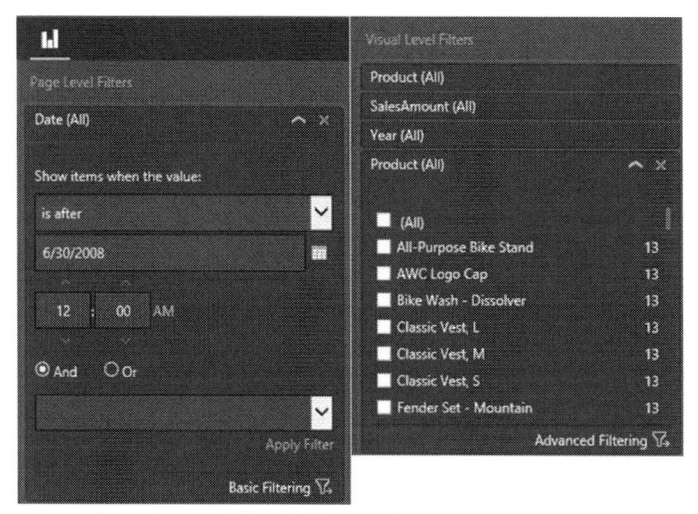

Figure 3.27 The Advanced Filter mode (left screenshot) allows you to specify more complex criteria and multiple conditions for filtering, such as filter dates where the Date field is after June 30th, 2008. The Visual Level Filters area (right screenshot) includes by default all the fields that are used in the visualization.

4. To work with visual-level filters, click the fifth (Matrix) visualization. To practice another way to create a filter besides drag and drop, hover on the Product field in the Fields pane. Then expand the ellipsis menu and click Add Filter.

Because there's an activated visualization, this action configures a visual-level filter. Notice that the Visual Level Filters (see the right screenshot in **Figure 3.27**) already includes the three fields used in the visualization so that you can filter on these fields without explicitly adding them as filters.

Creating a Treemap

Let's add a second page to the report that will help you analyze product sales using a Treemap visualization (see **Figure 3.28**).

1. At the bottom of the report, click the plus sign to add a new page. Rename the page in place to *Treemap*.
2. In the Fields list, check the SalesAmount and Product fields.
3. Change the visualization type to Treemap.
4. By default, Power BI uses arbitrary colors for the tree map tiles. Assuming you want to color the bestselling products in green and worst-selling products in red, drag the SalesAmount field to the Color Saturation area of the Visualizations pane.
5. In the Format tab of the Visualizations pane, change the Data Colors settings, as shown in **Figure 3.28**. Turning off the Diverging option allows you to specify a color for the values that fall in the middle. You can use the Minimum, Center, and Maximum fields to fine tune the ranges.
6. Save your report.

3.2.2 Getting Quick Insights

Let's face it, slicing and dicing data to perform root cause analysis (RCA) could be time consuming and tedious. For example, a report might show you that sales are increasing or decreasing, but it won't tell you why. Retrospectively, such tasks required you to produce more detailed reports, to explain sudden data fluctuations. And this gets even more difficult if you're analyzing a model created by someone else because you don't know which fields to use and how to use them to get answers. Enter Quick Insights!

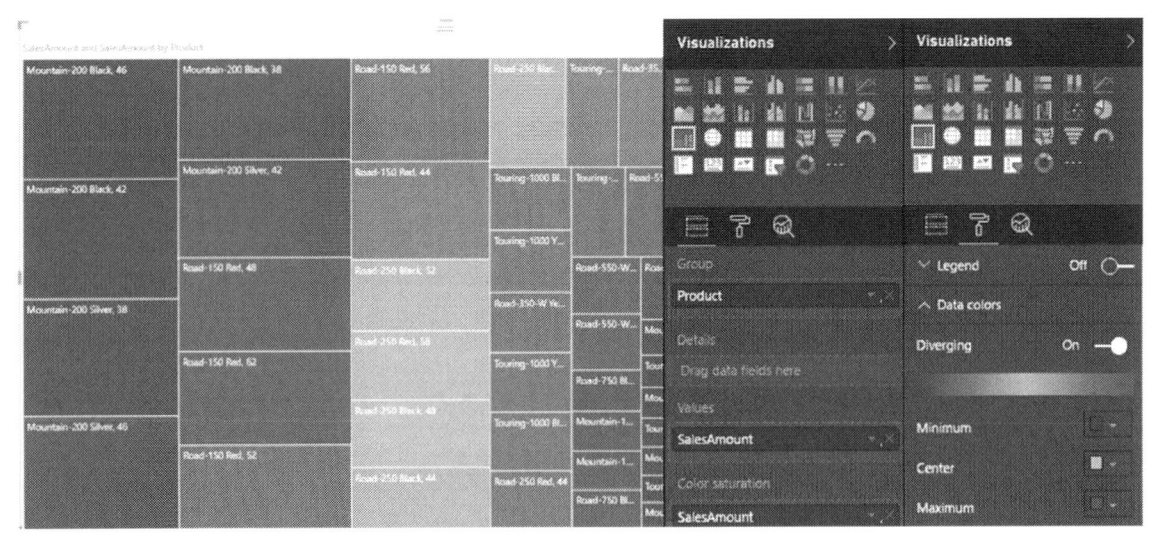

Figure 3.28 The Treemap visualization helps you analyze product sales.

Understanding Quick Insights

Power BI Quick Insights gives you new ways to find insights hidden in your data. With a click of button, Quick Insights run various sophisticated algorithms on your data to search for interesting fluctuations. Originating from Microsoft Research, these algorithms can discover correlations, outliers, trends, seasonality changes, and change points in trends, automatically and within seconds. **Table 3.2** lists some of the insights that these algorithms can uncover.

Table 3.2 This table summarizes the available insights.

Insight	Explanation
Major factors(s)	Finds cases where a majority of a total value can be attributed to a single factor when broken down by another dimension.
Category outliers (top/bottom)	Highlights cases where, for a measure in the model, one or two members of a dimension have much larger values than other members of the dimension.
Time series outliers	For data across a time series, detects when there are specific dates or times with values significantly different than the other date/time values.
Overall trends in time series	Detects upward or downward trends in time series data.
Seasonality in time series	Finds periodic patterns in time series data, such as weekly, monthly, or yearly seasonality.
Steady Share	Highlights cases where there is a parent-child correlation between the share of a child value in relation to the overall value of the parent across a continuous variable.
Correlation	Detects cases where multiple measures show a correlation between each other when plotted against a dimension in the dataset

By default, Quick Insights queries as much of the dataset as possible in a fixed time window (about 20 seconds). Quick Insights requires data to be imported in Power BI. Quick Insights isn't available for datasets that connect directly to data.

Working with Quick Insights

Let's find what insights we can uncover by applying Quick Insights to the Retail Analysis Sample dataset:

1. In the navigation bar, expand My Workspace. In the Datasets section, right-click the "Retail Analysis Sample" dataset and click Quick Insights (or click the ellipsis menu). Alternatively, click My Workspace in the navigation pane. In the workspace content page, select the Datasets tab. Click the ellipsis (…) button to the right of the "Retail Analysis Sample" dataset, and the click "Get quick insights".
2. While Power BI runs the algorithms, it displays a "Searching for insights" message. Once it's done, it shows "Insights are ready" message.
3. Click the ellipsis next to the "Retail Analysis Sample" dataset again. Note that the Quick Insights link is renamed to View Insights. Click View Insights.

Power BI opens a "Quick Insights for Retail Analysis Sample" page that shows many auto-generated insights. **Figure 3.29** shows the first report. It has found a correlation between the "Count of Segment" and "Count of Buyer" measures. This is an example of a Correlation insight. As you can see, Quick Insights can really help understand data changes. Currently, Power BI deactivates the generated reports when you close your browser. However, if you find an insight useful, you can click the pin button in the top-right corner to pin to a dashboard. (I discuss creating dashboards in more detail in the next chapter.

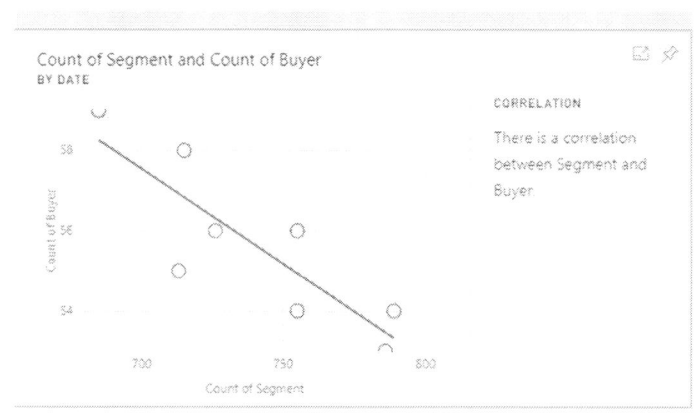

Figure 3.29 The first Quick Insight report shows a correlation between two measures.

3.2.3 Subscribing to Reports

In the previous chapter, I walked you through the steps to create the Adventure Works report from an Analysis Services model. Suppose that Maya would like to subscribe to a report so that she receives the report by email when the underlying data has changed.

> **NOTE** You might wonder why not use the Internet Sales report that you just created. Recall that this report imports data from an Excel file and you created it directly in Power BI Service (without using Power BI Desktop). As I explained in section 2.3.1, Power BI can't refresh these types of reports or the included sample reports, such as Retail Analysis Sample. Although you can subscribe to such reports, you won't get an email because there will be nothing to trigger the subscription. If you haven't created the Adventure Works report in the previous chapter but you want to practice subscriptions, fast forward and follow the instructions in section 11.2.3 to deploy the Adventure Works Power BI Desktop model and schedule it for refresh. Then, create and test a subscription to the Adventure Works report.

Creating a subscription
Follow these steps to create a subscription to an existing report.

1. In Power BI Service, expand My Workspace and click the Adventure Works report in the Reports section.

2. Click the Adventure Works report to open it in Reading View. Click the Subscribe menu.
3. In the "Subscribe to emails" window, leave the default settings to subscribe to the first page of the report. Or, if the report has multiple pages and you want to subscribe to them, click the "Add another subscription" button to create more subscriptions, one page at the time.
4. Click "Save and close" to create the subscription.

Receiving reports

When the Analysis Services model is refreshed, you'll get an email with screenshots of all report pages that you subscribed to. Power BI will determine the exact time when this will happen.

> **TIP** If you've subscribed to a report connected to a dataset with imported data and you've scheduled the dataset for refresh, you can manually refresh the dataset to get the email faster. To do so, go to the workspace content page, click the Datasets tab, and then click the "Refresh Now" icon next to the dataset name.

1. Check your mail inbox for an email from no-reply@email.powerbi.com. **Figure 3.30** shows the content of a sample email. The email includes screenshots of all subscribed pages. In this case, I've subscribed to only one page, so I get only one screenshot.
2. Suppose you want to open the report and interact with it. Click the "Go to Report" button and Power BI navigates you to the report.
3. Back to the email, click the "Manage subscription" link. This navigates you to the report and opens the "Subscribe to emails" window so that you can review and make changes to your report subscription.
4. In the "Subscribe to emails" window, click the "Manage all subscriptions" link. This navigates you to the Settings page that shows all your subscriptions that exist in the current workspace.

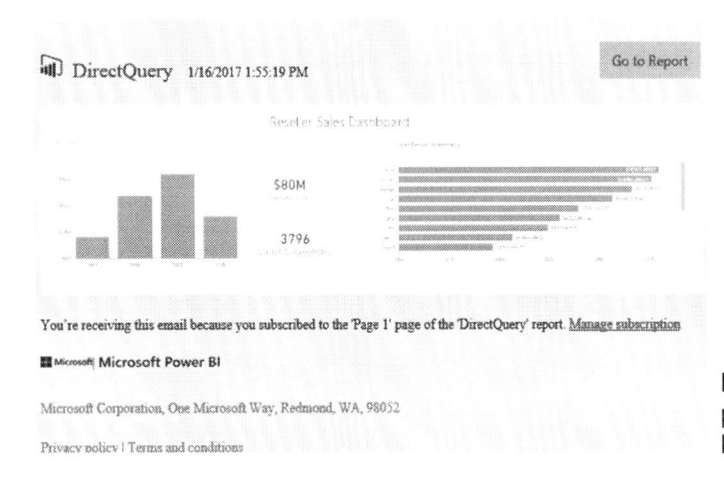

Figure 3.30 The subscription email includes page screenshots, a link to the report, and a link to change the subscription settings.

3.3 Working with Excel Reports

Ask a business user what tools they currently use for analytics and Excel comes on top. Thanks to its integration with SharePoint Online, Power BI can connect to existing Excel table or pivot reports and render them online (without importing the Excel file). In addition, business users can connect Excel desktop to Power BI datasets and create Excel pivot reports, just like they can connect Excel to Analysis Services models. Let's take a more detailed look at these two integration options with Excel.

3.3.1 Connecting to Excel Reports

Before you connect to your Excel reports, you need to pay attention to where the Excel file is stored:

- Excel files stored locally – If the Excel file is stored on your computer, Power BI needs to upload the file before Excel Online can connect to it. Because Excel Online can't synchronize the uploaded version with the local file (even if you set up a gateway), you have to re-upload the file after you make changes if you want the connected reports to show the latest.
- Excel files stored in the cloud – If your Excel file is saved to OneDrive for Business or SharePoint Online, Power BI doesn't have to upload the file because it can connect directly to it. As long as you save changes to the same location in the cloud, Power BI will always show the latest.

OneDrive for Business is a place where business users can store, sync, and share work files. While the personal edition of OneDrive is free, OneDrive for Business requires an Office 365 plan. For example, Maya might maintain an Excel file with some calculations. Or, Martin might give her an Excel file with Power Pivot model and pivot reports. Maya can upload these files to her OneDrive for Business and then add these reports to Power BI, and even pin them to a dashboard!

> **NOTE** Online Excel reports have limitations which are detailed in the "Bring Excel files in Power BI" article by Microsoft at https://powerbi.microsoft.com/en-us/documentation/powerbi-service-excel-workbook-files. One popular and frequently requested scenario that Power BI still doesn't support is Excel reports connected to external data, such as Analysis Services, although Excel workbooks with Power Pivot data models work just fine. That's because currently SharePoint Online doesn't support external connections, even if you have a gateway set up. This might be a serious issue if you plan to migrate your BI reports from on-premises SharePoint Server to Power BI.

Connecting to Excel

In this exercise, you'll connect an Excel file saved to OneDrive for Business and you'll view its containing reports online. As a prerequisite, your organization must have an Office 365 business plan and you must have access to OneDrive for Business. If you don't have access to OneDrive for Business, you can use a local Excel file. The Reseller Sales.xlsx file in the \Source\ch03 folder includes a Power Pivot data model with several tables. The first two sheets have Excel pivot tables and chart reports, while the third sheet has a Power View report. While all reports connect to an embedded Power Pivot data model, they don't have to. For example, your pivot reports can connect to Excel tables.

1. Copy and save the Reseller Sales.xlsx to your OneDrive for Business. To open OneDrive, click the Office 365 Application Launcher button (the yellow button in the upper-left corner in the Power BI portal) and then click OneDrive. If you don't see the OneDrive icon, your organization doesn't have an Office 365 business plan (to complete this exercise, go back to Get Data and choose the Local File option).
2. In Power BI, click Get Data. Then click the Get button in the Files tile.
3. In the next page, click the "One Drive – Business" tile. In the "OneDrive for Business" page, navigate to the folder where you saved the Reseller Sales.xlsx file, select the file, and then click Connect.

   Power BI prompts you how to work with the file (see **Figure 3.31**). You practiced importing from Excel in Chapter 2. If you take this path, Power BI will import only the data from the Excel file. If there are any pivot reports in the Excel workbook, they won't be added to Power BI.
4. Click the Connect button to connect directly to the Excel file. Power BI processes the Excel file and notifies you that it's added to your list of workbooks.

> **NOTE** If you've selected the Local File option in Get Data, the button caption will read "Upload" instead of "Connect". This is to emphasize the fact that Power BI will upload the file to its cloud storage before it connects to it.

OneDrive for Business

Choose how to connect to your Excel workbook

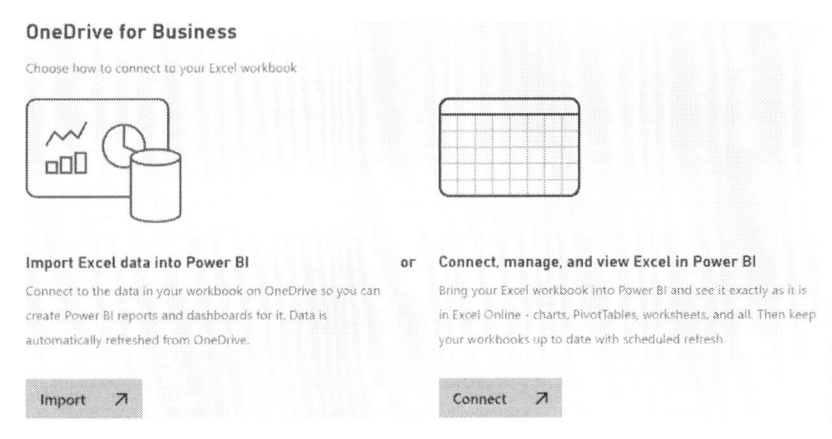

Import Excel data into Power BI or **Connect, manage, and view Excel in Power BI**

Connect to the data in your workbook on OneDrive so you can create Power BI reports and dashboards for it. Data is automatically refreshed from OneDrive.

Bring your Excel workbook into Power BI and see it exactly as it is in Excel Online - charts, PivotTables, worksheets, and all. Then keep your workbooks up to date with scheduled refresh.

Figure 3.31 When you connect to an Excel file stored on OneDrive for Business, Power BI asks you how you want to work with the file.

[Import]   [Connect]

Interacting with Excel reports

Excel Online (a component of SharePoint Online) renders the Excel reports in HTML so you don't need Excel on the desktop to view the Excel reports added to Power BI. And not only can you view the Excel reports, but you can also interact with them, just as you can do so in Excel Desktop.

1. In the Power BI portal, expand My Workspace. You should see Reseller Sales listed in the Workbooks section. Alternatively, in the navigation pane click My Workspace. In the workspace content page, click the Workbooks tab. You should see Reseller Sales listed. This represents the Excel file that is now available to Power BI.

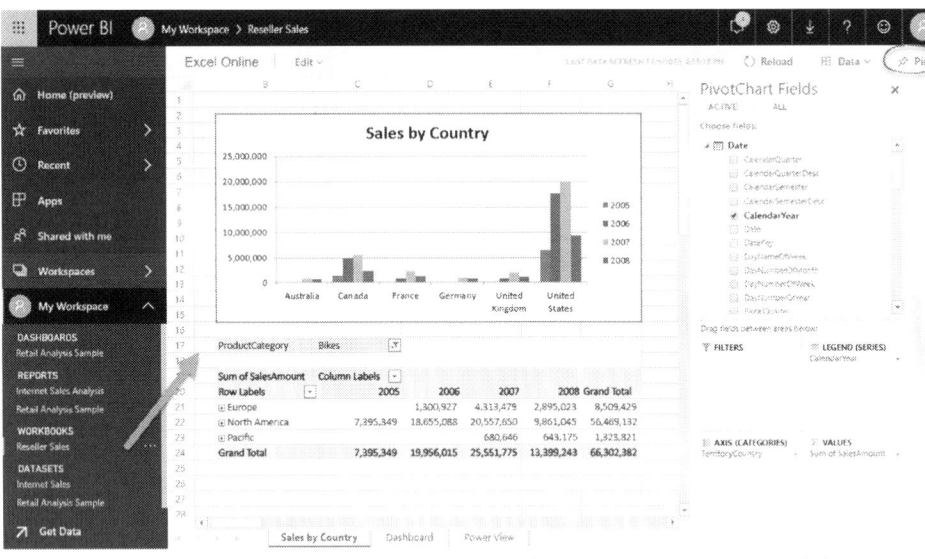

Figure 3.32 Power BI supports rendering Excel reports online if the Excel file is stored in OneDrive for Business.

2. Click the Reseller Sales workbook. Power BI renders the pivot reports and the Power View report online (Power View rendering requires a web browser that supports Microsoft Silverlight, such as Internet Explorer) via Excel Online (see **Figure 3.32**).
3. (Optional) Try some interactive features, such as changing the report filters and slicers, and notice that they work the same as they work in SharePoint Server or SharePoint Online. For example, you can change report filters and slicers, and you can add or remove fields.

TIP You can pin a range from an Excel report as a static image to a Power BI dashboard. To do so, select the range on the report and then click the Pin button in the upper-right corner of the report (see again **Figure 3.32**). The Pin to Dashboard window allows you to preview the selected section and prompts you if you want to pin it to a new or an existing dashboard. For more information about this feature, read the "Pin a range from Excel to your dashboard!" blog at https://powerbi.microsoft.com/en-us/blog/pin-a-range-from-excel-to-your-dashboard. Q&A is not available for Excel tiles.

3.3.2 Analyzing Data in Excel

Besides consuming existing Excel reports, business users can create their own Excel pivot reports connected to Power BI datasets. This feature, called Analyze in Excel, brings you another option to explore Power BI datasets (besides creating Power BI reports). For example, Maya knows Excel pivot reports and she wants to create a pivot report that's connected to the Retailer Analysis Sample dataset. She can use the Analyze in Excel feature to connect to her data in Power BI, just like she can do so by connecting Excel to a multidimensional cube. She can then use the Power BI Publisher for Excel add-in to pin her report as an image to a dashboard. Analyze in Excel is a Power BI Pro feature.

Creating Excel reports
Follow these steps to create an Excel report connected to the Retailer Analysis Sample dataset:

1. In Power BI portal, expand My Workspace in the navigation pane. Under the Datasets section, click the ellipsis menu (…) next to the Retail Analysis Sample dataset and then click Analyze in Excel. Alternatively, in the navigation pane click My Workspace. In the workspace content page, click the Datasets tab. Expand the ellipsis (…) menu next to the Retailer Analysis Sample dataset and click Analyze in Excel.
2. You'll be asked to install some updates to enable this feature. Accept to install these updates. They will install a newer version of the MSOLAP OLEDB provider that Excel needs to connect to Power BI. Then your web browser downloads a Retailer Analysis Sample.odc file which includes the connection details to connect Excel to the Power BI dataset.
3. Click the download file. Excel opens and prompts you to enable the connection. Once you confirm the prompt, Excel adds an empty pivot table report connected to the Power BI dataset.

NOTE As far as Excel is concerned, Analyze in Excel connects to Power BI using the same mechanism as it uses to connect to cubes. Excel parses the dataset metadata and it looks for measures and dimensions. Therefore, if you want to aggregate data you must define explicit measures in the datasets. In other words, the dataset must be created in Power BI Desktop and it must have explicit DAX measures. In fact, Analyze in Excel won't work if you have created the dataset directly in Power BI Service (as you did with the Internet Sales file).

Besides creating ad-hoc Excel pivot reports, another practical benefit of using Analyze in Excel is that it doesn't limit the number of rows when drilling through data (just double-click an aggregated cell in the pivot report to drill through).

Using Power BI Publisher for Excel
If you like Analyze in Excel, consider installing the "Power BI publisher for Excel" add-in. The tool adds the ability to connect to Power BI datasets directly from Excel (without downloading the *.odc file from Power BI portal) and to pin Excel ranges as static images to Power BI dashboards.

1. In Power BI portal, expand the Downloads menu in the top right corner and then click "Power BI publisher for Excel". Run the setup to install the tool.
2. Open Excel. Notice that the add-in adds a Power BI menu to the Excel ribbon (see **Figure 3.33**).
3. Click the "Connect to Data" button. Log in to Power BI and connect to the Retailer Analysis Sample datasets in My Workspace. The publisher will create an empty PivotTable report connected to the dataset.

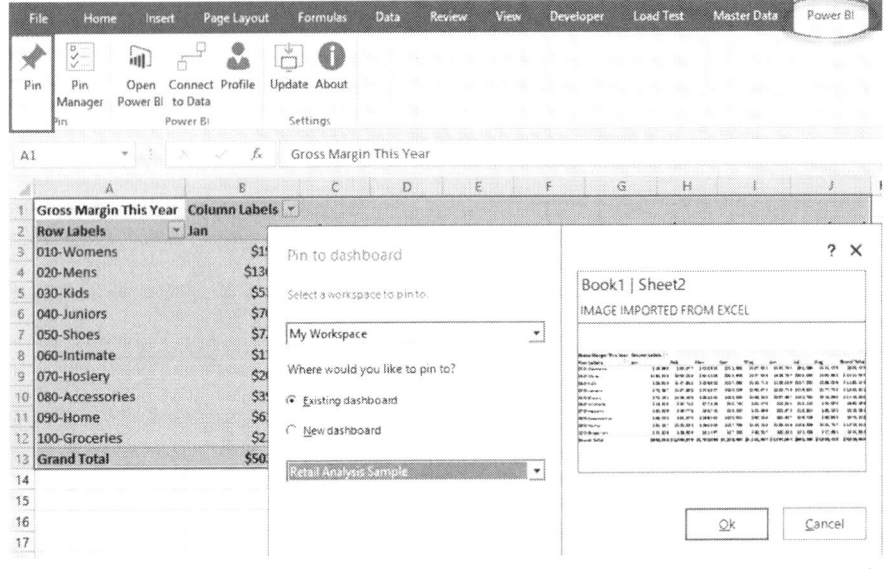

Figure 3.33 Power BI publisher for Excel lets you pin reports to dashboards.

4. Drag some fields on the report, such as the "Gross Margin This Year" measure (Sales Table) in the Values area, Category (Item table) in the Rows area, and Fiscal Year (Time table) in the Columns area.
5. Let's pin this report to a dashboard. Select the entire report and then click Pin. In the "Pin to dashboard" window, select My Workspace and then select the "Retail Analysis Sample" dashboard.
6. In Power BI Service, open the "Retail Analysis Sample" dashboard and notice that it includes an image of the Excel pivot report. Unlike connecting to an Excel file, you can't open the report online and interact with it. That's because the report was produced on the desktop.

For more information about the Power BI publisher for Excel, read the "Power BI publisher for Excel" article at https://powerbi.microsoft.com/documentation/powerbi-publisher-for-excel.

NOTE Unfortunately, the report interactive features won't work if you upload the Excel workbook to OneDrive or SharePoint Online and use Get Data to connect to it. The report will open but you won't be able to interact with it. That's because the report has an external connection to the dataset. This is the same limitation as connecting to Analysis Services.

3.3.3 Comparing Excel Reporting Options

At this point, you might be confused about which option to use when working with Excel files. **Table 3.3** should help you make the right choice. To recap, Power BI offers three Excel integration options.

Table 3.3 This table compares the Power BI options to work with Excel.

Criteria	Import Excel files	Connect to Excel files	Analyze in Excel
Data acquisition	Power BI parses the Excel file, imports data, and creates a dataset.	Power BI doesn't parse and import the data. Instead, Power BI connects to the Excel file hosted on OneDrive or SharePoint Online.	Connects to existing dataset in Power BI
Data model (Power Pivot)	Power BI imports the model and creates a dataset.	Power BI doesn't import the data model.	N/A
Pivot reports	Power BI doesn't import pivot reports.	Power BI renders pivot reports via Excel Online.	Create your pivot reports

Criteria	Import Excel files	Connect to Excel files	Analyze in Excel
Power View reports	Power BI imports Power View reports and adds them to Reports section in the left navigation bar.	Power BI renders Power View reports via Excel Online (requires Silverlight).	N/A
Change reports	You can change the imported Power View reports but the original reports in the Excel file remain intact.	You can't change reports. You must open the file in Excel, make report changes, and upload the file to OneDrive.	You can change reports saved in the Excel file.
Publish reports	Import or create new Power BI reports	Reports are available in the Workbooks tab; you can pin Excel ranges as static images to Power BI dashboards.	Pin Excel ranges as static images to Power BI dashboards
Data refresh	Scheduled dataset refresh (automatic refresh if saved to OneDrive or OneDrive for Business).	Dashboard tiles from Excel reports are refreshed automatically every few minutes.	N/A

Importing Excel files

Use this option when you need only the Excel data and you'll later create Power BI reports to analyze it. As a prerequisite for importing Excel files directly in Power BI Service, the data must be formatted as an Excel table (Power BI Desktop doesn't have this limitation). If the Excel file has Power View reports, Power BI will create a corresponding Power BI report, but it won't import any pivot reports. Because data is imported, you'd probably need to set up a data refresh. However, a scheduled refresh is not required if the workbook is saved in OneDrive or SharePoint Online because Power BI synchronizes changes every hour.

Connecting to Excel files

Use this option when you need to bring in existing Excel pivot reports and Power View reports to Power BI. In this case, Power BI doesn't import the data. Instead, it leaves the Excel file where it is, and it just connects to it. However, you must upload the file to OneDrive for Business or SharePoint Online. All connected Excel workbooks appears under the Workbooks tab in the workspace content page.

When you open the workbook, you can see its reports online without needing Excel on the desktop. You'll be able to interact with the reports if the data is imported in the Excel workbooks. At this point, external connections are not supported. You can select a range and pin to a dashboard as an image.

Analyze in Excel

Use this option when you want to create your own PivotTable and PivotChart reports connected to datasets published to Power BI Service. If you use Power BI publisher for Excel, you can pin the pivot reports as images to dashboards, just like you can do when connecting to Excel files.

3.4 Summary

As a business user, you don't need any special skills to gain insights from data. With a few clicks, you can create interactive reports for presenting information in a variety of ways that range from basic reports to professional-looking dashboards.

You can create a new report by exploring a dataset. Power BI supports popular visualizations, including charts, maps, gauges, cards, and tables. When those visualizations just won't do the job, you can import custom visuals from Microsoft AppSource.

Because Excel is a very pervasive tool for self-service, BI supports several integration options with Excel. You can import data from Excel tables. To preserve your investment in Excel pivot and Power View reports, save the Excel files in OneDrive for Business and connect to these files to view the included reports in Excel Online. Finally, you can connect Excel to Power BI datasets and create ad-hoc pivot reports.

Now that you know how to create reports, let's learn more about Power BI dashboards.

Chapter 4

Creating Dashboards

4.1 Understanding Dashboards 96
4.2 Adding Dashboard Content 105
4.3 Working with Dashboards 111
4.4 Summary 113

In Chapter 2, I introduced you to Power BI dashboards and you learned that dashboards are one of the three main Power BI content items (the other two are datasets and reports). I defined a Power BI dashboard as a summarized view of important metrics that typically fit on a single page. You need a dashboard when you want to combine data from multiple reports (datasets), or when you need dashboards-specific features, such as data alerts or real-time tiles.

This chapter takes a deep dive into Power BI dashboards. I'll start by discussing the anatomy of a Power BI dashboard. I'll walk you through different ways to create a dashboard, including pinning visualizations, using natural queries by typing them in the Q&A box, from predictive insights, and from SSRS reports. You'll also learn how to share dashboards with your co-workers.

4.1 Understanding Dashboards

Like an automobile's dashboard, a digital dashboard enables users to get a "bird's eye view" of the company's health and performance. A dashboard page typically hosts several sections that display data visually in charts, graphs, or gauges, so that data is easier to understand and analyze. You can use Power BI to quickly assemble dashboards from existing or new visualizations.

NOTE Power BI isn't the only Microsoft-provided tool for creating dashboards. For example, if you need an entirely on-premises dashboard solution, dashboards can be implemented with Excel (requires SharePoint Server or Power BI Report Server for sharing) and Reporting Services (requires SQL Server). While Power BI dashboards might not be as customizable as SSRS reports, they are by far the easiest to implement. They also gain in interactive features, the ability to use natural queries, and even to get real-time updates (when data is streamed to Power BI)!

4.1.1 Understanding Dashboard Tiles

A Power BI dashboard has one or more tiles. Each tile shows data from one source, such as from one report. For example, the Total Stores tile in the Retail Analysis Sample dashboard (see **Figure 4.1**) shows the total number of stores. The Card visualization came from the Retail Analysis Sample report. Although you can add as many tiles as you want, as a rule of thumb try to limit the number of tiles so that they can fit into a single page and so the user doesn't have to scroll horizontally or vertically.

A tile has a resize handle that allows you to change the tile size to one of the predefined tile sizes (from 1x1 tile units up to 5x5). Because tiles can't overlap, when you enlarge a tile it pushes the rest of the content out of the way. If the tile flow setting is enabled, when you make the tile smaller, adjacent tiles "snap in" to occupy the empty space.

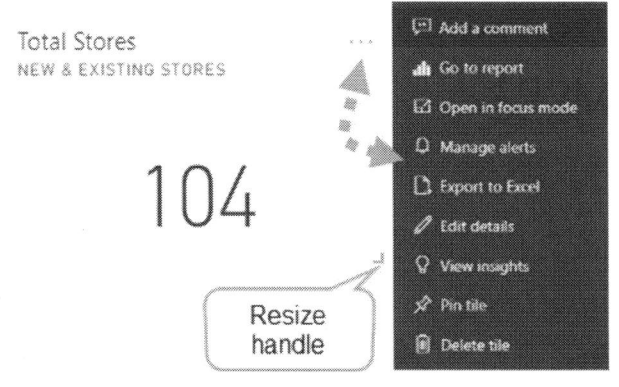

Figure 4.1 When you hover on a tile, the ellipsis menu (…) allows you to access the tile settings.

If the tile flow setting is not enabled, Power BI won't reclaim the empty space. To turn on tile flow, open the dashboard, click the ellipsis menu in the upper-right corner of the dashboard (next to the Share button), click Settings, and then slide the "Dashboard tile flow" slider to On. You can move a tile by just dragging it to a new location. Unlike reports, you don't need to explicitly save the layout changes you've made to a dashboard when you resize or move its tiles because Power BI automatically saves dashboard changes.

Understanding tile actions

When you hover on a tile, an ellipsis menu (…) shows up in the top-right corner of the tile. When you click the ellipsis menu, a context menu pops up with a list of tile-related actions. What actions are included in the menu depends on where the tile came from. For example, if the tile was produced by pinning an Excel pivot report, you won't be able to set alerts, export to Excel, and view insights. Or, if the dataset has row-level security applied, you won't see "View insights" because this feature is not available with RLS. Let's quickly describe the actions:

1. Add a comment – You can start a conversation at a dashboard or tile level. For example, you can post a question about the data shown in the tile.
2. Go to report – By default, when you click a tile, Power BI "drills through" it and navigates you to the underlying source. For example, if the tile is pinned from a report, you'll be taken to the underlying report. Another way to navigate to the report is to invoke "Go to report" from the context menu.
3. Open in focus mode – Like popping out visualizations on a report, this action pops out the tile so that you can examine it in more detail.
4. Manage alerts – A tile pinned from a visualization showing a scalar value (Single Card, Gauge, KPI) can have one or more data alerts, such as to notify you when the number of stores reaches 105.
5. Export to Excel – Exports the tile data to a Comma-separated values (CSV) text file. You can then open the file in Excel and examine the data.
6. Edit details – Allows you to change the tile settings, such as the tile title and subtitle.
7. View insights – Like Quick Insights but targets the specific tile for discovering insights. Power BI will search the tile and its related data for correlations, outliers, trends, seasonality, change points in trends, and major factors automatically, within seconds.
8. Pin tile – Pins a tile to another dashboard. Why would you pin a tile from a dashboard instead of from the report? Pinning it from a dashboard allows you to apply the same customizations, such as the title, subtitle, and custom link, to the other dashboard, even though they're not shared (once you pin the tile to another dashboard, both titles have independent customizations).
9. Delete tile – Removes the tile from the dashboard.

Some of these actions deserve more attention so I'll explain them next in more detail.

Understanding comments

Available in Power BI Service and Power BI Mobile, comments are a collaboration feature that allows you to start a conversation for something that peaked your interest. To post a dashboard comment, open the dashboard and click the Comments main menu. You can also post comments for a specific tile by clicking the tile ellipsis menu and then choosing "Add a comment". This will open the Comments pane (see **Figure 4.2**) where you can post your comments. You know that a tile has comments when you see the "Show tile conversations" button on the tile. Clicking this button brings you to the Comments pane where you can see and participate in the conversation.

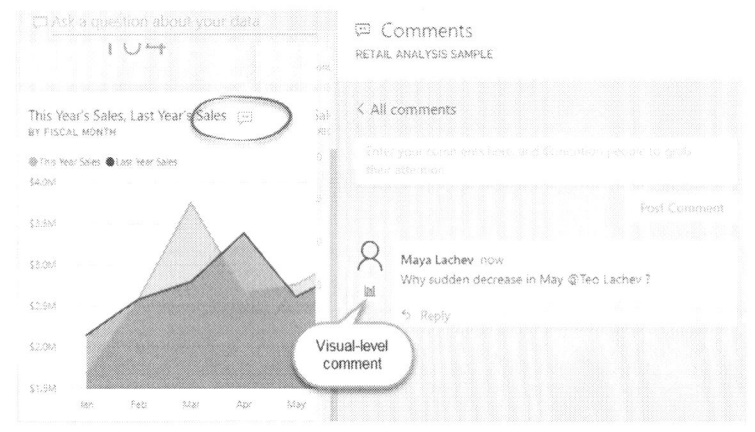

Figure 4.2 You can post a comment for a specific dashboard tile and include someone in the conversation.

For tile-related comments, you can click the icon below the person in the Comments pane, to navigate to the specific tile that the comment is associated with. To avoid posting a comment and waiting for someone to see it and act on it, you can @mention someone as you can do on Twitter. When you do this, the other person will get an email and in-app notification in Power BI Mobile. You can navigate to the Comments pane to participate in the conversation.

Power BI doesn't currently support retention policies for comments, so your comments don't expire. Comments don't save the state of the tile, such as a screenshot, if it changes after data refresh. Consequently, there is no way to recreate what the tile looked like when the comment was posted if the data changed.

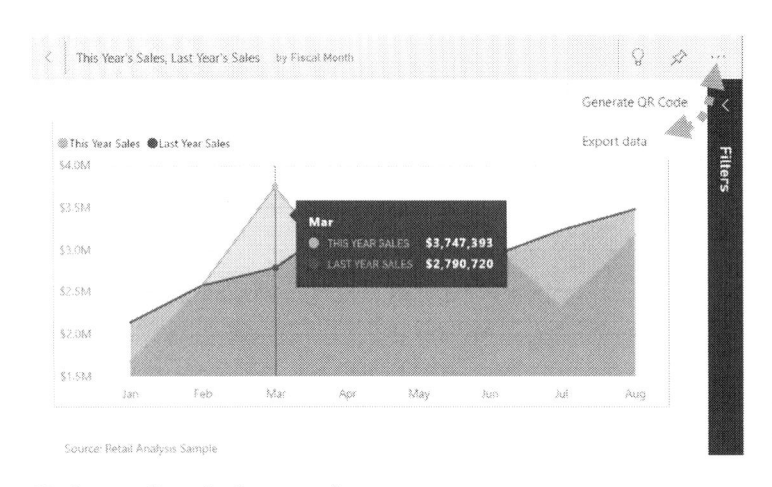

Figure 4.3 The focus mode page allows you to examine the tile in more detail, generate a QR code, and export the tile data.

Understanding the focus mode

When you click the "Open in focus mode" button, Power BI opens another page and enlarges the visualization (see **Figure 4.3**). Tooltips allow you to get precise values. If you pop out a line chart, you can also click a data point to place a vertical line and see the precise value of a measure at the intersection of the vertical bar and the line. The Filter pane is available so that you can filter the displayed data by specifying visual-level filters.

The focus page has an ellipsis menu (…) in the top-right corner. When you click it, a "Generate QR Code" menu appears. A QR Code (abbreviated from Quick Response Code) is a barcode that contains information about the item to which it is attached. In the case of a Power BI tile, it contains the URL of the tile. How's this useful, you might wonder? You can download the code, print it, and display it somewhere or post the image online. When other people scan the code (there are many QR Code reader mobile apps, including the one included in the Power BI iPhone app), they'll get the tile URL. Now they can quickly navigate to the dashboard tile. So QR codes give users convenient and instant access to dashboard tiles.

For example, suppose you're visiting a potential customer and they give you a pamphlet. It starts gushing about all these stats about how great their performance has been. You have a hard time believing what you hear or even understanding the numbers. You see the QR Code. You scan it with your phone. It pops up Power BI Mobile on your phone, and rather than just reading the pamphlet, now you're sliding the controls around in Power BI and exploring the data. You go back and forth between reading the pamphlet and then exploring the associated data on your phone.

Or, suppose you're in a meeting. The presenter is showing some data but wants you to explore it independently. He includes a QR Code on their deck. He also might pass around a paper with the QR Code on it. You scan the code and navigate to Power BI to examine the data in more detail. As you can imagine, QR codes open new opportunities for getting access to relevant information that's available in Power BI. For more information about the QR code feature, read the blog "Bridge the gap between your physical world and your BI using QR codes" at http://bit.ly/1lsVGJ5.

Understanding tile insights

In the previous chapter, you saw how Quick Insights makes it easy to apply brute-force predictive analytics to a dataset and discover hidden trends. Instead of examining the entire dataset, you can scope Quick Insights to a specific tile. You can do so by clicking the "View insights" action found in the tile's properties and in the upper-right corner of the tile while it's in focus.

Power BI will scan the data related to the tile and display a list of visualizations you may want to explore further. **Figure 4.4** shows two of the Insights visuals for the Total Stores card of the Retail Analysis Sample dashboard. To get even more specifics insights, you can click a data point in the visual, and Related Insights will focus on that data point when searching for insights. If you find a given insight useful, you can hover on the visual and click the pin button to pin it to a dashboard.

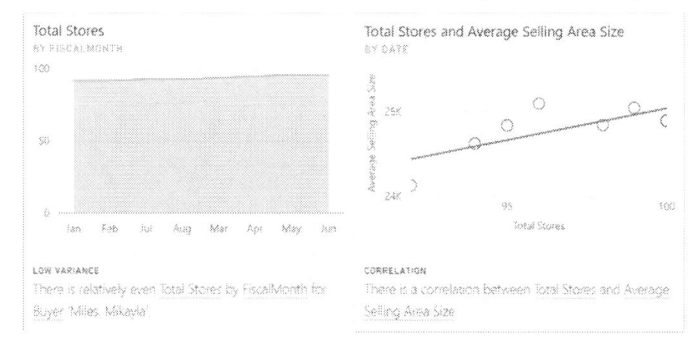

Figure 4.4 Insights applies the same predictive algorithms as Quick Insights but limits their scope to a specific tile.

Understanding data alerts

Wouldn't it be nice to be notified for important data changes, such as when this year's revenue reaches a specific goal? Now you can be with Power BI data alerts! You can create alerts on Single Card, Gauge, and KPI tiles because they show a single value. A tile can have multiple alerts, such as to notify you when the value is both above and below certain thresholds. You can create a data alert in Power BI Service (click

"Manage alerts" in the tile properties) or in Power BI Mobile native applications for mobile devices. This brings you to the "Manage alerts" window (see **Figure 4.5**) where you can create one or more alerts.

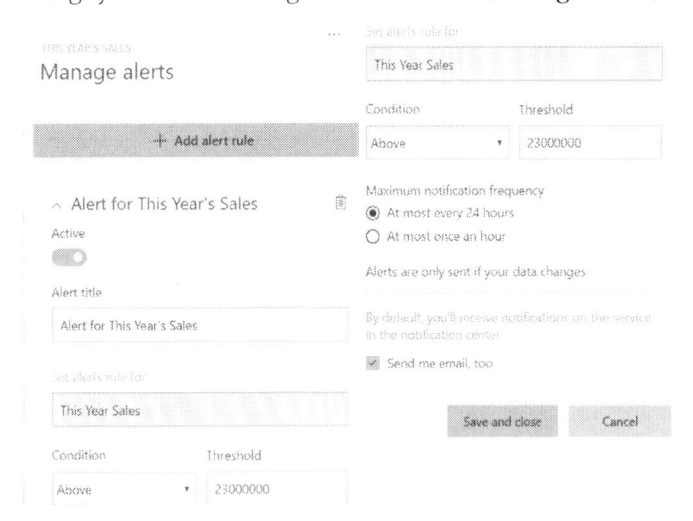

Figure 4.5 When you create an alert, you specify a condition and notification frequency.

Currently, Power BI supports two conditions (Above and Below) and two notification intervals (daily and hourly). By default, you'll get an email when the condition is met in addition to a notification in the Power BI Notification Center. If you have Power BI Mobile installed on your mobile device, you'll also get an in-app notification.

> **TIP** To view all data alerts that you defined for dashboards in My Workspace, in Power BI Portal expand the Settings menu, click Settings, and then select the Alerts tab. There you can deactivate the alert, edit it, or delete it. Currently, like the limitations for subscriptions, there isn't a way for the tenant admin to see alerts by other users.

Understanding tile details

Additional tile configuration options are available when you click "Edit details" (the fifth option in **Figure 4.1**). It brings you to the "Tile details" window (see **Figure 4.6**). Since report visualizations might have Power BI-generated titles that might not be very descriptive, the Tile Details window allows you to specify a custom title and subtitle for the tile.

Figure 4.6 The Tile Details window lets you change the tile's title, subtitle, and specify a custom link.

As you know by now, clicking a tile brings you to the report where the tile was pinned from. However, if you want the user to be navigated to another report or even a web page, you can overwrite this behavior by checking the "Set custom link" checkbox. Then you can specify if this is an external link (you need to enter the page URL) or a link to an existing dashboard and report in the workspace where your dashboard is in (you can pick the target dashboard or report from a drop-down). You can also configure the link to open in a new browser tab.

> **TIP** An external link could navigate the user to any URL-based resource, such as to an on-premises SSRS report. This could be useful if you want to link the tile to a more detailed report. Unfortunately, you can't pass the field values as report parameters.

This completes our discussion about tile-related actions. Let's now see what dashboard-relates tasks are available in Power BI.

Understanding dashboard actions

Additional dashboard-related actions are available to you from the menu in the upper-right corner of the dashboard, as shown in **Figure 4.7**. Starting from the left, the "Add tile" menu is yet another way to add a tile to a dashboard. It allows you to add media, such as web content, image, video, and custom streaming data (streamed datasets are covered in Chapter 14).

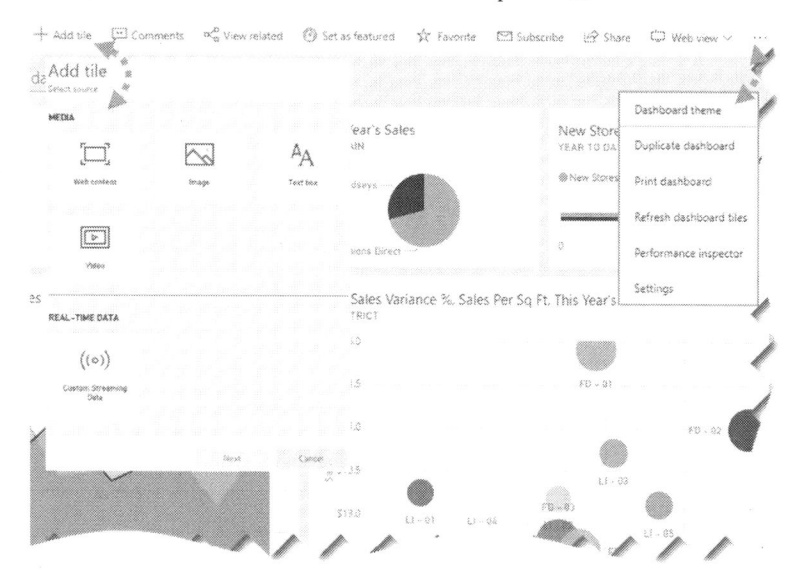

Figure 4.7 Additional actions are available from the menus in the upper-right corner of the open dashboard.

The Comments menu lets you add dashboard-related comments. "View related" shows reports (and their related datasets) from which the dashboard tiles originate. "Set as featured" marks the dashboard as featured so that you see this dashboard when you log in to Power BI instead of Power BI Home. If you don't have a featured dashboard, you'll be navigated to the last dashboard you visited. Clicking the Favorite button adds the dashboard to the Favorites section of the Power BI navigation bar and Power B Home.

Like report subscriptions, the Subscribe menu lets you create a dashboard-level subscription to get an email with a snapshot image of the dashboard when Power BI detects that the underlying data has changed. Let's skip the Share button for now. Power BI supports two dashboard views. The default Web view is for large screens. However, when you view dashboards in the Power BI Mobile app on a phone, you'll notice the dashboard tiles are laid out one after another, and they're all the same size. You can switch to Phone view to create a customized view that targets the limited display capabilities of phones. When you're in Phone view, you can unpin, resize, and rearrange tiles to fit the display. Changes in Phone view don't affect the web version of the dashboard.

CREATING DASHBOARDS

Clicking the ellipsis menu (...) opens a list of dashboard-related tasks. Going quickly through the list, "Dashboard theme" allows you to apply a Microsoft-provided or custom theme to change how the dashboard looks. For example, a visually impaired person could benefit from the "Color-blind friendly" theme. "Duplicate dashboard" clones the dashboard with a new name. Duplicating a dashboard could be useful if you want to retain the existing dashboard customization settings, but make layout changes to the new dashboard, such as to add or remove tiles. "Print dashboard" prints the dashboard content exactly as it appears on the screen. By default, Power BI updates the cache for dashboard tiles every fifteen minutes to synchronize them with data changes. You can force a tile refresh by clicking "Refresh dashboard tiles".

No one likes to wait for a report to show up. "Performance inspector" helps you inspect and diagnose why the dashboard loading time is excessive. A window pops up with alerts to help you identify the potential issue and tips about how to fix it. The last action is Settings and it deserves more attention.

Understanding dashboard settings

The Settings menu brings you to the dashboard settings window (see **Figure 4.8**), which is also accessible from the Dashboard tab in the workspace content page. You can rename the dashboard, disable Q&A and comments, and turn on tile flow. If your tenant administrator has enabled data classification (discussed in Chapter 12), you can assign a data classification category to a dashboard. For example, Maya's dashboard might show some sensitive information. Maya goes to the dashboard settings and tags the dashboard as Confidential Data. When Maya shares the dashboard with co-workers, they can see this classification next to the dashboard name.

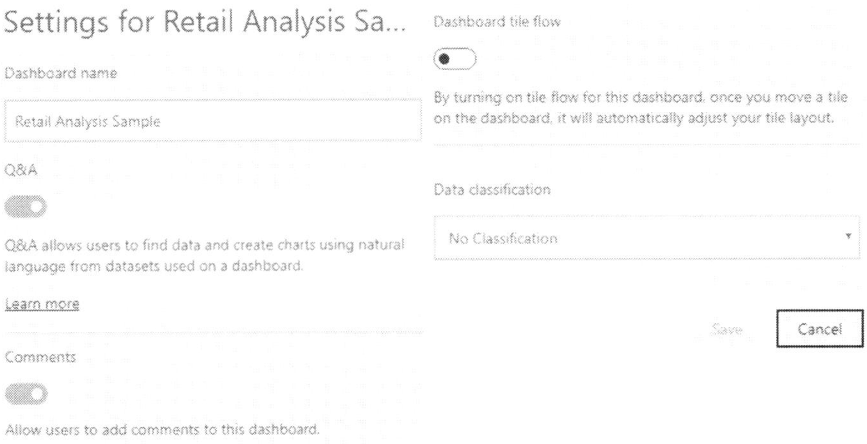

Figure 4.8 Use the dashboard Settings window to make dashboard-wide configuration changes.

You can also find the dashboard settings in the Power BI Service Settings page (click the Settings menu in the upper-right side of the Power BI portal main menu and then click Settings), as shown in **Figure 4.9**.

4.1.2 Sharing Dashboards

Power BI allows you to share dashboards easily with your coworkers. This type of sharing let other people see the dashboards you've created. Remember that all Power BI sharing options, including dashboard sharing, require the user who shares content to have a Power BI Pro or Power BI Premium license. Shared dashboards and associated reports are ready-only to recipients.

> **NOTE** Besides simple dashboard sharing, Power BI supports two other sharing options: workspaces and apps. Workspaces allow groups of users to contribute to shared content and apps are for broader content sharing, such as to share content with many viewers who can't make changes. Because these options require more planning, I discuss them in Chapter 12.

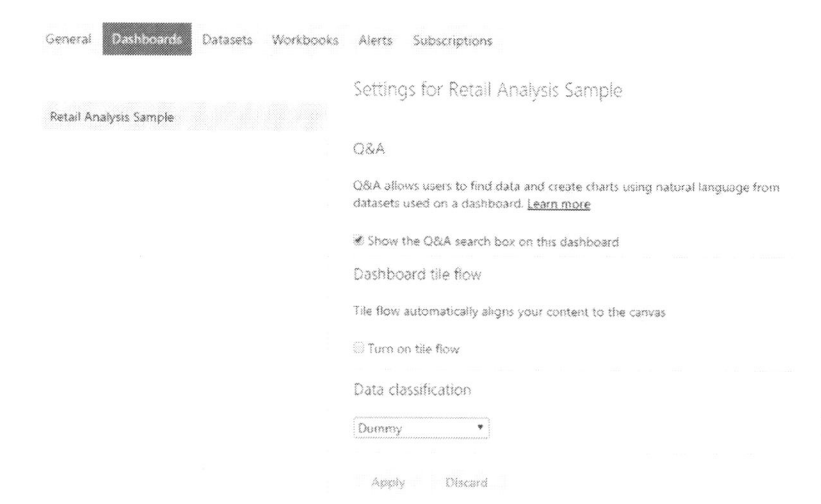

Figure 4.9 Dashboard settings are also available in the Power BI Service Settings page.

Understanding sharing access

Consider dashboard sharing when you need a quick and easy way to share your dashboard but don't go overboard because you may quickly loose track what was shared when you share specific dashboards and reports. When sharing a dashboard with your coworkers, they can still click the dashboard tiles and interact with the underlying reports in Reading View (the Edit Report menu will be disabled). They can't create new reports or make changes to existing reports nor can they make layout changes to the dashboard. When the dashboard author makes changes, the recipients can immediately see the changes. They can access all shared dashboards in the "Shared with me" section of the Power BI navigation pane (see **Figure 4.10**). They can further filter the list of shared dashboards for a specific author by clicking that person's name.

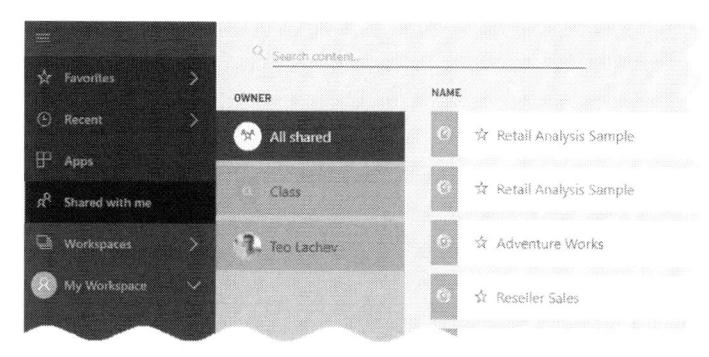

Figure 4.10 Recipients can find shared dashboards in the "Shared with me" section.

Sharing a dashboard

To share a dashboard, click the Share link in the upper-right corner of an open dashboard (see **Figure 4.7** again). This brings you to the "Share dashboard" window, as shown in **Figure 4.11**. Enter the email addresses of the recipients separated by comma (,) or semi-colon (;). You can even use both. Power BI will validate the emails and inform you if they are incorrect.

> **TIP** Want to share with many users, such as with everyone in your department? You can type in the email of an Office 365 distribution list or security group. If you are sharing a dashboard from a workspace in a Power BI Premium capacity, you can also share the dashboard with Power BI Free users.

Next, enter an optional message. To allow your coworkers to re-share your dashboard with others, check "Allow recipients to share your dashboard". If you change your mind later and you want to stop sharing,

CREATING DASHBOARDS   103

click the Access tab. This tab allows you to stop sharing and/or disable re-shares for each coworker you shared the dashboard with.

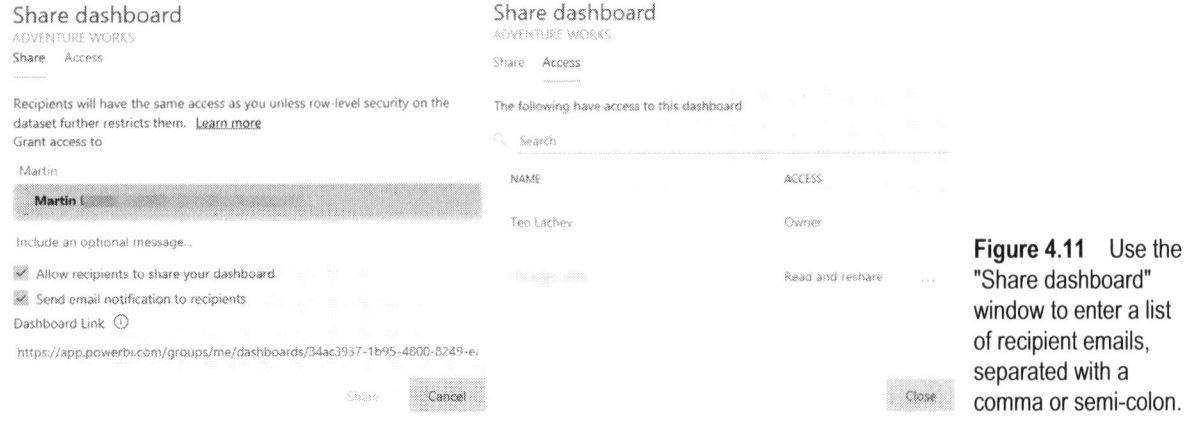

Figure 4.11 Use the "Share dashboard" window to enter a list of recipient emails, separated with a comma or semi-colon.

By default, the "Send email notification to recipients" checkbox is checked. When you click the Share button, Power BI will send an e-mail notification with a link to your dashboard. When the recipient clicks the dashboard link and signs in to Power BI, the shared dashboard will be added to the "Shared with me" section in the navigation bar. You might not always want the person you share a dashboard with to go through the effort of checking their email and clicking a link just for your dashboard to show up in their workspace. If you uncheck the "Send email notification to recipients" checkbox, you can share dashboards directly without them having to do anything. Now when you click Share, the dashboard will just show up in the other users' " Shared with me" section with no additional steps required on their end.

Sharing with external users
You can share dashboards with people within your organization and external users. For example, if Maya's email is maya@adventureworks.com, she can share with martin@adventureworks.com. If Maya wants to share with Matthew who works for Contoso (an external organization), she can do so by just typing in Matthew's business email address. Matthew will receive a notification with a link to the dashboard (Matthew should save that link as it has important encrypted information attached). When he clicks the link, he'll be asked to sign in to Power BI with his work email (or create a Power BI account if he doesn't have one). In other words, external recipients need to be Power BI users for their organization. From a licensing perspective, external users can gain access to shared content under one of these three options:

- They have a Power BI Pro license in their tenant – If Matthew has a Power BI Pro license in his (Contoso) tenant, that license will propagate to other organizations that share content with him.
- They have a Power BI Pro license in the other organization tenant – If Matthew has a Power BI Pro license in the AdventureWorks tenant, he can see the shared content.
- The workspace is in a Power BI Premium capacity – A premium workspace can share content out to Power BI Free internal and external users. The recipients need not be licensed.

Once Matthew has signed in, he'll see the shared dashboard in the web browser without the Power BI left navigation pane. Like internal sharing, Matthew can drill through tiles and access the underlying reports. All interactive features work but the reports are real-only. Maya can see all the external users who have access to this dashboard and revoke their permission from the Access tab in the "Share dashboard" window. All the external users who have access to this dashboard are marked as "Guest". External sharing works also with Power BI Desktop models that have Row-Level Security (RLS) and with dynamic data security in Analysis Services semantic models because the user email is passed on to the data source.

> **NOTE** For more information and a step-by-step guide to distributing BI content with Power BI and Azure AD B2B read the "Distribute Power BI content to external guest users using Azure Active Directory B2B" whitepaper at https://aka.ms/powerbi-b2b-whitepaper.

4.2 Adding Dashboard Content

You can create as many dashboards as you want. One way to get started is to create an empty dashboard by clicking the plus sign (+) in the upper-right corner of the workspace content page and then giving the new dashboard a name. Then you can add content to the dashboard. Or, instead of creating an empty dashboard, you can tell Power BI to create a new dashboard when pinning content. You can add content to a dashboard in several ways:

- Pin visualizations from existing Power BI reports or other dashboards
- Pin ranges from Excel Online reports or from Power BI publisher for Excel
- Pin visualizations from Q&A
- Pin visualizations from Quick Insights or Related Insights
- Pin report items from Power BI Report Server reports
- Add tiles from media and streamed datasets (click the "+Add tile" dashboard menu)

I showed in Chapter 3 how to add content from Excel ranges. I mentioned about adding tiles from media in the "Understanding Dashboard Tiles" section. I'll cover streamed datasets in Chapter 14 because they require programming. Next, I'll explain the rest of the options for adding content to dashboards.

4.2.1 Adding Content from Power BI Reports

The most common way to add dashboard content is to pin visualizations from existing reports or dashboards. This allows you to implement a consolidated summary view that spans multiple reports and datasets. Users can drill through the dashboard tiles to the underlying reports.

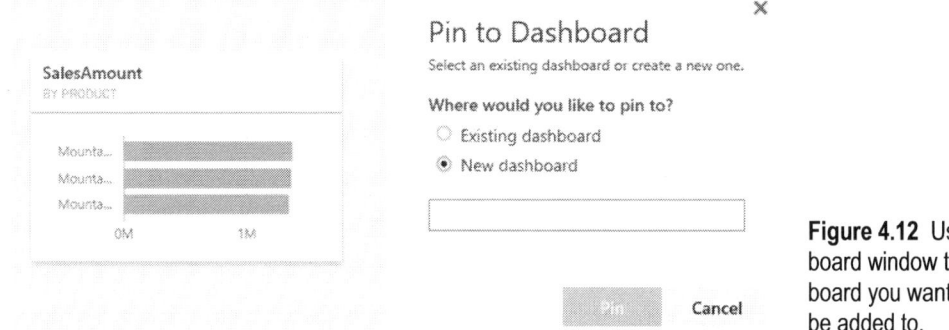

Figure 4.12 Use the Pin to Dashboard window to select which dashboard you want the visualization to be added to.

Pinning visualizations
To pin a visualization to a dashboard from an existing report, you hover on the visualization and click the pushpin button (📌). This opens the Pin to Dashboard window, as shown in **Figure 4.12**. This window shows a preview of the selected visualization and asks if you want to add the visualization to an existing dashboard or to create a new dashboard. If you choose the "Existing dashboard", you can select the target dashboard from a drop-down list. Power BI defaults to the last dashboard that you open. If you choose a new dashboard, you need to type in the dashboard name and then Power BI will create it for you.

Think of pinning a visualization like adding a shortcut to the visualization on the dashboard. You can't make layout changes to the visualization on the dashboard once it's pinned as a dashboard tile. You must make such changes to the underlying report where the visualization is pinned from. Interactive features, such as automatic highlighting and filtering, also aren't available in dashboards. You'll need to click the visualization to drill through the underlying report to make changes or use interactive features.

> **TIP** When pinning a visualization to a dashboard, you might want to show a subset of its data. You can do this by applying a filter (or a slicer) to the report prior to pinning the visualization. If the visualization is filtered, the filter will propagate to the dashboard.

Pinning report pages

As you've seen, pinning specific visualizations allows you to quickly assemble a dashboard from various reports in a single summary view. However, the pinned visualizations "lose" their interactive features, including interactive highlighting, sorting, and tooltips. The only way to restore these features is to drill the dashboard tile through the underlying report. In addition, when you pin individual visualizations you lose filtering capabilities because the Filtering pane won't be available, and you can't pin slicers.

> **NOTE** Currently Power BI doesn't support filtering across dashboard tiles when you pin individual visuals from a report. And the Filter pane is not available in dashboards. Cross-tile filtering is a frequently requested feature and it's on the Power BI roadmap.

However, besides pinning specific report visualizations, you can pin entire report pages. This has the following advantages:

- Preserve report interactive features – When you pin a report page, the tile preserves the report layout and interactivity. You can fully interact with all the visualizations in the report tile, just as you would with the actual report. You'll also get all the page visuals including slicers.
- Reuse existing reports for dashboard content – You might have already designed your report as a dashboard. Instead of pinning individual report visualizations one by one, you can simple pin the whole report page.
- Synchronize changes – A report tile is always synchronized with the report layout. So, if you need to change a visualization on the report, such as from a Table to a Chart, the dashboard tile is updated automatically. No need to delete the old tile and re-pin it.

Figure 4.13 You can pin report pages to your dashboards to preserve interactive features, reuse reports as dashboards, and synchronize layout changes.

Follow these steps to pin a report page to a dashboard:

1. Open the report in Reading View or Editing View.

2. Click "Pin Live Page" in the top menu.
3. In the "Pin to Dashboard" window, select a new or existing dashboard to pin the report page to, as you do when pinning single visualizations. Now you have the entire report page pinned and interactivity works! For example, **Figure 4.13** shows the "New Stores Analysis" page from the "Retail Analysis Sample" report that is now pinned to a dashboard.

4.2.2 Adding Content from Q&A

Another way to add dashboard content is to use natural questions (Q&A). Natural queries let data speak for itself by responding to questions entered in natural language, like how you search the Internet. The Q&A box appears on top of every dashboard that connects to datasets with imported data.

> **NOTE** As of the time of writing, natural queries are available only with datasets created by importing data and datasets with direct connections to Analysis Services Tabular models. Also, Q&A currently supports English only (supports for Spanish is currently in preview).

Understanding natural questions

When you click the Q&A box, it suggests questions you could ask about the dashboard data (see **Figure 4.14**). If the dashboard uses content from multiple datasets, there will be suggested questions from all datasets.

Figure 4.14 The Q&A box has predefined questions which are derived from the dataset metadata.

Of course, these suggestions are just a starting point. Power BI inferred them from the table and column names in the underlying dataset. You can add more predefined questions by following these steps:

1. In Power BI portal, click the Settings (cog) menu in the upper-right corner, and then click Settings.
2. Click the Datasets tab (see **Figure 4.9** again) and then select the desired dataset.
3. In the dataset settings, expand the "Featured Q&A Questions" section.
4. Click "Add a question" and then type a statement that uses dataset fields, such as "sales by country".

Users aren't limited to predefined questions. They can ask for something else, such as "what were this year sales", as shown in **Figure 4.15**. As you type a question, Power BI shows suggestions from a drop-down list. These suggestions correspond to fields in the dataset tables. The drop-down list also shows which table and field correspond to the suggestion. Q&A shows you how it interpreted the question below the visualization. By doing so, Power BI searches the datasets used in the dashboard. So that you can understand which dataset answers your question, Power BI displays the source dataset below the visualization. **Figure 4.15** shows "Source: Retail Analysis Sample" because this question was answered from the Retail Analysis Sample dataset.

CREATING DASHBOARDS

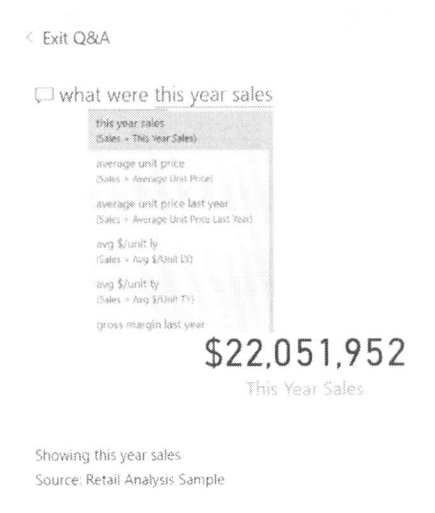

Figure 4.15 The Q&A box interprets the natural question and defaults to the best visualization.

Understanding Q&A reports

Power BI attempts to use the best visualization, depending on the question and supporting data. In this case, Power BI has interpreted the question as "Showing this year sales" and decided to use a card visualization. If you continue typing so the question becomes "what were this year sales by product", it would probably switch over to a Bar Chart. However, if you don't have much luck visualizing the data the way you want, you can always use the Visualizations and Fields panes to customize the visualization, as you can do with reports.

In other words, think of Q&A as a way to jump start your data exploration by creating a report that you can customize further, such as changing the color of the lines, adding labels to the axes, or even choosing another visualization type! Once you're done with the visualization, you can click the pushpin button to add the visualization to the dashboard. Once the tile is added, you can click it to drill through into the dataset. Power BI brings you the visualization you created and shows the natural question that was used. If you change the visual and you want to apply the changes to the dashboard, you'd need to pin the visual again. Power BI will add it as a new tile, so you might want to delete the previous tile.

So how smart is Q&A? Can it answer any question you might have? Q&A searches metadata, including table, column, and field names. It also has built-in smarts on how to filter, sort, aggregate, group, and display data. For example, the Internet Sales dataset you imported from Excel has columns titled "Product", "Month", "SalesAmount", and "OrderQuantity". You could ask questions about any of these terms, such as SalesAmount by Product or by Month. You should also note that Q&A is smart enough to interpret that SalesAmount is actually "sales amount", and you can use both interchangeably.

> **NOTE** Data analysts creating Power BI Desktop and Excel Power Pivot data models can fine tune the model metadata for Q&A. For example, Martin can create a synonym (discussed in Chapter 8) to tell Power BI that State and Province mean the same thing. Or, the data analyst can use Power BI Desktop to change the linguistic schema that drives Q&A.

4.2.3 Adding Content from Predictive Insights

Recall from the previous chapter that Power BI includes an interesting predictive feature called Quick Insights. When you apply Quick Insights at a dataset level it runs predictive algorithms on the entire dataset to find hidden patterns that might not be easily discernable, such as outliers and correlations. A similar feature can be applied to a dashboard tile to limit the data to whatever is shown in the tile. In both cases,

Quick Insights results are available within the current session. Once you close Power BI, they are removed but you can regenerate them quickly when you need them (they only take 20 or so seconds to create).

Adding Quick Insights
To generate Quick Insights at the dataset level, go to the workspace content page, click the Datasets tab, expand the ellipsis menu (…) next to the dataset name, and then click "Get quick insights". Or, click the ellipsis menu (…) next to the dataset name in the navigation bar and then click "Quick Insights". Once Quick Insights are ready, the menu changes to View Insights. You can add one or more of the resulting reports to a dashboard by pinning the visualization (hover on the visualization and click the pin button).

Once the visualization is added to the dashboard it becomes a regular dashboard tile. However, when you click it, Power BI opens the visualization in focus mode so that you can examine it in more detail and apply visual-level filters.

Adding Tile Insights
To generate insights for a specific dashboard tile, hover on the tile, click the ellipsis menu (…) in the upper-right corner of the tile, and then click "View insights". Then click the Related Insights (bulb) icon. This pops up the tile and shows the related insights in the Insights window on the right. You can add one or more of the resulting visualizations you like to a dashboard by pinning the visualization (hover on the visualization in the Insights pane and click the pushpin button).

Like tiles produced by Quick Insights at the dataset level, once a tile insight is added to the dashboard it becomes a regular dashboard tile. When you click it, Power BI opens the visualization in focus so that you can examine it in more detail and apply visual-level filters.

4.2.4　Adding Content from Power BI Report Server

The chances are that your organization uses SQL Server Reporting Services for distributing paginated reports and it's looking for ways to integrate different report types in a single portal. Recall from Chapter 1 that Power BI Report Server extends SSRS and allows you to deploy Power BI reports on an on-premises report server. If your report administrator has configured the Power BI Report Server for Power BI integration, you can add report items to Power BI dashboards. I'll provide general guidance to the administrator about this integration scenario and explain its limitations in Chapter 13. In this section, I'll show you how you can add content from SSRS reports to Power BI dashboards.

> **TIP** Besides pinning specific report items, Power BI Premium supports publishing SSRS paginated (RDL) reports to Power BI Service. I discuss this integration scenario in Chapter 14.

Pinning report items
Follow these steps to pin a report item:

1. Open the Power BI Report Server portal, such as http://<servername>/reports. Open a report you want to pin content from. The report's data source(s) must use stored credentials to connect to data (verify this with your report administrator).
2. Click the "Pin to Power BI Dashboard" toolbar button (see **Figure 4.16**). If you don't see this button, the report server is not configured for Power BI integration. If you see it and click it but you get a message that the report is not configured for stored credentials, you need to change the report data sources(s) to used stored credentials instead of other authentication options. Ask your SSRS administrator for help.
3. If you are not already signed in to Power BI, you'll be prompted to do so.
4. The report page background changes to black and the report items you can pin on the current page are highlighted while the items that you cannot pin, will be shaded dark. Currently, you can pin only image-

generating report items, including charts, gauges, maps, and images. You can't pin tables and lists. Continuing the list of limitations, items must be in the report body (you can't pin from page headers and footers).

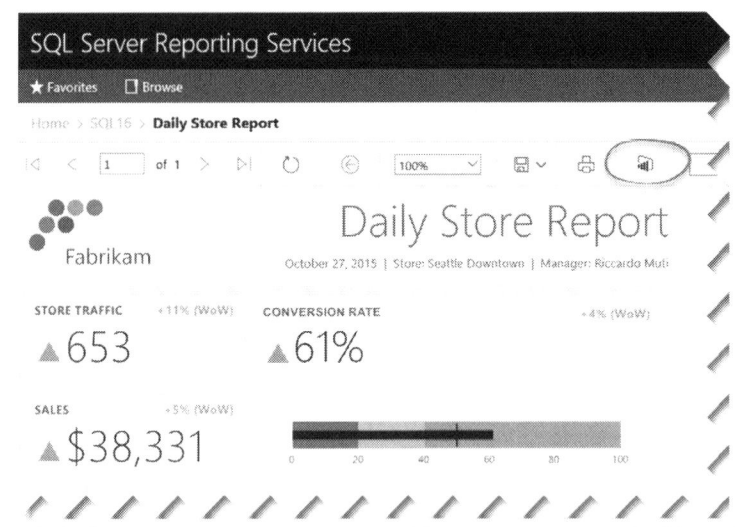

Figure 4.16 If Power BI Report Server is configured for Power BI integration, you can click the "Pin to Power BI Dashboard" toolbar button to pin report items.

5. Click the report item you want to add to your Power BI dashboard.
6. In the "Pin to Power BI Dashboard" window (see **Figure 4.17**), choose a workspace, dashboard, and update frequency (Hourly, Daily, or Weekly). The frequency interval specifies how often the dashboard tile will check for changes in the report data.

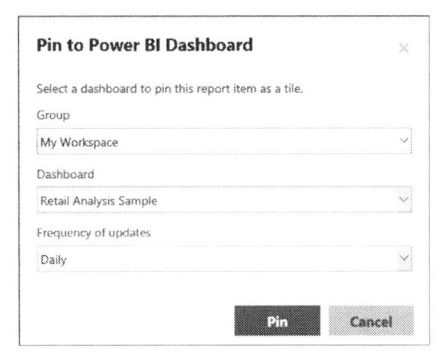

Figure 4.17 When you pin an SSRS item, you can specify the frequency of updates.

7. Click Pin. You should see a Pin Successful dialog. Click the provided link to open the Power BI dashboard.

> **NOTE** Behind the scenes to synchronize changes, the report server creates an individual subscription with the same frequency. You can see the subscription in the Power BI Report Server portal (expand the Settings menu and then click My Subscriptions). It's important to know that the report server doesn't remove the subscription when you remove the tile from the dashboard. To avoid performance degradation to the report server, you must manually remove your unused subscriptions.

Understanding tile changes

Once the report item is pinned to a dashboard, its tile looks just like any other tile except that it's subtitle shows the date and time the tile was pinned or when the report was last refreshed. If you open the tile actions (click the ellipsis menu (…) in the upper-right corner of the tile), you'll see that Power BI Report Server tiles don't have all the features of regular tiles (see **Figure 4.18**). For example, Insights and Focus Mode are not available. Continuing the list of limitations, Q&A is also not available.

Figure 4.18 The dashboard tile with a pinned report item has a link to the original report.

If you click Tile Details, you can see that the custom link includes the report URL. Consequently, when you click the tile, you'll be navigated to the report in the report portal. However, you must be on your corporate network for this to work. Otherwise, the report server won't be reachable, and you'll get an error in your web browser.

> **TIP** Your organization can set up a web application proxy to view Power BI Report Server reports outside the corporate network. The Chris Finlan's "Leveraging Web Application Proxy in Windows Server 2016 to provide secure access to your SQL Server Reporting Services environment" blog has the details at bit.ly/ssrsproxy.

4.3 Working with Dashboards

Next, you'll go through an exercise to create the Internet Sales dashboard shown in **Figure 4.19**. You'll create the first three tiles by pinning visualizations from an existing report. Then you'll use Q&A to create the fourth tile that will show a Line Chart.

Figure 4.19 The Internet Sales dashboard was created by pinning visualizations and then using a natural query.

4.3.1 Creating and Modifying Tiles

Let's start implementing the dashboard by adding content from a report. Then you'll customize the tiles and practice drilling through the content. Compared to reports, one difference you'll discover is that you can't manually save your changes to dashboard tiles as Power BI saves layout changes automatically every time you make a change (there is no Save menu).

Pinning visualizations
Follow these steps to pin visualizations from the Internet Sales Analysis report that you created in the previous chapter:

1. In the navigation bar, click the Internet Sales Analysis report to open it in Reading View or Editing View.
2. Hover on the SalesAmount card and click the pushpin button.
3. In the Pin to Dashboard window, select the "New dashboard" option, enter *Internet Sales*, and click Pin.

4.3.2 Creating and Modifying Tiles

Let's start implementing the dashboard by adding content from a report. Then you'll customize the tiles and practice drilling through the content. Compared to reports, one difference you'll discover is that you can't manually save your changes to dashboard tiles as Power BI saves layout changes automatically every time you make a change (there is no Save menu).

Pinning visualizations

Follow these steps to pin visualizations from the Internet Sales Analysis report that you created in the previous chapter:

1. In the navigation bar, click the Internet Sales Analysis report to open it in Reading View or Editing View.
2. Hover on the SalesAmount card and click the pushpin button.
3. In the Pin to Dashboard window, select the "New dashboard" option, enter *Internet Sales*, and click Pin.

   This creates a new dashboard named *Internet Sales*. You can find the dashboard in the workspace content page (Dashboards tab). Power BI shows a message that the visualization has been pinned to the Internet Sales dashboard.
4. In the Internet Sales Analysis report, pin also the OrderQuantity Card and the "SalesAmount and OrderQuantity by Date" Combo Chart, but this time pin them to the Internet Sales existing dashboard.
5. In the navigation bar under Dashboards, click the Internet Sales dashboard. Hover on the SalesAmount Card and click the ellipsis menu (…). Click "Edit details". In the Tile Details window, enter *Sales* as a title.
6. Change the title for the second Card to *Orders*. Configure the Combo Chart tile to have *Sales vs Orders* as a title and *BY DATE* as a subtitle.
7. Rearrange the tiles to recreate the layout shown back in **Figure 4.19**.

Drilling through the content

You can drill through the dashboard tiles to the underlying reports to see more details and to use the interactive features.

1. Click any of the three tiles, such as the Sales card tile. This action navigates to the Internet Sales Analysis report which opens in Reading View.
2. To go back to the dashboard, click its name in the Dashboards section of the navigation bar or click your Internet browser's Back button.
3. (Optional) Pin visualizations from other reports or dashboards, such as from the Retail Analysis Sample report or dashboard.
4. (Optional) To remove a dashboard tile, click its ellipsis (…) button, and then click "Delete tile".

4.3.3 Using Natural Queries

Another way to create dashboard content is to use natural queries. Use this option when you don't have an existing report or dashboard to start from, or when you want to add new visualizations without creating reports first.

Using Q&A to create a chart

Next, you'll use Q&A to add a Line Chart to the dashboard.

1. In the Q&A box, enter "sales amount by date". Note that Power BI interprets the question as "Showing sales amount sorted by date" and it defaults to a Line Chart, as shown in **Figure 4.20**.

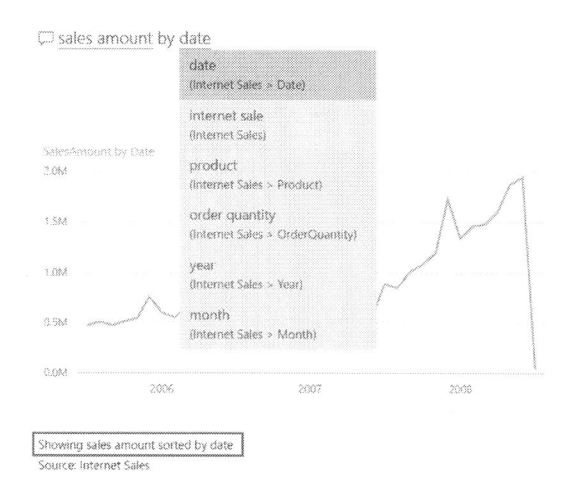

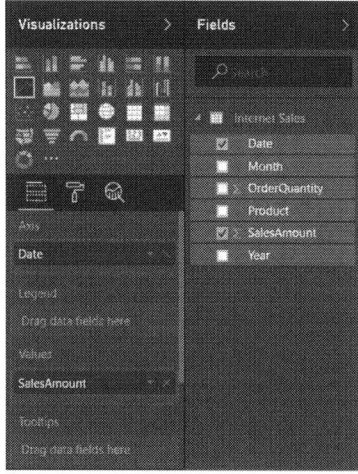

Figure 4.20 Create a Line Chart by typing a natural question.

2. You should also notice that you can use the Visualizations pane to change the visualization. Another way to use a specific visualization is to specify the visualization type in the question. Change the question to "sales amount by date as column chart". Power BI changes the visualization to a Column Chart.

3. (Optional) Practice your reporting skills to customize the visualization using the Visualizations and Fields pane. For example, use the Format tab of the Visualizations pane to turn on data labels.

4. Click the pushpin button to pin the visualization as a new dashboard tile in the Internet Sales dashboard.

Drilling through content

Like tiles bound to report visualizations, Power BI supports drilling through tiles that are created by Q&A:

1. Back in the dashboard, click the new tile that you created with Q&A. Power BI brings you back to the visualization as you left it (see **Figure 4.20**). In addition, Power BI shows the natural question you asked in the Q&A box.

2. (Optional) Use a different question or make some other changes, and then click the pushpin button again. This will bring you to the Pin to Dashboard window. If you choose to pin the visualization to the same dashboard, Power BI will add a new tile to the dashboard.

4.4 Summary

Consider dashboards for displaying important metrics at a glance. You can easily create dashboards by pinning existing visualizations from reports or from other dashboards. Or, you can use natural queries to let the data speak for itself by responding to questions, such as "show me sales for last year". You can drill through to the underlying reports to explore the data in more detail.

You can add content to your dashboards from predictive reports generated by Quick Insights or Related Insights. If your organization has invested in Power BI Report Server, you can pin report items from your reports to Power BI dashboards. Remember that you can also pin ranges from Excel reports and from pivot reports created in Power BI Publisher for Excel, as I showed you in the previous chapter.

Besides using the Power BI portal, you can access reports and dashboards on mobile devices, as you'll learn in the next chapter.

Chapter 5

Power BI Mobile

5.1 Introducing Mobile Apps 114
5.2 Viewing Content 117
5.3 Sharing and Collaboration 124
5.4 Summary 127

To reach its full potential, data analytics must not only be insightful but also pervasive. Pervasive analytics is achieved by enabling information workers to access actionable data from anywhere. Mobile computing is everywhere, and most organizations have empowered their employees with mobile devices, such as tablets and smartphones. Preserving this investment, Power BI Mobile enriches the user's mobile data analytics experience. Not only does it allow viewing reports and dashboards on mobile devices, but it also enables additional features that your users would appreciate. It does so by providing native mobile applications for iOS, Android, and Windows devices.

This chapter will help you understand the Power BI Mobile capabilities. Although native applications differ somewhat due to differences in device capabilities and roadmap priorities, there's a common set of features shared across all the applications. I'll demonstrate most of these features with the iPhone native application.

5.1 Introducing Mobile Apps

Power BI is designed to render reports and dashboards in HTML5. As a result, you can view and edit Power BI content from most modern Internet browsers. Currently, Power BI officially supports Microsoft Edge, Microsoft Explorer 10 and 11, the Chrome desktop version, the latest version of Safari for Mac, and the latest Firefox desktop version.

To provide additional features that enrich the user's mobile experience outside the web browser, Power BI currently offers three native applications that target the most popular devices: iOS (iPad and iPhone), Android, and Windows devices. These native applications are collectively known as Power BI Mobile (https://powerbi.microsoft.com/mobile). These apps are for viewing dashboard and reports; you can't use them to make changes. That's understandable considering the limited display capabilities of mobile devices. Next, I'll introduce you briefly to each of these applications.

> **TIP** Your organization can use Microsoft Intune to manage devices and applications, including the Power BI Mobile apps. Microsoft Intune provides mobile device management, mobile application management, and PC management capabilities from the Microsoft Azure cloud. For example, your organization can use Microsoft Intune to configure mobile apps to require an access pin, control how data is handled by the application, and encrypt application data when the app isn't in use. For more information about Microsoft Intune, go to https://www.microsoft.com/cloud-platform/microsoft-intune.

5.1.1 Introducing the iOS Application

Microsoft released the iOS application on December 18th, 2014, and it was the first native app for Power BI. Initially, the application targeted iPad devices but was later enhanced to support iPhone, Apple Watch, and iPod Touch. Users with these devices can download the Power BI iOS application from the Apple App Store. Realizing the market realities for mobile computing, the iOS app receives the most attention and it's prioritized to be the first to get any new features.

Viewing content

The iOS application supports an intuitive, touch optimized experience for monitoring business data on iPad or iPhone. You can view your dashboards, interact with charts and tiles, explore additional data by browsing reports, and share dashboard images with your colleagues by email. **Figure 5.1** shows the Retail Sales Analysis dashboard in landscape mode on iPhone.

Figure 5.1 The iOS application targets iPad and iPhone devices.

In portrait mode, the app shows dashboard tiles positioned one after another. Remember that if this is not desired, you can go to Power BI Service and open the dashboard in Phone edit view (click the ellipsis button in the upper-right corner of the dashboard and then click Phone in the Edit View section). Then, you can optimize the dashboard layout for portrait mode. Landscape mode lets you view and navigate your dashboards in the same way as you do in the Power BI portal. To view your dashboard in landscape, open it and simply rotate your phone. The dashboard layout changes from a vertical list of tiles to a "Bird's eye" landscape view. Now you can see all your dashboard's tiles as they are in the Power BI portal.

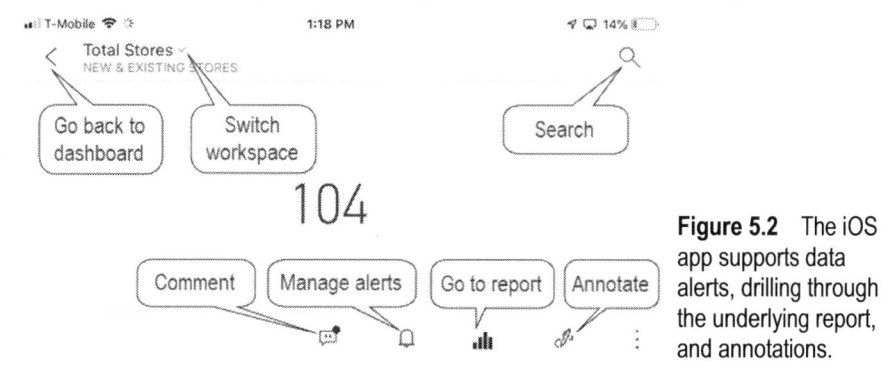

Figure 5.2 The iOS app supports data alerts, drilling through the underlying report, and annotations.

Understanding tile actions

While you're viewing a dashboard with the iPhone app, let's see what happens when you click a tile. Clicking a tile opens it in focus mode (see **Figure 5.2**) as opposed to going to the underlying report in

Power BI Service. This behavior applies to all mobile apps. The buttons at the bottom are for the three most common tile actions: comment, manage data alerts (remember that alerts are available for Single Card, Gauge, and KPI visuals only), go to the underlying report, and annotate. The ellipsis (…) menu in the bottom-right corner gives you access to the same actions.

5.1.2 Introducing the Android Application

Microsoft released the Power BI Mobile Android application in July 2015 (see **Figure 5.3**). This application is designed for Android smartphones and Android tablets (Android 5.0 operating system or later) and it's available for download from Google Play Store.

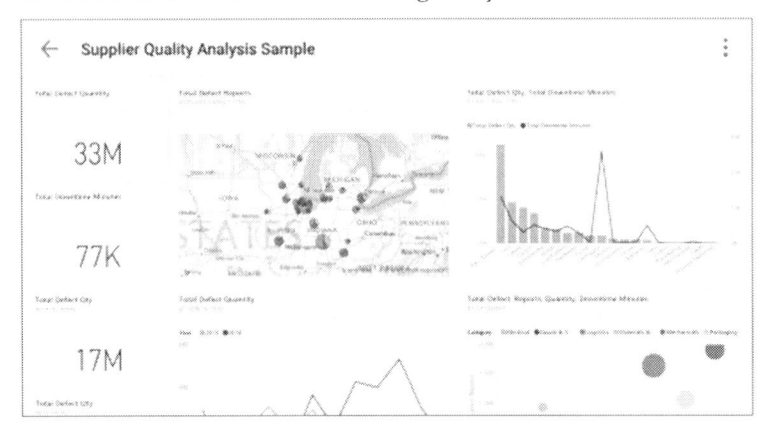

Figure 5.3 The Android application targets Android phones and tablets.

Android users can use this app to explore dashboards, invite colleagues to view data, add annotations, and share insights over email.

5.1.3 Introducing the Windows Application

In May 2015, Power BI Mobile added a native application for Windows 8.1 and Windows 10 devices, such as Surface tablets (see **Figure 5.4**). Microsoft has enhanced the app for Windows 10 phones. You can download the app from Windows Store (search for *Microsoft Power BI*). Your Windows device needs to be running Windows 10 and Microsoft recommends at least 2 GB RAM.

Figure 5.4 The Windows application targets Windows 10 devices and phones.

For the most part, the Windows app has identical features as the other Power BI Mobile apps. One feature that was originally included but Microsoft later removed was annotations. However, the Windows Ink Sketch Tool (only available in touch-enabled devices) has similar features, including taking a snapshot, annotating and sharing. For more information about how to use the Sketch Tool, refer to the "Windows Ink: How to use Screen Sketch" article at http://windowscentral.com/windows-ink-how-use-screen-sketch.

5.2 Viewing Content

Power BI Mobile provides simple and intuitive interface for viewing reports and dashboards. As it stands, Power BI Mobile doesn't allow users to edit the published content. This shouldn't be viewed as a limitation because mobile display capabilities are limited, and mobile users would be primarily interested in viewing content. Next, you'll practice viewing the BI content you created in the previous two chapters using the iPhone native app. As a prerequisite, install the iOS Power BI Mobile app from AppStore.

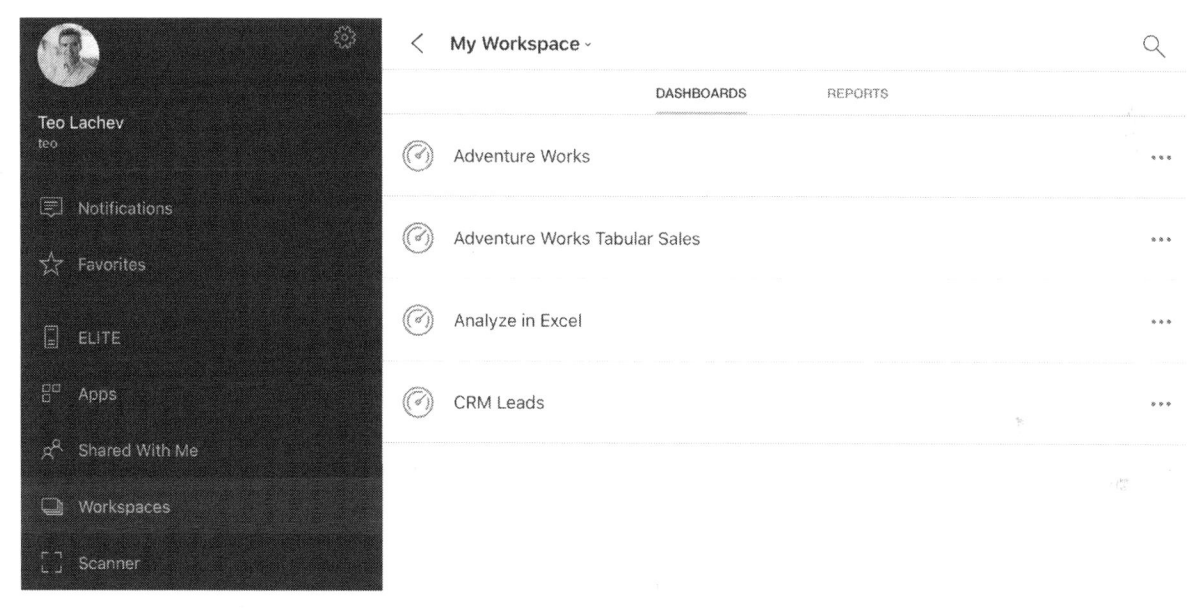

Figure 5.5 The navigation experience of the iPhone app.

5.2.1 Getting Started with Power BI Mobile

When you open the iPhone Power BI app and sign in to Power BI, you'll be presented with a landing page. If you have previously marked dashboards as favorites, the landing page will show a list of these dashboards. Or, if you have subscribed to apps, the landing page will show these apps. Otherwise, the landing page will let you know that you have no apps and encourage you to go to Power BI Service and add apps. When you expand the menu in the top-left corner, you'll see the navigation bar shown in **Figure 5.5**. Let's go quickly through the links starting from the top.

Understanding settings
Clicking the Settings (gear) menu in the top-right corner opens the Settings page (see **Figure 5.6**). The Accounts section allows you to sign in to Power BI. If your organization has installed Power BI Report Server,

the "Connect to server" link allows you to add one or more report servers. To do so, you need to provide the server address, such as https://<ServerName>/reports, and an optional friendly name so you can tell the servers apart.

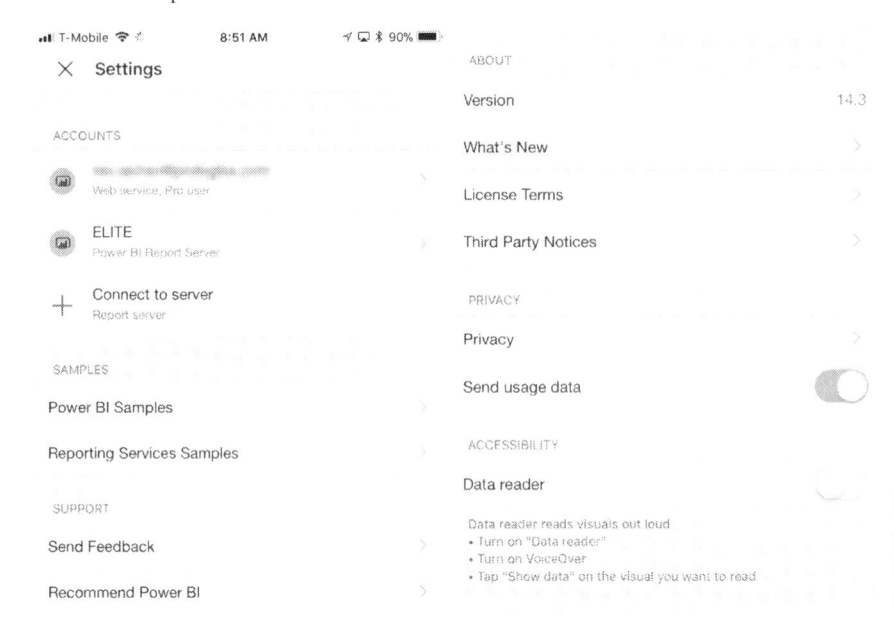

Figure 5.6 The iPhone Settings page allows you to sign in to Power BI, connect to report servers, and control app settings.

The samples section is to view sample Power BI and SSRS reports. Unlike Power BI Service, samples are ready to browse, and you don't have to install them. The Support section has links to send feedback to Microsoft and recommend Power BI to other people via email. The About section shows details about the Power BI app. You can use the Privacy section to read the Microsoft privacy statement and allow the Power BI app to send usage data to Microsoft. Finally, the Accessibility section allows people with accessibility needs to turn on data reader and hear information about visuals.

TIP Looking for an easy way to demonstrate Power BI content in mobile apps? Currently, there are six dashboards available for VP Sales, Director of Operations, Customer Care, Director of Marketing, CFO, and HR Manager. And, if you connect your mobile app to a Power BI Report Server, you can get Reporting Services samples as well.

Understanding navigation bar
Next, let's explore the navigation menus starting from the top:

- Notifications – Shows the notifications from the Power BI Service Notification Center.
- Favorites – Shows dashboards that you marked as favorites.
- Power BI Report servers – If your organization has integrated Power BI Report Server with Power BI, the next links will show the friendly names of the report server(s) you've added. You can click a link to navigate the report catalog, and to view Power BI reports, SSRS mobile reports and KPIs.
- Apps – Allows you to access your Power BI apps that you have previously installed.
- Shared With Me – Shows the list of dashboards that other people have shared with you.
- Workspaces – Shows the workspaces you are a member of so that you can select a workspace to work with. My Workspace is the default workspace.
- Scanner – This link shows only on mobile phones. It allows you to scan a Power BI QR code so that you can navigate to the report tagged with that code.

Browsing workspace content

Once you select a menu in the navigation bar, the relevant content shows in the right pane. Back to **Figure 5.5**, I've clicked the Workspaces menu, and then I've selected My Workspace. The Dashboards tab lists all dashboards in the selected workspace. The ellipsis (…) menu to the right of the dashboard name allows me to mark the dashboard as a favorite and to share the dashboard with others. And the Reports tab lists all reports hosted in the workspace.

Use the Search button to view most recent content you've visited and to search for content, such as to type "sales" to see all sales-related reports and dashboards. Matches are organized in dashboards, reports, and groups (workspaces) sections.

5.2.2 Viewing Dashboards

Mobile users will primarily use Power BI Mobile to view dashboards that they've created or that are shared with them. Let's see what options are available for viewing dashboards.

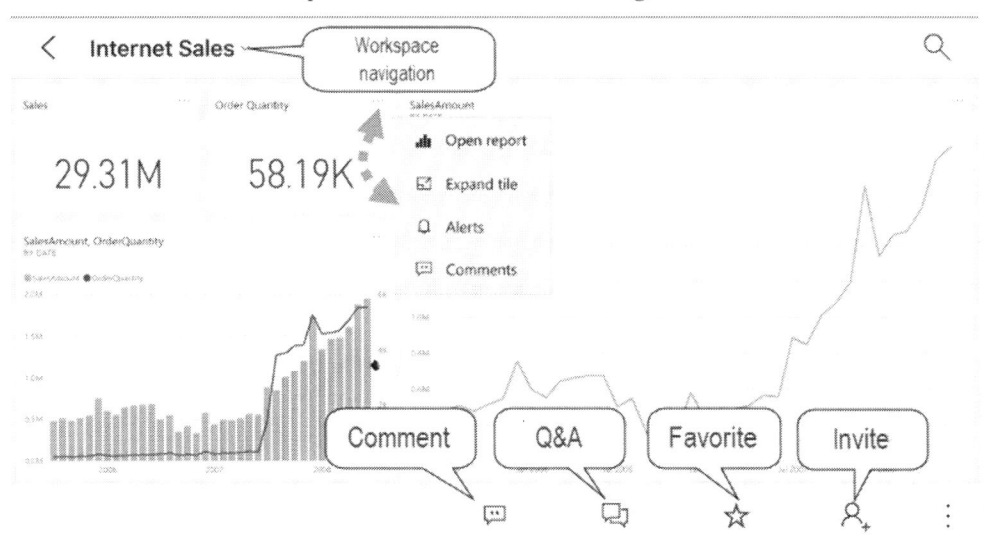

Figure 5.7 The Internet Sales dashboard open in Power BI Mobile.

Working with dashboards

This exercise uses the Internet Sales dashboard that you created in the previous chapter.

1. On your iPhone, open the Power BI app.
2. From the navigation bar, click Workspaces and select My Workspace.
3. In the Dashboards tab, click the Internet Sales dashboard to open it (see **Figure 5.7**). Power BI Mobile renders the dashboard content as it appears in the Power BI portal.
4. Click the Q&A icon at the bottom of the page and notice that you can type or speak natural questions. As you type your question, the app shows suggestions just like Power BI Service. Unlike Power BI Service, however, when you submit your question, the app shows not only a report but also narrated quick insights. For example, if you type "sales by year", you'll get a line chart and related insights, such as "There is a correlation between product and internet sales". When you click the insight, it shows it as a visual.
5. Back to the dashboard, if you'd like to mark the dashboard as a favorite, click the Favorite icon.
6. If you want to share the dashboard with someone else, click the Invite icon.
7. Click the Comment icon to access the dashboard conversation and type a comment.

8. Expand the Workspace Navigation drop-down and notice that it shows which workspace the dashboard is located in. The back arrow lets you navigate backward to the content. For example, if you click it, the mobile app will navigate you to My Workspace.

Working with tiles
There are additional features specific to tiles. You can click the ellipsis (…) menu to access the most popular actions: drill: Open Report (drill to the underlying report), Expand Tile (opens the tile in focus), Manage Alerts (set up and manage alerts).

1. Click the Sales tile. As you would recall, clicking a tile in Power BI Portal drills the tile through the underlying visualization (which could originate from several sources, including pinning a visual from a report or Q&A). However, instead of drilling through, Power BI Mobile pops the tile out so that you can examine the tile data (see **Figure 5.8**).

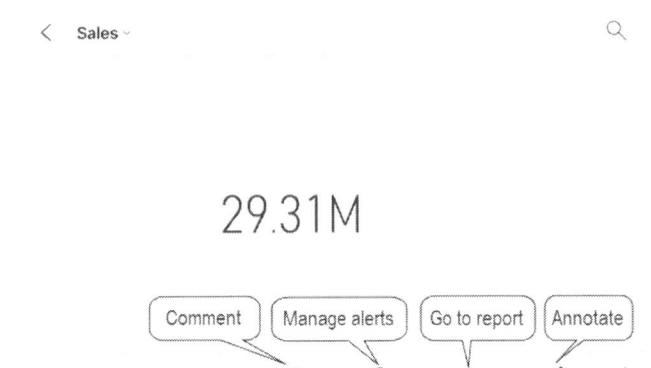

Figure 5.8 Clicking a tile opens the tile in focus mode.

Power BI refers to this as "focus" mode. Because the display of mobile devices is limited, the focus mode makes it easier to view and explore the tile data. That's why this is the default action when you click a tile.

Understanding tile actions
When a tile is in focus, users can take several actions. Click "Comment" to enter a comment associated with the tile. You can click "Manage alerts" to create and manage alerts for visualizations that display a single value (Single Card, Gauge, and KPIs). It has the identical settings as in Power BI Service to allow mobile users to create alerts while they are on the go. But when the underlying data meets the condition, you'll get an in-app notification on your phone instead of an email.

The "Go to report" button bring you to the underlying report which the visualization was pinned from. This action opens the report in Reading View (Power BI Mobile doesn't support Editing View). The Reports menu is available only for tiles created by pinning visualizations from existing reports. You won't see the Report menu for tiles created with Q&A.

I'll postpone discussing annotations to the Sharing and Collaboration section.

Examining the data
It might be challenging to understand the precise values of a busy chart on a mobile device. However, Power BI Mobile has a useful feature that you might find helpful.

1. Navigate back to the Internet Sales dashboard and click the line chart.
2. In the line chart, drag the vertical bar to intersect the chart line for Jan 2006, as shown in **Figure 5.9**.

Notice that Power BI Mobile shows the precise value of the sales amount at the intersection. If you have a Scatter Chart (the Retail Analysis Sample dashboard has a Scatter Chart), you can pop out a chart and select a bubble by positioning the intersection of a vertical line and a horizontal line. This allows you to see the values of the fields placed in the X Axis, Y Axis, and Size areas of the Scatter visualization. And for a Pie Chart, you can spin the chart to position the slices so that you can get the exact values.

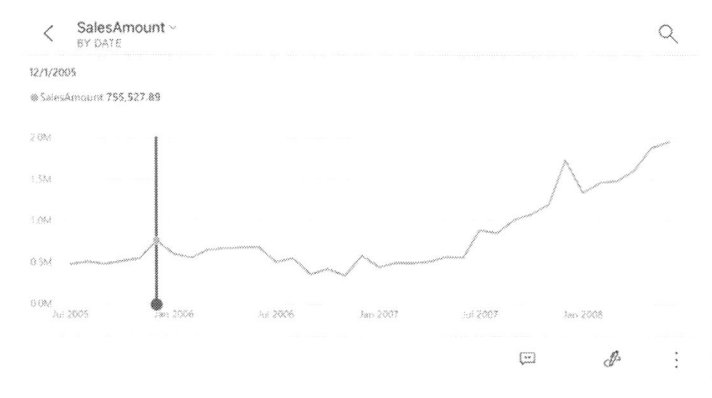

Figure 5.9 You can drag the vertical bar to see the precise chart value.

5.2.3 Viewing Reports

As you've seen, Power BI Mobile makes it easy for business users to view dashboards on the go. You can also view reports. As I mentioned, Power BI Mobile doesn't allow you to edit reports; you can only open and interact with them in Reading View.

> **TIP** As you'll discover, regular Power BI reports don't reflow when you turn your phone in a portrait mode. Unlike dashboards which reflow, reports always render in landscape. However, you can use Power BI Desktop to create a special phone-optimized view for each page on the report. Phone-optimized reports have a special icon in the Reports tab. For more information about how to create phone-optimized report layouts, refer to the "Create reports optimized for the Power BI phone apps" topic at https://powerbi.microsoft.com/documentation/powerbi-desktop-create-phone-report/.

Viewing Power BI reports

Let's open the Internet Sales Analysis report in Power BI Mobile. **Figure 5.10** shows the report.

Figure 5.10 Power BI Mobile opens reports in Reading View but supports interactive features.

1. Navigate to your workspace. You can do this by clicking the Back button in the top-left area of the screen.

POWER BI MOBILE   121

2. Under the Reports section, click the Internet Sales Analysis report to open it. Power BI Mobile opens the report in Reading View. Notice that you can't switch to Editing View to change the report. You shouldn't view this as a limitation because the small display size of mobile devices would probably make reporting and editing difficult anyway. Although you can't change the report, you can interact with it.

3. Click any bar in the Bar Chart or a column in the Column Chart. Notice that automatic highlighting works, and you can see the contribution of the selected value to the data shown in the other visualizations. However, the other interactive features, such as drilling through or exporting data, are not available.

4. Click a column header in the Matrix visualization and note that every click toggles the column sort order.

5. The Pages button shows you a list of the report pages, so you can navigate to another page. You can also swipe the report to the right or left to go to the next or previous page.

The icons at the bottom are for report-specific tasks as follows:

- Favorite – To mark the report as a favorite report so that you can find it in the Favorites section.
- Reset – If the report has filters and you've overwritten the default filter values, you can click the Reset icon to reset the filters to their default values.
- Annotate – To add an annotation to the report, such as some text or a smiley.
- Pages – To navigate the report pages.

NOTE Reports with map visuals add a "Geo filter" icon. Use it to filter a map to your current location. For example, imagine a sales person visiting customers. He opens a report that shows customer sales by state. He's in Georgia and he only wants to filter the report to show customers in Georgia. He can click Geo filter which will discover his location so that he can filter the map to show only Georgia.

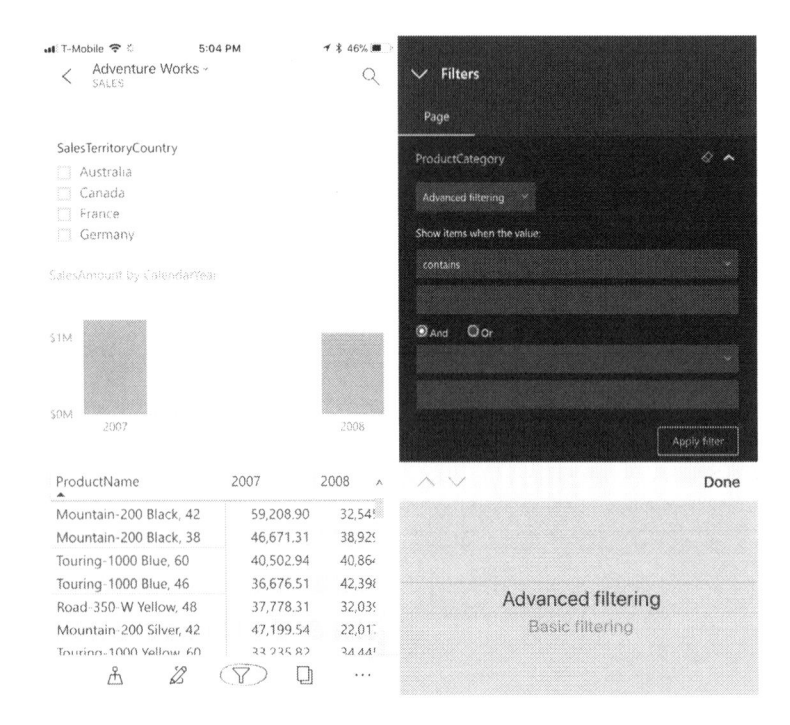

Figure 5.11 Available in phone-optimized report layouts only, the Filters pane lets you apply visual, page, and report filters.

Filtering report data

Recall that Power BI reports allow you to specify visual, page, and report filters. You might wonder why the Filter pane is nowhere to be found in the iPhone app. As it turns out, you need a phone-optimized report to get the filtering options. If you use Power BI Desktop to create a phone-optimized layout, then you'll discover that the Filters icon is available at the bottom of the report (see **Figure 5.11**).

The Filters icon will bring you to the Filters page that will show the page and report filters. And when you tap a visual on the report, it will also show visual-level filters. As in Power BI, the Filters page supports Basic and Advanced filtering options. As you'd recall, prefiltering the report content at design time (by setting slicers or filtering options in the Filter pane) preserves the filters when users view the reports. When you view a prefiltered report, the app will show a status bar at the top of the page, notifying you that there are active filters on the report.

Viewing Excel reports

Remember that Power BI allows you to connect existing Excel reports. Let's see what happens when you open an Excel report.

1. Navigate to My Workspace.
2. In the Reports section of the workspace content page, click the Reseller Sales report.

Notice that the report won't open inside the app. Instead, the app informs you that to view an Excel workbook, it must be saved to OneDrive. That's because Excel reports are rendered in Excel Online, which is a cloud service and it's not available in the mobile app. To view the workbook, you must either open the browser and navigate to powerbi.com or save the workbook to OneDrive before you connect to it.

Viewing reports in Power BI Report Server

If your organization uses Power BI Report Server, you can view content from a report server running in native mode. Currently, you can view three types of content:

- Power BI reports – Power BI Report Server allows users to upload Power BI Desktop files to the report catalog. If the file has a report and you have permissions, you can view the report in Power BI Mobile.
- KPIs – Starting with SQL Server 2016 Reporting Services, you can define key performance indicators (KPIs) directly in a SSRS folder (without creating a report). These KPIs will show up in the Power BI mobile apps.
- Mobile reports – A new report type in SQL Server 2016 Reporting Services, mobile reports are optimized for mobile devices. When you navigate to a report folder that has mobile reports, you'll see thumbnail images of the reports. Clicking a report opens it inside the mobile app.

NOTE Currently, traditional paginated (RDL) Reporting Services reports won't show up in the mobile apps. You can navigate the report catalog, but you can't see them.

Before you can access SSRS content, you need to register your report server:

1. In the navigation bar, click Settings. On the Accounts tab click "Connect to server".
2. Fill in the server address, such as http://<servernname/reports.
3. (Optional) Under "Advanced options", give the server a user-friendly name, such as Reporting Services. This is the name you'll see when you click the global navigation button (the yellow home button in the top-left corner).

Figure 5.12 Access KPIs, Power BI reports, and mobile reports in your mobile app.

4. Click Connect.

Once you are connected, you can view the reports that you're authorized to access.

5. In the navigation bar, tap your report server.
6. Navigate to the folder as instructed by your administrator. If the folder has Power BI reports, mobile reports, or KPIs, they'll show up in Power BI Mobile. You can tell Power BI reports by a special icon that looks like a column chart.
7. Click a Power BI report. **Figure 5.12** shows a Power BI report that I've previously deployed to Power BI Report Server. It renders online, just like when you view the report in Power BI Service.

> **TIP** If you mark reports or KPIs as favorites on your Power BI Report Server portal, they'll appear in the Power BI Favorites folder and you can access them by clicking Favorites in the navigation bar.

5.3 Sharing and Collaboration

Power BI Mobile goes beyond just content viewing. It lets mobile workers share BI content and collaborate while on the go. Specifically, Power BI Mobile supports three collaboration options:

- Comments – As in Power BI Service, you can post dashboard and tile comments.
- Content sharing – If you have a Power BI Pro subscription, you can share your dashboards and reports with a colleague.
- Annotations – A Power BI Mobile-only feature, annotations allow you to add some text or graphics to dashboard tiles and reports.

Let's examine these three features in more detail.

5.3.1 Posting Comments

As with Power BI service, you can directly add comments to dashboards and specific tiles to discuss your data. You can also pull people into your conversation by @mentioning your coworkers (see **Figure 5.13**).

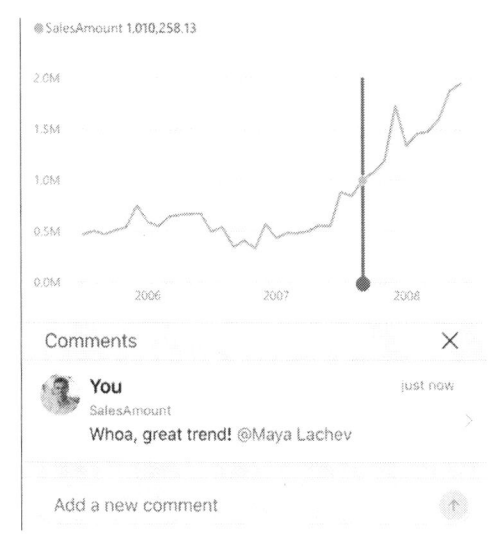

Figure 5.13 You can start a conversation at a dashboard or tile level by posting comments.

To post a comment, just press the Comment icon below a dashboard or in-focus tile. If there is no existing conversation, Power BI Mobile will let you know that you can start a conversation by posting a comment. You can then use both Power BI Mobile and Power BI Service to see the posted comments.

5.3.2 Sharing Content

Remember from the previous chapter that Power BI Service allows you to share reports dashboards with your colleagues by sending email invitations. You can do the same with Power BI Mobile. Both options are interchangeable. For example, if you initiate dashboard sharing in Power BI Service, you can see the sharing settings in Power BI Mobile, and vice versa. Let's share a dashboard but remember that all sharing options require a Power BI Pro license:

1. Back to the Home page, click the Internet Sales dashboard to open it.
2. Click the Invite button in the bottom-right corner.

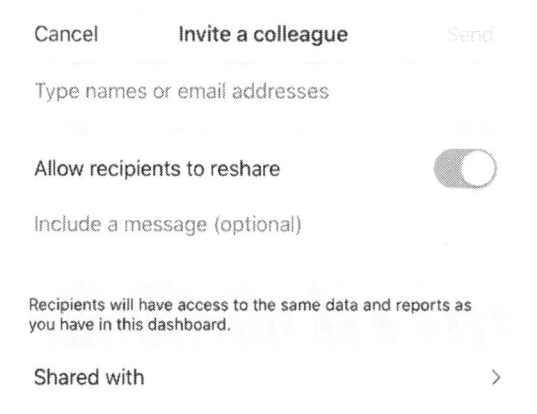

Figure 5.14 Power BI Mobile lets you share dashboards with your coworkers.

This action opens the "Invite a colleague" flyout window (see **Figure 5.14**). You need to enter the recipient email addresses, type in an optional message, and decide if you want them to be able to re-share the dashboards. You can find whom you've shared the dashboard with by using the "Shared with" section.

5.3.3 Annotating Visuals

While you're viewing the dashboard content, you might want to comment on some data and then share the comment with your coworkers. For example, after sharing her dashboard with a manager, Maya might ask the manager to formally approve that the data is correct. Her manager can open the dashboard on his mobile device, sign the dashboard, and then send a screenshot to Maya. Annotations allow you to enter text, simple graphics, or a smiley, and then share a screenshot of the annotated content. Annotations aren't saved in the Power BI content. Once you exit the annotation mode, all annotations are lost.

Adding annotations

You can annotate dashboard tiles, entire reports, or specific report visualizations. Let's annotate a dashboard tile:

1. With the Retail Analysis Sample dashboard open, click the "This Year's Sales, Last Year's Sales" surface chart to open it in focus mode.
2. Click the Annotate (pencil) button in the bottom-right corner. This switches the tile to annotation mode.
3. Click the Smiley button and then click the first smiley icon to add a smiley to the tile. Position the smiley as shown in **Figure 5.15**.

Figure 5.15 You can annotate a tile by typing text, drawing lines, or placing stamps.

4. Click the curve icon to the right of the smiley icon and type some text on the tile. If you make a mistake, you can click the Undo button in the bottom-right corner. The eraser button discards all your annotations.

Sharing screenshots

You can send screenshots to your colleagues by a text message or email. Let's send a screenshot of your annotations:

1. In annotation mode, click the Share link in the top right corner of the screen.
2. A flyout window asks you if you want to choose a delivery mechanism. Click Mail or whatever application you use as email client.
3. Power BI Mobile captures a screenshot of the annotated item (tile, report, or specific report visualization), and attaches it to the email (see **Figure 5.16**). It also includes a link to the item. Enter the recipient addresses separated by a semi-colon (;) and click the Send button.

If the recipients have rights to view the annotated item, such as when you've already shared the dashboard with them or you share the same workspace, they can click the link to go straight to the item.

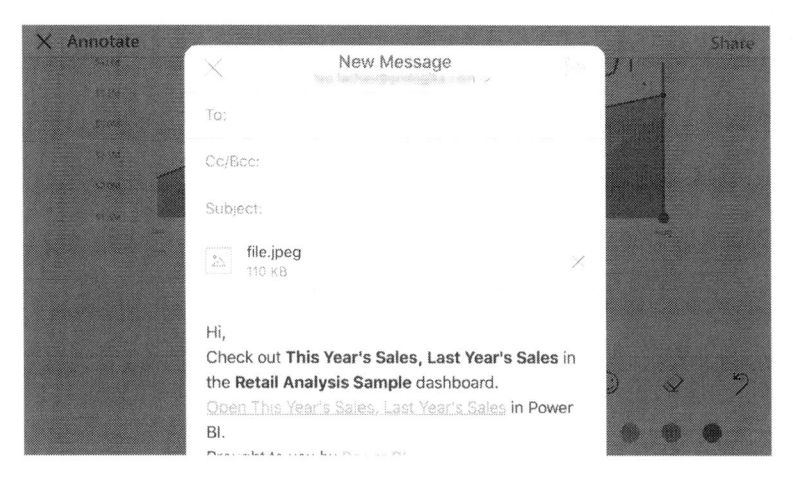

Figure 5.16 You can share screenshots of your annotations with your coworkers by email.

5.4 Summary

Power BI Mobile is a collective name of three native applications for iOS, Android, and Windows devices. Power BI Mobile enriches the data analysis experience of mobile workers. Besides dashboard and report viewing, it supports collaboration features, including comments, content sharing, and annotating reports and dashboard tiles. You can also create a data alert and get a notification when data meets specific thresholds that you specify.

This chapter concludes our Power BI tour for business users. Power BI has much more to offer than what you've seen so far, but it requires more knowledge. In the next part of the book, you'll see how data analysts (also referred to as power users) can create sophisticated data models to address more complicated data analytics needs.

PART 2

Power BI for Data Analysts

If you consider yourself a data analyst or power user, welcome! This part of the book teaches you how to implement self-service models with Power BI Desktop. If you're new to self-service data analytics, I recommend you review the first part of the book "Power BI for Business Users" beforehand as it explains important self-service BI and Power BI fundamentals.

As you've seen in the first part of the book, Power BI lets business users perform rudimentary data analysis without requiring data models. However, once the self-service BI path goes beyond apps and one-table datasets, you'll need a data model. Although you can still implement models with Excel, Power BI Desktop is the Power BI premium modeling tool for self-service BI. Packed with features, Power BI Desktop is a free tool that you can download and start using immediately to gain insights from your data.

If you have experience with Excel data modeling, you'll find that Power BI Desktop combines the best of Power Pivot, Power Query, and Power View in a simplified and standalone desktop tool. In this part of the book, I'll introduce you to Power BI Desktop and fundamental data modeling concepts. Next, you'll learn how to connect to data from a variety of data sources, ranging from relational databases, text files, Excel files, and cloud services.

Data quality is a big issue with many organizations and chances are that your data is no exception. Fortunately, Power BI has features that allow you to prepare, stage, cleanse and transform data before it enters your model, so you might not have to rely on someone else to do these tasks for you. A self-service data model is rarely complete without important business metrics. Thanks to its Data Analysis Expressions (DAX) language, Power BI Desktop lets you implement sophisticated calculations using Excel-like formulas. Then you can explore your data by creating interactive reports as you can do in Power BI Service.

If you're already a Power Pivot user, you'll undoubtedly breeze through the content of this part of the book (this will be a review with some important new changes). As you'll find out, you can almost seamlessly transfer your Excel data modeling knowledge to Power BI Desktop. Again, that's because the underlying technology is the same. However, with Power BI Desktop, you'll always have the latest Power BI features because Microsoft updates it every month.

Also, know that Power BI Desktop and Analysis Services Tabular share the same foundation – the in-memory xVelocity data engine. Therefore, a nice bonus awaits you ahead. While you're learning Power BI Desktop, you're also learning Analysis Services Tabular. So, if one day you decide to upgrade your self-service model from Power BI Desktop to a scalable organizational model powered by Analysis Services Tabular, you'll find that you already have most of the knowledge. You're now a BI pro!

To practice what you'll learn, the book includes plenty of exercises that will walk you through the steps for implementing a self-service model for analyzing sales data.

Chapter 6

Data Modeling Fundamentals

6.1 Understanding Data Models 129
6.2 Understanding Power BI Desktop 139
6.3 Importing Data 148

6.4 Advanced Storage Configurations 162
6.5 Summary 168

As a first step to building a data model, you need to acquire the data that you'll analyze and report on. Power BI Desktop makes it easy to access data from a variety of data sources, ranging from relational databases, such as a SQL Server database, to text files, such as a comma-delimited file extracted from a mainframe system. The most common way of bringing data into Power BI Desktop is by importing it from relational databases. When the data isn't in a database, Power BI Desktop supports other data acquisition methods, including text files, cubes, data feeds, and much more. And for some fast databases, Power BI Desktop allows you to connect directly to the data source without importing the data.

In this chapter, you'll learn the fundamentals of self-service data modeling with Power BI Desktop. To put your knowledge in practice, you'll implement a raw data model for analyzing the Adventure Works reseller sales. You'll exercise a variety of basic data import options to load data from the Adventure Works data warehouse, a cube, an Excel workbook, a comma-delimited file, and even from a Reporting Services report. You'll also learn how to work with advanced storage options and how to improve query performance by using predefined data summaries (aggregations). You'll find the resulting Adventure Works model in the \Source\ch06 folder.

6.1 Understanding Data Models

When you work with Power BI Desktop, you create a self-service data model with the data you need to analyze. As a first step, you need to obtain the data. The primary data acquisition option that supports all Power BI features is importing the data. For example, Martin could import some CRM data from Salesforce, finance data from Excel reports, and sales data from the corporate data warehouse. Once Martin relates all this data into a single model, he can then create a report that combines these three business areas. Power BI also supports hybrid (composite) models. For example, if Martin wants real-time access to an ERP table that stores sales orders, he could configure that table in DirectQuery, while the rest are imported. As you might realize, Power BI Desktop gives you tremendous power and flexibility for creating self-service data models!

Power BI Desktop allows you to acquire data from a variety of data sources with a few mouse clicks. While getting data is easy, relating data in your model requires some planning on your side to avoid inconsistent or even incorrect results. For example, you might have a Customer table and a Sales table, but if there isn't a way to relate the data in these tables, you'll get the same sales amount repeated for each customer. Therefore, before you click the Get Data button, you should have some basic understanding about the Power BI data modeling requirements and limitations. So, let's start by learning some important fundamentals of data modeling. Among other things, they will help you understand why having a single monolithic dataset is not always the best approach and why you should always have a date table.

6.1.1 Understanding Schemas

I previously wrote that Power BI Desktop organizes data in tables, like how Excel allows you to organize data into Excel lists. Each table consists of columns, also referred to as *fields* or *attributes*. If all the data is provided to you as just one table, then you could congratulate yourself and skip this section altogether. In fact, as you've seen in Part 1 of this book, you can skip Power BI Desktop and modeling because you can analyze a single dataset directly with Power BI Service. Chances are, however, that you might need to import multiple tables from the same or different data sources. This requires learning some basic database and schema concepts. The term "schema" here is used to describe the table definitions and how tables relate to each other. I'll keep the discussion light on purpose to get you started with data modeling as fast as possible. I'll revisit table relationships in the next chapter.

> **NOTE** Having all data in a single table might not require modeling, but it isn't a best practice. Suppose you initially wanted to analyze reseller sales and you've got a single dataset with columns such as Reseller, Sales Territory, and so on. Then you decide to extend the model with direct sales to consumers to consolidate reporting that spans now two business areas. Now you have a problem. Because you merged business dimensions into the reseller sales dataset, you won't be able to slice and dice the two datasets by the same lookup tables (Reseller, Sales Territory, Date, and others). In addition, a large table might strain your computer resources as it'll require more time to import and more memory to store the data. At the same time, a fully normalized schema, such as modeling a product entity with Product, Subcategory, and Category tables, is also not desirable because you'll end up with many tables and the model might become difficult to understand and navigate. When modeling your data, it's important to find a good balance between business requirements and normalization, and that balance is the star schema.

Understanding star schemas
For a lack of better terms, I'll use the dimensional modeling terminology to illustrate the star schema (for more information about star schemas, see http://en.wikipedia.org/wiki/Star_schema). **Figure 6.1** shows two schema types. The left diagram illustrates a star schema, where the ResellerSales table is in the center. This table stores the history of the Adventure Works reseller sales, and each row represents the most atomic information about the sale transaction. This could be a line item in the sales order that includes the order quantity, sales amount, tax amount, discount, and other numeric fields.

Dimensional modeling refers to these tables as *fact tables*. As you can imagine, the ResellerSales table can be very long if it keeps several years of sales data. Don't be alarmed about the dataset size though. Thanks to the state-of-the art underlying storage technology, your data model can still import and store millions of rows!

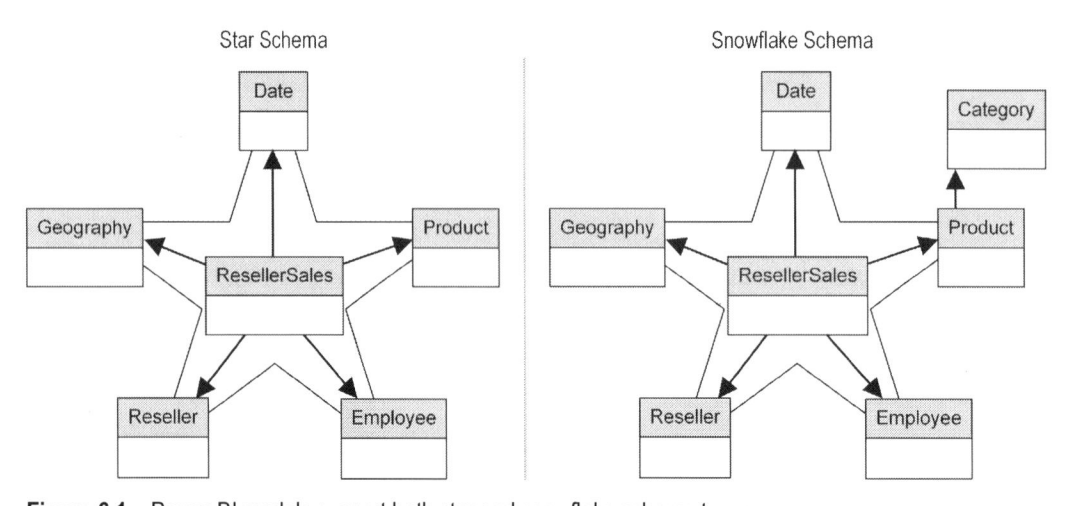

Figure 6.1 Power BI models support both star and snowflake schema types.

The ResellerSales table is related to other tables, called *lookup* or *dimension* tables. These tables provide contextual information to each row stored in the ResellerSales table. For example, the Date table might include date-related fields, such as Date, Quarter, and Year columns, to allow you to aggregate data at day, quarter, and year levels, respectively. The Product table might include ProductName, Color, and Size fields, and so on.

The reason why your data model should have these fields in separate lookup tables, is that, for the most part, their content doesn't need a historical record. For example, if the product name changes, this probably would be an in-place change. By contrast, if you were to continue adding columns to the ResellerSales table, you might end up with performance and maintenance issues. If you need to make a change, you might have to update millions of rows of data as opposed to updating a single row. Similarly, if you were to add a new column to the Date table, such as FiscalYear, you'll have to update all the rows in the ResellerSales table.

Are you limited to only one fact table with Power BI? Absolutely not! For example, you can add an InternetSales fact table that stores direct sales to individuals. In the case of multiple fact tables, you should model the fact tables to share some common lookup tables so that you could match and consolidate data for cross-reporting purposes, such as to show reseller and Internet sales side by side and grouped by year and product. This is another reason to avoid a single monolithic dataset and to have logically related fields in separate tables (if you have this option). Don't worry if this isn't immediately clear. Designing a model that accurately represents requirements is difficult even for BI pros, but it gets easier with practice.

> **NOTE** Another common issue that I witness with novice users is creating a separate dataset for each report, e.g. one dataset for a report showing reseller sales and another dataset for a report showing direct sales. Like the "single dataset" issue I discussed above, this design will lead to data duplication and inability to produce consolidated reports that span multiple areas. Even worse would be to embed calculations in the dataset, such as calculating Profit or Year-to-Date in a SQL view that is used to source the data. Like the issue with defining calculations in a report, this approach will surely lead to redundant calculations or calculations that produce different results from one report to another.

Understanding snowflake schemas

A *snowflake* schema is where some lookup tables relate to other lookup tables but not directly to the fact table. Going back to **Figure 6.1**, you can see that for whatever reason, the product categories are kept in a Category table that relates to the Product table and not directly to the ResellerSales table. One strong motivation for snowflaking is that you might have another fact table, such as SalesQuota, that stores data not at a product level but at a category level. If you keep categories in their own Category table, this design would allow you to join the Category lookup table to the SalesQuota table, and you'll still be able to have a report that shows aggregated sales and quota values grouped by category.

Power BI supports snowflake schemas just fine. However, if you have a choice, you should minimize snowflaking when it's not needed. This is because snowflaking increases the number of tables in the model, making it more difficult for other users to understand your model. If you import data from a database with a normalized schema, you can minimize snowflaking by merging snowflaked tables. For example, you can use a SQL query that joins the Product and Category tables. However, if you import text files, you won't have that option because you can't use SQL. However, when you use Power BI Desktop, you can still handle denormalization tasks in the Power Query, or by adding calculated columns that use DAX expressions to accomplish the same goal, such as by adding a column to the Product table to look up the product category from the Category table. Then you can hide the Category table.

To recap this schema discussion, you can view the star schema as the opposite of its snowflake counterpart. While the snowflake schema embraces normalization as the preferred designed technique to reduce data duplication, the star schema favors denormalization or data entities and reducing the overall number of tables, although this process results in data duplication (a category is repeated for each product that has the same category). Demormalization (star schemas) and BI go hand in hand. That's because star schemas reduce the number of tables and required joins. This makes your model faster and more intuitive.

Understanding date tables

Even if the data is given to you as a single dataset, you should strongly consider having a separate date table. A date table stores a range of dates that you need for data analysis. A date table typically includes additional columns for flexible time exploration, such as Quarter, Year, Fiscal Quarter, Fiscal Year, Holiday Flag, and so on. It may also include fiscal and manufacturing calendars. DAX time calculations, such as TOTALYTD, TOTALQTD, and so on, require a separate date table or auto-generated date tables but they are not a best practice.

> **NOTE** To avoid requiring date tables, Power BI Desktop is configured to automatically generate date tables and hierarchies (the Auto Date/Time setting in File ⇨ Options and Settings ⇨ Options (Data Load tab) is on). This feature generates a date table with a Year-Quarter-Month-Day hierarchy for *every* date field. This can severely bloat your data model if you have millions of rows and dates with large time spans. If you plan to use auto-generated tables, leave this feature on, but monitor the size of your data model. A best practice is to have a separate date table and write time calculations to use this table.

There are many ways to create a date table. You can import it from your corporate data warehouse, if you have one. You can maintain it in an Excel file and import it from there. You can also use the DAX CALENDAR and CALENDARAUTO functions to auto generate a date table. You can even generate it in Power Query using custom code written in the query language (referred to as "M"), as I'll show you in the next chapter. And you can have more than one date table in your model. This could be useful if you want to aggregate the same fact table by multiple dates, such as order date, ship date, and due date.

6.1.2 Introducing Relationships

Once you import multiple tables, you need a way to relate them. If two tables aren't related, your model won't aggregate data correctly when you use both tables on a report. To understand how to relate tables, you need to learn about Power BI relationships. Let's cover quickly the fundamentals.

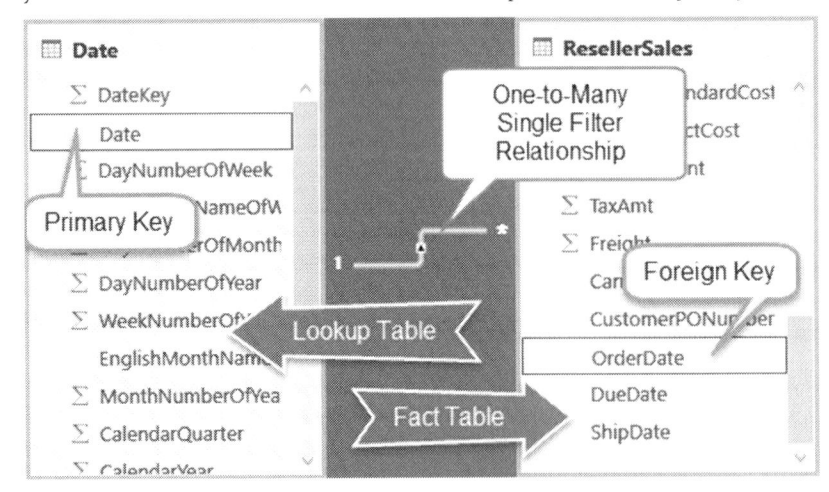

Figure 6.2 The Date column (primary key) in the Date table is related to the matching OrderDate column (foreign key) in the ResellerSales table.

Understanding relationships

In order to relate two tables, there must be data commonalities between the two tables. This isn't much different than joins in relational databases, such as Microsoft Access or SQL Server. For example, you won't be able to analyze sales by product if there isn't a common column between the ResellerSales and Date tables that ties a date to a sale (see **Figure 6.2**).

If the underlying data source has relationships (referential integrity constraints) defined, Power BI Desktop will detect and carry them to the model (this is controlled by the "Import relationships from data sources" setting in File ⇨ Options and setting ⇨ Options ⇨ Data Load under the Current File session). If not, Power BI is capable of auto-detecting relationships using internal rules (this is controlled by the "Autodetect new relationships after data is loaded" setting in the same section). Of course, you can also create relationships manually. It's important to understand that your data model is layered on top of the original data. No model changes affect the original data source and its design. You only need rights to read from the data source so that you can import the data you need.

Understanding keys
Common columns in each pair of tables are called *keys*. A *primary key* is a column that uniquely identifies each row in a table. A primary key column can't have duplicate values. For example, the Date column uniquely identifies each row in the Date table and no other row has the same value. An employee identifier or an e-mail address can be used as a primary key in an Employee table. To join Date to ResellerSales, in the ResellerSales table, you must have a matching column, which is called a *foreign key*. For example, the OrderDate column in the ResellerSales table is a foreign key.

A matching column means a column in the fact table that has matching values in the lookup table. The column names of the primary key and foreign key don't have to be the same (values are important). For example, if the ResellerSales table has a sale recorded on 1/1/2015, there should be a row in the Date table with date in the Date column of 1/1/2016. If there isn't, the data model won't show an error, but all the sales that don't have matching dates in the Data table would appear under an unknown (blank) value in a report that groups ResellerSales data by some column in the Date table.

Typically, a fact table has several foreign keys, so it can be related to different lookup tables. For performance reasons, you should use shorter data types, such as integers or dates. For example, the Date column could be a column of a Date data type. Or if you're importing from a data warehouse database, it might have an Integer data type, with values such as 20110101 for January 1st, 2011, and 20110102 for January 2nd, 2011, and so on.

> **NOTE** Relationships from fact tables to the same lookup table don't have to use the same column. For example, ResellerSales can join Date on the Date column but InternetSales might join it on the DateKey column, for example in the case where there isn't a column of a Date data type in InternetSales. If a column uniquely identifies each row, the lookup table can have different "primary key" columns.

Typically, you'll join a dimension (reference) table to a fact table and the dimension table will have a primary (unique) key that you'll relate to the corresponding column in the fact table. But a primary key is not required. For example, you might have Invoices and Orders tables, where the Orders table has the invoice number, which may not be unique in the Invoices table (an invoice can have several lines). However, you can still join these two tables unless you run into some of the Power BI relationship limitations, such as that redundant relationship paths are not allowed. For example, A ⇨ C and A ⇨ B ⇨ C form redundant relationships between tables A and C.

About relationship cardinality
The relationship cardinality reflects the number of rows in one table that are associated with the number of rows in the related table. Power BI uses the relationship carnality for data validation. Note back in in **Figure 6.2**, the number 1 is shown on the left side of the relationship towards the Date table and an asterisk (*) is shown next to the Reseller Sales table. This denotes a one-to-many cardinality. To understand this better, consider that one row (one date) in the Date table can have zero, one, or many recorded sales in ResellerSales, and one product in the Product table corresponds to one or many sales in ResellerSales, and so on. The important word here is "many".

Although not a common cardinality, Power BI also supports a one-to-one relationship type. For example, you might have Employee and SalesPerson tables in a snowflake schema, where a sales person is a type of an employee and each sales person relates to a single employee. By specifying a one-to-one relationship between Employee and SalesPerson, you're telling Power BI to check the data cardinality and show an error if the one-to-many relationship is detected on data refresh. A one-to-one relationship also brings additional simplifications when working with DAX calculations, such as to let you interchangeably use the DAX RELATED and RELATEDTABLE functions.

Lastly, Power BI supports a many-to-many relationship cardinality but don't confuse it with the many-to-many relationship type that typically requires a bridge table and it's discussed in Chapter 8. The Orders-Invoices relationship that I just mentioned is an example of a many-to-many cardinality because the invoice number is not unique in the Invoices table.

About relationship cross filter direction
While the relationship cardinality is useful to validate the expected association between two tables, a more important characteristic is the filter direction. Note also that in **Figure 6.2**, there's an arrow indicator pointing toward the ResellerSales table. This indicates that this relationship has a single cross filtering direction between the Date and Reseller tables. In other words, the ResellerSales table can be analyzed using the Date table, but not the other way around. For example, you can have a report that groups sales by any of the fields of the Date table. However, you can't aggregate dates, such as to count them, by a field in the ResellerSales table, which is probably meaningless anyway.

Now suppose you want to know how many times a product is sold by date. You might be able to find the answer by counting on a ProductKey field in the ResellerSales table without involving the Product table at all. However, what if you need to find how many times a product model (the ModelName column in the Product table) was sold on a given date? To avoid adding this column to the ResellerSales table, you'd want to count on the ModelName field in the Product table. However, this will cause the relationship direction to reverse. First, you need to follow the Date ⇨ ResellerSales relationship (no problems here because the filter direction points to the ResellerSales table), but then to get to the Product table, you need to propagate the filter from ResellerSales to Product. However, by default the filter direction is reversed. Although Power BI Desktop won't show any error, the report will return meaningless results because the relationship filter won't propagate from ResellerSales to Product.

This is where a cross filtering direction set to Both can help. It has a double arrow indicator (see **Figure 6.3**) to indicate that the filter can propagate either way between tables ResellerSales and Product.

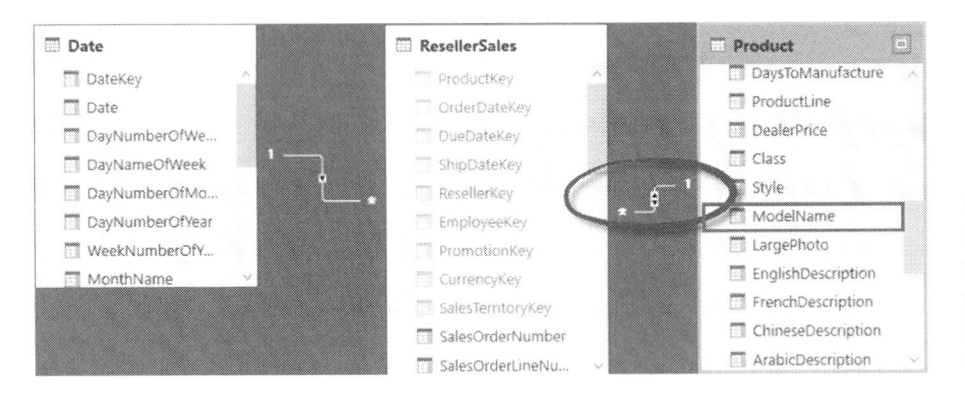

Figure 6.3 The relationship between the ResellerSales and Product table has a cross filtering direction set to Both.

NOTE Bidirectional relationships may also result in redundant paths which Power BI Desktop will detect and disallow. As a best practice, start with a unidirectional model and turn on bi-directional cross filtering only when needed. To learn more about bidirectional cross filtering, read the related whitepaper by Kasper De Jonge at http://bit.ly/2eZUQ2Z.

That's all you need to know about data modeling for now. Next, let's see what options you have for connecting to your data.

6.1.3 Understanding Data Connectivity

In Chapter 2, I mentioned that Power BI supports two options for accessing data: data import and live connections, but this was a simplified statement. Technically, Power BI Service and Power BI Desktop support three main options to connect to your data. There is also a hybrid option (dual storage), but I'll defer discussing it in section 6.4. Let me explain these three options to you now, because it's important to understand how they differ and when to use each one (if you have a choice). **Figure 6.4** should help you understand their differences.

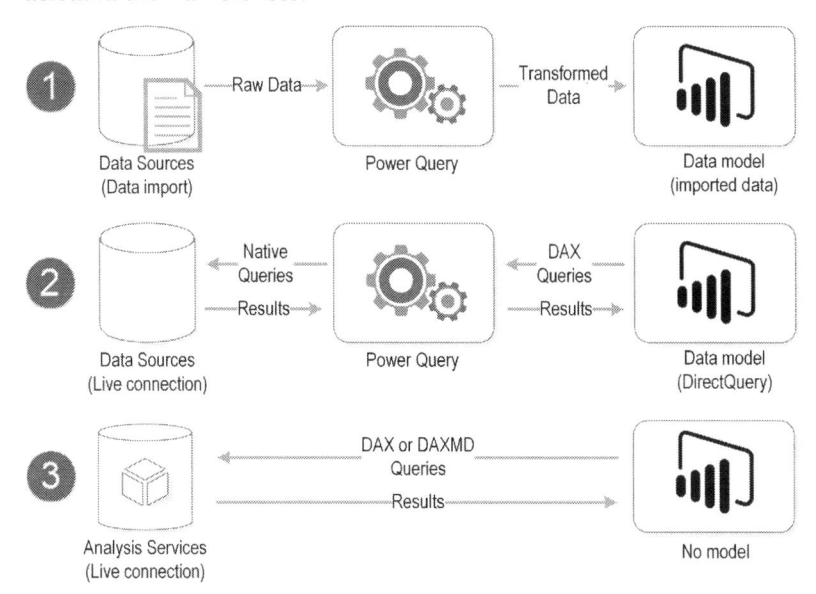

Figure 6.4 Power BI supports three main connectivity options.

Importing data

The first option (option 1 in the **Figure 6.4** diagram) is to import data. When Power BI imports the data, it stores the data in the xVelocity in-memory data engine. The in-memory engine is hosted in an out-of-process Analysis Services instance that is distributed with Power BI Desktop. So, the report performance is fast and predictable. You can pack millions of rows because data is stored in a highly compressed format and loaded in memory when you analyze the data.

When you import data, you can transform and clean it before it's loaded into the model. Power BI Desktop always connects to raw data that you import via a connectivity component called Power Query or just a "query". Think of Power Query as a layer between the raw data and your data model. Yes, the Power BI Desktop query is a successor of Excel Power Query, which you might be familiar with. However, unlike Excel, queries aren't optional when you import data in Power BI Desktop.

> **NOTE** Data analysts experienced with Excel data modelling might know that Excel has at least three ways to import data into a data model – Excel native import, Power Pivot Table Import Wizard, and Power Query. There hasn't been a way in Excel to switch easily from one import option to another without recreating your table, such as from Table Import Wizard to Power Query, to use the Power Query transformation features. To simplify this, in Power BI Desktop, all the data import roads go through queries, which are the equivalent of Power Query in Excel. On the downside, even if you don't transform the data, Power Query might add some performance overhead when extracting the data from the data source.

Unless you use advanced transformation features, such as query functions to automate importing data from multiple files, each imported table has a corresponding Power Query. So, if you import three tables from a database and then import two files, you'll end up with five queries. Power Query is your insurance against current and future data quality issues. Even if the data is clean, such as when you load it from a data warehouse, it might still require some shaping later, and the query is the best place to perform these transformations.

Once the data is imported, the data is cached inside the Power BI Desktop file. Data exploration queries are handled internally by Power BI Desktop (or Power BI Service when the model is deployed). In other words, once the data is imported, Power BI doesn't open connections and query the original data source unless you refresh the data.

> **NOTE** Similar to Microsoft Office files, a Power BI Desktop file (*.pbix) is an archive zip file. If you rename it to have a zip extension and open it, you'll see that the imported data is stored in the DataModel folder. xVelocity (the storage engine that powers Excel data models), Power BI, Analysis Services Tabular and SQL Server columnstore indexes) uses internal algorithms to compress the data. Depending on the cardinality of the data you import, expect a compression ratio of 5:1 or higher.

Because data is cached, you must periodically refresh the dataset to synchronize it with changes to the original data source and Power BI Service allows you to schedule published datasets for automatic refresh. However, if the data source is on premises, you need to install a special software called a gateway on your company's network so that Power BI can tunnel in and reach the data source to extract the data.

> **NOTE** A Power BI gateway is only required when Power BI Service needs to connect to on-premises data sources. The gateway can be installed for personal use, such as on the data analyst's laptop, or for enterprise (standard) use, such as on a dedicated server, to provide access to corporate data sources, such as a data warehouse. Both modes support refreshing published datasets.

Connecting live via DirectQuery

You might decide to connect Power BI Desktop to fast data sources that support direct (live) connectivity and then create reports that send native queries directly to these data sources (no data is cached in the model). This is option 2 in the **Figure 6.4** diagram. DirectQuery is a natural choice when you want real-time access to data. However, only a subset of the data sources supports direct connectivity. The list includes Analysis Services (on premises or Azure), datasets published to Power BI Service (they are hosted and processed by Analysis Services), SQL Server, Oracle, Azure SQL Database, Azure SQL Data Warehouse, Teradata, Amazon Redshift, Spark on Azure HDInsight, Impala, or SAP Hana, but the list is growing as Power BI evolves. When you connect directly to any of the supported data sources (other than Analysis Services), Power BI Desktop configures xVelocity in a special DirectQuery mode.

With DirectQuery, Power BI Desktop doesn't import any data, and xVelocity doesn't store any data. Instead, xVelocity generates DAX queries that the query layer translates to native queries. For example, if you connect Power BI Desktop to SQL Server with DirectQuery, the model will send T-SQL queries to SQL Server every time you interact with the report. Note that because Power BI uses Power Query in between, you can still perform basic data transformation tasks, such as column renaming. You can also create DAX calculations with some limitations. For example, DAX time calculations, such as TOTALYTD, are currently not supported with DirectQuery.

> **NOTE** Compared to importing data, DirectQuery has modeling limitations related to the complexity of auto-generating queries on the fly. To understand all DirectQuery limitations in Power BI Desktop, please read the document "Use DirectQuery in Power BI Desktop" at https://powerbi.microsoft.com/documentation/powerbi-desktop-use-directquery/.

When you connect to a data source that supports DirectQuery and before you load a table, Power BI Desktop will ask you how you want to get data: by importing data or by using DirectQuery (see **Figure 6.5**). In this case, I'm connecting to SQL Server and Power BI Desktop asks me if I want to import the data or use DirectQuery. If I select DirectQuery, Power BI Desktop will auto-generate native queries as I explore data and will show me the results it gets from SQL Server. DirectQuery supports limited modeling capabilities using the Data View and the Fields pane. However, you can create and manage relationships, rename the metadata (table and column names), and perform basic data transformations.

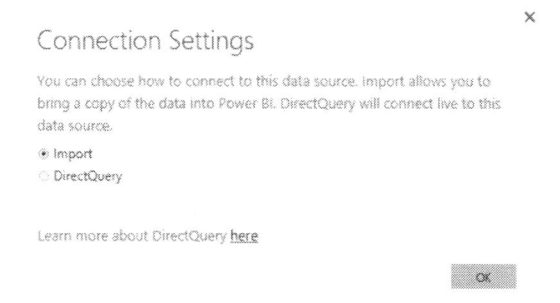

Figure 6.5 When connecting to a data source that supports DirectQuery, you need to decide how to access the data.

If you publish a DirectQuery model to Power BI Service, the dataset needs the Power BI on-premises data gateway to be installed on premises in standard mode (not personal) to connect live to the original data source. If the gateway is not configured, the dataset will be published but it will be disabled (it will show grayed out in the Power BI navigation bar) and you won't be able to use it.

Connecting live to multidimensional data sources
Finally, a special live connectivity option exists when you connect live to Analysis Services in all its flavors (Multidimensional, Tabular, and published datasets) and SAP (SAP Hana and SAP Data Warehouse) as option 3 in the **Figure 6.4** diagram shows. In this case, the xVelocity engine isn't used at all. Instead, Power BI connects directly to the data source and sends native queries. For example, Power BI generates DAX queries when connected to Analysis Services (Multidimensional handles DAX queries through a special DAXMD interop mechanism). There is no Power Query in between Power BI Desktop and the data source, and data transformations and relationships are not available.

In other words, Power BI becomes a presentation layer that is connected directly to the source, and the Fields pane shows the metadata from the model. This is conceptually very similar to connecting Excel to Analysis Services. When connecting to Analysis Services Tabular, you can create report-level DAX measures in Power BI Desktop on top of the model just like you can create MDX calculations in Excel. The measure formulas will be stored in the Power BI Desktop file and the original model is not affected.

Figure 6.6 shows the connectivity options when you connect to Analysis Services. The "Explore live" option connects you directly to the model.

Figure 6.6 When connecting to Analysis Services, Power BI allows you to connect live or import the data.

Like DirectQuery, if you publish a model that connects live to on-premises model, the dataset needs the Power BI on-premises data gateway to be installed in standard mode (personal mode doesn't support DirectQuery or live connections) to connect to Analysis Services. If the gateway is not configured, the dataset will be published, but it will be disabled (it will be grayed out in the Power BI navigation bar) and you won't be able to use it.

NOTE Analysis Services is also available as a Platform as a Service (PaaS) Azure service. If you use Azure Analysis Services, you don't need a gateway to connect Power BI reports to Azure Analysis Services. However, you'd still need a gateway to process (refresh) your cloud model from an on-premises data source if this is where the model gets data from.

Table 6.1 summarizes the key points about the three data connectivity options. Because most real-life needs would require importing data, this chapter focuses on this option exclusively. If you plan to connect to live data sources, your experience would be very similar to how you would do this in Power BI Service (refer to the section "Using Live Connections" in Chapter 2).

Table 6.1 This table compares the three connectivity options.

Feature	Data import	Connecting Live (DirectQuery)	Connecting Live (Analysis Services)
Data sources	Any data source	SQL Server (on premises), Azure SQL Database, Azure SQL Data Warehouse, Spark on Azure HDInsight, Azure SQL Data Warehouse, Oracle, Teradata, Amazon Redshift, Impala	Analysis Services (Tabular and Multidimensional), published Power BI datasets, SAP Hana and DW (multidimensional connection)
Usage scenario	When you need all Power BI features and predicable performance	When you connect to fast or large database that supports DirectQuery and you don't want to import data	When you connect to a single Analysis Services model
Power Query for data transformations	Available (all features)	Available (basic transformations only)	Not available
Connect to multiple data sources	Yes	Yes	No
Implement hybrid storage (import and DirectQuery)	Yes	Yes	No
Data storage	Data imported in xVelocity	Data is left at the data source	Data is left at the model
Connect to on-premises data from published models	Personal or standard gateway is required to refresh data	Standard (not personal) gateway is required to connect to data	Standard gateway is required to connect to SSAS models
Data modeling	Available	Available with limitations	Not available
Relationships	Available	Available with limitations	Not available
Business calculations in a data model	All DAX calculations	DAX calculations with limitations	DAX calculations both in the model and report (Tabular only)
Data exploration	Handled internally by Power BI Desktop or Power BI Service when the model is deployed without making connections to the original data sources	Power BI Desktop/Power BI Service (published models) autogenerates native queries, sends them to the data source, and shows the results	Power BI Desktop/Power BI Service (published models) autogenerates queries, sends them to the data source, and shows the results

Now that you've learned the modeling fundamentals, let's see how you can apply them in practice using Power BI Desktop. But let me introduce you first to Power BI Desktop and its design environment.

6.2 Understanding Power BI Desktop

As I mentioned in Chapter 1, data analysts have two tool options for creating self-service data models. If you prefer Excel, you can continue using the Excel data modeling capabilities and deploy Excel workbooks to Power BI Service, Power BI Report Server, or SharePoint Server. Be aware though that Excel has its own roadmap, so its BI features lag Power BI. By contrast, if you prefer to stay always on the latest BI features, consider Power BI Desktop, which combines the best of Excel Power Pivot, Power Query, and Power View in a standalone, freely available tool that Microsoft updates every month.

6.2.1 Installing Power BI Desktop

Power BI Desktop is available only on Windows operating system, but Mac users have options to run Windows apps. They can configure their Macs for dual boot, or run Windows in a virtual environment, such as by using Parallel Desktop for Mac.

Understanding bitness
Power BI Desktop is available as 32-bit and 64-bit Windows installations. The download page determines what version of Windows you have (32-bit or 64-bit) and downloads the appropriate executable. Nowadays, you can't buy a 32-bit computer (not easily, anyway). However, even if you have a 64-bit computer and 64-bit Windows OS, you can still install 32-bit applications. The problem is that 32-bit applications are limited to 2 GB of memory. By contrast, 64-bit computing enables applications to use more than 2 GB of memory. This is especially useful for in-memory databases that import data, such as xVelocity (remember that xVelocity is the storage engine of Power BI Service and Power BI Desktop).

In general, if you have a 64-bit version of Windows, you should install the 64-bit version of any software if a 64-bit version is available. Therefore, the 64-bit version of Power BI Desktop is a better choice. However, although your model on the desktop can grow and grow until it exhausts all the memory, remember that Power BI Pro won't let you upload a file that is larger than 1 GB (Power BI Premium supports files up to 10 GB) so keep this in mind as well if you plan to publish the model.

> **NOTE** Readers familiar with Excel data modeling might remember that the Office setup installs the 32-bit version of Office by default and getting IT to install the 64-bit version has been a struggle. The Office setup favors the 32-bit version in case you use 32-bit add-ins. Because Power BI Desktop doesn't depend on Office, you can go ahead and install the 64-bit version even if you have the 32-bit version of Office installed.

Choosing an installation option
You can download and install Power BI Desktop from https://powerbi.microsoft.com/desktop or from the Downloads menu in Power BI. This option requires you to be proactive and update Power BI Desktop periodically. In addition, you must have local admin rights to install it. Instead, if you have Windows 10, I recommend you install Power BI Desktop from Microsoft Store because of the following benefits:

- Automated updates – All data analysts within the company use the latest and greatest version. This avoids the issue of someone attempting to open a model created with more recent version of Power BI Desktop. While Power BI Desktop will automatically upgrade older files, it doesn't support downgrading to a previous version.
- You don't need admin rights – Many users don't have local admin rights to their computers.
- Faster installation – Because you don't have to run a setup, upgrading is much faster.

For more information about Power BI Desktop availability and minimum requirements, check the "Get Power BI Desktop" article at https://powerbi.microsoft.com//documentation/powerbi-desktop-get-the-desktop/.

6.2.2 Understanding Design Environment

Let's get familiar with the Power BI Desktop design environment. **Figure 6.7** shows its main elements numbered in the typical order of steps you'd take to create and refine self-service data models.

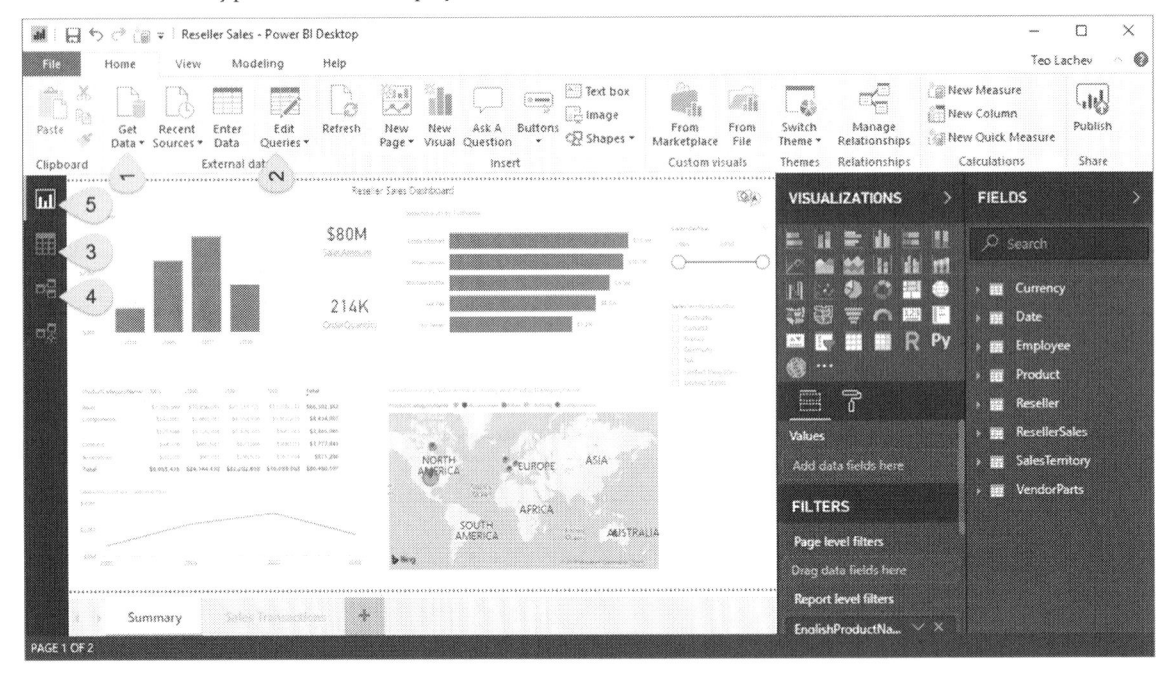

Figure 6.7 Power BI Desktop has five commonly used areas that correspond to the main modeling steps.

Understanding data modeling steps

A typical self-service data modeling workflow consists of the following five main steps (each step refers to the numbers in **Figure 6.7**):

1. Get data – The process starts with connecting to your data by clicking the Get Data button. Remember that when you import the data or use DirectQuery, Power BI Desktop creates a query for each table you import (except when you connect to Analysis Services, in which case there is no underlying query).
2. Transform data – If the data requires cleansing or transformations, click the Edit Queries button to open Power Query Editor and perform data transformation tasks, such as replacing column values.
3. Explore and refine data – Switch to the Data View tab to explore and refine the imported data, such as to see what data is loaded in a table and to change column data types. The Data View isn't available with DirectQuery and live connections. However, in the case of DirectQuery data sources, you can still use the Power Query Editor to shape and transform the data although not all transformations are available.
4. Create relationships – As a part of refining the data model, if you import multiple tables you need to relate them either using the Relationships View or the Manage Relationships button in the ribbon's Home tab. Relationships aren't available when connecting live to Analysis Services.

> **NOTE** Currently, Microsoft is upgrading the Relationships view with new features, such as a new tabbed interface. Therefore, the screenshot shows two Relationships tabs. To test the new features, go to File ⇨ Options and Settings ⇨Options, select "the Preview features" tab, and check Modeling View. Once the preview period is over, the new Relationships tab will take over the old one.

5. Visualize data – Finally, you build reports to visualize your data by switching to the Report View, which is available with all the data connectivity options.

Visualizations and Fields panes

When the Report tab is active, the Visualizations and Fields panes (on the right) should be familiar to you by now, as you've already worked with them in the first part of the book. The Fields pane shows the model metadata consisting of tables and fields. A field can be a table column or a calculation, such as Sales YTD. You can also use the Fields pane to create DAX calculations. The Fields pane is available when you're in the Report and Data views.

The Visualizations pane is only available when the Report View is active. It includes Microsoft-provided and custom visualizations. You can click the ellipsis menu (…) below the visualization icons to import custom visualizations from Microsoft AppSource or distributed as files. You can use the Visualizations pane to configure the visual data options and formatting.

6.2.3 Understanding Navigation

Power BI Desktop has a simplified navigation experience using a ribbon interface that should be familiar to you from other Microsoft products, such as Excel. But if you come from Excel data modeling, you'll undoubtedly appreciate the change toward simplicity. There is no more confusion about which ribbon to use and which button to click! By the way, if you need more space, you can minimize the ribbon by clicking the chevron button in the top-right corner or by pressing Ctrl-F1.

Understanding the ribbon's Home tab

The ribbon's Home tab (see **Figure 6.7** again) is your one-stop navigation for common tasks. The Clipboard group allows you to copy and paste text, such as a DAX calculation formula. It doesn't allow you to create tables by pasting data as you can with Excel Power Pivot (to do this, you can use the Enter Data button). However, you can use the Enter Data button in the External Data group to create tables by pasting or entering data. Like other Microsoft Office applications, you can use the Format Painter to copy and apply limited format settings from one selection to another. Let's say you've changed the format settings, such as colors and fonts, of a chart and you want to apply the same settings to another chart. Click the first chart to select it, click the Format Painter button to copy the settings, and then click the other chart to apply the settings.

The External Data group allows you to connect to data (the Get Data button). The Recent Sources button lets you bypass the first Get Data steps, such as when you want to import additional tables from the same database. The Enter Data button allows you to create your own tables by either pasting tabular data or typing in the data manually. The latter could be useful to enter some reference data, such as KPI goals. The Edit Queries button opens a separate Power Query Editor window so that you can apply cleansing or transformation steps. For models with imported data, the Refresh button deletes the data in all tables and re-imports the data. For DirectQuery models, it only refreshes the metadata.

The Insert ribbon group is available when the Report View is active. It allows you to insert new report pages or visuals to a report (alternatively, you can click the visual icon in the Visualizations pane). You can also insert graphical elements, such as text boxes, images, and shapes. The "Ask a Question" button (Q&A is currently in preview) brings Q&A from Power BI Service to the desktop. It creates a report from a natural question you ask! The Buttons drop-down is for adding predefined images that look like buttons to trigger actions, such as navigate to a bookmark or Q&A.

Fulfilling the same role as the ellipsis (…) menu in the Visualizations pane, the "Custom visuals" ribbon group lets you insert custom visuals from Microsoft AppSource or from a file.

Use the "Switch Theme" drop-down to change the report appearance to a predefined theme. For example, a visually impaired person might find "High contrast" theme useful. You can also create a report theme to apply consistent colors to your report, such as corporate colors or seasonal coloring. You specify the color theme by hand in a file described in JavaScript Object Notation (JSON) format. Then, you use the Switch Theme button to import the file. For more information about the color theme specification, read the "Use Report Themes in Power BI Desktop" article at https://powerbi.microsoft.com/documentation/powerbi-desktop-report-themes/. You can also find ready-to-use themes contributed by the community at https://community.powerbi.com/t5/Themes-Gallery/bd-p/ThemesGallery.

The Manage Relationships button allows you to relate tables in your model. The Calculations group is for creating DAX measures, calculated columns, and quick measures (predefined DAX measures that Microsoft has provided). And the Publish button lets you publish your model to Power BI Service.

Understanding the ribbon's View tab

The ribbon's View tab allows you to optimize the page layout for phone devices. Recall from the previous chapter that the Power BI Mobile apps favor phone-optimized report layouts. Power BI reports typically have a lot of visualizations and this is fine if users view them on laptops or tablets. But phones have much smaller displays. To avoid excessive scrolling, you can use the Change Layout button to define a layout optimized for phones.

In **Figure 6.8**, I toggled the Phone Layout button to switch to a phone layout. Then, I dragged an existing visualization from the Visualizations pane, dropped it to the phone layout, and resized it accordingly. Now when users view this page on their phones, the Power BI Mobile native app will detect and apply the phone view. It will also enable report filtering. If there isn't a phone-optimized view, the report will open in the non-optimized, landscape view and the filtering pane will be missing. Note that when you define a phone layout, you can't make changes to the visualizations; you can only resize them. Clicking the Desktop Layout button one more time toggles to the master layout, as you defined it in the Report View.

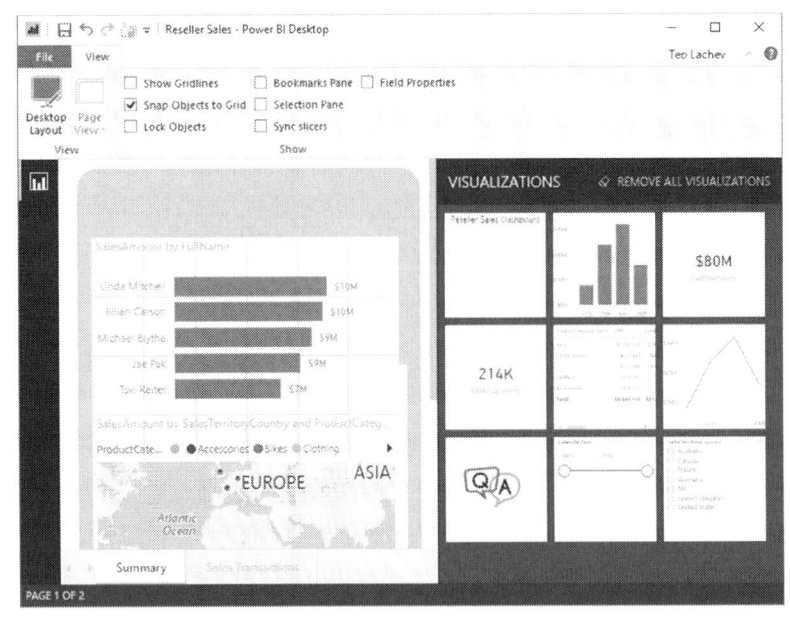

Figure 6.8 Use the Phone Layout to define a phone-optimized views of your report pages.

Continuing the list of menu options, the Page View button zooms the report in desktop layout. It has three options: Fit to Page, Fit to Width, and Actual Size. When checked, the "Show gridlines" shows a grid in the Report View to help you arrange elements on the report canvas. If you want to snap items to the grid to align them precisely, check "Snap objects to grid". When enabled "Lock Objects" prevents you from making accidental changes to visuals on the report.

The Selection pane allows you to toggle the visibility of report elements. This could be useful during design time and it's particularly useful when used together with the Bookmarks Pane. Important for data storytelling, the Bookmarks Pane lets you capture the current view of a report page, including applied filters and visibility state of the visual, and later go back to that state by clicking the saved bookmark. The "Sync slicers" pane allows to configure report slicers, such as to filter visuals in other pages. Finally, when enabled, Field Properties opens another pane that lets you configure properties, such as the description, for the field selected in the Fields pane.

> **TIP** As your data model grows in complexity, users might find it difficult to understand the model metadata, such as which field to use and what's the purpose of a given field or measure. However, if you're disciplined to enter informative descriptions, they will show in a tooltip when the user hovers the field in the Fields list. Now you have a self-documented model!

Understanding the ribbon's Modeling tab

The ribbon's Modeling tab (**Figure 6.9**) allows you to extend and refine your data model. Which are options are enabled depends on the active view. For example, if the Report View tab is active the New Parameter is available but not "Mark as Data Table".

Figure 6.9 The ribbon's Modeling tab is for performing data modeling tasks, such as creating calculations and defining data security.

The Manage Relationships button is available here as well. The Calculations group gives you access to DAX features to create calculated columns, measures, and tables. The New Parameter button in the What If ribbon group is for what-if analysis, such as to see how changes to a product discount affects sales. The "Sort by Column" button is for defining custom column sorting, such as to sort a Month Name column by the ordinal month number instead of the default alphanumeric sorting. The Formatting group lets you change the data type and formatting of a table column, such as to format a sales amount with two decimal places. The Properties group is for changing the purpose of specific columns, such as to tell Power BI Desktop that a Country column has a Country category so that a map knows how to plot it. In addition, it allows you to change the default aggregation behavior or a column, such as to mark a Year column as "Don't summarize" since it meaningless to aggregate years as numbers.

The Security group allows you to define data security, also known as Row-Level Security (RLS). Suppose that while Martin can see all the data in the model, Elena can see United States sales. You can define a role that grants Elena rights only to United States in the Sales Territory table. Then, when Elena views the published model, she can see only the data related to the United States as though the other countries don't exist in the model. The Groups group allow you to define new custom groups, such as to group all European countries in a "European Countries" group so they can be shown as one bar on a chart (groups are discussed in more detail in Chapter 10).

"Mark as Data Table" lets you inform Power BI that you have a custom date table and mark it as such, so that DAX time intelligence functions can use it. The Synonyms button in the Q&A is for defining field synonyms, such as SalesAmount and Revenue, so that Q&A can interpret both terms are equivalent. Speaking of tuning Q&A, the Language Linguistic Schema drop-downs help you refine Q&A even further as explained in the "Editing Q&A linguistic schemas" article at https://powerbi.microsoft.com/blog/editing-q-a-linguistic-schemas.

Understanding the ribbon's Help tab

The Help tab includes several useful resources divided into Help, Community, and Resources sections. The Help section includes shortcuts to access guided learning, documentation (Power BI has an excellent documentation!), training videos, support and the About submenu. Use the About button to see the version and monthly release (recall that Power BI Desktop is updated every month!) of the installed Power BI Desktop.

The Community section has shortcuts to the Power BI blog, community forums, samples, report an issue, and submit an idea about improving Power BI. The "Power BI for Developers" button brings you to the Power BI Developer Center, which contains useful resources for developers interested in implementing Power BI-centric solutions. The "Submit an idea" submenu is a shortcut for submitting a suggestion for improving Power BI.

The Solution Templates button in the Resources section navigates to Microsoft AppSource (appsource.microsoft.com) where you can find working end-to-end enterprise-ready Power BI solutions. Suppose your company uses Salesforce.com for customer relationship management. You already know that you can use the Salesforce apps (content packs) in Power BI Service to get prepackaged datasets, reports and dashboards. Or, you can use Power BI Desktop if you want to have more control over what's imported. But what if you work for a large organization and your dataset exceeds the Power BI maximum dataset size (1 GB for Power BI and up to 10 GB for Power BI Premium)? You can use the Salesforce solution template to schedule incremental data extraction from Salesforce to a local SQL Server database or an Azure SQL Database. The solution template even includes an Analysis Services semantic layer! For more information about Power BI solution templates, watch the "Rapid Deployments with Power BI Solution Templates" video by Richard Tkachuk and Justyna Lucznik at bit.ly/2y1J2Hv.

And if you need help with implementing the solution templates or Power BI consulting and training, click the Partner Showcase. It brings you to https://powerbi.microsoft.com/partners/ where consulting partners, such as Prologika, demonstrates their Power BI-based solutions.

Understanding the ribbon's Format tab

Two additional tabs become available when you select a visualization in the Report View and you select a visual: Format and Drill tabs (**Figure 6.10**). The Format tab allows you to control the placement of the selected visualization. For example, you might decide to add a background image to a report page that appears behind all visualizations. To do so, you can select the image, expand the Send Backwards button and then click Send to Back. Or, if you want to align specific visualizations, you can hold the Ctrl key to select them one by one, and then use the Align button to align them.

Figure 6.10 The ribbon's Format tab is for controlling placement and interaction behavior of selected visualization.

Like the Power BI Service Visual Interactions menu in report edit mode, the Edit Interactions button controls how visualizations on a report page interact with each other, such as in the case when you want to disable the default cross-highlighting to other charts on the page when you select a category in a chart. When checked, "Drilling filters other visuals" propagates the visual filters to other visuals on the page when you drill down. Let's say you have a report page with multiple charts and visualizations. One of the charts shows Sales by Year and you drill down into 2017 to see the sales by month in 2017. When this checkbox is checked, the drill-down will affect the other visuals so they also show data for just 2017.

Understanding the ribbon's Data/Drill tab
Some visualizations, such as charts, maps and Matrix, allow users to interactively drill down data. For example, if you add Year and Month fields to the chart's Axis area, you can drill down from year to month. However, because by default clicking a chart column invokes the highlighting feature, you can use the buttons in the ribbon's Drill tab (or the indicators in the chart) to tell Power BI Desktop that you want to drill down or up instead (see **Figure 6.11**). Or, you can right-click a bar and then use the context menu.

The See Data button opens a table below the visualization that shows the data behind the visualization at the current aggregation level. By contrast, See Records allows you to drill through to the lowest of level of detail behind a given chart. To do so, click the See Records button, and either click a chart element or right-click it and then click See Records.

Figure 6.11 The ribbon's Drill tab is to see the levels of detail behind a visualization, such as to drill down.

"Show next level" groups data by the next level. For example, if the Month field shows the name of the month, "Show next level" at the year level would now shows data grouped by each month, so the X-axis will show January to December. "Expand the next level" will group the data by the combination of year and month. In this case, the X-axis will show 2005 January, 2005 February...2005 December, 2006 January, 2006 February...2006 December, and so on.

The Drillthrough button is to drill through another report page that is specifically configured as a drillthrough target. For example, you might want to start with a summary matrix showing sales data by country for a specific date but allow the user to right-click a cell and drill through another page that shows orders for customer for that date and country.

Understanding the File menu
The File menu gives you access to additional tasks. To save space, **Figure 6.12** shows the bottom half of the menu side by side.

Figure 6.12 Use the Power BI Desktop File menu to work with files and change application settings.

Use the New menu to create a new Power BI Desktop (*.pbix) file and the Open menu to open an existing file. The Save menu saves changes to the current file, and the Save As menu saves the file as another file. If you're transitioning to Power BI Desktop from Excel, the Import menu allows you to import the Excel Power Pivot data model into Power BI Desktop (the reverse is not supported). You can also use the Import menu as another way to import custom visuals into the open Power BI Desktop file. Finally, you can use the Import menu to import an existing Power BI template file.

DEFINITION A Power BI template (.pbit) file includes all the main elements of an existing Power BI Desktop file (report, data model and queries) but not the actual data. This could be useful if you want to send your existing model to someone without giving them access to the data, such as in the case where the user might have restricted access to a subset of the data based on the user's Windows credentials. The user can instantiate the template (create a Power BI Desktop file from it) either by double-clicking on the template file or by using the Import menu.

The Export menu allows you to export your existing model to a Power BI template. The Publish menu is for publishing the data model to Power BI Service (same as the Publish button in the ribbon's Home tab). Remember that although Power BI Desktop can load as much data as it can fit in your computer memory, Power BI Service caps the file size, so be aware of this limitation. If you plan to target larger data volumes, you should consider Analysis Services. When you have an Analysis Services model, your data remains on the server, while you publish only the definitions of your reports and dashboards to Power BI Service, so the dataset size is not an issue. Chapter 14 provides more details when an Analysis Services semantic model could be a better choice than Power BI Desktop. The "Options and settings" menu lets you configure certain program and data source features, as I'll discuss in the next section.

NOTE Why there is no option to publish to Power BI Report Server? Because Power BI Report Server updates less frequently than Power BI Desktop. Therefore, the Power BI Report Server download page includes its version of Power BI Desktop. So, there are two Power BI Desktop versions: the untethered version, which will add features at a monthly cadence, and a version locked to Power BI Report Server and updated when a new report server release is available. The unfortunate side effect is that if you want to publish to both Power BI Service and Power BI Report Server, you need to install and keep both versions.

"Export to PDF" exports all visible report pages to PDF into what-you-see-is-what-you-get (WYSIWYG) PDF pages. The Help menu fulfills the same role as the Help ribbon tab. The "Get started" menu opens the Power BI Desktop startup screen, which has shortcuts (Get Data, Recent Sources, and recent files), video tutorials, and links to useful resources. If you haven't signed in to Power BI, you can do this right from the startup screen. Signing in to Power BI Desktop helps later when you are publishing to Power BI Service. Continuing the menu list, the "What's new" menu brings you to the Power BI blog to read about the new features in the installed release of Power BI Desktop. The Sign Out menu signs you out of Power BI Service in case you want to sign under another account when you publish the model to Power BI. And the Exit menu closes Power BI Desktop.

Understanding Options and Settings menu

Currently, the "Options and settings" menu has two submenus: Options and Data Source Settings. The Data Source Settings menu lets you change certain security settings of the data sources in the current model (you initially specified these settings when you used Get Data). For example, you can use the Data Source Settings menu to switch from SQL Server Windows authentication to standard authentication (requires a login and password). For data sources that support encrypted connections, such as SQL Server, it also allows you to change the connection encryption settings.

The Options menu brings you to the Options window (see **Figure 6.13**) that allows you to change various program features and settings. I'll cover most of them in appropriate places in this and subsequent chapters, but I'd like to explain some now. The Updates tab allows you to configure Power BI Desktop to receive a notification when there's a Power BI Desktop update (enabled by default). Recall that you can install Power BI Desktop from the Windows Store, so you are always on the latest. If you experience issues with Power BI Desktop, you can enable tracing from the Diagnostics tab and send the trace to Microsoft. An interesting setting is Preview Features. It allows you to test "beta" features that Microsoft makes available for testing. The goal is to get your feedback to help Microsoft improve these features.

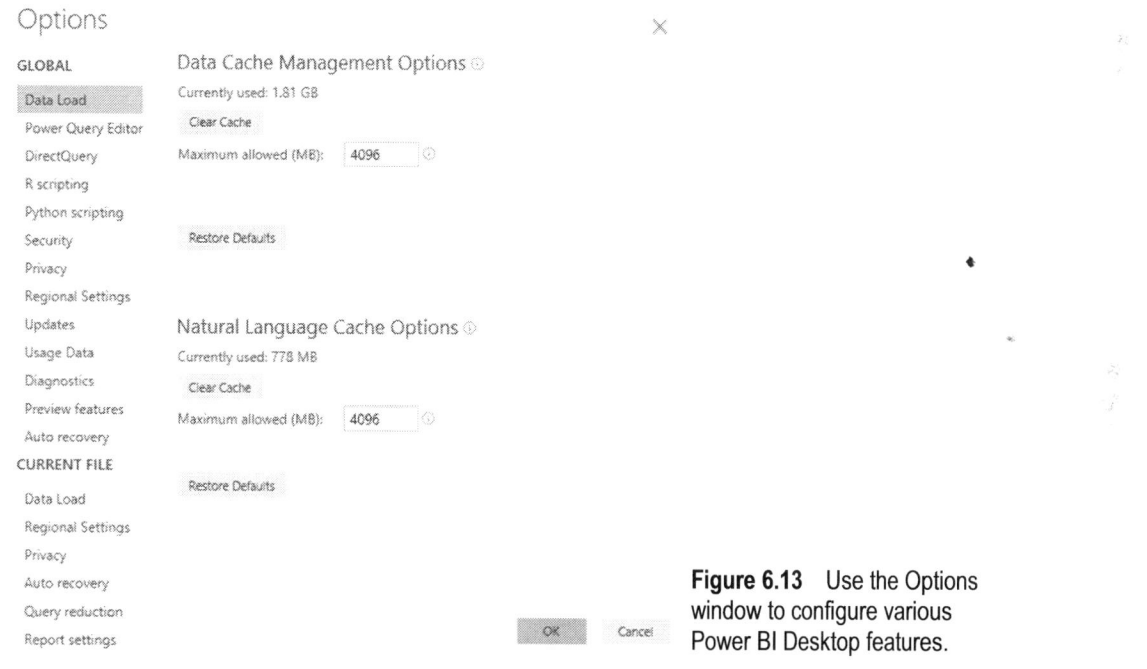

Figure 6.13 Use the Options window to configure various Power BI Desktop features.

Like automatic recovery in other Microsoft Office applications, Auto Recovery has settings that allow you to recover your model in the case of an application or operating system crash. Use the Query Reduction tab to disable some interactive settings, such as cross-highlighting, slicer and filter selection. This could be useful with DirectQuery connections to slow data sources to avoid querying the data source each time you change a filter. Instead, you can set filters and chose when to apply them. Lastly, visit the "Report settings" tab to control what report features, such as to disallow Power BI Service from persisting changes to filters, are enabled in the published report.

Now that I've introduced you to Power BI Desktop and data modeling, let's start the process of creating a self-service data model by getting the data!

6.3 Importing Data

Now let's go back to Martin, who's a data analyst with Adventure Works. Martin realizes that to perform comprehensive sales analysis, he needs data from different data sources. He'll implement a self-service data model and he'll import data from multiple data sources, including data residing in the data warehouse, an Analysis Services cube, flat files, and so on.

6.3.1 Understanding Data Import Steps

Power BI Desktop makes it easy to import data. For those of you who are familiar with Excel data modeling, the process is very similar to using Power Query in Excel. Importing data involves the following high-level steps (you'll repeat for each new data source you use in your model):

1. Choose a data source
2. Connect to the data
3. (Optional) Transform the raw data if needed
4. Load the data into the data model

Choosing a data source

Power BI Desktop can import data from a plethora of data sources with a few clicks and without requiring any scripting or programming skills. You can start the process by clicking the Get Data button in the Power BI Desktop ribbon (or in the splash screen). The most common data sources are shown in the drop-down menu (see **Figure 6.14**), but many more are available when you click the "More…" menu.

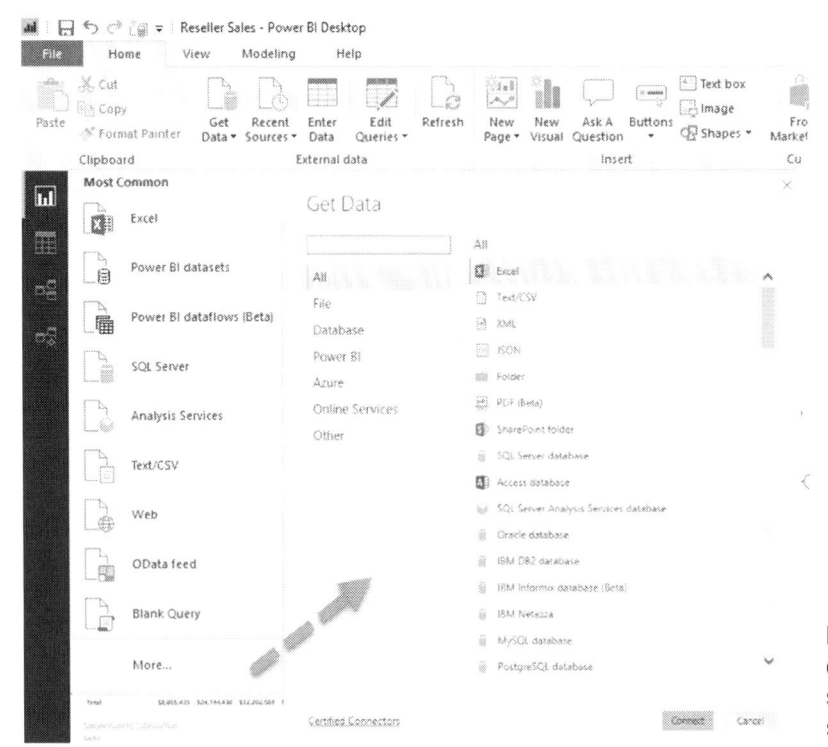

Figure 6.14 Power BI Desktop can connect to a variety of data sources without requiring any scripting or programming.

> **TIP** You might wonder what are the "Power BI datasets" and "Power BI dataflows" sources and why they have such a prominent place in Get Data (after Excel). Like Analyze in Excel, which allows you to connect Excel on your desktop to published datasets, the "Power BI datasets" option allows you to connect to a dataset deployed in Power BI Service and create reports in Power BI Desktop. Why not create reports directly in Power BI Service? One good reason could be that if someone deletes the dataset, Power BI will remove dependent reports, but you could still back up the file if you create them in Power BI Desktop. Another reason is to treat a published dataset as a "semantic layer" so that other users don't have to reimport the same data. "Power BI dataflows" is for connecting to data extracts created from a "dataflow", which I discuss in the next chapter.

To make it easier to find the appropriate data source, the Get Data window organizes them in File, Database, Azure, Online Services, and Other categories. Table 6.2 summarizes the currently supported data sources but expect the list to grow because Microsoft adds new data sources on a regular basis.

Table 6.2   This table summarizes the data sources supported by Power BI Desktop.

Data Source Type	Data Sources
File	Excel, CSV, XML, other delimited and fixed-width text files, JSON, PDF, a list of files in a Windows or SharePoint folder
Database	SQL Server, Microsoft Access, Analysis Services (Multidimensional, Tabular, PowerPivot workbooks deployed to SharePoint), Oracle, IBM DB2, IBM Informix, IBM Netezza, MySQL, PostgreSQL, Sybase, Teradata, SAP HANA, SAP Business Warehouse, Amazon Redshift, Impala, Google BigQuery, Snowflake, BI Connector, Dremio, Exasol, Jethro, Kyligence Enterprise, and other OLEDB and ODBC-compliant databases
Power BI	Power BI datasets and dataflows
Azure	SQL Database, SQL Data Warehouse, Analysis Services, Blob Storage, Table Storage, Cosmos DB, Data Lake Storage, HDInsight, Spark, HDInsight Interactive Query, Data Explorer
Online Services	SharePoint Online list, Microsoft Exchange Online, Dynamics 365, Common Data Service for Apps, Azure Consumption Insights, Azure DevOpps, Salesforce, Google Analytics, Adobe Analytics, appFigures, comScore, Data.World, Facebook, Github, MailChimp, Marketo, Mixpanel, Planview Projectplace, Quickbooks Online, SparkPost, Stripe, SweetIQ, Planview Enterprise, Twillio, tyGraph, Webtrends, Zendesk, TeamDesk
Other	Vertica, Web, SharePoint list, OData feed, Active Directory, Microsoft Exchange, Hadoop File from HDFS, Spark, R script, Python script, ODBC, OLEDB, Denodo, Paxata, and Blank Query

It's important to note that every data source requires installing appropriate connectivity software (also called provider or driver). Chances are that if you use Microsoft Office or other Microsoft applications, you already have drivers to connect to SQL Server, Excel files, and text files. If you need to connect to the data sources from other vendors, you need to research what connector (also called driver or provider) is needed and how to install it on your computer. For example, connecting to Oracle requires Oracle client software v8.1.7 or greater on your computer.

> **TIP** Because Power BI Desktop borrowed Power Query from Excel, you can find more information about the prerequisites related to connectivity in the "Import data from external data sources (Power Query)" document by Microsoft at http://bit.ly/1FQrjF3.

What if you don't find your data source on the list? If the data source comes with an ODBC connector, try connecting to it using the ODBC option. Although the data source might not be officially supported by Microsoft, chances are that you will be able to connect via ODBC. Or, if it comes with an OLE DB driver, try the generic OLE DB connector. Finally, remember that you can create your own connectors using the Power BI Data Connector SDK.

Connecting to data
Once you select your data source you want to connect to, the next step depends on the type of the data source. For example, if you connect to a database, such as SQL Server, you'll see a window that looks like the one in **Figure 6.15**. The only required field is the database server name that will be given to you by

your database administrator. You can also specify the database name, but it's not required because you can do this in the next step unless you use the advanced options to specify a custom query.

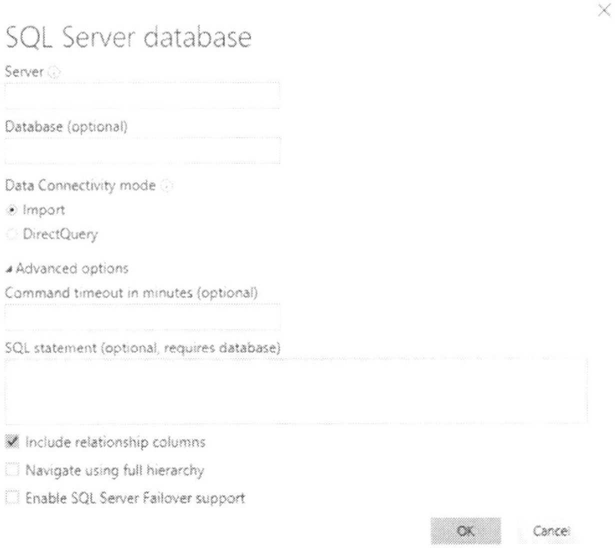

Figure 6.15 Connecting to a database requires a server name but additional options are available.

If the Power BI Desktop supports direct connectivity to the data source, you'll be able to specify how you want to access the data: import it in the Power BI Desktop file or connect to it directly using DirectQuery. Moving to the advanced options for relational databases, you can specify a command timeout in minutes to tell Power BI Desktop how long to wait before it times out the query. Instead of selecting a table or view in the next step, you can enter a custom SQL statement (also called a native database query). For example, if you need to execute a SQL Server stored procedure, you can enter the following statement:

exec <StoredProcedureName> parameter1, parameter 2, ...

If the data source supports referential integrity and you leave "Include relationship column" checked, in the next step (Navigator window) you can let Power BI Desktop preselect the related tables. If you check the "Navigate using full hierarchy", the Navigator window will organize tables in roles and schemas defined in the database (for data sources that support these features). For example, the Adventure-Works2012 database has all sales-related tables in the Sales schema. If this checkbox is checked, the Navigator window will show the database schemas. It'll also show the tables within the Sales schema when you expand it.

There could be additional data source-specific options. For example, if you connect to SQL Server configured in an Always On availability group, you can check "Enable SQL Server Failover support" so that Power BI can connect to the secondary replica when a failover occurs.

Specifying credentials

If you connect to a database for the first time, the next step asks you to enter credentials as instructed by your database administrator. For example, if you connect to SQL Server, you can use Windows credentials (behind the scenes it uses your Windows login) or database authentication (user name and password).

TIP Once you've connected to a data source, you don't need to use Get Data to import additional tables. Instead, use the Recent Sources button in the Power BI ribbon. If you need to change the data source credentials or encryption options, use the File ⇨ Options and Settings ⇨ Data Source Settings menu.

Power BI Desktop shows the "Access a SQL Server Database" window (see **Figure 6.16**) to let you specify how you want to authenticate. Note the Windows tab allows you specify alternative Windows credentials.

This could be useful if the database administrator has given you the credentials of a trusted Windows account. The Database tab lets you use standard (database) authentication.

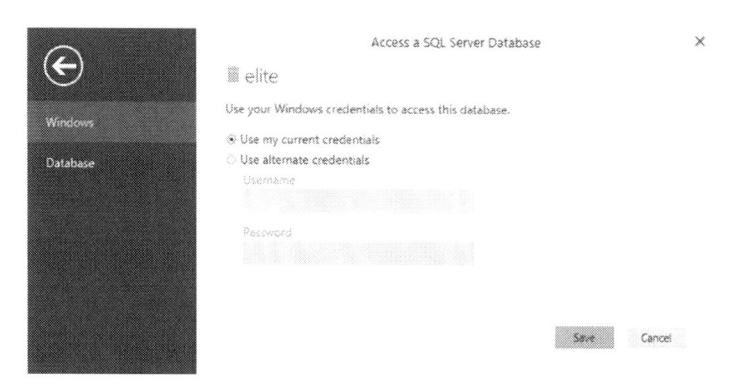

Figure 6.16 SQL Server supports Windows and standard authentication.

If you connect to a data source that is configured for encrypted connections, such as SQL Server, you'll be asked if you want to encrypt the connection while data is imported. If the data source doesn't support encrypted connections, Power BI Desktop will warn you about it.

If the data source has multiple entities, such as a relational database that has multiple tables, or an Excel file with multiple sheets, Power BI Desktop will open the Navigator window (see **Figure 6.17**). Use this window to navigate the data source objects, such as databases and tables, and select one or more tables to import. If the database has many objects, you can search the database metadata to find objects by name. To select a table or a SQL view to import, check its checkbox. The Navigator window shows a preview of the data in the right pane.

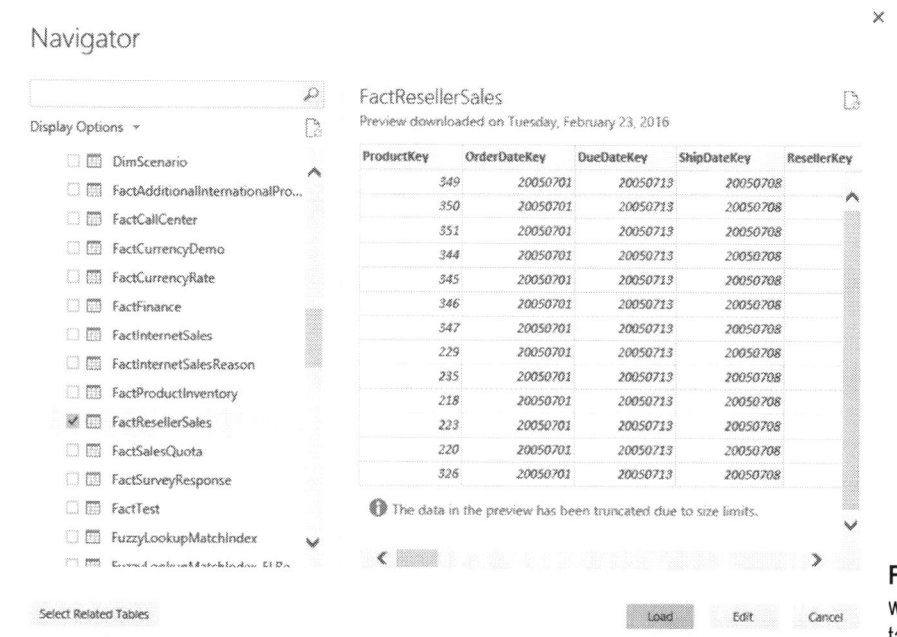

Figure 6.17 The Navigator window allows you to select tables and preview data.

Understanding the Navigator window

If the database has table relationships (the AdventureWorks databases have relationships), the "Select Related Tables" button allows you to include related tables (if the "Include relationship column" setting was

DATA MODELING FUNDAMENTALS

left checked in the previous step) so that you can import multiple tables in one step. There are two refresh buttons. The refresh button in the Navigator left pane, refreshes the metadata. This could be useful if someone makes a definition change, such as adding a column, and you don't want to close the Navigator window to start over. The refresh button on top of the preview pane refreshes the data preview so you can see the latest data changes or the effect of making column changes to the table whose data you're previewing, such as removing, adding, or renaming columns. Again, queries (and everything you do in Power BI Desktop) never make changes to the original data source, so don't worry about breaking something.

The Edit button launches the Power Query Editor, and this unlocks a whole new world to shape and transform data, such as if you want to replace values, merge data, unpivot columns, and so on. (I'll cover Power Query in detail in Chapter 7.) The Load button in the Navigator window adds a new table to the data model and loads it with the data from the selected table. If you click the Edit button, Power BI Desktop opens the Power Query Editor to let you define transformation steps before data is loaded.

> **NOTE** Readers familiar with Excel data modeling might know that the Power Pivot Table Import Wizard allows you to filter the data before it's imported. The Navigator window doesn't support filtering. However, you can click the Edit button to edit the query. Among many transformation options, you can apply necessary filtering in the Power Query Editor, such as removing columns and filtering rows for a given date range.

Next, let's go through a series of exercises to practice importing data from the most common data sources (the ones listed when you drop down the Get Data button), including databases, Excel files, text files, Web, and OData feeds.

6.3.2 Importing from Databases

Nowadays, most corporate data resides in databases, such as SQL Server and Oracle. In this exercise, you'll import two tables from the Adventure Works data warehouse database. The first table, FactResellerSales, represents a fact table and it keeps a historical record of numeric values (facts), such as Sales Amount and Order Quantity. You'll also import the DimDate table from the same database so that you can aggregate data by date periods, such as month, quarter, year, and so on. As a prerequisite, you need to install the Power BI Desktop (read Chapter 1 for installation considerations), and you need to have the AdventureWorks2012 (or later) database installed locally or on a remote SQL Server instance.

> **NOTE** Installing the AdventureWorks databases too complicated? If you don't have a SQL Server to install the AdventureWorks databases, you can import the FactResellerSales.txt and DimDate.txt files from the \Source\ch06 folder to complete this practice.

Connecting to the database
Follow these steps to import data from the FactResellerSales table:

1. Open Power BI Desktop. Close the splash screen. Click File ⇨ Save (or press Ctrl-S) and then save the empty model as *Adventure Works* in a folder on your local hard drive.
2. Expand the Get Data button in the ribbon and then click SQL Server. This opens the SQL Server Database window.
3. In the Server field, enter the name of the SQL Server instance, such as *ELITE*, if SQL Server is installed on a server called ELITE, or *ELITE\2012* if the SQL Server is running on a named instance 2012 on a server called ELITE. Confirm with your database administrator (DBA) what the correct instance name is. Leave the "Import" option selected. Because you're importing data from multiple sources, you can't use DirectQuery anyway. Click OK.

> **TIP** If the AdventureWorksDW database is installed on your local computer, you can enter localhost, (local), or dot (.) instead of the machine name. However, I recommend that you always enter the machine name. This will avoid connectivity issues that will require you to change the connection string if you move the file to another computer and then try to refresh the data.

4. If this is the first time you connect to that server, Power BI Desktop opens the "Access a SQL Server Database" window to ask you for your credentials. If you have access to the server via Windows security, leave the default "Use my current credentials" option selected. Or if the database administrator (DBA) has created a login for you, select the "Use alternate credentials" option, and then enter the login credentials. Click Connect, and then click OK to confirm that you want to use unencrypted connections.

Loading tables

If you connect successfully, Power BI Desktop opens the Navigator window. Let's load some tables:

1. Expand the AdventureWorksDW2012 database. It's fine if you have an older or later version of the database, such as AdventureWorksDW2014.
2. Scroll down the table list and check the FactResellerSales table. The data preview pane shows the first few rows in the table (see **Figure 6.17** again). Although the Navigator doesn't show row counts, this table is relatively small (about 60,000 rows), so you can go ahead and click the Load button to import it.

If the source table is large and you don't want to import all the data, you might want to filter the data before it's imported (as I'll show you how in the next step) so that you don't have to wait for all the data to load and end up with a huge data model.

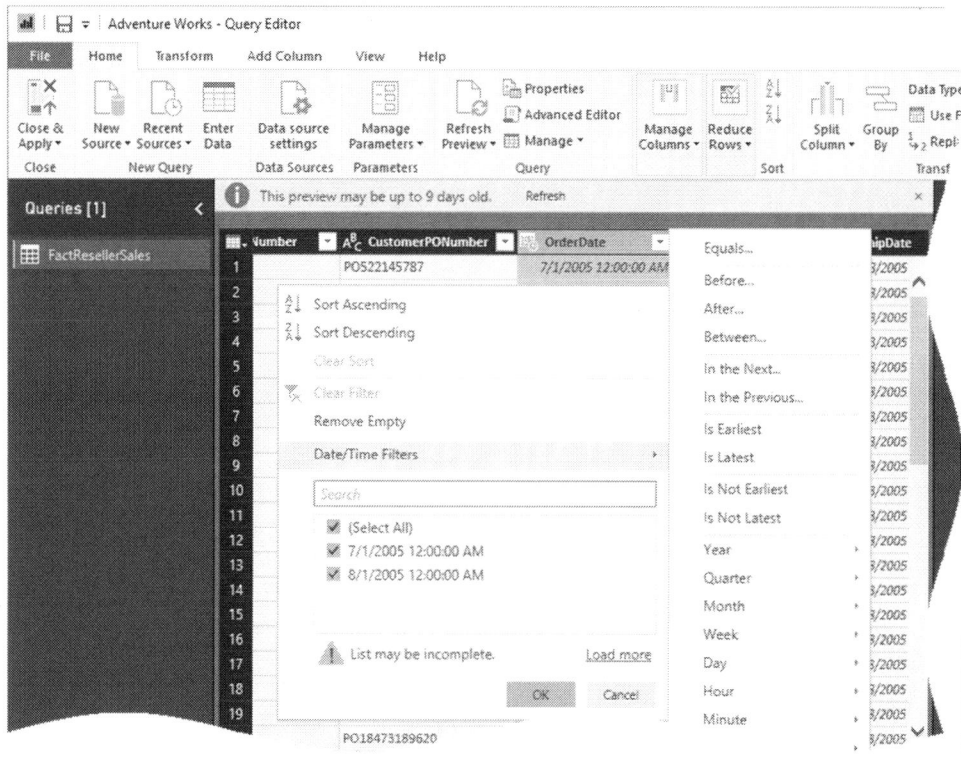

Figure 6.18 Use Power Query Editor to filter rows and columns.

Filtering data

As a best practice, don't import data you don't immediately need for analysis to avoid a large memory footprint and spending an unnecessary long time to load and refresh the data. The Power Query Editor makes it easy to filter the data before it's imported. While Power Query deserves much more attention (Chapter 7 has the details), let me quickly show you how to filter rows and columns:

1. While you're in the Navigator window, click Edit to open Power Query Editor in a new window.
2. In the data preview pane, scroll horizontally to the right until you find the OrderDate column.
3. Assuming you want to filter rows by date, expand the drop-down in the OrderDate column header, as shown in **Figure 6.18**. Notice that you can filter by checking or unchecking specific dates. For more advanced filtering options, click the "Date/Time Filters" context menu and notice that you can specify date-related filters, such as After (to filter after a given date) and Between (to filter rows between two dates).
4. You can also remove columns that you don't need. Besides simplifying the model metadata, this also helps keep your model more compact, especially columns that have many unique values because they can't compress well. Right-click a column in the preview window. Note that the context menu includes a Remove option, which you can use to delete a column. Don't worry if you need this column later; you can always bring back removed columns by undoing the Remove Column step.

> **TIP** A more intuitive option for removing and bringing columns back is Choose Columns. The Choose Columns button is in the Home ribbon of Power Query Editor. It allows you to search columns by name, which is very useful for wide tables. And you can bring columns back by just checking the column name.

5. If you've decided to open the Power Query Editor, click the "Close & Apply" button in the Power Query Editor ribbon to import FactResellerSales.

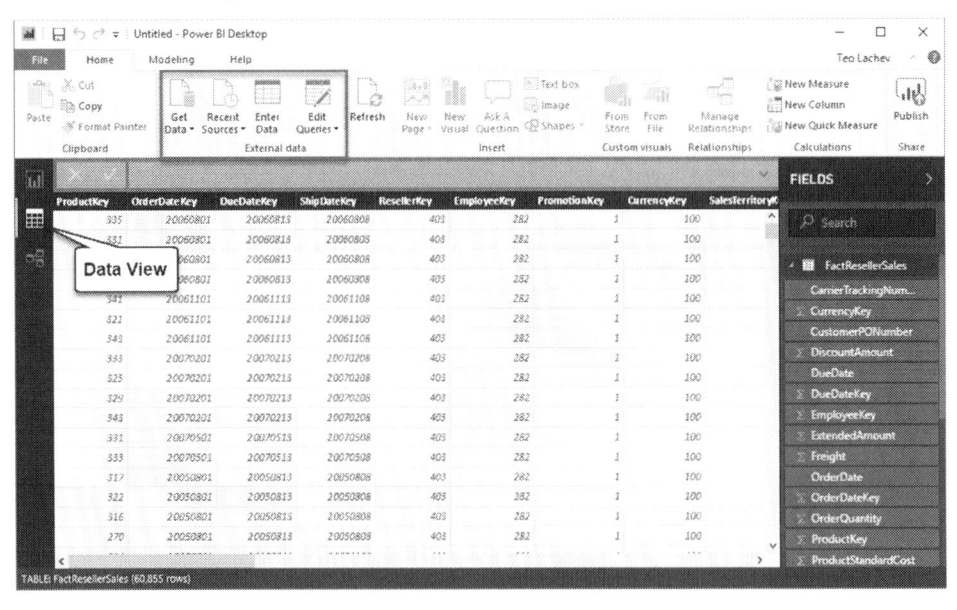

Figure 6.19 The Data View shows the tables in the model and preview of the data.

Understanding changes

Irrespective of which path you took (loading the table from the Navigator or from Power Query Editor), Power BI Desktop does the following behind the scenes:

1. It creates a query that connects to the database.
2. It adds a FactResellerSales table to the model.
3. It runs the query to extract the data from the FactResellerSales table in the AdventureWorksDW database.
4. It applies all transformations you defined in the Power Query Editor as the data streams from the source to the model.

5. It compresses the data and loads it into the FactResellerSales table inside the model.
6. Power BI Desktop switches to the Data View to show you the new table and read-only view of the loaded data (**Figure 6.19**). The Fields pane shows you the table fields.

Don't confuse the Data View, which represents your data model, with the Power Query Editor, which represents the query used to load a table in the model. While both show a read-only view of the same data, it comes from different places. The Power Query Editor opens in another window to show you the source data after all transformations you applied but *before* it's loaded to the data model. The Data View shows the data after it's loaded into the data model. In other words, the Power Query Editor shows what will happen to the data after you transform it, while the Data View shows what actually happened after the query was applied and data is loaded.

The External Data ribbon group in the Home ribbon of Power BI Desktop is your entry point for data-related tasks. You already know about the Get Data button. You can use the Recent Sources menu if you need to import another table from the data source that you've already used and if you want to jump directly to the Navigator. The Edit Queries button opens the Power Query Editor. And the Refresh button reloads all the data, so you can get the latest data changes.

> **NOTE** When you work with Power BI Desktop, the only way to synchronize the imported data with the data source changes is to manually refresh the data. You can do so by clicking the Refresh button to refresh all the tables. Or, you can right-click a table in the Field List and click "Refresh data" to reload only the selected table. Recall that once you publish the model to Power BI, you have the option to schedule an automatic data refresh, such as to reimport all the data daily.

Importing another table

As I explained at the beginning of this chapter, most models would benefit from a date table. The chances are that your data warehouse database has a date dimension table already. Let's import the DimDate table from the AdventureWorksDW2012 database:

1. In the External Data ribbon group, expand the Recent Sources button. Click the name of the database server that you specified when you connected to SQL Server. This opens the Navigator window.
2. Expand the AdventureWorksDW2012 node and check the DimDate table. Click the Load button. Power BI adds a table with the same name to the model and to the Fields pane.

As I pointed out, you should exclude columns you don't need for analysis. You can do this in the Power BI Desktop window or in Power Query Editor. In Power BI Desktop, you can right-click a column in Data View (or the Field List) and click Delete. Alternatively, you can delete the column in the Data View. In both cases, the Power Query Editor will add a "Removed Columns" transformation step to the Applied Steps list. However, as I mentioned, I prefer to use the Choose Columns transformation in the Power Query Editor, so I can see which columns are available and which ones are excluded.

3. Click the Edit Queries button. In the Power Query Editor, select DimDate in the Queries pane, and then click the Choose Columns button in the Power Query Editor ribbon's Home tab.
4. Uncheck all columns whose names start with "Spanish" and "French", and then click OK.
5. Click the "Close & Apply" button to apply the query changes and to reload the data. Note that these columns are removed from the DimDate table in the model.
6. Press Ctrl-S to save your data model or click File ⇨ Save. Unless you trust the auto recovery feature, get in a habit to save regularly so you don't lose changes if something unexpected happens and Power BI Desktop shuts down.

6.3.3 Importing Excel Files

Like it or not, much of corporate data ends up in Excel, so importing data from Excel files is a common requirement. If you have a choice, ask for an Excel file that has only the data in an Excel list with no formatting. If you must import an Excel report, things might get more complicated because you'll have to use the Power Query Editor to strip unnecessary rows and clean the data. In this exercise, I'll show you the simple case for importing an Excel list. In Chapter 7, I'll show you a more complicated case that requires parsing and cleansing an Excel report.

Understanding source data

Suppose that you're given a list of resellers as an Excel file. You want to import this list in the model.

1. Open the Resellers file from \Source\ch06 in Excel (see **Figure 6.20**).

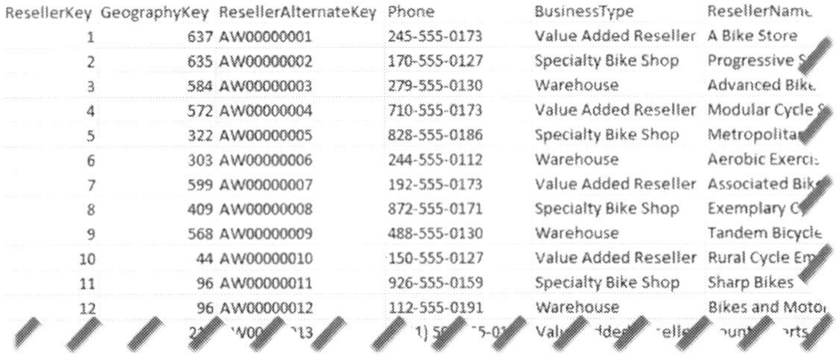

ResellerKey	GeographyKey	ResellerAlternateKey	Phone	BusinessType	ResellerName
1	637	AW00000001	245-555-0173	Value Added Reseller	A Bike Store
2	635	AW00000002	170-555-0127	Specialty Bike Shop	Progressive S
3	584	AW00000003	279-555-0130	Warehouse	Advanced Bik
4	572	AW00000004	710-555-0173	Value Added Reseller	Modular Cycle S
5	322	AW00000005	828-555-0186	Specialty Bike Shop	Metropolita
6	303	AW00000006	244-555-0112	Warehouse	Aerobic Exerci
7	599	AW00000007	192-555-0173	Value Added Reseller	Associated Bik
8	409	AW00000008	872-555-0171	Specialty Bike Shop	Exemplary C
9	568	AW00000009	488-555-0130	Warehouse	Tandem Bicycl
10	44	AW00000010	150-555-0127	Value Added Reseller	Rural Cycle E
11	96	AW00000011	926-555-0159	Specialty Bike Shop	Sharp Bikes
12	96	AW00000012	112-555-0191	Warehouse	Bikes and Moto

Figure 6.20 The Resellers file represents a list of resellers and it only has the data, without formatting.

2. Notice that the Excel file includes only data on the first sheet. This Excel list includes all the resellers that Adventure Works does business with. Close Excel.

> **TIP** Consider saving the source text files on a network share or even better on OneDrive for Business. If you import local files and you need to schedule your published dataset to refresh from Power BI Service, you'll be restricted to use a gateway installed on your machine. The chances are that neither Power BI Report Server nor a gateway on another server will be able to reach your local files.

Importing from Excel

Follow these steps to import from an Excel file:

1. With the Adventure Works model open in Power BI Desktop, expand Get Data, and then select Excel.
2. Navigate to the \Source\ch06 folder and double-click the Resellers file.
3. In the Navigator window, check Sheet1. The Navigator parses the Excel data and shows a preview of the data in Sheet1 (see **Figure 6.21**).

As you've seen, importing Excel files isn't much different than importing from a database. If the Excel file has multiple sheets with data, you can select and import them in one step. Power BI Desktop will create a query and a corresponding table for each sheet.

> **TIP** Don't like "Sheet1" as a table name in your data model? While you can rename the table in the Data View, you can also rename the query before the data is loaded. Power BI Desktop uses the name of the query as a default table name. While you're still in the Navigator, click the Edit button to open the Power Query Editor, and change the query name in the Query Settings pane.

4. Click the Edit button. In the Query Settings pane of the Power Query Editor, change the query name from Sheet1 to *Resellers*. Alternatively, you could click the Load button to load the table with the default name and then right-click the Sheet1 table in the Fields pane and click rename (or just double-click the name to enter the Edit mode).

5. Click the "Close & Apply" button. Power BI Desktop adds a third table (Resellers) to the data model.

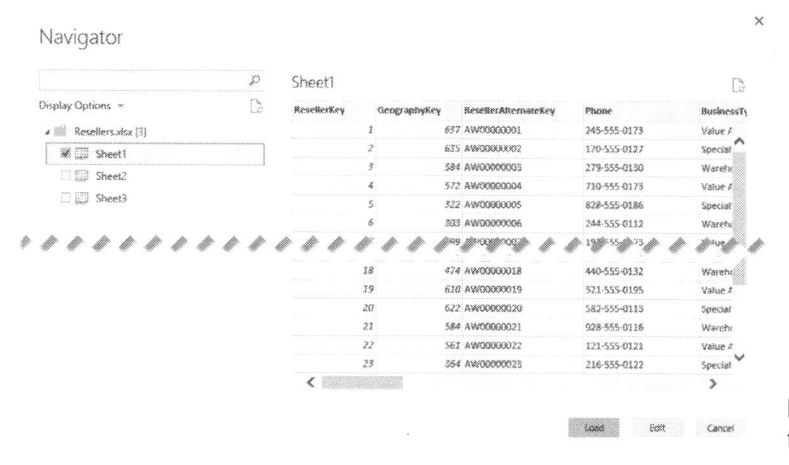

Figure 6.21 The Navigator parses the Excel data and shows a preview.

6.3.4 Importing Text Files

Importing from text files (delimited and fixed-length) is another common requirement. Security and operational requirements might prevent you from connecting directly to a database. In such cases, data could be provided to you as text files. For example, your database administrator might give you a data extract as a file as opposed to granting you direct access to a production database.

Importing from CSV files

Suppose that Adventure Works keeps the employee information in an HR mainframe database. Instead of having direct access to the database, you're given an extract as a comma-separated values (CSV) file. Follow these steps to import this file:

1. Expand the Get Data button and click CSV.
2. Navigate to the \Source\ch06 folder and double-click the Employees file.
3. Because a text file only has a single dataset, Power BI doesn't open the Navigator window. Instead, it just shows you a preview of the data, as shown in **Figure 6.22**.

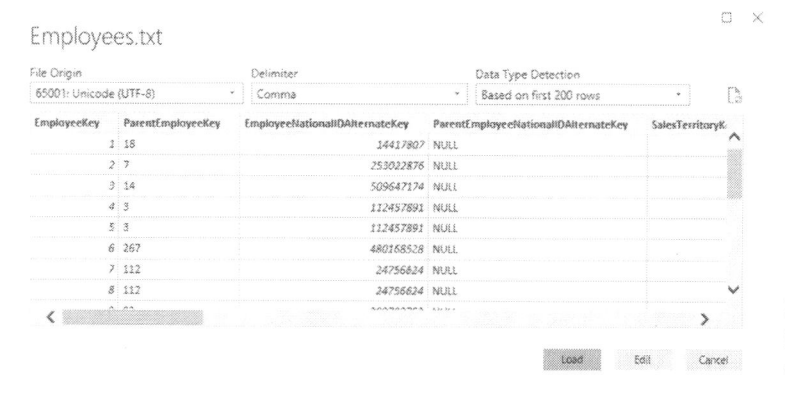

Figure 6.22 When importing from files, Power BI Desktop shows a data preview without opening the Navigator pane.

As you can see, it parses the file content and separates it in columns. Notice Power BI has detected that a comma is used as a column separator. Also notice that by default Power BI parses the first 200 rows in the file to detect the column data types.

DATA MODELING FUNDAMENTALS

> **NOTE** What happens if a column has numeric data in the first 200 rows but some text values, such as "N/A" in rows after that? Power BI will flag the column data type as numeric, but it will fail the import for rows with the inconsistent data types and it will show you which rows have failed. Then, you can use the Power Query Editor to address the data quality issue, such as by replacing the text values with "null".

4. Click Load to create a new Employees table and to load the data. At this point, the Adventure Works model should have four tables: DimDate, Employees, FactResellerSales, and Resellers.

Importing other formats

You might be given a file format other than CSV. For example, the file might use a pipe character (|) as a column separator. Or you might be a given a fixed-length file format, such as the one I demonstrate with the Employees2.txt file in the \Source\ch06 folder (see **Figure 6.23**).

```
EmployeeID  FirstName  LastName    Title
14417807    Guy        Gilbert     Production Technician - WC60
253022876   Kevin      Brown       Marketing Assistant
509647174   Roberto    Tamburello  Engineering Manager
112457891   Rob        Walters     Senior Tool Designer
```

Figure 6.23 The Employees2 file has a fixed-length format where each column starts at a specific position.

You can use either CSV or Text import options to parse such formats. To make it easier on you, Power BI Desktop will use its smarts to detect the file format. If it's successful, it will detect the delimiters automatically and return a multi-column table. If not, it'll return a single-column table that you can subsequently split into columns using Split Columns and other column tasks in the Power Query Editor.

> **NOTE** Readers familiar with Power Pivot in Excel might know that Power Pivot was capable of parsing more complicated file formats using a schema.ini file if it's found in the same folder as the source file. The Power BI Desktop queries don't support schema.ini files.

6.3.5 Importing from Analysis Services

If your organization has invested in Microsoft Analysis Services, you have two ways to access Multidimensional or Tabular models:

- Connect live – Choose this option when you want to create interactive reports connected to an Analysis Services model without importing the data, just like you would do it in Excel. For this to work, your Power BI Desktop file must not have any other connections or imported data. If you decide to connect live, the Data and Relationships views, and the Power Query Editor are not available. This makes sense because you wouldn't want to have a model on top of another model.
- Import – Choose this option if you want to mash up data from multiple data sources, including Analysis Services models or Power Pivot models deployed to SharePoint. This is especially useful when your model needs the results from business calculations or from KPIs defined in a multidimensional cube or a Tabular model.

Next, you'll import the Sales Territory dimension data and a key performance indicator (KPI) from the Adventure Works cube. (The book front matter includes steps for installing the Adventure Works cube.)

> **NOTE** If you don't have an Analysis Services instance with the Adventure Works cube, you can import the DimSalesTerritory CSV file found in the \Source\ch06 folder. Importing DimSalesTerritory won't import the Revenue KPI because it's only defined in the cube and that's OK. When going through subsequent exercises, ignore steps that reference the Revenue KPI.

Connecting to Analysis Services

Start by connecting to the Adventure Works multidimensional cube as follows:

1. Expand the Get Data button and click Analysis Services to open the "SQL Server Analysis Services Database" window. Remember that Analysis Services supports live connectivity, but it must be the only data source in your Power BI Desktop model. Therefore the "Connect live" option is disabled.

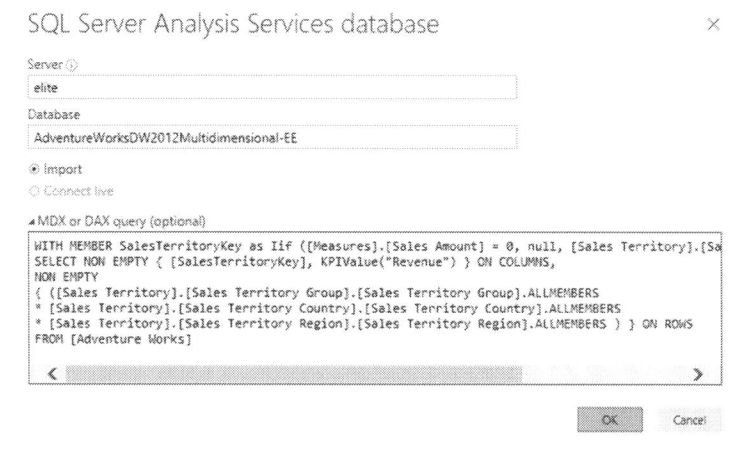

Figure 6.24 Power BI Desktop allows you to import data from SSAS.

If you don't specify a custom MDX or DAX query (or leave the Database field empty) and click OK, the Navigator window will pop up, allowing you to select the dimensions and measures. Once you are done, the Navigator window will auto-generate the MDX query for you. However, unlike the MDX Designer included in Excel, the Navigator doesn't let you create calculated members (business calculations in cubes). In this case, we need a simple calculation member that returns the key property of the "Sales Territory Region" dimension attribute so that we can subsequently relate the SalesTerritory table to FactResellerSales. Therefore, we need a custom MDX query that includes a SalesTerritoryKey calculated member.

2. In the "SQL Server Analysis Services Database" window, enter the name of your SSAS database, such as *AdventureWorksDW2012Multidimensional-EE*.
3. In the "MDX or DAX Query" field, enter the MDX query, which you can copy from the \Source\ch06\Queries file. Compare your results with **Figure 6.24**.
4. Click OK. Power BI Desktop shows a data preview window (see **Figure 6.25**).

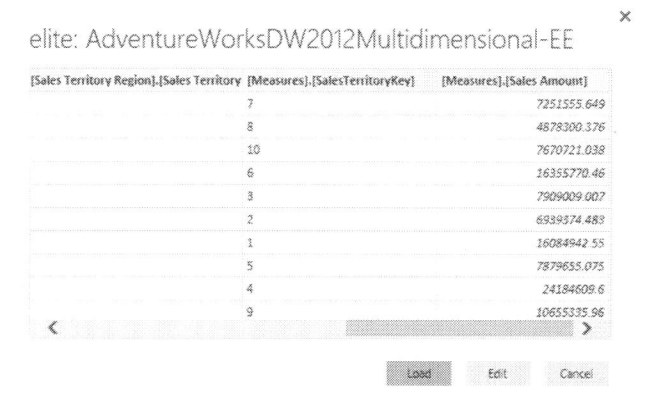

Figure 6.25 The SalesTerritoryKey column returns the key value of the Sales Territory Region attribute which you'll subsequently use as a primary key for creating a relationship.

Renaming metadata
If you click the Load button, you'll end up with "Query1" as a table name and system-generated column names. You can fix this later, but let's refine the metadata before the data is loaded.
1. Click the Edit button.

DATA MODELING FUNDAMENTALS

2. In the Query Settings pane, rename the query from "Query1" to *SalesTerritories*.
3. To rename the columns, double-click the column header of each column, and rename the columns to *SalesTerritoryGroup*, *SalesTerritoryCountry*, *SalesTerritoryRegion*, *SalesTerritoryKey*, and *SalesAmount*.
4. Click the "Close & Apply" button to create and load a new SalesTerritories table.

6.3.6 Importing from the Web

A wealth of information is available on the Web. Power BI Desktop can import tabular data that's accessible by URL. One popular Web-enabled data source is SQL Server Reporting Services (SSRS). Once a report is deployed to a report server, it's accessible by URL, which is exactly what the Web import option requires. Next, I'll show you how to import an SSRS report deployed to Microsoft Reporting Services.

> **NOTE** Readers familiar with the Power Pivot import capabilities might recall that Power Pivot supports importing SSRS reports as data feeds. Unfortunately, as it stands, the Power BI Desktop (and Power Query) OData import option doesn't support the ATOM data feed format that SSRS generates. However, the report URL can export the report as CSV, and the output then can be loaded using the Power BI Web import option.

Deploying the report

You can find a sample report named Product Catalog in the \Source\ch06 folder. This report must be deployed to a Reporting Services server that is version 2008 R2 or higher.

> **NOTE** If configuring Reporting Services isn't an option, you can import the required data from the AdventureWorksDW database using the custom SQL query I provided in the DimProduct.sql file, or from the \Source\ch06\DimProduct.txt file. The query doesn't return the exact results as the Product Catalog report, and that's okay.

1. Upload the Product Catalog.rdl file from the \Source\ch06 folder to your report server, such as to a folder called *PowerBI* in the SSRS catalog. Please note that the report data source uses the AdventureWorks2012 database (see the book front matter for setup instructions), and you probably need to change the connection string in the report data source to reflect your specific setup.
2. To test that the report is functional, open the Report Manager by navigating to its URL in your Web browser (assuming SSRS is running in native mode).
3. Navigate to the PowerBI folder. Click the Product Catalog report to run the report. The report should run with no errors.

Importing the report

Follow these steps to import the Product Catalog report in the Adventure Works data model:

1. In Power BI Desktop, expand the Get Data button and click Web.
2. In the "From Web" window that pops up, enter the following URL, but change it to reflect your SSRS server URL (tip: if you test the URL in your Web browser, it should execute fine and it should prompt you to download Product Catalog.csv file):

http://localhost/ReportServer?/PowerBI/Product Catalog&rs:Command=Render&rs:Format=CSV

This URL requests the Product Catalog report that's located in the PowerBI folder of my local report server. The Render command is an optimization step that tells SSRS that the requested resource is a report. The Format command instructs the server to export the report in CSV.

3. Click OK. Power BI Desktop shows a preview of the report data.
4. Click the Edit button. In the Power Query Editor, rename the query to *Products*.

5. Use the Choose Columns feature to remove all the columns whose names start with "Textbox". Click the "Close & Apply" button to load the Products table.

> **TIP** You can also use the Web connector to import files stored in OneDrive for Business. The main benefit from storing your files in the cloud is that you can avoid gateways to refresh data. To learn more, read the "Use OneDrive for Business links in Power BI Desktop" article at https://docs.microsoft.com/power-bi/desktop-use-onedrive-business-links.

6.3.7 Entering Static Data

As a best practice, you should store and maintain reference data outside your data model, such as in an Excel file or relational database. This allows you to make changes to the reference data without changing and redeploying your Power BI Desktop file. In addition, you can use the tool capabilities for data enrichment, such as Excel formulas or macros.

Using Enter Data

Sometimes, however, it might be preferable to enter or paste some static data directly in the model. For example, you might need a few KPI goals, and creating a separate data source could be an overkill. Or, you might need a quick way to copy and paste a list of currencies. This is where the Power BI Enter Data feature might be useful.

1. In the Home ribbon, click Enter Data. Power BI Desktop creates a table with one column and one row.
2. Double-click Column1 and enter the desired column header.
3. If you need another column, click the second cell and give it a name.
4. Then, enter the table rows and values (see **Figure 6.26**).

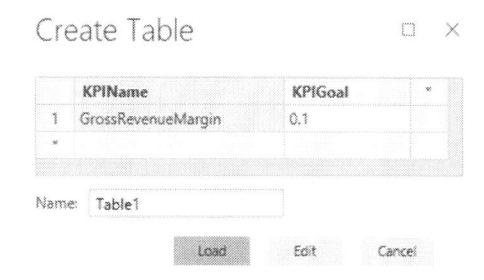

Figure 6.26 Use the Enter Data feature to enter data manually or paste it from somewhere.

5. Give the table a name.
6. Since you won't be using this data in the Adventure Works model, click Cancel to discard the static table.

> **TIP** You can also copy and paste to create a static table. If you want to practice this feature, open the Curencies.txt file in Notepad, press Ctrl+A to select all content and then press Ctrl+C to copy it to the Windows clipboard. Then, in Power BI Desktop, click Enter Data and press Ctrl+V to paste. If the copied data has a tabular format, Enter Data should recognize it and create a table.

Managing static tables

Power BI won't refresh static tables as they don't have associated data sources. You must manually make changes, but it's not immediately obvious how.

1. In the Fields pane, right click your static table and click "Edit query" to open the Power Query Editor.
2. In the Query Settings pane, click the gear button next to the first step (Source) in the Applied Steps list. This will bring you to the Create Table window where you can make your changes.
3. Enter your changes and click OK.

This practice completes the import process of the initial set of tables that you'll need to analyze the Adventure Works sales. At this point, the Fields list should have six tables: FactResellerSales, DimDate, SalesTerritories, Resellers, Employees, and Products.

6.4 Advanced Storage Configurations

To recap what you've learned so far about data storage, Power BI has three main data connectivity options:

- Data import – supported for all data sources.
- DirectQuery – supported for a limited set of "fast" data sources.
- Live connection – when you connect to Analysis Services, Power BI published datasets, and SAP.

Power BI supports more data storage options to help you meet more advanced requirements, including composite models and aggregations.

6.4.1 Understanding Composite Models

The choice between DirectQuery and imported data doesn't have to be exclusive. In fact, many business requirements could be better addressed by a hybrid model that imports some tables but leaves others configured for DirectQuery. For example, you might decide to import most data to get predicable query performance but configure certain tables in DirectQuery to gain real-time access to their data. Models with hybrid storage are known as composite models. **Figure 6.27** shows a model where the FactSalesQuota table is configured for DirectQuery (see the "Storage mode" setting in the Properties page), where the other three tables import data. You can find this model in the \Source\ch06\Composite.pbix file.

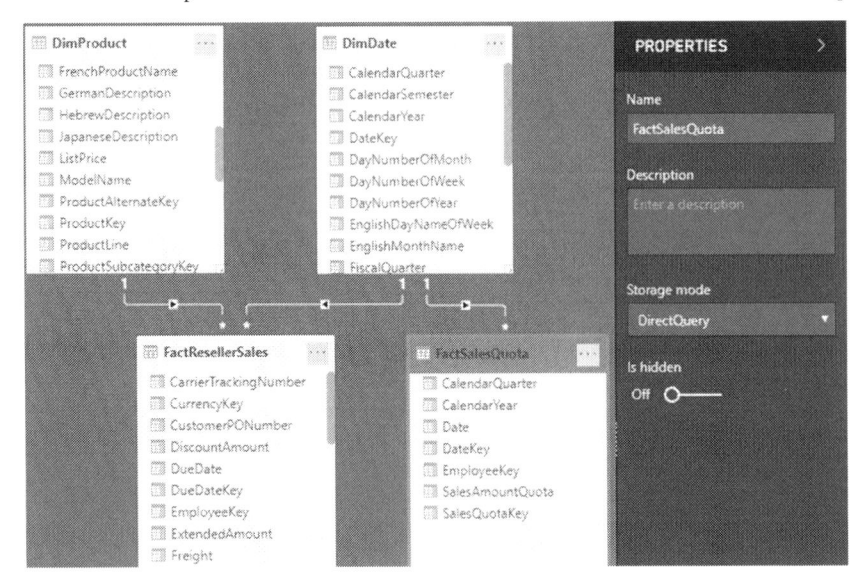

Figure 6.27 This composite model mixes import and DirectQuery storage modes.

Creating composite models

Before composite models were introduced, one Power BI Desktop file could access only one data source in DirectQuery. Composite models enable the following data acquisition options:

- Combine tables from multiple databases from the same server in DirectQuery – For example, your model can have DirectQuery tables from two or more databases on the same server instance.

- Combine multiple data sources configured for DirectQuery – For example, your model can include DirectQuery tables from your on-premises Oracle database and Azure SQL Database.
- Combine a DirectQuery table with imported table from the same data source – For example, you prefer most tables to be imported but some in DirectQuery for real-time analysis.
- Implement a hybrid storage model that combines a data source with imported data with another data source configured for DirectQuery – For example, you import data from Excel (the only storage supported for files) and combine this data with DirectQuery table from another database.

There is nothing special you need to do to configure your Power BI Desktop file as a composite model. You simply indicate what storage mode (import or DirectQuery) you prefer when you connect to a source that supports both.

Understanding dual storage

When you create a report that involves a heterogenous relationship between two tables, such as between an imported table and a DirectQuery table, the Power BI mashup engine must decide how to join the data. Microsoft hasn't disclosed the exact rules but if the imported table is relatively small (a few hundred rows), the mashup engine might decide to group the imported data at the relationship grain and include it in the query sent to the DirectQuery data source. For example, if DimProduct is imported but FactResellerSales is DirectQuery and you request a report that shows sales grouped by ProductCategory, Power BI might resolve the join as follows:

1. Serialize all rows from DimProduct as a subquery in the native SQL statement.
2. Rewrite the native query to include a join between the subquery and FactInternetSales on ProductKey.
3. Sends the native query to the DirectQuery data source.

However, if the join involves larger tables, Power BI might decide that it's more efficient to group the DirectQuery table at the relationship grain, retrieve the aggregated data and then perform the join internally. You can help Power BI make a better choice in some cases by using a dual storage mode. As the name implies, the dual storage mode is a hybrid between Import and DirectQuery. Like importing data, the dual storage mode caches the data in the table. However, it leaves it up to Power BI to determine the best way to query the table depending on the query context. Consider the schema and storage configuration shown in **Figure 6.28**.

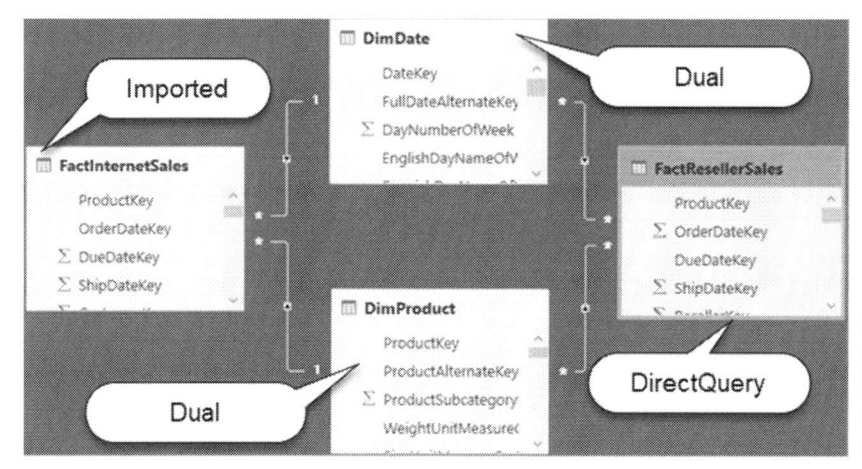

Figure 6.28 Power BI determines the best way to join tables configured for dual storage depending on the query context.

Power BI will attempt the most efficient way to resolve the table joins. For example, if a query involves FactInternetSales and DimDate, the query could use the DimDate cache. However, if the query involves

FactResellerSales, Power BI will probably pass through the join. That's because it could be much more efficient to let the data source join the two tables in DirectQuery as opposed to bringing all the FactResellerSales table at the join granularity and then joining it to the DimDate cache.

Understanding strong and weak relationships

There is more to dual storage than just performance. It also determines if a many-to-one relationship is strong or week. A strong relationship can push the join to the source. In addition, a strong relationship is considered for aggregation hits (discussed in the next section). The following storage mode configurations between any two tables participating in M:1 join from the same data source result in a strong relationship.

Table 6.3 Storage configurations between two tables from the same source that result in a strong relationship.

Storage Mode of Table on Many Side	Storage Mode of Table on One Side Must Be
Dual	Dual
Import	Import or Dual
DirectQuery	DirectQuery or Dual

Here are configurations that result in weak relationships:

- The table on the many side (fact table) is DirectQuery while the dimension table is Import.
- A cross-source relationship with mixed storage modes. The only case when a cross-source relationship is considered strong is if both tables are Import.
- Many-to-many relationships are always weak.

NOTE As a best practice, change the storage of a shared (conformed) dimension table to Dual if it joins an imported fact table and a DirectQuery fact table from the same data source to ensure that the relationship is strong.

Switching storage modes

You can use the "Storage mode" setting on the table properties (see again **Figure 6.27**) to switch the table storage mode at any time. However, currently Power BI doesn't allow switching from Import to Dual or DirectQuery, so these options are disabled for tables with imported data. If Power BI detects that changing the table storage mode will result in a weak relationship, such as starting with all tables in DirectQuery and changing one fact table to Import, it'll warn you and suggest you change the storage mode of a shared dimensions to Dual.

NOTE Why Power BI doesn't handle the dual storage mode on its own? There are two reasons to delegate this task to the modeler and to make the Dual storage configuration explicit: a) like Import, Dual requires refresh, whereas DirectQuery doesn't, and b) apart from being able to revert to DirectQuery mode, Dual is subject to the same restrictions as DirectQuery. Therefore, the modeler needs to be aware that the switch may result in requiring a data refresh or may result in removing the data.

Understanding limitations of composite models

Some of the limitations of composite models stem from the DirectQuery limitations:

- As I just mentioned, imported tables can't be converted to DirectQuery. You must delete the table and connect to it choosing DirectQuery.
- Dual storage has the same limitations as DirectQuery.
- DirectQuery can't return more than one million rows. This has been a long standing DirectQuery limitation. Consider a DimCustomer table (from same or different source) that joins FactSales configured for DirectQuery and you request a report that shows sales by customer. At a certain (undisclosed by Microsoft) point it becomes inefficient to send the entire customer list to the

WHERE clause of the FactSales direct query. Instead, the query will group FactSales at the Customer field used for the join, and then internally aggregate the results. However, if that query exceeds one million, it will fail.

- Only a subset of data sources, such as popular relational databases and "fast" databases, support DirectQuery. I hope Microsoft extends DirectQuery to more sources, such as Excel and text files.
- You can't pass parameters to custom SQL SELECT statement or stored procedure, such as to pass the value that the user selects in a slicer to a stored procedure configured for DirectQuery.
- Live connections cannot participate in composite models – Composite models can't include live connections to Analysis Services (MD and Tabular), published Power BI datasets, and SAP (multi-dimensional). This limitation stems from the fact that there isn't a DirectQuery layer when Power BI uses a live connection. Therefore, a single Power BI desktop file is still limited to connecting to a single multidimensional data source.

6.4.2 Understanding Aggregations

Ask end users which connectivity option they prefer and most of them will answer real-time access, which translates to DirectQuery. The biggest issue with DirectQuery though is that because Power BI passes queries to the source, the report performance will depend on the underlying data source. And once you start dealing with millions of rows, reports might take a while to render. Aggregations let you implement fast summarized queries on top of large datasets (imported or DirectQuery) at the expense of creating summarized tables.

NOTE Currently, Power BI aggregations are a Power BI preview feature. To enable them in Power BI Desktop, go to File ⇨ Options and Settings ⇨ Options, and check Manage Aggregations.

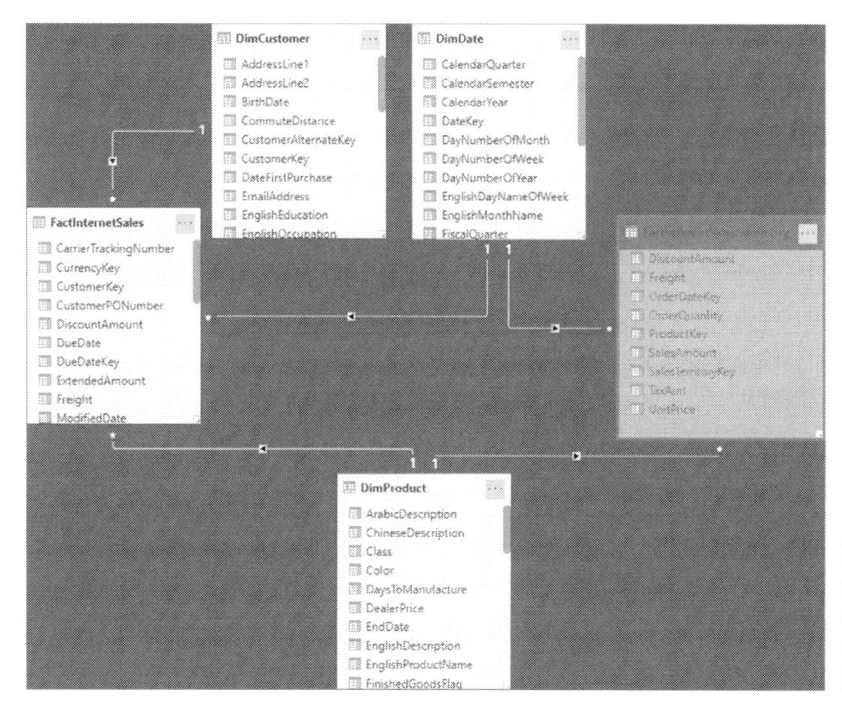

Figure 6.29 The FactInternetSalesSummary aggregates data to speed up summarized queries that group by Date and Product.

DATA MODELING FUNDAMENTALS 165

When to use aggregations?
Consider the schema shown in **Figure 6.29** (you can find the corresponding Aggregations.pbix file in the \Source\ch06 folder). This model has a FactInternetSales fact table (DirectQuery storage) and three dimensions: DimCustomer, DimProduct, and DimDate. Suppose that most queries request data at the Product and Date levels (not Customer) but such queries don't give you the desired performance. This is where aggregations might help (contrary reasons for using aggregations is to compensate for bad design or inefficient DAX).

Understanding aggregation tables
As a first step for setting up aggregations, you need to add a summarized (aggregation) table to your model. It's up to you how you want to design and populate the summarized table. It's also up to you which measures you want to aggregate and at what grain. And the summarized table doesn't have to be imported (it could be left in DirectQuery) although for best performance it probably should. You can also have multiple aggregations tables (more on this in a moment).

In this case I've decided to base the FactInternetSalesSummary table on a SQL view that aggregates the FactInternetSales data, but I could have chosen to use a DAX calculated table or load it with ETL. In my case, FactInternetSalesSummary aggregates sales at the Product and Date level because I want to speed up queries at that grain. In real life, FactInternetSalesSummary would be hidden to end users so they are not confused which table to use.

> **NOTE** Recall that a strong relationship has specific requirements for configuring a shared dimension table that connects to fact tables in different storage configurations. For example, if FactInternetSalesSummary is imported but FactInternetSales is DirectQuery (our configuration), DimProduct and DimDate must be configured in Dual storage mode for a strong relationship and aggregation hits.

Configuring aggregations
Once the aggregation table is in place, the next step is to define the actual aggregations. Note that this must be done for the aggregation table (not the detail table) so in my case this would be FactInternetSalesSummary. To do so, right-click the aggregation table in the Fields pane and select "Manage aggregations". Configuring aggregations involves specifying the following configuration details in the "Manage aggregations" window (see **Figure 6.30**):

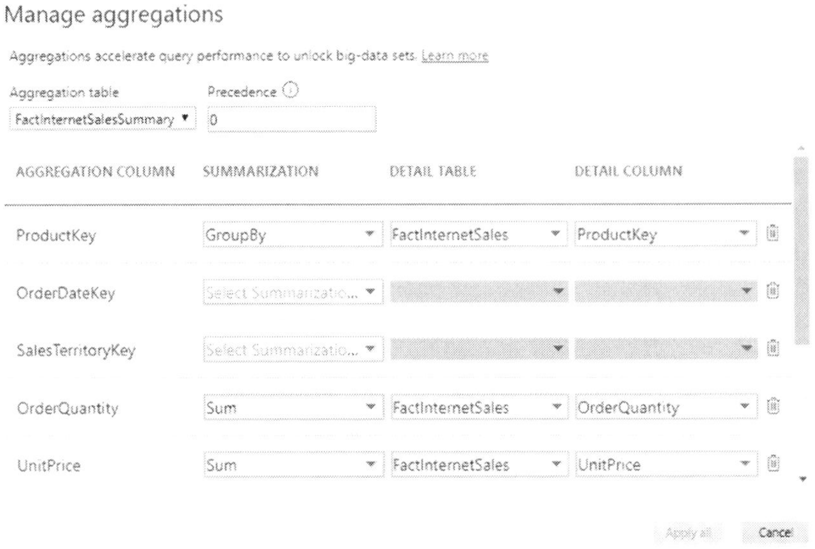

Figure 6.30 Use the "Manage aggregations" window to configure the aggregation design.

- Aggregation table – the aggregation table that you want to use for the aggregation design. You might have multiple aggregations tables and this drop-down should be populated with the table that you selected in the Fields pane.
- Precedence – in the case of multiple aggregation tables that aggregates the same data at a different level, you can define which aggregation table will take precedence (the server will probe the aggregation table that has a highest precedence first).
- Summarization function – Supported are Count, GroupBy, Max, Min, Sum, Count Table Rows. Note that except for Count and "Count table rows", the data type of the aggregated column must match the data type in the detail table. If the aggregation table has relationships to dimension tables, there is no need to specify GroupBy. However, if the aggregation table can't be joined to the dimension tables in a Many:One relationship, GroupBy is required. For example, you might have a huge DirectQuery table where all dimension attributes are denormalized and there are no dimension tables, in which case GroupBy is required.

> **NOTE** Another usage scenario for GroupBy is for speeding up DistinctCount measures. If the column that the distinct count is performed on is defined as GroupBy, then the query should result in an aggregation hit. Finally, note that derivative DAX calculations that directly or indirectly reference the aggregate measure would also benefit from the aggregation.

- Detail table – which table should answer the query for aggregation misses. Note that you can redirect to a different fact table for each measure in the aggregated table.
- Detail column – what is the underlying column in the fact table in case of an aggregation miss.

How do you refresh the aggregation table once you publish the model to Power BI Service? The answer depends on how the table was created. A DirectQuery aggregation table won't require a refresh. However, if the table is imported, then you need to refresh it just like a regular table. Finally, if the aggregation table is created in DAX, then Power BI will update it when the dataset is refreshed. Larger aggregation tables with imported data would probably require incremental refresh (discussed in chapter 8). The important thing to remember is that the aggregation table must be synchronized with the detail table to avoid inconsistent results.

Monitoring aggregation hits

Once the aggregations are configured and dataset deployed, Power BI determines which queries can be answered by the aggregation table. In the presence of one or more aggregation tables, the server would probe for a suitable summarized table that can answer the query resulting in an aggregation hit. As it stands, Power BI Desktop doesn't have monitoring features but if you have SQL Server Management Studio (SSMS) installed, you can use SQL Server Profiler to monitor aggregation hits during development, as follows:

1. Find which port the Analysis Services instance associated with the Power BI Desktop file listens on. Power BI doesn't make this easy on you too so use one of the techniques described in the blog "Four Different Ways to Find Your Power BI Desktop Local Port Number" at https://biinsight.com/four-different-ways-to-find-your-power-bi-desktop-local-port-number/.
2. Open SQL Server Profiler and choose to Analysis Services. Enter localhost:<portnumber" as a server name.
3. In the Trace Properties window, select the "Aggregate Table Rewrite Query" event under the "Query Processing" section and start the trace. In the case of the aggregation hit, the event will look like this (note the matchFound setting in the matchingResult property).

```
{
"table": "FactInternetSales",
"mapping": {
"table": "FactInternetSalesSummary"
},
```

```
"matchingResult": "matchFound",
"dataRequest": [
}
```

To get an aggregation hit at the joined dimensions granularity, the DAX query must involve one or more of the actual dimensions. For example, this query would result in an aggregation hit because it involves the DimDate dimension which joins FactInternetSalesSummary.

```
EVALUATE
SUMMARIZECOLUMNS (
'DimDate'[CalendarYear],
"Sales", SUM ( FactInternetSales[SalesAmount] )
)
```

However, this DAX query won't result in an aggregation hit because it aggregates a column from the InternetSales table, even though this column is used for the relationship to DimDate and the aggregation is at the OrderDateKey grain.

```
EVALUATE
SUMMARIZECOLUMNS (
FactInternetSales[OrderDateKey],
"Sales", SUM ( FactInternetSales[SalesAmount] )
)
```

6.5 Summary

A Power BI model is a relational-like model and represents data as tables and columns. This chapter started by laying out fundamental data modeling concepts (such as table schemas, relationships, and keys) that you need to understand before you import data. It also explained data connectivity options supported by Power BI Desktop and introduced you to the Power BI premium tool for self-service data modeling.

Next, the chapter explained the data import capabilities of Power BI Desktop. As you've seen, you can acquire data from a wide variety of data sources, including relational and multidimensional databases, Excel files, text files, Web, and data feeds. Once the data is imported in the model, every table is an equal citizen and it doesn't matter where the data came from!

The choice between data import and DirectQuery doesn't have to be exclusive. You can implement a composite model with hybrid storage, such as when you need to import most tables but leave some in DirectQuery to access their data in real time. You can also speed queries to large datasets by summarizing data and implementing aggregations.

Source data is seldom clean. Next, you'll learn how to use queries to shape and transform raw data when needed.

Chapter 7

Transforming Data

7.1 Understanding the Power Query Editor 169
7.2 Shaping and Cleansing Data 177
7.3 Using Advanced Power Query Features 182

7.4 Staging Data with Dataflows 192
7.5 Summary 201

As you've seen, it doesn't take much effort to import data from wherever it might reside. Importing data is one thing but transforming arbitrary or dirty data is quite another. Fortunately, Power BI Desktop has a query layer (many still refer to it as Power Query) that allows you to clean and transform data before it's loaded in the model. Remember that this layer is available when you import data or when you connect live to data sources using the DirectQuery connectivity mechanism. The query layer isn't available when you connect live to multidimensional data sources.

This chapter explores the capabilities of the Power Query Editor component of Power BI Desktop (I'll use the terms Power Query and Query Editor interchangeably). The chapter starts by introducing you to the Power Query Editor design environment. Next, it walks you through an exercise to practice its basic transformation steps. It also teaches you about its more advanced transformation features that require custom code. Lastly, it shows you how you can use dataflows to prepare and stage the data.

Since you won't need the results from these exercises in the Adventure Works model, you'll practice with a new Power BI Desktop file. You can find the finished query examples that you'll do in this chapter in the Query Examples.pbix file located in the \Source\ch07 folder.

7.1   Understanding the Power Query Editor

The Power Query Editor is packed with features that let you share and transform data before it enters the data model. The term "transformation" here includes any modification you apply on the raw data. All transformations are repeatable, meaning that if you import another data extract that has the same structure, Power BI Desktop will apply the same transformation steps when you refresh the data.

> **NOTE** You might have heard of BI pros implementing Extraction, Transformation, and Loading (ETL) processes to clean data in an automated way. Think of the Power Query Editor (or Excel Power Query) relationship to self-service BI as what ETL is to organizational BI. Although not as flexible and powerful as professional ETL tools, the Power Query features (Query Editor and datapools) should be able to help when issues with source data require basic to moderate preparation, staging and shaping. If your data requires more complex integration and transformation steps, such as when integrating data from multiple systems, consider the organization BI architecture (discussed in Chapter 2) and plan for dedicated ETL.

7.1.1   Understanding the Power Query Environment

Before I dive into the Power Query Editor's plethora of features, let's take a moment to explore its environment. As I mentioned, you launch the Power Query Editor when you click the Edit Queries button in the Power BI Desktop ribbon's Home tab or when you right-click a table in the Fields pane and then click

"Edit Query". The Power Query Editor opens in a new window, side by side with the Power BI Desktop main window. **Figure 7.1** shows the main elements of Query Editor when you open it in the Adventure Works model that you implemented in the previous chapter.

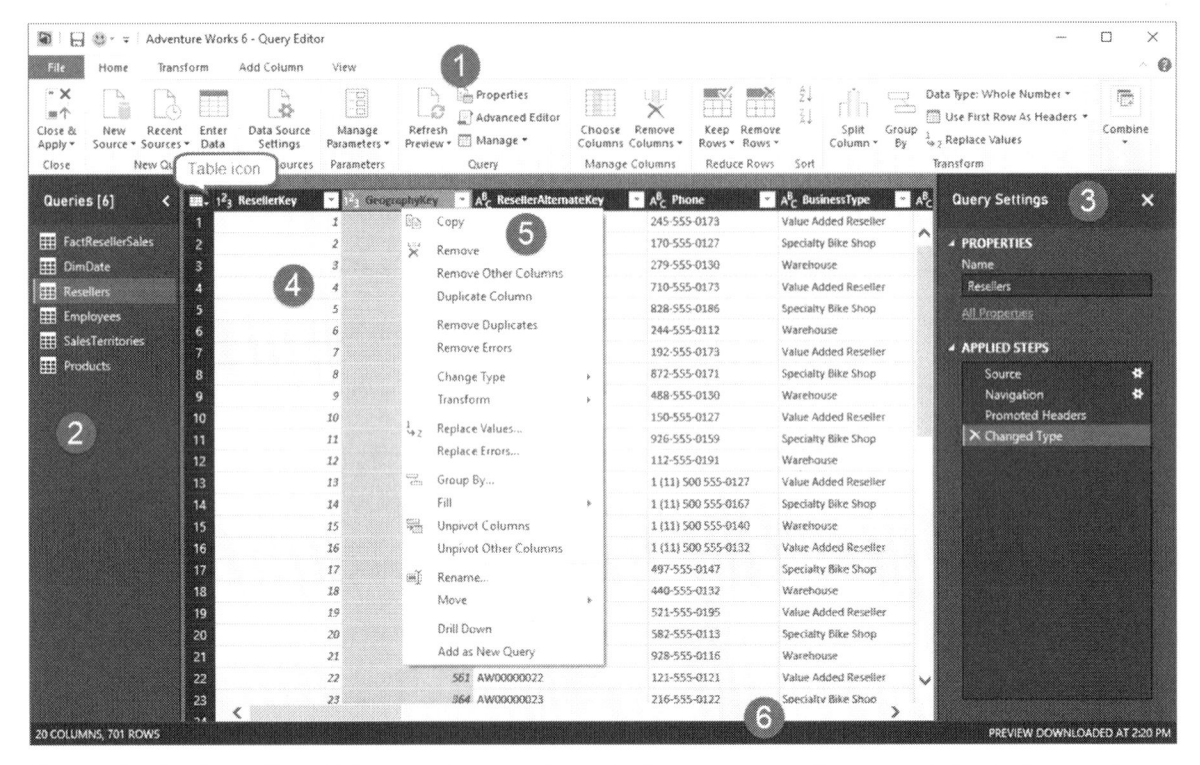

Figure 7.1 The Power Query Editor opens in a new window to give you access to the queries defined in the model.

Understanding the ribbon's Home tab

The Home tab in the ribbon (see item 1 in **Figure 7.1**) includes buttons for common tasks and some frequently used columns and table-level transformations. Starting from the left, you're already familiar with the Close & Apply button. When expanded, this button has three values, giving you options to close the Power Query Editor without applying the query changes to the data model (Close menu), to apply the changes without closing the editor (Apply), and both (Close & Apply). If you choose to close the editor without applying the changes, Power BI Desktop will display a warning that pending query changes aren't applied.

> **NOTE** Some structural changes, such as adding a new column, must reload the data in the corresponding table in the data model. Other changes, such as renaming columns, are handled internally without data refresh. Power BI Desktop (more accurately the xVelocity engine) always tries to apply the minimum steps for a consistent model without unnecessary data refreshes.

The New Query ribbon group is another starting point for creating new queries if you prefer to do so while you're in the Power Query Editor as opposed to Power BI Desktop. The New Source button is equivalent to the Get Data button in the Power BI Desktop's ribbon. The Recent Sources and Enter Data buttons are the Editor Query counterparts of the same buttons in the Power BI Desktop ribbon's Home tab.

The "Data Source Settings" button in the Data Sources ribbon's group brings the "Data Source Settings" window (you can also open it from the Power BI Desktop File ⇨ "Options and settings" ⇨ "Data source settings" menu) allows you to see what data sources are used in the current Power BI Desktop file, as well as change their authentication, encryption, and privacy settings (all these settings that you specified when you connected to the data source the first time). For example, you can go to the properties of a data source to change the authentication properties, such as to switch from Windows to standard authentication that requires a username and password to connect to a database.

> **NOTE** The data source privacy level determines its level of isolation from other data sources. Suppose you import a list of customers that has some sensitive information, such as contact details. To prevent inadvertently sending this information to another data source, such as a data feed, set the data source privacy level to Private. For more information about privacy levels, read the "Power BI Desktop privacy levels" blog at https://docs.microsoft.com/power-bi/desktop-privacy-levels.

The Managed Parameters button is to define query parameters to customize conveniently certain elements of the data models, such as a query filter, a data source reference, a measure definition, and others. For example, a parameter can change the data source connection information so that you refresh data from Production or Testing environments based on the selected parameter value. I'll postpone discussing the Manage Parameters button to the "Using Advanced Feature" section in this chapter.

The ribbon's Query group is to perform query-related tasks. Specifically, the Refresh Preview button refreshes the preview of the query results, such to see a new column that you just added to an underlying table in the database. Not to be confused with the Refresh button in Power BI Desktop's Home ribbon, it doesn't refresh the data in the model. The Properties button opens a Query Properties window (**Figure 7.2**) that allows you to change the query name. Alternatively, you can change the query name in the Query Settings pane or double-click the query in the Queries pane (or right-click and click Rename).

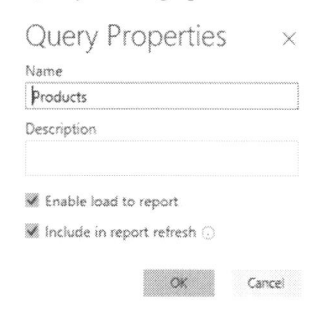

Figure 7.2 Use the Query Properties pane to change the query name, to enable data load to report, and to include in report refresh.

Sometimes, you might not want to load the query data in the data model, such as when you plan to append the query results to another query or use them as a source to another query. If you don't want the query to generate a table in the data model, uncheck the "Unable load to report" checkbox. And, if you don't want to refresh the query results when you click the Refresh button in Power BI Desktop, uncheck "Include in report refresh". Unfortunately, this setting applies only to Power BI Desktop (therefore, it refers to "report" refresh). Power BI Service will refresh all queries with manual or automated refresh.

Continuing the list of Home tab's buttons, the Advanced Editor button gives you access to the query source. You can use Manage drop-down button to delete, duplicate, and reference a query. These tasks are also available when you right-click a query in the Queries navigation pane.

> **NOTE** Queries are described in a formula language (informally known as "M"). Every time you apply a new transformation, the Power Query Editor creates a formula and adds a line to the query source. For more information about the query formula language, read "Microsoft Power Query for Excel Formula Language Specification" at http://go.microsoft.com/fwlink/p/?linkid=320633.

The rest of the buttons on the Home tab let you perform common transformations, including removing columns, reducing rows, grouping by and replacing values, and combining queries. We'll practice many of these in the lab exercise that follows.

Understanding the ribbon's Transform tab

The Transform tab (see **Figure 7.3**) includes additional table and column transformations. Many of the column-level transformations from the context menu (see item 5 in **Figure 7.1**) are available when you right-click a column in the data preview pane. And, many of the table-level transformations are available when you expand or right-click the Table icon (▦) in the top-left corner of the data preview pane.

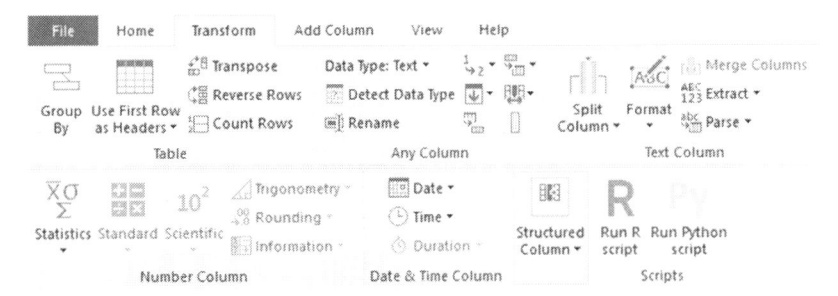

Figure 7.3 The Transform ribbon (split in the screenshot to reduce space) includes many table and column transformations.

Some transformations apply to columns that have specific data types (see the second row in **Figure 7.3**). For example, the Split Column transformation applies only to text columns, while the Rounding transformation applies only to number columns. If you have experience in R or Python and you prefer to use them for data cleansing and shaping, the last two buttons are for this purpose. To learn about data shaping with R, check the "Data Cleansing with R in Power BI" blog by Sharon Laivand at http://bit.ly/2eZ6f4R and to learn how to do this with Python, check the "Using Python in Query Editor" article at https://docs.microsoft.com/power-bi/desktop-python-in-query-editor.

Understanding the ribbon's Add Column tab

The Add Column ribbon tab (see **Figure 7.4**) lets you create custom columns. For example, I'll show you later how you can create a custom column that returns the last day of the month from a date.

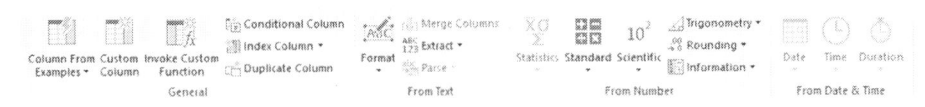

Figure 7.4 Use the Add Column tab in the ribbon to create custom columns.

NOTE Don't confuse query custom columns with data model calculated columns. Added to the query, query custom columns are created using the Power Query formula language called "M" and they can't reference fields in the data model. On the other hand, calculated columns in the data model are described in DAX and they can reference other fields in the model.

Another interesting variant of a custom column is a conditional column (the Conditional Column button in the General section) that lets you define different values depending on a condition (see **Figure 7.5**).

Figure 7.5 The CostBand conditional column evaluates the StandardCost column to assign each value to a band.

Like a SWITCH CASE statement in programming languages, this example creates a conditional column that examines the product cost and assigns each row in the Product table to a cost band which values Low, Medium, or High.

A very powerful feature awaits you in the "Column From Examples" button. As you probably realize, the Power Query Editor is a great tool, but it might be difficult for a novice user to understand which transformation to apply to get the desired result. No worries, you can let Query Editor take a guess! Let's say I want a column that shows the employee's first name and their department, such as "Guy from Production" (see **Figure 7.6**). I selected the Employees table in Query Editor. Next, I expanded "Column From Examples", chose "From Selection", and checked the FirstName and Department columns.

Then, In the first cell of the new Merged column, I typed *Guy from Production* and pressed Ctrl-Enter. Query Editor understood what I want to do and filled in all rows with the desired results. For more information about this excellent feature, read the "Add a column from an example in Power BI Desktop" article at https://powerbi.microsoft.com/documentation/powerbi-desktop-add-column-from-example/.

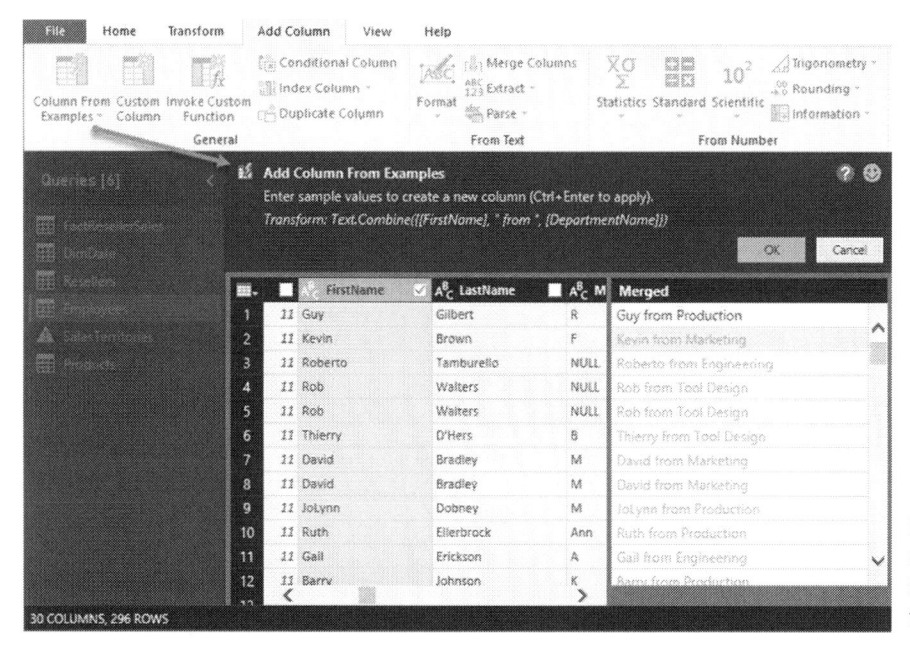

Figure 7.6 You can create custom columns by giving Query Editor an example of the desired outcome.

Understanding the ribbon's View tab

Figure 7.7 shows the ribbon's View tab. The Query Settings button in the Layout group toggles the visibility of the Query Settings pane (item 3 in **Figure 7.1**). The Formula Bar checkbox toggles the visibility of the formula bar that shows you the "M" formula behind the selected transformation step in the Applied Steps list. Checking the Monospace checkbox in the Data Preview tab changes the text font in the Data Preview window (the window that shows the query results) to Monospace. When checked, the "Show whitespace" checkbox shows whitespace and newline characters in the Data Preview window.

Data quality is a big problem that reduces the business value of data analytics. Currently in preview, "Column profiling" aims to help you get valuable statistics about the data behind each column. Currently, column profiling examines only the first 1,000 rows. If you enable the "Column quality" checkbox, you'll get a percentage of Valid (non-error and non-empty values), Error (values with errors, such as when the column data type is Date, but you have a non-date value), and Empty (empty values). And if you enable "Column distribution", you'll get a column chart that shows the value distribution. That's all the profiling you get for now, but Microsoft has promised more features, such as profiling all values, more statistics, such as Min, Max, Std, Median.

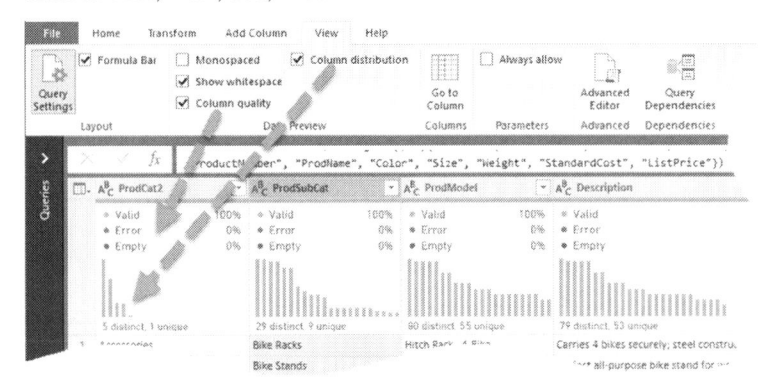

Figure 7.7 The View tab gives you access to the query source.

The "Go to Column" is for quick navigation to a column that you select from a list of columns in the active table. Query parameters allow refactor certain properties, such as the server name in the connection string, as a parameter. If "Always allow" is off, you must define a parameter first before you see the option to specify the parameter value in properties that support parameters. If it's on, users will see that they can use parameters for these properties without having to create a parameter beforehand. The Advanced Editor button does the same thing as the button with the same name (also called Advanced Editor) in the Home tab. It shows the source code of the query and allows you to change it. Lastly, clicking the Query Dependencies button shows a diagram that can help visualize the dependencies between queries, such as when a query combines data from other queries.

So, what does this "M" query language do for you anyway? It allows you to implement more advanced data manipulation. For example, Martin needs to load multiple Excel files from a given folder. Looping through files isn't an out-of-box feature. However, once Martin applies the necessary transformations to a single file, he can use the Advanced Editor to modify the query source to define a query function. Now Martin can automate the process by invoking the query function for each file, passing the file path. I'll show you some of these capabilities later in this chapter.

7.1.2 Understanding Queries

Recall that there's a query behind every table you import or access directly via DirectQuery (except when you connect live to multidimensional sources, such as Analysis Services). The whole purpose of the Power Query Editor is to access to these queries so that you can add additional transformation steps if needed.

> **TIP** A quick way to navigate to the underlying query for a table is to right-click the table in the Fields list and then click Edit Query. This will open the Power Query Editor and select the query in the Queries pane.

Understanding the Queries pane

The Queries pane (see item 5 in **Figure 7.1**) shows you all the queries that exist in the Power BI Desktop file. In the Adventure Works model, there are six queries because you've loaded six tables. In general, the number of queries correspond to the number of tables you use in the model, unless you've created queries for other more advanced tasks, such as to merge results from two queries.

You can right-click a query to open a context menu with additional tasks, such as to delete, duplicate, reference (reuse another query so you can apply additional steps), enable or disable load (controls if the query produces a table in the model), move the query up or down, and organize queries in groups.

Understanding the Query Settings pane

As you've seen, the Query Settings pane allows you to change the query name. Renaming the query changes the name of the table in the data model and vice versa. The more significant role of Query Settings is to list all the steps you've applied to load and shape the data (see **Figure 7.8**). The query shown in the screenshot is named Products and it has four applied steps. The Source step represents the connection to the data source. A step that have a window to help you change its settings has a cog icon (✿) to the right.

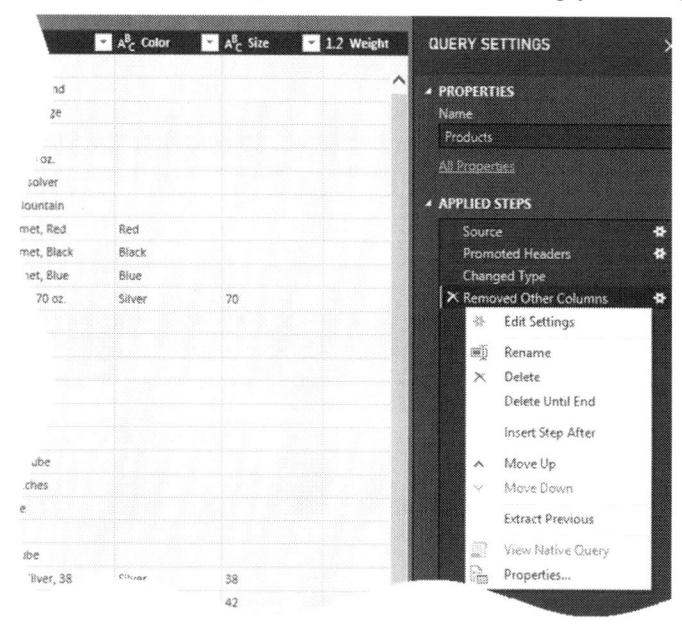

Figure 7.8 The Applied Steps section of Query Setting show all the steps applied to load and shape the data.

For example, when you click this icon for the Source step, a window opens to let you view and change the source settings, such as the name of the file and what delimiter will be used to parse the columns. If the Get Data wizard used the Navigator window, such as to let you select a database table or an Excel sheet, Power BI will a second step (Navigation) so that you can view or change the source table if needed. However, you imported the Products table from an SSRS report or file, and there is no Navigation step in the Products query.

Although you didn't specifically do this, Power BI Desktop applied the Promoted Headers step to promote the first row as column headers. Power BI Desktop applies the Change Type step when it discovers that it needs to overwrite the column data types. Finally, you applied the "Removed Other Columns" step when you removed some of the source columns when you imported the Product Catalog report.

You can click a step to select it. If the formula bar is enabled (you can check the Formula checkbox in the ribbon's View tab to enable it), you'll see the query language formula behind the step. In addition, selecting a step updates the data preview to show you how the step affected the source data. When you select a step in the Applied Steps list, the Data Preview pane shows the transformed data after that step is applied. So, you can always go back in the step history to check the effect of every step!

If the step is not needed, click the (X) button that appears to the left of the step name when you hover on it, or press the Delete key to remove a step. The Power Query Editor will ask you to confirm deleting intermediate steps because there might be dependent downstream steps and removing a prior step might result in breaking changes. You can also right-click a step to get additional options, such as to rename a step to make its name more descriptive, to delete it, to delete the current steps and all subsequent steps, to move the step up or down in the Applied Steps list, and to extract previous steps in a separate query.

TRANSORMING DATA

7.1.3 Understanding Data Preview

The data preview pane (see item 4 back in **Figure 7.1**) shows a read-only view of the source schema and the data as of the time the query was created, or the data preview was last refreshed. Each column has a drop-down menu that lets you sort and filter the data before it's imported. Icons in the column headers indicate the column data type, such as a calendar icon for Date/Time columns.

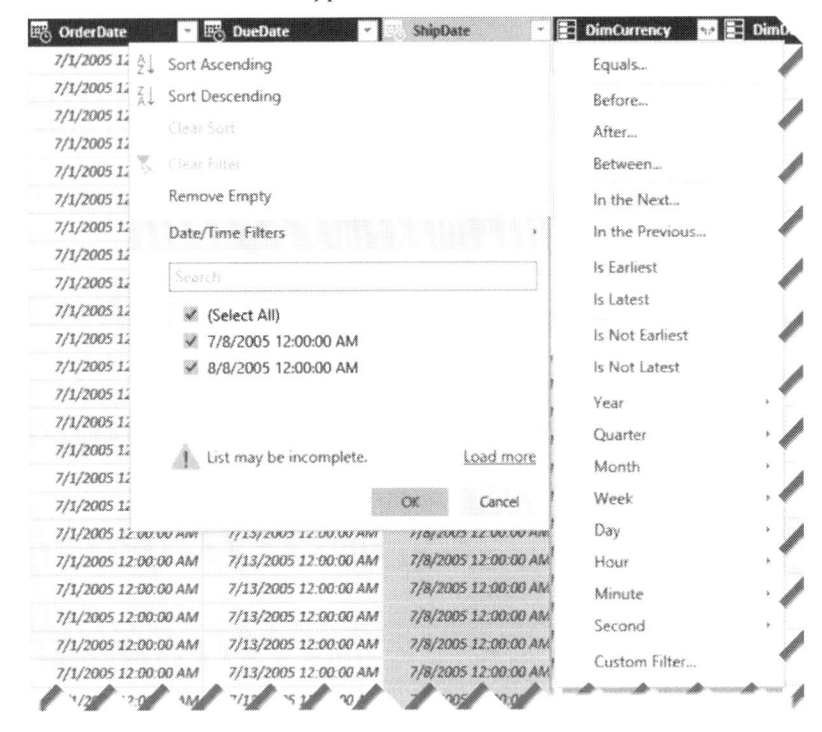

Figure 7.9 The column drop-down allows you to sort and filter the source data before it's loaded in the model.

Understanding data filtering

Filtering allows you to exclude rows, so you don't end up with more data than you need. The filtering options differ, based on the data type of the column. **Figure 7.9** shows the filtering options available for date/time columns.

> **NOTE** Power BI queries have smarts to push as much processing as possible to some data sources. This is called query folding. For example, if you filter a column in a table that was imported from a relational database, the query would append a WHERE clause and pass it on to the data source. This is much more efficient than filtering the results after all the data is loaded. Filters, joins, groupings, type conversions, and column removal are examples of work that gets folded to the source. What gets folded depends on the capabilities of the source, level of support, internal logic, and the data source privacy level. If a transformation step results in query folding, you can right-click the step in the Applied Steps pane, and then click "View Native Query" to see what query is generated. You can't change the native query that Power Query generates.

For example, if I filter the ShipDate column in FactResellerSales for the last year, this will create a new transformation step that will load only the data for last year based on the system date.

> **TIP** Do you want to export the data shown in the preview pane? While waiting for Microsoft to implement the "Export to Excel" feature, you can expand the Table icon in the top-left corner of the preview pane and click "Copy Entire Table". Then you can paste the data in Excel. Note, however, that this will copy only the first 1,000 rows that are shown in the preview. If you want to copy all the rows, right-click the table in the Power BI Desktop Data View tab, and then click "Copy table".

Understanding preview caching

The Power Query Editor status bar (see item 6 in the figure) informs you when the data preview of the selected query was last refreshed. A cached copy of the query preview results is stored on your local hard disk for faster viewing later. You can control the size of the data cache from File ⇨ Options and Settings ⇨ Options (Data Load tab). Because the preview results are cached, the data preview might get out of sync with schema and data changes in the data source. Click the Refresh Preview button to update the data preview.

If the data preview hasn't been refreshed for more than two days, a warning will be displayed above the preview pane. Don't confuse data preview refresh with table refresh in the data model (the Refresh button in the Power BI Desktop ribbon). The data model refresh executes the queries and reloads the data, while the query preview shows you what the data would look like after a step is applied.

> **NOTE** By default, every time you refresh the model, Power BI will refresh the data previews for all query steps. This could become expensive with many queries or slow data sources. Try mitigating the performance hit by disabling "Allow data preview to download in the background" option from File ⇨ Options and Settings ⇨ Options (Data Load tab).

Auto-discovering relationships

When you import data from a database that has relationships defined between tables, the query discovers these relationships and adds corresponding columns to let you bring columns from the related tables. For example, if you select FactResellerSales and scroll the data preview pane all the way to the right, you'll see "split" columns for DimCurrency, DimDate (three columns for each relationship), DimEmployee, and all the other tables that FactResellerSales has relationships with in the AdventureWorksDW database. If you click the split button (↔) in the column header, Query Editor opens a list that allows you to add columns from these tables. This handy feature saves you steps to create custom queries to join tables and to look up values in related tables.

> **NOTE** The relationships in the Power Query Editor are different than the relationships in the model (discussed in detail in the next chapter). The former result in lookup joins between database tables. The later let you analyze data in one table by another. When you import tables, Power BI Desktop checks for database relationships during the auto-discovery process and it might add corresponding relationships to both the query as split columns and to the data model.

As you've seen, you can also rename columns in the Power Query Editor and in the Data View interchangeably. No matter which view you use to rename the column, the new name is automatically applied to the other view. However, I encourage you to check and fix the column data types (use the Transform group in the ribbon's Home tab) in the Power Query Editor so you can address data type issues before your data is loaded.

For example, you might expect a sales amount field to be a numeric column. However, when Query Editor parsed the column, it changed its data type to Text because of some invalid entries, such as "N/A" or "NULL". It would be much easier to fix these data type errors in the Power Query Editor, such as by using the Remove Errors, Replace Errors, and Replace Values column-level transformations, than to use DAX formulas in the data model.

7.2 Shaping and Cleansing Data

Suppose that the Adventure Works Finance department gives Martin periodically (let's say every month or year) an Excel file that details accessories and parts that Adventure Works purchases from its vendors. Martin needs to analyze spending by vendor. The problem is that the source data is formatted in Excel tables that the Finance department prepared for its own analysis. This makes it very difficult for Martin to load the data and relate it to other tables that he might have in the model. Fortunately, the Power Query

Editor component of Power BI Desktop allows Martin to transform and extract the data he needs. For the purposes of this exercise, you'll use the Vendor Parts.xlsx file that's located in the \Source\ch07 folder.

7.2.1 Applying Basic Transformations

Figure 7.10 shows the first two report sections in the Vendor Parts file. This format is not suitable for analysis and requires some preprocessing before data can be analyzed. Specifically, the data is divided in sections and each section is designed as an Excel table. However, you need just the data as a single Excel table, like the Resellers Excel file that you imported in the previous chapter. Another issue is that the data is presented as crosstab reports, making it impossible to join the vendor data to a Date table in the data model. Further, the category appears only in the first row of every section and each section has a subtotal row that you don't need.

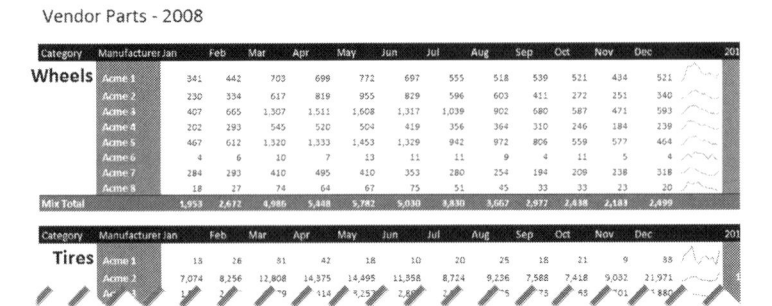

Figure 7.10 The Vendor Parts Excel file includes crosstab reports, which present a challenge for relating this data to other tables in the model.

Exploring source data

Let's follow familiar steps to connect to the Excel file. However, this time you'll launch the Power Query Editor before you import the data.

1. If the Vendor Parts file is open in Excel, close it so that Excel doesn't lock the file and prevent importing.
2. Open a new instance of Power BI Desktop. Save the file as *Query Examples*.
3. Expand the Get Data menu and click Excel because you'll import an Excel file.
4. Navigate to the \Source\Ch07 folder and select the Vendor Parts.xlsx file. Then click Open.
5. In the Navigator window, check Sheet1 to select it and preview its data. The preview shows how the data would be imported if you don't apply any transformations. As you see, there are many issues with the data, including mixed column content, pivoted data by month, and null values.
6. Click the Edit button to open the Power Query Editor.

Removing rows

First, let's remove the unnecessary rows:

1. Right-click the first cell in the Column1 column, and then click Text Filters ➪ "Does Not Equal" to filter only rows where the text in the first column doesn't equal "Vendor Parts – 2008". The net effect after applying this step is that the "Filtered Rows" step will all rows with that text (in our case only the first row will be excluded).
2. Locate the *null* value in the first cell of Column3 and apply the same filter (Text Filters ➪ "Does Not Equal") to exclude all the rows that have *null* in Column3.
3. Promote the first row as headers so that each column has a descriptive column name. To do so, in the ribbon's Transform tab, click the "Use First Row as Headers" button. Alternatively, you can expand the table

icon (in the top-left corner of the preview window), and then click "User First Row as Headers". Compare your results with **Figure 7.11**.

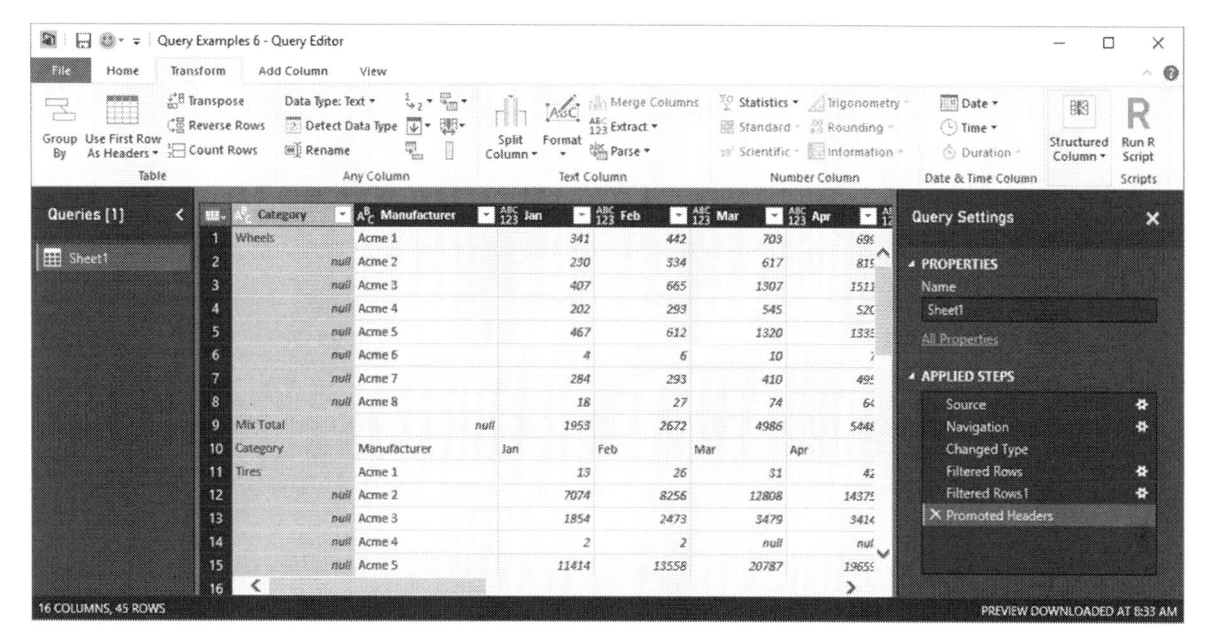

Figure 7.11 The source data after filtering unwanted rows.

4. Note that the first column (Category) has many null values. These empty values will present an issue when relating the table to other tables, such as Product. Click the first cell in the Category column (that says Wheels), and then click the ribbon's Transform tab. Click the Fill ⇨ Down button. This fills the null values with the actual categories.

5. Let's remove rows that represent report subtotals. To do so, right-click a cell in the Category column that contains the word "Category" (should be the first cell in the tenth row). Click Text Filters ⇨ "Does Not Equal" to remove all the rows that have "Category" in the first column.

6. Next, you will need to filter all the rows that contain the word "Total". Expand the column drop-down in the column header of the Category column. Click Text Filters ⇨ "Does Not Contain". In the Filter Rows dialog box, type "Total", and then click OK.

7. Hold the Ctrl key and select the last two columns, Column15 and 2014 Total. Right-click the selection, and then click Remove Columns.

Un-pivoting columns

Now that you've cleansed most of the data, there's one remaining task. Note how the months appear on columns. This makes it impossible to join the table to a Date table because you can't join on multiple columns. To make things worse, as new periods are added, the number of columns might increase. To solve this problem, you need to un-pivot the months from columns to rows. Fortunately, this is very easy to do with the Power Query Editor!

1. Hold the Shift key and select all the month columns, from Jan to Dec.

2. Right-click the selection, and then click Unpivot Columns. The Power Query Editor un-pivots the data by creating new columns called Attribute and Value, as shown in **Figure 7.12**.

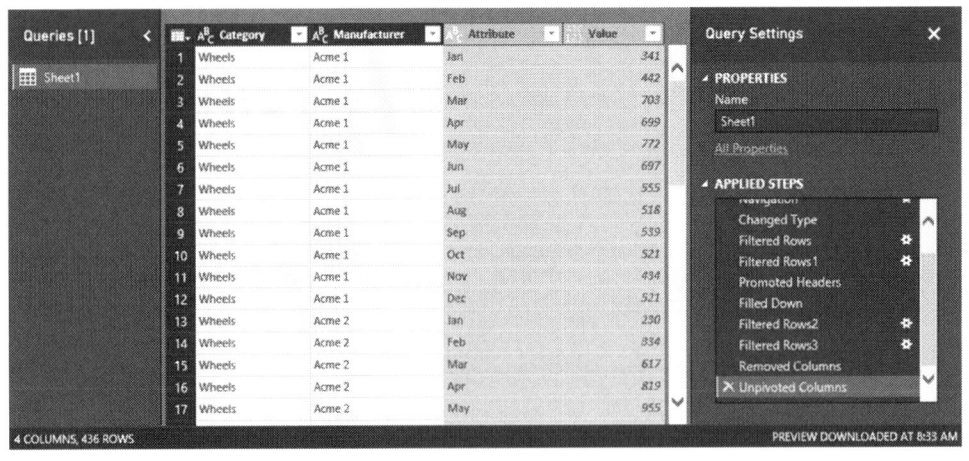

Figure 7.12 The un-pivoted dataset includes Attribute and Value columns.

1. Double-click the column header of the Attribute column and rename it to *Month*. Rename the Value column to *Units*.

7.2.2 Working with Custom Columns

Since you have a Date table in the model, you might want to join the vendor data to it. As you know by now, a Date table must have a row for each date. To create the VendorParts ⇨ Date relationship, you need to convert the Month column to a date. Next, I'll show you two ways to accomplish this task: using the "Column from Examples" feature and creating a custom column by typing in an M formula.

Adding a column from examples
As I mentioned, Power Query describes steps in a language called "M". You can add custom columns described in M but learning yet another language might be too much. Instead, you can let Power Query auto-generate the M code by showing it an example of what the result should look like. It's such a cool feature!

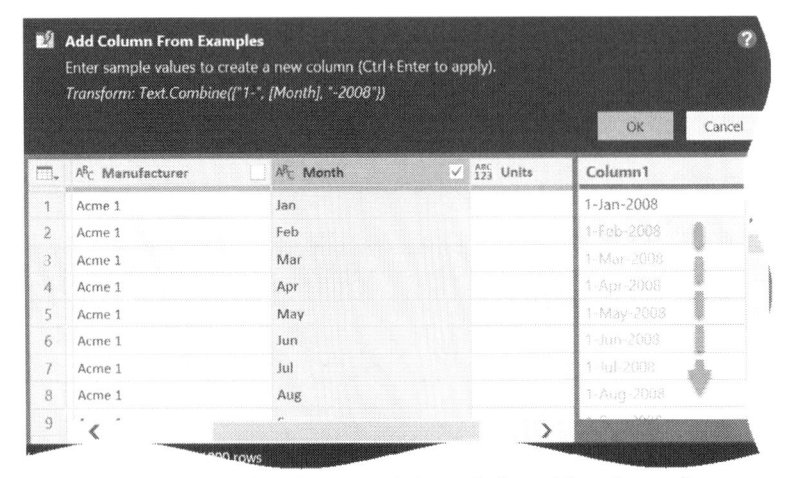

Figure 7.13 Use the "Column from Examples" feature to auto-generate a custom column from an example you provide to Power Query.

1. Right-click the Month column and then click "Add Column from Examples…" in the context menu. Or, with the Month column selected, click the Add Column ribbon, expand the Column from Examples dropdown, and click "From Selection". This tells Power Query to use the selected column(s) when figuring the custom formula.

2. In the "Add Column from Examples" window, enter *1-Jan-2008* in the cell below Column1 to tell Power Query what the value you expect for the first row. Press Enter. Press Enter. If all is well, Power BI will infer that you want the first day of the month and will fill down the expected results for each row (see **Figure 7.13**).
3. Double-click the Column1 column header and rename it to *FirstDayOfMonth*. Click OK.
4. Select the FirstDayOfMonth column. Expand the Data Type drop-down in the Home ribbon and select Date to change the column data type for the date data type.
5. Assuming you need the month end date instead of the first date of the month, select the FirstDayOfMonth column in the data preview pane. In the ribbon's Transform tab, expand the Date drop-down button, and then select Month ⇨ "End of Month". Rename the new column to *Date*.

(Optional) Adding a custom column with M formula
You can achieve the same result by adding a custom formula with a M formula you enter.

1. Click the ribbon's Add Column tab, and then click "Custom Column".
2. In the "Add Custom Column" dialog box, enter *FirstDayOfMonth1* as the column name. Then enter the following formula (be careful because the "M" query language is case sensitive):

=Date.FromText([Month] & " 1, 2008")

3. Compare your results with **Figure 7.14**. Click OK to close the "Add Custom Column" window.

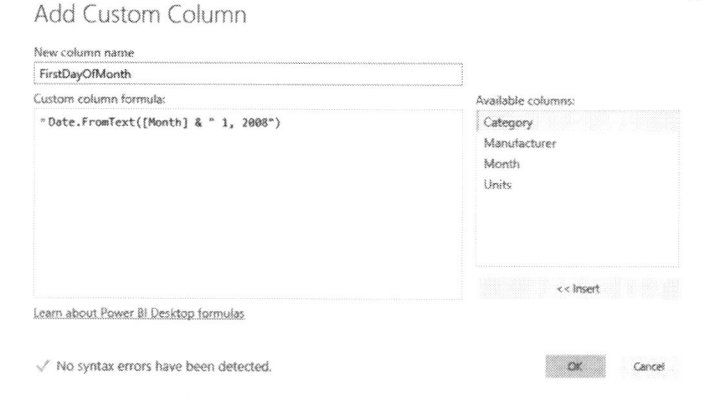

Figure 7.14 Create a custom column that converts a month to the first day in that month for year 2008.

This formula converts the month value to the first day of the month in year 2008. For example, if the Month value is Jan, the resulting value will be 1/1/2008. The formula hardcodes the year to 2008 because the source data doesn't have the actual year. If you need to default to the current year, you can use the formula Date.Year(DateTime.LocalNow()). Or, had the year been present in a column, you could simply reference that column in the expression.

> **NOTE** Unfortunately, as it stands, the "Add Custom Column" window doesn't have IntelliSense or show you the formula syntax, making it difficult to work with formulas and forcing a "trial and error" approach. If you've made a mistake, the custom column will display "Error" in every row. You can click the Error link to get more information about the error. Then in the Applied Steps pane, click the gear (Settings) icon next to the step to get back to the formula, and try again. Or, right-click the query and go to the Advanced Editor which shows all the steps in one place and supports IntelliSense.

That's it! With a few clicks you added steps to transform and cleanse the source data into a format that is suitable for reporting. But the data is not loaded yet. What you just did was defining the steps that will be executed in the order that the steps are listed in the "Applied Steps" pane once you refresh the data.

7.2.3 Loading Transformed Data

As I explained before, you have used the "Close & Apply" button to load the data. Recall that the first option "Close & Apply" closes the Power Query Editor and applies the changes to the model. You can close the Power Query Editor without applying the changes, but the model and queries aren't synchronized. Finally, you can choose to apply the changes without closing the Power Query Editor so that you can continue working on the queries.

Renaming steps and queries

Before loading the data, consider renaming the query to apply the same name to the new table. You can also rename transformation steps to make them more descriptive. Let's rename the query and a step:

1. In the Query Settings pane, rename the query to *VendorParts*. This will become the name of the table in the model.
2. In the Applied Steps pane, right-click the last step and click Rename. Change the step name to "*Renamed Column to Date*" and click Enter.
3. (Optional) Right-click any of the steps in the Applied Steps pane and click Properties. Notice that you can enter a description. Then when you hover on the step, the description will show in a tooltip. This is a great way to explain what a step does in more detail.

Loading transformed data

Let's load the transformed data into a new table:

1. Click the Close & Apply button in the ribbon's Home tab. Power BI Desktop imports the data, applies all the steps as the data streams into the model, closes the Power Query Editor, and adds the VendorParts table to the Fields pane.
2. In the ribbon's Home tab, click the Edit Queries button. This brings you to the Power Query Editor in case you want to apply additional transformation steps.
3. (Optional) You can disable loading query results. This could be useful if another query uses the results from the VendorParts query and it doesn't make sense to create unnecessary tables in the model. To demonstrate this, open Query Editor, right-click the VendorParts query in the Queries pane, and then uncheck "Enable Load". Accept the warning that follows that disabling the query load will delete the table from the model and break existing reports. Click Close & Apply and notice that the VendorParts table is removed from the Fields list.

> **TIP** Sometimes things go bad, such when an input file is not found in the expected source folder. Power BI doesn't have native capabilities for error handling or branching so the query would just fail. However, with some coding effort, you can handle errors gracefully. Chris Webb demonstrates a possible approach in his "Handling Data Source Errors in Power Query" blog at https://blog.crossjoin.co.uk/2014/09/18/handling-data-source-errors-in-power-query/.

7.3 Using Advanced Power Query Features

The Power Query Editor has much more to offer than just basic column transformations. In this section, I'll walk you through more advanced scenarios that you might encounter so that you handle them yourself instead of asking for help. First, you'll see how you can join and merge datasets. Then I'll show you how query functions can help you automate mundane data processing tasks. You'll find how to use the "M" query language to auto-generate date tables and how to parameterize connections to data sources.

7.3.1 Combining Datasets

As I mentioned previously, if relationships exist in the database, the query will discover these relationships. This allows you to expand a table and reference columns from other tables. For example, if you open the Adventure Works model (Adventure Works.pbix) and examine the data preview pane of the FactResellerSales query, you'll see columns that correspond to all the tables that are related to the FactResellerSales table in the AdventureWorksDW database. These columns show the text "Value" for each row in FactResellerSales and have an expansion button (⁂) in the column header (see **Figure 7.15**).

When you click the expansion button, the Power Query Editor opens a window that lists all the columns from the related table so that you can include the columns you want in the query. This is a useful feature, but what if there are no relationships in the data source? As it turns out, if you have matching columns, you can merge (join) queries.

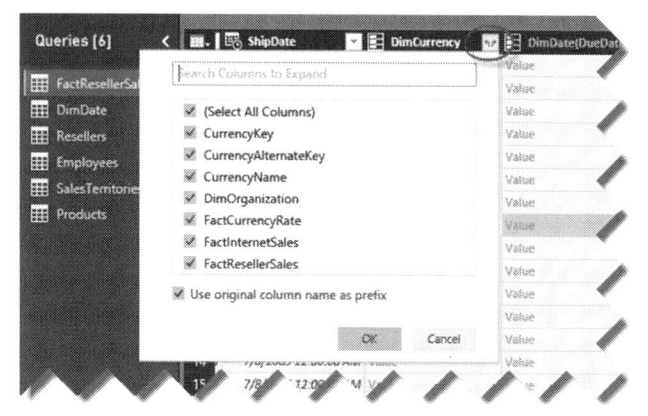

Figure 7.15 Create a custom column that converts a month to a date.

Merging queries

We're back to the Query Examples.pbix file. Suppose you have another query that returns a list of vendors that Adventure Works does business with. Let's import this list.

1. If the Power Query Editor is closed, click the Edit Queries button in the Power BI Desktop's ribbon to open it. In the Power Query Editor's Home ribbon, expand Get Data and then click Excel.
2. Navigate to the \Source\ch07 folder and select the Vendor Parts file.
3. In the Navigator window, check the Vendors sheet and then click Load. This creates a Vendors query that load the data from the Vendors sheet in the Excel file.
4. In the Queries pane, make sure the Vendors query is selected. Select the Transform ribbon tab and then click "Use First Row as Headers" button to promote the first row as column headers.
5. Compare your results with **Figure 7.16**.

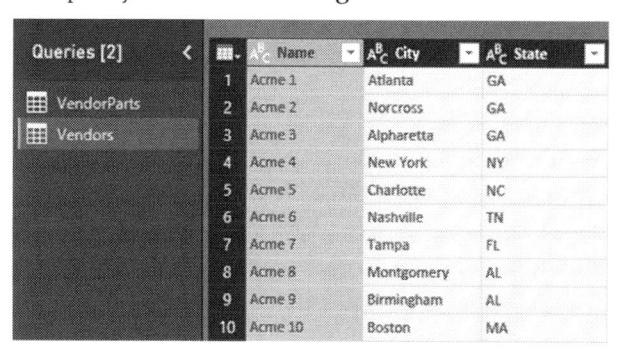

Figure 7.16 The Vendors query returns a list of vendors imported from the Vendors sheet in the Vendor Parts Excel file.

TRANSORMING DATA

Now I'd like to join the VendorParts query to the Vendors query so that I can look up some columns from the Vendor query and add them to the VendorParts query. If two queries have a matching column(s) you can join (merge) them just like you can join two tables in SQL.

6. In the Queries pane, select the VendorParts query because this will be our base query.

7. In the ribbon's Home tab, click Merge Queries (in the Combine group).

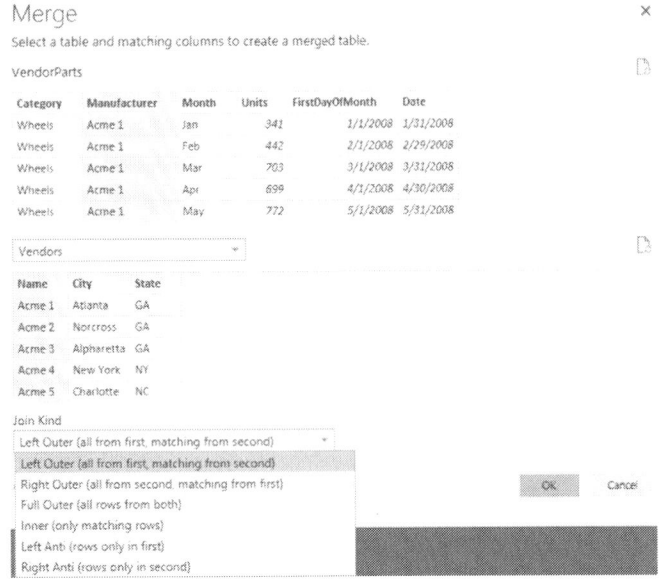

Figure 7.17 You can merge queries by one or more matching columns.

8. Configure the Merge window as shown in **Figure 7.17**. This setup joins the Manufacturer column from the VendorParts query to the Name column of the Vendors query. Notice that the Join Kind list has different types of joins. For example, a Left Outer Join will keep all the rows from the first query and only return the matching values from the second query, or null if no match is found. By contrast, the Inner Join will only return matching rows.

> **TIP** Sometimes, the column values in the two queries might not match exactly because of data quality issues. You can use the fuzzy matching settings at the bottom of the Merge window (not shown in **Figure 7.17**) to specify a similarity threshold and other settings for fuzzy matching.

9. Click OK. The Power Query Editor adds a NewColumn column to the end of the VendorParts query.

10. Click the expansion button in the column header of the new column. Notice that now you can add columns from the Vendors query (see **Figure 7.18**). You can also aggregate these columns, such as by using the Sum or Count aggregation functions.

Figure 7.18 Once you merge queries, you can add columns to the source query from the merged query.

184 CHAPTER 7

Appending queries

Suppose that some time has passed, and Martin gets another Vendors Parts report, for the year 2009. Instead of overwriting the existing data for 2008 in the data model, which will happen if Martin refreshes the data, Martin wants to append the second dataset to the VendorParts table, so he can analyze data across several years. If Martin is given a new file occasionally, such as in a month or year, he can use the "Append Queries" feature to append datasets manually. This will work if the dataset format (schema) is the same. To simulate a second dataset, you'll clone the existing VendorParts query.

> **TIP** If Martin knows that he'd be importing multiple files, instead of appending queries he can just use the Get Data ⇨ Folder data source. I'll demonstrate the Folder data source in "Using Functions" section. The Append Query feature is useful when you want to combine a limited number of datasets, especially if they require different transformations before appending them.

1. In the Queries pane, right-click the VendorParts query, and then click Duplicate. The Power Query Editor adds a VendorParts (2) query.
2. In the Queries pane, select the VendorParts (2) query. Click the cog icon (✿) to the right of "Added Custom" step, and then change the formula to use year 2009. You do this to simulate that this dataset has data for the year 2009.

   =Date.FromText([Month] & " 1, 2009")

3. In the Query Settings pane, rename the VendorsParts (2) query to *VendorParts 2009*.
4. Right-click *VendorParts 2009* and turn off Enable Load because you'll append this query and you don't want it to create a new table when you click Close & Apply.
5. In the Queries pane, select the VendorParts query.
6. In the ribbon's Home tab, click Append Queries (in the Combine group).
7. In the Append window, expand "Table to append" and select the VendorParts 2009 query. Click OK. The Power Query Editor appends VendorParts 2009 to VendorParts. As a result, the VendorParts query returns a combined dataset for years 2008 and 2009. If two queries have the same columns, you can append them.

> **TIP** If you need more complicated logic to look up values from another table you might find my blog "Implementing Lookups in Power Query" at http://prologika.com/implementing-lookups-in-power-query/ useful. It demonstrates a query function that uses a range filter for the lookup.

7.3.2 Using Functions

Appending datasets manually can get tedious quickly as the number of files increase. What if Martin is given Excel files every month and he needs to combine 100 files? Or, what if he needs to extract data from many pages in a paged table on a web page? Well, when the going gets tough, you write some automation code, right? If you have a programming background, your first thought might be to write code that loops through files, to check if the file is an Excel file, to load it, and so on. However, the "M" language that Power BI queries are written in is a functional language, and it doesn't support loops and conditional logic. What it does support is functions and they can be incredibly useful for automation.

Using the Folder data source

Think of a query function as a query that can be called repeatedly from another query. Like functions in programming languages, such as C# and Visual Basic, a function can take parameters. To understand how query functions work, we'll create a query that combines some files in folder using the Folder data source.

1. In the Power Query Editor, expand the New Source button (in the ribbon's Home tab), and then click More.

2. In the Get Data window, click the File tab and select Folder. The Folder data source returns a list of files in a specific folder. Click Connect.
3. In the Folder window, specify the folder path where the Excel source files are located. For your convenience, I saved two Excel files (with same definition) in the \Source\ch07\Files folder. Click OK.
4. A window opens to show a list of files in that folder. Click the "Combine & Edit" button.
5. In the Combine Files window, select Sheet1. Notice that the preview window shows what the data would look like after the files are appended. Notice also that without any transformations, the data will have the same issues that we've addressed in the Vendor Parts query. Click OK.

Query Editor does several things. First, it creates a new query called Files. Then it creates a new query group "Transform File from Files" (see **Figure 7.19**). A query group shows related items together and makes it easier to work with functions. For example, the "Transform File from Files" group has a Sample Query subgroup that shows the definition of one of the files in the source folder. Then, there is a "Transform Sample File from Files" query, which has a dependent function "Transform File from File" (prefixed with *fx*). When you make changes to the "Transform Sample File from Files" query, Query Editor updates the function automatically to match changes to the source file.

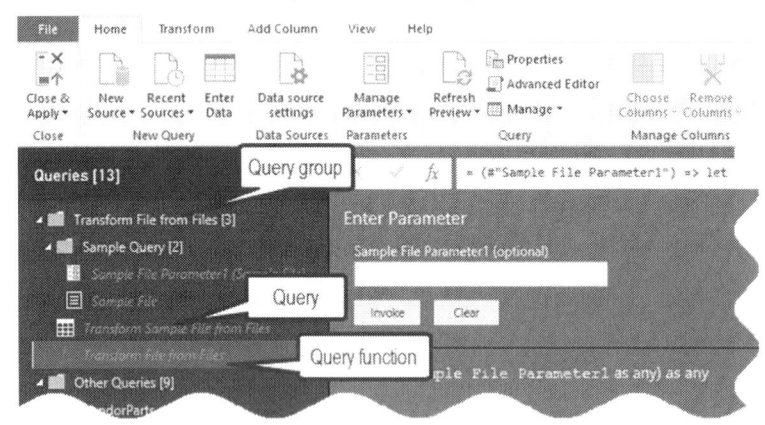

Figure 7.19 A query group facilitates testing query functions.

6. From the View ribbon, click Query Dependencies to visualize how these objects related to each other. Click Close in the Query Dependencies window.

Understanding functions
Let's take a moment to understand how the "Transform File from Files" function works.

1. In the Query Pane, click the "Transform File from Files" function. Notice that it takes a parameter that represents the full path to a file. The Enter Parameter dialog allows you to pass a value for the parameter and test the function. However, in this case the function expects the binary content of the file, which is what the Folder data source creates, so you can't really test the function using the Enter Parameter feature.
2. In the Queries pane, rename the "Transform File from Files" function to *fnProcessFile*.
Right-click *fnProcessFile* and click Advanced Editor to see the function source described in the M programming language (see **Figure 7.20**). Notice that function takes a parameter called #"Sample File Parameter1" that represents the file binary content. Then it loads Sheet1 from the Excel file.
3. In the Queries pane, click the Files query at the bottom of the list. Note that the second step invokes the fnProcessFile function for each file in the folder.

> **TIP** Do you want to process only files with a specific file extension? Click the Source step in the Applied Steps pane. In the data preview pane, expand the drop-down in the column header of the Extension column, and select only the file extension(s) you need.

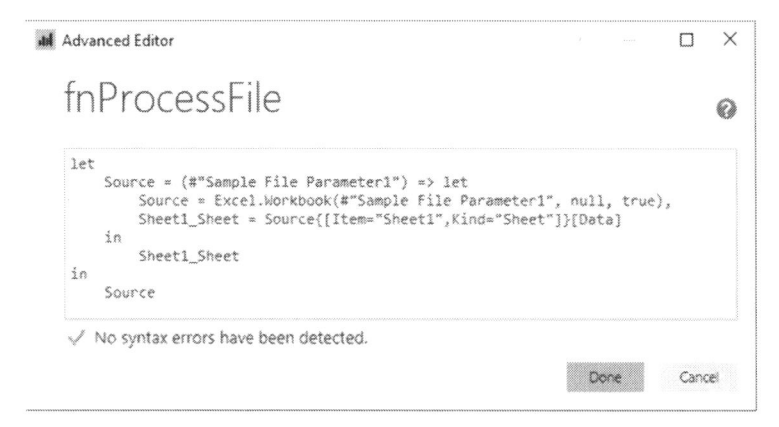

Figure 7.20 The fnProcessFile function takes the file content as an argument and loads the file.

Modifying functions

As useful as the fnProcessFile query function is, it doesn't apply the transformations we did in the Vendor Parts query. Let's fix this now.

1. In the Queries pane, right-click the Vendor Parts query and then click Advanced Editor. Copy all rows starting with Sheet1_Sheet line and ending with the #"Appended Query" line (before the *in* operator).
2. In the Queries pane, right-click the fnProcessFile function and then click Advanced Editor. Replace the content of the function, as shown below.

```
let
    Source = (#"Sample File Parameter1") => let
    Source = Excel.Workbook(#"Sample File Parameter1", null, true),
    Sheet1_Sheet = Source{[Item="Sheet1",Kind="Sheet"]}[Data],
    #"Changed Type" = Table.TransformColumnTypes(Sheet1_Sheet,{{"Column1", type text}, {"Column2", type text}, {"Column3", type any}, {"Column4", type any}, {"Column5", type any}, {"Column6", type any}, {"Column7", type any}, {"Column8", type any}, {"Column9", type any}, {"Column10", type any}, {"Column11", type any}, {"Column12", type any}, {"Column13", type any}, {"Column14", type any}, {"Column15", type any}, {"Column16", type any}}),
    #"Filtered Rows" = Table.SelectRows(#"Changed Type", each [Column1] <> "Vendor Parts - 2008"),
    #"Filtered Rows1" = Table.SelectRows(#"Filtered Rows", each [Column3] <> null),
    #"Promoted Headers" = Table.PromoteHeaders(#"Filtered Rows1"),
    #"Filled Down" = Table.FillDown(#"Promoted Headers",{"Category"}),
    #"Filtered Rows2" = Table.SelectRows(#"Filled Down", each [Category] <> "Category"),
    #"Filtered Rows3" = Table.SelectRows(#"Filtered Rows2", each not Text.Contains([Category], "Total")),
    #"Removed Columns" = Table.RemoveColumns(#"Filtered Rows3",{"Column15", "2014 Total"}),
    #"Unpivoted Columns" = Table.UnpivotOtherColumns(#"Removed Columns", {"Category", "Manufacturer"}, "Attribute", "Value"),
    #"Renamed Columns" = Table.RenameColumns(#"Unpivoted Columns",{{"Attribute", "Month"}, {"Value", "Units"}}),
    #"Added Custom" = Table.AddColumn(#"Renamed Columns", "FirstDayOfMonth", each Date.FromText([Month] & " 1, 2008")),
    #"Inserted End of Month" = Table.AddColumn(#"Added Custom", "EndOfMonth", each Date.EndOfMonth([FirstDayOfMonth]), type date),
    #"Renamed Column to Date" = Table.RenameColumns(#"Inserted End of Month",{{"EndOfMonth", "Date"}}),
    #"Merged Queries" = Table.NestedJoin(#"Renamed Column to Date",{"Manufacturer"},Vendors,{"Name"},"NewColumn",JoinKind.LeftOuter),
    #"Appended Query" = Table.Combine({#"Merged Queries", #"VendorParts 2009"})
in
    #"Appended Query"
in
    Source
```

TRANSORMING DATA

3. (Optional) Change the #"Sample File Parameter1" to *FileContent* to describe better its purpose. For your convenience, I provided the source code of the fnProcessFile function in the fnProcessFile.txt file in the \Source\ch07 folder.
4. Click OK to close the Advanced Editor.
5. Notice in the Queries pane that the Files query shows a warning sign.
6. Click the Files query. Click each of the applied steps (unfortunately, there isn't a better way to discover which steps has failed) and find that the issue is with the last step Changed Type. This step is looking for Column1 which the code from Vendor Parts doesn't have. Delete this step.
7. Rename the Files query to *ProcessExcelFiles*.

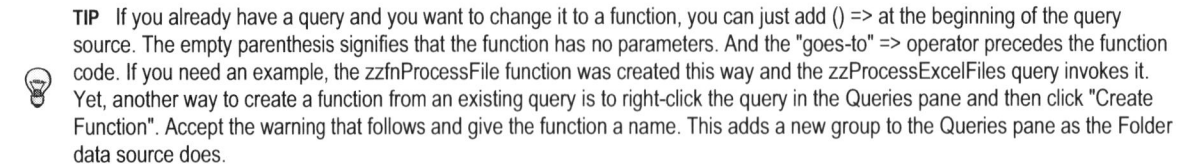

> **TIP** If you already have a query and you want to change it to a function, you can just add () => at the beginning of the query source. The empty parenthesis signifies that the function has no parameters. And the "goes-to" => operator precedes the function code. If you need an example, the zzfnProcessFile function was created this way and the zzProcessExcelFiles query invokes it. Yet, another way to create a function from an existing query is to right-click the query in the Queries pane and then click "Create Function". Accept the warning that follows and give the function a name. This adds a new group to the Queries pane as the Folder data source does.

For each file in the folder, the ProcessExcelFiles query calls the fnProcessFile function. Each time the function is invoked, it loads the file passed as argument and appends the results. So, the function does the heavy work, but you need a query to invoke it repeatedly.

> **NOTE** If you expand the drop-down of the Date column in the ProcessExcelFiles results, you'll only see dates for year 2008, which might let you believe that you have data from one file only. This is not the case, but it's a logical bug because year 2008 is hardcoded in the query. If the year is specified in the file name, you can add another custom column that extracts the year, passes it to a third parameter in the fnProcessFile function, and uses that parameter instead of hardcoded references to "2008".

7.3.3 Generating Date Tables

Now that you know about query functions, I'm sure you'll think of many real-life scenarios where you can use them to automate routine data crunching tasks. Let's revisit a familiar scenario. As I mentioned in Chapter 6, even if you import a single dataset, you should strongly consider a separate date table. I also mentioned that there are different ways to import a date table, and one of them was to generate it in the Power Query Editor. The following code is based on an example by Matt Masson, as described in his "Creating a Date Dimension with a Power Query Script" blog post (https://mattmasson.com/2014/02/creating-a-date-dimension-with-a-power-query-script/).

Generating dates
The Power Query Editor has useful functions for manipulating dates, such as for extracting date parts (day, month, quarter), and so on. The code uses many of these functions.

1. Start by creating a new blank query. To do so, in the Power Query Editor, expand the New Source button (the ribbon's Home tab) and click Blank Query. Rename the blank query to *GenerateDateTable*.
2. In the Queries pane, right-click the GenerateDateTable query and click Advanced Editor.
3. In the Advanced Editor, paste the following code which you can copy from the GenerateDateTable.txt file in the \Source\ch07 folder:

```
let GenerateDateTable = (StartDate as date, EndDate as date, optional Culture as nullable text) as table =>
  let
    DayCount = Duration.Days(Duration.From(EndDate - StartDate)),
    Source = List.Dates(StartDate,DayCount,#duration(1,0,0,0)),
    TableFromList = Table.FromList(Source, Splitter.SplitByNothing()),
```

```
    ChangedType = Table.TransformColumnTypes(TableFromList,{{"Column1", type date}}),
    RenamedColumns = Table.RenameColumns(ChangedType,{{"Column1", "Date"}}),
    InsertYear = Table.AddColumn(RenamedColumns, "Year", each Date.Year([Date])),
    InsertQuarter = Table.AddColumn(InsertYear, "QuarterOfYear", each Date.QuarterOfYear([Date])),
    InsertMonth = Table.AddColumn(InsertQuarter, "MonthOfYear", each Date.Month([Date])),
    InsertDay = Table.AddColumn(InsertMonth, "DayOfMonth", each Date.Day([Date])),
    InsertDayInt = Table.AddColumn(InsertDay, "DateInt", each [Year] * 10000 + [MonthOfYear] * 100 + [DayOfMonth]),
    InsertMonthName = Table.AddColumn(InsertDayInt, "MonthName", each Date.ToText([Date], "MMMM", Culture), type text),
    InsertCalendarMonth = Table.AddColumn(InsertMonthName, "MonthInCalendar", each (try(Text.Range([MonthName],0,3))
       otherwise [MonthName]) & " " & Number.ToText([Year])),
    InsertCalendarQtr = Table.AddColumn(InsertCalendarMonth, "QuarterInCalendar", each "Q" & Number.ToText([QuarterOfYear]) & " "
& Number.ToText([Year])),
    InsertDayWeek = Table.AddColumn(InsertCalendarQtr, "DayInWeek", each Date.DayOfWeek([Date])),
    InsertDayName = Table.AddColumn(InsertDayWeek, "DayOfWeekName", each Date.ToText([Date], "dddd", Culture), type text),
    InsertWeekEnding = Table.AddColumn(InsertDayName, "WeekEnding", each Date.EndOfWeek([Date]), type date)
  in
    InsertWeekEnding
in
  GenerateDateTable
```

This code creates a GenerateDateTable function that takes three parameters: start date, end date, and optional language culture, such as "en-US", to localize the date formats and correctly interpret the date parameters. The workhorse of the function is the List.Dates method, which returns a list of date values starting at the start date and adding a day to every value. Then the function applies various transformations and adds custom columns to generate date variants, such as Year, QuarterOfYear, and so on.

Invoking the function

Remember that you need an outer query to invoke the GenerateDateTable function even if don't have to execute it repeatedly. Fortunately, Query Editor can do this for you.

1. In the Queries pane, select the GenerateDateTable function.
2. In the Enter Parameters window (see **Figure 7.21**), enter StartDate and EndDate parameters. Click OK to invoke the function. Query Editor adds an Invoked Function query to wrap the function call.
3. Click the Invoked Function query and notice that it has the desired results. If you want to regenerate the table with a different range of values, simply delete the "Invoked Function" query in the Queries pane, and then invoke the function again with different parameters, or change the query's Source step.

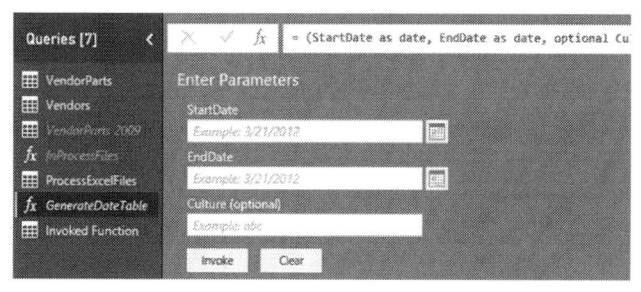

Figure 7.21 Invoke the GenerateDateTable function and pass the required parameters.

7.3.4 Working with Query Parameters

As you've seen, query functions can go a long way to help you create reusable queries. However, sometimes you might need a quick and easy way to customize the query behavior. Suppose you want to change the data source connection to point to a different server, such as when you want to switch from your development server to a production server. Or, you might need a convenient way to pass parameters to a stored procedure. This is where query parameters can help.

A query parameter externalizes certain query settings, such as a data source reference, a column replacement value, a query filter, and others, so that you can customize the query behavior without having to change the query itself. How do you know what query settings can be parameterized? If a step in the Applied Steps pane has a cog icon next to it (has a window that let you change its settings), click it and look for settings that are prefixed with a drop-down A^B_C ▼. If you see it, then that setting can be parameterized.

TIP Even if you don't see the "abc" drop-down, you can still parameterize they query but you need to change the code manually. My blog "Power BI DirectQuery with Parameterized Stored Procedure" at http://prologika.com/power-bi-directquery-with-parameterized-stored-procedure/ demonstrates how this can done to pass parameters to a stored procedure.

Don't confuse query parameters with what-if parameters (the New Parameter in the Modeling ribbon). The former is for parameterizing queries to the data source. The latter is for parameterizing DAX measures for runtime what-if analysis.

Creating query parameters

Suppose you're given access to a development SQL Server and you have created a model with many tables. Now, you want to load data from another server, such as your production server. This isn't as bad as it sounds because you can click the "Data Source Settings" button found in the Power Query Editor's Home ribbon group and change the server name. But suppose you want to switch back and forth between development and production environments and you don't want to remember (and type in) the server names (they can get rather cryptic sometimes). Instead, you'll create a query parameter that will let you change the data source with a couple of mouse clicks.

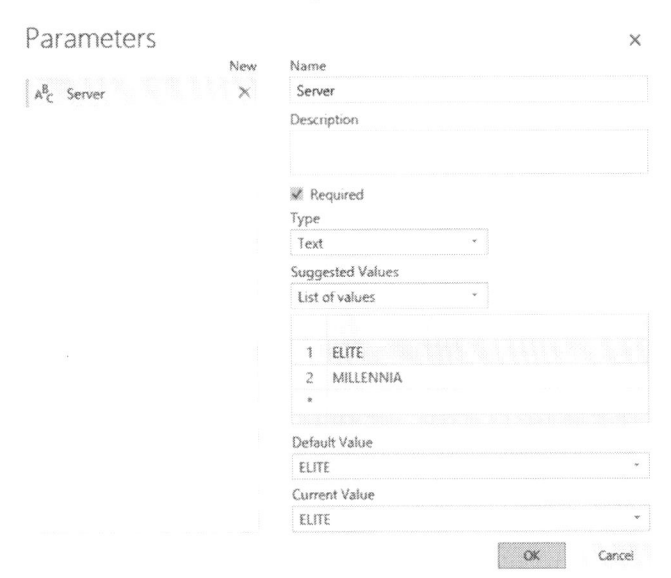

Figure 7.22 When setting up a parameter, specify its name, type, and suggested values.

1. To have a test query, in the Power Query Editor (Home ribbon), expand Get Data and import a table, such as DimProduct, from the AdventureWorksDW database. You can import any table you want. If you don't have access to SQL Server, you can import the \Source\ch07\DimProduct file and then follow similar steps to parameterize the query connection string.

2. In the Home ribbon's tab, click the Manage Parameters button.

3. In the Parameters window, click the New link and create a new parameter (see **Figure 7.22**).

    I've created a required parameter named *Server*. The parameter data type is Text. I've decided to choose the parameter value from a pre-defined list that includes two servers (ELITE and MILLENNIA). You can also type in the parameter value or load it from an existing query. The parameter will default to ELITE and the parameter current value is ELITE. Consequently, I'll be referencing the ELITE server in my queries.

4. Click OK to create the parameter.

Using query parameters

Now that we have the Server parameter defined, let's use it to change the data source in all queries. The following steps assume that you want to change the server name in all queries that reference the SQL Server. If you want to change only specific queries, instead of using Data Source Settings, change the Source step in the Applied Steps pane for these queries.

1. In the Home ribbon, click the Data Source Settings button.
2. In the Data Source Settings window, select the data source that references your server, and then click the Change Source button. If the data source is SQL Server, the familiar "SQL Server Database" window opens.
3. Expand the drop-down to the left of the server name and choose Parameter. Then expand the drop-down to the right and select the Server parameter (see **Figure 7.23**). Click OK.

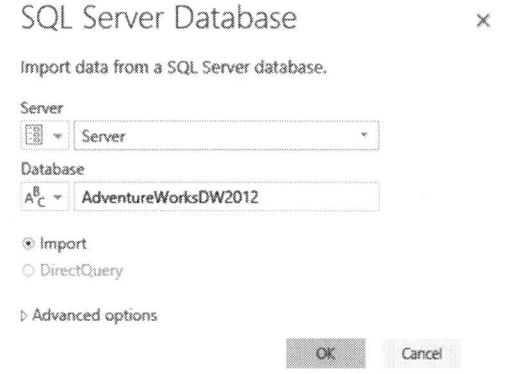

Figure 7.23 You can parameterize every query setting that has a drop-down.

4. In the Power Query Editor, observe that a new query named Server is added to the query list. By default, the query results won't be loaded in a table, but you can right-click the query and click Enable Load.

> **TIP** What makes query parameters even more useful is that you can reference the selected parameter value in DAX formulas, such as to show on the report which server is being used to load the data from. If you've enabled the loading of the Server query and have a Server table added to the model, you can use this DAX measure to show the server name:
> ServerName = "The current server is " & FIRSTNONBLANK('Server'[Server], TRUE)

5. Besides entering the parameter value in the Power Query Editor, you can do so directly in Power BI Desktop without having to open Query Editor. In the Power BI Desktop window (Home ribbon's tab), expand the Edit Queries tab and then click Edit Parameters. Notice that you can change the Server parameter.

> **NOTE** Unfortunately, Power BI doesn't expose the query parameters in reports. Therefore, there is no way for the end user viewing a report in Power BI Service or Power BI Report Server to set the query parameter, such as to pass a different value to a stored procedure with DirectQuery connection to SQL Server. You can change query parameters only in Power BI Desktop.

7.4 Staging Data with Dataflows

You've seen how Power Query can help you shape the data *inside* Power BI Desktop by applying transformations to the raw data as it moves from the source to the model. Wouldn't it be nice to have the same technology available *outside* the desktop for preparing and staging the data so it's available for everyone? Of course, it would! Dataflows (think of them as "Power BI in the Cloud") extend the Power BI Service capabilities to do just that. But before I delve into the dataflow technical details, let me explain the much broader vision that Microsoft has for dataflows as a part of the Common Data Model initiative.

7.4.1 Understanding the Common Data Model

Many years ago, I worked for a large provider of financial software products. All software apps we developed ingested the same data from our clients: Accounts, Customers, Balances. We were set to develop a common model for the financial industry with a standardized set of entities. Once the data was staged, it would be ready to be loaded by different apps. Besides standardization, the obvious advantage was reducing the data integration effort among apps. Because the data was staged in a predefined format, every app could just read it from the same place. The Microsoft Common Data Model has the same goal but on a much larger scale.

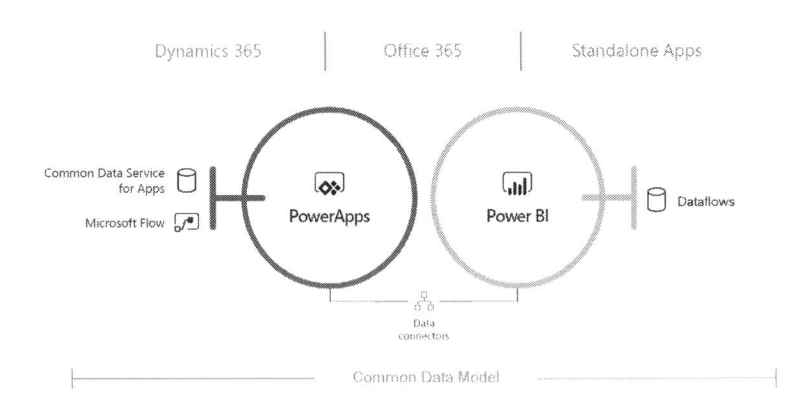

Figure 7.24 The Microsoft Business Application Platform includes Common Data Services for Apps and Dataflows with both layered on top of Common Data Model.

What's Microsoft Common Data Model (CDM)?
Recall from chapter 1, that Microsoft considers Power BI as a component of the Business Application Platform (see **Figure 7.24**), which also includes Microsoft Dynamics 365, PowerApps, and Flow. The Common Data Model is a specification that seeks to standardize common entities and how they relate to each other. Currently, CDM defines several core entities, such as Account, Activity, Organization, and entities for CRM, Sales, Service and Solutions domains. The entity schemas are based on the corresponding entities in Microsoft Dynamics and the experience Microsoft has harvested from implementing business apps under the Dynamics portfolio.

Microsoft has provided the CDM specification in the CDM repo on GitHub at https://aka.ms/cdmrepo. Once you're there, navigate to the CDM/schemaDocuments/core/applicationCommon/ folder if you want to examine the schemas of the available entities (described in JSON format), such as Account.cdm.json.

What does the Common Data Model mean for you?
At this point, not much and you don't have to use its entities for CDS-A or dataflows. However, Microsoft has a bold vision for standardizing the industry data. As part of the Open Data Initiative (http://bit.ly/opendatainitiative), Microsoft is working with other major vendors and partners to evolve CDM and to develop apps that are layered on top of CDM for delivering instant features and insights. For

example, if you use conformed CRM entities, such an app can work similarly to a Power BI service app and deploy predefined datasets, reports and apps to Power BI.

Personally, I'm somewhat skeptical about how well CDM can fulfill this vision, as I know from experience that creating a standard data model is not easy. Even in well-defined business segments, such as Finance or Insurance, every company does business in its own unique way, so achieving data standardization might remain an unattainable dream. I'd love to be proven wrong though.

7.4.2 Understanding Common Data Service for Apps

Glancing back at **Figure 7.24**, we see Common Data Service for Apps (CDS-A) layered on top of CDM CDS-A is designed to be used as a data repository for Microsoft PowerApps and Flow. For example, if a business user creates an app to automate something, instead of requesting IT to provision an Azure SQL Database (with all the hurdles surrounding the decision), the app can save and read data from CDS-A, which by the way is powered by Azure SQL Database. In fact, if you use Dynamics 365 your data is saved in CDS-A.

What's to like about CDS-A?
There is a lot to like about CDS-A. Let's start with pricing. Other vendors have similar repositories, but their offerings are very expensive. The CDS-A pricing is included in the PowerApps licensing model because PowerApps is the primary client for creating CDS-centric solutions. But CDS-A is more than just a data repository. It's a business application platform with a collection of data, business rules, processes, plugins and more. With CDS-A you can:

- Define and change entities, fields, relationships, and constraints – For example, you can define your own entity and how it relates to other entities, just like you can do with Microsoft Access.
- Business rules – For example, you can define a business rule that prepopulates Ship Date based on Order Date.
- Apply security – You can secure data to ensure that users can see it only if you grant them access. Role-based security allows you to control access to entities for different users within your organization.

Besides the original PowerApps canvas apps (like InfoPath forms), CDS-A also opens the possibility to create model-driven PowerApps apps (model-driven apps require a PowerApps P2 licensing plan). Model-driven apps are somewhat like creating Access data forms but more versatile. Because PowerApps knows CDS-A, you can create the app bottom-up, such as by starting with your data model and then generating the app based on the actual schema and data. For example, you can use PowerApps to build a model-driven app for implementing the workflow for approving a certain process.

Understanding CDS-A limitations
A potential downside is that Microsoft doesn't allow a direct access to the underlying Azure SQL Database of CDS-A. Back to the subject of this book, Power BI Desktop has a connector for importing data from CDS-A, such as to import data from Microsoft Dynamics 365. However, this connector uses the ODATA v4 Web API and it's slow.

To make things worse, the connector doesn't support query folding, so Power BI must download the entire dataset before Power Query applies any filters. Because the connector doesn't support REST filters and select predicates, so you can't filter data or select a subset of columns at the source. Microsoft is actively working on improving the connector performance and it should get better in time.

7.4.3 Understanding Dataflows

Back to **Figure 7.24**, we see that dataflows are another component of the Business Application Platform data architecture, side by side with CDS-A. Previously, this component was known as Common Data Services for Analytics but was renamed to *dataflows* to avoid similar names. We also see that unlike CDS-A, which is meant to be used for operational data (think of it as OLTP), dataflows are meant for data analytics and their main consumer is Power BI.

What's a dataflow?
Let's define a dataflow as a collection of Power Query queries that are scheduled and executed together. It's up to you how you group entities in dataflows. For example, if you need to stage some tables from Dynamics 365, you can create one dataflow that has a query for each table you want to stage. So, dataflows allow you to logically group related Power Query queries. This could be helpful for larger and more complex data integration projects.

> **NOTE** For the BI pros reading this book who are familiar with SSIS projects for ETL, think of a dataflow as a project and queries as SSIS packages. Just like you can deploy an SSIS project and schedule it to run at a specific time, you can schedule a dataflow, and this will execute all its queries.

When to use dataflows?
In general, you should use dataflows whenever you believe the data you collect and manage is valuable enough that it could be used by other models. Consider dataflows to address the following data integration and governance scenarios:

- Data staging – Many organizations implement operational data stores (ODS) and staging databases before the data is processed and loaded in a data warehouse. As a business user, you can use dataflows for a similar purpose. For example, one of our clients is a large insurance company that uses Microsoft Dynamics 365 for customer relationship management. Various data analysts create data models from the same CRM data, but they find that refreshing the CRM data is time consuming. Instead, they can create a dataflow to stage some CRM entities before importing them in Power BI Desktop. Even better, you could import the staged CRM data into a single dataset or in an organizational semantic model to avoid multiple data copies and duplicated business logic.

- Certified datasets – One way to improve data quality and promote better self-service BI is to prepare a set of certified common entities, such as Organization, Product, and Vendor. A data steward can be responsible for designing and managing these entities. Once in place, data analysts can import the certified entities in their data models.

- Data enrichment – As I mentioned, Power BI Premium lets you bring your own data lake storage. This opens interesting possibilities because now you have direct access to the staged data to use it both as an input to or output from other processes.

- Packaged insights – An independent software vendor can use dataflows to distribute packaged data preparation routines and reports to clients.

Understanding the dataflow architecture
The Power BI dataflow architecture consists of:

- Entities – The equivalent of a query in Power BI Desktop.
- Dataflow calculation engine (Power BI Premium) – A scalable cloud M engine that orchestrates and processes dataflows.
- Data storage – Unlike Power Query in Power BI Desktop which saves the query output in the model, a dataflow saves its output in the Microsoft Azure Data Lake Store (ADLS).

For example, **Figure 7.25** shows one dataflow hosted in a Power BI workspace which has two entities. Let's discuss these components in more detail.

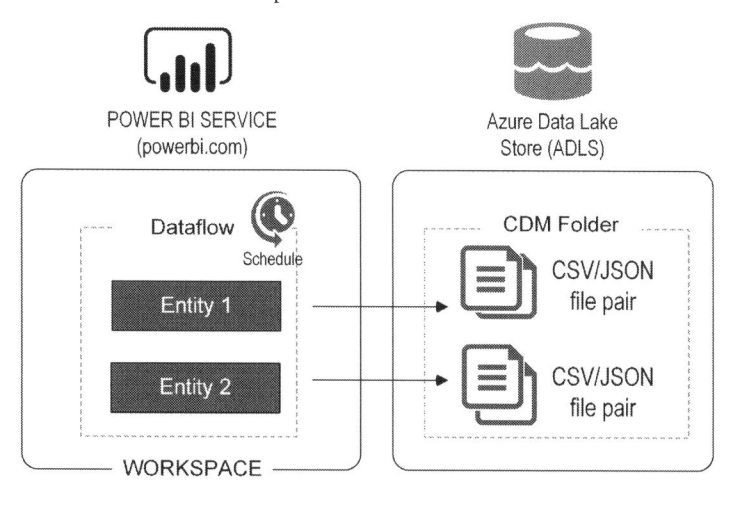

Figure 7.25 Hosted in a workspace, a dataflow consists of one or more entities that save data in Azure Data Lake Store.

Understanding entities

I defined a dataflow as a collection of Power Query queries. Now let's substitute the term "query" with "entity" to denote that the output of a dataflow is a data structure that you can import in Power BI Desktop, just like the output of a query in Power BI Desktop is a table in your data model. In fact, the dataflow user interface uses the terms "tables", "queries", and "entities" interchangeably. A dataflow entity has one and only one query described in M.

Like Power BI Desktop, the underlying query can have multiple transformation steps. Consider a CRM dataflow with an Account entity that stages an Account table from Dynamics Online. You can apply multiple steps to shape and transform the data, such as replacing values, unpivoting columns, deduplicating rows, and so on. Each step adds an M formula. The Account dataflow entity will include the entire query with all its steps. Like Power BI Desktop, you can view the entity M code in the Advanced Editor.

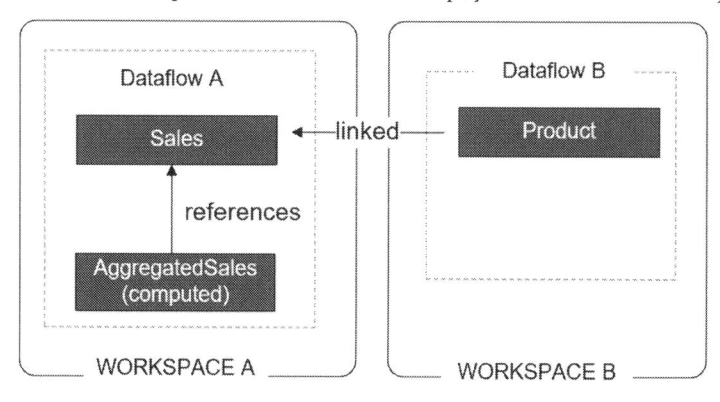

Figure 7.26 Dataflows can have computed and linked entities to create more complicated data preparation processes.

Power BI Premium brings more flexibility to dataflows by supporting two entity types:

- Computed entity – A computed entity is a reference to data that is already saved by another entity. For example, **Figure 7.26** shows that the AggregatedSales computed entity references the Sales entity in the same workflow, such as to aggregate its data like summary, average, or distinct count. You can also configure an entity not to load data, such as in the case when an entity appends other entities. In this case, you might not need to import the dependent entities, so you can disable their "Enable load" entity setting.

- Linked entity -- A linked entity is a special computed entity that references another entity residing in a different dataflow and even in a different workspace. In **Figure 7.25**, Dataflow A links to the Product entity in Dataflow B so that it can use its data. The linked entity is read-only, you cannot change it in the consuming dataflow (Dataflow A) but only in the source dataflow (Dataflow B). When creating a linked entity, Power BI first creates a link to the target entity and then creates a computed entity on top.

Computed entities are different than appending or merging queries in Power Query. The big difference is that Power BI Premium monitors the source entity for changes. If the source entity changes, Power BI Premium recomputes the computed entities so that the dataflow is always up to date with changes in the source systems. In addition, computed and linked entities let you chain dataflows to create more complicated data preparation and staging processes, such as to use the Product entity staged by one dataflow in another dataflow. Power BI Pro doesn't support computed and linked entities.

Understanding dataflow calculation engine
Currently, dataflows are executed by the M engine that's behind Power Query. In a Power BI Pro app workspace, the M engine refreshes entities within a dataflow sequentially with no guarantee regarding the order. However, Power BI Premium refreshes entities in parallel. The Power BI Premium calculation engine is more scalable. Because Power BI Pro doesn't support linked and computed entities, it uses the Power Query (M) engine which executes in a shared environment and it's not designed to scale.

You don't need to know much about what's executing your dataflows because the engine is a backend service that you can't manage or configure, at least not now. But to cover the essentials, the engine is responsible for orchestrating and processing dataflow entities. Specifically, it analyzes the M code of each entity, finds references to computed or linked entities (if any), and uses the information to build a dependency graph between the entities that might look like the Query Dependencies graph in the Power BI Desktop Query Editor. Using the dependency graph, the engine determines the order of execution and parallelism (entities can be processed in parallel). As I mentioned, the calculation engine is responsible for updating the dataflow when a referenced entity is refreshed.

The dataflow calculation engine also ensures data consistency. The dataflow either succeeds (when all entities are processed successfully) or fails (if one or more of its entities fail). The main conceptual difference between Power BI Pro and Power BI Premium is that in Premium, dataflows are refreshed within a "transaction" which maintains the consistency between all entities. This also applies to any linked entities within the same workspace.

Understanding dataflow storage
Where does a dataflow entity output its data? As you know by now, Power Query in Power BI Desktop saves the query output in the model. However, a dataflow saves its output in the Microsoft Azure Data Lake Store Gen2 (ADLS) although you can't directly access it. Azure Data Lake Store is a scalable cloud repository for storing data of any type (structured or unstructured). Specifically, each entity saves its output in a special Common Data Model (CDM) folder, which Microsoft has documented in the "Dataflows in Power BI" whitepaper at http://bit.ly/dataflowpaper. The data is saved in at least two files (see again **Figure 7.25**):

- A comma separated values (CSV) file that has the actual data. Microsoft settled on CSV because it's the most popular format and it's the fastest to load. The dataflow output is saved as one file if the corresponding entity is *not* configured for incremental refresh. An entity configured for incremental refresh will save its data to more CSV files (one per each partition).
- A file in a JSON format that defines the schema, such as the data type for each field.

Microsoft provides the data lake storage, but its quota counts towards the quota of the workspace that hosts the dataflow. For example, Power BI Pro limits the workspace storage to 10 GB, which includes all data including datasets and dataflow entities in that workspace. However, if your organization is on Power

BI Premium, you can bring your own data lake storage to replace the Microsoft storage. Besides allowing access the CDM folders and files directly, bringing your own storage opens interesting integration scenarios. For example, a data scientist can apply a machine learning algorithm after a dataflow stages the data.

> **NOTE** Currently, bringing your own storage is in preview and it's configurable under the "Dataflow settings (preview)" tab in the Power BI Admin Portal. Switching stores is done through a simple action, like moving workspaces to a dedicated (premium) capacity. Microsoft has also promised an SDK to help you create CDM folders through Azure programmatically. The SDK is not necessary (all the files are CSV and JSON, so you can create them without an SDK), but it can save you time and troubleshooting effort. In store are also tools to help you monitor and troubleshoot the dataflow execution.

The Microsoft vision behind dataflows is that data is valuable and can be used and reused in a variety of ways, both inside Power BI and outside it. The idea is that good data has life of its own outside of a specific BI model. Once created, it is expected that over its lifespan the data will be used in many ways, such as a feed to multiple models or combined with other data or enriched by other tools. To take the most out of dataflows, you'd need Power BI Premium and you must replace the Microsoft-provided storage with your own data lake so that you could have direct access to the staged data. Currently, the only way to consume the dataflow output with Power BI Pro is to use the "Power BI dataflows" connector in Power BI Desktop. This limits dataflow consumers to only Power BI Desktop.

Comparing features between editions
Table 7.1 shows the feature differences between Power BI Pro and Power BI Premium.

Table 7.1   Comparing dataflow features between Power BI Pro and Power BI Premium.

Feature	Power BI Pro	Power BI Premium
Storage quota	10 GB per workspace	100 TB across all capacities (P1 or higher)
Parallelism	Serial execution of entities	Parallel execution of entities whenever possible
Incremental refresh	No	Yes
Computed entities	No	Yes
Linked entities	No	Yes
Dataflow engine	M engine in shared capacity	Calculation engine in dedicated capacity
Refresh rates	Up to 8 times/day	Up to 48 times/day

Now that you know the dataflow concepts, let's create one. You'll need to sign in to Power BI Service (powerbi.com) with a Power BI Pro license. I'll explicitly state features that require Power BI Premium.

7.4.4   Working with Dataflows

Suppose that your company uses Salesforce for customer relationship management. Several data analysts import CRM data in personal data models. While doing this, they import the same data and apply the same transformations. They report performance issues with the Power BI Desktop Query Editor. Specifically, because they apply transformations on top of thousands of rows, they complain about long wait times for data previews to render. As a data steward, you'll address these challenges by creating a dataflow to stage the CRM data.

> **NOTE** The dataflow in this practice connects to Salesforce.com. If you don't have a Salesforce account but you want to follow along, start a free trial at https://www.salesforce.com/editions-pricing/sales-cloud/. When configuring the tenant, choose the option to populate it with sample data. You also need to be a member of a Power BI organizational workspace because dataflows are not available in My Workspace.

Getting started with dataflows
Follow these steps to create a dataflow with one entity that stages the Leads Salesforce entity:

1. Go to powerbi.com and sign in. Navigate to an organizational workspace. Make sure you have edit permissions to this workspace so that you can contribute content.
2. In the workspace content page, click the Create button in the top-right corner, and then select Dataflow.
3. In the "New dataflow" page, click the "Add new entities" button.
4. The "Choose data source" page shows all available Power Query connectors. Click "Salesforce objects".

> **TIP** As you will notice, currently only a subset of the Power Query connectors is available in dataflows, but Microsoft is working hard to bring the rest. Meanwhile, if you're missing a connector, you can use it in the Power BI Desktop and copy the M code behind the query in the Advanced Editor. Then, back to the dataflow, choose "Blank query" and paste the code. This might be a workaround for some data sources while waiting for Microsoft to port the connectors and provide user interface.

5. In the "Connect to a data source" page, sign in to Salesforce, and then click Next.

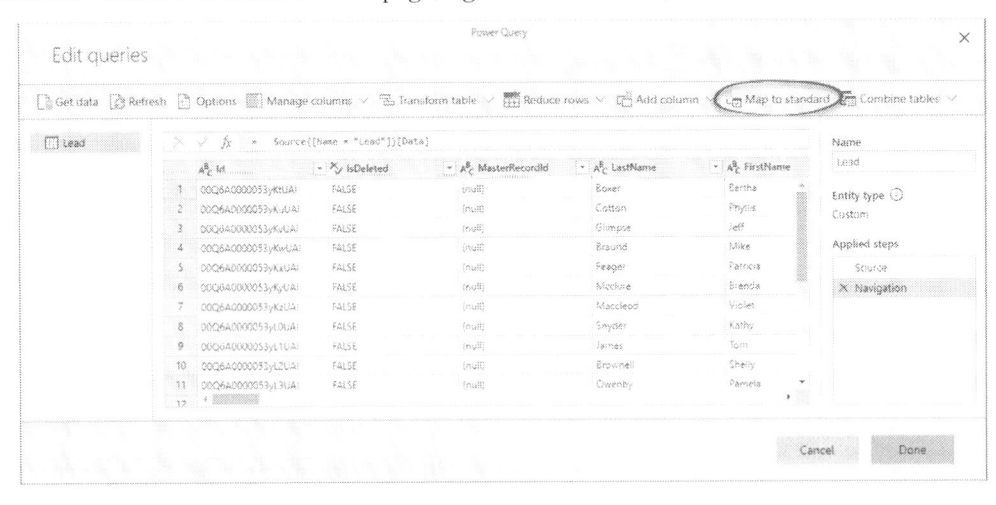

Figure 7.27 Use the "Edit queries" to apply transformations.

Creating an entity
Next, you'll create an entity to stages the Lead entity from Salesforce.

1. In the "Choose data" page, check the Lead entity and click Next.

    The "Edit queries" page should look familiar to you because it resembles the Power Query Editor in Power BI Desktop. This is where you apply transformation steps (only a subset is currently available). This is also where you can map the entity to a common data model entity by clicking the "Map to standard" button.

2. Click the "Map to standard" button to open the "Map to standard entity" window. Expand the "Entity type" drop-down and select the Lead CDM entity. Note that the "Field mapping" page allows you to map columns from your entity to the standard one. Click Cancel to ignore your changes.

> **TIP** Should you bother mapping your entity to a standard one if you can map only a few fields? For example, you won't be able to map many fields from the Salesforce Lead entity to the Lead standard entity, which is surprising given that both Salesforce and Dynamics are CRM systems! As I mentioned, we're yet to see the business value of the Common Data Model so for now you could just ignore it. Should one day CDM become irresistible, you can always change your entity and map it to a standard entity.

3. Back to the "Edit queries" page, let's practice a simple transformation. Click the "Manage columns" menu and then click "Choose columns". Unselect all columns and check only id, lastName, firstName, Name, State, Country, Email and Status. Click Done.

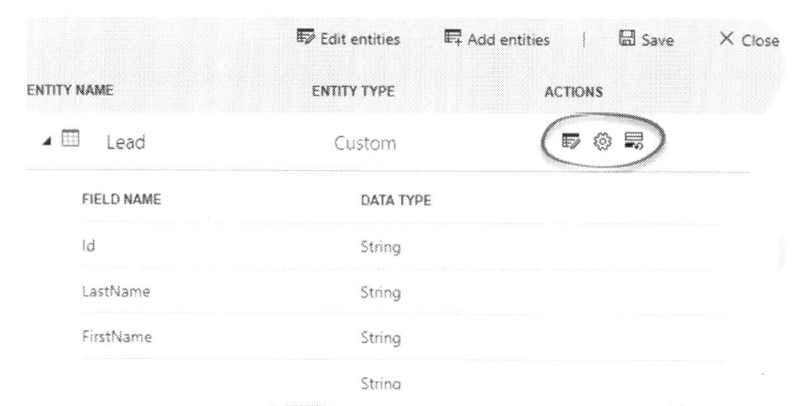

Figure 7.28 Use the dataflow page to see the list of entities.

4. Notice that the dataflow page lists the Lead entity. You can expand the Lead entity to see its fields and data types. The buttons next to the entity let you edit, set settings (Description is currently the only setting), and schedule the entity for incremental refresh.

> **NOTE** A larger entity (with millions of rows) can benefit from an incremental refresh. Like Power BI dataset incremental refresh (discussed in the next chapter), you configure an entity to refresh only a subset of rows. Incremental refresh (datasets and entities) is a Power BI Premium feature.

5. Click the Save button and name the dataflow "Salesforce staging". This should prompt you to refresh the entity which I'll discuss next.

Loading data

At this point the Lead entity is created but it's not loaded with data. Like datasets, you need to refresh the dataflow (manually or automated) to load entities with data. Refreshing a dataflow refreshes all its entities.

1. In the Power BI navigation bar, click the workspace to navigate to the workspace content page. Click the Dataflows tab. Notice that it lists the Salesforce Staging dataflow (see **Figure 7.29**).

2. Click the first icon (Refresh now) next to the dataflow name. Power BI runs the dataflow and populates the Lead entity with data. The Last Refreshed column updates to show the date and time the dataflow was most recently refreshed

Going quickly through the other task, the "Schedule refresh" allows you to set up an automated refresh. Note that like datasets, loading data from on-premises data sources requires a gateway. The Settings menu lets you edit the data flow, change its properties, see the refresh history, export the dataflow definition as a JSON file, and delete the dataflow.

> **TIP** The JSON file could be useful to automate importing dataflows using the dataflow REST APIs, such as to back up dataflows for disaster recovery. The dataflow APIs are documented at https://docs.microsoft.com/power-bi/service-dataflows-developer-resources. Currently, the UI doesn't support importing dataflows from JSON files.

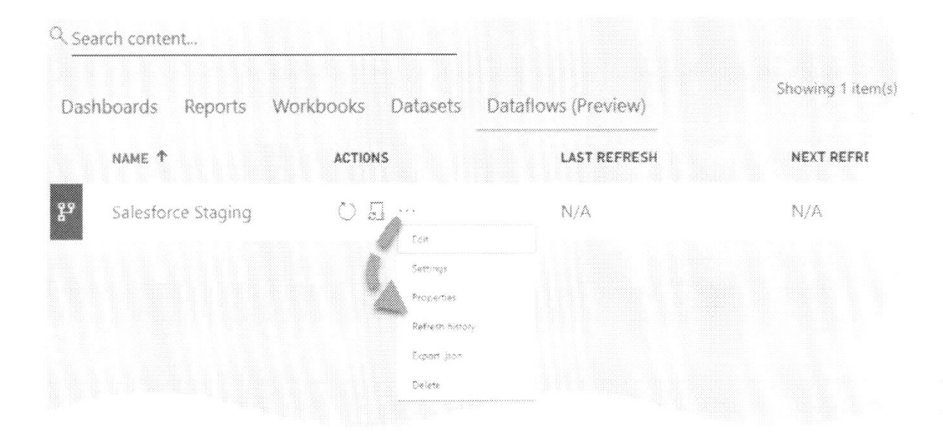

Figure 7.29 Use the Dataflows tab to manage the dataflows in the workspace.

Connecting to dataflows

Now that the Lead entity is staged, data analysts can use it. They should be delighted because performance will be faster, and the entity is managed and certified by the data steward.

1. Open Power BI Desktop. Make sure that the top-right corner shows your organizational account. If not, sign in to Power BI Service.
2. Click Get Data and choose the "Power BI dataflows" connector.
3. In the Navigator window, expand the Salesforce Staging dataflow and select the Lead entity.
4. Click Load to load its data or Edit to apply additional transformations.

Adding entities

Now that data analysts realize the business value of dataflows, they request you stage more entities.

1. In the Dataflows tab, click the Salesforce Staging dataflow.
2. In the dataflow content page, click Add Entity. Alternatively, click "Edit entity" next to the Lead entity to open the "Edit queries" page, and then click "Get data". Both approaches lead to the "Choose data source" page where you can select a connector for the next entity.

Currently, adding linked entities (a Power BI Premium feature) requires that both the source and target dataflow must be in an "improved" workspace. "Improved" workspaces are currently in preview (when creating a workspace, click "Try now" when you see the Preview Improved Workspaces message). Then follow these steps to add a linked entity:

3. In the dataflow content page, expand the "Add entities" drop-down and "Add linked entities". Or, click "Add entities" and then select the "Power BI dataflows" connector.
4. In the "Connect to data source" step, leave the "Organizational account" selected for authentication and click Next. If asked, authenticate to Power BI.
5. In the "Choose data" window (see **Figure 7.30**), navigate to the desired dataflow and entity, check it, and click Next.
6. In the "Edit queries" window, notice that the linked entity has a special icon and a message that informs you that it can't be modified.

Choose data

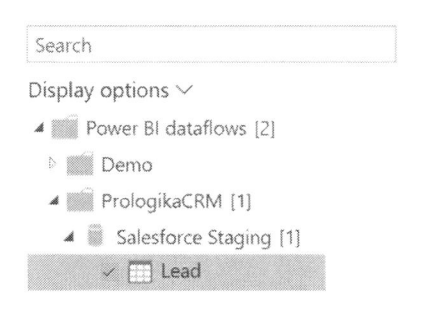

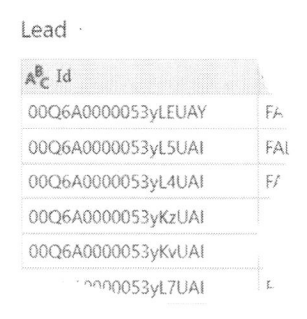

Figure 7.30 Power BI Premium supports linked entities that let you reference an entity from another dataflow.

7.5 Summary

Behind the scenes, when you import data, Power BI Desktop creates a query for every table you import or connect to with DirectQuery. Not only does the query give you access to the source data, but it also allows you to shape and transform data using various table and column-level transformations. To practice this, you applied a series of steps to shape and clean a crosstab Excel report so that its results can be used in a self-service data model.

You also practiced more advanced query features. You learned how to join, merge, and append datasets. Every step you apply to the query generates a line of code described in the M query language. You can view and customize the code to meet more advanced scenarios and automate repetitive tasks. You learned how to use query functions to automate importing files. And you saw how you can use custom query code to generate date tables if you can't import them from other places. You can also define query parameters to customize the query behavior.

Dataflows are to self-service BI as what ETL is to organizational BI. Use them to prepare and stage data before it's ingested in data models. A dataflow is a logic container of entities. Think of entity as "Power Query in the cloud". Power BI Premium lets you link entities to create more advanced dataflows.

Next, you'll learn how to extend and refine the model to make it more feature-rich and intuitive to end users!

Chapter 8

Refining the Model

8.1   Understanding Tables and Columns 203
8.2   Managing Schema and Data Changes 212
8.3   Relating Tables 219
8.4   Refining Metadata 232
8.5   Summary 236

In the previous two chapters, you learned how to import and transform data. The next step is to explore and refine your data model before you start gaining insights from it. Typical tasks in this phase include making table and field names more intuitive, exploring data, and changing the column type and formatting options. When your model has multiple tables, you must also set up relationships to join tables.

In this chapter, you'll practice common tasks to enhance the Adventure Works model. First, you'll learn how to explore the imported data and how to refine the metadata. Next, I'll show you how to do schema and data changes, including managing connections and tables, and refreshing the model data to synchronize it with changes in the data sources. I'll walk you through the steps needed to set up table relationships so that you can perform analysis across multiple tables. Lastly, you'll learn about some features that can help you refine the model metadata to make it more user friendly.

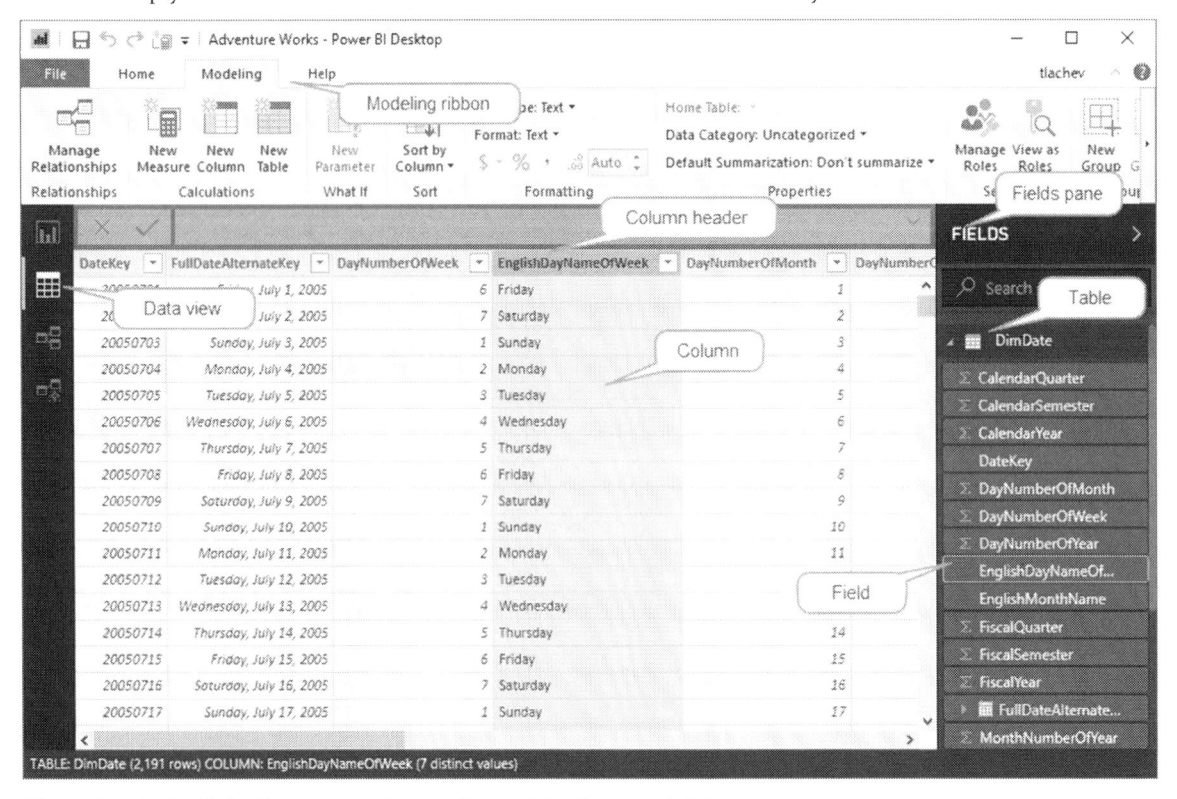

Figure 8.1   In the Data View, you can browse the model schema and data.

8.1 Understanding Tables and Columns

Recall from Chapter 6 that the most common connectivity options are importing data or connecting directly with DirectQuery. If you decide to import, Power BI stores imported data in tables. Although the data might originate from heterogeneous data sources, once it enters the model, it's treated the same regardless of its origin. Like a relational database, a table consists of columns and rows. You can use the Data View (only available for models that import data) to explore the table schema and data (see **Figure 8.1**).

8.1.1 Understanding the Data View

The Power BI Desktop navigation bar (the vertical bar on the left) has three view icons: Report, Data, and Relationships (the second Relationships view is currently in preview, but it will become the default one when it ships). As its name suggests, the Data View is for browsing the model data. In contrast, the Relationships View only shows a graphical representation of the model schema. And the Report View is for creating visualizations that help you analyze the data. In Chapter 6, I covered how the Data View shows the imported data from the tables in the model. This is different from the Power Query Editor data preview, which shows the source data and how it's affected by the transformations you've applied.

Understanding tables

The Fields pane shows you the model metadata that you interact with when creating reports. When you select a table in the Fields pane, the Data View shows you the first rows in the table. As it stands, the Adventure Works model has six tables. The Data View and the Fields pane shows the metadata (table names and column names) sorted alphabetically. You can also use the Search box in the Fields pane to find fields quickly, such as type in *sales* to filter all fields whose name include "sales".

> **NOTE** What's the difference between a column and a field anyway? A field in the Fields pane can be a table column or a calculated measure, such as SalesYTD. However, a calculated measure doesn't map to a table column. So, fields include both physical table columns and calculations.

The table name is significant because it's included in the model metadata, and it's shown to the end user. In addition, when you create calculated columns and measures, the Data Analysis Expressions (DAX) formulas reference the table and field names. Therefore, spend some time to choose suitable names and to rename tables and fields accordingly.

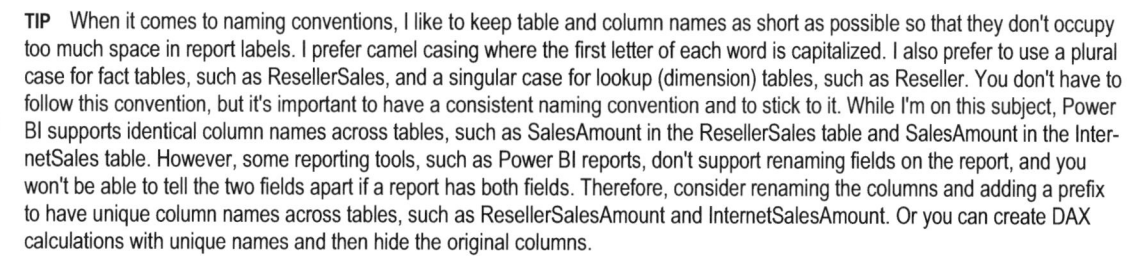

> **TIP** When it comes to naming conventions, I like to keep table and column names as short as possible so that they don't occupy too much space in report labels. I prefer camel casing where the first letter of each word is capitalized. I also prefer to use a plural case for fact tables, such as ResellerSales, and a singular case for lookup (dimension) tables, such as Reseller. You don't have to follow this convention, but it's important to have a consistent naming convention and to stick to it. While I'm on this subject, Power BI supports identical column names across tables, such as SalesAmount in the ResellerSales table and SalesAmount in the InternetSales table. However, some reporting tools, such as Power BI reports, don't support renaming fields on the report, and you won't be able to tell the two fields apart if a report has both fields. Therefore, consider renaming the columns and adding a prefix to have unique column names across tables, such as ResellerSalesAmount and InternetSalesAmount. Or you can create DAX calculations with unique names and then hide the original columns.

The status bar at the bottom of the Data View shows the number of rows in the selected table. When you select a field, the status bar also shows the number of its distinct values. For example, the EnglishDayNameOfWeek field has seven distinct values. This is useful to know because that's how many values the users will see when they add this field to the report.

Understanding columns

The vertical bands in the table shown in the Data View represent the table columns. You can click any cell to select the entire column and to highlight the column header. The Formatting group in the ribbon's

Modeling tab shows the data type of the selected column. Like the Power Query Editor data preview, Data View is read-only. You can't change the data – not even a single cell. Therefore, if you need to change a value, such as when you find a data error that requires a correction, you must make the changes either in the data source or in the query. I encourage you to make data transformations, such as replacing values, in the query (that's what it is for).

Another way to select a column is to click it in the Fields pane. The Fields pane prefixes some fields with icons. For example, the sigma (Σ) icon signifies that the field is numeric and can be aggregated using any of the supported aggregate functions, such as Sum or Average. If the field is a calculated measure, it'll be prefixed with a calculator icon (▣). Even though some fields are numeric, they can't be meaningfully aggregated, such as CalendarYear. The Properties group in the ribbon's Modeling tab allows you to change the default aggregation behavior, such as to change the CalendarYear default aggregation to "Do not aggregate". This is just a default; you and other users can still overwrite the aggregation type on reports.

The Data Category property in the Properties group (ribbon's Modeling tab) allows you to change the column category. For example, to help Power BI understand that this is a geospatial field, you can change the data category of the SalesTerritoryCountry column to Country/Region. This will prefix the field with a globe icon. More importantly, this helps Power BI to choose the best visualization when you add the field on an empty report, such as to use a map visualization when you add a geospatial field. Or, if a column includes hyperlinks and you would like the user to be able to navigate by clicking the link, set the column's data category to Web URL.

8.1.2 Exploring Data

If there were data modeling commandments, the first one would be "Know thy data". Realizing the common need to explore the raw data, the Power BI team has added features to both the Power Query Editor and Data View to help you become familiar with the source data.

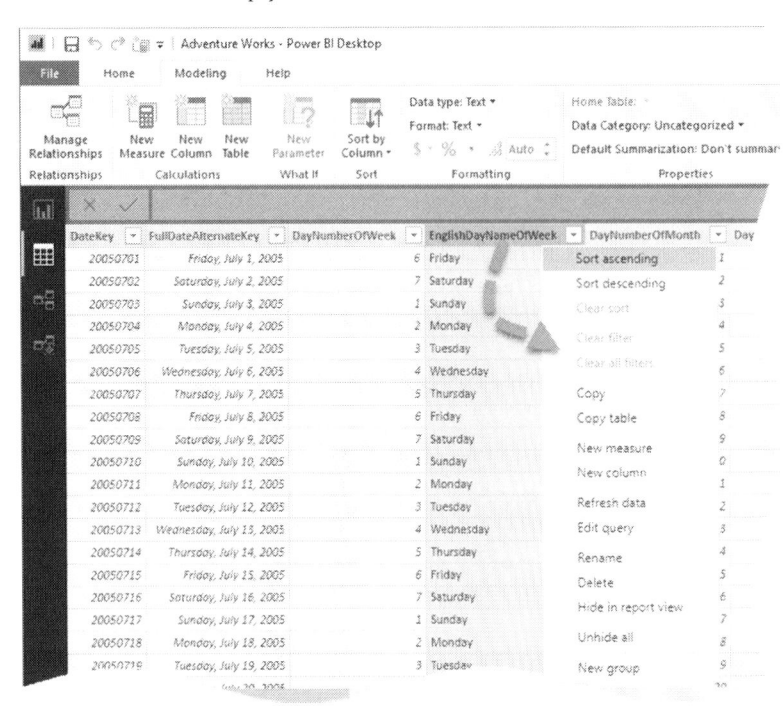

Figure 8.2 You can sort the field content in ascending or descending order.

Sorting data

Power BI doesn't sort data by default. As a result, Data View shows the imported data as it's loaded from the source. You can right-click a column and use the sort options (see **Figure 8.2**) to sort the data. You can sort the content of a table column in an ascending or descending order. This type of sorting is for your benefit, because it allows you to get familiar with the imported data, such as to find what's the minimum or maximum value. Power BI doesn't apply the sorting changes to the way the data is saved in the model, nor does it propagate the column sort to reports. For example, you might sort the EnglishDayNameOfWeek column in a descending order. However, when you create a report that uses this field, the visualization would ignore the Data View sorting changes and it will sort days in an ascending order (or whatever sort order the reporting tool prefers).

When a column is sorted in the Data View, you'll see an up or down arrow in the column header, which indicates the sort order. You can sort the table data by only one column at a time. To clear sorting and to revert to the data source sort order, right-click a column, and then click Clear Sort.

> **NOTE** Power BI Desktop automatically inherits the data collation based on the language selection in your Windows regional settings, which you can overwrite in the Options and Settings ⇨ Option ⇨ Data Load (Current File section). The default collations are case-insensitive. Consequently, if you have a source column with the values "John" and "JOHn", then Power BI Desktop imports both values as "John" and treats them the same. While this behavior helps the xVelocity storage engine compress data efficiently, sometimes a case-sensitive collation might be preferable, such as when you need a unique key to set up a relationship, and you get an error that the column contains duplicate values. However, currently there isn't an easy way to change the collation and configure a given field or a table to be case-sensitive. So, you'll need to try to keep the column names distinct.

Custom sorting

Certain columns must be sorted in a specific order on reports. For example, calendar months should be sorted in their ordinal position (Jan, Feb, and so on) as opposed to alphabetically. This is where custom sorting can help. Custom sorting allows you to sort a column by another column, assuming the column to sort on has one-to-one or one-to-many cardinality with the sorted column.

Let's say you have a column MonthName with values Jan, Feb, Mar, and so on, and you have another column MonthNumberOfYear that stores the ordinal number of the month in the range from 1 to 12. Because every value in the MonthName column has only one corresponding value in MonthNumberOfYear column, you can sort MonthName by MonthNumberOfYear. However, you can't sort MonthName by a Date column because there are multiple dates for each month.

Compared to field sorting for data expiration, custom sorting has a reverse effect on data. Custom sorting doesn't change the way the data is displayed in the Data View, but it affects how the data is presented in reports. **Figure 8.3** shows how changing custom sorting will affect the sort order of the month name column on a report.

EnglishMonthName	EnglishMonthName
April	January
August	February
December	March
February	April
January	May
July	June
June	July
March	August
May	September
November	October
October	November
September	December

Figure 8.3 The left table shows the month with the default alphabetical sort order while the right table shows it after custom sorting was applied by MonthNumberOfYear.

REFINING THE MODEL

Filtering data

You can also filter data in the Data View by using the drop-down in the column header. For example, you might need to explore a specific row(s) in more detail. You could expand the column drop-down and apply a filter just like you can do in an Excel table. The available filter options depend on the column data type. For example, you have date-specific filters to date columns, such as before or after a specific date.

Like sorting, filtering data doesn't affect the data shown in reports. You might filter the FactResellerSales table in Data View to show only one row, but reports will still show or aggregate all the rows. You can click "Clear filter" in the column context menu to remove a filter from the selected column or "Clear all filters" to remove all filters applied to a table.

Copying data

Sometimes you might want to copy the content of a column (or even an entire table) and paste it in Excel or send it to someone. You can use the Copy and Copy Table options from the context menu (see **Figure 8.2** again) to copy the content to Windows Clipboard and paste it in another application. You can't paste the copied data into the data model. Again, that's because the data model is read-only. The Copy Table option is also available when you right-click a table in the Fields pane. Copying a table preserves the tabular format, so pasting it in Excel produces a list instead of a single column.

Understanding additional column tasks

Going quickly through the rests of the column tasks in the context menu, "New measure" and "New column" are for creating DAX measures and calculated columns respectively. "Refresh data" reimports the data in the table. "Edit query" opens the Power Query Editor so you can apply transformations. "Rename" puts the column header in Edit mode so you can rename the column. "Delete" removes the column from the data model.

"Hide in report view" for hiding the column when creating reports, such as a system column that's not useful for reporting. "Unhide all" makes all hidden columns visible. And "New group" is for creating custom groups (also called bins or buckets), such as to group southern states in a "South Region". I'll revisit some of these tasks and provide more details in the relevant sections that follow.

8.1.3 Understanding the Column Data Types

A table column has a data type associated with it. When Power Query connects to the data source, it attempts to infer the column data type from the data provider and then maps it to one of the data types it supports. Although it seems redundant to have data types in two places (Power Query and data model), it gives you more flexibility. For example, you can keep the source data type in the query but change it in the model.

Currently, there isn't an exact one-to-one mapping between query and storage data types. Instead, Power BI Desktop maps the query column types to the ones that the xVelocity storage engine supports. **Table 8.1** shows these mappings. Power Query supports a couple of more data types (Date/Time/Timezone and Duration) than table columns.

Table 8.1 This table shows how query data types map to column data types.

Query Data Type	Storage Data Type	Description
Text	String	A Unicode character string with a max length of 268,435,456 characters
Decimal Number	Decimal Number	A 64 bit (eight-bytes) real number with decimal places
Fixed Decimal Number	Fixed Decimal Number	A decimal number with four decimal places of fixed precision useful for storing currencies.

Query Data Type	Storage Data Type	Description
Whole Number	Whole number	A 64-bit (eight-bytes) integer with no decimal places
Percentage	Fixed Decimal Number	A 2-digit precision decimal number
Date/Time	Date/Time	Dates and times after March 1st, 1900
Date	Date	Just the date portion of a date
Time	Time	Just the time portion of a date
Date/Time/Timezone	Date	Universal date and time
Duration	Text	Time duration, such as 5:30 for five minutes and 30 seconds
TRUE/FALSE	Boolean	True or False value
Binary	Binary data type	Blob, such as file content (supported in Query Editor but not in the data model)

How data types get assigned

The storage data type has preference over the source data type. For example, the query might infer a column date type as Decimal Number from the data provider, and this type might get carried over to storage. However, you can overwrite the column data type in the Data View to Whole Number. Unless you change the data type in the query and apply the changes, the column data type remains Whole Number.

The storage engine tries to use the most compact data type, depending on the column values. For example, the query might have assigned a Fixed Decimal Number data type to a column that has only whole numbers. Don't be surprised if the Data View shows the column data type as Whole Number after you import the data. Power BI might also perform a widening data conversion on import if it doesn't support certain numeric data types. For example, if the underlying SQL Server data type is tinyint (one byte), Power BI will map it to Whole Number because that's the only data type that it supports for whole numbers.

Power BI won't import data types it doesn't recognize and won't import the corresponding columns. For example, Power BI won't import a SQL Server column of a geography data type that stores spatial data. If the data source doesn't provide schema information, Power BI imports data as text and uses the Text data type for all the columns. In such cases, you should overwrite the data types after import when it makes sense.

Changing the column data type

As I mentioned, the Formatting group in ribbon's Modeling tab and the Transform group in the Power Query Editor indicate the data type of the selected column. You should review and change the column type when needed, for the following reasons:

- Data aggregation – You can sum or average only numeric columns.
- Data validation – Suppose you're given a text file with a SalesAmount column that's supposed to store decimal data. What happens if an 'NA' value sneaks into one or more cells? The query will detect it and might change the column type to Text. You can examine the data type after import and detect such issues. As I mentioned in the previous chapter, I recommend you address such issues in the Power Query Editor because it has the capabilities to remove errors or replace values. Of course, it's best to fix such issues at the data source, but probably you won't have this security permission.

NOTE What happens if all is well with the initial import, but a data type violation occurs the next month when you are given a new extract? What really happens in the case of a data type mismatch depends on the underlying data provider. The text data provider (Microsoft ACE OLE DB provider in this case) replaces the mismatched data values with blank values, and the blank values will be imported in the model. On the query side of things, if data mismatch occurs, you'll see "Error" in the corresponding cell to notify you about dirty data, but no error will be triggered on refresh.

- Better performance – Smaller data types have more efficient storage and query performance. For example, a whole number is more efficient than text because it occupies only eight bytes irrespective of the number of digits.

Sometimes, you might want to overwrite the column data type in the Data View. You can do so by expanding the Data Type drop-down list in the Formatting ribbon group and then select another type. Power BI Desktop only shows the list of the data types that are applicable for conversion. For example, if the original data type is Currency, you can convert the data type to Text, Decimal Number, and Whole Number. If the column is of a Text data type, the Data Type drop-down list would show all the data types. However, you'll get a type mismatch error if the conversion fails, such as when trying to convert a non-numeric text value to a number.

Understanding column formatting
Each column in the Data View has a default format based on its data type and Windows regional settings. For example, my default format for Date columns is MM/dd/yyyy hh:mm:ss tt because my computer is configured for English US regional settings (such as 12/24/2011 13:55:20 PM). This might present an issue for international users. However, they can overwrite the language from the Power BI Desktop's File ⇨ "Options and settings" ⇨ Options ⇨ Regional Settings (Current File section) menu to see the data formatted in their culture.

Use the Formatting group in the ribbon's Modeling tab to overwrite the default column format settings, as shown in **Figure 8.4**. Unlike changing the column data type, which changes the underlying data storage, changing column formatting has no effect on how data is stored because the column format is for visualization purposes only. As a best practice, format numeric and date columns that will be used on reports using the Formatting group in the ribbon's Modeling tab. If you do this, all reports will inherit these formats and you won't have to apply format changes to reports.

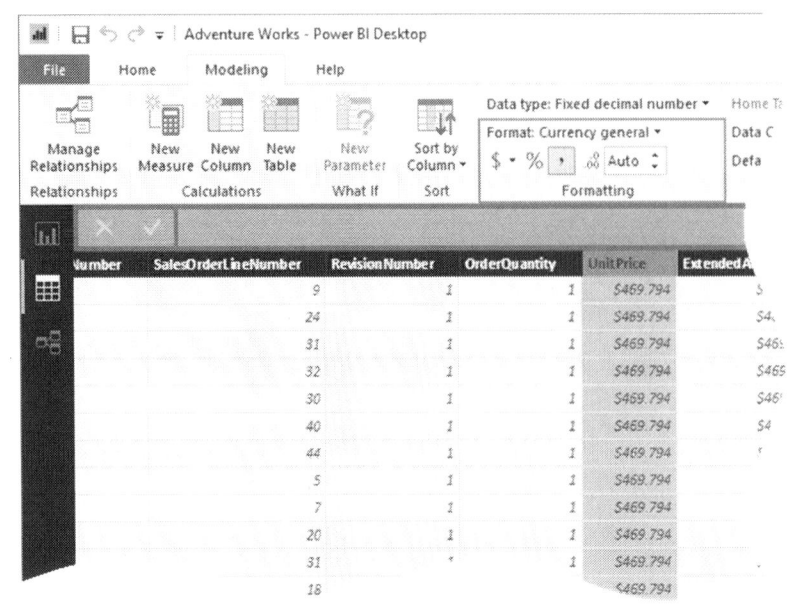

Figure 8.4 Use the Formatting ribbon group to change the column format.

CHAPTER 8

You can use the format buttons in the Formatting ribbon group to apply changes interactively, such as to add a thousand separator or to increase the number of decimal places. Formatting changes apply automatically to reports the next time you switch to the Report View. If the column width is too narrow to show the formatted values in Data View, you can increase the column width by dragging the right column border. Changing the column width in Data View has no effect on reports.

8.1.4 Understanding Column Operations

You can perform various column-related tasks to explore data and improve the metadata visual appearance, including renaming columns, removing columns, and hiding columns.

Renaming columns
Table columns inherit their names from the underlying query that inherits them in turn from the data source. These names might be somewhat cryptic, such as TRANS_AMT. The column name becomes a part of the model metadata that you and the end users interact with. You can make the column name more descriptive and intuitive by renaming the column. You can rename a column interchangeably in three places: Data View, Query Editor, and Fields pane. For example, if you rename a column in the Data View and then switch to the Power Query Editor, you'll see that Power BI Desktop has automatically appended a Rename Column transformation step to apply the change to the query.

> **NOTE** No matter where you rename the column, the Power BI "smart rename" applies throughout all the column references, including calculations and reports to avoid broken references. You can see the original name of the column in the data source by inspecting the Rename Column step in the Power Query Editor formula bar or by looking at the query source.

To rename a column in the Data View, double-click the column header to enter edit mode, and then type in the new name. Or, right-click the column, and then click Rename Column (see **Figure 8.2** again). To rename a column in the Fields pane (in the Data and Report Views), right-click the column and click Rename (or double-click the column).

Removing and hiding columns
In Chapter 6, I advised you to not import a column that you don't need in the model. However, if this ever happens, you can always remove a column in the Data View, Power Query Editor, and Fields pane. I also recommended you use the Choose Columns transformation in Power Query Editor as a more intuitive way to remove and add columns. If the column participates in a relationship with another table in the data model, removing the column removes the associated relationship(s).

Suppose you need the column in the model, but you don't want to show it to end users. For example, you might need a primary key column or foreign key column to set up a relationship. Since such columns usually contain system values, you might want to exclude them from showing up in the Fields pane by simply hiding them. The difference between removing and hiding a column is that hiding a column allows you to use the column in the model, such as in hierarchies or custom sorting, and in DAX formulas.

To hide a column in Data View, right-click any column cell and then click "Hide in Report View". A hidden column appears grayed out in Data View. You can also hide a column in the Fields pane by right-clicking the column and clicking Hide. If you change your mind later, you can unhide the column by toggling "Hide in Report View" (see **Figure 8.5**). Or, you can click Unhide All to unhide all the hidden columns in the selected table. Unfortunately, Power BI Desktop doesn't currently support selecting multiple columns, so you must apply column tasks, such as renaming or hiding, to one column at the time.

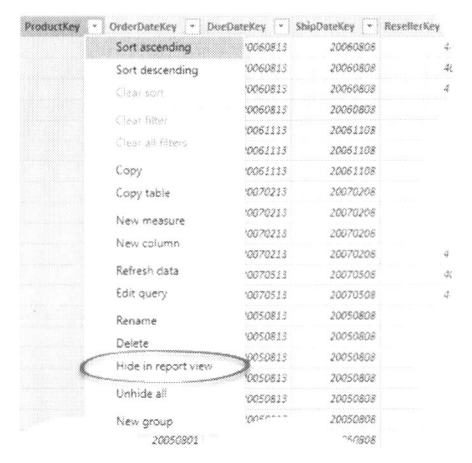

Figure 8.5 Toggle the "Hide in Report View" menu to hide or unhide a column.

8.1.5 Working with Tables and Columns

Now that you're familiar with tables and columns, let's turn our attention again to the Adventure Works model and spend some time exploring and refining it. The following steps will help you get familiar with the common tasks you'll use when working with tables and columns.

> **NOTE** I recommend you keep on working and enhancing your version of the Adventure Works model. However, if you haven't completed the Chapter 6 exercises, you can use the Adventure Works file from the \Source\Ch06 folder. However, remember that my samples import data from several local data sources, including the Adventure Works cube and the Product Catalog report. If you decide to refresh the data, you need to update all the data sources to reflect your specific setup. To do so, open the Power Query Editor, and then click the Data Source Settings button in the ribbon's Home tab and click the Change Source button for each data source. Or, double-click the Source step in the Applied Steps section (Query Settings pane) for each data source that fails to refresh. Then, change the server name and database name as needed.

Sorting data

You can gain insights into your imported data by sorting and filtering it. Suppose that you want to find which employees have been with the company the longest:

1. In Power BI Desktop, open the Adventure Works.pbix file that you worked on in Chapter 6.
2. Click Data View in the navigation bar. Click the Employees table in the Fields pane to see its data in Data View.
3. Right-click the HireDate column, and then click Sort Ascending. Note that Guy Gilbert is the first person on the list, and he was hired on 7/31/1998.
4. Right-click the HireDate column again, and then click the Clear Sort menu to remove the sort and to revert to the original order in which data was imported from the data source.

Implementing a custom sort

Next, you'll sort the EnglishMonthName column by the MonthNumberOfYear column so that months are sorted in their ordinal position on reports.

1. In the Fields pane, click the DimDate table to select it.
2. Click a cell in the EnglishMonthName column to select this column.
3. In the ribbon's Modeling tab, click the "Sort by Column" button, and then select MonthNumberOfYear.

4. (Optional) Switch to the Report View. In the Fields pane, check the EnglishMonthName column. This creates a Table visualization that shows months. The months should be sorted in their ordinal position.

Renaming tables

The name of the table is included in the metadata that you'll see when you create reports. Therefore, it's important to have a naming convention for tables. In this case, I'll use a plural naming convention for fact tables (tables that keep a historical record of business transactions, such as ResellerSales), and a singular naming convention for lookup tables.

1. Double-click the DimDate table in the Fields pane (or right-click the DimDate table and then click Rename) and rename it to *Date*. You can rename tables and fields in any of the three views (Report, Data, and Relationships).
2. To practice another way for renaming a table, click the Edit Queries button to open the Power Query Editor. In the Queries pane, select the Employees query. In the Query Settings pane, rename the query to *Employee*. Click the "Apply & Close" button to return to the Data View.
3. Rename the rest of the tables using the Fields pane. Rename FactResellerSales to *ResellerSales*, Products to *Product*, Resellers to *Reseller*, and SalesTerritories to *SalesTerritory*.

Working with columns

Next, let's revisit each table and make column changes as necessary.

1. In the Fields pane (in the Data View), select the Date table. Double-click the column header of the FullDateAlternateKey column, and then rename it to *Date*. In the data preview pane, increase the Date column width by dragging the column's right border so it's wide enough to accommodate the content in the column. Rename the EnglishDayNameOfWeek column to *DayNameOfWeek* and EnglishMonthName to *MonthName*. Right-click the DateKey column and click "Hide in Report View" to hide this column.
2. You can also rename and hide columns in the Fields pane. In the Fields pane, expand the Employee table. Right-click the EmployeeKey column and then click "Hide in Report View". Also hide the ParentEmployeeKey and SalesTerritoryKey columns. Using the Data View or Fields pane, delete the columns EmployeeNationalIDAlternateKey and ParentEmployeeNationalIDAlternateKey because they're sensitive columns that probably shouldn't be available for end-user analysis.
3. Click the Product table. If you've imported the Product table from the Product Catalog report, rename the ProdCat2 column to *ProductCategory*. Increase the column width to accommodate the content. Rename ProdSubCat column to *ProductSubcategory*, ProdModel to *ProductModel*, and ProdName to *ProductName*. Hide the ProductKey column. Using the ribbon's Modeling tab (Data View), reformat the StandardCost and ListPrice columns as Currency. To do so, expand the Format drop-down and select Currency ⇨ $ English (United States). Hide the ProductKey column.
4. Select the Reseller table. Hide the ResellerKey and GeographyKey columns. Rename the ResellerAlternateKey column to *ResellerID*.
5. Select the ResellerSales table. The first nine foreign key columns (with the "Key" suffix) are useful for data relationships but not for data analysis. Hide them.
6. To practice formatting columns again, change the format of the SalesAmount column to two decimal places. To do so, select the column in the Data View (or in the Fields pane), and then enter 2 in the Decimal Places field in the Formatting group on the ribbon's Modeling tab. Press Enter.
7. Select the SalesTerritory table in the Fields pane. Hide the SalesTerritoryKey column. If you have imported the SalesTerritory table from the cube, rename the SalesAmount column to Revenue and format the Revenue column as Currency ⇨ $ English (United States).
8. Press Ctrl-S (or click File ⇨ Save) to save the Adventure Works data model.

8.2 Managing Schema and Data Changes

To review, once Power BI Desktop imports data, it saves a copy of the data in a local file with a *.pbix file extension. The model schema and data are *not* automatically synchronized with changes in the data sources. Typically, after the initial load, you'll need to refresh the model data on a regular basis, such as when you receive a new source file or when the data in the source database is updated. Power BI Desktop provides features to keep your model up to date.

8.2.1 Managing Data Sources

It's not uncommon for a model to have several tables connected to different data sources so that you can integrate data from multiple places. As a modeler, you need to understand how to manage connections and tables, such as to rebind a table to another server when you move from test to production.

Managing data source settings
Suppose you need to import additional tables from a data source that you've already set up a connection to. One option is to use Get Data again. If, you connect to the same server and database, Power BI Desktop will reuse the same data source definition. To see and manage all data sources defined in the current file, expand the Edit Queries button in the ribbon's Home table and then click "Data Source Settings". For example, if the server or security credentials change, you can use the "Data Source Settings" window (see **Figure 8.6**) to update the connection. Recall that you can also open the Data Source Settings window from File ⇨ "Options and settings" ⇨ "Data source settings".

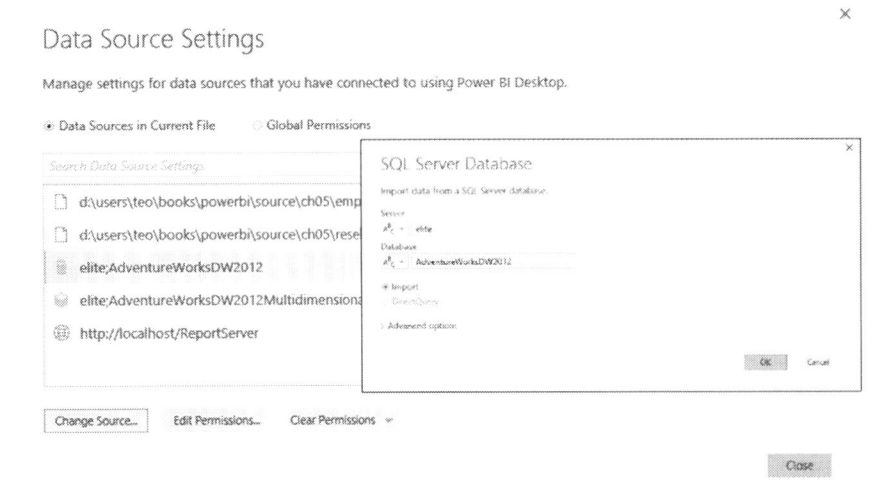

Figure 8.6 Use the "Data Source Settings" window to view and manage data sources used in the current Power BI Desktop file.

For data sources in the current file, you can select a data source and click the Change Source button to change the server, database, and advanced options, such as a custom SQL statement (the SQL Statement is disabled if you didn't specify a custom query in the Get Data steps). As you can see in **Figure 8.6**, there are drop-downs in front of the server and database fields. Recall from Chapter 7, that you can further simplify data source maintenance by using query parameters instead of typing in names.

Managing sensitive information
Power BI Desktop encrypts the connection credentials and stores them in the local AppData folder on your computer. Use the Edit Permissions button to change credentials (see **Figure 8.7**), such as to switch from Windows to standard security (username and password) or encryption options if the data source supports encryptions.

For security reasons, Power BI Desktop allows you to delete cached credentials by using the Clear Permissions button which supports two options. The first (Clear Permissions) option deletes the cached credentials of the selected data source. For local data sources, this option removes the credentials and privacy settings. For non-local data sources, this option does the same but also removes the data source from the Global Permissions list. The second option (Clear All Permissions) deletes the cached credentials for all data sources in the current file (if the Data Sources in Current File option is selected), or all data sources used by Power BI Desktop (if the Global Permissions option is selected).

Figure 8.7 Use the "Edit Permissions" window to change the data source credentials and privacy options.

Although deleting credentials might sound dangerous, nothing really gets broken and models are not affected. However, the next time you refresh the data, you'll be asked to specify credentials and encryption options as you did the first time you used Get Data to connect to that data source.

Finally, if you used custom SQL Statements (native database queries) to import data, another security feature allows you to revoke their approval. This could be useful if you have imported some data using a custom statement, such as a stored procedure, but you want to prevent other people from executing the query if you intend to share the file with someone else.

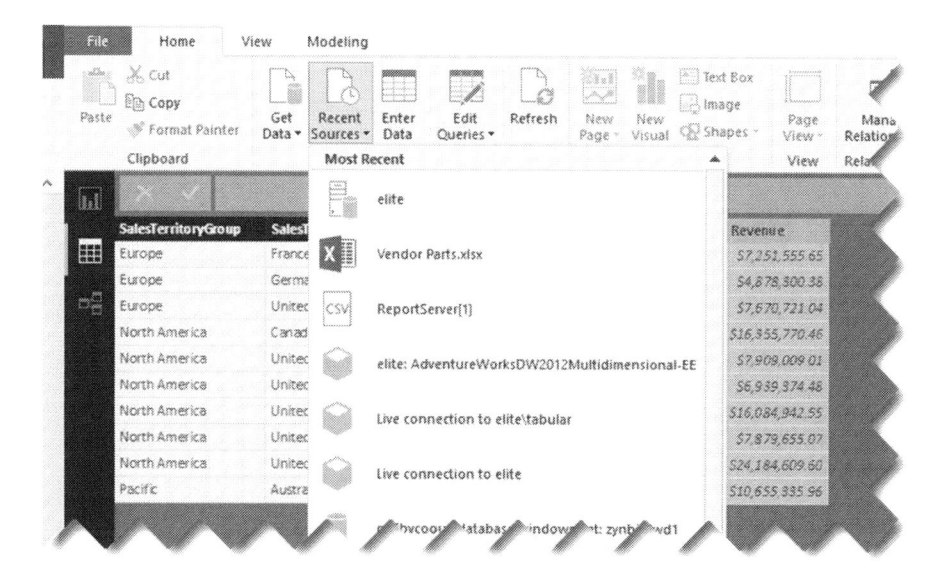

Figure 8.8 Use the Recent Data Sources window to manage the data source credentials and encryption options in one place.

REFINING THE MODEL

Using recent data sources

If you need more tables from the same database, instead of going through the Get Data steps and typing in the server name and database, there is a shortcut: use the Recent Sources button in the ribbon's Home tab (see **Figure 8.8**).

If you connect to a data source that has multiple entities, such as a relational database, when you click the data source in Recent Sources, Power BI Desktop will bring you straight to the Navigator window so that you can select and import another table.

Importing additional tables

Besides wholesale data, the Adventure Works data warehouse stores retail data for direct sales to individual customers. Suppose that you want to extend the Adventure Works model to analyze direct sales to customers who placed orders on the Internet.

> **NOTE** Other self-service tools on the market restrict you to analyzing single datasets only. If that's all you need, feel free to skip this exercise as the model has enough tables and complexity already. However, chances are that you might need to analyze data from different subject areas side by side. This requires you to import multiple fact tables and join them to common dimensions. And this is where Power BI excels because it allows you to implement self-service models whose features are on a par with professional models. I encourage you to stay with me as the complexity cranks up and learn these features, so you never say "I can't meet this requirement".

Follow these steps to import three additional tables:

1. In the ribbon's Home tab, expand the Recent Sources button, and then click the SQL Server instance that hosts the AdventureWorksDW database. Or, use Get Data to connect to it.

> **NOTE** If you don't have a SQL Server with AdventureWorksDW, I provide the data in the DimCustomer.csv, DimGeography.csv and FactInternetSales.csv files in the \Source\ch08 folder. Import them using the CSV or TEXT option in Get Data.

2. In the Navigator window, expand the AdventureWorksDW database, and then check the DimCustomer, DimGeorgraphy, and FactInternetSales tables. In the AdventureWorksDW database, the DimGeography table isn't related directly to the FactInternetSales table. Instead, DimGeography joins DimCustomer, which joins FactInternetSales. This is an example of a snowflake schema, which I covered in Chapter 6.

3. Click the Edit button. In the Queries pane of the Power Query Editor, select DimCustomer and change the query name to *Customer*.

4. In the Queries pane, select DimGeography and change the query name to *Geography*.

5. Select the FactInternetSales query and change its name to InternetSales. Use the Choose Columns transformation to exclude the RevisionNumber, CarrierTrackingNumber, and CustomerPONumber columns.

6. Click "Close & Apply" to add the three tables to the Adventure Works model and to import the new data.

7. In the Data View, select the Customer table. Hide the CustomerKey and GeographyKey columns. Rename the CustomerAlternateKey column to *CustomerID*.

8. Select the Geography table and hide the GeographyKey and SalesTerritoryKey columns.

9. Select the InternetSales table and hide the first eight columns (the ones with "Key" suffix).

8.2.2 Managing Data Refresh

When you import data, Power BI Desktop caches it in the model to give you the best performance when you visualize the data. The only option to synchronize data changes on the desktop is to refresh the data manually.

> **NOTE** Unlike Excel, Power BI Desktop doesn't support automation and macros. At the same time, there are scenarios that might benefit from automating data refresh on the desktop. While there is an officially supported way to do so, my blog "Automating Power BI Desktop Refresh" (http://prologika.com/automating-power-bi-desktop-refresh/) lists a few options if you have such a requirement.

Refreshing data

Refreshing entire tables in Power BI Desktop is simple. You just need to click the Refresh button in the Report View or in the Data View. This executes all the table queries, discards the existing data, and imports all the tables from scratch. If you need to refresh a specific table, right-click the table in the Fields pane (Report View or Data View) and click "Refresh data". Suppose that you've been notified about changes in one or more of the tables, and now you need to refresh the data model.

1. In Power BI Desktop, click the Data View icon (or the Report View icon) in the navigation bar.
2. In the ribbon's Home tab, click the Refresh button to refresh all tables. When you initiate the refresh operation, Power BI Desktop opens the Refresh window to show you the progress, as shown in **Figure 8.9**.

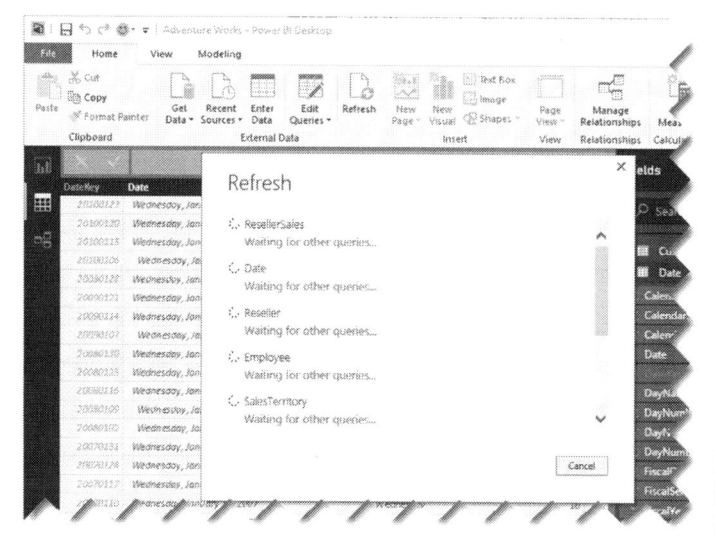

Figure 8.9 Power BI Desktop refreshes tables sequentially and cancels the entire operation if a table fails to refresh.

3. Press Ctrl-S to save the Adventure Works data model.

Power BI Desktop refreshes tables in parallel (the "Enable parallel loading of tables" setting in File ⇨ Options and Settings ⇨ Options (Data Load tab) controls this). The Refresh window shows the number of rows imported. You can't cancel the refresh once it has started. The xVelocity storage engine can import thousands of rows per second. However, the actual data refresh speed depends on many factors, including how fast the data source returns rows, the number and data type of columns in the table, the network throughput, your machine hardware configuration, and so on.

> **REAL LIFE** I was called a few times to troubleshoot slow processing issues with Power BI. In all the cases, I've found that the external factors impacted the processing speed. In one case, it turned out that the IT department had decided to throttle the network speed on all non-production network segments in case a computer virus takes over.

Troubleshooting data refresh

If a table fails to refresh, such as when there's no connectivity to the data source, the Refresh window shows an error indicator and displays an error message, as shown in **Figure 8.10**.

Refresh

Figure 8.10 If the refresh operation fails, the Refresh window shows which table failed to refresh and shows the error description.

When a table fails to refresh, the entire operation is aborted because it runs in a transaction, and no data is refreshed. At this point, you need to troubleshoot the error.

8.2.3 Refreshing Data Incrementally

A Power BI Premium feature, incremental refresh allows Power BI Service to refresh a subset of a table with imported data typically on a schedule. The main goal is to reduce the refresh time so that new data becomes available online faster.

> **NOTE** Currently, incremental refresh is a preview feature so make sure to enable it from File ⇨ Options and Settings ⇨ Options ⇨ Preview Features (Incremental Refresh Policies).

When to use incremental refresh?
Consider using incremental refresh in the following scenarios:

- Large tables – The table might have millions of rows and it might be impractical to process the entire table every time.
- Slow data sources – The data source might be slow for whatever reasons and it might not return all rows fast enough.
- Reduced impact on the source system – By reducing the number of rows to load you reduce the performance impact on the data source.

At a high level, configuring incremental refresh requires two steps: a) at design time you implement an incremental refresh policy in Power BI Desktop and b) you publish the model to Power BI Service. Only Power BI Service can refresh data incrementally; you can't do this in Power BI Desktop.

Implementing parameters
Start by implementing two query parameters: RangeStart and RangeEnd. Power BI Service will automatically populate and use these parameters to filter the data to be loaded.

1. In Power BI Desktop, click Edit Queries in the Home ribbon to open the Power Query Editor.
2. In the Home ribbon of Power Query Editor, click Manage Parameters.
3. Create RangeStart and RangeEnd parameters. Note they are case sensitive, so you must enter their exact names. You must also set their type to Date/Time. If you make a mistake here, you won't be able to set up a date filter in the next step.
4. During development, it might make sense to define the parameter current value. For example, if during development you want to load only data for year 2008, set the Current Value of the RangeStart parameter to *1/1/2008* and RangeEnd parameter to *12/31/2008* (see **Figure 8.11**)

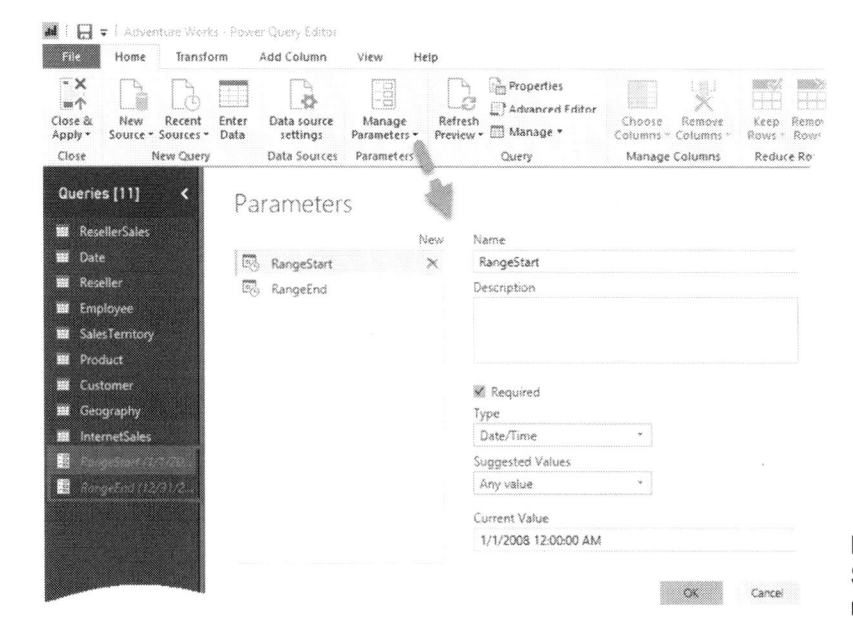

Figure 8.11 Configure Range-Start and RangeEnd query parameters.

Setting up a table filter

Next, set up a date filter on the table that you want to refresh incrementally. For example, follow these steps to filter the InternetSales fact table for incremental refresh:

1. In Power Query Editor, select Internet Sales in the Queries pane.
2. Scroll to the list of columns until you find the OrderDate column. Expand the column drop-down, choose Date/Time Filters, and then select Custom Filter.

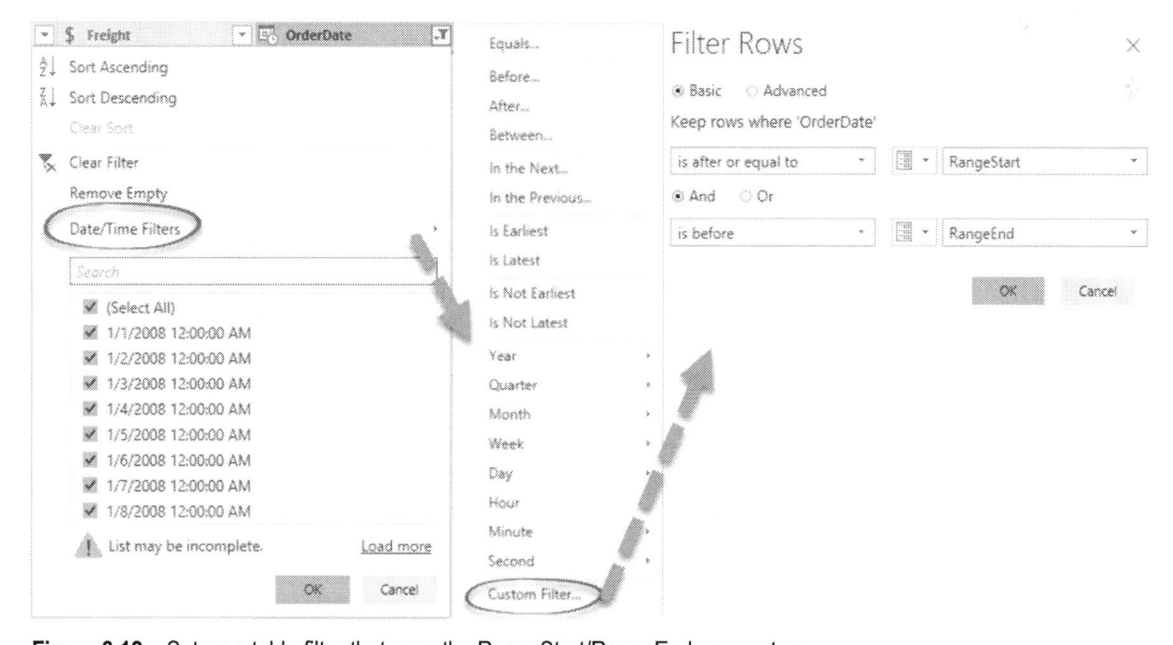

Figure 8.12 Set up a table filter that uses the RangeStart/RangeEnd parameters.

REFINING THE MODEL 217

3. Configure the Filter Rows dialog, as shown in **Figure 8.12**. Triple verify the filter range to ensure that rows don't overlap. For example, if you make a mistake and set the second condition to "is before or equal to", then you'll get overlapping rows for the end period because both left and right boundaries will qualify the same rows.

4. Once the table filter is ready, you can click the Close & Apply button to return to Power BI Desktop.

> **TIP** While the RangeStart/RangeEnd parameters must be of the Date/Time type, you can support the scenario where the filtered column is not a date column, such as when the filtered column is a "smart" integer in the format YYYYMMMDD. To do so, specify a filter condition, then open the table query in Advanced Editor and change the filter to convert the parameter values to integers:
> #"Filtered Rows" = Table.SelectRows(#"Removed Other Columns", each [OrderDateKey] >= RangeStart.Year*10000 + RangeStart.Month*100 + RangeStart.Day and [OrderDateKey] < RangeEnd.Year*10000 + RangeEnd.Month*100 + RangeEnd.Day)

Incremental refresh works great with data sources that support query folding. Recall that query folding passes some transformation steps, such as filtering and grouping, to the data source. Data sources that support SQL should support query folding. To check, right-click the Filtered Rows step in the Applied Steps pane of the Power Query Editor and check if the "View Native Query" option is enabled. It's important to check query folding because if the data source doesn't support it, Power BI Desktop doesn't prevent incremental refresh, but it will load all the data before the filter is applied. Specifically, the query mashup (M) engine will apply the filter as it reads the rows before it gets loaded, which is probably not what you want.

> **TIP** You might be able to mitigate this performance issue with non-foldable sources by applying the RangeStart/RangeEnd filter when the initial query is sent to the data source. For example, Dynamics Online supports a $filter clause that will work with incremental refresh:
> = OData.Feed("<endpoint url>/sales?$filter=CreatedDate ge " & Date.ToText(RangeStart) & " and CreatedDate lt " & Date.ToText(RangeEnd)")

Defining a refresh policy

The last step in Power BI Desktop is to set up a refresh policy that defines the refresh granularity.

1. In the Power BI Desktop window, right-click the InternetSales table in the Fields pane and click Incremental Refresh. Turn on the Incremental Refresh slider (see **Figure 8.13**).

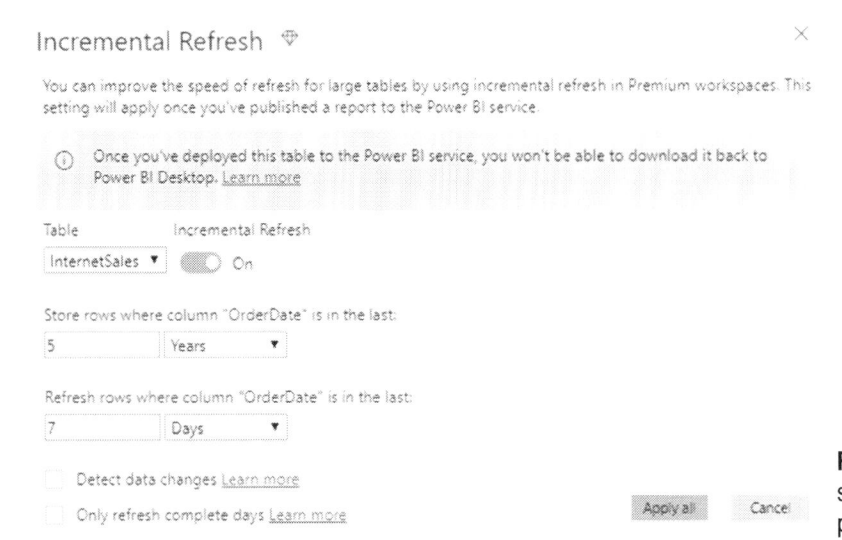

Figure 8.13 A refresh policy specifies historical periods and periods for incremental refresh.

2. Specify how many periods to retain. The example in the screenshot defines the following retention policy:
   - It retains five full years of data, plus the data for the current year up to the current date.
   - It refreshes the last seven days of data up to the current date.
   - It removes years prior to the current date. For example, once the current date is past 12/31/2018, year 2013 will be removed.
3. Once the policy is in place, the last step is to publish your Power BI Desktop file to Power BI Service and schedule it for automated refresh.

Understanding advanced policy settings
The last two checkboxes deserve more attention. The "Detect data changes" allow you to further limit the refresh to only data that has changed. Without this option, Power BI will refresh the last seven days every time even if data hasn't changed. However, if there is a timestamp column, such as LastUpdatedDate, you can enable "Detect data changes" and specify that column. Power BI Service would then automatically cache the latest timestamp value and ask for rows after that date.

The "Only refresh complete <periods>" checkbox could be useful when refreshing data at a lower granularity doesn't make sense. For example, if your model depends on closing the fiscal month, it doesn't make sense to refresh it daily. If you set the "Refresh rows" period to Month and check "Only refresh complete months", Power BI Service won't refresh days until the beginning of next month.

What happens under the hood?
As you can see, Power BI incremental refresh is very easy to set up. You only need to configure a refresh policy and Power BI Service takes care of the rest. Behind the scenes, Microsoft introduced a special table partition definition that has a refresh policy and parameterized query using the RangeStart and RangeEnd parameters. When the model is refreshed, Power BI creates the actual table partitions. Considering the above setup and current date of May 5, 2018, it creates five yearly partitions, one quarter partition (for Q1 2018), and 35 daily partitions. These partitions get consolidated and merged over time. For example, once Q2 is full, all daily partitions are merged into a monthly partition, and when the quarter is complete, monthly partitions get merged into a quarterly partition, then quarters get merged into years. Power BI also takes care of removing older partitions when they fall off the range (sliding window).

Remember that full load happens once the first time you initiate manual or scheduled refresh of the published dataset. Once the dataset is fully loaded, subsequent refreshes load the dataset incrementally (the last seven days with the above configuration). Currently, there isn't a way to reload the published dataset (full refresh), such as when you discover the historical data has data quality issues and you need to reload the history, except deleting the dataset and republishing it.

8.3 Relating Tables

One of the most prominent Power BI strengths is that it can help an analyst analyze data across multiple tables. Back in Chapter 6, I covered that as a prerequisite for aggregating data in one table by columns in another table, you must set up a relationship between the two tables. When you import tables from a relational database that supports referential integrity and has table relationships defined, Power BI Desktop detects these relationships and applies them to the model. However, when no table joins are defined in the data source, or when you import data from different sources, Power BI Desktop might be unable to detect relationships upon import. Because of this, you must revisit the model and create appropriate relationships before you analyze the data.

8.3.1 Relationship Rules and Limitations

A relationship is a join between two tables. When you define a table relationship with a One-to-Many cardinality, you're telling Power BI that there's a logical one-to-many relationship between a row in the lookup (dimension) table and the corresponding rows in the fact table. For example, the relationship between the Reseller and ResellerSales tables in **Figure 8.14** means that each reseller in the Reseller table can have many corresponding rows in the ResellerSales table.

Indeed, Progressive Sports (ResellerKey=1) recorded a sale on August 1st, 2006 for $100 and another sale on July 4th 2007 for $120. In this case, the ResellerKey column in the Reseller table is the primary key in the lookup (dimension) table. The ResellerKey column in the ResellerSales table fulfills the role of a foreign key in the fact table.

Figure 8.14 There's a One-to-Many cardinality between the Reseller table and the ResellerSales table because each reseller can have multiple sales recorded.

Understanding relationship rules

A relationship can be created under the following circumstances:

- The two tables have matching columns, such as a ResellerKey column in the Reseller lookup table and a ResellerKey column in the ResellerSales table. The column names don't have to be the same, but the columns must have matching values. For example, you can't relate the two tables if the ResellerKey column in the ResellerSales table has reseller codes, such as PRO for Progressive Sports.
- To create a relationship with a One-to-Many cardinality, the key column in the lookup (dimension) table must have unique values, like a primary key in a relational database. The key column can't have (empty) null values. In the case of the Reseller table, the ResellerKey column fulfills this requirement because its values are unique across all the rows in the table. However, this doesn't mean that all fact tables must join the lookup table on the same primary key. If the column is unique, it can serve as a primary key. And some fact tables can use one column while others can use another column.

If you create a relationship to a column that doesn't contain unique values in the other table, Power BI Desktop will create the relationship with a Many-to-Many cardinality and you'll get a warning in the "Create relationship" window. This might be a valid business case, but it could very well be a data quality issue that must address and change the cardinality to One-to-Many.

> **NOTE** Most of the relationships that you'll ever create will be with a One-to-Many cardinality, such as when you join dimension (lookup) tables to a fact table. Not to be confused with Many-to-Many relationships, such as a customer can have many accounts and an account can be owned by multiple customers, the Many-to-Many cardinality should be rare.

220 CHAPTER 8

Interestingly, Power BI doesn't require the two columns to have matching data types. For example, the ResellerKey column in the Reseller table can be of a Text data type while its counterpart in the fact table could be defined as the Whole Number data type. Behind the scenes, Power BI resolves the join by converting the values in the latter column to the Text data type. However, to improve performance and to reduce storage space, use numeric data types whenever possible.

Understanding relationship limitations
Relationships have several limitations. To start, only one column can be used on each side of the relationship. If you need a combination of two or more columns (so the key column can have unique values), you can add a custom column in the query or a calculated column that uses a DAX expression to concatenate the values, such as =[ResellerKey] & "|" & [SourceID]. I use the pipe delimiter here to avoid combinations that might result in the same concatenated values. For example, combinations of ResellerKey of 1 with SourceID of 10 and ResellerKey of 11 and SourceID of 0 result in "110". To make the combinations unique, you can use a delimiter, such as the pipe character. Once you construct a primary key column, you can use this column for the relationship.

Moving down the list, you can't create relationships forming a closed loop (also called a diamond shape). For example, given the relationships Table1 ⇨ Table2 and Table2 ⇨ Table3, you can't set an active relationship Table1 ⇨ Table3. Such a relationship probably isn't needed anyway, because you'll be able to analyze the data in Table3 by Table1 with only the first two relationships in place. Power BI will let you create the Table1 ⇨ Table3 relationship, but it will mark it as inactive. This brings to the subject of role-playing relationships and inactive relationships.

As it stands, Power BI doesn't support role-playing relationships. A role-playing lookup table is a table that joins the same fact table multiple times, and thus plays multiple roles. For example, the InternetSales table has the OrderDateKey, ShipDateKey, and DueDateKey columns because a sales order has an order date, ship date, and due date. Suppose you want to analyze sales by these three dates. Here are the two most common approaches to handle role-playing lookup tables:

- Reimport the same table – One approach is to import the Date table three times with different names and to create relationships to each date table. This approach gives you more control because you now have three separate Date tables and their data doesn't have to match. For example, you might want the ShipDate table to include different columns than the OrderDate table. On the downside, you increase your maintenance effort because now you must maintain three tables.

- Create calculated tables – Another approach is to create calculated tables by clicking the New Table button in the Modeling ribbon. A calculated table is a table that uses a DAX table-producing formula. Like a calculated column, a calculated table is updated when the model is refreshed and then its results are saved. For example, the DAX formula ShipDate = 'Date' creates a ShipDate calculated table from the Date table. Then you can use the ShipDate just like any other table.

REAL WORLD About date tables, AdventureWorksDW uses a "smart" integer primary key for the Date table in the format YYYYMMDD. This is a common practice for data warehousing, but you should use a date field (Date data type) instead. Not only is it more compact (3 bytes vs. 4 bytes for Integer) but it's also easier to work with. For example, if a business user imports ResellerSales, he can filter easier on a Date data type, such as to import data for the current year, than to parse integer fields. That's why in the practice exercises that follow, you'll recreate the relationships to the date column of the Date table.

Understanding active and inactive relationships
Another approach is to join the three date columns in InternetSales to the Date table. This approach allows you to reuse the same date table three times. However, Power BI supports only one active role-playing relationship. An active relationship is a relationship that Power BI follows to automatically aggregate the data between two tables. A solid line in the Relationships View indicates an active relationship while a dotted line is for inactive relationships (see **Figure 8.15**).

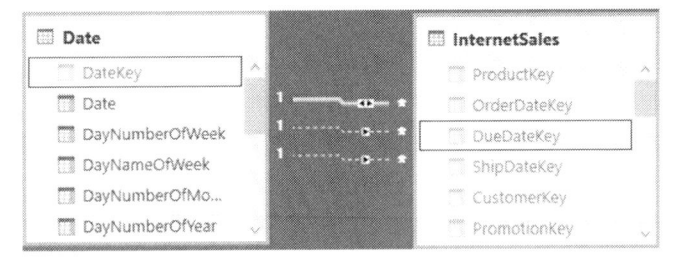

Figure 8.15 Power BI supports only one active relationship between two tables and marks the other relationships as inactive.

You can also open the Manage Relationships window (click the Manage Relationships button in ribbon's Home or Modeling tabs) and inspect the Active flag. When Power BI Desktop imports the relationships from the database, it defaults the first one to active and marks the rest as inactive. In our case, the InternetSales[DueDateKey] ⇨ DimDate[DateKey] relationship is active because this happens to be the first of the three relationships between the DimDate and FactInternetSales tables that you imported. Consequently, when you create a report that slices Internet dates by Date, Power BI automatically aggregates the sales by the due date.

> **NOTE** I'll use the TableName[ColumnName] notation as a shortcut when I refer to a table column. For example, InternetSales[DueDateKey] means the DueDateKey column in the InternetSales table. This notation will help you later with DAX formulas because DAX follows the same syntax. When referencing relationships, I'll use a right arrow (⇨) to denote a relationship from a fact table to a lookup table. For example, InternetSales[OrderDateKey] ⇨ DimDate[DateKey] means a relationship between the OrderDateKey column in the InternetSales table to the DateKey column in the DimDate table.

If you want the default aggregation to happen by the order date, you must set InternetSales[OrderDateKey] ⇨ DimDate[DateKey] as an active relationship. To do so, first select the InternetSales[ShipDateKey] ⇨ DimDate[DateKey] relationship, and then click Edit. In the Edit Relationship dialog box, uncheck the Active checkbox, and then click OK. Finally, edit the InternetSales[OrderDateKey] ⇨ DimDate[DateKey] relationship, and then check the Active checkbox.

What if you want to be able to aggregate data by other dates without importing the Date table multiple times? You can create DAX calculated measures, such as ShippedSalesAmount and DueSalesAmount, that force Power BI to use a given inactive relationship by using the DAX USERELATIONSHIP function. For example, the following formula calculates ShippedSalesAmount using the ResellerSales[ShipDateKey] ⇨ DimDate[DateKey] relationship:

ShippedSalesAmount=CALCULATE(SUM(InternetSales[SalesAmount]), USERELATIONSHIP(InternetSales[ShipDateKey], 'Date'[DateKey])

Cross filtering limitations
In Chapter 6, I explained that the relationship cross-filter direction is more important than the relationship cardinality and that a relationship can be set to cross-filter in both directions. This is a great out-of-box feature that allows you to address more advanced scenarios that previously required custom calculations, such as many-to-many relationships. However, bi-directional filtering doesn't make sense and should be avoided in the following cases:

- When you have two fact tables sharing some common dimension tables – In fact, to avoid ambiguous join paths, Power BI Desktop won't let you turn on bi-directional filtering from multiple fact tables to the same lookup table. Therefore, if you start from a single fact table but anticipate additional fact tables down the road, you may also consider a uni-directional model (Cross filtering set to Single) to keep a consistent experience to users, and then turn on bi-directional filtering only if you need it.

> **NOTE** To understand this limitation better, let's say you have a Product lookup table that has bi-directional relations to ResellerSales and InternetSales tables. If you define a DAX measure on the Product table, such as Count of Products, but have a filter on a Date table, Power BI won't know how to resolve the join: count of products through ResellerSales on that date, or count of products through InternetSales on that date.

- Relationships toward the date table – Relationships to date tables should be one-directional so that DAX time calculations continue to work.
- Closed-loop relationships – As I just mentioned, Power BI Desktop will automatically inactivate one of the relationships when it detects a closed loop, although you can still use DAX calculations to navigate inactive relationships. In this case, bi-directional relationships would produce meaningless results.

> **BEST PRACTICE** Start with a unidirectional model (Cross Filter Direction = Single) and then turn on cross filtering to Both when needed, such as when you need a many-to-many relationship between tables.

8.3.2 Auto-detecting Relationships

When you create a report that uses unrelated tables, Power BI Desktop can auto-detect and create missing relationships. This behavior is enabled by default, but you can disable it by turning it off from the File ⇨ Options and Settings ⇨ Options menu, which brings you to the Options window (see **Figure 8.16**).

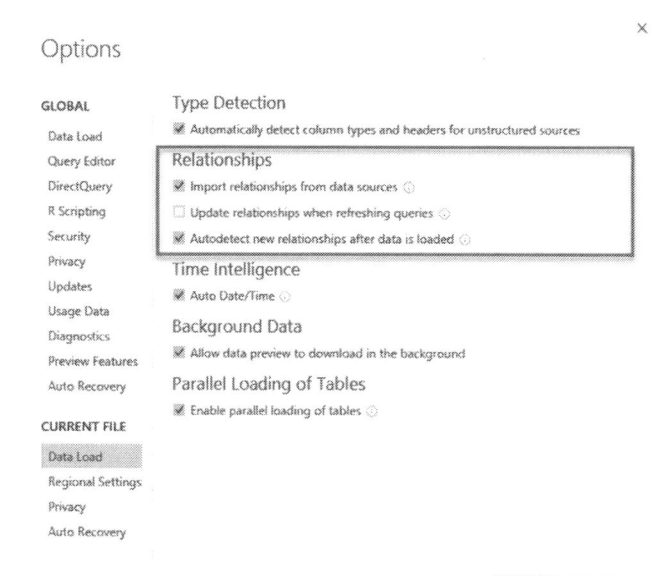

Figure 8.16 You can use the Relationships options in the Data Load section to control how Power BI Desktop discovers relationships.

Configuring relationships detection
There are three options that control how Power BI desktop detects relationships. The "Import relationships from data sources" option (enabled by default) instructs Power BI Desktop to detect relationships from the data source *before* the data is loaded. When this option is enabled, Power BI Desktop will examine the database schema and probe for existing relationships.

The "Update relationships when refreshing queries" option will attempt to discover missing relationships when refreshing the imported data. Because this might result in dropping existing relationships that you've created manually, this option is off by default. Finally, "Autodetect new relationships after data is loaded" will attempt to auto-detect missing relationships *after* the data is loaded. Because this option is on by default, Power BI Desktop was able to detect relationships between the InternetSales and Date tables, as well as between other tables. The auto-detection mechanism uses an internal algorithm that considers column data types and cardinality.

Understanding missing relationships

What happens when you don't have a relationship between two tables and attempt to analyze the data in a report? You'll get repeating values (see **Figure 8.17**).

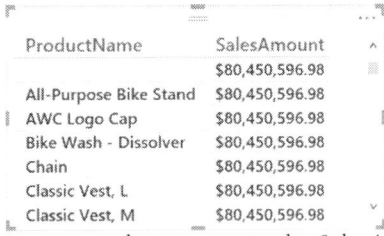

Figure 8.17 Reports show repeating values in the case of missing relationships.

I attempted to aggregate the SalesAmount column from the ResellerSales table by the ProductName column in the Product table, but there's no relationship defined between these two tables. If reseller sales should aggregate by product, you must define a relationship to resolve this issue.

Autodetecting relationships

The lazy approach to handle missing relationships is to let Power BI Desktop create them by clicking the Autodetect button in the Manage Relationship window. If the internal algorithm detects a suitable relationship candidate, it creates the relationship and informs you, as shown in **Figure 8.18**.

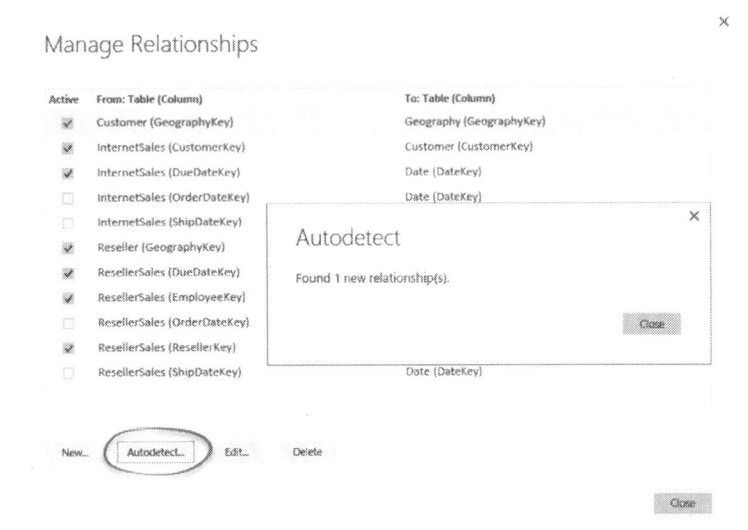

Figure 8.18 The Autodetect feature of the Manage Relationship window shows that it has detected and created a relationship successfully.

In the case of an unsuccessful detection process, the Relationship dialog box will show "Found no new relationships". If this happens and you're still missing relationships, you need to create them manually.

8.3.3 Creating Relationships Manually

Since table relationships are very important, I'd recommend that you configure them manually. You can do this by using the Manage Relationships window or by using the Relationships View. Because relationships are very important, you can find the Manage Relationships button in the ribbon in all views (Report, Data, and Relationships).

Steps to create a relationship
Follows these steps to set up a relationship with a One-to-Many cardinality:
1. Identify a foreign key column in the table on the Many side of the relationship.
2. Identify a primary key column that uniquely identifies each row in the lookup (dimension) table.
3. In the Manage Relationship window, click the New button to open the Create Relationship window. Then create a new relationship with the correct cardinality. Or you can use the Relationships View to drag the foreign key from the fact table onto the primary key of the lookup table.

Understanding the Create Relationship window
You might prefer the Create Relationship window when the number of tables in your model has grown and using the drag-and-drop technique in the Relationships View becomes impractical. **Figure 8.19** shows the Create Relationship dialog box when setting up a relationship between the ResellerSales and Product tables. Note that if you have imported the Product table from the SSRS Product Catalog report, it will have an empty row with a null value in the ProductKey column. As a mentioned before, a key column can't have a null value. To fix this issue, open Power Query Editor, expand the drop-down in the ProductKey column header of the Product table, and uncheck the null value.

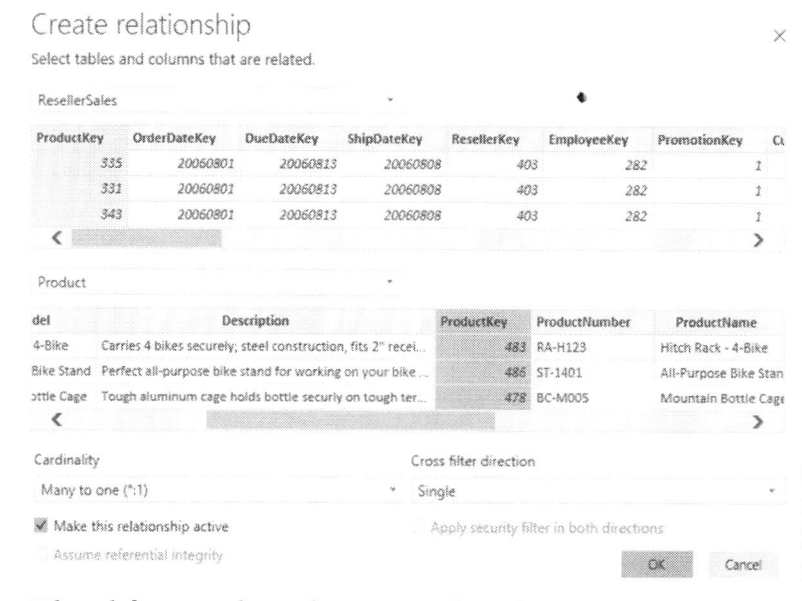

Figure 8.19 Use the Create Relationship window to specify the columns used for the relationship, cardinality and cross filter direction.

When defining a relationship, you need to select two tables and matching columns. The Create Relationships window will detect the cardinality for you. For example, if you start with the table on the many side of the relationship (ResellerSales), it'll choose the Many to One cardinality; otherwise it selects One to Many. If you attempt to set up a relationship with the wrong cardinality, you'll get an error message ("The Cardinality you selected isn't valid for this relationship"), and you won't be able to create the relationship. And if you choose a column that doesn't uniquely identify each row in the lookup table, you'll end up with a Many-to-Many cardinality and the warning message "The relationship has cardinality Many-Many.

This should only be used if it is expected that neither column contain unique values, and that the significantly different behavior of Many-many relationship is understood."

Because there isn't another relationship between the two tables, Power BI Desktop defaults the "Make this relationship active" to checked. This checkbox corresponds to the Active flag in the Manage Relationship window. "Cross filter direction" defaults to Single. The "Assume Referential Integrity" checkbox is disabled because it applies only to DirectQuery. When checked, it auto-generates queries that use INNER JOIN as opposed to OUTER JOIN when joining the two tables. Don't worry for now about "Apply security filter in both direction". I'll explain it when I discuss row-level security (RLS) in the next chapter.

> **NOTE** When data is imported, all Power BI joins are treated as outer joins. For example, if ResellerSales had a transaction for a reseller that doesn't exist in the Reseller table, Power BI won't eliminate this row, as I explain in more detail in the next section.

Understanding unknown members

Consider the model shown in **Figure 8.20**, which has a Reseller lookup table and a Sales fact table. This diagram uses an Excel pivot report to demonstrate unknown members, but a Power BI Desktop report will behave the same. The Reseller table has only two resellers. However, the Sales table has data for two additional resellers with keys of 3 and 4. This is a common data integrity issue when the source data originates from heterogeneous data sources and when there isn't an ETL process to validate and clean the data.

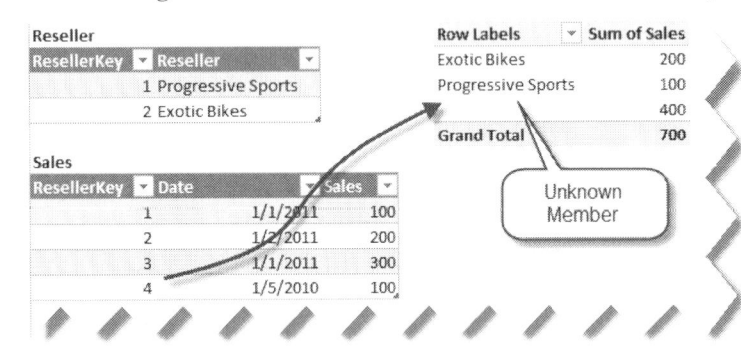

Figure 8.20 Power BI enables an unknown member to the lookup table when it encounters missing rows.

Power BI has a simple solution for this predicament. When creating a relationship, Power BI checks for missing rows in the lookup table. If it finds any, it automatically configures the lookup table to include a special unknown (Blank) member. That's why all unrelated rows appear grouped under a blank row in the report. This row represents the unknown member in the Reseller table.

> **NOTE** If you have imported the Product table from the SSRS Product Catalog report in Chapter 6, you'll find that it has a subset of the Adventure Works products. Therefore, when you create a report that shows sales by product, a large chunk of sales will be associated with a (Blank) product.

What about the reverse scenario where there are resellers with no sales and you want to show all resellers irrespective if they have sales or not in the Sales table? Once you add the desired field from the Reseller table to the report, expand the drop-down next to the field in the Fields tab of the Visualizations pane and then click "Show items with no data" in the drop-down menu.

Managing relationships

You can view and manage all the relationships defined in your model by using the Manage Relationships window (see **Figure 8.18** again). In this case, the Manage Relationships window shows that there are 11 relationships defined in the Adventure Works model from which four are inactive, plus one relationship that was just discovered using the Autodiscover feature.

The Edit button opens the Edit Relationship window, which is the same as the Create Relationship window but with all the fields pre-populated. Finally, the Delete button removes the selected relationship. Don't worry if your results differ from mine. You'll verify the relationships in the lab exercise that follows and will create the missing ones.

8.3.4 Understanding the Relationships View

Another way to view and manage relationships is to use the Relationships View. Microsoft is replacing the Relationship View with an updated version (to try it out, check the Modeling View setting in File ⇨ Options and Settings ⇨ Options ⇨ Preview Features tab). I'll use the new Relationships view so that I can demonstrate the forthcoming features. You can use the Relationships View to:

- Visualize the model schema and create diagrams
- Create and manage relationships
- Make other schema changes, such as renaming, hiding, deleting objects, changing field properties and table storage.

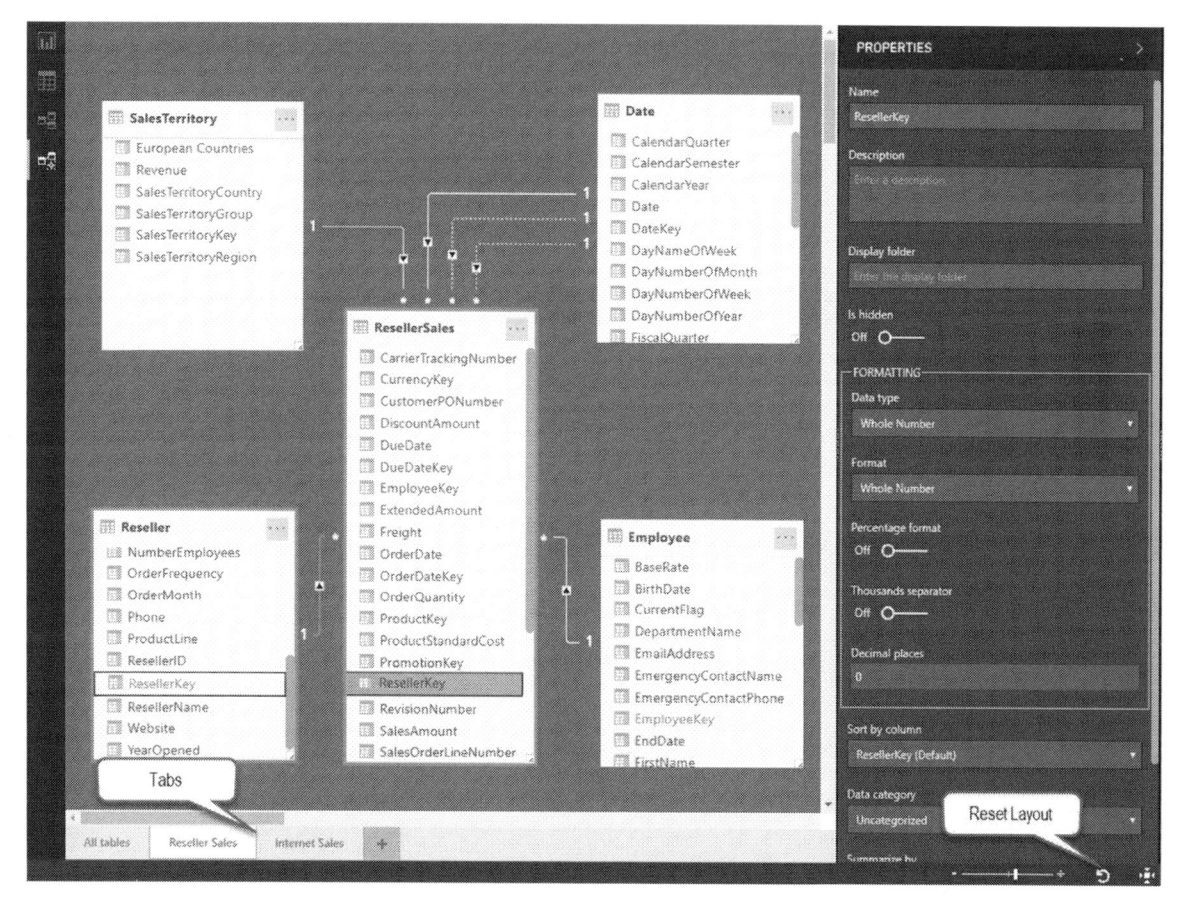

Figure 8.21 The Relationships View helps you understand the model schema and work with relationships.

Recall that the Relationships view is available in models with imported data or in models that connect directly to data sources (DirectQuery), but it's not available when connecting live to multidimensional data

REFINING THE MODEL

sources, such as Analysis Services or published Power BI datasets. One of the strengths of the Relationships View is that you can quickly visualize and understand the model schema and relationships. **Figure 8.21** shows a subset of the Adventure Works model schema (Internet Sales fact table and related tables) open in the Relationships View. Glancing at the model, you can immediately see what relationships exist in the model!

Organizing metadata
Your data model schema can get busy with many tables. You can add tabs to divide the model schema into logical diagrams. Just add a tab, drag a fact table from the Fields pane, then right-click the table in the diagram and click "Add related tables". The default "All tables" table shows all the tables in the model. In **Figure 8.21**, I added Reseller Sales and Internet Sales tabs that include only the tables in these subject areas.

The slider in the bottom-right corner lets you zoom in and out of the diagram. The Reset Layout button is useful to auto-arrange the tables in the active tab in a more compact layout. Lastly, click the "Fit to screen" button to the right of "Reset Layout" to fit the diagram to screen.

Making schema changes
You can make schema changes in the Relationships View. When you right-click an object, a context menu opens to show the supported tasks. And when you select an object, the Properties pane shows its properties. **Table 8.2** lists the supported tasks that you can perform in the Relationships View.

Table 8.2 This table shows the schema tasks by object type.

Object Type	Supported Operations	Object Type	Supported Operations
Table	Delete, hide, rename, synonyms, change storage mode, enter description	Measure	Delete, hide, rename, display folder, change format
Column	Delete, hide, rename, sort by column, enter description, assign display folder, change data type and format, set data category and default aggregation, set nullability	Relationship	Delete

Managing relationships
Back to the subject of relationships, let's take a closer look at how the Relationships View represents them. A relationship is visualized as a connector between two tables. Symbols at the end of the connector help you understand the relationship cardinality. The number one (1) denotes the table on the One side of the relationship, while the asterisk (*) is shown next to the table on the Many side of the relationship. For example, after examining **Figure 8.21**, you can see that there's a relationship between the Reseller table and ResellerSales table and that the relationship cardinality is One to Many with the Reseller table on the One side of the relationship and the ResellerSales table on the many.

When you click a relationship to select it, the Relationships View highlights it in an orange color. When you hover your mouse over a relationship, the Relationships View highlights columns in the joined tables to indicate visually which columns are used in the relationship. For example, pointing the mouse to the highlighted relationship between the ResellerSales and Reseller tables reveals that the relationship is created between the ResellerSales[ResellerKey] column and Reseller[ResellerKey].

As I mentioned, Power BI has a limited support of role-playing relationships where a lookup table joins multiple times to a fact table. The caveat is that only one role-playing relationship can be active. The Relationships View shows the inactive relationships with dotted lines. To make another role-playing relationship active, first you need to deactivate the currently active relationship. To do so, double-click the active relationship, and then in the Edit Relationship window, uncheck the "Make this relationship active" checkbox. Next, you double-click the other role-playing relationship and then check its "Make this relationship active" checkbox.

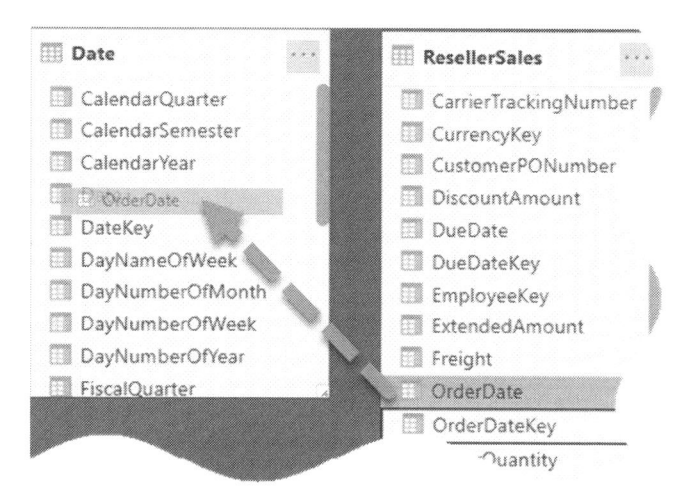

Figure 8.22 The Relationships View lets you create a relationship by dragging a column.

A great feature of Relationships View is creating relationships by dragging a column from one table and dropping it onto a column in another table. For example, to create a relationship between the ResellerSales and Date tables, drag the OrderDate column in the ResellerSales table and drop it onto the Date column in the Date table (see **Figure 8.22**). Doing this in the reverse direction will work as well (Power BI automatically detects the cardinality). To delete a relationship, simply click the relationship to select it, and then press the Delete key. Or right-click the relationship line, and then click Delete.

Understanding synonyms

Remember the fantastic Q&A feature that let business users gain insights in dashboards by asking natural queries? The Relationships View allows you to fine tune Q&A by defining synonyms. A synonym is an alternative name for a field. Suppose you want to allow natural queries to use "revenue" and "sales amount" interchangeably. Follow these steps to define a synonym:

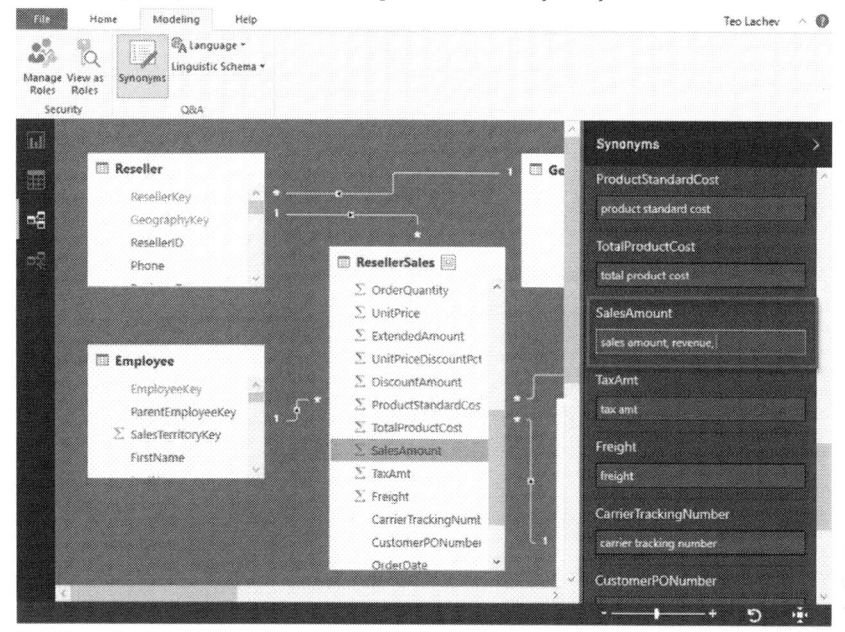

Figure 8.23 The "sales amount" and "revenue" are synonyms for the SalesAmount field.

1. In the Relationships View, select the ResellerSales table.

REFINING THE MODEL

2. In the ribbon's Modeling tab, click the Synonyms button. A Synonyms pane opens. Notice that Power BI Desktop has already defined a synonym "sales amount" for the SalesAmount field.

3. Next to "sales amount", type in *revenue* (see **Figure 8.23**). That's all it takes to define a synonym. Once you deploy your model to Power BI Service or use Q&A in Power BI Desktop, you can use the synonym in in your natural questions, such as by typing "revenue by product".

8.3.5 Working with Relationships

As it stands, the Adventure Works model has nine tables and 11 relationships. Power BI has done a great job detecting the relationships. Next, you'll practice different ways to change and create relationships.

Auto-detecting relationships

Let's see how far you can get by letting Power BI Desktop auto-detect relationships:

1. In the Data View (or Report View), click the Manage Relationships button in the ribbon's Home tab to open the Manage Relationships window.

2. Click the Autodetect button. If there's no relationship between the Customer and Geography tables, the auto-detection finds one new relationship. Click OK. Notice that a relationship Reseller[GeographyKey] ⇨ Geography[GeographyKey] is added. This relationship reflects the underlying snowflake schema consisting of the ResellerSales, Reseller, and Geography tables. The new relationship allows us to analyze reseller sales by geography using a cascading relationship spanning three tables (ResellerSales ⇨ Reseller ⇨ Geography).

> **NOTE** Usually a byproduct of a snowflake schema, a cascading relationship joins a fact table to a lookup table via another referenced lookup table. Power BI supports cascading relationships that can traverse multiple lookup tables.

Now let's clean up some existing relationships. As it stands, the InternetSales table has three relationships to the Date table (one active and two inactive) which Power BI Desktop auto-discovered from the underlying database. All these relationships join the Date table on the DateKey column. As I mentioned before, I suggest you use a column of a Date data type in the Date table. Luckily, both the Reseller Sales and InternetSales tables have OrderDate, ShipDate, and DueDate date columns. And the Date table has a Date column which is of a Date data type.

3. While still in the Manage Relationships window, delete the two inactive relationships (the ones with an unchecked Active flag) from the InternetSales table to the Date table. You can press and hold the Ctrl key to select multiple relationships and delete them in one step.

4. Delete also the three relationships from ResellerSales to Date: ResellerSales[DueDateKey] ⇨ Date[DateKey], ResellerSales[ShipDateKey] ⇨ Date[DateKey] and ResellerSales[OrderDateKey] ⇨ Date[DateKey].

Using the Manage Relationships window

The Adventure Works model has two fact tables (ResellerSales and InternetSales) and seven lookup tables. Let's start creating the missing relationships using the Manage Relationships window:

> **TIP** When you have multiple fact tables, join them to common dimension tables. This allows you to create consolidated reports that include multiple subject areas, such as a report that shows Internet sales and reseller sales side by side grouped by date and sales territory.

1. First, let's rebind the InternetSales[OrderDateKey] ⇨ Date[DateKey] relationship to use another set of columns. In the Manage Relationship window, double-click the InternetSales[OrderDateKey] ⇨ Date[DateKey] relationship (or select it and click Edit). If this relationship doesn't exist in your model, click the New button to create it. In the Edit Relationship window, select the OrderDate column (scroll all the way to the right) in the InternetSales table. Then select the Date column in the Date table and click OK.

NOTE When joining fact tables to a date table on a date column, make sure that the foreign key values contain only the date portion of the date and not the time portion. Otherwise, the join will never find matching values in the date table. If you don't need it, the easiest way to discard the time portion is to change the column data type from Date/time to Date. You can also apply query transformations to strip the time portion or to create custom columns that have only the date portion.

2. Back in the Manage Relationship window, click New. Create a relationship ResellerSales[OrderDate] ⇨ Date[Date]. Leave the "Cross filter direction" drop-down to Single, and click OK.
3. Create ResellerSales[SalesTerritoryKey] ⇨ SalesTerritory[SalesTerritoryKey] and ResellerSales[ProductKey] ⇨ Product[ProductKey] relationships. However, change the "Cross filtering direction" option to *Single* to avoid errors related to ambiguous relationships later.
4. Click the Close button to close the Manage Relationship window.

Creating relationships using the Relationships View
Next, you'll use the Relationships View to create relationships for the InternetSales table.
1. Click the Relationships View icon in the navigation bar.
2. Add a Reseller Sales tab. Drag the ResellerSales table from the Fields pane and drop it on the Reseller Sales tab. Right-click the ResellerSales table in the tab and click "Add related tables" to create a diagram showing only the Reseller Sales subject area. Repeat these steps to create an Internet Sales tab showing only the tables related to the InternetSales table.
3. If this relationship doesn't exist, drag the InternetSales[ProductKey] column and drop it onto the Product[ProductKey] column.
4. Drag the InternetSales[SalesTerritoryKey] column and drop it onto the SalesTerritory[SalesTerritoryKey] column.
5. Click the Manage Relationships button. Compare your results with **Figure 8.24**. As it stands, the Adventure Works model has 11 relationships. For now, let's not create inactive relationships. I'll revisit them in the next chapter when I cover DAX.

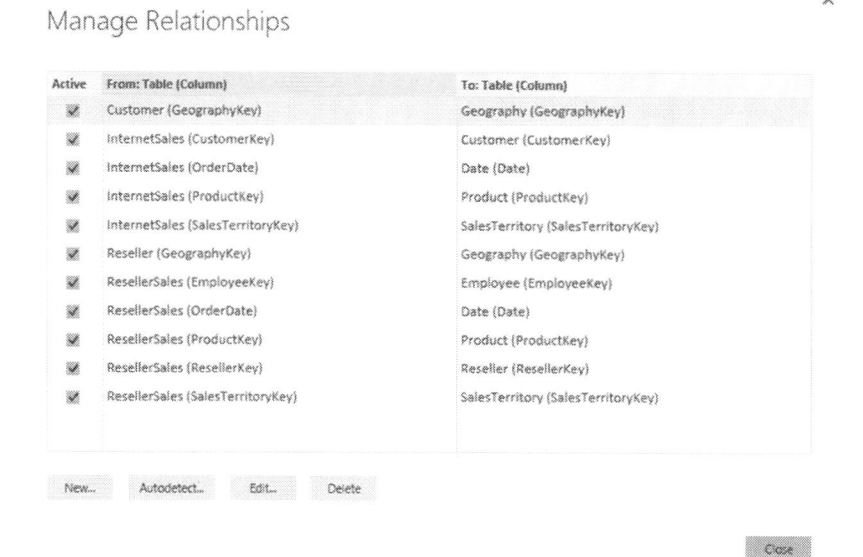

Figure 8.24 The Manage Relationships dialog box shows 11 relationships defined in the Adventure Works model.

REFINING THE MODEL

6. If there are differences between your relationships and **Figure 8.24**, make the necessary changes. Don't be afraid to delete wrong relationships if you must recreate them to use different columns.
7. Once your setup matches **Figure 8.24**, click Close to close the Manage Relationships window. Save the Adventure Works file.

8.4 Refining Metadata

Power BI Desktop has additional modeling capabilities for you to implement end-user features that further enrich the model. This section discusses features that don't require the Data Analysis Expressions DAX experience and are not available in Power BI Service.

8.4.1 Working with Hierarchies

A hierarchy is a combination of fields that defines a navigational drilldown path in the model. As you've seen, Power BI allows you to use any column for slicing and dicing data in related tables. However, some fields form logical navigational paths for data exploration and drilling down. You can define hierarchies to group such fields.

Understanding hierarchies
A hierarchy defines a drill-down path using fields from a table. When you add the hierarchy to the report, you can drill down data by expanding its levels. A hierarchy can include fields from a single table only. If you want to drill down from different tables, just add the fields (don't define a hierarchy). A hierarchy offers two important benefits:

- Usability – You can add all fields for drilling down data in one click by adding the hierarchy instead of individual fields.
- Performance – Suppose you add a high-cardinality column, such as CustomerName, to a report. You might end up with a huge report. This might cause unnecessary performance degradation. Instead, you can hide the Customer field and you can define a hierarchy with levels, such as State, City, and Customer levels, to force end users to use this navigational path when browsing data by customers.

Typically, a hierarchy combines columns with logical one-to-many relationships. For example, one year can have multiple quarters and one quarter can have multiple months. This doesn't have to be the case though. For example, you can create a reporting hierarchy with ProductModel, Size, and Product columns, if you wish to analyze products that way.

Once you have a hierarchy in place, you might want to hide high-cardinality columns to prevent the user from adding them directly to the report and to avoid performance issues. For example, you might not want to expose the CustomerName column in the Customer table, to prevent users from adding it to a report outside the hierarchies it participates in.

Understanding in-line date hierarchies
The most common example of hierarchy is the date hierarchy, consisting of Year, Quarter, Month, and Date levels. In Chapter 6, I encouraged you to have a separate Date table so that you can define whatever date-related columns you need and implement DAX time calculations, such as YTD, QTD, and so on. But what if you didn't follow my advice and you want a quick and easy date hierarchy? Fortunately, Power BI Desktop can generate an in-line date hierarchy. All you need to do is add a column of a Date data type to the report. For example, **Figure 8.25** shows that I've added a Date field to the Values area of a Table report. Power BI has automatically generated a hierarchy with levels Year, Quarter, Month, and Day.

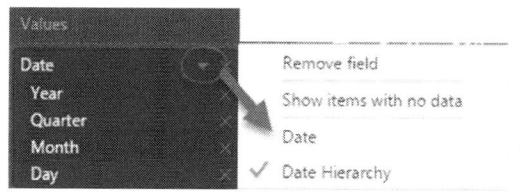

Figure 8.25 Power BI Desktop creates an inline hierarchy when you add a date field to the report.

If you don't want any of the levels, you can delete them by clicking the X button next to the level. And if you want to see just the date and not the hierarchy on the report, simply click the drop-down next to the Date hierarchy and then check the Date field.

> **NOTE** One existing limitation of the automatic in-line date hierarchy feature is that it doesn't generate time levels, such as Hour, Minute, and so on. If you need to perform time analysis, you need to create a Time table with the required levels and join it to the table with the data. Also, keep in mind that in-line hierarchies might increase your model size substantially, as I explained in Chapter 6. To remove them, go to File ⇨ Options and Settings ⇨ Options and uncheck the "Auto Date/Time" setting on the Data Load tab.

Implementing user-defined hierarchies

Follow these steps to implement a Calendar Hierarchy consisting of CalendarYear, CalendarQuarter, Month, and Date levels:

1. In the Fields pane (Report View or Data View), click the ellipsis button next to the CalendarYear field in the Date table, and then click New Hierarchy. This adds a CalendarYear Hierarchy to the Date table.
1. Click the ellipsis button next to the CalendarYear Hierarchy and then click rename. Rename the hierarchy to *Calendar Hierarchy*.
2. Click the ellipsis button next to the CalendarQuarter field and then click Add to Hierarchy ⇨ Calendar Hierarchy.
2. Repeat the last step to add MonthName and Date fields to the hierarchy. If you didn't add the fields in the correct order, you can simply drag a level in the hierarchy and move it to the correct place.
3. The name of the hierarchy level doesn't need to match the name of the underlying field. Click the ellipsis button next to the MonthName level of the Calendar Hierarchy (not to the MonthName field in the table) and rename it to *Month*. Compare you results with **Figure 8.26**.

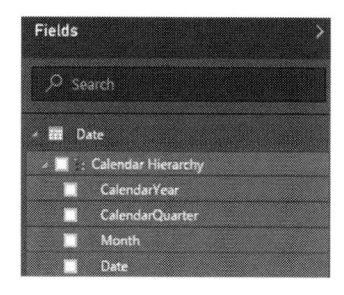

Figure 8.26 The Calendar Year hierarchy includes CalendarYear, CalendarQuarter, Month and Date levels.

4. (Optional) Create a chart report to add the Calendar Hierarchy to the Axis area of the chart. Enable drill-down behavior of the chart and test your new hierarchy.

> **TIP** A quick way to create a hierarchy is simply to drag a field and drop onto another within the same table. The resulting hierarchy will have two levels with the lower level corresponding to the field that you dragged.

REFINING THE MODEL

8.4.2 Working with Field Properties

When Power BI Desktop imports data, not only does it get the actual data, it also gets additional metadata such as the table and column names, data types, and column cardinality. This information also helps Power BI Desktop to visualize the field when you add it to a report. A data category is additional metadata that you assign to a field to inform Power BI Desktop about the field content so that it can be visualized even better. You assign a data category to a field by using the Data Category drop-down in the ribbon's Modeling tab.

Assigning geo categories
When you expand the Data Category drop-down, you'll find that most of the data categories are geo-related, such as Address, City, Continent, and so on. When you use a geo-related field on a report, Power BI Desktop tries its best to infer the field content and geocode the field. For example, if you add the AddressLine1 field from the Customer table to an empty Map visualization, Power BI Desktop will correctly interpret it as an address and plot it on the map. So, in most cases, specifying a data category is not necessary.

In some cases, however, Power BI might need extra help. Suppose you have a field with abbreviated values such as AZ, AL, and so on. Do values represent states or countries? This is where you'd need to specify a data category. For more information about Power BI geocoding and geo data categories, read my blog "Geocoding with Power View Maps" at prologika.com/geocoding-with-power-view-maps.

> **TIP** Maps show cities in wrong locations? Cities with the same name can exist in different states and countries. If cities end up in the wrong place on the map, consider adding Country, State and City fields (or create a hierarchy with these levels) to the map's Location area and enabling drilling down. When you do this, Power BI will attempt to plot the location within the parent territory. Of course, another solution to avoid ambiguity is to use latitude and longitude coordinates instead of location names.

Configuring navigation links
Sometimes, you might want to show a clickable navigation link (URL) to allow the user to navigate to a web page or another report. For example, the Table visual in **Figure 8.27** shows a list of reseller names and their websites (I fabricated a Website field from the Reseller Name with empty spaces removed). The user can click the website URL to navigate to it in the browser. Assuming you have a field with the links, you can simply assign it to the Web URL data category.

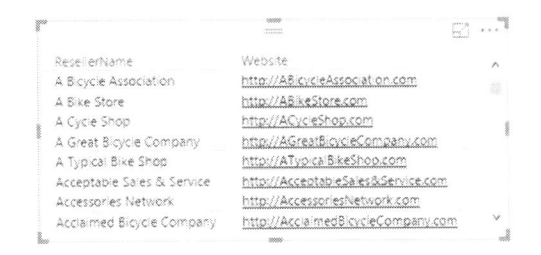

Figure 8.27 Assign the Web URL data category to implement clickable links.

And if you have a field that stores links to images, you can assign the Image URL category to it so that the images show in a Table or Card visuals.

Configuring default summarization
When you add a field to the Value area of the Visualizations pane, Power BI determines how to aggregate the field. If the field is numeric (indicated by the sigma icon in front of the field in the Fields pane), Power BI sums the field, otherwise it defaults to the Count aggregation function. Some fields are meaningless when aggregated, such as Year, Quarter, OrderLineNumber. Instead of overwriting the field aggregation function in the Value area each time you add the field to a report, you can configure the field's default summarization behavior.

1. In Report View or Data View, select the field in Fields pane.
2. In the Modeling tab, expand the Default Summarization drop-down and choose the appropriate aggregation function. For example, if you don't want the field to summarize at all, set its default summarization to "Don't summarize".

Organizing fields in display folders
A table might have many fields. Instead of asking the user to scroll up and down the Fields list, you can organize fields in display folders to improve the end user experience.

1. Switch to the Relationships View and expand the Customer table in the Fields pane.
2. Hold the Ctrl key and click a few fields, such as EnglishEducation, EnglishOccupation, Gender, and HouseOwnerFlag.
3. In the Properties pane, type *Demographics* in the "Display folder" property.

> **TIP** You can nest display folders by using a backspace ("\"). For example, Demographic\Education will create a subfolder Education under the Demographics folder. Just like the rest of the metadata, display folders are sorted alphabetically in Report View. If you want them to be listed immediately after the table name, you can prefix their names with an underscore ("_").

4. Select only the Gender field in the Fields pane. In the Properties pane, type *M for male, F for female*.
5. Switch to the Reports view. Expand the Customer table in the Fields list. Observe that the selected fields are now located in the Demographics folder (see **Figure 8.28**).
6. Hover over the Gender field. Notice that the tooltip shows the field description you entered. Now you have a self-documented model!

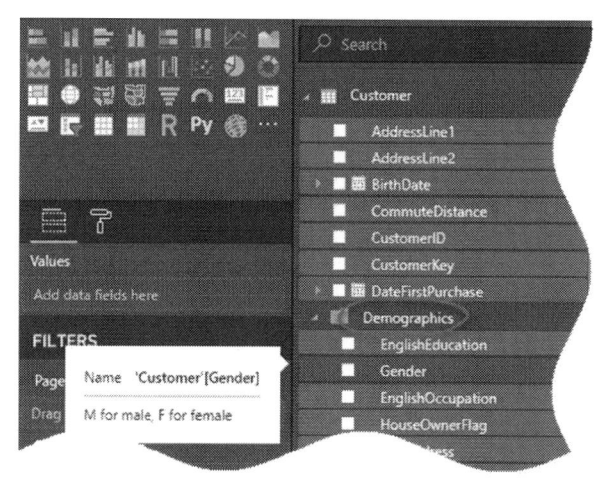

Figure 8.28 You can organize fields in display folders and enter a description for each field.

8.4.3 Configuring Date Tables

As I discussed in Chapter 6, as a best practice you should have one or more date tables instead of relying on the Power BI auto-generated date tables for each date field. You can go one step further by telling Power BI about your date table(s).

Marking a date table
Follow these steps to mark the Date table:

1. In the Fields list, right-click the Date table and then click "Mark as date table" ⇨ "Mark as date table".

2. Expand the "Date column" drop-down and select the Date column (you must select a column that has a Date data type), as shown in **Figure 8.29**. Press OK once Power BI validates the date table.

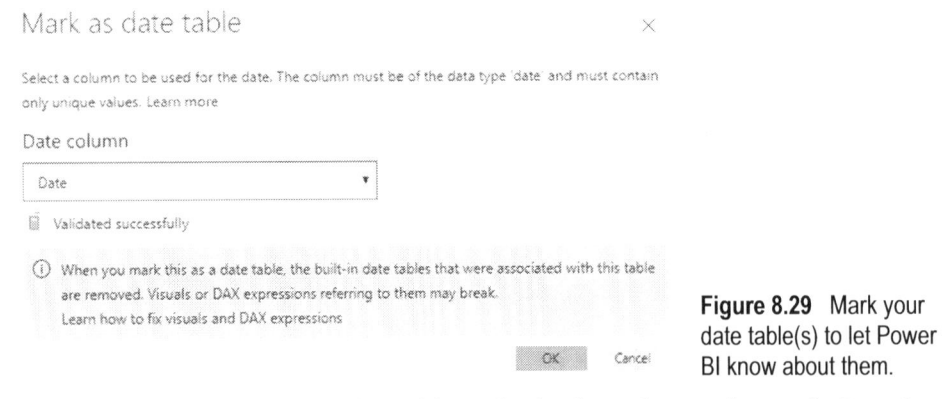

Figure 8.29 Mark your date table(s) to let Power BI know about them.

When Power BI validates your date table, it checks that it has a column of a Date data type. It must also have a day granularity, where each row in the table represents a calendar day. And it must contain a consecutive range of dates you need for analysis, such as starting from the first day with data to a few years in the future, without any gaps.

Understanding changes
Marking a date table accomplishes several things:
- Disables the Power BI-generated date table for the Date field in the Date table. Note that it doesn't remove them from the other tables unless you disable the Auto Date/Time setting in File ⇨ Options and Settings ⇨ Options (Data Load tab).
- Allows you to use your Date table for time calculations in Quick Measures.
- Makes DAX time calculations work even if the relationship between a fact table and the Date table is created on a field that is not a date field, such as a smart integer key (YYYYMMDD).
- When Analyze in Excel is used, enables special Excel date-related features when you use a field from the Date table, such as date filters.

You can unmark a date table by toggling click "Mark as date table" ⇨ "Mark as date table". If you want to change the settings, such as to use a different column, go to "Mark as date table" ⇨ "Date table settings".

8.5 Summary

Once you import the initial set of tables, you should spend time exploring the model data and refining the model schema. The Data View supports various column operations to help you explore the model data and to make the necessary changes. You should make your model more intuitive by having meaningful table and column names. Revisit each column and configure its data type and formatting properties.

Power BI excels in its data modeling capabilities. Relationships are the cornerstone of self-service data modeling that involves multiple tables. You must have table relationships to integrate data across multiple tables. Power BI supports flexible relationships with different cardinalities and filtering behavior.

As Power BI Desktop evolves, it adds more features to address popular analytical needs. Hierarchies let you explore data following natural paths. Data categories help Power BI Desktop interpret the field content. Display folders and comments let you make your model more intuitive to end users.

You've come a long way in designing the Adventure Works model! Next, let's make it even more useful by extending it with business calculations.

Chapter 9

Implementing Calculations

9.1 *Understanding Data Analysis Expressions 237*
9.2 *Implementing Calculated Columns 248*
9.3 *Implementing Measures 251*
9.4 *Implementing Advanced Relationships 258*
9.5 *Implementing Data Security 262*
9.6 *Summary 270*

Power BI promotes rapid personal business intelligence (BI) for essential data exploration and analysis. Chances are, however, that in real life you might need to go beyond just simple aggregations. Business needs might require you to extend your model with calculations. Data Analysis Expressions (DAX) gives you the needed programmatic power to travel the "last mile" and unlock the full potential of Power BI.

DAX is a big topic that deserves much more attention, and this chapter doesn't aim to cover it in depth. However, it'll lay down the necessary fundamentals so that you can start using DAX to extend your models with business logic. The chapter starts by introducing you to DAX and its arsenal of functions. Next, you'll learn how to implement custom calculated columns and measures. I'll also show you how to handle more advanced scenarios with DAX, such as Many-To-Many relationships and data security.

9.1 Understanding Data Analysis Expressions

Data Analysis Expressions (DAX) is a formula-based language in Power BI, Power Pivot, and Tabular that allows you to define custom calculations using an Excel-like formula language. DAX was introduced in the first version of Power Pivot (released in May 2010) with two major design goals:

- Simplicity – To get you started quickly with implementing business logic, DAX uses the Excel standard formula syntax and inherits many Excel functions. As a business analyst, Martin already knows many Excel functions, such as SUM and AVERAGE. When he uses Power BI, he appreciates that DAX has the same functions.

- Relational – DAX is designed with data models in mind and supports relational artifacts, including tables, columns, and relationships. For example, if Martin wants to sum up the SalesAmount column in the ResellerSales table, he can use the following formula:
=SUM(ResellerSales[SalesAmount]).

DAX also has query constructs to allow external clients to query organizational Tabular models. As a data analyst, you probably don't need to know about these constructs. This chapter focuses on DAX as an expression language to extend self-service data models. If you need to know more about DAX in the context of organizational BI, you might find my book "Applied Microsoft SQL Server 2012 Analysis Services: Tabular Modeling" useful.

You can use DAX as an expression language to implement custom calculations that range from simple expressions, such as to concatenate two columns together, to complex measures that aggregate data in a specific way, such as to implement weighted averages. Based on the intended use, DAX supports two types of calculations: calculated columns and measures.

9.1.1 Understanding Calculated Columns

A calculated column is a table column that uses a DAX formula to compute the column values. This is conceptually like a formula-based column added to an Excel list, although DAX formulas reference columns instead of cells.

How calculated columns are stored

When a column contains a formula, the storage engine computes the value for each row and saves the results, just like it does with a regular column. To use a techie term, values of calculated columns get "materialized" or "persisted". The difference is that regular columns import their values from a data source, while calculated columns are computed from DAX formulas and saved after the regular columns are loaded. Because of this, the formula of a calculated column can reference regular columns and other calculated columns.

The storage engine might not compress calculated columns as much as regular columns because they don't participate in the re-ordering algorithm that optimizes the compression. So, if you have a large table with a calculated column that has many unique values, this column might have a larger memory footprint.

Understanding row context

Every DAX formula is evaluated in a specific context. The formulas of calculated columns are evaluated for each row (row context). Let's look at a calculated column called FullName that's added to the Customer table, and it uses the following formula to concatenate the customer's first name and last name:

FullName=[FirstName] & " " & [LastName]

Because its formula is evaluated for each row in the Customer table (see **Figure 9.1**), the FullName column returns the full name for each customer. Again, this is very similar to how an Excel formula works when applied to multiple rows in a list, so this should be easy to understand.

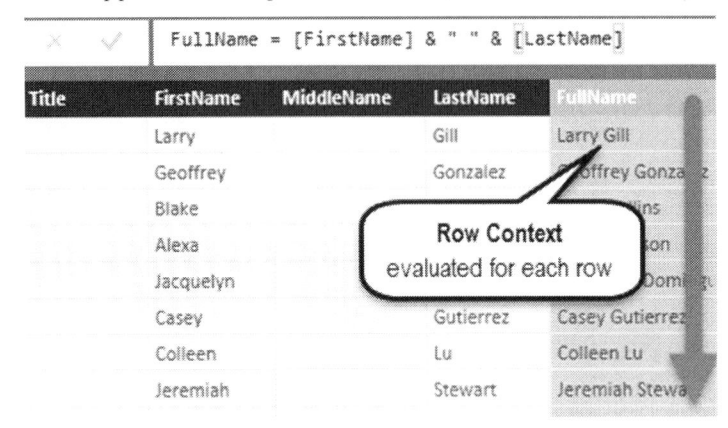

Figure 9.1 Calculated columns operate in row context, and their formulas are evaluated for each table row.

In terms of reporting, you can use calculated columns to group and filter data, just like you can use regular columns. For example, you can add a calculated column to any area of the Visualizations pane.

When to use calculated columns

In general, use a calculated column when you need to use a DAX formula to derive the column values. Because DAX formulas can reference other tables, a good usage scenario might be to look up a value from another table, just like you can use Excel VLOOKUP to reference values from another sheet. For example, to calculate the profit for each line item in ResellerSales, you might need to look up the product cost from the Product table. In this case, using a calculated column might make sense because its results are stored for each row in ResellerSales.

TIP You should be able to implement even this cross-table lookup scenario in the Power Query Editor either by merging datasets or using query functions (see my blog "Implementing Lookups in Power Query" at http://prologika.com/implementing-lookups-in-power-query/ for an example). Whether to use a DAX calculated column or another approach is a tradeoff between convenience and performance. As a best practice, implement your calculated columns as downstream as possible: in the data source, view, Power Query Editor, and finally DAX.

When shouldn't you use calculated columns? In general, you can't use calculated columns when the expression result depends on the user selection because the column formula is evaluated before the report is produced. For example, you can't use a calculated column for time calculations that depend on the date the user selects in a report slicer.

From a performance standpoint, I mentioned that because calculated columns don't compress well, they require more storage than regular columns. Therefore, if you can perform the calculation at the data source or in Power Query, I recommend you do it there instead of using calculated columns. This is especially true for high-cardinality calculated columns in large tables because they require more memory for storage. For example, you might need to concatenate a carrier tracking number from its distinct parts in a large fact table. It's better to do so in the data source or in the table query before the data is imported. Continuing this line of thought, the example that I gave for using a calculated column for the customer's full name should probably be avoided in real life because you can perform the concatenation in the query.

Sometimes, however, you don't have a choice. For example, you might need a more complicated calculation that can be done only in DAX, such as to calculate the rank for each customer based on sales history. In these cases, you can't easily apply the calculation at the data source or the query. This is a good scenario for using DAX calculated columns.

9.1.2 Understanding Measures

Besides calculated columns, you can use DAX formulas to define measures. Unlike calculated columns, which might be avoided by using other implementation approaches, measures typically can't be replicated in other ways – they need to be written in DAX. DAX measures are very useful because they are used to produce aggregated values, such as to summarize a SalesAmount column or to calculate a distinct count of customers who have placed orders. Although measures are associated with a table, they don't show in the Data View's data preview pane, as calculated columns do. Instead, they're accessible in the Fields pane. When used on reports, measures are typically added to the Value area of the Visualizations pane.

Table 9.1 Comparing implicit and explicit measures.

Criterion	Implicit Measures	Explicit Measures
Design	Automatically generated	Manually created or by using Quick Measures
Accessibility	Use the Visualization pane to change the aggregation	Use the formula bar to change the expression
DAX support	Standard aggregation functions only	Any valid measure-producing DAX expression

Understanding measure types
Power BI Desktop supports two types of measures:

- Implicit measures – To get you started as quickly as possible with data analysis, Microsoft felt that you shouldn't have to write formulas for basic aggregations. Any field added to the Value area of the Visualizations pane is treated as an implicit measure and is automatically aggregated, based on the column data type. For example, numeric fields are summed while text fields are counted.

- Explicit measures – You'll create explicit measures when you need an aggregation behavior that goes beyond the standard aggregation functions. For example, you might need a year-to-date (YTD) calculation. Explicit measures are measures that have a custom DAX formula you specify. **Table 9.1** summarizes the differences between implicit and explicit measures.

Implicit measures are automatically generated by Power BI Desktop when you add a field to the Value area of the Visualizations pane. By contrast, you must specify a custom formula for explicit measures. Once the implicit measure is created, you can use the Visualizations pane to change its aggregation function. By contrast, explicit measures become a part of the model, and their formula must be changed in the formula bar. Implicit measures can only use the DAX standard aggregation functions: Sum, Count, Min, Max, Average, Distinct Count, Standard Deviation, Variance, and Median. However, explicit measures can use any DAX formula, such as to define a custom aggregation behavior.

Understanding filter context

Unlike calculated columns, DAX measures are evaluated *at run time* for each report *cell* as opposed to once for each table row. DAX measures are always dynamic, and the result of the measure formula is never saved. Moreover, measures are evaluated in the filter context of each cell, as shown in **Figure 9.2**.

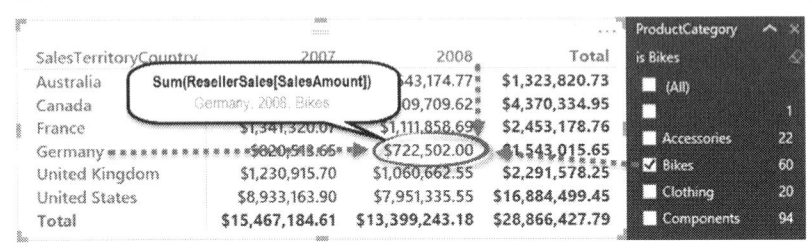

Figure 9.2 Measures are evaluated for each cell, and they operate in filter context.

This report summarizes the SalesAmount measure by countries on rows and by years on columns. The report is further filtered to show only sales for the Bikes product category. The filter context of the highlighted cell is the Germany value of the SalesTerritory[SalesTerritoryCountry] fields (on rows), the 2008 value of the Date[CalendarYear] field (on columns), and the Bikes value of the Product[ProductCategory] field (used as a filter).

If you're familiar with the SQL language, you can think of the DAX filter context as a WHERE clause that's determined dynamically and then applied to each cell on the report. When Power BI calculates the expression for that cell, it scopes the formula accordingly, such as to sum the sales amount from the rows in the ResellerSales table where the SalesTerritoryCountry value is Germany, the CalendarYear value is 2008, and the ProductCategory value is Bikes.

> **NOTE** Strictly speaking every DAX measure is evaluated in both row and filter contexts. However, there is no filter context for calculated columns because their expressions are evaluated before reports are created. Simple measure formulas might not have row context but measures that use iterators do. For example, as SUMX(<table>, <expression>) iterates through the rows in the table passed as the first argument, it propagates the row context to the expression passed as the second argument.

When to use measures

In general, measures are most frequently used to aggregate data. Explicit measures are typically used when you need a custom aggregation behavior, such as for time calculations, aggregates over aggregates, variances, and weighted averages. Suppose you want to calculate year-to-date (YTD) of reseller sales. As a first attempt, you might decide to add a SalesAmountYTD calculated column to the ResellerSales table. But now you have an issue because each row in this table represents an order line item. It's meaningless to calculate YTD for each line item.

As a second attempt, you could create a summary table in the database that stores YTD sales at a specific grain, such as product, end of month, reseller, and so on. While this might be a good approach for report performance, it presents issues. What if you need to lower the grain to include other dimensions?

What if your requirements change and now YTD needs to be calculated as of any date? A better approach would be to use an explicit measure that's evaluated dynamically as users slice and dice the data. And don't worry too much about performance. Thanks to the memory-resident nature of the storage engine, most DAX calculations are instantaneous!

> **NOTE** The performance of DAX measures depends on several factors, including the complexity of the formula, your knowledge of DAX (whether you write inefficient DAX), the amount of data, and even the hardware of your computer. While most measures, such as time calculations and basic filtered aggregations, should perform very well, more involved calculations, such as aggregates over aggregates or the number of open orders as of any reporting date, are more expensive.

Comparing calculated columns and measures

Beginner DAX practitioners often confuse calculated columns and measures. Although both use DAX, their behavior and purpose are completely different. **Table 9.2** should help you understand these differences.

Table 9.2 Comparing calculated columns and measures.

	Calculated Column	Measure
Evaluation	Design time (before reports are run)	Run time (when reports are run)
Typical context	Row context	Filter context (and row context with iterators, such as SUMX)
Alternative implementation	Possibly Power Query or database views (unless DAX formulas are required)	Usually no alternatives
Typical usage	Row-based expressions, lookups	Custom aggregation, such as YTD, QTD, weighted averages

> **NOTE** You might be able to avoid DAX calculated columns by using Power Query custom columns or calculations further downstream, such as expression-based fields in database views, if they don't negatively impact data refresh times. But you almost never can replace DAX measures because no alternatives can depend on runtime conditions, such as filters and slicers.

9.1.3 Understanding DAX Syntax

As I mentioned, one of the DAX design goals is to look and feel like the Excel formula language. Because of this, the DAX syntax resembles the Excel formula syntax. The DAX formula syntax is case-insensitive. For example, the following two expressions are both valid:

=YEAR([Date])
=year([date])

That said, I suggest you have a naming convention and stick to it. I personally prefer the first example where the function names are in uppercase and the column references match the column names in the model. This convention helps me quickly identify functions and columns in DAX formulas, and so that's what I use in this book.

Understanding expression syntax

A DAX formula for calculated columns and explicit measures has the following syntax:

Name=expression

Name is the name of the calculated column or measure. The expression must evaluate to a scalar (single) value. Expressions can contain operators, constants, or column references to return literal or Boolean values. The FullName calculated column that you saw before is an example of a simple expression that concatenates two values. You can add as many spaces as you want to make the formula easier to read.

Expressions can also include functions to perform more complicated operations, such as aggregating data. For example, back in **Figure 9.2**, the DAX formula references the SUM function to aggregate the SalesAmount column in the ResellerSales table. Functions can be nested. For example, the following formula nests the FILTER function to calculate the count of line items associated with the Progressive Sports reseller:

=COUNTROWS(FILTER(ResellerSales, RELATED(Reseller[ResellerName])="Progressive Sports"))

DAX supports up to 64 levels of function nesting but going beyond two or three levels makes the formulas more difficult to understand. When you need to go above two or three levels of nesting, I recommend you break the formula into multiple measures or variables. This also simplifies testing complex formulas.

Table 9.3 DAX supports the following operators.

Category	Operators	Description	Example
Arithmetic	+, -, *, /, ^	Addition, subtraction, multiplication, division, and exponentiation	=[SalesAmount] * [OrderQty]
Comparison	>, >=, <, <=, <>	For comparing values	=FILTER(RELATEDTABLE(Products),Products[UnitPrice]>30))
Logical	||, &&	Logical OR and AND	=FILTER(RELATEDTABLE(Products),Products[UnitPrice]>30 && Products[Discontinued]=TRUE())
Concatenation	&	Concatenating text	=[FirstName] & " " & [LastName]
Unary	+, -, NOT	Change the operand sign	= - [SalesAmount]

Understanding operators

DAX supports a set of common operators to support more complex formulas, as shown in **Table 9.3**. DAX also supports TRUE and FALSE as logical constants.

Referencing columns

One of DAX's strengths over regular Excel formulas is that it can traverse table relationships and reference columns. This is much simpler and more efficient than referencing Excel cells and ranges with the VLOOKUP function. Column names are unique within a table. You can reference a column using its fully qualified name in the format <TableName>[<ColumnName>], such as in this example:

ResellerSales[SalesAmount]

If the table name includes a space or is a reserved word, such as Date, enclose it with single quotes:

'Reseller Sales'[SalesAmount] or 'Date'[CalendarYear]

When a calculated column references a column from the same table, you can omit the table name. The AutoComplete feature in the formula bar helps you avoid syntax errors when referencing columns.

> **TIP** The formula bar has a comprehensive editor (referred also as "DAX editor") that supports color coding, indentation, syntax checking and more. The "Formula editor in Power BI Desktop" article (https://docs.microsoft.com/power-bi/desktop-formula-editor) lists the supported keyboard shortcuts.

As **Figure 9.3** shows, the moment you start typing the fully qualified column reference in the formula bar, it displays a drop-down list of matching columns.

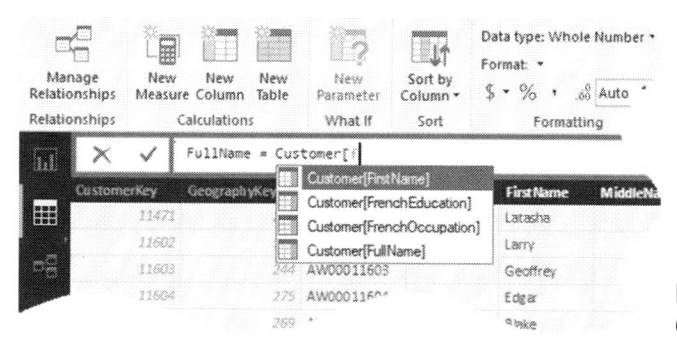

Figure 9.3 AutoComplete helps you with column references in the formula bar.

9.1.4 Understanding DAX Functions

DAX supports over a hundred functions that encapsulate a prepackaged programming logic to perform a wide variety of operations. If you type in the function name in the formula bar, AutoComplete shows the function syntax and its arguments. For the sake of brevity, this book doesn't cover the DAX functions and their syntax in detail. For more information, please refer to the DAX language reference by Ed Price (this book's technical editor) at http://bit.ly/daxfunctions, which provides a detailed description and examples for most functions. Another useful resource is "DAX in the BI Tabular Model Whitepaper and Samples" by Microsoft (http://bit.ly/daxwhitepaper) and DAX Guide (https://dax.guide) by SQLBI.

Functions from Excel

DAX supports approximately 80 Excel functions. The big difference is that DAX formulas can't reference Excel cells or ranges. References such as A1 or A1:A10, which are valid in Excel formulas, can't be used in DAX functions. Instead, when data operations are required, the DAX functions must reference columns or tables. **Table 9.4** shows the subset of Excel functions supported by DAX with examples.

Table 9.4 DAX borrows many functions from Excel.

Category	Functions	Example
Date and Time	DATE, DATEVALUE, DAY, EDATE, EOMONTH, HOUR, MINUTE, MONTH, NOW, SECOND, TIME, TIMEVALUE, TODAY, WEEKDAY, WEEKNUM, YEAR, YEARFRAC	=YEAR('Date'[Date])
Information	ISBLANK, ISERROR, ISLOGICAL, ISNONTEXT, ISNUMBER, ISTEXT	=IF(ISBLANK('Date'[Month]), "N/A", 'Date'[Month])
Logical	AND, IF, NOT, OR, FALSE, TRUE	=IF(ISBLANK(Customers[MiddleName]),FALSE(),TRUE())
Math and Trigonometry	ABS,CEILING, ISO.CEILING, EXP, FACT, FLOOR, INT, LN, LOG, LOG10, MOD, MROUND, PI, POWER, QUOTIENT, RAND, RANDBETWEEN, ROUND, ROUNDDOWN, ROUNDUP, SIGN, SQRT, SUM, SUMSQ, TRUNC	=SUM(ResellerSales[SalesAmount])
Statistical	AVERAGE, AVERAGEA, COUNT, COUNTA, COUNTBLANK, MAX, MAXA, MIN, MINA	=AVERAGE(ResellerSales[SalesAmount])
Text	CONCATENATE, EXACT, FIND, FIXED, LEFT, LEN, LOWER, MID, REPLACE, REPT, RIGHT, SEARCH, SUBSTITUTE, TRIM, UPPER, VALUE	=SUBSTITUTE(Customer[Phone],"-", "")

IMPLEMENTING CALCULATIONS 243

Aggregation functions

As you've seen, DAX "borrows" the Excel aggregation functions, such as SUM, MIN, MAX, COUNT, and so on. However, the DAX counterparts accept a table column as an input argument instead of a cell range. Since only referencing columns can be somewhat limiting, DAX adds X-version of these functions: SUMX, AVERAGEX, COUNTAX, MINX, MAXX. These functions are also called *iterators* and take two arguments. The first one is a table to iterate through and the second is an expression that is evaluated for each row.

Suppose you want to calculate the total order amount for each row in the ResellerSales table using the formula [SalesAmount] * [OrderQuantity]. You can accomplish this in two ways. First, you can add an OrderAmount calculated column that uses the above expression and then use the SUM function to summarize the calculated column. However, a better approach is to perform the calculation in one step by using the SUMX function, as follows:

=SUMX(ResellerSales, ResellerSales[SalesAmount] * ResellerSales[OrderQuantity])

Although the result in both cases is the same, the calculation process is very different. In the case of the SUM function, DAX simply aggregates the column. When you use the SUMX function, DAX will compute the expression for each of the detail rows behind the cell and then aggregate the result. What makes the X-version functions flexible is that the table argument can also be a function that returns a table of values. For example, the following formula calculates the simple average (arithmetic mean) of the SalesAmount column for rows in the InternetSales table whose unit price is above $100:

=AVERAGEX (FILTER(InternetSales, InternetSales[UnitPrice] > 100), InternetSales[SalesAmount])

This formula uses the FILTER function, which returns a table of rows matching the criteria that you pass in the second argument.

Statistical functions

DAX adds new statistical functions. The COUNTROWS(Table) function is similar to the Excel COUNT functions (COUNT, COUNTA, COUNTX, COUNTAX, COUNTBLANK), but it takes a table as an argument and returns the count of rows in that table. For example, the following formula returns the number of rows in the ResellerSales table:

=COUNTROWS(ResellerSales)

Similarly, the DISTINCTCOUNT(Column) function, counts the distinct values in a column. DAX includes the most common statistical functions, such as STDEV.S, STDEV.P, STDEVX.S, STDEVX.P, VAR.S, VAR.P, VARX.S, and VARX.P, for calculating standard deviation and variance. Like Count, Sum, Min, Max, and Average, DAX has its own implementation of these functions for better performance instead of just using the Excel standard library.

Filter functions

This category includes functions for navigating relationships and filtering data, including the ALL, ALLEXCEPT, ALLNOBLANKROW, CALCULATE, CALCULATETABLE, DISTINCT, EARLIER, EARLIEST, FILTER, LOOKUPVALUE, RELATED, RELATEDTABLE, and VALUES functions. Next, I'll provide examples for the most popular filter functions.

You can use the RELATED(Column), RELATEDTABLE(Table), and USERELATIONSHIP (Column1, Column2) functions for navigating relationships in the model. The RELATED function follows a many-to-one relationship, such as from a fact table to a lookup table. Consider a calculated column in the ResellerSales table that uses the following formula:

=RELATED(Product[StandardCost])

For each row in the ResellerSales table, this formula will look up the standard cost of the product in the Product table. The RELATEDTABLE function can travel a relationship in either direction. For example, a calculated column in the Product table can use the following formula to obtain the total reseller sales amount for each product:

=SUMX(RELATEDTABLE(ResellerSales), ResellerSales[SalesAmount])

For each row in the Product table, this formula finds the corresponding rows in the ResellerSales table that match the product and then it sums the SalesAmount column across these rows. The USERELATIONSHIP function can use inactive role-playing relationships, as I'll demonstrate in section 9.4.1.

The FILTER (Table, Condition) function is useful to filter a subset of column values, as I've just demonstrated with the AVERAGEX example. The DISTINCT(Column) function returns a table of unique values in a column. For example, this formula returns the count of unique customers with Internet sales:

=COUNTROWS(DISTINCT(InternetSales[CustomerKey]))

When there is no table relationship, the LOOKUPVALUE (ResultColumn, SearchColumn1, SearchValue1 [, SearchColumn2, SearchValue2]...) function can be used to look up a single value from another table. The following formula looks up the sales amount of the first line item bought by customer 14870 on August 1st, 2007:

=LOOKUPVALUE(InternetSales[SalesAmount],[OrderDateKey],"20070801",[CustomerKey],"14870", [SalesOrderLineNumber],"1")

If multiple values are found, the LOOKUPVALUE function will return the error "A table of multiple values was supplied where a single value was expected". If you expect multiple values, use the FILTER function instead.

Understanding CALCULATE

The CALCULATE(Expression, [Filter1],[Filter2]..) function is a very popular and useful function because it allows you to overwrite the filter context. It evaluates an expression in its filter context that could be modified by optional filters. Suppose you need to add a LineItemCount calculated column to the Customer table that computes the count of order line items posted by each customer. On a first attempt, you might try the following expression to count the order line items:

=COUNTROWS(InternetSales)

However, this expression won't work as expected (see the top screenshot in **Figure 9.4**). Specifically, it returns the count of all rows in the InternetSales table instead of counting the line items for each customer.

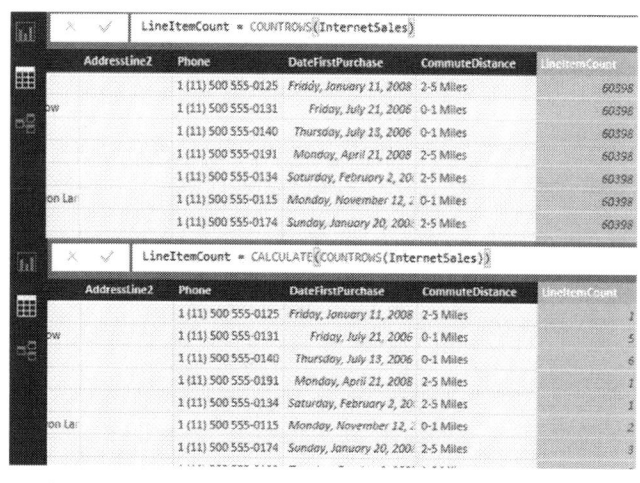

Figure 9.4 This calculated column in the second example uses the CALCULATE function to pass the row context to the InternetSales table.

To fix this, you need to force the COUNTROWS function to execute in the current row context. To do this, I'll use the CALCULATE function as follows:

IMPLEMENTING CALCULATIONS

=CALCULATE(COUNTROWS(InternetSales))

The CALCUATE function determines the current row context and applies the filter context to the formula. Because the Customer table is related to InternetSales on CustomerKey, the value of CustomerKey for each row is passed as a filter to InternetSales. For example, if the CustomerKey value for the first row is 11602, the filter context for the first execution is COUNTROWS(InternetSales, CustomerKey=11602).

The CALCULATE function can also take one or more filters as optional arguments. The filter argument can be a Boolean expression or a table. The following expression returns the transaction count for each customer for the year 2007 and the Bikes product category:

=CALCULATE(COUNTROWS(InternetSales), 'Date'[CalendarYear]=2007, Product[ProductCategory]="Bikes")

The following expression counts the rows in the InternetSales table for each customer where the product category is "Bikes" or is missing:

=CALCULATE(COUNTROWS(InternetSales), FILTER(Product, Product[ProductCategory]="Bikes" || ISBLANK(Product[ProductCategory])))

The FILTER function returns a table that contains only the rows from the Product table where ProductCategory="Bikes". When you pass the returned table to the CALCULATE function, it'll filter away any combination of column values that doesn't exist in the table.

> **TIP** When the expression to be evaluated is a measure, you can use the following shortcut for the CALCULATE function: =MeasureName(<filter>). For example, =[SalesAmount1]('Date'[CalendarYear]=2006)

Time intelligence functions

One of the most common analysis needs is implementing time calculations, such as year-to-date, parallel period, previous period, and so on. The time intelligence functions require a Date table. The Date table should contain one row for every date that might exist in your data. You can add a Date table using any of the techniques I discussed in Chapter 6 but remember also to mark it as a date table, as I showed you in the previous chapter. DAX uses the Data table to construct a set of dates for each calculation depending on the DAX formula you specify. For more information about how DAX uses a date table, read the blog post, "Time Intelligence Functions in DAX" by Microsoft's Howie Dickerman (http://bit.ly/daxtifunctions).

Recall that Power BI doesn't limit you to a single date table. For example, you might decide to import three date tables, so you can do analysis on order date, ship date, and due date. If they are all related to the ResellerSales table, you can implement calculations such as:

SalesAmountByOrderDate = TOTALYTD(SUM(ResellerSales[SalesAmount]), 'OrderDate'[Date])
SalesAmountByShipDate = TOTALYTD(SUM(ResellerSales[SalesAmount]), 'ShipDate'[Date])

DAX has about 35 functions for implementing time calculations. The functions that you'll probably use most often are TOTALYTD, TOTALQTD, and TOTALMTD. For example, the following formula calculates the YTD sales. The second argument tells DAX which Date table to use as a reference point:

= TOTALYTD(SUM(ResellerSales[SalesAmount]), 'Date'[Date])
-- or the following expression to use fiscal years that end on June 30th
= TOTALYTD(SUM(ResellerSales[SalesAmount]), 'Date'[Date], ALL('Date'), "6/30")

Another common requirement is to implement variance and growth calculations between the current and previous time period. The following formula calculates the sales amount for the previous year using the PREVIOUSYEAR function:

=CALCULATE(SUM(ResellerSales[SalesAmount]), PREVIOUSYEAR('Date'[Date]))

There are also to-date functions that return a table with multiple periods, including the DATESMTD, DATESQTD, DATESYTD, and SAMEPERIODLASTYEAR. For example, the following measure formula returns the YTD reseller sales:

=CALCULATE(SUM(ResellerSales[SalesAmount]), DATESYTD('Date'[Date]))

Finally, the DATEADD, DATESBETWEEN, DATESINPERIOD, and PARALLELPERIOD functions can take an arbitrary range of dates. The following formula returns the reseller sales between July 1st 2005 and July 4th 2005.

=CALCULATE(SUM(ResellerSales[SalesAmount]), DATESBETWEEN('Date'[Date], DATE(2005,7,1), DATE(2005,7,4)))

Ranking functions

You might have a need to calculate rankings. DAX supports ranking functions. For example, the RANK.EQ(Value, Column, [Order]) function allows you to implement a calculated column that returns the rank of a number in a list of numbers. Consider the Rank calculated column in the SalesTerritory table (see **Figure 9.5**).

Figure 9.5 The RANK.EQ function ranks each row based on the value in the REVENUE column.

The formula uses the RANK.EQ function to return the rank of each territory, based on the value of the Revenue column. If multiple territories have the same revenue, they'll share the same rank. However, the presence of duplicate numbers affects the ranks of subsequent numbers. For example, had Southwest and Canada had the same revenue, their rank would be 1, but the Northwest rank would be 3. The function can take an Order argument, such as 0 (default) for a descending order or 1 for an ascending order.

Creating calculated tables

An interesting Power BI Desktop feature is creating calculated tables using DAX. A calculated table is just like a regular table, but it's populated with a DAX function that returns a table instead of using a query. I mentioned in the previous chapter that a good use for calculated tables is implementing role-playing lookup tables, such as ShipDate, OrderDate, DueDate. You can create a calculated table by clicking the New Table button in the ribbon's Modeling tab. For example, you can add a SalesSummary table (see **Figure 9.6**) that summarizes reseller and Internet sales by calendar year using the following formula:

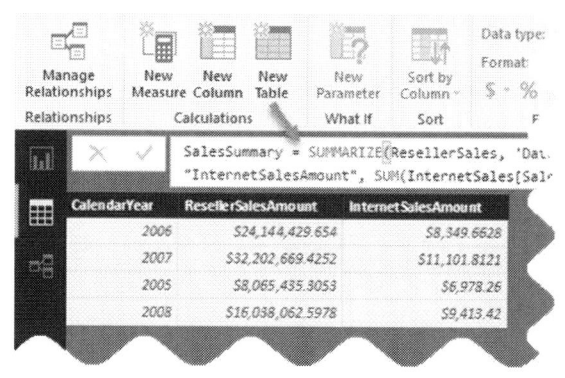

Figure 9.6 You can use the New Table button in the ribbon's Modeling tab to create a calculated table that uses a DAX formula.

SalesSummary = SUMMARIZE(ResellerSales, 'Date'[CalendarYear], "ResellerSalesAmount", SUM(ResellerSales[SalesAmount]), "InternetSalesAmount", SUM(InternetSales[SalesAmount]))

This formula uses the SUMMARIZE function which works similarly to the SQL GROUP BY clause. It summarizes the ResellerSales table by grouping by Date[CalendarYear] and computing the aggregated ResellerSales[SalesAmount] and InternetSales[SalesAmount]. Unlike SQL, you don't have to specify joins because the model has relationships from the ResellerSales and InternetSales tables to the Date table. Another practical scenario for using a calculated table is for implementing aggregations (see Chapter 6).

Now that I've introduced you to the DAX syntax and functions, let's practice creating DAX calculations. You'll also practice creating visualizations in the Report View to test the calculations, but I won't go into the details because you've already learned about visualizations in Chapter 3. If you don't want to type in the formulas, you can copy them from the dax.txt file in the \Source\ch09 folder.

9.2 Implementing Calculated Columns

As I previously mentioned, calculated columns are columns that use DAX formulas for their values. Unlike the regular columns you get when you import data, you add calculated columns after the data is imported, by entering DAX formulas. When you create a report, you can place a calculated column in any area of the Visualizations pane, although you'd typically use calculated columns to group and filter data on the report.

9.2.1 Creating Basic Calculated Columns

DAX includes various operators to create basic expressions, such as expressions for concatenating strings and for performing arithmetic operations. You can use them to create simple expression-based columns.

Concatenating text
Suppose you need a visualization that shows sales by employee (see **Figure 9.7**). Since you'd probably need to show the employee's full name, which is missing in the Employee table, let's create a calculated column that shows the employee's full name:

1. Open the Adventure Works file with your changes from the previous chapter.

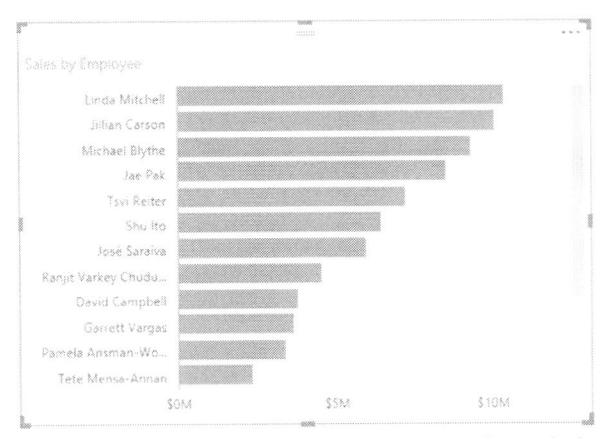

Figure 9.7 This visualization shows sales by the employee's full name.

2. Click the Data View icon in the navigation bar. Click the Employee table in the Fields pane to select it.
3. In the Modeling bar, click the New Column button. This adds a new column named "Column" to the end of the table and activates the formula bar. In the formula bar, enter the following formula:

FullName = [FirstName] & " " & [LastName]

This formula changes the name of the calculated column to *FullName*. Then, the DAX expression uses the concatenation operator to concatenate the FirstName and LastName columns and to add an empty space in between them. As you type, AutoComplete helps you with the formula syntax, although you should also follow the syntax rules, such as that a column reference must be enclosed in square brackets.

4. Press Enter or click the checkmark button to the left of the formula bar. DAX evaluates the expression and commits the formula. Power BI Desktop adds the FullName field to the Employee table in the Fields pane and prefixes it with a special *fx* icon.

Implementing custom columns in Power Query

Instead of DAX calculated columns, you can implement simple expression-based columns in Power Query. This is the technique you'll practice next.

1. Right-click the Customer table in the Fields pane and then click Edit Query.

2. Add a FullName custom column (in the ribbon's Add Column tab, click Custom Column) to the Customer query with the following formula:

=[FirstName] & " " & [LastName]

In this case, the formula has a similar syntax as the DAX calculated column but make no mistake: M is a separate language than DAX.

> **TIP** Instead of writing an M formula, another way to accomplish the same task in Power Query is to click the Add Column ⇨ Column from Example button and simply type the expected result using the data in the first row. For example, because Jon Yang is the first customer listed, simply type Jon Yang and press Enter. Power Query will figure out the formula!

3. In the Queries pane of the Power Query Editor, select the Date query. Add the custom columns shown in **Table 9.5** to assign user-friendly names to months, quarters, and semesters. In case you're wondering, the Text.From() function is used to cast a number to text. An explicit conversion is required because the query won't do an implicit conversion to text, and so the formula will return an error.

Table 9.5 Add the following calculated columns in the Date query.

Column Name	Expression	Example
MonthNameDesc	=[MonthName] & " " & Text.From([CalendarYear])	July 2007
CalendarQuarterDesc	="Q" & Text.From([CalendarQuarter]) & " " & Text.From([CalendarYear])	Q1 2008
FiscalQuarterDesc	="Q" & Text.From([FiscalQuarter]) & " " & Text.From([FiscalYear])	Q3 2008
CalendarSemesterDesc	="H" & Text.From([CalendarSemester]) & " " & Text.From([CalendarYear])	H2 2007
FiscalSemesterDesc	="H" & Text.From([FiscalSemester]) & " " & Text.From([FiscalYear])	H2 2007

4. Click the "Close & Apply" button to apply the changes to the data model.

5. In the Fields pane, expand the Date table, and click the MonthNameDesc column to select it in the Data View. Click the "Sort By Column" button (ribbon's Modeling tab) to sort the MonthNameDesc column by the MonthNumberOfYear column. You do this so that month names are sorted in the ordinal order when MonthNameDesc is used on a report.

6. To reduce clutter, hide the CalendarQuarter, CalendarSemester, FiscalQuarter and FiscalSemester columns in the Date table. These columns show the quarter and semester ordinal numbers, and they're not that useful for analysis.

7. In the Reports tab, create a Bar Chart using the SalesAmount field from the ResellerSales table (add it to Value area) and the FullName field from the Employee table (add it to the Axis area).
8. Hover on the chart and click the ellipsis (…) menu in the upper-right corner. Sort the visualization by SalesAmount in descending order. Compare your results with **Figure 9.7** to verify that the FullName calculated column is working. Save the Adventure Works model.

Performing arithmetic operations

Another common requirement is to create a calculated column that performs some arithmetic operations for each row in a table. Follow these steps to create a LineTotal column that calculates the total amount for each row in the ResellerSales table by multiplying the order quantity, discount, and unit price:

1. Another way to add a calculated column is to use the Fields pane. In the Fields pane, right-click the ResellerSales table, and then click New Column.
2. In the formula bar, enter the following formula and press Enter. I've intentionally misspelled the OrderQty column reference to show you how you can troubleshoot errors in formulas.

LineTotal = [UnitPrice] * (1-[UnitPriceDiscountPct]) * [OrderQty]

This expression multiplies UnitPrice times UnitPriceDiscountPrc times OrderQty. Notice that when you type in a recognized function in the formula bar and enter a parenthesis "(", AutoComplete shows the function syntax. Notice that the formula bar shows the error "Column 'OrderQty' cannot be found or may be used in this expression". In addition, the LineTotal column shows "Error" in every cell (see **Figure 9.8**).

3. In the formula bar, replace the OrderQty reference with OrderQuantity as follows:

LineTotal = [UnitPrice] * (1-[UnitPriceDiscountPct]) * [**OrderQuantity**]

4. Press Enter. Now, the column should work as expected.

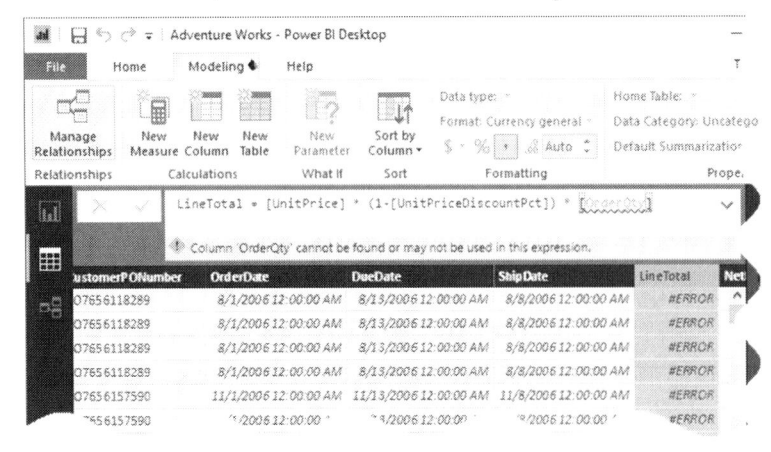

Figure 9.8 The formula bar displays an error when the DAX formula contains an invalid column reference.

9.2.2 Creating Advanced Calculated Columns

DAX supports formulas that allow you to create more advanced calculated columns. For example, you can use the RELATED function to look up a value from a related table. Another popular function is the SUMX function, with which you can sum values from a related table.

Implementing a lookup column

Suppose you want to calculate the net profit for each row in the ResellerSales table. For the purposes of this exercise, you'd calculate the line item net profit by subtracting the product cost from the line item total. As a first step, you need to look up the product cost in the Product table.

1. In the Fields pane, add a new NetProfit calculated column to the ResellerSales table that uses the following expression:

   NetProfit = RELATED(Product[StandardCost])

   This expression uses the RELATED function to look up the value of the StandardCost column in the Product table. Since a calculated column inherits the current row context, this expression is evaluated for each row. Specifically, for each row DAX gets the ProductKey value, navigates the ResellerSales[ProductKey] ⇨ Product[ProductKey] relationship, and then retrieves the standard cost for that product from the Product[StandardCost] column.

2. To calculate the net profit as a variance from the line total and the product's standard cost, change the expression as follows:

   NetProfit = [LineTotal] - (RELATED(Product[StandardCost]) * ResellerSales[OrderQuantity])

   Note that when the line item's product cost exceeds the line total, the result is a negative value.

   Aggregating values
   You can use the SUMX function to aggregate related rows from another table. Suppose you need a calculated column in the Product table that returns the reseller sales for each product:

3. Add a new ResellerSales calculated column to the Product table with the following expression:

   ResellerSales = SUMX(RELATEDTABLE(ResellerSales), ResellerSales[SalesAmount])

   The RELATEDTABLE function follows a relationship in either direction (many-to-one or one-to-many) and returns a table containing all the rows that are related to the current row from the specified table. In this case, this function returns a table with all the rows from the ResellerSales table that are related to the current row in the Product table. Then, the SUMX function sums the SalesAmount column.

4. Note that the formula returns a blank value for some products because these products don't have any reseller sales.

   Ranking values
   Suppose you want to rank each customer based on the customer's overall sales. The RANKX function can help you implement this requirement:

5. In the Fields pane, right-click the Customer table and click New Column.
6. In the formula bar, enter the following formula:

   SalesRank = RANKX(Customer, SUMX(RELATEDTABLE(InternetSales), [SalesAmount]),,,Dense)

   This function uses the RANKX function to calculate the rank of each customer, based on the customer's overall sales recorded in the InternetSales table. Like the previous example, the SUMX function is used to aggregate the [SalesAmount] column in the InternetSales table. The Dense argument is used to avoid skipping numbers for tied ranks (ranks with the same value).

9.3 Implementing Measures

Measures are typically used to aggregate values. Unlike calculated columns whose expressions are evaluated at design time for each row in the table, measures are evaluated at run time for each cell on the report. DAX applies the row, column, and filter selections when it calculates the formula. DAX supports implicit and explicit measures. An implicit measure is a regular column that's added to the Value area of the Visualizations pane. An explicit measure has a custom DAX formula. For more information about the differences between implicit and explicit measures, see **Table 9.1** again.

9.3.1 Implementing Implicit Measures

In this exercise, you'll work with implicit measures. This will help you understand how implicit measures aggregate and how you can control their default aggregation behavior.

Changing the default aggregation behavior
I explained before that by default, Power BI Desktop aggregates implicit measures using the SUM function for numeric columns and the COUNT function for text-based columns. When you add a column to the Value area, Power BI Desktop automatically creates an implicit measure and aggregates it based on the column type. For numeric columns Power BI Desktop uses the DAX SUM aggregation function. If the column date type is Text, Power BI Desktop uses COUNT. Sometimes, you might need to overwrite the default aggregation behavior. For example, the CalendarYear column in the Date table is a numeric column, but it doesn't make sense to sum it up on reports.

1. Make sure that the Data View is active. In the Fields pane, click the CalendarYear column in the Date table. This shows the Date table in the Data View and selects the CalendarYear column.
2. In the ribbon's Modeling tab, expand the Default Summarization drop-down and change it to "Do Not Summarize". As a result, the next time you use CalendarYear on a report, it won't get summarized.

Working with implicit measures
Suppose need to check if there's any seasonality impact to your business. Are some months slower than others? If sales decrease, do fewer customers purchase products? To answer these questions, you'll create the report shown in **Figure 9.9**. Using the Line and Clustered Column Chart visualization, this report shows the count of customers as a column chart and the sales as a line chart that's plotted on the secondary axis. You'll analyze these two measures by month.

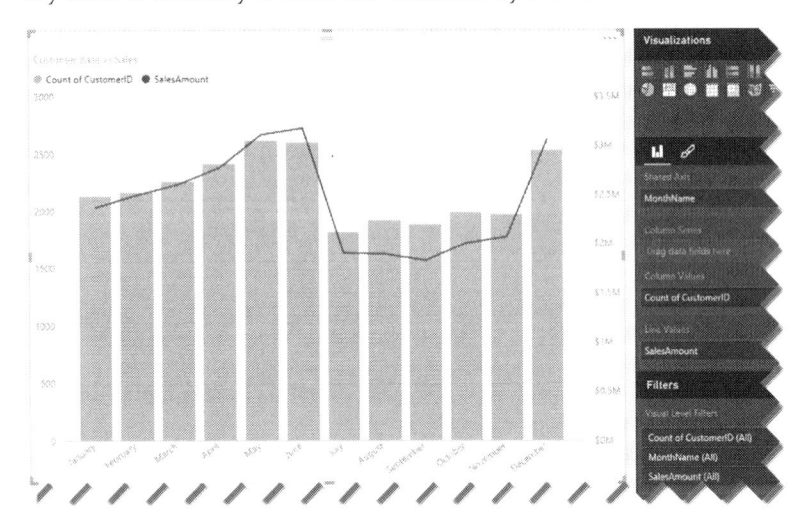

Figure 9.9 Implemented as a combo chart, this visualization shows the correlation between count of customers and sales.

Let's start with visualizing the count of customers who have purchased products by month. Traditionally, you'd add some customer identifier to the fact table and you'd use a Distinct Count aggregation function to only count unique customers. But the InternetSales table doesn't have a CustomerID column. Can you count on the CustomerID column in the Customer table?

1. Switch to the Report View. From the Fields pane, drag the CustomerID column from the Customer table, and then drop it in an empty area in the report canvas.
2. Power BI Desktop defaults to a table visualization that shows all customer identifiers. Switch the visualization type to "Line and Clustered Column Chart".

3. In the Visualizations pane, drag CustomerID from the Shared Axis area to the Column Values area.

> **NOTE** Why not count on the CustomerKey column in InternetSales? This will work if the Customer table handles Type 1 changes only. A Type 1 change results in an in-place change. When a change to a customer is detected, the row is simply overwritten. However, chances are that business requirements necessitate Type 2 changes as well, where a new row is created when an important change occurs, such as when the customer changes address. Therefore, counting on CustomerKey (called a surrogate key in dimensional modeling) is often a bad idea because it might lead to overstated results. Instead, you'd want to do a distinct count on a customer identifier that is not system generated, such as the customer's account number.

4. Expand the drop-down in the "Count of CustomerID" field. Note that it uses the Count aggregation function, as shown in **Figure 9.10**.

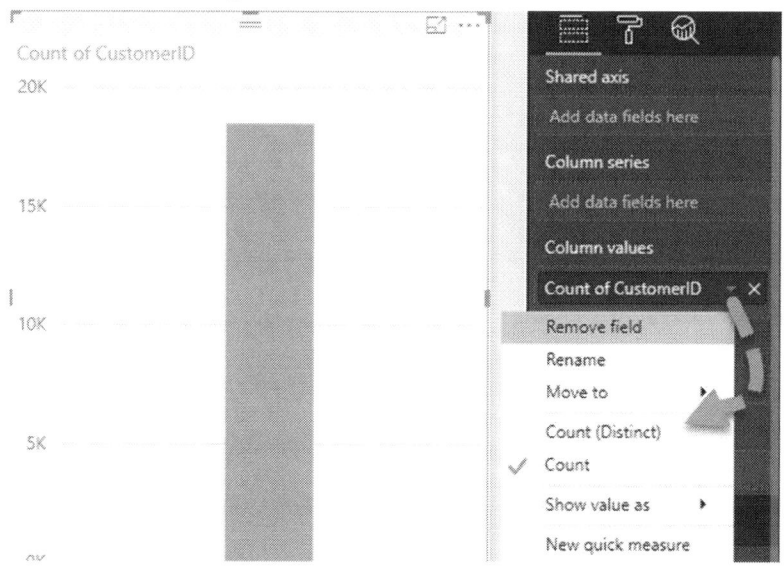

Figure 9.10 Text-based implicit measures use the Count function by default.

5. A product can be sold more than once within a given time period. If you simply count on CustomerID, you might get an inflated count. Instead, you want to count customers uniquely. Expand the drop-down next to the "Count of CustomerID" field in the "Column values" area and change the aggregation function from Count to Count (Distinct).

6. (Optional) Use the ribbon's Modeling tab to change the CustomerID default summarization to Count (Distinct) so you don't have to overwrite the aggregation function every time this field is used on a report.

7. With the new visualization selected, check the MonthName column of the Date table in the Fields pane to add it to the Shared Axis area of the Visualizations pane.

At this point, the results might be incorrect. Specifically, the count of customers might not change across months. The issue is that the aggregation happens over the InternetSales fact table via the Date ⇐ InternetSales ⇒ Customer path (notice that the relationship direction changes). Furthermore, the cardinality of the Date and Customer tables is Many-to-Many (there could be many customers who purchased something on the same date, and a repeating customer could buy multiple times).

8. Switch to the Relationships View. Double-click the InternetSales ⇒ Customer relationship. In the Advanced Options properties of the relationship, change the cross-filter direction to Both.

9. Switch to the Report View. Note that now the results vary by month.

10. Drag the SalesAmount field from the InternetSales table to the Line Values area of the Visualizations pane. Note that because SalesAmount is numeric, Power BI Desktop defaults to the SUM aggregation function.

IMPLEMENTING CALCULATIONS

Note also that indeed, seasonality affects sales. Specifically, the customer base decreases during the summer. And as the number of customers decreases, so do sales.

9.3.2 Implementing Quick Measures

As you've started to realize, DAX is a very powerful programming language. The only issue is that there is a learning curve involved. At the same time, there are frequently used measures that shouldn't require extensive knowledge of DAX. This is where "showing values as" and quick measures could help.

Showing value as

A common requirement is to show a value as a percent of total. Fortunately, there is a quick and easy way to meet this requirement.

1. Create a new Table visualization that has SalesTerritoryCountry (SalesTerritory table) and SalesAmount (ResellerSales table) fields in the Values area. Add the SalesAmount field one more time to the Values area.
2. In the Values area of the Visualizations pane, expand the drop-down next to the second SalesAmount field and choose "Show value as". Select "Percent of column total". Compare your results with **Figure 9.11**. Notice that the "%CT SalesAmount" now shows the contribution of each country to the column total.
3. (Optional) In the Visualizations pane (Fields tab), double-click the "%CT Sales Amount" field and rename it to *% of Total Sales*.

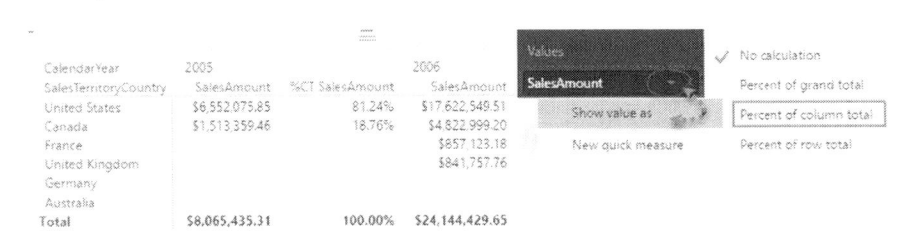

Figure 9.11 The %CT SalesAmount field shows each value as a percent of the column total.

"Show value as" changes an existing measure in place to show its results as a percentage of a column, row, or grand total. It doesn't create a new measure. Power BI implements this feature internally so don't try to find or change the DAX formula. If you require more control, I'll walk you through implementing an explicit measure in the next section that does the same thing but this time with a DAX formula.

Creating quick measures

Before further honing your DAX skills, let's look at another feature that may help you avoid, or at least help you learn DAX. Quick measures are prepackaged formulas for common analytical requirements, such as time calculations, aggregates, and totals. Unlike "show value as", quick measures are implemented as DAX explicit measures, so you can see and change the quick measure formula. Suppose you want to implement a running sales total across years (see **Figure 9.12**).

Figure 9.12 The second measure accumulates sales over years and it's produced by the "Running total" quick measure.

1. Create a new Table visualization that has CalendarYear (Date table) and SalesAmount (ResellerSales table) fields in the Values area.
2. Right-click the ResellerSales table in the Fields pane and then click "New quick measure". Alternatively, you expand the drop-down next to SalesAmount in the Values area and then click "New Quick Measure".
3. In the "Quick measures" window (see **Figure 9.13**), expand the Calculation drop-down. Observe that Power BI supports various measure types. Select "Running total" under the Totals section.

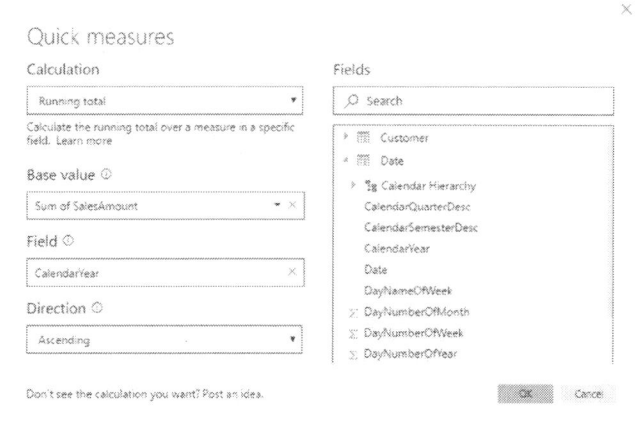

Figure 9.13 Power BI supports various quick measures to meet common analytical requirements.

4. Drag the SalesAmount field from the ResellerSales table to the "Base value" area. Drag the CalendarYear field from the Date table to the Field area. Click OK.
5. Power BI adds a new "SalesAmount running total in CalendarYear" field to the ResellerSales table in the Fields pane. Click this field. Notice that the formula bar shows the DAX formula behind the measure.

Once you create the quick measure, it becomes just like any explicit DAX measure. You can rename it or use it on your reports. However, you can't go back to the "Quick measures" dialog. To customize the measure, you must make changes directly to the formula, so you still need to know some DAX.

9.3.3 Implementing Explicit Measures

Explicit measures are more flexible than implicit measures because you can use custom DAX formulas. Like implicit measures, explicit measures are typically used to aggregate data and are usually placed in the Value area in the Visualizations pane.

> **TIP** DAX explicit measures can get complex and it might be preferable to test nested formulas step by step. To make this process easier, you can test measures outside Power BI Desktop by using DAX Studio. DAX Studio (http://daxstudio.codeplex.com) is a community-driven project to help you write and test DAX queries connected to Excel Power Pivot models, Tabular models, and Power BI Desktop models. DAX Studio features syntax highlighting, integrated tracing support, and exploring the model metadata with Dynamic Management Views (DMVs). If you're not familiar with DMVs, you can use them to document your models, such as to get a list of all the measures and their formulas.

Implementing a basic explicit measure
A common requirement is implementing a measure that filters results. For example, you might need a measure that shows the reseller sales for a specific product category, such as Bikes. Let's implement a BikeResellerSales measure that does just that.

1. In Fields pane (Data View or Report View), right-click the ResellerSales table, and click New Measure.
2. In the formula bar, enter the following formula and press Enter:

IMPLEMENTING CALCULATIONS 255

BikeResellerSales = CALCULATE(SUM(ResellerSales[SalesAmount]), 'Product'[ProductCategory]="Bikes")

Power BI Desktop adds the measure to the ResellerSales table in the Fields pane. The measure has a special calculator icon in front of it.

> **TIP** Added a measure to a wrong table? Instead of recreating the measure in the correct table, you can simply change its home table. To do this, click the measure in the Fields pane to select it. Then, in the ribbon's Modeling tab, use the Home Table dropdown (Properties group) to change the table. Because measures are dynamic, they can be anchored to any table.

3. (Optional) Add a map visualization to show the BikeResellerSales measure (see **Figure 9.14**). Add both SalesTerritoryCountry and SalesTerritoryRegion fields from the SalesTerritory table to the Location area of the Visualizations pane. This enables the drill down buttons on the map and allows you to drill down sales from country to region!

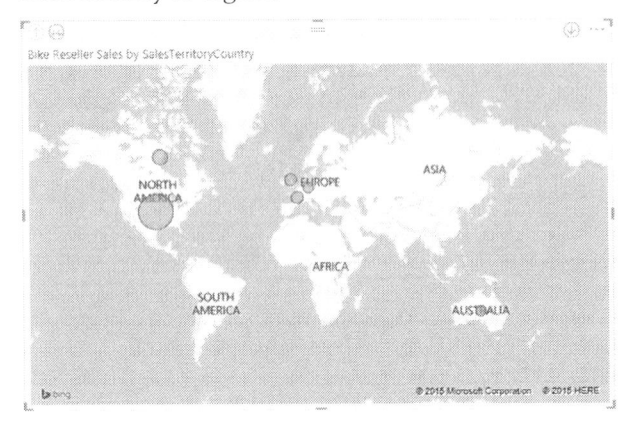

Figure 9.14 This map visualization shows the "Sum of Bike Reseller Sales" measure.

Implementing a percent of total measure

Suppose you need a measure for calculating a ratio of current sales compared to overall sales across countries. Previously, you've used the "show value as" feature. As easy as it was, this feature doesn't give you control over the calculation formula. Next, I'll show you how to implement an explicit measure that accomplishes the same (see **Figure 9.15**).

SalesTerritoryCountry	2005	2006	2007	2008	Total
Australia			2.63 %	4.66 %	1.98 %
Canada	18.76 %	19.98 %	17.55 %	14.90 %	17.87 %
France		3.55 %	7.37 %	8.58 %	5.73 %
Germany			3.41 %	5.52 %	2.47 %
United Kingdom		3.49 %	6.71 %	7.96 %	5.32 %
United States	81.24 %	72.99 %	62.33 %	58.37 %	66.63 %
Total	100.00 %	100.00 %	100.00 %	100.00 %	100.00 %

Figure 9.15 The PercentOfTotal measure shows the contribution of the country sales to the overall sales.

1. Another way to create a measure is to use the New Measure button. Make sure that the Data View is selected. In the Fields pane, click the ResellerSales table.
2. Click the New Measure button in the Modeling ribbon.
3. In the Formula field, enter the following formula:

PercentOfTotal = DIVIDE (SUM(ResellerSales[SalesAmount]), CALCULATE (SUM(ResellerSales[SalesAmount]), ALL(SalesTerritory)))

To avoid division by zero, the expression uses the DAX DIVIDE function, which performs a safe divide and returns a blank value when the denominator is zero. The SUM function sums the SalesAmount column for the current country. The denominator uses the CALCULATE and ALL functions to ignore the current context so that the expression calculates the overall sales across *all* the sales territories.

4. Click the Check Formula button to verify the formula syntax. You shouldn't see any errors. Press Enter.
5. In the Formatting section of the ribbon's Modeling tab, change the Format property to Percentage, with two decimal places.
6. (Optional). In the Report View, add a matrix visualization that uses the new measure (see **Figure 9.15** again). Add the SalesTerritoryCountry to the Rows area and CalendarYear to the Columns area to create a crosstab layout.

Implementing a YTD calculation

DAX supports many time intelligence functions for implementing common date calculations, such as YTD, QTD, and so on. These functions require a column of the Date data type in the Date table. The Date table in the Adventure Works model includes a Date column that meets this requirement. In the previous chapter, you also marked the Date table.

> **NOTE** Remember that if you don't mark the date table, the DAX time calculations will work only if the relationships to the Date table use a column of a Date type. So, in our case ResellerSales[OrderDate] ⇨ 'Date'[Date] will work but ResellerSales[OrderDateKey] ⇨ 'Date'[DateKey] won't.

Let's implement an explicit measure that returns year-to-date (YTD) sales:

1. In the Fields pane, right-click the ResellerSales table, and then click New Measure.
2. In the formula bar, enter the following formula:

SalesAmountYTD =TOTALYTD(Sum(ResellerSales[SalesAmount]), 'Date'[Date])

This expression uses the TOTALYTD function to calculate the SalesAmount aggregated value from the beginning of the year to date. Note that the second argument must reference the column of the Date data type in the date table. It also takes additional arguments, such as to specify the end date of a fiscal year.

3. To test the SalesAmountYTD measure, create the matrix visualization shown in **Figure 9.16**. Add CalendarYear and MonthName fields from the Date table in the Rows area and SalesAmount, and SalesAmountYTD fields in the Values area.

CalendarYear	MonthName	SalesAmount	SalesAmountYTD
2005	July	$489,328.58	$489,328.5787
	August	$1,538,408.31	$2,027,736.8909
	September	$1,165,897.08	$3,193,633.9687
	October	$844,721.00	$4,038,354.965
	November	$2,324,135.80	$6,362,490.7625
	December	$1,702,944.54	$8,065,435.3053
	Total	$8,065,435.31	$8,065,435.3053
2006	January	$713,116.69	$713,116.6943
	February	$1,900,788.93	$2,613,905.6247
	March	$1,455,280.41	$4,069,186.0

Figure 9.16 The SalesAmountYTD measure calculates the year-to-date sales as of any date.

If the SalesAmountYTD measure works correctly, its results should be running totals within a year. For example, the SalesAmountYTD value for 2005 ($8,065,435) is calculated by summing the sales of all the previous months since the beginning of the year 2005. Notice also that the formula works as of *any* date and the date fields don't have to be added to the visual. For example, if the report has a slicer, the user can pick a date, and as any other measure, SalesAmountYTD will recalculate as of that date. This brings a tremendous flexibility to reporting and avoids saving the results of time calculations in the database!

9.4 Implementing Advanced Relationships

Besides regular table relationships where a lookup table joins the fact table directly, you might need to model more advanced relationships, including role-playing, parent-child, and many-to-many relationships. Next, I'll show you how to meet such requirements with DAX.

9.4.1 Implementing Role-Playing Relationships

In Chapter 6, I explained that a lookup table can be joined multiple times to a fact table. The dimensional modeling terminology refers to such a lookup table as a role-playing dimension. For example, in the Adventure Works model, both the InternetSales and ResellerSales tables have three date-related columns: OrderDate, ShipDate, and DueDate. However, you only created relationships from these tables to the OrderDate column. As a result, when you analyze sales by date, DAX follows the InternetSales[OrderDate] ⇨ Date[Date] and ResellerSales[OrderDate] ⇨ Date[Date] paths.

Creating inactive relationships

Suppose that you'd like to analyze InternetSales by the date the product was shipped (ShipDate):

1. Click the Manage Relationships button. In the Manage Relationships window, click New.
2. Create the InternetSales[ShipDate] ⇨ Date[Date] relationship, as shown in **Figure 9.17**. Note that this relationship will be created as inactive because Power BI Desktop will discover that there's already an active relationship (InternetSales[OrderDate] ⇨ Date[Date]) between the two tables.

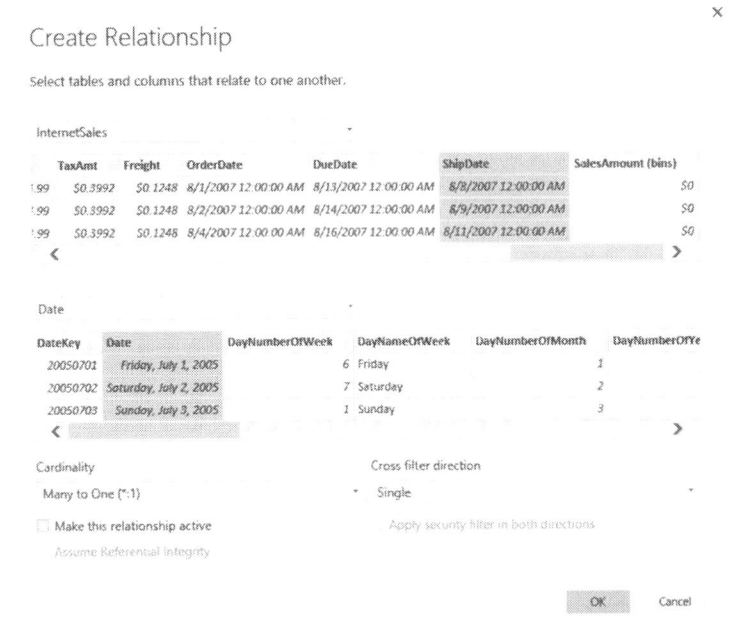

Figure 9.17 The InternetSales[ShipDate] ⇨ Date[Date] relationship will be created as inactive because there is already a relationship between these two tables.

3. Click OK and then click close.
4. In the Relationships View, confirm that there's a dotted line between the InternetSales and Date tables, which signifies an inactive relationship.

Navigating relationships in DAX
Let's say that you want to compare the ordered sales amount and shipped sales amount side by side, such as to calculate a variance. To address this requirement, you can implement measures that use DAX formulas to navigate inactive relationships. Follow these steps to implement a ShipSalesAmount measure in the InternetSales table:

1. Switch to the Data View. In the Fields pane, right-click InternetSales, and then click New Measure.
2. In the formula bar, enter the following expression:

ShipSalesAmount = CALCULATE(SUM([SalesAmount]), USERELATIONSHIP(InternetSales[ShipDate], 'Date'[Date]))

The formula uses the USERELATIONSHIP function to navigate the inactive relationship between the ShipDate column in the InternetSales table and the Date column in the Date table.

3. (Optional) Add a Table visualization with the CalendarYear (Date table), SalesAmount (InternetSales table) and ShipSalesAmount (InternetSales table) fields in the Values area. Notice that the ShipSalesAmount value is different than the SalesAmount value. That's because the ShipSalesAmount measure is aggregated using the inactive relationship on ShipDate instead of OrderDate.

9.4.2 Implementing Parent-Child Relationships

A parent-child relationship is a hierarchical relationship formed between two entities. Common examples of parent-child relationships include an employee hierarchy, where a manager has subordinates who in turn have subordinates, and an organizational hierarchy, where a company has offices and each office has branches. DAX includes functions that are specifically designed to handle parent-child relationships.

Understanding parent-child relationships
The EmployeeKey and ParentEmployeeKey columns in the Employee table have a parent-child relationship, as shown in **Figure 9.18**.

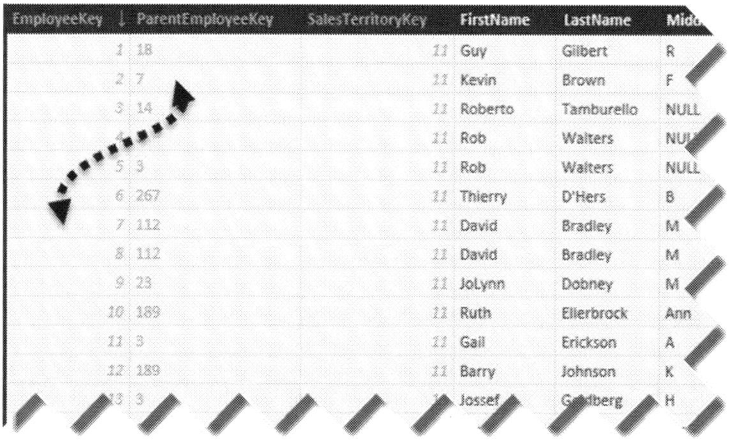

Figure 9.18 The ParentEmployeeKey column contains the identifier for the employee's manager.

Specifically, the ParentEmployeeKey column points to the EmployeeKey column for the employee's manager. For example, Kevin Brown (EmployeeKey = 2) has David Bradley (EmployeeKey=7) as a manager, who in turn reports to Ken Sánchez (EmpoyeeKey=112). (Ken is not shown in the screenshot.) Ken Sánchez's ParentEmployeeKey is blank, which means that he's the top manager. Parent-child hierarchies might have an arbitrary number of levels. Such hierarchies are called *unbalanced* hierarchies.

Implementing a parent-child relationship

Next, you'll use DAX functions to flatten the parent-child relationship before you can create a hierarchy to drill down the organizational chart:

1. Start by adding a Path calculated column to the Employee table that constructs the parent-child path for each employee. For the Path calculated column, use the following formula:

Path = PATH([EmployeeKey], [ParentEmployeeKey])

> **NOTE** At this point, you might get an error "The columns specified in the PATH function must be from the same table, have the same data type, and that type must be Integer or Text". The issue is that the ParentEmployeeKey column has a Text data type. This might be caused by a literal text value "NULL" for Ken Sánchez's while it should be a blank (null) value. To fix this, open the Power Query Editor (right-click the Employee table and click Query Editor), right-click the ParentEmployeeKey column, and then click Replace Values. In the Replace Value dialog, replace NULL with blank. Then, in the Power Query Editor (Home ribbon tab), change the column type to Whole Number and click the "Close & Apply" button.

The formula uses the PATH DAX function, which returns a delimited list of IDs (using a vertical pipe as the delimiter) starting with the top (root) of a parent-child hierarchy and ending with the current employee identifier. For example, the path for Kevin Brown is 112|7|2. The rightmost part is the ID of the employee on that row and each segment to the right follows the organizational path.

The next step is to flatten the parent-child hierarchy by adding a column for each level. This means that you need to know beforehand the maximum number of levels that the employee hierarchy might have. To be on the safe side, add one or two more levels to accommodate future growth.

2. Add a Level1 calculated column that has the following formula:

Level1 = LOOKUPVALUE(Employee[FullName], Employee[EmployeeKey], VALUE(PATHITEM([Path],1)))

This formula uses the PATHITEM function to parse the Path calculated column and return the first identifier, such as 112 in the case of Kevin Brown. Then, it uses the LOOKUPVALUE function to return the full name of the corresponding employee, which in this case is Ken Sánchez. The VALUE function casts the text result from the PATHITEM function to Integer so that the LOOKUPVALUE function compares the same data types.

3. Add five more calculated columns for Levels 2-6 that use similar formulas to flatten the hierarchy all the way down to the lowest level. Compare your results with **Figure 9.19**. Note that most of the cells in the Level 5 and Level 6 columns are empty, and that's okay because only a few employees have more than four indirect managers.

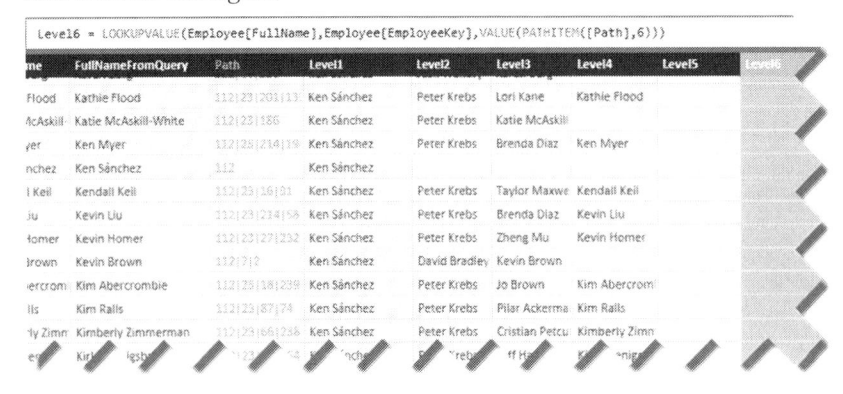

Figure 9.19 Use the PATHITEM function to flatten the parent-child hierarchy.

4. Hide the Path column in the Employee table as it's not useful for analysis.
5. (Optional) Create an Employees hierarchy consisting of six levels based on the six columns.
6. (Optional) Create a table visualization to analyze sales by any of the Level1-Level6 fields.

7. (Optional) Deploy the Adventure Works model to Power BI Service. To do this, click the Publish button in the ribbon's Home tab, or use the File ⇨ Publish ⇨ "Publish to Power BI" menu. This will add an Adventure Works dataset and Adventure Works report to the navigation bar in the Power BI portal. Once the model is published, go to Power BI Service (powerbi.com) and test the visualizations you've created. Use your knowledge from Part 1 of this book to explore and visualize the Adventure Works dataset.

9.4.3 Implementing Many-to-Many Relationships

Typically, a row in a lookup table relates to one or more rows in a fact table. For example, a given customer has one or more orders. This is an example of a one-to-many relationship that most of our tables have used so far. Sometimes, you might run into a scenario where two tables have a logical many-to-many relationship. Not to be confused with the many-to-many cardinality, a many-to-many relationship typically require a bridge table, such as to resolve the relationship between customers and bank accounts.

Understanding many-to-many relationships

The M2M.pbix sample in the \Source\ch09 folder demonstrates a popular many-to-many scenario that you might encounter if you model joint bank accounts. Open it in another Power BI Desktop and examine its Relationship View. It consists of five tables, as shown in **Figure 9.20**. The Customer table stores the bank's customers. The Account table stores the customers' accounts. A customer might have multiple bank accounts, and a single account might be owned by two or more customers, such as a savings account.

The CustomerAccount table is a bridge table that indicates which accounts are owned by which customer. The Balances table records the account balances over time. Note that the relationship CustomerAccount[AccountNo] ⇨ Account[AccountNo] is bi-directional so that the filter on the Customer table can pass through the CustomerAccount table and to the Account table.

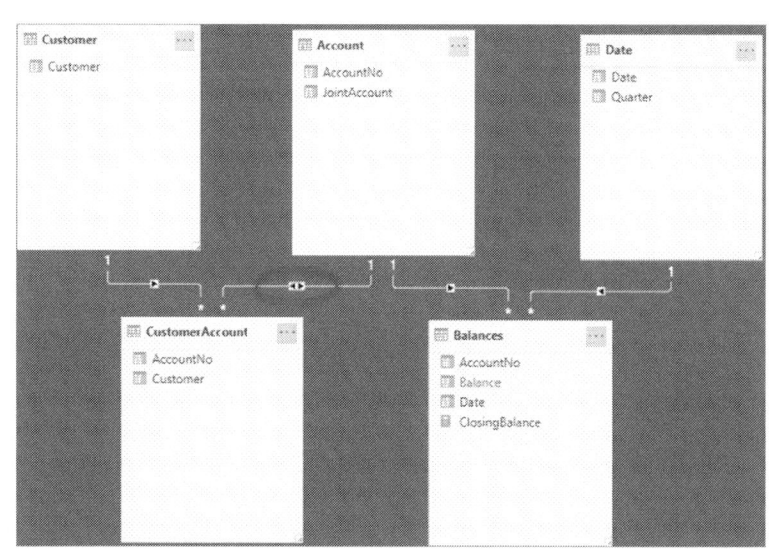

Figure 9.20 The M2M model demonstrates joint bank accounts.

Implementing closing balances

If the Balance measure is fully additive (can be summed across all lookup tables that are related to the Balances table), then you're done. However, semi-additive measures, such as account balances and inventory quantities, are trickier because they can be summed across all the tables except for the Date table. To understand this, examine the report shown in **Figure 9.21**.

Quarter	Q1 2011				Q2 2011			Total
Customer	1/1/2011	2/1/2011	3/1/2011	Total	4/1/2011	5/1/2011	Total	
Alice	100	200	300	300				300
Bob	600	700	300	300				300
John	100	200		200				200
Sam		100	100	100	200	50	50	50
Total	700	1000	400	400	200	50	50	50

Figure 9.21 This report shows closing balances per quarter.

If you create a report that simply aggregates the Balance measure (hidden in Report View), you'll find that the report produces wrong results. Specifically, the grand totals at the customer or account levels are correct, but the rest of the results are incorrect. Instead of using the Balance column, I added a ClosingBalance explicit measure to the Balances table that aggregates his account balance correctly. The measure uses the following formula:

ClosingBalance = CALCULATE(SUM(Balances[Balance]), LASTNONBLANK('Date'[Date], CALCULATE(SUM(Balances[Balance]))))

This formula uses the DAX LASTNONBLANK function to find the last date with a recorded balance. This function travels back in time, to find the first non-blank date within a given time period. For John and Q1 2011, that date is 2/1/2011 when John's balance was 200. This becomes the first quarter balance for John, as you can see in the Matrix visualization. He didn't have an account balance for Q2 (perhaps, his account was closed) so the Q2 balance is empty. His overall balance matches the Q1 balance of 200.

9.5 Implementing Data Security

Do you have a requirement to allow certain users (internal or external) to see only a subset of data that they're authorized to access? For example, as a model author Martin can see all the data he imported. However, when he deploys the model to Power BI Service, he wants Elena to see only sales for a specific geography. Or, Martin would like to restrict external partners to access only their data in a multi-tenant model that he created. This is where the Power BI data security (also known as row-level security or RLS) can help.

9.5.1 Understanding Data Security

Data security is supported for models that import data and that connect live to data, except when connecting live to Analysis Services, which has its own security model. At a high level, implementing data security is a two-step process:

- Modeling step – This involves defining roles and table filters inside the model to restrict access to data. Because more involved security scenarios require DAX knowledge for filters, I discuss data security in this chapter.
- Operational step – Once roles are defined, you need to deploy the model to Power BI Service to assign members to roles. Configuring membership is the operational aspect of RLS that needs to be done in Power BI Service.

It's important to understand that data security is only enforced in Power BI Service, that is when the model is deployed and shared with other users who have view-only rights (they don't have Admin or Edit Content permissions to a workspace) to shared content. Such users won't be able to access any data unless they are assigned to a role. However, if you email the Power BI Desktop file to another user and he opens it in Power BI Desktop, data security is *not* enforced, and the user can see all the data.

Understanding roles

A role allows you to grant other users restricted access to data in a secured model. **Figure 9.22** is meant to help you visualize a role.

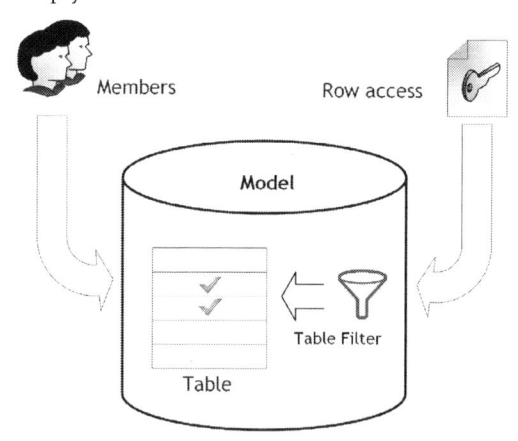

Figure 9.22 A role grants its members permissions to a table, and it optionally restricts access to table rows.

In a nutshell, a role gives its members permissions to view the model data. To create a new role, click the Manage Roles button in the ribbon's Modeling tab. Then click the Create button in the "Manage roles" window and name the role. As I mentioned, after you deploy the model to Power BI Service, you must assign members to the role. You can type in email addresses of individual users, security groups, and workspace groups.

What happens if a user with view-only rights to shared content in Power BI Service attempts to view a report in a secured model, and the user is not assigned to a role, either individually or via a group membership? When they view a report, all report visualizations show errors (see **Figure 9.23**).

Figure 9.23 If a user with view-only rights is not added to a role when data security is enabled, report visualizations show errors with details "Couldn't load the data for this visual".

Understanding table filters

By default, a role can access all the data in all tables in the model. However, the whole purpose of implementing data security is to limit access to a subset of data, such as to allow Maya to see only sales for the United States. This is achieved by specifying one or more table filters. As its name suggests, a table filter defines a filter expression that evaluates which table rows the role can see. To set up a row filter in Role Manager, enter a DAX formula next to the table name.

The DAX formula must evaluate to a Boolean condition that returns TRUE or FALSE. For example, when the user connects to the published model and the user is a member of the role, Power BI applies the row filter expression to each row in the SalesTerritory table. If the row meets the criteria, the role is authorized to see that row. For example, **Figure 9.24** shows that "US" role applies a row filter to the SalesTerritory table to return only rows where the SalesTerritoryCountry column equals "United States".

> **TIP** As it stands, Power BI doesn't support object security to hide entire tables. Even if the table filter qualifies no rows, the table will show in the model metadata. The simplest way to disallow a role from viewing any rows in a table is to set up a table filter with a FALSE() expression. If no table filter is applied to a table, TRUE() is assumed and the user can see all of its data.

Figure 9.24 This table filter grants the US role access to rows in the SalesTerritory table where SalesTerritoryCountry is United States.

Roles are additive. If a user belongs to multiple roles, the user will get the superset of all the role permissions. For example, suppose Maya is a member of both the Sales Representative and Marketing roles. The Sales Representative role grants her rights to United States, while the Marketing role grants her access to all countries. Because roles are additive, Maya can see data for all countries.

How table filters affect related tables

From an end-user perspective, rows the user isn't authorized to view and their related data in tables on the many side of the relationship simply don't exist in the model. Imagine that a global WHERE clause is applied to the model that selects only the data that's related to the allowed rows of all the secured tables.

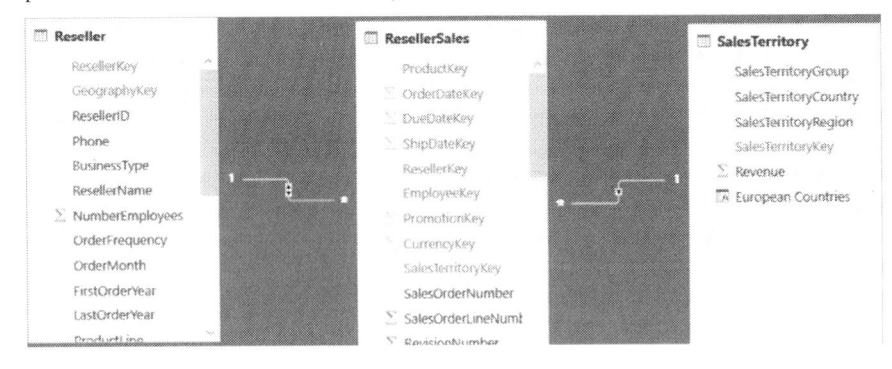

Figure 9.25 A table filter can propagate to related tables depending on the relationship type and cross filter direction.

Given the model shown in **Figure 9.25**, the user can't see any other sales territories in the SalesTerritory table except United States. Moreover, because of the SalesTerritory ⇨ ResellerSales filter direction, the user can't see sales for these territories in the ResellerSales table or in any other tables that are directly or indirectly (via cascading relationships) related to the SalesTerritory table if the filter direction points to these tables. In other words, Power BI propagates data security to related tables following the filter direction.

What about the Reseller table? Should the user see only Resellers with sales in the United States? The outcome depends on the relationship cross-filter direction. If it's Single (there is a single arrow pointing from Reseller to ResellerSales), the security filter is not propagated to the Reseller table and the user can see all resellers. To clarify, the user can see the list of all resellers, but he can see only sales for the US resellers because sales come from the filtered ResellerSales table. However, if the cross filter direction is Both and the "Apply security filter in both directions" setting (see again **Figure 9.17**) is checked, then the security filter propagates to the Reseller table and the user can see only resellers with sales in the United States.

9.5.2 Implementing Basic Data Security

In the exercise that follows, you'll add a role that allows the user to view only the United States. Then, I'll show you how to test the role on the desktop and how to add members to the role after you deploy your model to Power BI Service.

Creating a role
Start by creating a new role in the Adventure Works model.

1. In the ribbon's Modeling tab, click the Manage Roles button.
2. In the Manage Roles window, click the Create button. Rename the new role to *US*.
3. Click the ellipsis button next to the SalesTerritory table, and then click "Add filter…" ⇨ [SalesTerritoryCountry] to filter the values in this column.
4. Change the "Table Filter DAX Expression" content with the following formula (see again **Figure 9.24**):

[SalesTerritoryCountry] = "United States"

5. Click Save.

> **TIP** Consider adding an Open Access role that doesn't have any table filter. This role is for users who need full access to data. Recall that by default a role has unrestricted access unless you defined a table filter.

Testing data security
You don't have to deploy the model to Power BI Service to test the role. Power BI Desktop lets you do this conveniently on the desktop. Recall that you can add yourself to a role in Power BI Desktop (even if you were able to, you'll still gain unrestricted access as a model author). However, you can test the role as though you're a user who is a member of the role.

1. In the ribbon's Modeling tab, click the "View as Roles" button.
2. In the "View as roles" window, make sure that that US role is selected (see **Figure 9.26**). Click OK.

Figure 9.26 The "View as roles" lets you test a role inside Power BI Desktop.

3. You should see a status bar showing "Now viewing report as: US". Create a report that includes the SalesTerritoryCountry column from the SalesTerritory table, such as the one shown in **Figure 9.27**. The report should show only data for US.

Figure 9.27 The report shows only data for United States.

4. (Optional) Add a Table visualization showing the ResellerName column from the Reseller table. You should see all resellers. However, if you add a measure from the ResellerSales table, you should see only resellers with sales in the USA. If you want to prevent the role to see non-US resellers, change the cross filter direction of the ResellerSales[ResellerKey] ⇨ Reseller[ResellerKey] to Both.

IMPLEMENTING CALCULATIONS   265

Defining role membership

Now that the role is defined, it becomes a part of the model, but its setup is not complete yet. Next, you'll deploy the model to Power BI Service and add members to the role.

1. In the ribbon's Home tab, click Publish. If prompted, log in to Power BI and deploy the Adventure Works model to My Workspace.
2. Open your browser and navigate to Power BI Service (powerbi.com). Click My Workspace.
3. In the workspace content page, click the Datasets tab. Click the ellipsis button next to the Adventure Works dataset, and then click Security from the drop-down menu.

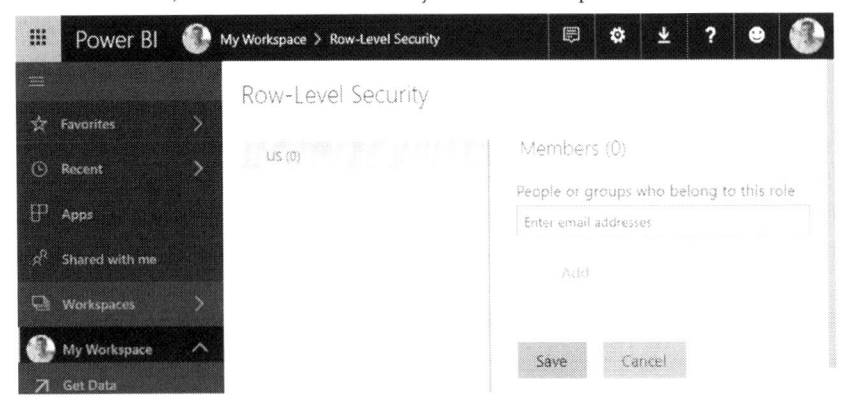

Figure 9.28 You set up the role membership in Power BI Service.

4. In the "Row-Level Security" window, add the emails of individuals or groups who you want to add to the role (**Figure 9.28**). You can also add external users that you have previously shared content with as members to the role. Click Save.
5. (Optional) Create a dashboard that uses visualizations from the Adventure Works report and share the dashboard with users who belong and don't belong to the role (you and the recipients must have Power BI Pro or Power BI Premium subscriptions). Ask them to view the dashboard and report their results.
6. (Optional) Republish the Adventure Works model. Power BI Desktop will ask you to replace the dataset. In Power BI Service, go to the Adventure Works dataset security settings and notice that the role membership is preserved. That's because the role membership is external to the Adventure Works model and re-publishing the file doesn't overwrite it. However, if you delete the dataset in Power BI Service, you'll lose its role membership.

> **NOTE** As a model author, you always have admin rights to model so don't be surprised that you see all the data irrespective of your role membership. If you publish the model to a workspace (workspaces are discussed in the next chapter), the workspace administrators and members who can edit content also gain unlimited access.

9.5.3 Implementing Dynamic Data Security

The row filter example securing on a territory that I've just shown you returns a fixed (static) set of allowed rows. This works well if you have a finite set of unique permissions. For example, if there are three regions, you can build three roles. Static filters are simple to implement and work well when the number of roles is relatively small. However, suppose you must restrict managers to view only the sales data of the employees that are reporting directly or indirectly to them. If static filters were the only option, you'd have no choice except to set up a database role for each manager. This might lead to a huge number of roles and maintenance issues. Therefore, Power BI supports dynamic data security.

Understanding dynamic data security

Dynamic security relies on the identity of the interactive user to filter data. For example, if Maya logs in to Power BI as maya@adventure-works.com, you can filter the Employee table to allow Maya to access herself and her subordinates. You need only a single role with the following table filter applied to the Employee table:

PATHCONTAINS(Employee[Path], LOOKUPVALUE(Employee[EmployeeKey], Employee[EmailAddress], USERPRINCIPALNAME()))

This expression uses the USERPRINCIPALNAME() DAX function (specifically added to support Power BI) which returns the user principal name (UPN) in both Power BI Service and Power BI. If you have set up dynamic security with Analysis Services Multidimensional or Tabular, you have probably used the USERNAME() function. However, this function returns the user domain login in Power BI Desktop (see **Figure 9.29**). You can use the WhoAmI.pbix Power BI Desktop file in the \Source\ch09 folder to verify the results.

Figure 9.29 USERPRINCIPALNAME() and USERNAME() return different results on the desktop.

To avoid using an OR filter to support both Power BI and Power BI Desktop, use USERPRINCIPALNAME() but make sure that the EmailAddress column stores the user principal name (typically but not always UPN corresponds to the user's email address) and not the user's Windows login (domain\login). To explain the rest of the filter, the DAX expression uses the DAX LOOKUPVALUE function to retrieve the value of the EmployeeKey column that's matching the user's login. Then, it uses the PATHCONTAINS function to parse the Path column in the Employee table in order to check if the parent-child path includes the employee key. If this is the case, the user is authorized to see that employee and the employee's related data because the user is the employee's direct or indirect manager.

> **NOTE** If your computer is not joined to a domain, both USERPRINCIPALNAME() and USERNAME() would return your login (NetBIOS name) in the format MachineName\Login in Power BI Desktop. In this case, you'd have to use an OR filter so that you can test dynamic security in both Power BI Service and Power BI Desktop.

Setting up the test environment

Next, I'll walk you through the steps required to implement dynamic data security for the manager-subordinate scenario. Ideally, you would have two Power BI accounts to test dynamic security in Power BI. Since you're not on the adventure-works domain, start by making changes to the Employee table:

1. In the Adventure Works model, right-click the Employee table in the Fields pane, and then click Edit Query to open the Power Query Editor.
2. Find the row for Stephen Jiang (EmployeeKey = 272). Right-click the EmailAddress cell for that row and click Copy to copy his email (it should be stephen0@adventure-works.com). In the next step, you'll replace this email with your email address.
3. Right-click the EmailAddress column and then click "Replace Values…". In the Replace Values window, paste the copied email address in the "Value to Find" field. In the "Replace With" field, type in your email address (the one you use to log in to Power BI).
4. (Optional) Right-click the EmailAddress column and then click "Replace Values…" again. In the Replace Values window, enter *amy0@adventure-works.com* in the "Value to Find" field. In the "Replace With" field, type in the email address of someone else in your organization that has a Power BI Pro subscription.
5. In the ribbon's Home tab, click Close & Apply to reload the Employee table.

IMPLEMENTING CALCULATIONS 267

Creating a new role

Next, you'll create a new role that will filter the Employee table.

1. In the ribbon's Modeling tab, click Manage Roles.
2. In the "Manage roles" window create a new *Employee* role.
3. In the Table section, select the Employee table. Enter the following expression in the "Table Filter DAX Expression" field:

PATHCONTAINS(Employee[Path], LOOKUPVALUE(Employee[EmployeeKey], Employee[EmailAddress], USERPRINCIPALNAME()))

4. Click the checkmark button in the top right corner of the window to check the expression syntax. If there are no errors, click Save to create the role.

Testing the role

Now that the Employee role is in place, let's make sure it works as expected.

1. In the ribbon's Modeling tab, click "View As Roles" (see **Figure 9.30**).

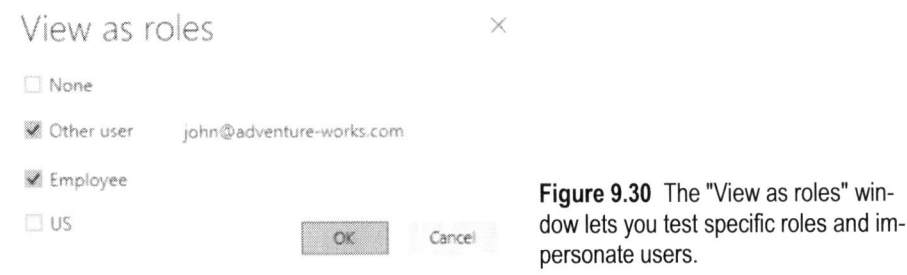

Figure 9.30 The "View as roles" window lets you test specific roles and impersonate users.

2. In the "View as roles" window check the Employee role to test it as though you're a member of the role.
3. If you'd like to impersonate another user to test his permissions, check the "Other user" checkbox and type in the user's UPN. As a result, USERPRINCIPALNAME() will return whatever you typed in. Click OK.
4. (Optional) Create a Table report that uses the Employees hierarchy (or Level1-Level6 fields), as shown in **Figure 9.31**. Notice that the report lets you access Stephen Jiang and his direct or indirect subordinates.

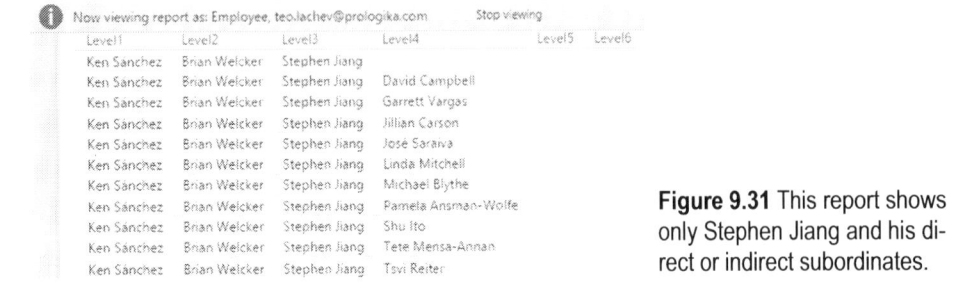

Figure 9.31 This report shows only Stephen Jiang and his direct or indirect subordinates.

9.5.4 Externalizing Security Policies

The final progression of data security is externalizing security policies in another table. Suppose that Adventure Works uses a master data management application, such as Master Data Services (MDS), to associate a sales representative with a set of resellers that she oversees. Your task is to enforce a security role that restricts the user to see only her resellers. This would require importing a table that contains the employee-reseller associations.

REAL LIFE This approach builds upon the factless fact table implementation that I demonstrated in my "Protect UDM with Dimension Data Security, Part 2" article (http://bit.ly/YBcu1d). I've used this approach in real-life projects because of its simplicity, performance, and ability to reuse the security filters across other applications, such as across operational reports that source data directly from the data warehouse.

Implementing the security filter table

A new SecurityFilter table is required to store the authorized resellers for each employee (see **Figure 9.32**).

Figure 9.32 The SecurityFilter bridge table stores the authorized resellers for each employee.

This table is related to the Reseller and Employee tables. If an employee is authorized to view a reseller, a row is added to the SecurityFilter table. In real life, business users or IT pros will probably maintain the security associations in a database or external application. For the sake of simplicity, you'll import the security policies from a text file (you can also enter the data directly using the Enter Data button in the ribbon's Home tab).

1. In the ribbon's Home tab, click Get Data. Choose CSV.
2. Navigate to the \Source\ch09 folder and select the SecurityFilter.csv file. Click Open.
1. Preview the data and compare your results with **Figure 9.33**. Click Load. Power BI Desktop adds a SecurityFilter table to the model.

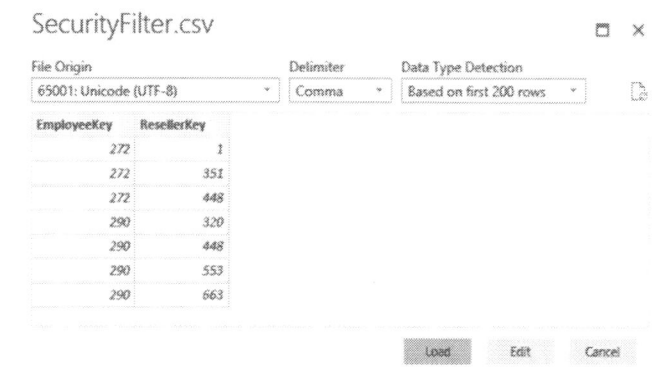

Figure 9.33 The SecurityFilter table specifies the resellers that an employee can access.

2. Because users shouldn't see this table, right-click the SecurityFilter table in the Fields pane (Data View) and click "Hide in Report View".
3. In the Relationships View, double-click the ResellerSales[ResellerKey]⇨Reseller[ResellerKey] relationship. If the "Apply security filter in both directions" checkbox is checked, uncheck it because it will conflict with the new relationships.
4. In the Relationships View, verify that the SecurityFilter[EmployeeKey]⇨Employee[EmployeeKey] and SecurityFilter[ResellerKey]⇨Reseller[ResellerKey] relationships exist and that they are active. If that's not the case, make the necessary changes to create these two relationships.

REAL LIFE Although in this case the SecurityFilter table is related to other tables, this is not a requirement. DAX is flexible and it allows you to filter tables using the FILTER() function even if they can't be related. For example, a real-life project required defining application security roles and granting them access to any level in an organization hierarchy. The DAX row filter granted the role access to a parent without explicit access to its children. The security table didn't have relationships to the tact table.

IMPLEMENTING CALCULATIONS 269

Implementing the Reseller role

Next, you'll add a role that will enforce the security policy. Follow these steps to set up a new Reseller role:

1. In the ribbon's Modeling tab, click Manage Roles.
2. In the "Manage roles" window create a new *Reseller* role.
3. In the Table section, select the Reseller table. Enter the following expression in the "Table Filter DAX Expression" field (you can copy it from \Source\ch09\dax.txt file):

CONTAINS(RELATEDTABLE(SecurityFilter), SecurityFilter[EmployeeKey], LOOKUPVALUE(Employee[EmployeeKey], Employee[EmailAddress], USERPRINCIPALNAME()))

Let's digest this expression one piece at a time. As you already know, the LOOKUPVALUE function is used to obtain the employee key associated with the email address. Because the table filter is set on the Reseller table, for each reseller, the CONTAINS function attempts to find a match for that reseller key and employee key combination in the SecurityFilter table. Notice the use of the RELATEDTABLE function to pass the current reseller. The net effect is that the CONTAINS function returns TRUE if there is a row in the SecurityFilter table that matches the ResellerKey and EmployeeKey combination.

Testing the Reseller role

Let's follow familiar steps to test the role:

1. In the ribbon's Modeling tab, click "View As Roles". In the "View as roles" window, check the Reseller role.
2. If you'd like to impersonate another user to test his permissions, check the "Other user" checkbox and type in the user's UPN. As a result, USERPRINCIPALNAME() will return whatever you typed in. Click OK.
3. (Optional) Create a Table report that uses the ResellerName field from the Reseller table. The report should show only the three resellers associated with Stephen.
4. In the Home ribbon, click the Publish button. Deploy the Adventure Works model to Power BI Service. Add members to the Employee and Reseller roles. Ask the role members to view reports and report results.

9.6 Summary

One of the great strengths of Power BI is its Data Analysis Expressions (DAX) programming language, which allows you to unlock the full power of your data model and implement sophisticated business calculations. This chapter introduced you to the DAX calculations, syntax, and formulas. You can use the DAX formula language to implement calculated columns and measures.

Calculated columns are custom columns that use DAX formulas to derive their values. The column formulas are evaluated for each row in the table, and the resulting values are saved in the model. The practices walked you through the steps for creating basic and advanced columns.

Measures are evaluated for each cell in the report. Power BI Desktop automatically creates an implicit measure for every column that you add to the Value area of the Visualizations pane. You can create explicit measures that use custom DAX formulas you specify.

More complex models might call for role-playing, parent-child, and many-to-many relationships. You can use DAX formulas to navigate inactive relationships, to flatten parent-child hierarchies, and to change the measure aggregation behavior.

Power BI supports a flexible data security model that can address various security requirements, ranging from simple filters, such as users accessing specific countries, to externalizing security policies and dynamic security based on the user's identity. You define security roles and table filters in Power BI Desktop and role membership in Power BI Service.

Chapter 10

Analyzing Data

10.1 Performing Basic Analytics 271
10.2 Getting More Insights 278
10.3 Data Storytelling 289

10.4 Integrating with PowerApps 298
10.5 Summary 302

Up until now in this part of the book, you have seen how a business analyst can implement a self-service model and mash up data from virtually everywhere. This is the ground work required when you don't have an organizational semantic model. Now that the model is complete, let's get some insights from it. After all, the whole purpose of creating a model is to derive knowledge from its data. I've already shown you in the first part of this book how to create meaningful and attractive reports with just a few mouse clicks. But Power BI has more to offer.

In this chapter, I'll walk you through more analytics features for data exploration. We'll start by creating a dashboard for analyzing the company performance. Then I'll demonstrate more advanced data visualization techniques and data storytelling capabilities. A Power BI prominent strength is that it can integrate with other products in the Microsoft Data Platform. To emphasize this, I'll show how you can integrate your reports with PowerApps so that you can change the data behind the report.

Think of this chapter as tips and tricks for report authoring. If after completing this chapter you feel like you need more practice to hone your report authoring skills, check the excellent Dashboard in a Day (DIAD) material by Microsoft at http://bit.ly/diahanddiad (download the DIAD Student Package zip file). Microsoft updates the training material periodically to keep up with the latest features!

10.1 Performing Basic Analytics

Let's start by creating the dashboard-looking report shown in **Figure 10.1** for analyzing the Adventure Works sales performance. Besides giving you another opportunity to work with reports, you'll use this report as a starting point to demonstrate more analytical features later in this chapter.

10.1.1 Getting Started with Report Development

Let's start with some basic report tasks, such as calibrating the report page, adding a company logo, and creating a report title.

Setting up the report page
If you're starting from scratch, follow these steps to set up a new report page:
1. In Report View, click the plus (+) button at the bottom to add a report page.
2. Double-click the tab and rename it to *Dashboard*.
3. Click the Dashboard tab to select it. In the Visualizations pane, click the Format tab and notice that you can apply different settings. For example, you can expand the Page Size section and specify a custom size.

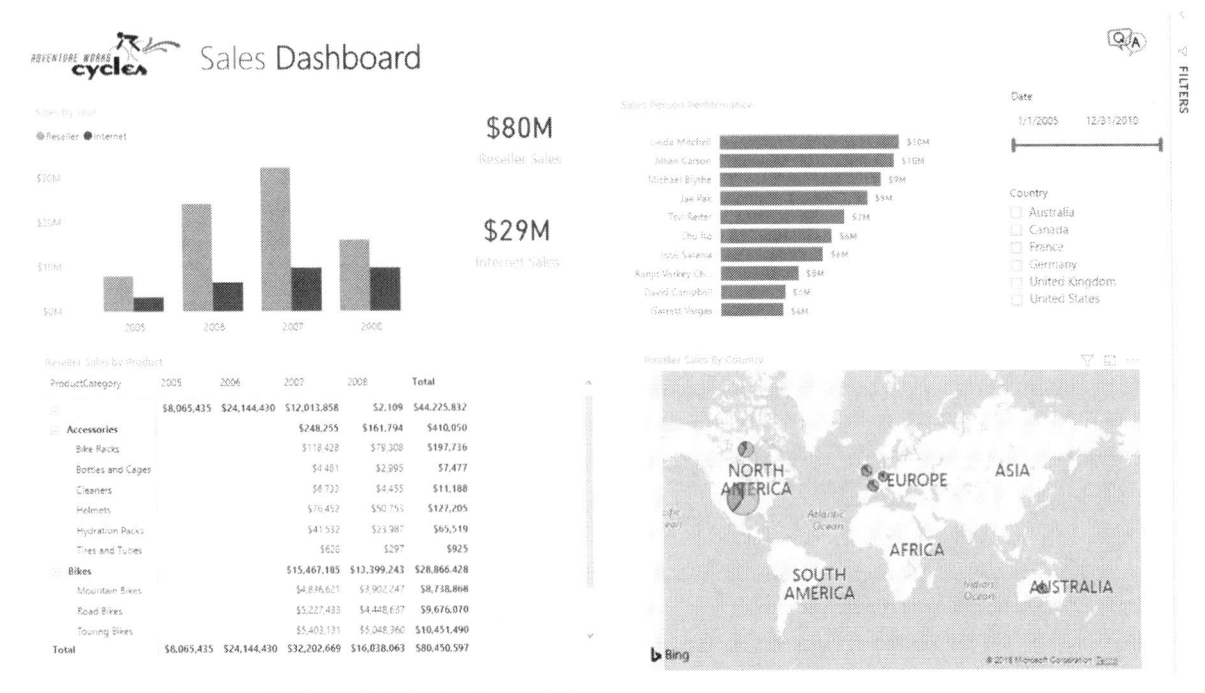

Figure 10.1 This report facilitates high-level sales analysis.

Adding the company logo and report title

Static images are typically used for logos, buttons, or report backgrounds. You can use the Image element (Home ribbon) to embed and display an image. Follow these steps to display the Adventure Works logo:

1. In the Home ribbon, click the Image element.
2. Navigate to the \Source\ch10 folder, select the awc.jpg file, and then click Open.
3. Position and resize the image as necessary.

Figure 10.2 Use the Image element to embed company logos, buttons, and report background images.

When you select the image, you'll see the Visualizations pane is replaced with the Format Image pane (see **Figure 10.2**). Use this pane to set various image options, such as scaling.

> **TIP** To use an image as a page background, click the corresponding page tab to activate the page. Then, go the Format tab in the Visualizations pane, expand the Page Background section, and then click Add Image.

4. In the Home ribbon, click the "Text box" element. Type *Sales Dashboard*. Format and position it as needed.

10.1.2 Working with Charts

Next, you'll implement the Sales by Year and Sales Person Performance charts.

Implementing the Sales by Year chart
This chart shows reseller and Internet sales by year. It's implemented as a column chart.

1. In the Fields pane, check the SalesAmount field in ResellerSales table. Power BI Desktop defaults to a clustered column chart visualization.
2. In the Fields pane, check the SalesAmount field in InternetSales table, or drag it and drop it onto the chart. Now the Value area of the Visualizations pane has two SalesAmount fields.
3. To avoid name confusion, double-click the first SalesAmount field in the Value area and rename it to *Reseller* (or expand the drop-down next to the field and click Rename). Rename the second field to *Internet*.
4. In the Fields pane, drag the Calendar Hierarchy (Date table) to the Axis area so that you explore the chart data by drilling down the hierarchy levels. Observe that the reseller sales exceed Internet sales.
5. In the Format tab of the Visualizations pane, turn on the Title property and enter *Sales by Year* as the chart title. Expand the "Data colors" section and change colors for the data series as desired.

Implementing the Sales Person Performance chart
Implemented as a bar chart, this graph shows sales for the top 10 sales people.

1. Click on an empty area on the report canvas.
2. In the Fields pane, check the SalesAmount field in the ResellerSales table.
3. In the Visualizations pane, change the visualization to Clustered Bar Chart.
4. In the Fields pane, check the FullName field (Employee table) to add it to the Axis zone.
5. In the Format tab of the Visualizations pane, turn on the Data Labels property.
6. Hover over the chart. In the upper right corner, click the More Options menu and then click Sort by ⇨ SalesAmount to sort the bar chart in a descending order by sales.
7. In the Format tab of the Visualizations pane, turn on the Title property and enter *Sales Person Performance* as the chart title.
8. Expand the "X-Axis" section and turn off "Concatenate labels" so that the chart show quarters grouped by year when you drill down. Move and resize the chart as needed.

10.1.3 Working with Cards

Recall that Power BI Desktop has a Card visual for displaying a single value, so you can draw attention to important measures, such as Profit.

Creating cards for sales revenue
Let's use the Card visualization to display the Adventure Works reseller and Internet sales side by side.

1. Click an empty area on the report canvas.
2. In the Fields pane, check the SalesAmount field in the ResellerSales table.
3. Change the new visualization to Card. Resize the card and position it between the two charts. Rename the SalesAmount field to *Reseller Sales* (in the Visualizations pane Fields tab, double-click SalesAmount in the Fields area).
4. Click the Reseller Sales card to select it. Press Ctrl+C to copy the card and Ctrl+V to paste it. Position the new card before the Reseller Sales card.

> **TIP** You can copy visuals between Power BI Desktop files too. Just select a visual and press Ctrl+C to copy it. Then, switch to the second Power BI Desktop instance and press Ctrl+V to paste the visual on the desired page.

5. In the Fields pane, drag the SalesAmount field from the InternetSales table and drop it to the Fields area of the Visualizations pane. Rename the field on the report to *Internet Sales*.

Configuring visual interactions

Suppose you don't want selections in other visuals to affect the cards. You can configure interactions between visuals to disable cross highlighting and filtering.

1. Select the Sales by Year chart. Click the Format ribbon and then click "Edit interactions".
2. Notice that additional icons appear on top of the other visuals. Click the "None" icon on each card so that filters applied to the chart, such as when the user clicks a bar, don't affect the cards (see **Figure 10.3**).

Figure 10.3 Configure visual interactions to control how selections in one visual affect another.

3. Click the "Edit interactions" button to turn it off.

10.1.4 Working with Table and Matrix Visuals

Recall that you can use the Table and Matrix visuals to create tabular reports.

Creating a tabular report

The Reseller Sales by Product crosstab report uses the Matrix visual but let's start with a Table first.

1. Click an empty area on the report canvas.
2. In the Fields pane, check the SalesAmount field in the ResellerSales table.
3. Change the visualization to Table. Resize the table and position it below the Sales by Year chart.
4. In the Fields pane, check the ProductSubcategory field in the Product table. In the Values area of the Visualizations pane, drag ProductSubcategory before SalesAmount.
5. In the Fields pane, check the ProductCategory field in the Product table. In the Values area of the Visualizations pane, drag ProductCategory before ProductSubcategory.

Converting to a crosstab report

To pivot the report by calendar year, you need to change the visualization from Table to Matrix.

1. With the Table visual, change it to Matrix. This adds a Columns area in the Visualizations pane.

2. Drag the CalendarYear field from the Date table to the Columns area. Then, drag the CalendarQuarter field from the Date table to the Columns area below CalendarQuarter.
3. Resize the visualization as needed to show more columns.
4. In the Visualizations Format tab, expand the Style section and choose the Minimal style.
5. Turn the Title setting to On and change the title to *Reseller Sales by Product*.
6. Expand the "Row headers" section and turn on "+/- icons" so that you can conveniently expand and collapse row groups.

10.1.5 Working with Maps

Recall that Power BI supports four geospatial visualizations: Map (plots measures as bubbles), Filled Map (fills regions on the map), Shape Map (supports custom map shapes), and ArcGIS (supports advanced features, such as overlaying layers, radius, driving distance and lassoing data points). In the next exercise, you'll use the Map visualization to plot sales on the map.

Implementing the Sales by Geography map
This map shows the reseller sales by geography. It uses the regular Map visualization.
1. Click on an empty area on the report canvas.
2. In the Fields pane, check the SalesAmount from the ResellerSales table.
3. In the Visualizations pane, change the visualization to Map.
4. In the Fields pane, drag the SalesTerritoryCountry field from the SalesTerritory table to Location area in the Visualizations pane.
5. In the Format tab, turn on the visualization Title property and change the title to *Reseller Sales by Country*.
6. In the Format tab, expand the "Map styles" section and change the theme to Grayscale.

Displaying pie charts
Let's break down the sales data plotted on the map as bubbles by product category:
1. Drag the ProductCategory field from the Product table to the Legend area in the Visualization pane. This changes each bubble to a pie chart with areas for each of the Adventure Works product categories.
2. To inform the user what each pie slice represents, consider turning on the map Legend property in the Format pane.
3. Move and resize the map as needed. Notice that you can hover on the map and click the Pop Out button to pop out the map.

10.1.6 Working with Slicers

Recall that besides the default cross-filtering behavior, Power BI has two main ways to filter report data: slicers and filters. Implemented as Power BI visuals, slicers are embedded on the report and support different configurations. Consider filters when you need more advanced filtering needs. Let's implement two slicers to let users filter the report data by date and country.

Implementing a Date slicer
Follow these steps to create and configure a date slicer:
1. Drag the Date[Date] field from the Fields pane to a blank area on the report.

2. Flip the visual to Slicer. Power BI recognizes that the slicer is bound to a field of the Date data type and defaults to Between configuration.
3. Hover over the slicer and expand the chevron in the top right corner (see **Figure 10.4**) and notice that you can change the slicer configuration. The configuration options depend on the data type of the field. For example, a date field supports a Relative option that lets you filter on relative dates, such as the last N periods. Experiment with different configurations.

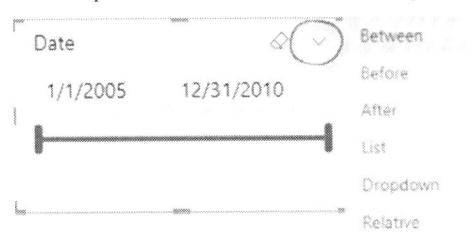

Figure 10.4 The Slicer visual supports different configurations depending on the field type.

Implementing a Country slicer

Let's implement another slicer to demonstrate additional options that Power BI slicers support.

1. Drag the SalesTerritory[SalesTerritoryCountry] field from the Fields pane to a blank area on the report.
2. Change the visual to Slicer. Double-click SalesTerriroryCountry in the Fields area of the Visualizations pane and rename it to *Country*.
3. The Country slicer defaults to a single selection. However, you can hold the Ctrl key to select multiple countries. Alternatively, in the Visualizations pane (Format tab), expand the Selection Controls section and change the Single Select slider to Off. While you are on the Format tab, notice the "Select All" option, which adds a new item to the slicer to let you conveniently select all items. Also, expand the General section and notice that you configure the slicer for vertical (default) and horizontal layouts.
4. What if the slicer displays a long list of items and it's difficult to scroll and locate items? Hover over the slicer and click the ellipsis (…) menu in the right corner. Click Search and notice that you can now search for items. As you type some text, the slicer filters the items that match the criteria.

Synchronizing slicers

The Slicer visual supports flexible configurations. By default, a slicer filters only the visuals on the current page. However, you can configure the slicer for cross-page filtering using the "Sync slicers" pane.

1. If you want to configure the Date slicer to filter multiple pages, select the Date slicer.
2. Expand the View menu and check "Sync slicers" to enable this pane (see **Figure 10.5**).

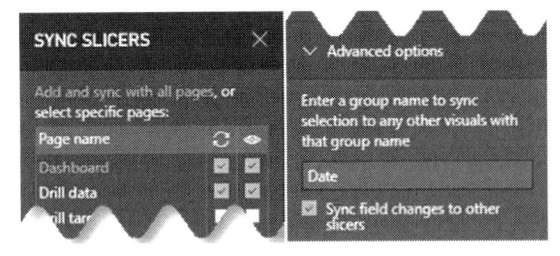

Figure 10.5 Use the "Sync slicers" pane to configure which pages will be filtered by the slicer.

Notice that there are two checkboxes next to each report page. When checked, the first checkbox configures the slicer to filter the data on that page. Behind the scenes, Power BI copies the slicer and adds it to any page that you check at the same location where the original slicer is (you can reposition the slicers later if you want). The second (eyeball) checkbox is to make the slicer visible on that page. For example, the configuration shown on the screenshot will configure the Date slicer to filter both the Dashboard and "Drill data" pages and to show on both pages.

Lastly, the "Sync field changes to other slicers" checkbox is to synchronize the slicer copies so that the same filter is applied to all slicers. When you have multiple pages, you can configure slicers in different groups to synchronize them independently. For example, if you want to set a relative filter to the last 3 months for the Date slicers on the first two pages, you can assign them to a "Last 3 months" group, while the rest could belong to another group.

> **TIP** Because Power BI slicers are implemented as visuals, you can use "Edit interactions" to configure a slicer to filter specific visuals instead of all the visuals on the page. To do this, select the slicer and enable "Edit interactions" from the Format menu. Then, click the None filter icon on the visuals that you don't want the slicer to filter.

10.1.7 Working with Filters

The second option for filtering data on the report is to use the Filters section in the Visualizations pane. Compared to slicers, filters have the following advantages:

- Filters supports different scopes (visual, page, report) – As the number of filtering needs grow, filters become more attractive because you don't need to keep on adding slicers and this can conserve space on the report.
- Filters support advanced filtering criteria – For example, you can use filters for top or bottom filtering, and multiple "and" and "or" criteria for the same field.
- Filters can be hidden or disabled – For example, you could let end users see what's filtered but prevent them from overwriting the filter.

Next, you'll implement two visual-level filters (see **Figure 10.6**).

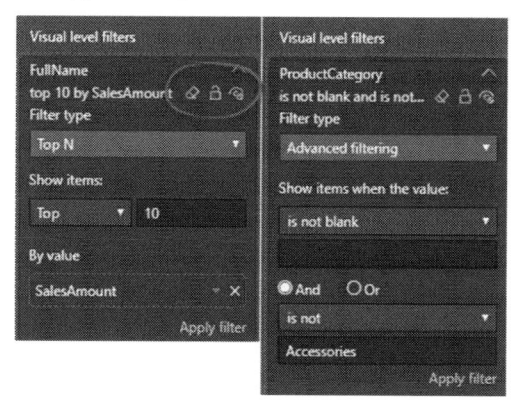

Figure 10.6 You can apply advanced filter conditions, such as Top N, and to configure filters as hidden or disabled.

Implementing filters

Follow these steps to filter the "Sales Person Performance" bar chart to show the top 10 sales people:

1. Click the "Sales Person Performance" bar chart to select it.
2. In the Visualizations pane (Fields tab) expand the FullName field in the "Visual level filters" area and change the "Filter type" to Top N. Enter *10* in the "Show items" area.
3. Drag ResellerSales[SalesAmount] from the Fields pane to the "By value" area to rank by this field. Click Apply Filter. Compare your filter configuration with the FullName configuration on the screenshot.

Next, let's implement another visual-level filter to exclude blank categories and Accessories in the "Reseller Sales by Product" matrix report.

4. Click the "Reseller Sales by Product" matrix to select it.
5. Configure the ProductCategory visual-level filter as shown on the right side of the screenshot.

Using the Filters pane

A potential downside of configuring filters in the past was that it was difficult for both the report author and end user to understand what was filtered because filters were not shown on the report. After you publish the report, the end user had to remember to expand the Filters pane in order to see and change filters. And there was no option to hide or disable filters. This all changes with the updated Filters pane, which is currently available as a preview feature.

6. Go to File ⇨ Options and Settings ⇨ Options (Preview features) and check "New filter experience". While you are in the Options window and if you work with a Power BI Desktop file created before November 2018, go to the "Report settings" tab and check "Enable the updated filter pane".

7. By default, only page-level and report-level filters show in the Filters pane, but you can choose to show visual-level filters as well. Select the "Sales person performance" bar chart. In the Filters section of the Visualizations pane, locate the "Visual level filters" section where you configured the Top 10 filter. Click the eyeball icon next to the FullName filter (see again **Figure 10.6**) to show the FullName filter on the Filters pane. Now when you select the bar chart, you can easily see what visual-level filters are applied.

8. Select the "Reseller sales by product" matrix and click the eyeball icon next to the ProductCategory visual-level filter to show it in the Filters pane.

9. Suppose you don't want the end user to change the ProductCategory filter. Click the "Lock filter" icon next to the eyeball icon. **Figure 10.8** shows what the Filters pane looks like when you select the bar chart and then the matrix. In the latter case, users can see the ProductCategory filter, but they can't change it.

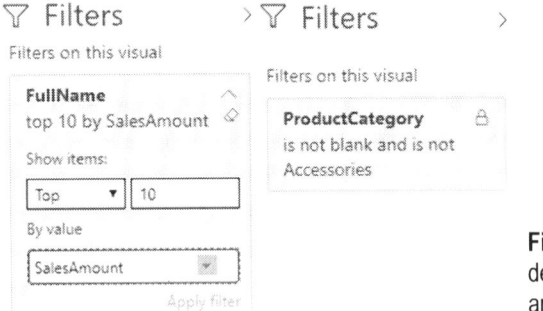

Figure 10.7 The Filters pane is visible by default on the report and shows what filters are applied to the selected visual.

10.2 Getting More Insights

Let's now demonstrate some additional analytical features that I haven't previously covered or haven't covered in enough detail, including drilling down and through, custom grouping and binning, conditional formatting, and working with images.

10.2.1 Drilling Down and Across Tables

Drilling down data is a common requirement. For example, you might have a chart, matrix, or map that shows some summary information, but you want to explore underlying data in more detail.

Drilling down the same table

As you've learned in Chapter 6 and 8, drilling down the same table can be achieved in two ways:

- Adding the required fields that form the drilldown path to the same area in the Visualizations pane (Data tab)
- Creating a hierarchy and dragging it to the appropriate area in the visualization.

Figure 10.8 shows a column chart with the Calendar Hierarchy in chart Axis area.

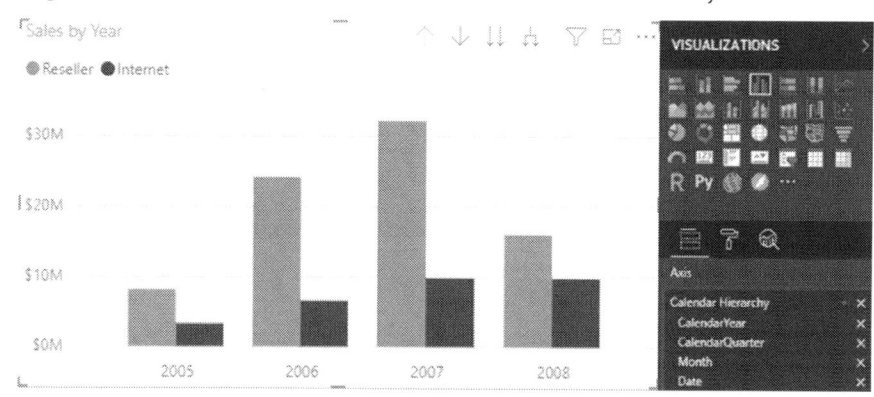

Figure 10.8 Drilling down data using a hierarchy.

To drill down data in both Power BI Desktop and Power BI Service, use the Data/Drill ribbon, the drill indicators on top of the chart, or right-click a bar and use the context menu.

> **TIP** Power BI Desktop files created before July 2018 show the old-style visual header when you hover over a visual, which takes up some space. As **Figure 10.8** shows, the new-style renders in line with the visual. This new design also makes it easier to align visuals. To switch older files to the new style, go File ⇨ Options and Settings ⇨ Options (Report Settings tab) and check "Use the modern visual header with updated styling options".

Drilling across tables

Now consider the matrix on the "Drill data" report page (see **Figure 10.9**). I've added two fields from different tables in the Rows area. You can start your analysis at the CalendarYear level. Then, you use one of the drill options, such as right-click a year and click "Expand to Next Level" to drill down to SalesTerritoryCountry (from SalesTerritory table). Or, you can right-click a year and then click "Drill Down" to expand only that year.

CalendarYear		Accessories	Bikes	Clothing
⊟ 2007		$12,013,858	$248,255	$15,467,185	$574,784
	Australia	$1,342	$15,588	$680,646	$26,122
	Canada	$2,360,726	$46,826	$2,460,625	$108,343
	France	$572,622	$24,027	$1,341,320	$48,613
	Germany	$831	$20,630	$820,514	$43,614
	United Kingdom	$565,437	$21,724	$1,230,916	$46,761
	United States	$8,512,900	$119,460	$8,933,164	$301,332
⊟ 2008		$2,109	$161,794	$13,399,243	$386,013
	Australia	$447	$8,360	$643,175	$16,793
	Canada	$64	$32,356	$1,909,710	$77,497
	France	$192	$16,296	$1,111,859	$33,664
	Germany	$320	$14,453	$722,502	$28,006
	United Kingdom	$64	$14,303	$1,060,663	$32,462
Total		$44,225,832	$410,050	$28,866,428	$960,797

Figure 10.9 Drilling across tables can be achieved by using fields from different tables.

While we're discussing the matrix visual, notice that it defaults to a stepped layout. Fields added to the Rows area are stacked to occupy a single column and reduce horizontal space. However, some report types, such as financial reports, may require expanding the layout to separate columns. To configure this layout, go to the Format tab in the Visualizations pane, expand the "Row headers" section, and then turn off "Stepped layout".

ANALYZING DATA

TIP You may have a requirement to implement a master-detail report, such as a typical invoice header-details report. Currently, Power BI doesn't have a visual for a freeform layout to position fields at arbitrary locations, so you must resort to Card, Multi-row Card, Table, or Matrix visuals. However, cross-highlighting works across Table or Matrix visuals. Therefore, one approach is to use a Table or Matrix for the header and another for the details. Then, you can select a row in the "header" section and see the "details" in the second table or matrix.

10.2.2 Drilling Through Data

Another very popular requirement is drilling through data. For example, you might want to see the transactions (as they are imported) behind a cell, or to drill from a summarized view through another page. Power BI supports two drillthrough options:

- See records – Power BI generates a default drillthrough page. You can customize the layout, but you can't save the page.
- Drillthrough page – You create a drillthrough page and customize it just like any other page.

Using "See Records"

Drilling through a data point on chart, map, or matrix can be accomplished by using the "See Records" feature. While you drill *down* fields in (lookup) dimension tables, you drill *through* measures, such as fields added to the Values area of a chart or matrix. To drill through, right-click any data point and then click See Records or use the same menu in the Data/Drill ribbon. For example, right-click the 2006 bar in the column chart and then click "See Records". Power BI Desktop generates a new tabular report that displays the rows from the ResellerSales table that contribute to the cell value, as shown in **Figure 10.10**.

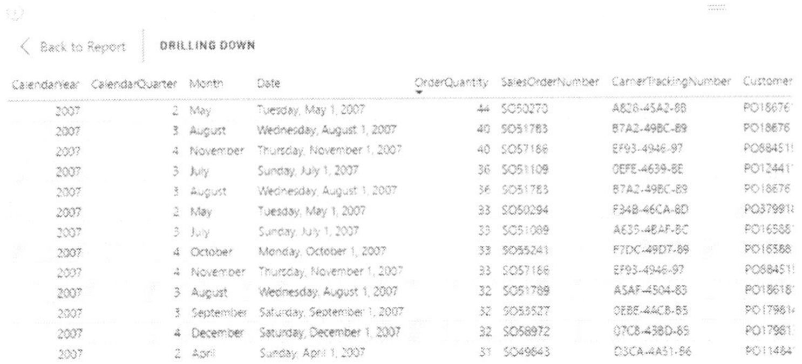

CalendarYear	CalendarQuarter	Month	Date	OrderQuantity	SalesOrderNumber	CarrierTrackingNumber	Customer
2007	2	May	Tuesday, May 1, 2007	44	SO50270	A826-45A2-8B	PO18676
2007	3	August	Wednesday, August 1, 2007	40	SO51783	B7A2-49BC-89	PO18676
2007	4	November	Thursday, November 1, 2007	40	SO57166	EF93-4946-97	PO68451
2007	3	July	Sunday, July 1, 2007	36	SO51109	0EFE-4639-8E	PO12441
2007	3	August	Wednesday, August 1, 2007	36	SO51783	B7A2-49BC-89	PO18676
2007	2	May	Tuesday, May 1, 2007	33	SO50294	F34B-46CA-8D	PO37991
2007	3	July	Sunday, July 1, 2007	33	SO51069	A635-4BAF-BC	PO16588
2007	4	October	Monday, October 1, 2007	33	SO55241	F7DC-49D7-89	PO16588
2007	4	November	Thursday, November 1, 2007	33	SO57166	EF93-4946-97	PO68451
2007	3	August	Wednesday, August 1, 2007	32	SO51789	A5AF-4504-83	PO18618
2007	3	September	Saturday, September 1, 2007	32	SO53527	0EBE-44CB-B5	PO17981
2007	4	December	Saturday, December 1, 2007	32	SO58972	07C8-43BD-65	PO17981
2007	2	April	Sunday, April 1, 2007	31	SO49843	D3CA-4A51-86	PO11484

Figure 10.10 "See Records" generates a new report that shows the individual rows from the underlying table.

By default, Power BI adds all text fields from the underlying table and fields from the other tables that are used in the main report. Currently, you can't choose default fields for the drillthrough report. However, you can add additional fields to the generated report with the caveat that your changes are not preserved when you click "Back to Report" to navigate to the main report. Continuing the list of limitations, "See Records" isn't available for DAX explicit measures. It's also currently limited to 1,000 rows and there is no way to increase the limit.

TIP If you need to see more than 1,000 records with the default drillthrough action, consider "Analyze in Excel" (expand the ellipsis menu next to the dataset name in Power BI Service and then click Analyze in Excel). Then, you can double-click a cell to initiate the default drillthrough action. This approach doesn't limit the detail rows.

Creating custom drillthrough pages

Do you need more customization over the drillthrough report? You can create your own page(s) as a drillthrough target! Going back to **Figure 10.9**, suppose you want a list of the customer orders behind a given cell. Start by adding a new page to the report that returns the required fields (refer to the "Drill target" page in the Adventure Works file, which is shown in **Figure 10.11**). This page shows detailed information about customer orders. There is nothing special about this page except that the SalesAmount measure came from a different table (InternetSales) than the calling page. I wanted to demonstrate that drilling through data doesn't have to target the same fact table.

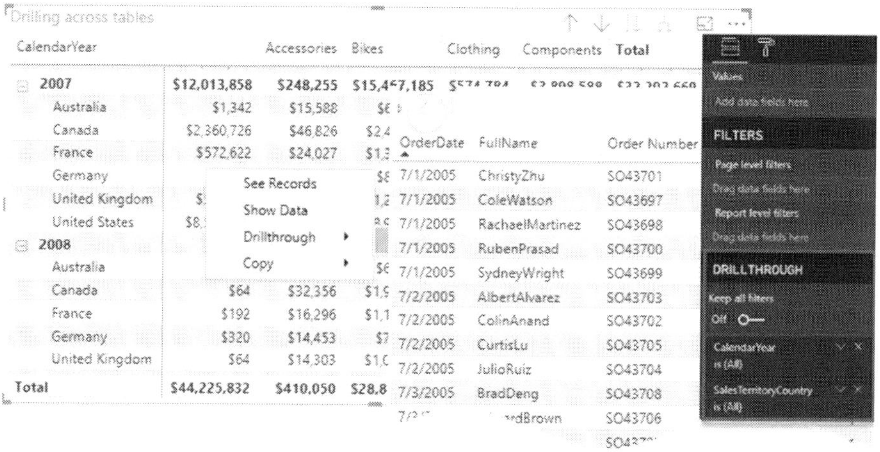

Figure 10.11 Unlike default drillthrough, a custom drillthrough page allows you to define the report layout.

The trick for configuring drillthrough is to add fields to the "Drillthrough" area in the Visualizations page. Interestingly, the main page automatically checks if its visual has one of the fields used in the Drillthrough filters area. If it does, it automatically enables the Drillthrough context menu. The context menu is activated even if the source page has a subset of the fields used as drillthrough filters. For example, if the Sales visual has only CalendarYear, the drillthrough page would show all customer orders for that year. If it has also SalesTerritoryCountry, the drillthrough page would show orders for that year and for that country. If the Sales visual has none of the fields used for drillthrough filters, then the Drillthrough context menu won't show up. In other words, Power BI automatically matches the source fields and drillthrough filters and this saves you a lot of configuration steps, such as to configure parameters, to check which fields exist, and to pass All to the parameters that don't exist!

When enabled, "Keep all filters" in the Drillthrough area passes through the entire filter context (including from fields added to the Drillthrough area or indirect filters or slicers) to the drillthrough page. When disabled (default value), Power BI filters on parameters only.

Once you add a field to the "Drillthrough filters" area, Power BI automatically adds an image (back arrow) to let you navigate back to the main page. You can use your own image if you don't like the Microsoft-provided one. To configure it as a back button, click the image, go to the image properties in the Format Image pane, expand the Link section, and then set its Type property to Back.

10.2.3 Configuring Tooltips

Power BI generates a default tooltip when you hover over a data point. This is helpful for graphs because you can see the exact value of the data point. You can add additional measures to the default tooltip. In addition, like drillthrough pages, you can create custom tooltip pages.

Implementing basic tooltip customization
Let's revisit the "Sales by year" chart on the Dashboard report page and customize its tooltips:
1. Hover over any bar on the chart. Notice that a default tooltip pops up that shows the calendar year and measure value.

2. Suppose that besides the sales amount you want the tooltip to show the order quantity. In the Visualizations pane, select the Fields tab. Notice that it has a Tooltips area which is empty.
3. Drag ResellerSales[OrderQuantity] from the Fields list to the Tooltips area. Hover over a chart data point again and notice that the tooltip now includes the order quantity.

Creating a custom tooltip page

Next, you'll implement a custom tooltip page that replaces the default tooltip with a crosstab report, as shown in **Figure 10.12**. This tooltip helps the user understand the sales breakdown by product category. Note that you can use any Power BI visual (or multiple visuals) to implement the tooltip page.

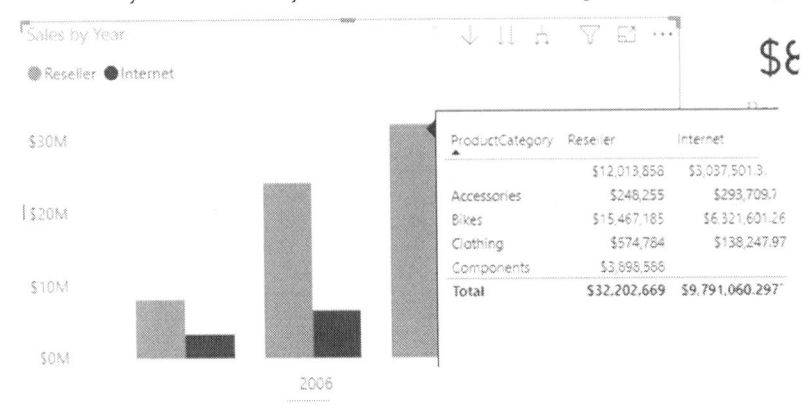

Figure 10.12 This custom tooltip page shows a matrix visual when you hover over a chart data point.

1. Add a new page to the report and name it *Tooltip*.
2. Click the new page to select it. In the Format tab of the Visualizations page, expand the Page Information section and turn on the Tooltip slider. This configures the new page as a tooltip page.
3. Expand the Page Size section. Expand the Type drop-down and select Tooltip. This changes the page size to a smaller predefined size that is suitable for tooltips.
4. Select the Fields tab of the Visualizations pane. Notice that it has a Tooltip area. Like a custom drill through page, you can add fields to this section. For example, if you want the tooltip to be available only if the source visual includes the calendar year, drag Date[CalendarYear] and drop it in the Tooltip area.
5. (Optional) Right-click the Tooltip page and click Hide Page so that end users don't see it.

Connecting the tooltip page

Next, configure the source visual to use the Tooltip page.

1. Switch to the Dashboard page and select the Sales by Year chart.
2. In the Visualizations page, select the Format tab. Expand the Tooltip section, then expand the Type drop-down and select "Report page". This tells Power BI to overwrite the default tooltip with a custom page.
3. If the Page setting is left to "Auto", Power BI will auto-detect suitable tooltip pages and show the first one. Assuming you want to specify a page, expand the Page drop-down and select the Tooltip custom page.
4. Switch to the Fields tab of the Visualizations page and notice that the Tooltips section now shows that the Tooltip page will be used. Test your setup by hovering over a chart data point.
5. (Optional) If you want to go back to the default tooltip, switch to the Format tab, expand the Tooltip section, and then change the Type drop-down to Default.

10.2.4 Grouping and Binning

Dynamic grouping allows you to create your own groups, such as to group countries with negligible sales in an "Others" category. In addition to grouping categories together, you can also create bins (buckets or bands) from numerical and time fields, such as to segment customers by revenue or create aging buckets.

Implementing groups

Consider the two charts shown in **Figure 10.13**. The chart on the left displays sales by country. Because European countries have lower sales, you might want to group them together as shown on the right. Follow these steps to implement the group:

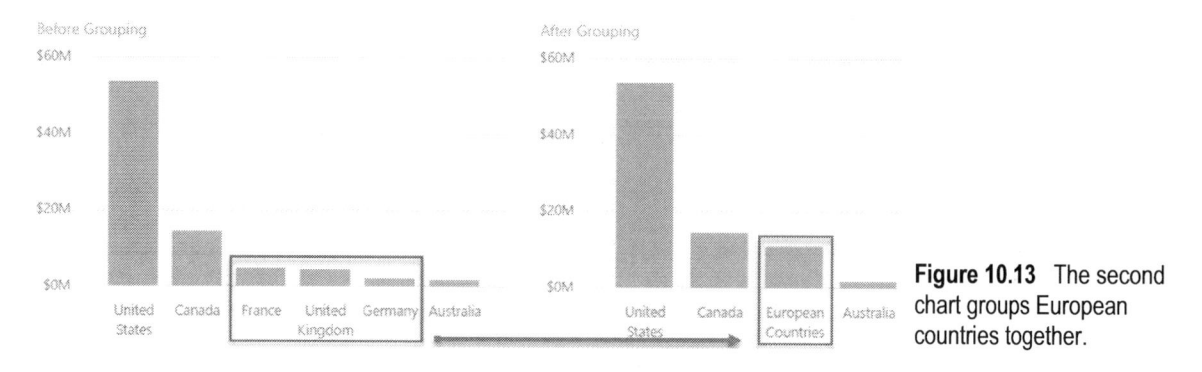

Figure 10.13 The second chart groups European countries together.

1. Create a Stacked Column Chart with SalesTerritoryCountry (SalesTerritory table) in the Axis area and SalesAmount (ResellerSales table) in the Values area.
2. Hold the Ctrl key and click each of the data categories you want to group. Only charts support this way of selecting group members. To group elements in tables or matrices, expand the drop-down next to the field in the Visualizations pane (or click the ellipses button in the Field list), and then click New Group.
3. Right-click any of the selected countries and click Group from the context menu. Power BI Desktop adds a new SalesTerritoryCountry (group) field to the SalesTerritory table. This field represents the group and it's prefixed with a special double-square icon. Power BI Desktop adds the field to the chart's Legend area.
4. In the Fields pane, click the ellipsis (…) button next to SalesTerritoryCountry (group). Click Rename and change the field name to *European Countries*.
5. Click the ellipsis (…) button next to the European Countries field and then click Edit Groups.

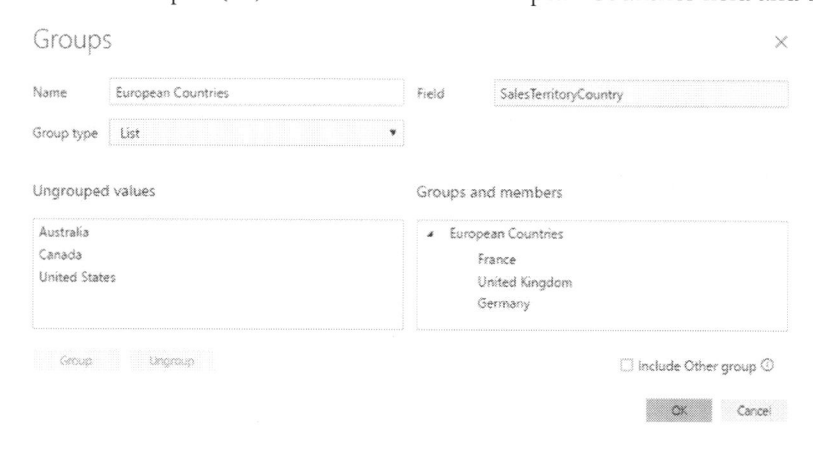

Figure 10.14 Use the Groups window to view the grouped values and control how the ungrouped values are shown.

ANALYZING DATA 283

6. In the Groups window (see **Figure 10.14**), you can change the group name and see the grouped and ungrouped members. If the "Include Other group" checkbox is checked (default setting), the rest of the data categories (Canada and United States) will be grouped into an "Other" group. Leave the "Include Other group" checkbox unchecked so that Canada and United States show as separate data categories. Click OK.
7. Back to the report, remove SalesTerritoryCountry from the Axis area. Add the European Countries field to the Axis area. Compare your report with the right chart shown in **Figure 10.13**.

> **TIP** Although Power BI Desktop doesn't currently support lassoing categories for as a faster way of selecting many items, you can use the Groups window to select and add values to the group. Instead of clicking elements on the chart, right-click the corresponding field in the Fields pane and then click New Group to open the Groups window. Select the values in the "Ungrouped values" (hold the Shift key for extended selection) and then click the Group button to create a new group.

Binning data

Besides grouping categories, Power BI Desktop is also capable of discretizing numeric values or dates in equally sized ranges called *bins*. Suppose you want to group customers in different bins based on the customer's overall sales, such as $0-$99, $100-$200, and so on (see the chart's X-axis in **Figure 10.15**).

Figure 10.15 This report counts customers in bin sizes of $100 based on the overall sales.

This report counts distinct values of the CustomerID field (Count Distinct aggregation function) in the Customer table which is related to the InternetSales table. This requires following the InternetSales[CustomerKey] ⇨ Customer[CustomerKey] relationship because the SalesAmount field in the InternetSales table will become the "dimension" while the measure (Count of Customers) comes from the Customer table. Follow these steps to create the report:

1. In the Relationships View, if the InternetSales[CustomerKey] ⇨ Customer[CustomerKey] relationship has a single arrow (cross filter direction is Single), double-click it to open Edit Relationship window and change the "Cross filter direction" drop-down to Both. Click OK.
2. Switch to the Report View (or Data View). In the Fields pane, click the ellipsis (…) button next to the SalesAmount field in the InternetSales table and then click New Group.
3. In the Groups window, change the bin size to 100 (you're grouping customers in bins of $100). Give the group a descriptive name, such as *SalesAmount (bins)*, and then click OK.
4. Add a Stacked Column Chart visualization. Add the SalesAmount (bins) field that you've just created to the Axis area of the Visualizations pane (you'll be grouping the chart data points by the new field).
5. Add the CustomerID field from the Customer table to the Value area. Expand the drop-down next to the CustomerID field in the Value area and switch the aggregation to Count (Distinct). Compare your results with **Figure 10.15**.

TIP The built-in binning feature creates equal bins based on the bin size you specify in the Groups window. If you need more control over the bin ranges, consider either using Power Query Editor to add a conditional column, as I explained in Section 7.1.1, or creating a separate lookup (dimension) table for the bins and then joining this table to the fact table.

10.2.5 Applying Conditional Formatting

You can apply conditional formatting to change the color of measures in Table and Matrix visuals based on different conditions, such as to color negative numbers in red. Power BI supports conditional formatting expressed as data bars, font, and background colors. The report in **Figure 10.16** uses conditional formatting to emphasize trends (see the "Conditional formatting" tab in Adventure Works.pbix).

Figure 10.16 This report demonstrates data bars, background, and foreground conditional formatting.

Applying data bars

I used the following steps to configure the SalesAmountYTD column to show data bars.

1. Add a Table with the FullName field (Employee table) and the SalesAmountYTD, SalesAmount, NetProfit, and OrderQuantity measures from the ResellerSales table.

2. In the Visualizations pane (Fields tab), right-click the SalesAmountYTD field and then click Conditional Formatting ⇨ Data Bars. Alternatively, click the ellipsis button (…) next to the SalesAmountYTD field in the Values area to see the Conditional Formatting menu.

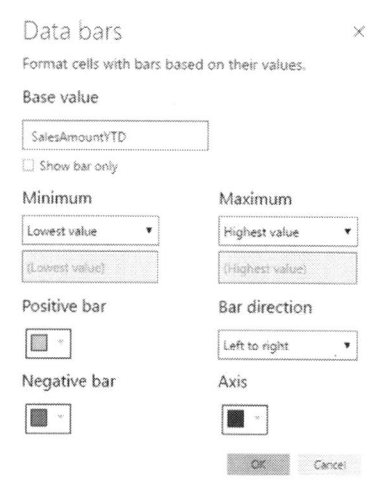

Figure 10.17 Use this window to configure the data bar configuration settings.

ANALYZING DATA   285

3. Accept the default settings in the "Data bars" window (see **Figure 10.17**). Going through them quickly, check "Show bar only" if you want to show only the data bar and not the data. By default, Power BI detects the data range for each cell but if you want to enter a specific range, expand the "Lowest value" (or Highest value) and enter a number for the lowest or highest boundary.
4. Click OK. You can now easily see that Linda Mitchel has the highest YTD sales.

Applying color formatting

Color (fore and background color) formatting allows you to vary the color by one of these three options:

- Color scale – Power BI determines the color ranges.
- Rules – You specify logical rules for the color ranges.
- Field value – You specify a field or DAX measure for the color ranges.

Back to the report, the SalesAmount measure uses conditional formatting to change its background cell color (Conditional Formatting ⇨ Background Color Scales). And the NetProfit measure conditionally changes the font color (Conditional Formatting ⇨ Font Color Scales). These options have similar settings to the data bars, but they support a diverging option so that you can specify a center value and color. The OrderQuantity measure brings conditional formatting one step further by using rules (the "Color by rules" checkbox is on), as shown in **Figure 10.18**.

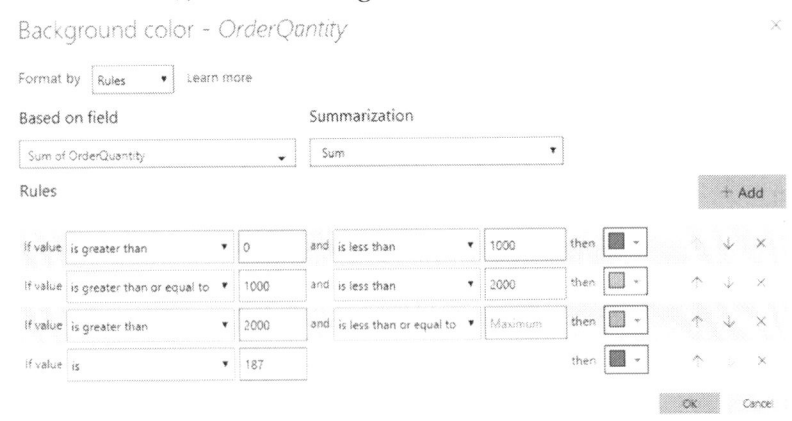

Figure 10.18 Conditional coloring lets you specify rules (the rules below win over rules above).

Specifically, the first three rules specify colors for different data ranges. The last rule checks for a specific value. Rules are evaluated in the order they are defined, and subsequent rules win over. Therefore, although the last rule checks for 187, which falls within the first rule, rows on the report with OrderQuantity = 187 will "win" over the rules above, and these cells will be colored in purple. You can change the rule precedence by clicking the up or down arrows.

The last column (TaxAmt) on the report demonstrates how you can make the color rules even more flexible by using a DAX measure (or a field value). The TaxColor DAX measure has the following formula:

TaxColor = SWITCH(TRUE(), SUM(ResellerSales[TaxAmt])>100000, "Red", SUM(ResellerSales[TaxAmt])>50000,"Yellow", SUM(ResellerSales[TaxAmt])>10000,"Green", BLANK())

Although the measure defines again three bands of colors, it can also check additional runtime conditions, such as what field is used on the report or what value the user has selected in a slicer.

> **TIP** Power BI is yet to deliver expression-based properties. Currently, besides conditional formatting, only chart data colors ("Data colors" section in the Format tab) have an "Advanced controls" setting to vary the data point color by a DAX measure. "Advanced controls" brings you to the same screen as conditional formatting, where you can vary the color by one of the three options: color scale, rules, or field value.

10.2.6 Working with Links

You saw in Chapter 4 how you can configure a custom URL for a dashboard tile to navigate the user to a web page, instead of navigating to the report where the visual was pinned from. You can also use links in your reports to implement navigation features.

Implementing static links

You can manually enter the link URL to navigate the user to a specific web page, as demonstrated by the "Working with links" page (see **Figure 10.19**).

Figure 10.19 Use the Text Box element to specify static links.

I used a text box for the report title (in the Home ribbon, click "Text box" in the Insert ribbon group). As you type the text, you can select the URL portion, and then click the Insert Link button to configure the link. After you publish the file to Power BI Service or Power BI Report Server, users can click the link. This opens another browser window that will navigate them to the web page.

Implementing web URLs

The Table visual on the same page builds upon the visual in the "Drill target" page by allowing the user to click a link next to the order number (see **Figure 10.20**). In real life, such a link can navigate the user to an ERP system to get more information about the order. Follow these steps to implement this scenario:

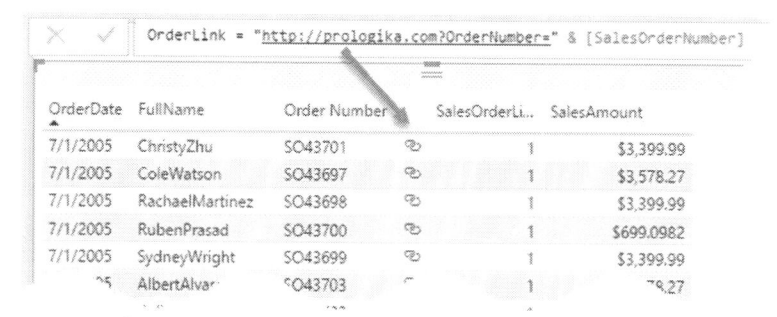

Figure 10.20 You can implement dynamic links with DAX calculated columns and measures.

1. To manufacture a link for every order, add a calculated column OrderLink to the InternetSales table with the following DAX formula:

OrderLink = "http://prologika.com?OrderNumber=" & [SalesOrderNumber]

2. Add the OrderLink column to the report. You can now see the URL for every order but it's not clickable.
3. In the Fields pane, click the OrderLink field to select it. In the Modeling ribbon, expand the Data Category drop-down and select Web URL. The link is now clickable, but it might not be desirable to show the URL.
4. With the Table visual selected, select the Format tab in the Visualizations pane, expand the Values area, and then turn on the "URL icon" slider.
5. (Optional) If you don't need a caption for the link column, rename the OrderLink field in the Values area of the Visualizations pane to an empty space (double click the field and then enter an empty space).

> **TIP** You can also configure links on DAX measures too, such as to enable or disable links depending on a report filter, or to make SalesAmountYTD "clickable". The OrderLinkMeasure measure fulfills the same purpose with the formula:
> IF (HASONEVALUE(InternetSales[SalesOrderNumber]), "http://prologika.com?OrderNumber=" & VALUES(InternetSales[SalesOrderNumber]))

ANALYZING DATA 287

10.2.7 Working with Images

A picture is sometimes better than a thousand words. Power BI supports various ways to work with images, ranging from static and web images, image areas, and Visio diagrams. One notable exception are images stored in a database table, which are not supported yet in Power BI.

Working with image URLs

You could have images stored on a web server or a web page that you may want to show on reports. For example, the Table visual in **Figure 10.21** shows three Power BI-related book images from their respective Amazon pages. Follow these steps to implement such reports:

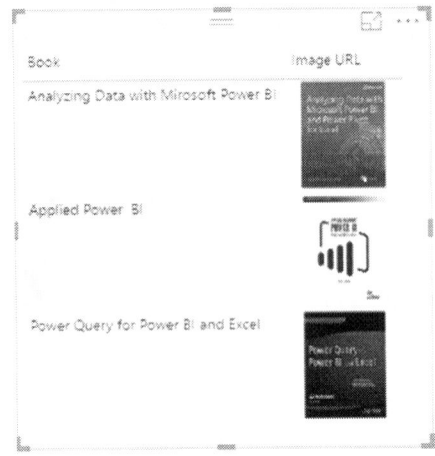

Figure 10.21 Table, Matrix, and Multi-row Card visuals can display images from URLs.

1. Obtain the image URLs and import them into a table. You can use the calculated column approach I demonstrated for link URLs to construct the image URLs. For this example, I used the "Enter Data" button in the Home ribbon to create a static table with two columns: Book and ImageURL. Then, I entered three rows in that table.
2. In the Fields list, click the ImageURL field to select it.
3. In the Modeling table, change the field data category to Image URL.
4. Use Table, Matrix, or Multi-row Card to visualize the images.

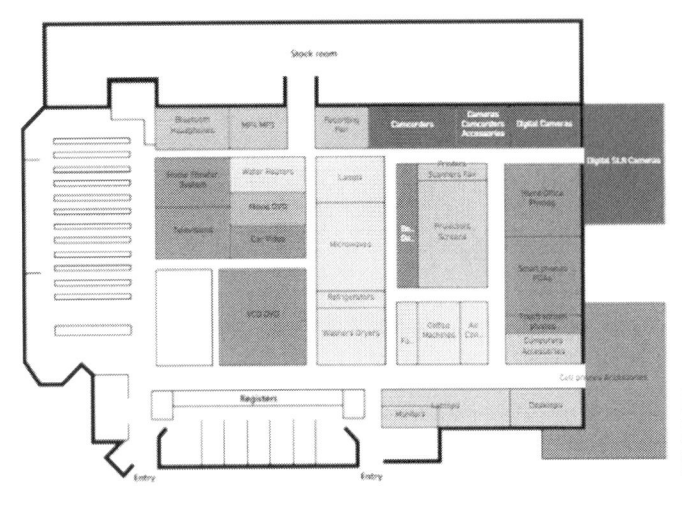

Figure 10.22 Use the Synoptic Panel custom visual to define clickable image areas.

288   CHAPTER 10

Working with image areas

Since the dawn of Internet, web designers have used image areas (called image maps) to create clickable locations in an image. You can use a similar technique to divide an image into clickable areas. Power BI doesn't natively support this feature, but a popular custom visual called Synoptic Panel by SQLBI can be used for this purpose. For example, **Figure 10.22** shows a floor plan where the colored areas are clickable.

As with the Power BI native visuals, when the user clicks an area, cross-highlighting filters other visualizations on the page. For more information about how to use Synoptic Panel, define image maps, and download a sample Power BI report, go to the product home page at http://okviz.com/synoptic-panel/.

Embedding Visio diagrams

Bringing image maps further, another custom visual (currently in preview) allows you to embed Visio diagrams in your Power BI reports. By using Visio and Power BI together, you can illustrate data as both diagrams and visualizations in one place to drive operational and business intelligence. I demonstrate this integration scenario in the Visio Demo.pbix file (see **Figure 10.23**), but make sure to follow the steps listed on the report to set it up for integration with Visio Online.

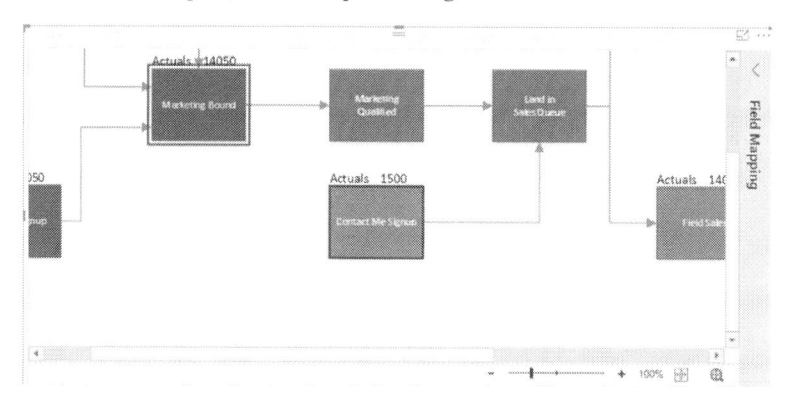

Figure 10.23 The Visio custom visual allows you to add interactive Visio diagrams to your reports.

This report imports data from an Excel file. The data represents different stages in the process of acquiring customers, starting from Trial Signup to Opportunity, like the typical sales funnel in CRM systems. Each stage has Target, Actual, and Gap numbers. The Visio diagram shows how these stages are related. During the process of configuring the custom visual, you specify which fields would be used and whether they will be used to change the shape text or color. Cross-highlighting works so that you can click a Power BI chart bar to zoom in the corresponding Visio shape.

The Visio custom visual requires the Visio file to be saved to Office 365 OneDrive for Business or SharePoint Online. That's because the diagram needs to be rendered online using O365 Visio Online. For more information about how to configure the Visio custom visual, refer to the "Add Visio visualizations to Power BI reports" article by Microsoft at http://bit.ly/powerbivisio.

10.3 Data Storytelling

Creating compelling and insightful reports goes a long way toward extracting value from your data. By combining analytics with narrative flow, data storytelling is the last mile for unlocking the full potential of your data. For a lack of a better definition, data storytelling is a way for communicating data insights that combines three key elements: data, visuals, and natural interfaces, such as Q&A and narratives. So far, our focus has been on the first two. Now you'll see how you can communicate your data story effectively with Power BI.

10.3.1 Asking Natural Questions

In Chapter 4, I showed you how you can ask natural questions for dashboards and reports in Power BI Service, such as "Show me sales by year". And in Chapter 5, I showed you how to use Q&A in the Power BI mobile apps. Wouldn't it be nice to do the same in the Power BI Desktop? Of course, it would! In fact, Q&A is available for you as a data analyst and for end users who will use your report. However, currently Q&A requires data to be imported (Q&A for data sources with live connections, such as Analysis Services, is currently in preview). It doesn't work with DirectQuery connections.

Q&A for data analysts
A data analyst can use Q&A to create new visuals. In fact, Q&A is the easiest way to get you started with visualizing your data if you're new to Power BI. There are two ways to invoke Q&A in Power BI Desktop:

1. Double-click an empty space anywhere on a page.
2. Click the "Ask A Question" button in the Home ribbon's tab.

This adds an empty "Stacked Column Chart" visual and a Q&A area above it that prompts you to ask a question about your data. On the desktop, Q&A works the same way as in Power BI Service (see **Figure 10.24**). As you type in your question, it guides you through the metadata fields and visualizes the data.

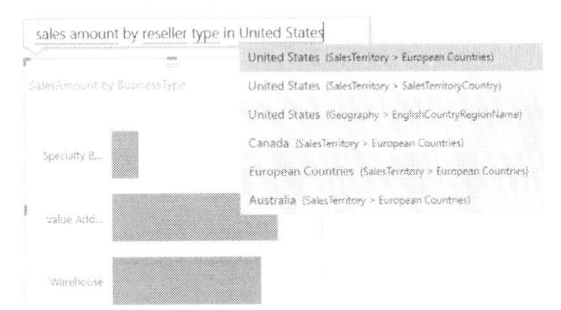

Figure 10.24 As you type your question, Power BI Desktop visualizes the data.

Once you're done with the question, you can use the visual just like any other visuals. Unlike Power BI Service, once you deactivate the visual, such as by clicking somewhere else on the page, the Q&A box disappears, and you can't bring it back to see what question was asked.

Q&A for the end user
What if end users don't have permissions to edit the published report (they can't use the "Ask a question" feature which is only available in the report's Edit view in Power BI Service), but you would like to encourage them to ask their own or predefined natural questions for data exploration? Besides creating visuals, you can let end users explore data with Q&A. This requires adding a button or image to the report to invoke the Q&A action, as follows:

1. With the report open in Power BI Desktop, expand the Buttons drop-down in the Home ribbon and select the Q&A button.

   TIP For your convenience, the Microsoft-provided Q&A button is preconfigured to invoke the Q&A action. However, you can use another button or a custom image. If you decide to do so, the only configuration steps required is to turn on the Action slider and set the action Type property (expand the Action section) in the Format Image pane. See the Q&A image on the Dashboard report page for an example.

2. Because the default click action is to select the object, to test Q&A at design time, hold the Ctrl key and click the button (once the report is published, you just click the button). This opens the Q&A Explorer where you can type in the question (see **Figure 10.25**).

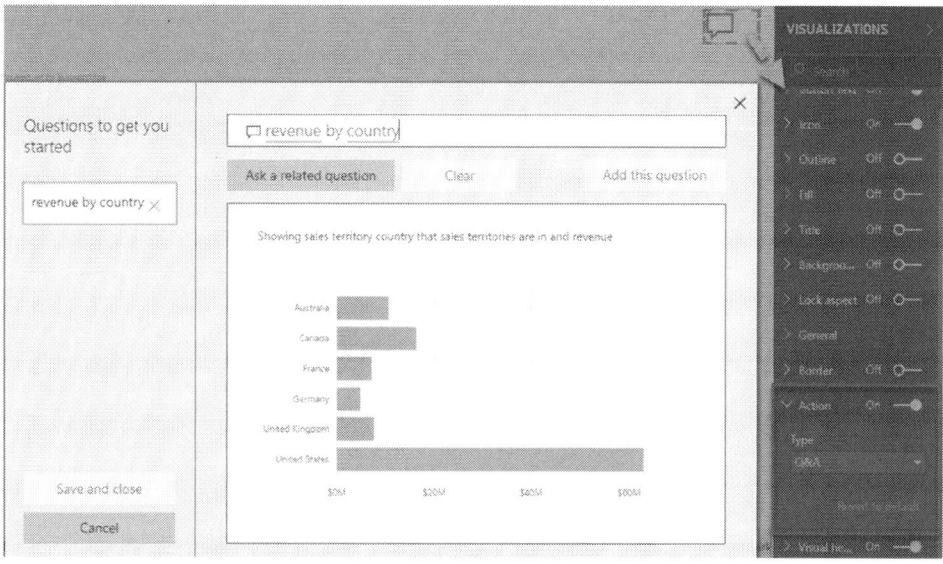

Figure 10.25 You can use Q&A Explorer to add predefined questions.

3. At design time you can predefine natural questions that might be of interest to end users. Suppose that users might be interested to see revenue by country. Type *revenue by country* in the Q&A box. Notice that you can't change the visualization type (the Visualizations pane is not available), but you can specify the visual as you type the question, such as *revenue by country as treemap*.

4. Click "Add this question" to add it as a predefined question. Power BI adds the question to the "Questions to get you started" pane. Notice that you can click the "Ask a Related Question" button to build upon the previous question by typing other related questions to narrow down your research.

10.3.2 Integrating with Windows Cortana

To recap, Q&A is available in Power BI Service, Power BI Mobile, and Power BI Desktop. But most of us still use laptops and most of them run Windows. Wouldn't it be nice to integrate data insights from Power BI directly in Windows? This is where Cortana comes in.

Cortana is an intelligent personal assistant that Microsoft included in Windows 10, Windows phones, and Xbox One. Cortana can help you update your schedule and answer questions using information from a variety of places, such as current weather and traffic conditions, sports scores, and biographies. For more information about Cortana's features, read "What is Cortana?" at http://windows.microsoft.com/windows-10/getstarted-what-is-cortana. And, of course, Cortana knows about Power BI. Who doesn't?

Configuring Cortana for Power BI
Follow these steps to integrate Cortana with Power BI:

1. Ensure that you have Windows 10. To check, in Windows press the hotkey Win+R to open the Run dialog, type *winver*, and then press Enter.
2. To find if Cortana is activated, type *Cortana* in the Windows search box (located in the taskbar on the left).
3. In the Search results window, click "Cortana & Search settings". In the Settings window, make sure that the first setting "Cortana can give you suggestions…" is on. If you want Cortana to respond to your voice when you say "Hey Cortana", turn on the "Hey Cortana" setting as well.
4. So that Cortana can reach out to Power BI and access your datasets, you must first add your work or school account to Windows. Right-click the Windows button to the left of the search box in the Windows

ANALYZING DATA

taskbar, and then click Settings. In the Settings window, click Accounts. In the next window, click "Access work or school".

5. Check if the work email you use to sign in to Power BI is listed (see **Figure 10.26**). If the account is not listed, click the "Add a Microsoft account" link, and then add the account.

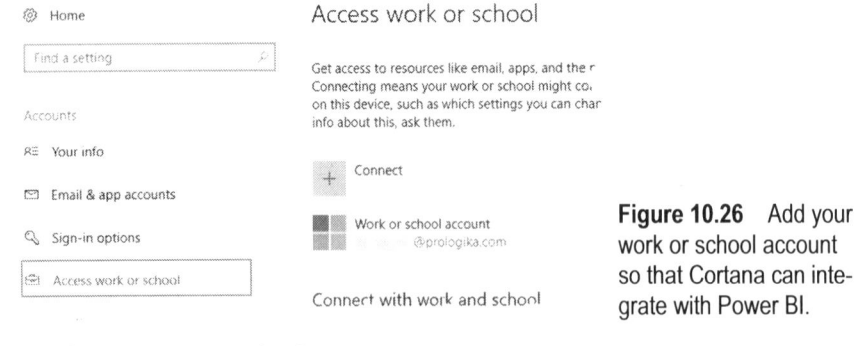

Figure 10.26 Add your work or school account so that Cortana can integrate with Power BI.

Configuring Power BI for Cortana

To get the most out Cortana, you need to add pages to your reports that are specifically optimized for Cortana (also known as Cortana answer cards). You can also use Cortana to search Power BI dashboards and reports by name.

NOTE Why doesn't Cortana just search all datasets when you ask a natural question? When the Power BI integration with Cortana was initially released, Cortana did this. However, Microsoft noticed there were a large percentage of cases where customers were enabling Q&A in Cortana simply to search for reports, without intending to ask natural questions. This was resulting in unexpected Q&A ad-hoc results showing up in Cortana answer lists, leading to user confusion. So, Microsoft decided it would be better to restrict results to Cortana answer cards until Power BI supports configuration settings to allow model authors to explicitly control whether ad-hoc answers should be enabled as well.

Let's start by allowing Cortana to access specific datasets.

1. By default, Power BI datasets are not enabled for Cortana. You need to turn on the Cortana integration for each dataset that you want Cortana to access. Open your web browser and log in to the Power BI portal. In the Application Toolbar at the top-right corner, expand the Settings (gear) menu, and then click Settings.
2. In the Settings page, click the Datasets tab (**Figure 10.27**).

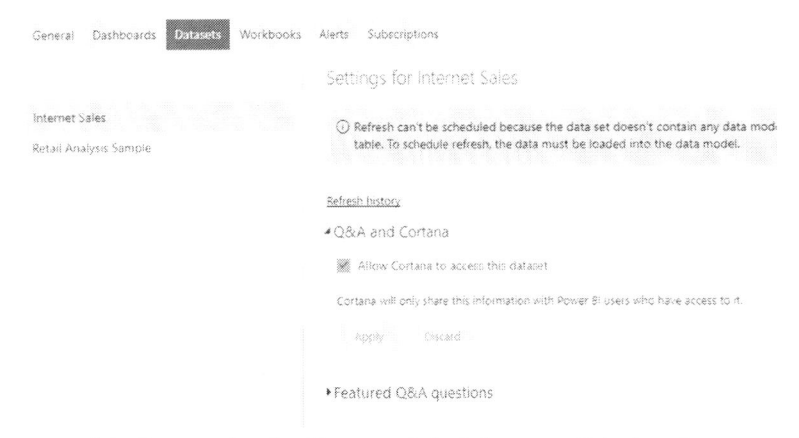

Figure 10.27 Use the Settings page to enable Cortana to access datasets.

3. To enable Cortana for the "Internet Sales" dataset, click that dataset, and then check the "Allow Cortana to access this dataset" checkbox. Click Apply. Now Cortana can access this dataset and its dependent reports and dashboards but give it some time to discover it and learn about its data.

4. On your desktop, type in the dashboard or report name. Once you see it in the Cortana list, click it and watch it open in a separate browser window.

Creating answer cards

If you want to get more from Cortana, you'd need to create Cortana answer cards. As of this time, Cortana answer cards work only if the dataset is created in Power BI Desktop. They don't work for the Power BI samples or for reports created from datasets that are imported directly in Power BI Service. Let's create quickly a Cortana answer card in Power BI Desktop (you can also do this directly in Power BI Service):

1. Add a new page to your report. Change the page name to *Internet Sales*.
2. Click the gray area outside the report canvas to unselect any visualization you might have selected. Select the Format tab in the Visualization pane to access the page properties.
3. Change the page type to Cortana. Power BI will reduce the page size, so it fits the Cortana window.
4. (Optional) In the Page Information section of the Visualization pane, enter additional synonyms if you want users to search by other phrases, such as *Cortana Sales answer card*. Remember that Cortana requires at least two words for questions.
5. Add and configure some visualizations to that card that you want to see in Cortana (see **Figure 10.28**).

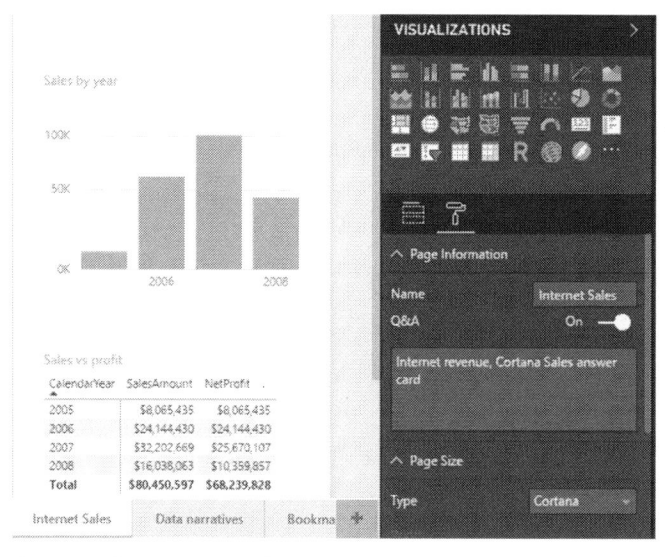

Figure 10.28 Create a Cortana answer card to provide preconfigured reports to Cortana questions.

6. (Optional) To require the user to specify a report filter, add a field to the Page Filters area, change the filter mode to Basic and check "Require single selection". Cortana will only display this report as an answer if the question includes one of the filter items.
7. Deploy the file to Power BI Service and remember to enable Q&A in the dataset settings. Give some time for Cortana to discover and index the card.

Getting data insights with Cortana

Now that the answer card is ready, let's take Cortana for a ride.

1. In the Windows search box, enter the page name or one of synonyms, such as "Internet revenue" or "what's Internet revenue". Cortana should show some matches under the Power BI category. Alternatively, you can say "Hey Cortana" to activate Cortana and dictate your question.
2. Click the match. Cortana shows the answer card as you've designed it (see **Figure 10.29**). Notice that the report includes interactive features, such as cross-highlighting and sorting!

ANALYZING DATA   293

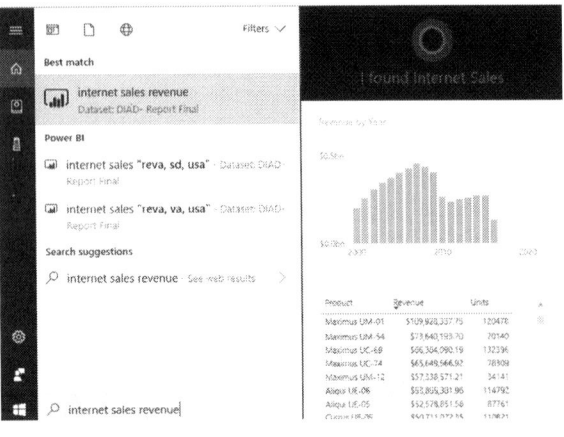

Figure 10.29 Cortana finds Power BI matches to your questions and visualizes your data.

3. (Optional) If you have enabled the answer card for Q&A, you can further explore the data by appending to the card name, such as "Internet revenue for 2010". To further explore an answer, click the "Open in Power BI" link under the visualization. This opens your Web browser and navigates you to the Power BI Q&A page that is prepopulated with the same question. From here, Q&A takes on.

Can't get enough from Cortana or get it to work at all? Try the "Troubleshoot Cortana for Power BI" article at https://powerbi.microsoft.com/documentation/powerbi-service-cortana-troubleshoot/?

As you can see, Cortana opens new opportunities to enable your business, and your customers' businesses, to get things done in more helpful, proactive, and natural ways.

10.3.3 Narrating Data

Power BI by itself doesn't have data narrating capabilities. But as an open platform, third-party vendors can extend it in versatile ways. Narrative Science has contributed a Narratives for Business Intelligence custom visual that explains the data in natural language. These narratives bring the following value:

- Tell stories from your data – Narratives can be generated from any data source.
- Act as a companion analyst – Dynamic narratives update as you change visualizations.
- Can be customized and shared – Narratives are updated when you set filters or apply cross-highlighting, extending the context of insights.

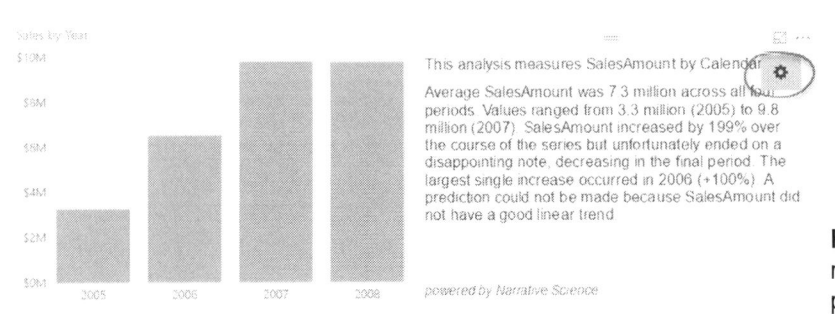

Figure 10.30 The narrative next to the column chart explains the data in the chart.

Getting started with data narratives

Let's examine the Sales by Year report shown in **Figure 10.30**. The Narratives for Business Intelligence custom visual explains the data. The chart and custom visual aren't connected. I just configured the custom visual the same way I configured the chart. As you can see, the custom visual explains the data in English. What's not so obvious is that if you filter the report, such as when you set a slicer or cross-filter it from another visual, the custom visual would pick the filter and change the narrative!

Configuring narratives

Configuring the Narratives for Power BI visual is not much different than configuring any other visual:

1. Click the ellipsis (…) in the Visualizations pane, and then click "Import from store". Find and import the Narratives for Business Intelligence visual.
2. Drop the visual on the report canvas. Drag CalendarYear (Date table) to the Dimensions area in the Visualizations pane. Drag SalesAmount (InternetSales table) to the Values area.
3. When the visual asks you "How would you describe your data?", leave the "Continues" data type selected, and then click Write Narrative.

This covers the basics but notice that you can customize the visual behavior by clicking the Settings button. For more information about the Narratives for Business Intelligence visual, refer to the "Narratives for Power BI Solution Overview" article at https://narrativescience.com/Resources/Resource-Library/Article-Detail-Page/narratives-for-power-bi-solution-overview.

10.3.4 Sharing Insights with Bookmarks

Imagine you're working on some an executive report that will provide insights into the sales performance of your organization. You end up with many visualizations on many pages. You're concerned that the message might be lost in the minutia of details. You need a way to communicate the data story step by step. This is where bookmarking can help. In Power BI, effective data storytelling with bookmarking involves three features:

- Bookmarks – A bookmark is a captured state of a report page that saves the visibility and applied filters, including cross highlighting from other visuals. For example, if Martin wants to start his presentation with the sales for the current year, he can apply a date filter and save the page as a bookmark. However, a bookmark is not a data snapshot. Although the filters are preserved, the visual would still query the underlying dataset because the data is not saved in the bookmark.
- Visual visibility – Sometimes less is more. When drawing attention to specific visuals, you could hide other visuals. You can configure the visual visibility using the Power BI Selection pane.
- Spotlight – Instead of hiding visuals, you might decide to fade some away by bringing others to the forefront (in the spotlight).

Creating bookmarks

You can create as many bookmarks as needed to communicate a story efficiently. Consider the Bookmarks page in the Adventure Works.pbix file. Suppose you want to start your presentation by showing the USA sales first.

1. Change the Country slicer to "United States".
2. In the View ribbon, check Bookmarks Pane. In the Bookmarks Pane, click Add to create a new bookmark.
3. Double-click "Bookmark 1" and change its name to *USA* (or expand its ellipsis menu and click Rename). Compare your results with **Figure 10.31**. Notice that you can further assign related bookmarks to groups if you have a lot of bookmarks.

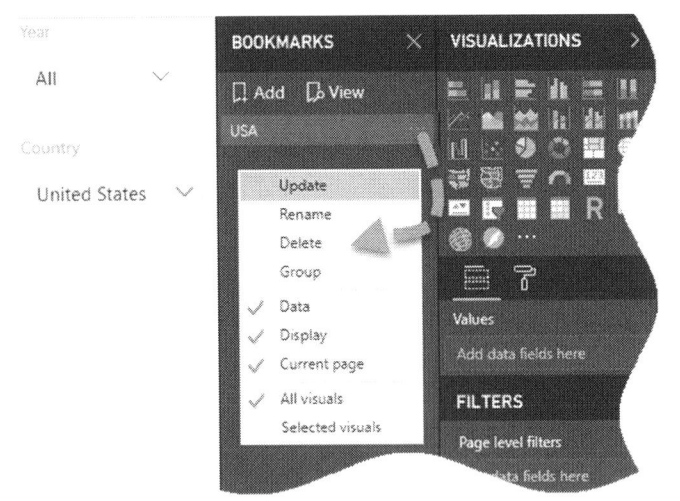

Figure 10.31 The Bookmarks Pane shows all bookmarks defined in the report and lets you specify which properties the bookmark saves.

4. To test the bookmark, clear the Country slider to show data for all countries. In the Bookmarks Pane, click the USA bookmark. Notice that the Country slider is filtered for USA.

5. (Optional) Navigate to another report page and then click the USA bookmark. Notice that Power BI navigates to the Bookmarks page. It's helpful to think about the Bookmarks Pane as a Table of Contents (TOC) of your report to help you navigate pages.

6. Click the ellipsis (…) menu next to the USA bookmark in the Bookmarks pane. Notice that you can configure what visual properties get saved in the bookmark. For example, when Data is selected, the data-related properties (filters and slicers) will be saved. The Display property is for saving the "visual" properties, such as visibility and spotlight. And "Current Page" is for the page change that moves users to the page that was visible when the bookmark was added.

By default, a bookmark saves all visuals on the page. However, if you want to save only specific visuals, you can hold the Ctrl key and select them one by one, and then enable the "Selected Visuals" option in the bookmark properties.

Hiding visuals
When you tell your data story, you might prefer to hide some visuals on a busy report so that a bookmark brings attention to the most important visuals. Suppose you want to hide the scatter chart when showing the USA sales.

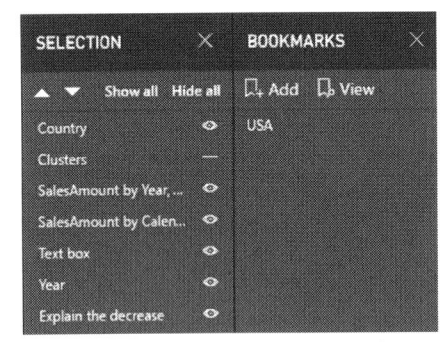

Figure 10.32 Use the Selection Pane to change the visibility of visuals.

1. In the View ribbon, check the Selection Pane to add it to the report. The pane lists all the visuals on the page and allows you to change their visibility.

2. Click the eye icon next to the Clusters visual to hide it. Notice that you can also reorder visuals. This could be useful if you have overlapping visuals and you want to change their display order.
3. Expand the ellipsis (...) menu next to the USA bookmark in the Bookmarks Pane and then click Update. This updates the bookmark to reflect the current state of the page, as shown in **Figure 10.32**.
4. In the Selection Pane, click "Show all" to show all visuals and clear the Country slider. Add another bookmark and name it *Default*. Drag the Default bookmark before the USA bookmark.
5. Click the Default bookmark and then click the USA bookmark. Notice that the Default bookmark shows all visuals without filters, while the USA bookmark doesn't show the Clusters visual and shows data only for USA.
6. In the Bookmarks Pane, click View. Notice that a slider is added to the bottom of the report that allows you to navigate your bookmarks. The same slider is available when you deploy a report with bookmarks to Power BI Service and view the report. Use the slider to tell your story one step at a time.
7. Click the Exit button in the Bookmarks pane to exit the View mode.

> **TIP** Although frequently used together with bookmarking, the Selection Pane is also useful during report authoring and analysis. For example, when analyzing data on a busy report page, you might want to focus on a specific visual and hide the rest.

Bringing visuals to spotlight

Instead of hiding visuals, you can fade them away by using the Spotlight feature that is available for every visual on the page. Suppose that you want to start your presentation by bringing focus to the "Explain the decrease" column chart.

1. In the Bookmarks Pane, click the Default bookmark.
2. Hover on the column chart, click the ellipsis (...) menu in the top-right corner, and then click Spotlight. The chart stands out while all other visuals fade away in the background.
3. In the Bookmarks pane, click the ellipsis (...) menu next to the Default bookmark and click Update. If you can't find the ellipsis menu, make sure to first click the Exit button to exit the View mode.

Using images to trigger bookmarks

Sometimes, you might want to allow users to click "buttons" to toggle visibility of visuals or to navigate them to different pages. You can use any image to trigger a bookmark.

1. In the Home ribbon, click the Image button and import the On.jpg image from the \Source\ch10 folder.
2. Size and position the image above the "Explain the decrease" chart.
3. Click the image to select it. The Visualizations Pane changes to Format Image pane.
4. Turn on the Link slider. Expand the Link section in the Format Image pane. Expand the Type drop-down and select Bookmark. Recall that the other option (Back) can be used to navigate the user from a drillthrough page to the calling page.
5. Expand the Bookmark drop-down and select the USA bookmark, as shown in **Figure 10.33**.
6. To test the changes, hold the Ctrl key and click the image. Notice that it navigates you to the USA bookmark.
7. (Optional) Add an "Off" image and position it behind the "On" image. Link the "Off" image to the Default bookmark. Hide the "Off" image in the selection pane and update the Default bookmark. Update the USA bookmark to show the "Off" image and hide the "On" image. The desired effect is to allow the user to toggle the image "button".

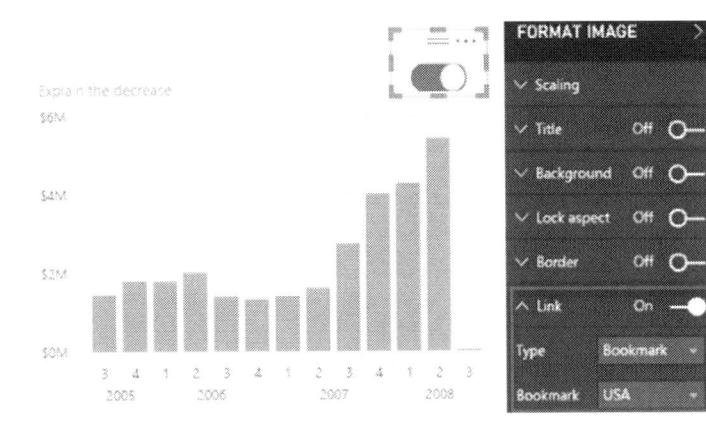

Figure 10.33 Configure an image to act as a button for navigating the user to a bookmark.

10.4 Integrating with PowerApps

In Chapter 1, I mentioned that Microsoft positions Power BI as a part of the Microsoft Power Platform (https://dynamics.microsoft.com/microsoft-power-platform/), which consists of three products: Power BI, PowerApps, and Flow. What's more exciting for data analysts is that these products are integrated! You can integrate Power BI with PowerApps to bridge the analytics and developer worlds. And you can use Flow to start workflows when a Power BI data alert is generated (to learn more about this integration scenario, read "Microsoft Flow and Power BI" at https://docs.microsoft.com/power-bi/service-flow-integration). Next, I'll demonstrate how you can integrate Power BI and PowerApps to make changes to the data behind the report (writeback).

10.4.1 Understanding PowerApps

Microsoft PowerApps is an Office 365 product that helps business users build no-code/low-code apps for automating business processes and creating data-driven apps. Every organization has business automation needs which traditionally have been solved by developers writing custom code. However, just like Power BI democratizes BI, PowerApps empowers business users like yourself to create their own apps without knowing a professional programming language, such as C#.

What can you do with PowerApps?
If your organization has an Office 365 business plan, you have everything you need to start using PowerApps. PowerApps supports two types of apps:

- Canvas apps – Perhaps you've used Microsoft Access or InfoPath to create data entry forms in the past? PowerApps allows you to implement similar forms but without requiring database or programming skills. And PowerApps are automatically web-enabled and mobile-ready! For example, you can quickly create apps for automating processing expense reports or handling customer support cases. You design the app by dragging and dropping elements onto a canvas, just as you would design a slide in PowerPoint. To get a feeling of the capabilities of canvas apps, go to https://docs.microsoft.com/powerapps/maker/canvas-apps/ and review the sample apps and tutorials provided by Microsoft.
- Model-driven apps – In Chapter 7, I introduced you to the Microsoft Common Data Model (CDM) in the context of dataflows. If you use CDM, PowerApps can auto-generate the app for you! Unlike canvas apps where you define the app layout and bind it to data, with model-driven apps much of the layout and data binding code is auto-generated.

How does Power BI integrate with PowerApps?

Power BI can pass data to PowerApps using the PowerApps custom visual. This visual is currently in preview and it can be obtained from the Microsoft Marketplace just like any other custom visual. As the interactive user selects data on the report, such as when clicking a row in a table to select it, Power BI passes the data behind the selection to a PowerApps canvas app. This data exchange is one-directional and currently there isn't a way for PowerApps to pass data directly back to Power BI (however both apps can exchange data via some data repository, such as a relational database and Common Data Services for Apps).

What can your PowerApps app do with the data it gets from the report? Anything you want it to. For example, it can retrieve data from an ERP system for the selected invoice and display it to the user. Or, in our case, the PowerApps canvas app could allow the end user to make corrections to the report data and write the changes to a database.

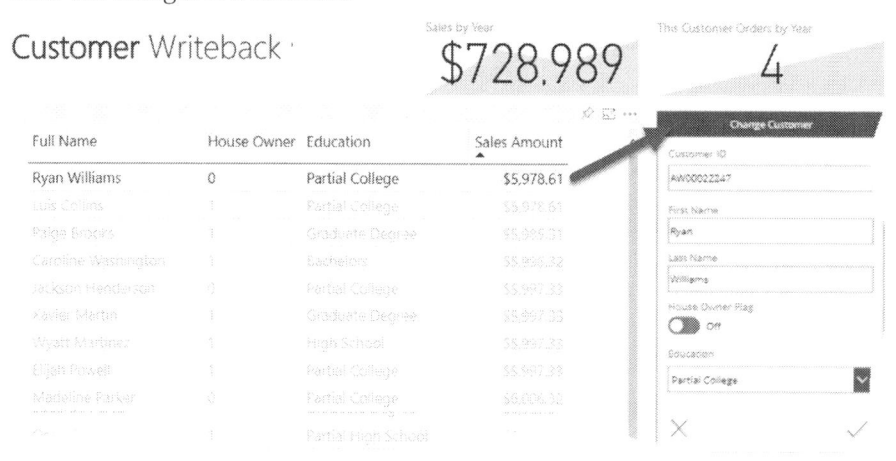

Figure 10.34 This report integrates with PowerApps to let the user make changes to the report data.

10.4.2 Implementing Report Writeback

The Power BI report in **Figure 10.34** shows a list of customers. For each customer, the report shows some demographics information and overall sales. When the user selects a customer in the Table visual, the report passes the context to the PowerApps app on the right. The user can make corrections in the data form and save the changes to the backend database. Then, the user can refresh the report to see the latest data. Let's go through the steps to implement this exciting scenario, which is known as report writeback.

Getting started with PowerApps

A preview limitation of the PowerApps custom visual is that in Power BI desktop you can only use it to reference an existing PowerApps app. If you want to create an app, you must use the visual in Power BI Service. The Customer Writeback Demo Start.pbix file in \Source\ch10 folder is the starting point for this practice. As a prerequisite, you need to have a subscription to an Office 365 business plan. To follow the steps, you'd need also the AdventureWorksDW2012 database hosted in an Azure SQL Database and read permissions to retrieve data.

1. Open the report in Power BI Desktop. Hover over any of the tables in the Fields pane and notice that they are configured for DirectQuery. Consequently, the report queries data in real time from the AdventureWorksDW database hosted in an Azure SQL Database instance. Publish the file to powerbi.com.
2. In Power BI Service, open the report in Edit mode.
3. Select the Table visual. In the Visualizations pane, notice that the first field is CustomerKey. The PowerApps app will use the value of this field to retrieve the data for the selected customer on the report.

4. In the Visualizations pane, click the ellipsis (…) menu, click Import from Marketplace, and import the PowerApps custom visual. Once the visual is added to the Visualizations pane, click its icon to add it to the report. Expand the Customer table and check CustomerKey to bind it to the PowerApps visual.

5. In the PowerApps visual, click "Create new" to create a new PowerApps app. If prompted, sign in to Office 365. Once PowerApps creates the app, click Skip on the welcome screen.

PowerApps has generated a fully functional app consisting of one screen and a gallery that shows the data that Power BI passes to the app. Notice the PowerBIIntegration connector in the Screens pane on the left. Power BI uses this connector to pass the selected data on the report to the app.

Creating a data entry form

Next, you'll replace the default gallery layout, which is for browsing data only, with a data entry form.

1. In the Screens pane, right-click the Gallery1 gallery and click Delete.
2. In the Insert ribbon, expand the Forms drop-down and click Edit. PowerApps adds an empty data entry form and opens the Data pane so that you can specify the data source for the form.
3. Expand the "Select a data source" drop-down and select "Add a data source". Create a new connection to the AdventureWorksDW2012 database. Select the DimCustomer table and click Connect.

> **NOTE** In this case, the report and PowerApps connects to the same database so that data changes are immediately shown on the report after you refresh the report. However, there is nothing stopping you from connecting to different databases.

4. Check the following fields to bind them to the form: CustomerKey, FirstName, LastName, HouseOwner-Flag, and EnglishEducation. Close the Data pane. Compare your results with **Figure 10.35**. Notice that PowerApps adds a card on the form for each database field. A card includes the field label, textbox, and another label to show an error in case something goes wrong. By default, the card is locked to prevent you from making accidental layout changes.

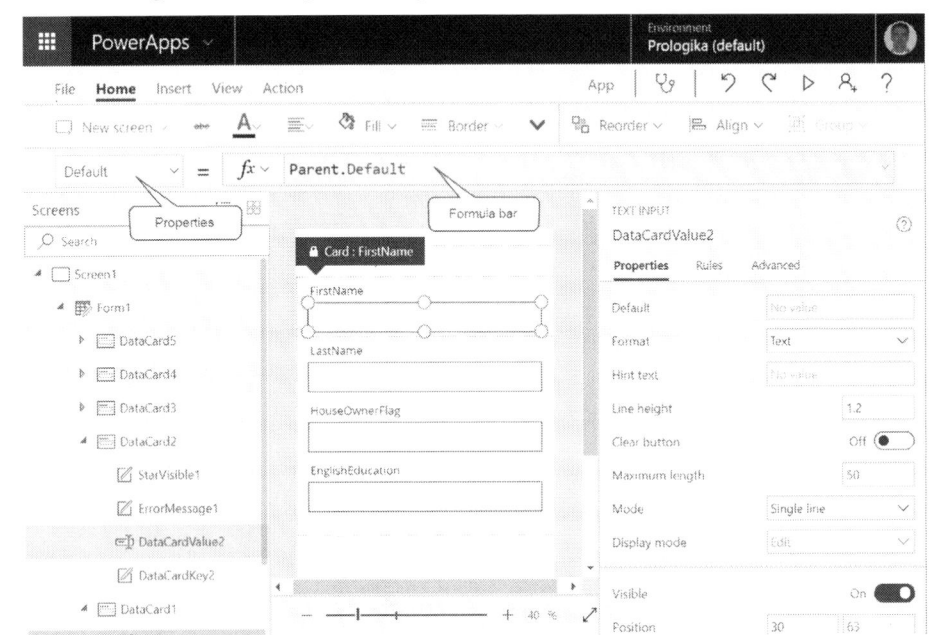

Figure 10.35 The app uses a form to let you make data changes.

5. In the Screens pane, select Form1. The Properties drop-down should default to the DataSource property.
6. In the formula bar, enter the following expression (PowerApps has its own expression language):

300   CHAPTER 10

First(Filter('[dbo].[DimCustomer]', CustomerKey = First(PowerBIIntegration.Data).CustomerKey))

This expression filters the data in the DimCustomer table where CustomerKey equals to the value of CustomerKey in the first row of the Power BI dataset. You need the First function because the Power BI connector exposes the data as a table even if there is just one row.

7. To test the changes, go back to the report and select a customer. Switch to PowerApps and notice that the form displays the selected customer.

Implementing a toggle

To make the form more user friendly and avoid data entry issues, let's implement the HouseOwnerFlag field as a toggle.

1. Select the HouseOwnerFlag card. In the Advanced properties of the Card pane on the right, switch to the Advanced tab and then click the padlock icon to unlock the card properties.
2. Select the HouseOwnerFlag textbox (not the card) and delete it.
3. Select the HouseOwnerFlag card. With the card selected, go to the Insert ribbon, expand the Controls drop-down, and then select Toggle.
4. With the toggle control selected, right-click Toggle1 in the Screens pane and click Rename. Rename the control to *tblHouseOwner*.
5. With the toggle control selected, expand the Properties drop-down and select the Default property. Enter the following expression in the formula bar *If(Parent.Default="1", true, false)*. This expression "translates" the database values (1 and 0) to Boolean values that the toggle expects.
6. To fix the two errors shown on the form, click the first error icon. This should select the Update property of the card. Change its expression to *tglHouseOwner.Value*. This expression will change the database value to the toggle value when you save the changes.
7. Click the second error icon and change the Y property to *tglHouseOwner.Y + tglHouseOwner.Height*.
8. Resize the card and position the fields as needed.

Implementing a drop-down

To make the form more user friendly and avoid data entry issues, let's implement the EnglishEducation field as a toggle.

1. Select the EnglishEducation card. In the Advanced properties of the Card pane on the right, switch to the Advanced tab and then click the padlock icon to unlock the card properties.
2. Select the EnglishEducation textbox (not the card) and delete it.
3. Select the EnglishEducation card. With the card selected, go to the Insert ribbon, expand the Controls drop-down, and then select "Drop down".
4. With the drop-down control selected, right-click Dropdown1 in the Screens pane and click Rename. Rename the control to *drpEducation*.
5. With the dropdown selected, expand the Properties drop-down and select the Items property. Enter the expression *Distinct('[dbo].[DimCustomer]', EnglishEducation)* in the formula bar. This expression populates the drop-down with the distinct values from the EnglishEducation column in the DimCustomer table.
6. Change the Default property to *Parent.Default*. This expression defaults the drop-down selection to the database value.
7. To fix the two errors shown on the form, click the first error icon. This should select the Update property of the card. Change its expression to *drpEducation.Selected.Value*. This expression will change the database value to the drop-down value when you save changes.
8. Click the second error icon and change the Y property to *drpEducation.Y + drpEducation.Height*.

9. Resize the card and position the fields as needed.

Canceling data changes

Follow these steps to implement a button that cancels the changes if the user decides to abandon them:

1. In the Screens pane, select the Form1 form.
2. In the Insert ribbon, expand the Icons drop-down and select the Cancel icon. Position the icon as needed.
3. Add the following code to the icon's OnSelect property.

   Revert('[dbo].[DimCustomer]', First(Filter('[dbo].[DimCustomer]', CustomerKey = First(PowerBIIntegration.Data).CustomerKey)))

   This expression uses the Revert function to ignore the user changes and display the original values.

Saving data changes

Follow these steps to implement a button that saves the changes to the database:

1. In the Screens pane, select the Form1 form.
2. In the Insert ribbon, expand the Icons drop-down and select the Check icon. Position the icon as needed.
3. Add the following code to the icon's OnSelect event

   Patch('[dbo].[DimCustomer]', First(Filter('[dbo].[DimCustomer]', CustomerKey = First(PowerBIIntegration.Data).CustomerKey)),{FirstName:txtFirstName.Text,LastName:txtLastName.Text,HouseOwnerFlag:If(tglHouseOwner.Value=true, "1", "0"), EnglishEducation:drpEducation.Selected.Value})

   This convoluted expression uses the Patch function to save the user changes to the database. In the simplest case, your app can just call the Update method to save changes. However, we need the Patch function to translate the selected value of the toggle control to a value (1 and 0) that the database expects.

Publishing the app

The app is now ready for prime time.

1. Click the File menu and click Save. Enter *CustomerWriteback* as the app name. At this point, your report should be fully functional. However, you must share the app so that other users can use it.
2. Click the File menu and click Share. Enter the names or emails of the users whom you want to share the app with.

10.5 Summary

Power BI is all about bringing your data to life and getting insights to make decisions faster. You can show more details behind a data point by drilling down, drilling across, and drilling through. You can create custom groups and bins. Conditional formatting helps change colors to spot trends easier. You can extend your reports with links that bring users to other systems and display web images.

Consider the Power BI data storytelling capabilities to communicate your insights more effectively. Get insights by asking natural questions on the desktop as you do in Power BI Service. Integrate Cortana on your Windows 10 computer with Power BI so that you can ask natural questions as you work without navigating to powerbi.com. Explain the story behind a visual with Narratives for Power BI. Walk your audience through your data story by creating bookmarks.

Power BI can integrate with the other products in the Microsoft Power Platform: PowerApps and Flow. Integrate Power BI with PowerApps to bridge the analytical and developer worlds. Integrate Power BI with Flow to start workflows when data alerts are triggered.

Power BI doesn't limit you to only descriptive analytics. It includes comprehensive predictive features for both data analysts and data scientists, as you'll discover in the next chapter.

Chapter 11

Predictive Analytics

11.1 Using Built-in Predictive Features 303
11.2 Using R and Python 306
11.3 Integrating with Azure Machine Learning 312
11.4 Summary 319

Predictive analytics, also known as data mining, machine learning, and artificial intelligence (AI), is an increasingly popular requirement. It also happens to be one of the least understood because it's usually confused with slicing and dicing data. However, predictive analytics is about discovering patterns that aren't easily discernible. These hidden patterns can't be derived from traditional data exploration, because data relationships might be too complex or because there's too much data for a human to analyze.

So, predictive analytics is concerned with what will happen in the future. It uses machine learning algorithms to determine probable future outcomes and discover patterns that might not be easily discernible based on historical data. With all the interest surrounding predictive analytics and machine learning, you may wonder what Power BI has to offer. You won't be disappointed by its predictive capabilities! As you'll discover in this chapter, they range from simple features that take a few clicks to building integrated solutions with Azure Machine Learning.

This chapter starts by introducing you to built-in predictive features in Power BI Desktop. Then, I'll show you how you can integrate R and Python for data visualization and machine learning. Lastly, I'll show you how you can integrate Power BI with Azure Machine Learning. You'll find the examples in the \Source\ch11 folder.

11.1 Using Built-in Predictive Features

You don't have to be a data scientist to get business value from predictive analytics. Power BI Desktop includes features that make it easy for a data analyst to apply predictive analytics without knowing too much about it. These features include explaining data fluctuations, linear forecasting, and clustering data.

11.1.1 Explaining Increase and Decrease

As you've seen, Power BI Desktop helps you quickly implement sophisticated models for descriptive analytics. But you can slice and dice all day long and still have unanswered questions, such as "Why there is drop in sales for this month?". You've already seen how Quick Insights helps you discover hidden trends in Power BI Service with a few clicks. A similar feature, called Explain Increase/Decrease is available in Power BI Desktop to help you perform root cause analysis (RCA) for unexpected variances.

Using Explain Increase/Decrease
Consider the column chart on page "Explain Decrease and Clustering" in the Adventure Works file (see **Figure 11.1**). As you examine the data, you see a decrease in sales for Q3 of 2016. Instead of trying to narrow down the cause on your own, you'll let Power BI do it. You right-click on the bar and then click Analyze ⇨ Explain the Decrease.

Figure 11.1 Use Explain Increase/Decrease to uncover hidden trends that are not easily discernible.

Power BI applies machine learning algorithms, finds possible insights, ranks them, and shows reports. For example, in this case Power BI has found that the most significant decrease was from customers who don't commute much to work. You can vote a report up and down to help Microsoft tune the algorithms, switch to another visual, or add the visual to the report if you like it.

> **TIP** Do you wonder how I configured the chart to group by year and then quarter? In the Visualizations pane (Format tab), I expanded the X-axis section and then turned off "Concatenate labels".

Understanding limitations
Explain Increase/Decrease isn't available if the visual has one of these features:
- Visual-level filters (top N filters, include/exclude filters, measure filters)
- Non-additive measures and aggregates, non-numeric measures, "show value as" measures
- Categorical columns on X-axis, unless it defines a sort by column that is scalar
- DirectQuery or live connection (only datasets with imported data are supported at this time)

11.1.2 Implementing Time Series Forecasting

Another common predictive task is forecasting, such as to show revenue over future periods. Power BI Desktop supports basic forecasting capabilities to address such requirements.

Understanding time series forecasting
Time series forecasting produces forecasts over data points indexed in time order. Power BI Desktop uses a built-in predictive algorithm to automatically detect the interval, such as monthly, weekly, or annually. It's also capable of detecting seasonality changes. Currently, forecasting is supported for single series line charts with a continuous (quantitative) axis. You can use the Analytics tab of the Visualization pane (see **Figure 11.2**) to add a forecast line.

You can customize certain aspects of the forecasting model. Change the "Forecast length" setting to specify the number of future intervals to forecast. Change the "Ignore last" setting to exclude a specified number of last points, such as when you know that the last period of data is incomplete. This is especially useful if you know the last month of data is still incomplete. "Confidence interval" lets you control the upper and lower boundaries of the forecasted results.

The Seasonality setting lets you override the automatically detected seasonality trend, such as 3 points if the seasonal cycle rises and falls every 3 months, assuming you're forecasting at the month level. When you hover over the line chart, you can see the exact values of the forecasted value, as well as the upper and lower bands (the shaded area width is controlled by the "Confidence interval" setting).

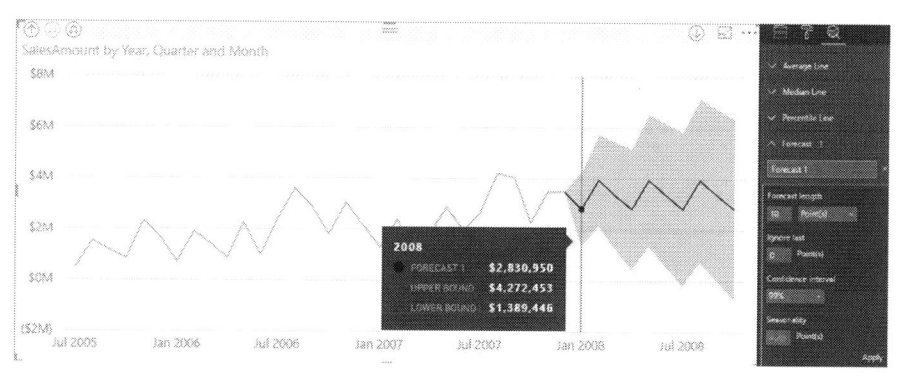

Figure 11.2 Time series forecasting uses a built-in model that supports limited customization.

Implementing forecasting

Follow these steps to implement time series forecasting:

1. Add the "Line Chart" visualization to the report.
2. Add the Calendar Hierarchy from the Date table to the Axis area of the Visualizations pane.
3. Add the SalesAmount field from the ResellerSales table to the Values area.
4. Click twice the "Expand one level down the hierarchy" button in the top-left corner of the chart to navigate to the Month level of the hierarchy.
5. In the Format tab of the Visualizations pane, change the Type setting of the X-Axis section to Continuous. You can only do this if the data type of the field added to the Axis area is Date or Numeric.
6. In the Analytics tab of the Visualizations tab, expand the Forecast section and click the Add link.
7. (Optional) Experiment with the settings to see how they affect the forecasted area in the chart.

11.1.3 Clustering Data

Clustering (also called segmentation) is another way for dynamic grouping (the others are custom groups and binning) that lets you quickly find groups of similar data points in a subset of your data. It uses predictive algorithms to group data points in similar clusters. You must use a scatter chart to detect clusters.

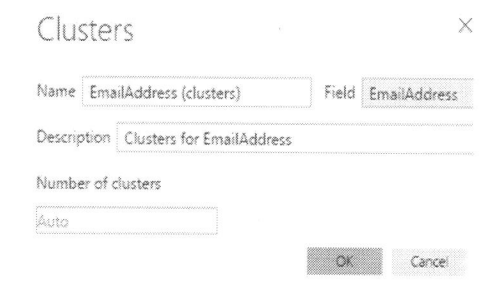

Figure 11.3 By default, Power BI would automatically detect the number of clusters.

Implementing clustering

Follow these steps to detect clusters that group customers by analyzing the correlation between the customer spend and number of items they bought.

1. Add the Scatter visual to an empty area of the report.
2. Add EmailAddress (Customer table) in the Details area, SalesAmount (InternetSales) in the X Axis area, and OrderQuantity (InternetSales table) in the Y Axis area. This configuration will see a correlation between the quantity of the items sold and generated revenue.

PREDICTIVE ANALYTICS

3. Hover over the visualization, click the ellipsis (…) menu in the top-right corner, and then click "Automatically find clusters".
4. In the Clusters window (see **Figure 11.3**), leave the default to auto-detect clusters to let Power BI automatically find clusters. Click OK.

> **NOTE** All Power BI charts and maps are high-density visuals that can plot efficiently thousands of points. If you click the information icon in the top left corner, you'll see that the algorithm prioritizes the most significant data points. For more information about how the algorithm works, read the "High Density Sampling in Power BI scatter charts" article at https://powerbi.microsoft.com//documentation/powerbi-desktop-high-density-scatter-charts/.

Interpreting results

The algorithm finds three clusters and shows them in different colors. After the clustering algorithm runs, it creates a new categorical field called "EmailAddress (clusters)" with the different cluster groups in it. This new field is added to your scatter chart's Legend field.

1. In the Visualizations pane, select the Format tab and turn on "Fill point". Rename the "EmailAddress (clusters)" to *CustomerClusters*. Compare your results with **Figure 11.4**.

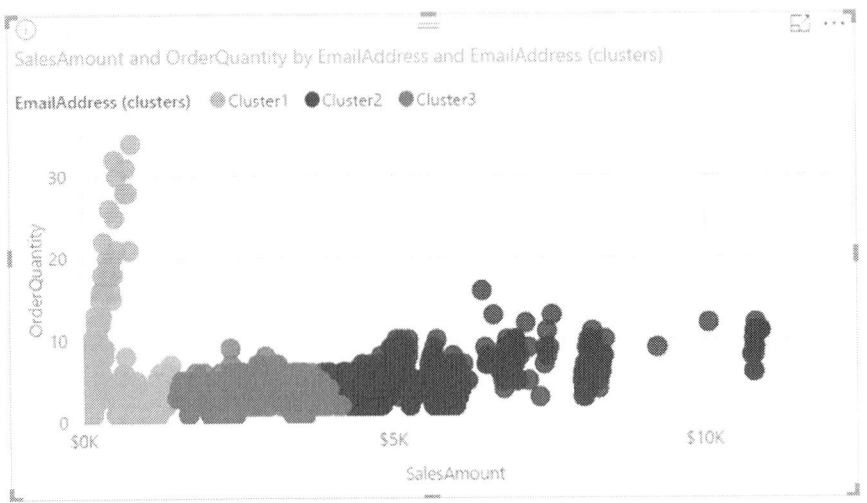

Figure 11.4 Automatic clustering found three clusters.

2. In the Fields pane, click the ellipsis next to CustomerClusters and then click "Edit clusters". This bring you back to the Clusters window where you can review the clusters and make changes, such as to increase the number of clusters. Now you understand that the first cluster (the one with low sales) has 6,230 customers, the second cluster has 1,439 customers, and the third cluster has 3,179 customers. Unfortunately, as it stands Power BI doesn't allow you to compare the cluster characteristics, such as to find similarities or differences between two clusters, nor does it allow you to rename the clusters.
3. (Optional) Create another visualization that uses the new CustomerClusters field. Although you must use a scatter chart to detect clusters, you can then use the clusters just like any other field.

11.2 Using R and Python

With all the buzz surrounding R and Python, data analysts and scientists might want to preserve their investment in these languages to import, transform, and analyze data with Power BI. Fortunately, Power BI supports R and Python (the latter is currently in preview). This integration brings the following benefits:

- Cleanse your data – If you prefer to do so, you can use R or Python (instead of or in addition to the Power Query Editor) to cleanse your data, such as to ensure that all the data points are in place, correct outliers, and normalize to uniform scales. To learn about data shaping with R, check the "Data Cleansing with R in Power BI" blog by Sharon Laivand at http://bit.ly/2eZ6f4R.
- Visualize your data – Once your script's data is imported in Power BI, you can use a Power BI visualization to present the data. That's possible because the R and Python data sources are not different than any other data source.
- Share the results – You can leverage the Power BI sharing and collaboration capabilities to disseminate the results computed in R or Python with everyone in your organization.
- Operationalize your script – Once the data is uploaded to Power BI Service, you can configure the dataset for a scheduled refresh, so that the reports are always up to date.
- Reuse your visualizations – You might use the R ggplot2 or Python pyplot packages to plot beautiful statistical graphs. Now you can bring these visuals into Power BI by using the corresponding script visuals in the Visualizations pane. You can also share your R visuals (or use the ones published by the community) at the R Script Showcase (https://community.powerbi.com/t5/R-Script-Showcase/bd-p/RVisuals/). This opens a whole world of new data visualizations! To learn more about how to create visuals, read the "Create Power BI visuals using R" blog by David Iseminger at http://bit.ly/2eQ5dHu and "Create Power BI Visuals using Python" at https://docs.microsoft.com/power-bi/desktop-python-visuals.

Data scientists also use R and Python for machine learning. Typical tasks include forecasting, customer profiling, and basket analysis. Machine learning can answer questions, such as, "What are the forecasted sales numbers for the next few months?", "What other products is a customer likely to buy along with the product he or she already chose?", and "What type of customer (described in terms of gender, age group, income, and so on) is likely to buy a given product?"

11.2.1 Using R

In this exercise, I'll show you how to use R to forecast time series and visualize it (see **Figure 11.5**). The first segment in the line chart shows the actual sales, while the second segment shows the forecasted sales that are calculated in R. Because we won't need the forecasted data in the Adventure Works data model, you'll find the finished example in a separate "R Demo.pbix" file located in the \Source\ch10 folder.

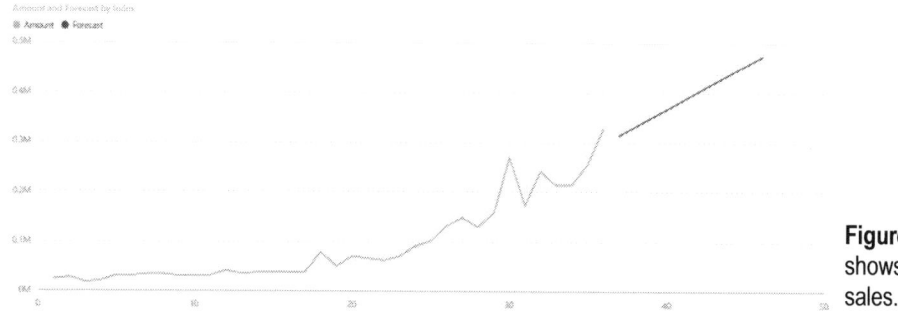

Figure 11.5 This visualization shows actual and forecasted sales.

Getting started with R

R is an open source programming language for statistical computing and data analysis. Over the years the community has contributed and extended the R capabilities through packages that provide various specialized analytical techniques and utilities. Besides supporting R in Power BI, Microsoft invested in R by acquiring Revolution Analytics, whose flagship product (Revolution R) is integrated with SQL Server 2016.

Before you can use the Power BI Desktop R integration, you must install R. Microsoft R Open, formerly known as Revolution R Open (RRO), is an enhanced distribution of R from Microsoft and it's a free open source platform for statistical analysis and data science. For more information about Microsoft R, go to https://aka.ms/microsoft-r-open-docs.

1. Open your web browser and navigate to https://mran.revolutionanalytics.com/download, and then download and install R for Windows.
2. I also recommend that you install RStudio Desktop (an open source R development environment) from http://www.rstudio.com. RStudio Desktop will allow you to prepare and test your R script before you import it in Power BI Desktop.

> **TIP** As I mentioned, you can also use R to visualize your data by using the R visual in the Visualization pane. In this scenario, you can configure Power BI Desktop to use an external IDE, such as R Studio or Visual Studio. For more information about how to do so, read the "Use an external R IDE with Power BI" article at https://powerbi.microsoft.com/documentation/powerbi-desktop-r-ide/.

3. Use the Windows ODBC Data Sources (64-bit) tool (or 32-bit if you use the 32-bit version of Power BI Desktop) to set up a new ODBC system data source AdventureWorksDW that points to the AdventureWorksDW2012 (or a later version) database.

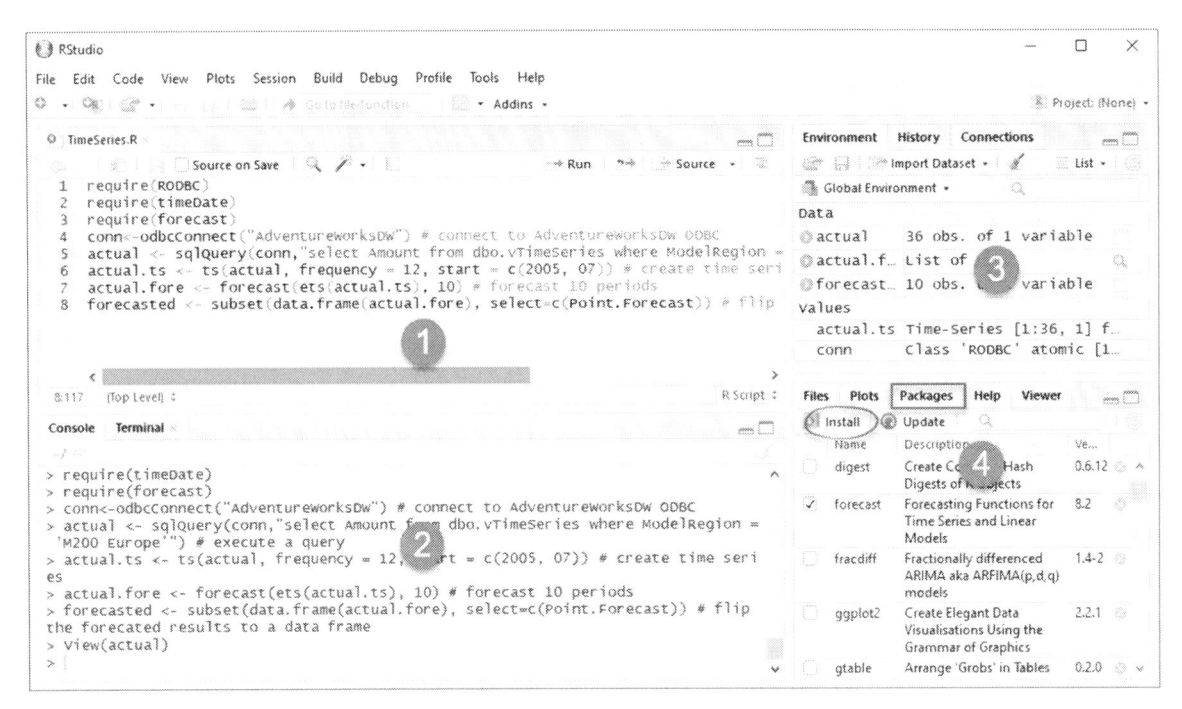

Figure 11.6 Use RStudio to develop and test R scripts.

Using R for time series forecasting

Next, you'll create a basic R script for time series forecasting using RStudio. The RStudio user interface has four areas (see **Figure 11.6**). The first area (shown as 1 in the screenshot) contains the script that you're working on. The second area is the RStudio Console that allows you to test the script. For example, if you position the mouse cursor on a given script line and press Ctrl-Enter, RStudio will execute the current script line and it will show the output in the console.

The Global Environment area (shown as 3 in **Figure 11.6**) shows some helpful information about your script variables, such as the number of observations in a time series object. Area 4 has a tabbed interface that shows some additional information about the RStudio environment. For example, the Packages tab shows you what packages are loaded, while the Plots tab allows you to see the output when you use the R plotting capabilities. Let's start by importing the packages that our script needs:

1. Click File ⇨ New File ⇨ R Script File (or press Ctlr+Shft+N) to create a new R Script. Or, if you don't want to type R code, click File ⇨ Open File, then open TimeSeries.R script from the \Source\ch11 folder.
2. In the area 4, select the Packages tab, and then click the Install tab.
3. In the Install Packages window, enter *RODBC* (IntelliSense helps you enter the correct name), and then click Install. This installs the RODBC package which allows you to connect to ODBD data sources.
4. Repeat the last two steps to install the "timeDate" and "forecast" packages.

Going through the code, lines 1-3 list the required packages. Line 4 connects to the AdventureWorksDW ODBC data source. Line 5 retrieves the Amount field from the vTimeSeries SQL view, which is one of the sample views included in the AdventureWorksDW database. The resulting dataset represents the actual sales that are saved in the "actual" data frame. Like a Power BI dataset, an R data frame stores data tables. Line 6 creates a time series object with a frequency of 12 because the actual sales are stored by month. Line 7 uses the R forecast package to create forecasted sales for 10 periods. Line 8 stores the Point.Forecast column from the forecasted dataset in a data frame.

> **NOTE** As of the time of writing, the R Source data source in Power BI only imports data frames, so make sure the data you want to load from an R script is stored in a data frame. Going down the list of limitations, columns that are typed as Complex and Vector are not imported and are replaced with error values in the created table. Values that are N/A are translated to NULL values in Power BI Desktop. Also, any R script that runs longer than 30 minutes will time out. Interactive calls in the R script, such as waiting for user input, halt the script's execution.

Using the R Script source

Once the R script is tested, you can import the results in Power BI Desktop.

1. Open Power BI Desktop. Click Get Data ⇨ More ⇨ R Script, and then click Connect.

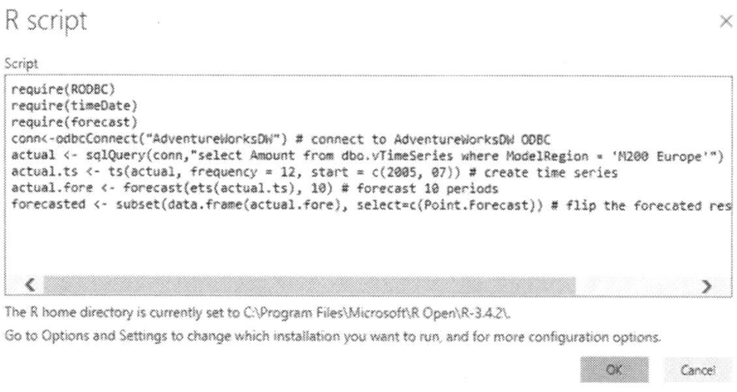

Figure 11.7 Enter the script in "R Script" window to use it as a data source.

2. In the "Execute R Script" window (see **Figure 11.7**), paste the R script. Expand the "R Installation Settings" section and make sure that the R installation location matches your R setup. Click OK.
3. In the Navigator window, notice that the script imports two tables (actual and forecasted) that correspond to the two data frames you defined in the R script. Click the Edit button to open Query Editor.
4. Click the "actuals" table. With the "actuals" query selected in the Queries pane, click the Append Queries button in ribbon's Home tab.

PREDICTIVE ANALYTICS

5. In the Append window, select the "forecasted" table, and then click OK. This appends the forecasted table to the actual table so that all the data (actual and forecasted) is in a single table.
6. Rename the "actual" table to *ActualAndForecast*. Rename the Point.Forecast column to *Forecast*.
7. (Optional) If you need actual and forecasted values in a single column, in the ribbon's Add Column tab, click "Add Custom Column". Name the custom column "Result" and enter the following expression:

   if [Amount]=null then [Forecast] else [Amount]

   This formula adds a new Result column that combines Amount and Forecast values into a single column.
8. In the ribbon's Add Column tab, click "Add Index Column" to add an auto-incremented column that starts with 1.
9. In the Home ribbon, click Close & Apply to execute the script and import the data.
10. To visualize the data, create a Line Chart visualization that has the Index field added to the Axis area, and Amount and Forecast fields added to the Values area.
11. (Optional) Deploy the Power BI Desktop file to Power BI Service and schedule the dataset for refresh.

> **TIP** What if instead of doing all data prepation in R or Python, you just need to apply a script for a transformation step while the rest are done in Power Query? You can use the Run R Script or Run Python Script transformation tasks in Power Query Editor Transform ribbon. They will insert a new step where you can apply your script.

11.2.2 Using Python

You can use Python for transforming or visualizing your data just like you can do with R. In this practice, you'll use Python to visualize the distribution of your data as a beeswarm plot, which is included in the Python seaborn package.

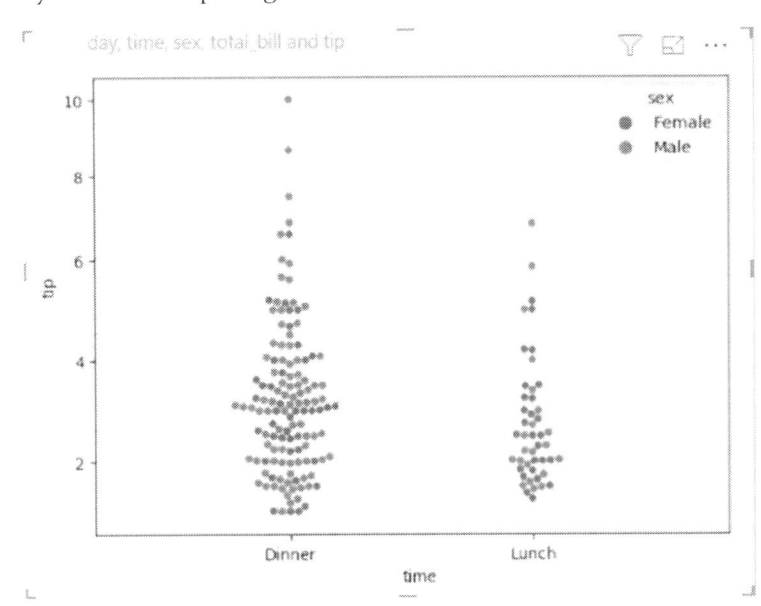

Figure 11.8 This beeswarm plot shows the distribution of bill tips by time and gender.

Getting started with Python
As a prerequisite, you need to install Python on your laptop.

1. Install Python from the Official Python download page (https://python.org/) or Anaconda (https://anaconda.org/anaconda/python/).
2. In Power BI Desktop, go to File ⇨ Options and Settings ⇨ Options and click the "Python scripting" tab. Ensure that the Python home directory is detected and references the folder where you installed Python.
3. Currently, Python scripting is in preview. Select the "Preview features" tab and check "Python support".
4. The Python script that you'll use next references three Python packages that you need to install. Open the Windows command prompt and enter the following commands (press Enter after each line).

```
py -m pip install pandas
py -m pip install matplotlib
py -m pip install seaborn
```

Visualizing data with Python

Next, you'll use a Python script to create a beeswarm plot for visualizing the distribution of bill tips by time of the day and gender (see **Figure 11.8**). The Python Demo.pbix file in \Source\ch10 demonstrates the final solution. Here are the implementation steps:

1. In Power BI Desktop, import the \Source\ch10\tips.csv file.
2. Click the Python visual (Py) in the Visualizations pane to add it to the report.
3. With the new visual selected, check the sex, time, and tip fields to add them to the visual.
4. Expand the drop-down next to each field in the Values area and change their aggregation to "Don't summarize". This is needed because you want to plot the data distribution without pre-aggregating the data.
5. In the Python script editor, enter the following script (see **Figure 11.9**):

```
import seaborn as sns
import matplotlib.pyplot as plt
sns.swarmplot (x="time", y="tip", hue="sex", data=dataset)
plt.show()
```

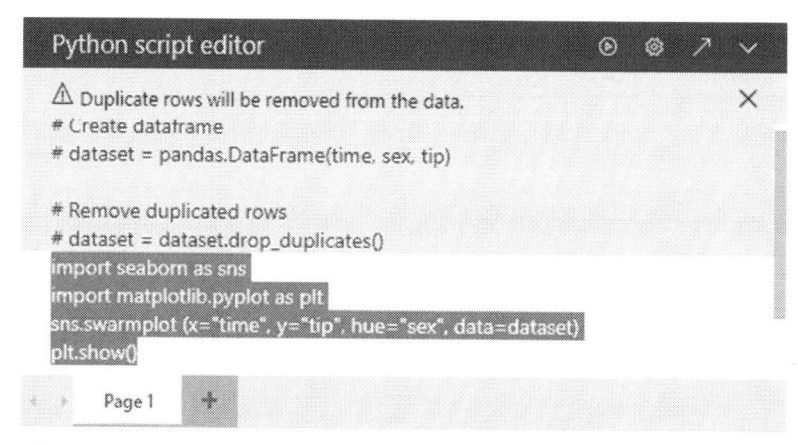

Figure 11.9 Enter the Python script in the script editor.

This script imports the seaborn and matplotlib packages and aliases them as sns and plt respectively. Then, it calls the swarmplot function to plot the data by placing *time* on the X axis, and *tip* on the Y axis. It then categorizes the results by the person's gender. For more information about the Python swarmplot package, read its documentation at https://seaborn.pydata.org/generated/seaborn.swarmplot.html.

6. Click the Run button in the editor top right corner to execute the script.

Power BI should render the graph. Analyzing the graph, we can deduce that in general women tend to be better tippers and most tips fall within the $2-4 range.

PREDICTIVE ANALYTICS

11.3 Integrating with Azure Machine Learning

Predictive analytics isn't new to Microsoft. Microsoft extended Analysis Services with data mining back in SQL Server 2000. Besides allowing BI pros to create data mining models with Analysis Services, Microsoft also introduced the Excel Data Mining add-in to let business users perform data mining tasks in Excel.

> **NOTE** With the focus shifting to Azure ML and R, we probably won't see future investments from Microsoft in SSAS Data Mining (and the Excel data mining add-in for that matter) which is currently limited to nine algorithms.

SQL Server 2016 added R Services that allow you to integrate the power of R with your T-SQL code. You've already seen that Power BI includes Quick Insights, time-series forecasting, and clustering as built-in predictive features. And in 2014, Microsoft unveiled a cloud-based service for predictive analytics called Azure Machine Learning or AzureML, which also originated from Microsoft Research.

11.3.1 Understanding Azure Machine Learning

In a nutshell, Azure Machine Learning makes it easy for data scientists to quickly create and deploy predictive models in the cloud. Once the predictive model is in place, client applications, such as Power BI, can integrate with it to obtain predictive results.

Understanding business value of Azure ML
The Azure ML value proposition includes the following appealing features:

- It provides an easy-to-use, comprehensive, and scalable platform without requiring hardware or software investments.
- It supports workflows for transforming and moving data. For example, AzureML supports custom code, such as R or Python code, to transform columns. Furthermore, it allows you to chain tasks, such as to load data, create a model, and then save the predictive results.
- It allows you to easily expose predictive models as REST web services, so that you can incorporate predictive features in custom applications.

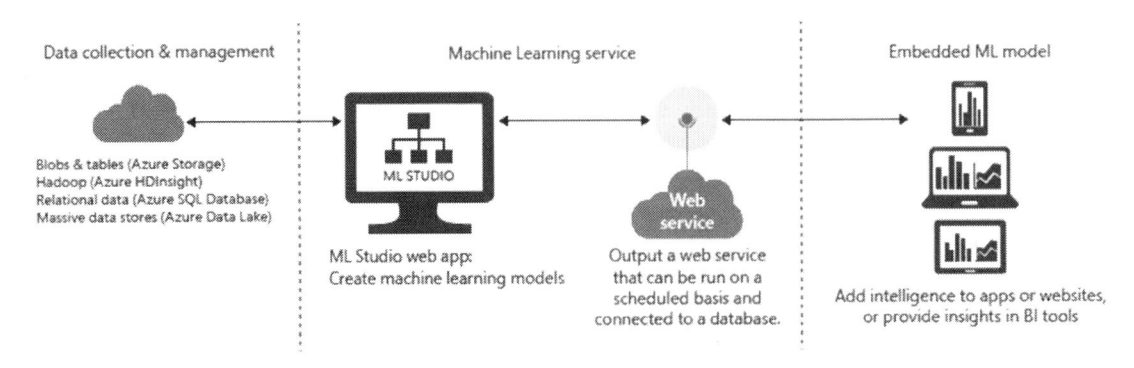

Figure 11.10 The diagram demonstrates a common flow to implement predictive models with AzureML.

Understanding workflows
Figure 11.10 shows a typical AzureML implementation. Because it's a cloud service, AzureML can obtain the input data directly from other cloud services, such as Azure tables, Azure SQL Database, or Azure

HDInsight. Alternatively, you can export on-premises data as a file and upload the dataset to AzureML or connect directly to an on-premises SQL Server database by using a data gateway.

Then you use ML Studio to build a workflow for creating and training a predictive model. ML Studio is a browser-based tool that allows you to drag, drop, and connect the building blocks of your solution. You can choose from a large library of Machine Learning algorithms to jump-start your predictive models! You can also extend the workflow with your own custom R and Python scripts.

Like Stream Analytics and Power BI, AzureML is an integral component of the Cortana Analytics Suite, although you can also use it as a standalone service. The Cortana Analytics Gallery (http://gallery.cortanaanalytics.com) is a community-driven site for discovering and sharing predictive solutions. It features many ready-to-go predictive models that have been contributed by Microsoft and the analytics community. You can learn more about Azure Machine Learning at its official site (https://azure.microsoft.com/en-us/services/machine-learning) and start using for free!

11.3.2 Creating Predictive Models

Next, I'll walk you through the steps to implement an AzureML predictive model for a familiar scenario. Our bike manufacturer, Adventure Works, is planning a marketing campaign. The marketing department approaches you to help them target a subset of potential customers who are the most likely to purchase a bike. You need to create a predictive model that predicts the purchase probability from some sales data accumulated in the past.

Understanding the historical dataset

To start, you'd need to obtain an order history dataset that you'd use to train the model:

1. In SQL Server Management Studio (SSMS), connect to the AdventureWorksDW2012 database and execute the following query:

```
SELECT
   Gender,YearlyIncome,TotalChildren,NumberChildrenAtHome,
   EnglishEducation,EnglishOccupation,HouseOwnerFlag,
   NumberCarsOwned,CommuteDistance,Region,Age,BikeBuyer
FROM [dbo].[vTargetMail]
```

This query returns a subset of columns from the vTargetMail view that Microsoft uses to demonstrate the Analysis Services data mining features. The last column, BikeBuyer, is a flag that indicates if the customer has purchased a bike. The model will use the rest of the columns as an input to determine the most important criteria that influences a customer to purchase a bike.

> **NOTE** The Adventure Works Analysis Services Multidimensional cube includes a Targeted Mailing data mining structure, which uses this dataset. The mining models in the Targeted Mailing structure demonstrate how the same scenario can be addressed with an on-premises Analysis Services solution.

2. Export the results to a CSV file. For your convenience, I included a Bike Buyers.csv file in the \source\ch11\AzureML folder.

Creating a predictive model

Next, you'll use AzureML to create a predictive model, using the Bike Buyers.csv file as an input:

1. Go to https://studio.azureml.net and sign in. If you don't have an Azure subscription, you can start a trial subscription, or just use the free version!

2. Once you are in Microsoft Azure Machine Learning (Azure ML) Studio, click New on the bottom of the screen, and then create a dataset by uploading the Bike Buyers.csv file. Name the dataset *Bike Buyers*.

PREDICTIVE ANALYTICS   313

3. Click the New button again and create a new experiment. An Azure ML experiment represents the workflow to create and train a predictive model. When you're done, your experiment will look like the one shown in **Figure 11.11**.

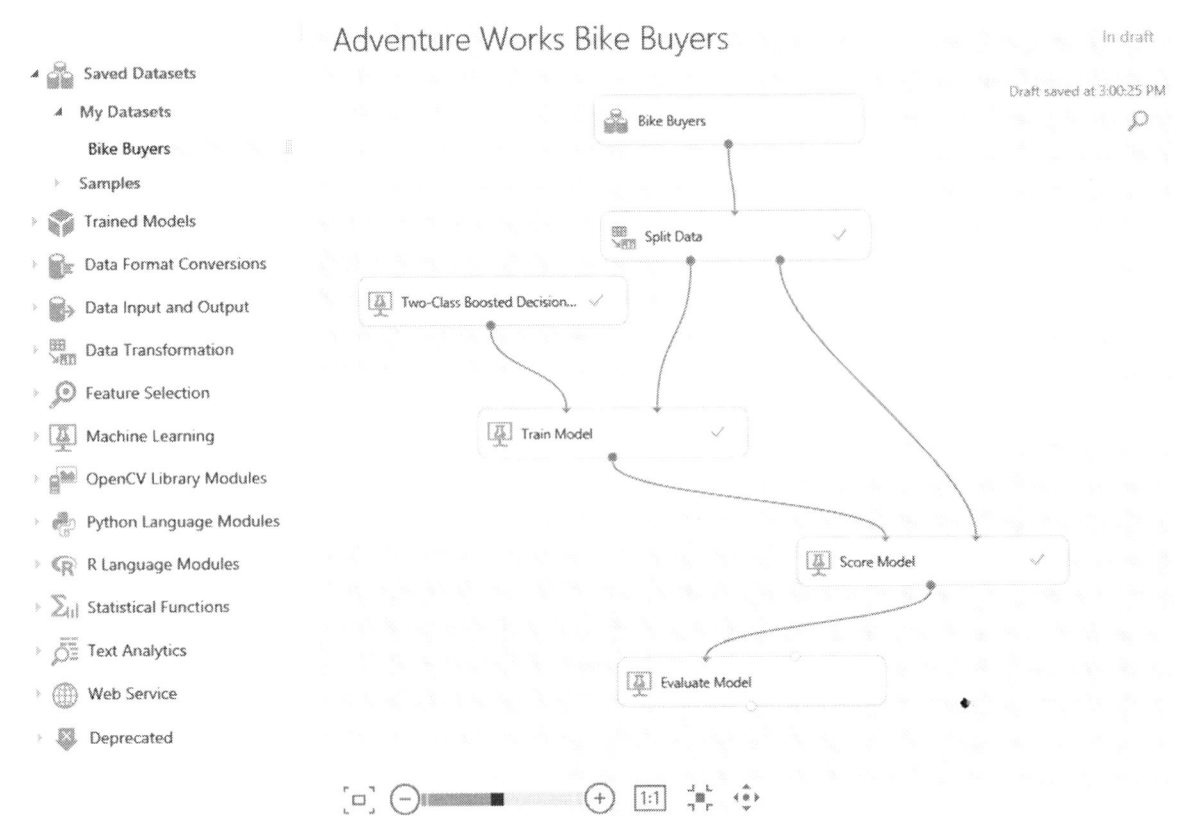

Figure 11.11 The Adventure Works Bike Buyer predictive model.

4. From the Saved Datasets section in the navigation bar, drag and drop the Bike Buyers dataset.
5. Using the search box, search for each of the workflow nodes shown in **Figure 11.11**. by typing its name, and then drop them on the workflow. Join them as shown in the diagram. For example, to find the Split Data task, type "Split" in the search box. From the search results, drag the Split Data task and drop it onto the workflow. Then connect the Bike Buyer dataset to the Split Data task.
6. The workhorse of the model is the Two-Class Boosted Decision Tree algorithm, which generates the predictive results. Click the Split Data transformation and configure its "Fraction of rows in the first output dataset" property for a 0.8 split. That's because you'll use 80% of the input dataset to train the model and the remaining 20% to evaluate the model accuracy.

Setting up a web service

A great AzureML feature is that it can easily expose an experiment as a REST web service. The web service allows client applications to integrate with AzureML and use the model for scoring. Setting up a web service is remarkably easy.

1. Click the Run button to run the experiment.

2. (Optional) Right-click the output (the small circle at the bottom) of the Evaluate Model task, and then click Visualize to analyze the model accuracy. For example, the Lift graph shows the gain of the model, compared to just targeting all the customers without using a predictive model.
3. At the bottom of the screen, click "Set up Web Service". AzureML creates a new experiment because it needs to remove the unnecessary tasks from the web service, such as the task to train the model. **Figure 13.12** shows the workflow of the predictive experiment after AzureML sets up the web service.

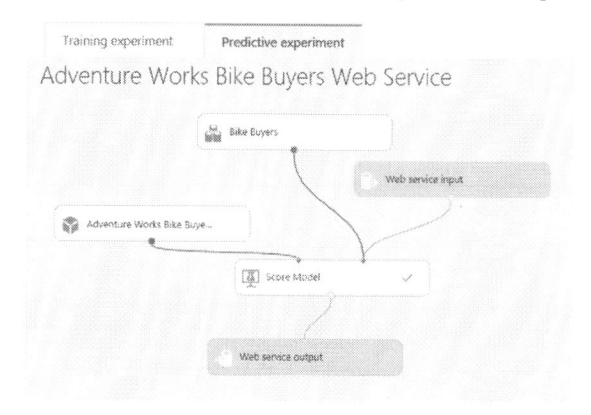

Figure 11.12 The predictive experiment is optimized for scoring.

4. Run the predictive experiment.
5. At the bottom of the screen, click "Deploy Web Service" to create the REST API endpoint.
6. In the navigation bar, click Web Services, and then click the new web service that you just created.
7. AzureML opens the web service page (see **Figure 11.13**).

Figure 11.13 The web service page allows you to obtain the API key and test the web service.

Your application will use the API key to authenticate against ML. Think of it as a password. Copy the API key because you'll need it later. The Request/Response link is for calling the web service in a singleton manner (one row at a time). The Batch Execution link is for scoring multiple rows in one batch.

> **TIP** The Microsoft Azure ML team has provided an Excel Azure Machine Learning Add-in (bit.ly/2g0oAgc) that allows you to integrate the Azure ML predictive web service with Excel. The add-in supports scoring multiple rows from an Excel range by calling the Azure ML batch API.

PREDICTIVE ANALYTICS

8. Click the Request/Response link to see the web service developer documentation and to test the web service. The documentation page includes the web service endpoint, which should look like this following example (I excluded the sensitive information):

https://ussouthcentral.services.azureml.net/workspaces/<...>/execute?api-version=2.0&details=true

The page also shows a simple POST request and response described in JSON (see **Figure 11.14**).

Sample Request
```
{
  "Inputs": {
    "input1": {
      "ColumnNames": [
        "Gender",
        "YearlyIncome",
        "TotalChildren",
        "NumberChildrenAtHome",
        "EnglishEducation",
        "EnglishOccupation",
        "HouseOwnerFlag",
        "NumberCarsOwned",
        "CommuteDistance",
        "Region",
        "Age",
        "BikeBuyer"
      ],
      "Values": [
        [
```

Sample Response
```
{
  "Results": {
    "output1": {
      "type": "DataTable",
      "value": {
        "ColumnNames": [
          "Gender",
          "YearlyIncome",
          "TotalChildren",
          "NumberChildrenAtHome",
          "EnglishEducation",
          "EnglishOccupation",
          "HouseOwnerFlag",
          "NumberCarsOwned",
          "CommuteDistance",
          "Region",
          "Age",
          "BikeBuyer",
          "Scored Labels",
```

Figure 11.14 A simple request and response from the Adventure Works Bike Buyers predictive web service.

Operationalizing the predictive service

While creating a web service is easy, operationalizing it takes more work. For example, you might be interested in automating your predictive solution, such as scheduling your experiment for retraining. Azure ML supports several ways of retraining your models, including retraining programmatically, using PowerShell, or by using Azure Data Factory.

For more information about operationalizing Azure ML models, check the "Azure Machine Learning Web Services: Deployment and consumption" article at https://docs.microsoft.com/en-us/azure/machine-learning/studio/deploy-consume-web-service-guide. Going back to the subject of this book, let's see next how you can derive insights from your predictive models in Power BI.

11.3.3 Integrating Machine Learning with Power BI

Currently, Power BI doesn't include a connector to connect directly to Azure Machine Learning. This leaves you with two integration options:

- Instead of publishing to a web service, save the predictive results to Azure Storage, such as to an Azure SQL Database. Then use Power BI Service's Get Data to visualize the predictive results.
- Publish the predictive model as a web service, and then use Power BI Desktop or Power Query to call the web service.

> **NOTE** At Ignite 2018 Microsoft demoed a forthcoming integration between Power Query and Azure ML and Azure Cognitive Services. To get a quick preview of this integration, watch the video "Fusing AI and data visualization" at https://youtube.com/watch?v=G3Vxys_jsqY.

The second option allows you to implement flexible integration scenarios, such as to call the web service for each customer from a dataset you imported in Power BI Desktop. Moreover, it demonstrates some of the advanced capabilities of Power BI Desktop queries and Power Query. This is the integration option I'll demonstrate next.

Understanding the input dataset

Let's get back to our Adventure Works scenario. Now that the predictive web service is ready, you can use it to predict the probability of new customers who could purchase a bike, if you have the customer demographics details. The marketing department has given you an Excel file with potential customers, which they might have downloaded from the company's CRM system.

1. In Excel, open the New Customers.xlsx file (in \ch11\Machine Learning folder), which includes 20 new customers (see **Figure 11.15**).

EMailAddress	Gender	YearlyIncome	TotalChildren	NumberChi	EnglishEducation	EnglishOccupation	HouseOwner	NumberC	CommuteDistance	Region	Age	BikeBuyer
jon24@adventur	M	90000	2	0	Bachelors	Professional	1	0	1-2 Miles	Pacific	49	0
eugene10@adve	M	60000	3	3	Bachelors	Professional	0	1	0-1 Miles	Pacific	50	0
ruben35@adven	M	60000	3	3	Bachelors	Professional	1	1	2-5 Miles	Pacific	50	0
christy12@adver	F	70000	0	0	Bachelors	Professional	0	1	5-10 Miles	Pacific	47	0
elizabeth5@adve	F	80000	5	5	Bachelors	Professional	1	4	1-2 Miles	Pacific	47	0
julio1@adventur	M	70000	0	0	Bachelors	Professional	1	1	5-10 Miles	Pacific	50	0
janet9@adventu	F	70000	0	0	Bachelors	Professional	1	1	5-10 Miles	Pacific	49	0
marco14@adven	M	60000	3	3	Bachelors	Professional	1	2	0-1 Miles	Pacific	51	0
rob4@adventure	F	60000	4	4	Bachelors	Professional	1	3	10+ Miles	Pacific	51	0
shannon38@adv	M	70000	0	0	Bachelors	Professional	0	1	5-10 Miles	Pacific	51	0
jacquelyn20@ad	F	70000	0	0	Bachelors	Professional	0	1	5-10 Miles	Pacific	51	0
curtis9@adventu	M	60000	4	4	Bachelors	Professional	1	4	10+ Miles	Pacific	51	0
lauren41@adven	F	100000	2	0	Bachelors	Management	1	2	1-2 Miles	North Am	47	0
ian47@adventur	M	100000	2	0	Bachelors	Management	1	3	0-1 Miles	North Am	47	0
sydney23@adver	F	100000	3	0	Bachelors	Management	0	3	1-2 Miles	North Am	47	0
chloe23@advent	F	30000	0	0	Partial College	Skilled Manual	0	1	5-10 Miles	North Am	36	0
wyatt32@advent	M	30000	0	0	Partial College	Skilled Manual	1	1	5-10 Miles	North Am	36	0
shannon1@adve	F	20000	4	0	High School	Skilled Manual	1	2	5-10 Miles	Pacific	71	0
clarence32@adv	M	30000	2	0	Partial College	Clerical	1	2	5-10 Miles	Pacific	71	0
luke18@adventu	M	40000	0	0	High School	Skilled Manual	0	2	5-10 Miles	Europe	37	0

Figure 11.15 The New Customers Excel file has a list of customers that need to be scored.

2. Note that the last column (BikeBuyer) is always zero. That's because at this point you don't know if the customer could be a potential bike buyer. That's what the predictive web service is for.

The predictive web service will calculate the probability for each customer to purchase a bike. This requires calling the web service for each row in the input dataset by sending a predictive query (a data mining query that predicts a single case is called a singleton query). To see the final solution, open the Predict Buyers.pbix file in Power BI Desktop.

Creating a query function

You already know from Chapter 7 how to use query functions. Like other programming languages, a query function encapsulates common logic so that it can be called repeatedly. Next, you'll create a query function that will invoke the Adventure Works predictive web service:

1. In Power BI Desktop, click Edit Queries to open the Power Query Editor.
2. In Query Editor, expand the New Source button and click Blank Query. Then in the ribbon's View tab, click Advanced Editor.
3. Copy the function code from the \source\ch11\real-time\fnPredictBuyer.txt file and paste in the query. The query function code follows:

```
1.  let
2.  PredictBikeBuyer = (Gender, YearlyIncome, TotalChildren, NumberChildrenAtHome, EnglishEducation, EnglishOccupation,
    HouseOwnerFlag, NumberCarsOwned, CommuteDistance, Region, Age, BikeBuyer) =>
3.  let
4.  //replace service Uri and serviceKey with your own settings
```

PREDICTIVE ANALYTICS

```
 5.    serviceUri="https://ussouthcentral.services.azureml.net/workspaces/.../execute?api-version=2.0&details=true",
 6.    serviceKey="<your service key>
 7.    RequestBody = "
 8.    {
 9.    ""Inputs"": {
10.    ""input1"": {
11.    ""ColumnNames"": [
12.    ""Gender"", ""YearlyIncome"", ""TotalChildren"", ""NumberChildrenAtHome"", ""EnglishEducation"", ""EnglishOccupation"",
13.    ""HouseOwnerFlag"", ""NumberCarsOwned"", ""CommuteDistance"", ""Region"", ""Age"", ""BikeBuyer""
14.    ],
15.    ""Values"": [
16.    [
17.    """&Gender&""", """&Text.From(YearlyIncome)&""", """&Text.From(TotalChildren)&""", """&Text.From(NumberChildren-
       AtHome)&""", """&EnglishEducation&""", """&EnglishOccupation&""", """&Text.From(HouseOwnerFlag)&""",
       """&Text.From(NumberCarsOwned)&""", """&Text.From(CommuteDistance)&""",
18.    """&Region&""", """&Text.From(Age)&""", """&Text.From(BikeBuyer)&"""
19.    ]]},
20.    ""GlobalParameters"": {}
21.    }
22.    ",
23.    Source=Web.Contents(serviceUri,
24.    [Content=Text.ToBinary(RequestBody),
25.    Headers=[Authorization="Bearer "&serviceKey,#"Content-Type"="application/json; charset=utf-8"]]),
26.    #"Response" = Json.Document(Source),
27.    #"Results" = Record.ToTable(#"Response")
28.    in
29.    #"Results"
30.    in
31.    PredictBikeBuyer
```

The code in line 2 defines a PredictBikeBuyer function with 12 arguments that correspond to the columns in the input dataset. Remember to update lines 5 and 6 with your web service URI and service key. Then the code creates a request payload described in JSON, as per the web service specification (see **Figure 11.14** again). Notice that the code obtains the actual values from the function arguments. Lines 23-25 invoke the web service. Line 26 reads the response, which is also described in JSON. Line 27 converts the response to a table.

4. Rename the query to *fnPredictBuyer* and save it.

Figure 11.16 The PredictedScore custom column calls the fnPredictBuyer function.

Creating a query

Now that you have the query function, let's create a query that will load the input dataset from the New Customers Excel file, and then call the function for each customer:

1. In Query Editor, expand New Source again and then click Excel.
2. Navigate to New Customers.xlsx and load Table1. Table1 is the Excel table that has the new customers.
3. Rename the query to *PredictedBuyers*.
4. Add a custom column called PredictedScore, as shown in **Figure 11.16**. This column calls the fnPredictBuyer function and passes the customer demographic details from each row in the input dataset.
5. The results of the custom column will be a table, which includes other nested tables, as per the JSON response specification (see **Figure 11.17**). You need to click the "expand" button four times until you see "List" showing in the PredictedScore column.

Region	Age	BikeBuyer	PredictedScore
Pacific	49	0	Table
Pacific	50	0	Table
Pacific	50	0	Table
Pacific	47	0	Table
Pacific	47	0	Table
Pacific	50	0	Table

Figure 11.17 Expand the PredictedScore column four times until you get to the list of values.

6. Once you get to the list, add another custom column to get the last value of the list. Because you have 12 input columns, the last value will always be at position 11. This value represents the score:

[PredictedScore.Value.output1.value.Values]{0}{13}

7. Change the column type to Decimal Number and remove any errors.
8. Create a table report that shows the customer e-mail and the probability for each customer to purchase a bike, as shown in **Figure 11.18**.

EMailAddress	PredictedScore
jon24@adventure-works.com	0.97
julio1@adventure-works.com	0.94
janet9@adventure-works.com	0.94
clarence32@adventure-works.com	0.88
lauren41@adventure-works.com	0.71
christy12@adventure-works.com	0.48
ian47@adventure-works.com	0.40
jacquelyn20@adventure-works.com	0.32

Figure 11.18 A table report that shows the predicted results.

11.4 Summary

Power BI doesn't limit you to only descriptive analytics. It includes comprehensive predictive features for both data analysts and data scientists. Use Explain Increase/decrease for root cause analysis. Use time-series forecasting to predict periods in the future. Find data similarities by detecting clusters. And use R and Python scripts for data cleansing, machine learning, and custom visuals.

If you need to predict future outcomes, you can implement on-premises or cloud-based predictive models. Azure Machine Learning lets business users and professionals build experiments in the cloud. You can save the predictive results to Azure, or you can publish the experiment as a predictive REST web service. Then Power BI Desktop and Power Query can call the predictive web service so that you can create "smart" reports and dashboards that transcend traditional data slicing and dicing!

By now, as a data analyst, you should have enough knowledge to implement sophisticated self-service data models. One important task though is publishing your model to Power BI Service and sharing it with your teammates, which I'll discuss in the next chapter.

PART

Power BI for Pros

BI and IT pros have much to gain from Power BI. Information technology (IT) pros are concerned with setting up and maintaining the necessary environment that facilitates self-service and organizational BI, such as providing access to data, managing security, data governance, and other services. On the other hand, BI pros are typically tasked to create backend services required to support organizational BI initiative, including data marts and data warehouses, cubes, ETL packages, operational reports, and dashboards.

We're back to Power BI Service now. This part of the book gives IT pros the necessary background to establish a trustworthy and collaborative environment! You'll learn how Power BI security works. You'll see how you can create workspaces to promote team BI where multiple coworkers can work on the same BI artifacts. Finally, you'll learn how to create apps so that you can push BI content to a larger audience and even to the entire company. And you'll discover how the on-premises data gateway can help you centralize data management and implement hybrid solutions where your data remains on premises, but you can still enjoy Power BI interactive dashboards and reports that connect to the data via the gateway.

Next, you'll see why Power BI Premium is preferred by larger organizations. You'll understand how to move workspaces to a premium capacity and how to secure them. You'll learn about features that are only available in Power BI Premium. I'll show you how to use Power BI Report Server to implement on-premises report portals for centralizing and managing different types of reports. And, if you are interested in migrating traditional (paginated) SSRS reports to the cloud, I'll show you how you can publish them to Power BI Premium.

I'll show BI pros how to integrate popular organizational BI scenarios with Power BI. If you've invested in on-premises Analysis Services models, you'll see how you can create reports and dashboards connected to these models without moving data to the cloud. If you plan to implement real-time BI solutions, I'll show how you can do that with Azure Stream Analytics and Power BI.

Chapter 12

Enabling Team BI

12.1 Power BI Management Fundamentals 321
12.2 Collaborating with Workspaces 332
12.3 Distributing Content 339

12.4 Centralizing Data Management 346
12.5 Summary 350

We all need to share information, and this is even more true with BI artifacts that help an organization understand its business. To accomplish this, an IT department (referred to as "IT" in this book) must establish a trustworthy environment where users have secure access to the BI content and data they need. While traditionally Microsoft has promoted SharePoint for sharing all your documents, including BI artifacts, Power BI doesn't have dependencies on SharePoint Server or SharePoint Online. Power BI has its own sharing and collaboration capabilities! Although these capabilities are available to all users, establishing a cooperative environment should happen under the guidance and supervision of IT. Therefore, I discuss sharing and collaboration in this part of the book.

Currently, Power BI doesn't have all the SharePoint data governance capabilities, such as workflows, taxonomy, self-service BI monitoring, versioning, retention, and others. Although a large organization might be concerned about the lack of such management features now, Power BI gains in simplicity and this is a welcome change for many who have struggled with SharePoint complexity, and for organizations that haven't invested in SharePoint. This chapter starts by laying out the Power BI management fundamentals. Next, it discusses workspaces and then explains how members of a department can share Power BI artifacts. Next, it shows you how IT can leverage Power BI organizational apps to bundle and publish content across your organization, and how to centralize management for on-premises data sources.

12.1 Power BI Management Fundamentals

Recall from Chapter 2 that Power BI makes it easy for users to sign up for Power BI. When the first user signs up, Power BI creates an unmanaged "shadow" tenant (yourcompany.onmicrosoft.com) in Azure AD. It's unmanaged because it's under Microsoft's management, not yours. I refer to this stage as "The Wild West". Everyone can sign up without any supervision. The next progression is to take over the unmanaged tenant in Office 365. This allows the Office 365 admin to manage certain aspects of the user enrollment and enables the Power BI Admin Center. The final step is to federate your organizational Active Directory to Azure Active Directory to achieve a single sign-on between your on-premises AD and Azure Active Directory. To accomplish this, you can use the DirSync tool to synchronize your on-premises AD with Azure, or you can federate (extend) your corporate AD to Azure.

Your data will be stored in a Microsoft data center in a specific geography. When the first user signs up, Power BI will ask the user which country your company is located in. Based on the country selection, Power BI will choose a regional data center. Unfortunately, once that data center is selected and associated with the tenant, it can't be changed although there are good scenarios to do so, such as a multinational company that prefers a data center closer to where most of the Power BI users will be located. If you're on Power BI Premium, you can create a capacity in a specific data region. If you're on Power BI Pro, however, your only option for changing the data region is to call Microsoft Support and ask them to recreate your tenant. For more information about Power BI data regions, read the "How the Power BI Data Region is selected" blog by Adam Saxton at https://guyinacube.com/2016/08/power-bi-data-region-selected.

12.1.1 Managing User Access

If your tenant is still unmanaged, I strongly suggest you or your system administrator take it over so that it can be actively managed by you. I said "system administrator" because the takeover process requires knowledge of your organization's domain setup and small changes to the domain registration so that Power BI can verify domain ownership. For more information about the specific takeover steps, refer to the blog "How to perform an IT Admin Takeover with O365" by Adam Saxton at https://powerbi.microsoft.com/en-us/blog/how-to-perform-an-it-admin-takeover-with-o365.

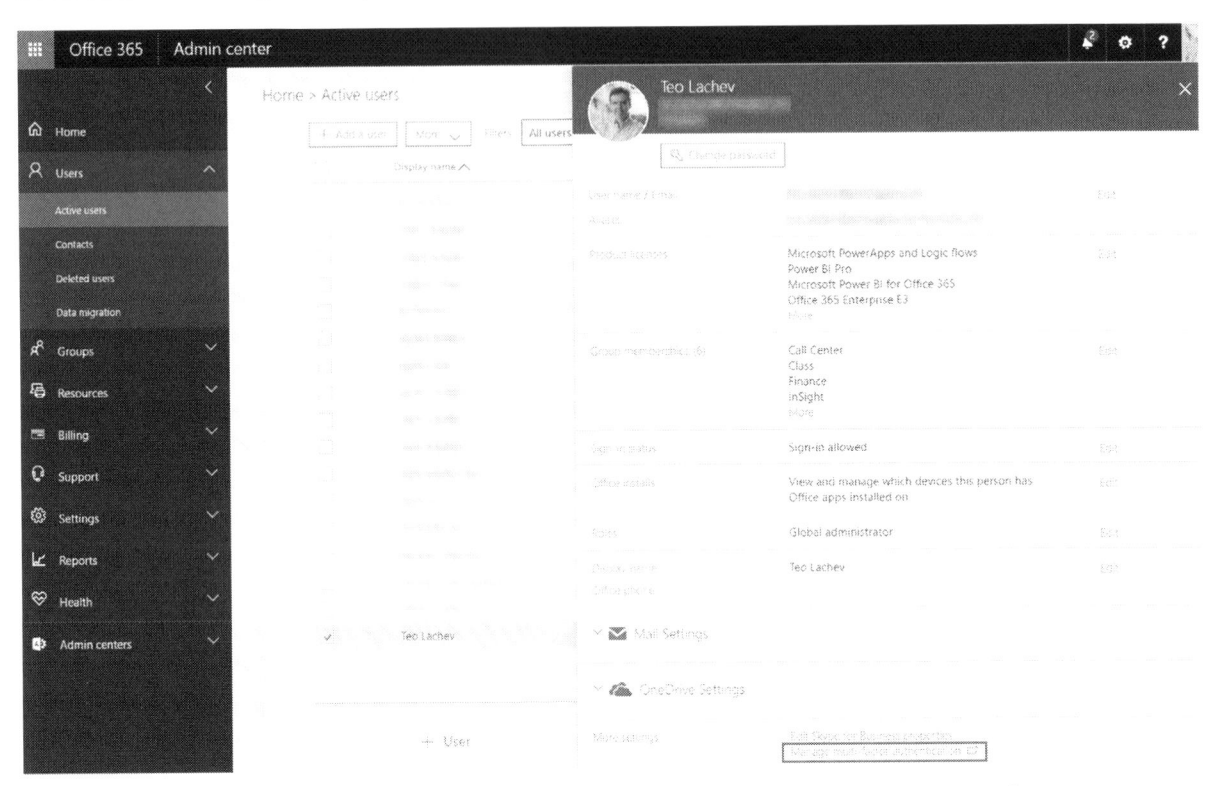

Figure 12.1 The global administrator can manage users and Power BI licenses in the Office 365 Admin Center.

Managing users
Once the admin takeover is completed, the Office 365 global administrator can use the Office 365 Admin Center (https://portal.office.com) to manage users and licenses (see **Figure 12.1**). Another way to navigate to the Office 365 Admin Center is to click the "Office 365 Application Launcher" icon in the top left corner of the Power BI portal and then click the Admin button. Only Office 365 global admins can see the Admin button. Finally, a third option to navigate directly to the "Active Users" section of the Office 365 Admin Center is from the "Manage users" area in the Power BI Admin Portal (discussed in the "Using the Admin Portal" section later in this chapter).

Unless you extend or synchronize your on-premises AD, the user chooses a password when the user signs up with Power BI. The Power BI password is independent of the password he uses to log in to the corporate network. As a best practice, it's a good idea to expire passwords on a regular basis. Switching to a managed client gives you a limited control over the password policy, which you can find under the Settings menu in the left toolbar ⇨ "Security & privacy". You can turn on the expiration policy using the "Days before password expire" setting. You can also specify if the users can reset their passwords.

Managing licenses
From a Power BI standpoint, one important task that the administrator will perform is managing Power BI Pro licenses for internal and external (B2B) users. Users don't need a license to access Power BI Free features. Yet, your organization might have concerns about indiscriminate enrolling to Power BI and uploading corporate data. Solutions can be found in the "Power BI in your organization" document by Microsoft at http://bit.ly/1IY87Qt.

Users contributing Power BI content require a Power BI Pro license. Unless the workspace is in a Power BI Premium capacity, recipients of shared content also require a Power BI Pro license. The Product Licenses section of the user properties (see again **Figure 12.1**) show what licenses the user has. Click the Edit link to grant the user a Power BI Pro license. This of course will entail a monthly subscription fee unless your organization is on the Office 365 E5 business plan which includes Power BI Pro.

Enabling conditional access
The cloud nature of Power BI could be both a blessing and a curse. Users can access Power BI reports and dashboards from anywhere and on any device if they're connected to Internet. However, unless you take additional steps, Power BI security hinges only on the user's password since the user email is not secure. One of the most important steps you can take to enforce an additional level of security is to restrict access to Power BI (and your organization's data) by enabling conditional access.

A multifactor authentication (MFA) is a security configuration that requires more than one method of authentication to verify the user's identity. For example, Office 365 could send an application password to the user's mobile device. The user will have to enter it in addition to the Power BI password when signing in to Power BI. You can enable MFA for all Office 365 services (see the corresponding link in the "More settings" section on the user properties page in **Figure 12.1**) or just for Power BI.

> **NOTE** Depending on the O365 business plan your organization has, tenant-level MFA might require an additional fee, or it might be included in the plan. For more information about MFA, read the "Getting started with Azure Multi-Factor Authentication in the cloud" article by Kelly Gremban at https://docs.microsoft.com/en-us/azure/multi-factor-authentication/multi-factor-authentication-get-started-cloud. Configuring application-level access (also known as conditional rules) requires a subscription to Azure Active Directory Premium. In addition, it requires a federated or managed Azure Active Directory tenant.

Follow these steps to enable MFA for Power BI only:

1. Open your browser and navigate to portal.azure.com and sign in with your account (you need to be an admin on the tenant).
2. In the left navigation bar, click Azure Active Directory.
3. In your AD organization page, click the Enterprise Applications tab, and then click All Applications.
4. Change the filter on top of the page to Microsoft Applications.
5. Scroll down the list and click Power BI Service (see **Figure 12.2**).
6. In the next page, click the Configure link.
7. In the next page, click Conditional Access and set rules. For more information about how to do this, read the "Conditional Access now in the new Azure portal" article by Microsoft at https://cloudblogs.microsoft.com/enterprisemobility/2016/12/15/conditional-access-now-in-the-new-azure-portal/.

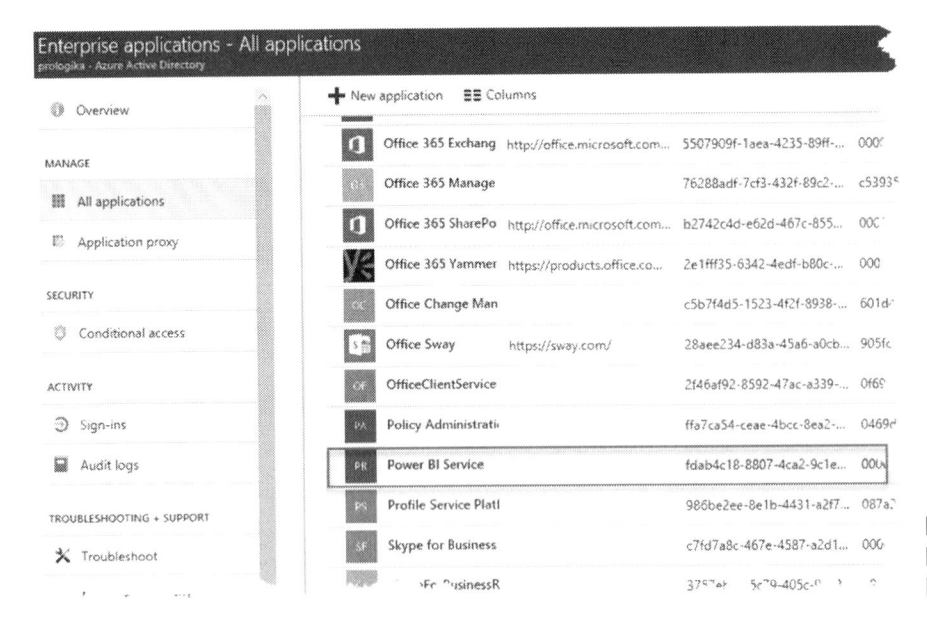

Figure 12.2 Use the Azure Portal to enable MFA for Power BI.

Understanding conditional rules

You can set up the following rules:

- Require Multi-factor authentication – Users to whom access rules apply will be required to complete multi-factor authentication before accessing the application affected by the rule.

- Require Multi-factor authentication when not at work – Users trying to access the application from a trusted IP address won't be required to perform multi-factor authentication. Click the link below to enter the trusted IP address ranges that define your work location.

- Block access when not at work – Users trying to access the application from outside your corporate network will not be able to access the application.

> **REAL LIFE** I helped a large organization to evaluate and adopt Power BI. One of the first questions their review committee asked was if they can limit access to Power BI only from the corporate network and from approved devices. I didn't have a good answer then. Conditional access can help you meet this requirement.

Once the rules are configured, Azure will apply them when a user attempts to sign in to Power BI. For example, let's say that Elena (Office 365 admin) has configured a conditional access policy requiring MFA for only Power BI. When Maya visits the Office 365 portal to check her email, she can log in (or automatically sign in if the active directory is federated to Azure) without using MFA. But when Maya tries to navigate to Power BI, she'll be asked to complete an MFA challenge irrespective of the device she uses. If the "Block access when not at work" rule is enabled, she can access Power BI only from the corporate network.

> **TIP** You can secure access to Power BI even further by enabling these conditional access policies alongside Risk Based Conditional Access policy available with Azure AD Identity Protection. Azure Identity Protection detects risk events involving identities in Azure Active Directory that indicate that the identities may have been compromised. For more information, read the "AzureAD Identity Protection adds support for federated identities" at bit.ly/2gwdTGu.

12.1.2 Understanding Office 365 Groups

Power BI security is interwoven with Azure Active Directory and Office 365 security. Sure, granting access to individual users by entering their emails works for all features that require Power BI security, but it quickly becomes counterproductive with many users. Suppose you'd like to grant report access to 250 users and integrate this report with Dynamics 365. If you secure individually, this will require entering 250 emails three times: Dynamics 365, Power BI, and possibly Row-level Security (RLS).

As an administrator, you should use groups to reduce the maintenance effort because if all users are added to a security group, we can just grant access to the group. And, when users no longer need access, you make changes to one place only: the group they belong to. At, least this is how the story goes on premises where administrators are typically use only Active Directory groups. However, things are more complicated with Office 365.

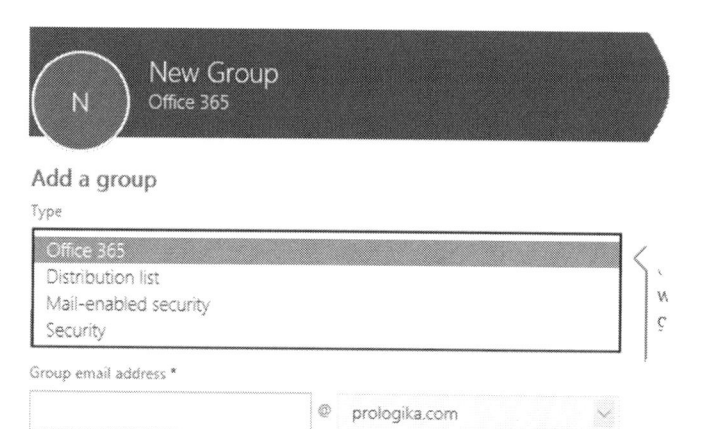

Figure 12.3 Office 365 supports four group types: Office 365 groups, distribution lists, mail-enabled security group, and security groups.

Understanding group types

Office 365 supports four group types, as shown in **Figure 12.3**.

- Office 365 groups – This is a newcomer and specific to Office 365. To understand why you need Office 365 groups consider that today every Office 365 online application (Exchange, SharePoint, OneDrive for Business, Skype for Business, Yammer, and others) has its own security model, making it very difficult to restrict and manage security across applications. Microsoft introduced Office 365 groups to unify security across apps and foster sharing and collaboration.

    NOTE Conceptually, an Office 365 group is like a Windows AD security group; both have members and can be used to simplify security. However, an Office 365 group has shared features (such as a mailbox, calendar, task list, and others) that Windows groups don't have. Unlike security groups, Office 365 groups can't be nested. To learn more about Office 365 groups, read the "Find help about groups in Office 365" document by Microsoft at http://bit.ly/1BhDecS.

- Distribution lists – Like Outlook contact groups you might be familiar with, they are only for sending an email to all members in the distribution list.
- Mail-enabled security groups – A security group with an assigned email address so that you can contact its members by sending an email.
- Security groups – Azure Active Directory security groups for users who need a common set of permissions. This is the Office 365 equivalent of an on-prem AD group.

ENABLING TEAM BI

How groups affect Power BI features

Currently, Power BI has a varying degree of supporting the four types of Office 365 groups. Most organizations prefer to use AD security groups which Power BI supports everywhere, except for membership in the original (v1) workspaces. **Table 12.1** shows how different Power BI features support groups.

Table 12.1   How Power BI security supports different Office 365 group types.

Feature	Office 365 Group	Distribution List	Mail-enabled Security Group	Security Group
Workspace v1 membership	Yes	No	No	No
Workspace v1 app membership	No	Yes	Yes	Yes
Workspace v2 membership (preview)	Yes	Yes	Yes	Yes
Workspace v2 app membership (preview)	No	Yes	Yes	Yes
Dashboard/report sharing	No	Yes	Yes	Yes
Subscriptions	No	Yes	Yes	Yes
Row-level security	No	Yes	Yes	Yes
Power BI tenant features	No	No	Yes	Yes

Now that you know how to manage users and groups, let's discuss how you can use the Power BI Admin Portal to control feature availability.

12.1.3 Using the Power BI Admin Portal

Power BI provides an admin portal to allow the administrator to monitor Power BI utilization and to control tenant wide settings. To access the Power BI Admin Portal, log in to Power BI Service, expand the Settings menu in the top-right corner, and then click Admin Portal. To see the Admin Portal menu, you have a member of one of these roles:

- Office 365 Global Administrator – The Office 365 global administrator can manage all aspects of Office 365, including Power BI.
- Power BI Service Administrator – Besides accessing the Power BI Admin Center, this user can modify users and licenses within the Office 365 admin center and access the audit logs.

Granting Power BI admin access

The Office 365 global administrator can use the Office 365 Admin Portal to delegate Power BI admin access to other users by following these steps:

1. In the Office 365 admin center (https://portal.office.com), click "Active users".
2. Select the user and dismiss the user properties window to return to the "Active users" page.
3. Expand the More drop-down and click "Edit roles".
4. In the "Edit user roles" window, select "Customized administrator" and check "Power BI service administrator". Click Save.

The global administrator could also run a PowerShell command (before you run the command, install Azure PowerShell from https://docs.microsoft.com/en-us/powershell/). For example, to grant Martin Power BI Administrator rights to the Adventure Works Power BI tenant, Elena would execute this command:

```
Add-MsolRoleMember -RoleMemberEmailAddress "martin@adventureworks.com" -RoleName "Power BI Service Administrator"
```

Now Martin can access the Power BI Admin Portal, which is shown in **Figure 12.4**. Currently, the portal has five management areas (Usage metrics, Manage Users, Audit logs, Tenant and Capacity settings).

Figure 12.4 Use the Power BI Admin Portal to view usage statistics and control tenant wide settings.

Monitoring usage metrics
The "Usage metrics" management area provides insights into the usage of Power BI within your organization. It opens a dashboard that has two sections of tiles:

- User-level information – The top three rows provide usage statistics for individual users, including the total number of dashboards, reports, and datasets, top users with most dashboards and reports, most consumed dashboards, and most consumed content packs.
- Group-level information – The bottom three rows provide the same information but for groups (I'll discuss workspaces and groups in the next section).

The "Usage metrics" is a good starting point to help you understand Power BI utilization but much more is needed to make it useful. I hope Microsoft extends it in the future with additional health monitoring features to help you proactively manage Power BI, such as CPU and memory utilization, data quotas, refresh failures, and others.

Users
The second management area (Users) includes a shortcut that brings you to the Office 365 Admin Center (see again **Figure 12.1**). Recall that you can use the Office 365 Admin Center to manage users, licenses, and groups.

Audit logs
The "Audit logs" management area provides another shortcut to the Office 365 portal where you view tenant activity and export the audit logs. I'll discuss the audit logs in the "Auditing User Activity" section.

Tenant settings
Go to the "Tenant settings" section of the Admin Portal to manage tenant-wide settings. Many of these settings can be enabled for specific security groups or the entire organization but some, such as dashboard tagging, are organization-level only. I'll discuss these settings in more detail in the "Managing tenant settings section".

ENABLING TEAM BI

Capacity settings

The "Capacity settings" is for managing Power BI Premium and Power BI Embedded capacities. I'll postpone discussing these settings to the next chapter which is dedicated to Power BI Premium.

Embed Codes

Recall that Power BI Service (powerbi.com) lets you publish a report for anonymous viewing (open a report and click File ⇨ "Publish to web"). Power BI will give you an embed code (iframe) and a link. Use the Embed Codes section to find which reports across the entire tenants were published to web.

Figure 12.5 Use the "Manage tenant settings" area to manage important tenant-wide security and functionality settings.

Organization visuals
One of the most prominent extensibility areas of Power BI is that it allows report authors to use custom visuals contributed by the community, Microsoft, and partners. Your organization can evaluate and vet certain custom visuals. The Power BI Administrator can use this section to add the approved custom visuals. Then, when the report authors click the ellipsis (...) button in the Visualizations pane and select "Import from marketplace", they will see these visuals on the "My Organization" tab.

Dataflow settings (preview)
Recall that Power BI Premium allows you to bring your own data lake storage to stage data from Power BI dataflows. You can use this tab to learn how to do it and to connect your data lake storage to Power BI.

Workspaces
Shows a list of all workspaces in the Power BI tenant. Each workspace has one of these three types:
- Workspace – This is a v2 workspace that's not backed by an Office 365 group.
- Group – This is a v1 workspace.
- PersonalGroup – This is a personal workspace (My Workspace) suffixed with the user name.

The "Read only" column shows True for v1 workspaces that are configured for "Members can only view Power BI content". The State column shows "Deleted" if the workspace has been deleted. Yes, removed workspaces are still there and Microsoft has promised a recovery feature. You can also rename v2 workspaces and modify their membership.

12.1.4 Understanding Tenant Settings

Let's go back to the "Tenant settings" section (see **Figure 12.5**). I'll explain each setting and provide recommendations. Every administrator should understand their purpose and configure them before rolling out Power BI. After all, you probably don't want users to expose sensitive data to everyone on Internet!

Workspace settings
Currently, Microsoft is previewing a new version of Power BI workspaces that doesn't depend on Office 365 groups. By default, every Power BI Pro user can create organizational workspaces which is probably not desired as it can lead to workspace explosion. I recommend you restrict this right to specific groups.

Export and sharing settings
Let's go quickly through these settings. The "Share content with external users" controls whether users can share content to users external to your organization (discussed in more detail in section 12.3.1). By default, Power BI Pro users can share content to both internal and external users, so consider disabling this setting for added data security if not needed. The "Publish to web" setting is even more dangerous. By default, your users will be able to share reports anonymously to anyone on the Internet, such as by embedding reports in blogs! This is *not* the setting you need to share with external users securely. Strongly consider turning this setting off.

"Export data" controls if users would be able to export data from report visuals. By default, users would be able to export summarized and underlying data. When off, the "Export reports as PowerPoint presentations" disables exporting to PowerPoint (this export option is in the report File menu). Similarly, "Print dashboards and reports" disables the corresponding menus. I recommend you leave these settings enabled.

Content pack and app settings
"Publish content packs and apps to the entire organization" controls the allowed audience for distributing organizational content packs (obsolete and superseded by apps) and apps (discussed in the "Packaging

and Publishing Content" section later in this chapter). By default, content packs and apps can be distributed to the entire organization, which is probably OK for your company.

Unless "Create template organizational content packs and apps" is off, when a user creates an organizational content with imported data, they can decide to remove the data and package the content as a template content pack. This works conceptually like Power BI Desktop templates.

Power BI allows app authors to push apps directly to consumers instead of asking the consumers to search and install the apps. "Push apps to end users" defaults to the entire organization. Consider disabling this setting or restricting it to specific security groups.

Integration settings

When off, the "Ask questions about data using Cortana" setting disables Power BI integration with Cortana. Consequently, a Windows 10 user can't use Cortana to ask Power BI questions on the desktop (they must go to Power BI Service). Recall that the "Analyze in Excel" feature allows users to create pivot reports in Excel Desktop connected to Power BI datasets, just like they'd use Excel to connect to cubes. Users can publish the Excel reports to Power BI Service dashboards. "Analyze in Excel with on-premises datasets" disables this feature for datasets connected directly to on-premises databases.

When off, "Use ArcGIS Maps for Power BI" removes this visual from the Visualizations pane in Power BI Service and disables usage of this visual. This control exists because ArcGIS maps may use the Esri cloud services that are outside of your Power BI tenant's geographic region.

You saw in Chapter 10 how you can use Cortana to get answers from Power BI without navigating to Power BI Service. Behind the scenes, the Cortana integration relies on the Azure Search Service (https://azure.microsoft.com/en-us/services/search/) because of its ranking, error correction, and auto complete capabilities. The "Use global search for Power BI" controls if the Azure Search Service can access Power BI Service and default setting of Enabled should be fine.

R visuals settings

"Interact with and share R visuals" is for custom visuals designed with R. R visuals can be created in Power BI Desktop, and then published to the Power BI Service. Unless this setting is off, R visuals behave like any other visual in the Power BI service; users can interact, filter, slice, and pin them to a dashboard, or share them with others. The default setting of Enabled should be fine.

Audit and usage settings

The "Audit and usage" section controls if Power BI generates auditing and usage data from user activity. I'll discuss auditing in more detail in the next section but by default Power BI records the user activity which can be monitored in Office 365. I just explained the Usage Metrics tab of the Audit Portal. The next two settings control what usage data Power BI captures. By default, these settings are enabled, and this should be OK for your organization.

Dashboard settings

When on, "Data classifications for dashboards" lets you tag dashboards. For example, your users might have dashboards that show some sensitive information and they might request a mechanism to inform the users about it. As the administrator, you can use the Admin Portal to create a "Confidential Data" tag. Then, your users can go to the dashboard settings in Power BI Service and select the tag from the "Data classification" drop-down. Once they choose a tag, it'll show next to the dashboard name when the user views the dashboard in the Power BI portal (see **Figure 12.6**).

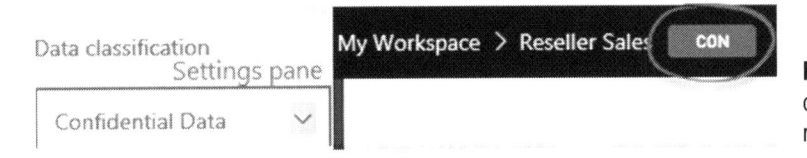

Figure 12.6 Users can use the data classification tags defined in the Admin Portal to tag dashboards.

If you mark a tag as a default tag in the Admin Portal (see again **Figure 12.5**), all new and existing dashboards will show this tag. To avoid this, create a dummy tag, set it as a default tag, and clear the "Show Tag" setting. Also, when setting up a tag, consider providing a tag URL so that users can click on the dashboard tag and learn more about why the dashboard was classified this way.

> **NOTE** Data classification tags could have been very useful for allowing IT to certify BI content. Unfortunately, every Power BI Pro user can access and change them from the dashboard settings because currently this feature is a tenant-level option. And it's limited to dashboards only.

Developer settings
Developers can call the Power BI REST APIs to support two main scenarios for embedding Power BI content: embedding for internal users and embedding for external customers. The "Embed content in app" setting controls if these REST APIs can be invoked. Consider restricting content embedding to specific security groups.

Dataflow settings
Recall from chapter 7 that Power BI Pro users can create dataflows for staging data in the Microsoft-provided Azure Data Lake store. However, the staged data counts toward the workspace storage. By default, this feature is enabled and unfortunately can't be restricted to specific security groups. Leave it enabled if you plan to let users create dataflows.

12.1.5 Auditing User Activity

Regulatory and compliance requirements are typically met with audit policies. Power BI can log certain user activities, such as creating, editing, printing, exporting, sharing reports and dashboards, and creating groups and content packs (for the full list, see "List of activities audited by Power BI" at http://bit.ly/power-biaudit).

Getting started with Power BI auditing
You can turn on Power BI auditing by flipping the "Create audit logs for internal activity auditing and compliance purposes" setting to On in the Power BI Admin Portal (see again **Figure 12.5**). Be patient though because audit logs can take up to 24 hours to show after you enable them. To see the actual logs, you need to use the Office 365 Admin Center again. A convenient shortcut is available in the "Audit Logs" area of the Power BI Admin Portal and it brings you directly to the "Audit search" page in the Office 365 Admin Center.

> **NOTE** Auditing is a Power BI Pro feature and auditing events are only available for Power BI Pro users. Users with Power BI (free) licenses will be displayed as Free User when you view the audit logs. In addition, to enable auditing for Power BI, you need at least one Exchange mailbox license in your tenant.

Viewing audit logs
The "Audit log search" page (see **Figure 12.7**) allows you to view and search all Office 365 audit logs. To view only the Power BI logs, expand the Activities drop-down and then select "Power BI activities" or choose specific Power BI activities, such as "Viewed Power BI dashboard". To search logs for a user, start typing in the user name and Power BI will show a drop-down to help you locate the user (you can enter multiple users). You can also subscribe to receive an alert that meets the search criteria.

If the search criteria result matches existing logs, the logs will be shown in the Results pane. You can see the date, the user IP address, user email, activity (corresponds to the items in the Activities drop-down), item (the object that was created or modified because of the corresponding activity) and Detail (some activities have more details). You can click a row to see more details, such as to see if the activity succeeded or failed. You can click the "Export results" to export the results as a CSV file.

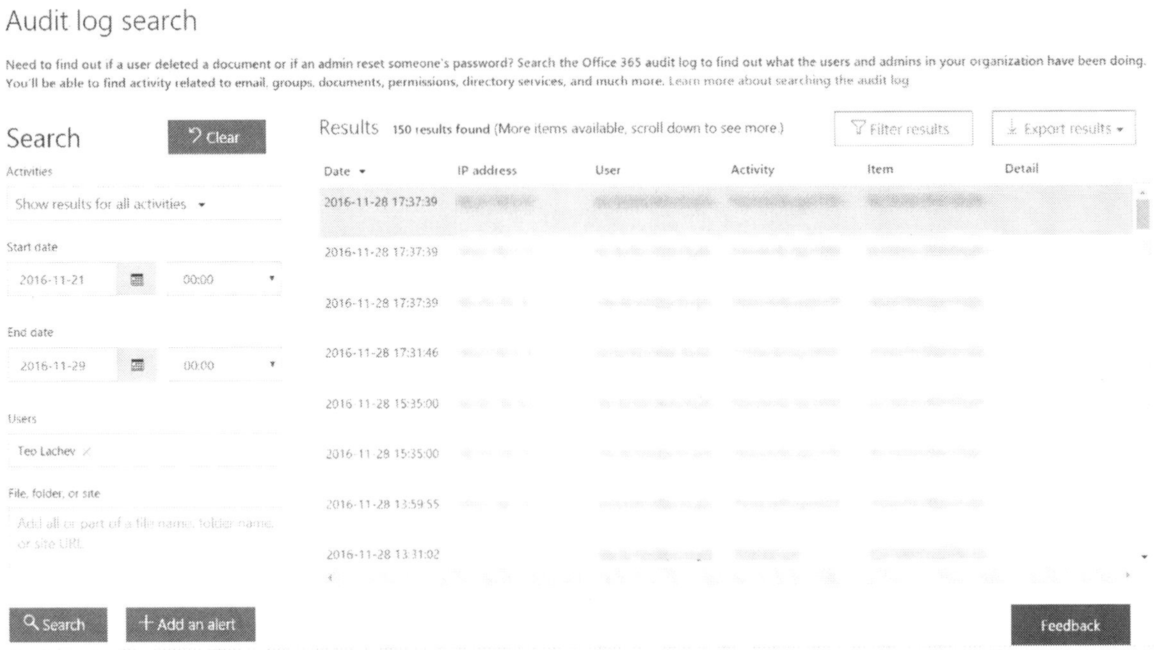

Figure 12.7 Use the "Audit log search" page to view Office 365 audit logs, including logs for Power BI.

12.2 Collaborating with Workspaces

Oftentimes, BI content needs to be shared within an organizational unit or with members of a project group. Typically, the group members require write access so that they can collaborate on the artifacts they produce and create new content. This is where Power BI workspaces can help. Remember that as with all sharing options, only Power BI Pro users can create workspaces.

For example, now that Martin has created a self-service data model with Power BI Desktop, he would like to share it with his coworkers from the Sales department. Because his colleagues also intend to produce self-service data models, Martin approaches Elena to set up a workspace for the Sales department. The workspace would only allow the members of his unit to create and share BI content.

12.2.1 Understanding Workspaces

A Power BI workspace is a container of BI content (datasets, reports, and dashboards) that its members share and collaborate on. By default, all the content you create goes to the default workspace called "My Workspace". Think of My Workspace as your private desk – no one can see its content unless you share it. By contrast, an app (organizational) workspace is shared by all the members. So, workspaces play important role for organizing and sharing content.

Up until August 2018, workspaces relied on Office 365 groups and had various limitations. Some of these limitations are lifted with the new workspaces that are currently in preview. Let's discuss both versions and compare their differences.

Understanding v1 workspaces

For a lack of better term, I'll refer to the original workspaces as version 1 (v1) workspaces. When you create a v1 workspace, Power BI creates an Office 365 group and vice versa, a group created in Office 365 shows up as a workspace in Power BI. So, there is one-to-one relationship between a v1 workspace and a group and you can't have one without the other.

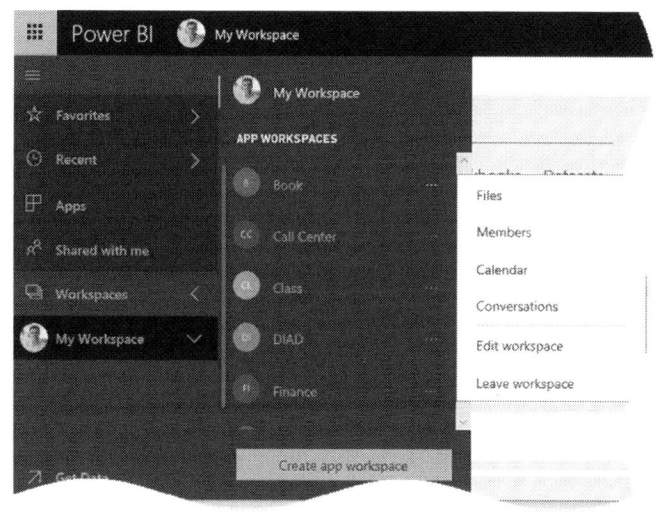

Figure 12.8 Use the Workspaces menu to see all workspaces you have access to.

Because the primary goal of Power BI workspaces was to facilitate communication and collaboration, v1 workspaces go beyond BI and support collaborative features. Workspaces members can access these features by clicking the ellipsis (…) menu next to the workspace name, as shown in **Figure 12.8**. Alternatively, click the workspace and from the workspace content page, click the ellipsis (…) menu in the top-right corner. Let's review the available collaboration features:

- Files – Brings you to the OneDrive for Business file storage that's dedicated to the workspace. That's right, a workspace gets its one Power BI storage quota (10 GB with Power BI Pro) and its OneDrive for Business cloud storage. While you can save all types of files to OneDrive, Excel workbooks used to import data to Power BI are particularly interesting. As I mentioned, that's because Power BI automatically refreshes the datasets you import from Excel files stored to OneDrive every ten minutes or when the file is updated.
- Calendar – This brings you to a shared group calendar that helps members coordinate their schedules. Everyone in the group sees meeting invites and other events posted to the group calendar. Events that you create in the group calendar are automatically added and synchronized with your personal calendar. For events that other members create, you can add the event from the group calendar to your personal calendar. Changes you make to those events automatically synchronize with your personal calendar.
- Conversations – Think of a conversation as a real-time discussion list. The Conversations page displays each message. If you use Outlook, conversations messages are delivered to a separate folder dedicated to the group. You can either use Outlook or the conversation page to reply to messages and you can include attachments.

Understanding v2 workspaces

To make workspaces more flexible, Power BI introduced a new workspace experience, which I'll refer to as "v2" workspaces. A v2 workspace has the following advantages:

- No dependency to Office 365 group – A v2 workspace doesn't need an Office 365 group.

ENABLING TEAM BI

- Security groups as members – You can add security groups when you set up membership.
- New toolset – The Power BI admin can control which security groups can create workspaces.
- Content security – Roles (Viewer, Contributor, Member, Admin) define content-level security.

Currently, v2 workspaces don't support the Files and Calendar collaboration features. Dashboard and report comments supersede Conversations.

Comparing workspaces

Table 12.2 compares features between the v1 and v2 workspaces. Currently, there isn't a way to upgrade a v1 workspace to v2. Moving forward, I recommend you create your workspaces to v2 and migrate v1 workspaces when Microsoft provides the toolset.

Table 12.2 Comparing v1 and v2 workspaces.

Feature	V1	V2
Can be created without Office 365 group	No	Yes
Control who can create workspaces	No	Yes
Add security groups as members	No	Yes
Support content security	No	Yes
Support collaboration features	Yes	No
Copy content between workspaces	No	No
Support nesting	No	No
Row-level security	No	Yes
Power BI tenant features	No	No

Understanding workspace limitations

The following workspace limitations continue to exist with v2 workspaces:

- No content copy between workspaces – Currently there isn't a way to move or copy content from one workspace, such as from My Workspace to another. Therefore, it makes sense to create a workspace before you start adding content to Power BI. If you're a Power BI Pro user, think of who you want to share the content with and create a workspace that includes these people. As I said, workspaces typically align with organizational departments.
- No nesting – Power BI workspaces can be nested. For example, you can't create a Sales workspace that further breaks down into Sales North America and Sales Europe. Therefore, you need resort to a "flattened" list of workspaces.
- One-to-one relationship with apps -- Sharing content outside the workspace requires an app. But you can't publish multiple apps from a workspace, such as to share some reports with one group of users and another set with a different group.
- Can't share with Power BI Free users – If you are on Power BI Premium and what to share content with viewers, you can't just add Power BI Free users as workspace members to share content in a premium workspace. Instead, you must share content out either using individual report/dashboard sharing or apps. I hope the forthcoming "Viewer" role will make this easier.

12.2.2 Managing Workspaces

Because the new workspace experience will become the norm once it's officially released, I'll show you how to manage v2 workspaces. Recall that you can use the Power BI admin portal to control who can create v2 workspaces. The user who creates the workspace becomes its administrator. The administrator has full control over the workspace, such as adding other users as members, renaming, or deleting the workspace. A Power BI user can be added to multiple workspaces. For example, **Figure 12.8** shows that besides My Workspace, I'm a member of several other workspaces, which I can access by clicking the Workspaces menu in the navigation bar.

Creating workspaces
Creating a workspace only takes a few mouse clicks:

1. Once you log in to Power BI Service, click Workspaces in the navigation bar. Click the "Create app workspace" button (see again **Figure 12.8**).
2. (Preview step) In the "Create an app workspace" window, click "Try now" in the Preview Improved Workspaces section.
3. Give your workspace a name (must be unique within the tenant) and an optional description.

Managing access
Once you create a v2 workspace, you're the administrator and the only user who can access it. Follow these steps to add workspace members:

1. In the Power BI navigation bar, expand the ellipsis (…) menu next to the workspace, and click "Workspace access" to open the Access window (shown in **Figure 12.9**).

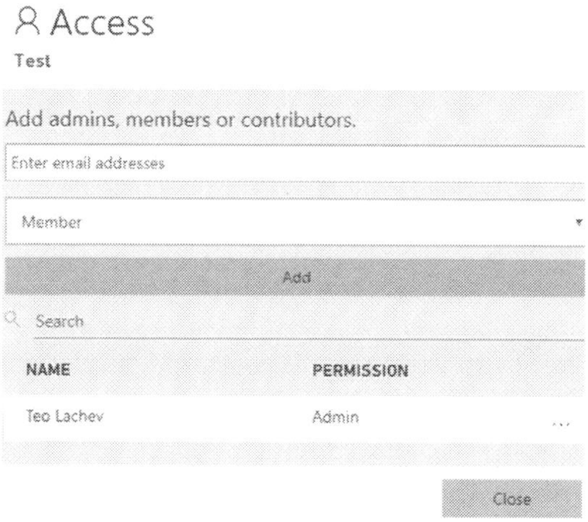

Figure 12.9 When defining the workspace access, you can enter individual users or groups, and assign a content role for each member.

2. In the "Enter email addresses" field, type individual email addresses of the members. You can also type the names of groups (all group types are supported). As you type, Power BI will attempt to resolve the email or group name and show you matches.
3. Expand the Member drop-down and choose a role that will determine the content permissions for the workspace member (individual user or group). **Table 12.3** enumerates the permissions assigned to roles for securing access to content.

> **NOTE** Microsoft views workspaces primarily to let teams collaborate on shared content, so the default role is Member. As a best practice, assign the member the minimum content permissions they need to get their job done.

ENABLING TEAM BI

If you need to overwrite the content permissions, click the ellipsis (...) menu next to the member and choose another role. Once the group is created, a welcome page opens that's very similar to the Get Data page, so that you can start adding content the group can work on.

Table 12.3   Content roles in v2 workspaces

Permission	Viewer (not available in preview)	Contributor	Member	Admin
View content	√	√	√	√
Add/edit/delete workspace content		√	√	√
Change workspace membership			√	√
Publish and update apps			√	√
Change and delete workspaces				√
Add workspace admins				√

Workspaces and data security

The main goal of workspaces is to allow all group members to access the same content. When the group members explore datasets with imported data, everyone sees the same data. If Elena creates and publishes the Adventure Works self-service model created by Martin to the Sales workspace, every member will have access to all the data that Martin imported. In other words, Martin and the workspace members have the same access to the data. If Martin has scheduled the Adventure Works model for data refresh, the consumers will also see the new data.

What if you want consumers to have different access rights to the data? For example, you might want Martin to have unrestricted access but want Maya to see data for only a subset of your customers. If you prefer to keep your model in Power BI Desktop, you can extend the model with row-level security (RLS), which I discussed in Chapter 9. Another option is to implement an Analysis Services model that applies data security based on the user identity. Then, in Power BI Service you need to create a dataset that connects live to the Analysis Services model. You can create this dataset by using Get Data in the Power BI Portal (see steps in Chapter 4) or by using Power BI Desktop to create reports and publishing the file to Power BI Service.

There are factors that might influence your decision to choose the implementation path, such as planning for a centralized data model, scalability, and others. But in both cases, when Maya opens the report, her identity will be passed to the model, and she'll get restricted access depending on how the model security is set up. So, users access content in the workspace under their identity. It's helpful to think of two levels of security: workspace security that grants permissions to content and model data security that determines if the user has access to the model and what subset of data they can see (if data security is implemented in the model).

12.2.3 Working with Workspaces

We're back to Martin, a data analyst from Adventure Works. Martin approached Elena, who oversees data analytics, to help him set up a workspace for the Sales Department. This workspace will be accessed only by members of his unit, and it'll contain BI content produced by Martin and his colleagues.

> **NOTE** Remember that with the default tenant security settings, there's nothing stopping Martin from creating a workspace on his own (if he has a Power BI Pro subscription) and becoming the new workspace admin. However, I do believe that someone needs to coordinate workspaces, because creating them indiscriminately could quickly become as useful as having no workspaces at all. So, as a Power BI admin, go to Power BI Admin Portal (Tenant Settings tab) and configure which groups can create workspaces.

Creating a workspace

As a first step, you need to create a Sales Department workspace:

1. Open your web browser and navigate to http://powerbi.com. Log in to Power BI Service.
2. In the left navigation bar, click Workspaces, and then click "Create app workspace".
3. (Preview task) In the "Create an app workspace", click "Try now" to create a v2 workspace.
4. In the "Create an app workspace" window, enter *Sales Department* as a workspace name and click Save.

Assigning workspace members

Now that the workspace is created, let's assign members. As a prerequisite, Elena should create an appropriate Sales Department security group in the Office 365 Admin Center and assign members to it.

1. In Power BI Service, expand Workspaces in the navigation bar, and click "..." next to the Sales Department workspace. Click "Workspace access".
2. In the "Access" window, enter *Sales Department* in the "Enter email addresses" field.
3. If the Member role provides the required permissions, leave the content role to Member and click Add to add the Sales Department group as a member of the workspace. Click Close.

In the navigation bar, the Workspaces section now includes the Sales Department workspace.

Uploading content

Once you create the workspace, Power BI opens a "Welcome to the Sales Department workspace" page so that you can start adding content immediately. Let's add the Adventure Works model (that you previously created) to the Sales Department workspace. Since you're in Power BI Service, the steps that follow show you how to upload the file by using Get Data. However, you can also publish it directly from Power BI Desktop by clicking the Publish button in the Home ribbon.

1. In the welcome page, click the Get button in the Files section. If you close your web browser and go back to Power BI, make sure that you click Workspaces and select Sales Department so that content is added to this workspace and not to your personal "My Workspace".
2. In the Files page, click Local File.
3. Navigate to the Adventure Works.pbix file you worked on in the previous part of the book and upload it in Power BI. If you decide to use the one included in the book source, make sure to change the data sources to reflect your setup. To do so, open the file in Power BI Desktop, in the Home ribbon expand Edit Queries, and click "Data source settings". Then verify and change the data source connection strings as needed.
4. Using your knowledge from reading this book, view and edit the existing reports, and create some new reports and dashboards. For example, open the Adventure Works.pbix dashboard. Click the Adventure Works.pbix tile to navigate to the underlying report, and then pin some tiles to the dashboard. Back to the dashboard, delete the Adventure Works.pbix tile, and rename the dashboard to *Adventure Works Sales Dashboard*.

Scheduling data refresh

Once a business user uploads a dataset with imported data, the user might want to schedule an automatic data refresh to keep a dataset with imported data synchronized with changes to the data source(s). If the dataset imports data from on-premises data sources (data sources hosted on physical or virtual machines side in your corporate network), such as our Adventure Works data model, you need to install a gateway. Recall that if the dataset imports data from cloud services, such as Azure SQL Server Database, then gateway is not needed.

Remember that you can install the gateway in one of two modes: personal and standard. As its name suggests, the personal mode is for your personal use. The idea here is to allow business users to refresh imported data without involving IT. The personal gateway installs as a Windows desktop app. You can install the gateway on your computer or another machine that has access to the data source(s) you want to refresh the data from. Each personal gateway installation is tied to the user who installs it and it can't be shared with other users. By contrast, the standard mode (discussed in section 12.4) is for centralizing access to important on-premises data sources.

NOTE Currently, Power BI doesn't offer an option to prevent users from installing gateways. The only option might be to set up a software restriction corporate policy as you would restrict installation of other unwanted software. For more information, read the article "Using Software Restriction Policies to Protect Against Unauthorized Software" at bit.ly/restrictsoftware.

If you haven't done so, start with installing the data gateway in personal mode:

1. From the Power BI portal, expand the Downloads menu in the top-right corner, and click Data Gateway. In the next page, click the "Download gateway" button (both gateways are included in the same setup).
2. Once the setup program starts, select "on-premises data gateway (personal mode)" when the setup asks you what type of gateway you want to install. For detailed setup steps, refer to the "On-premises data gateway (personal mode)" article at https://docs.microsoft.com/power-bi/personal-gateway. Note that the email address you use to sign in to Power BI is the one that Power BI will use to associate the gateway with the user who schedules the refresh. In other words, the user who installs the personal gateway must schedule the dataset refresh that uses the gateway.
3. Back in Power BI Service, click the ellipsis (…) button next to the Adventure Works dataset. In the properties window, click Schedule Refresh to open the Settings page (see **Figure 12.10**). The Gateway Status should show that the personal gateway is online on the computer where you installed it.

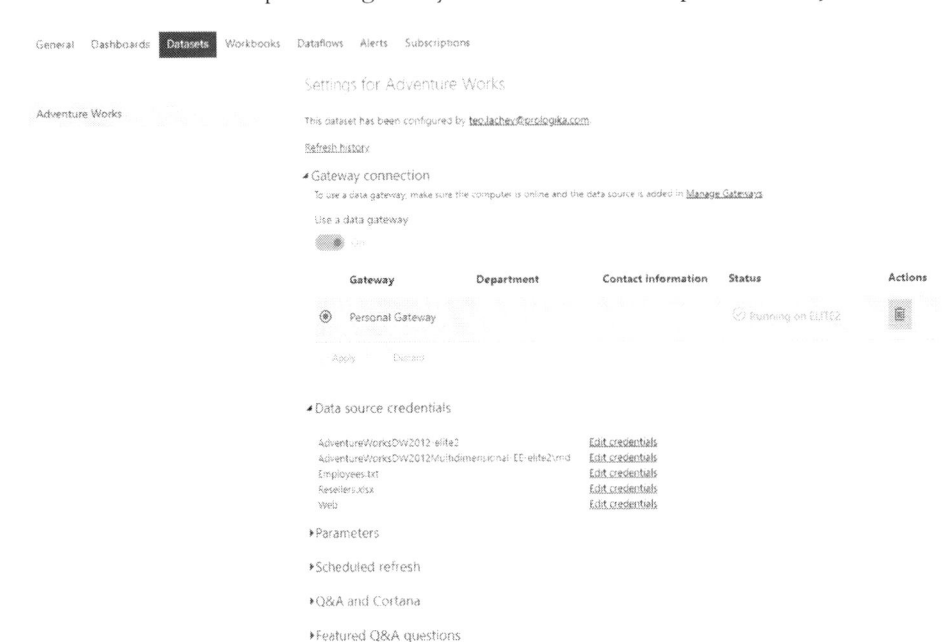

Figure 12.10 The dataset Settings page allows you to configure data refresh.

NOTE If you use the on-premises data gateway (standard mode) to schedule the refresh, make sure that the data sources in your Power BI Desktop model have the same connection settings as the data sources registered in the on-premises data gateway. For example, if you have imported an Excel file, make sure that the file path in the underlying query matches the file path in the gateway data source. If the connection settings differ, you won't be able to use the on-premises data gateway.

The "Data source credentials" section shows that the credentials are incorrect. Although this might look alarming, it's easy to fix, and you only need to do it once per data source. For added security, Power BI doesn't carry the credentials you used in Power BI Desktop. Connecting to relational databases and cloud services may require a user name and password to authenticate. The only authentication option to connecting to files is Windows authentication.

4. Click the "Edit credentials" link for each data source, specify the appropriate authentication, and then click the "Sign In" button (see **Figure 12.11**). Power BI will communicate with the gateway to ensure you have permissions to the data source.

Figure 12.11 The first time you configure scheduled data refresh, you need to specify credentials.

5. Expand the Scheduled Refresh section. Turn the "Keep your data up to date" slider to On. Specify the refresh details, including the refresh frequency, your time zone, time of the refresh (you can schedule up to 8 refreshes per day on specific times with Power BI Pro), and whether you want refresh failure email notifications. When you're finished, click Apply.

Now the Adventure Works is scheduled for an automatic refresh. When the schedule is up, Power BI will connect to the data gateway, which in turn will connect to all the data sources in the model and will reload the data. Currently, there isn't an option to refresh specific data sources or to specify data source-specific schedules. Once a model is enabled for refresh, Power BI will refresh all the data on the same schedule.

6. (Optional) A few minutes after the schedule is up, go back to the Settings page and click the "Refresh history" link to check if the refresh was successful. If another member in your group has scheduled a dataset refresh, go to the dataset Settings page and discover how you can take over the data refresh when you need to. Once you take over, you can overwrite the data source and the schedule settings.

12.3 Distributing Content

You saw how workspaces foster collaboration across team members. But what if you want to package and publish content to a broader audience, such as across multiple departments or even to the entire organization? Enter Power BI organizational apps. Your users no longer need to wait for someone else to share content and will no longer be left in the dark without knowing what BI content is available in your company! Instead, users can discover and open apps from a single place - the Power BI AppSource page by clicking the Apps link in the navigation bar.

NOTE Organizational apps supersede organizational content packs, which Power BI previously had for broader content delivery. The problem with content packs was that once installed, they lose their package identity and users couldn't tell them apart from other BI content. Organizational content packs are still available (under the Power BI Service Settings menu) but they are deprecated, and I won't discuss them.

12.3.1 Understanding Organizational Apps

In Chapter 2, I explained that Power BI comes with service apps that allow your information workers to connect to a variety of online services, such as Google Analytics, Dynamics CRM, QuickBooks, and many more. Microsoft and its partners provide these content packs to help you analyze data from popular cloud services. Not only do content packs allow you to connect easily to external data, but they also include pre-packaged reports and dashboards that you can start using immediately! Like Power BI service apps, organizational apps let data analysts and IT/BI pros package and distribute BI content within their organization or to external users.

What's an organizational app?
Consider an organizational app to distribute Power BI content (dashboards, reports, and workbooks) outside of a workspace to anyone who's interested in it. One of the prominent advantages of apps is that they isolate consumers from changes to content. Let's say Martin creates an app to distribute content from the Sales workspace and Maya installs the app. Now Maya gets a read-only copy of all reports and dashboards included in the app. Martin continues making changes to the workspace content, but Maya only get these changes when Martin republishes the app.

With the advances that Microsoft made to v2 workspaces, apps are somewhat less appealing for content sharing. Here are the most important scenarios where you currently must use apps:

- You must isolate content changes from consumers.
- You plan to distribute specific read-only content from a workspace, such as a workspace with certified reports to many users, groups, or the entire organization. For example, the Sales Department workspace might have many reports, but you want to publish only a subset.
- If you're on Power BI Premium, you plan to distribute read-only content to Power BI Free users or external users without incurring additional cost. Currently, the only other option is dashboard or report sharing but it's not a best practice because of the maintenance overhead.

You can create apps only from an organizational workspace (you can't create an app from My Workspace). There is a one-to-one relationship between an app and a workspace. Therefore, an app can't distribute content from another workspace.

Creating an app
It's easy to create an organizational app and here are the steps (remember that you need to have a Power BI Pro license to create an app and you must have Member or Admin rights to the workspace content):

1. In Power BI Service, click Workspaces, and then click the workspace whose content you want to distribute to other users.
2. In the workspace content page, visit the Dashboards, Reports, and Workbooks tabs and turn on the "Included in App" slider for each item you want to distribute with the app. Datasets don't have sliders because they will be automatically included when you select the dependent reports.
3. In the workspace content page, click the "Publish App" button in the top-right corner.
4. In the Details tab (see **Figure 12.12**), enter a description for the app. You can also specify a background color for the app menu (more on this in a moment).

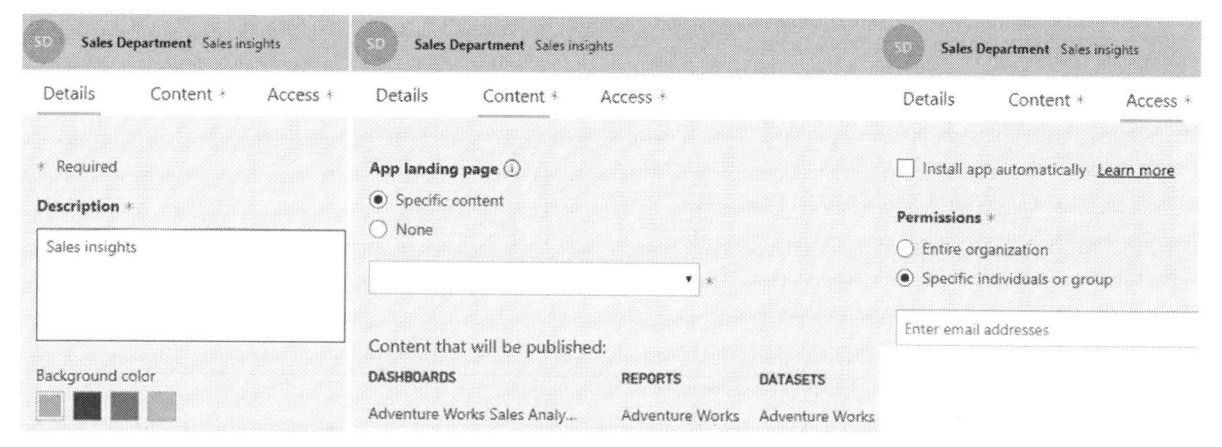

Figure 12.12 An organizational app includes all the workspace content.

5. Check that the Content tab shows the content you intend to distribute. As an optional step, select a specific dashboard or report as a landing page (the default item that users will see when they click the app).

> **NOTE** What happens when you publish a dashboard but exclude a report whose visuals were pinned to dashboard tiles? Power BI will let you publish the app (with warnings) but the recipients won't see these tiles.

Understanding content access

Next, you use the Access tab to specify who can consume the app. You can publish the app to the entire organization or restrict it to specific individuals or groups. Currently, app distribution supports Office 365 distribution lists and security groups (Office 365 groups are not supported). When checked, "Install app automatically" would add the app to the recipient's Apps folder in the Power BI navigation bar (the user doesn't have to discover and install the app).

Once you specify the recipients, click Publish to publish the app. You'll be given a link that you can distribute to recipients. They can add this link to their browser's favorites to go directly to the app. Of course, they can navigate to the app from within Power BI Service as well. As I mentioned, think of a published app as a snapshot of dashboard and report definitions (not data). Users won't get changes to content until you republish the app. To do so, go to the workspace content page, and click the same button that you used to publish the app, but it should now read "Update App". This will bring you to the same "Publish app" tabbed page and you follow the same steps to republish the app.

Discovering and consuming apps

On the consumer side of things, any Power BI Pro user can consume an app. In addition, if your organization is on Power BI Premium, Power BI Free recipients can also consume apps. If the app is restricted to specific groups, the user must be a member of one or more of these groups. All consumers get read-only access to the content and they can't personalize it or make copies. Unless the app was automatically distributed ("Install app automatically" was checked), the recipients must install the app using either one of these options:

1. Open the browser and enter the app link.
2. Click Apps in the Power BI Service navigation bar. If they haven't installed the app yet, they need to click the Get Apps button to navigate to AppSource. Find the app and click "Get it now"
3. Click Get Data and then click the My Organization tile to navigate to AppSource.

ENABLING TEAM BI

Figure 12.13 Use the app menu to navigate to other content included in the app.

The Apps tab in the navigation bar gives the user access to all apps they have installed. When they access the app, they will see the landing page you specified. The recipients can use the app menu to navigate to other content included in the app, as shown in **Figure 12.13**. If they have edit permissions to the app workspace, they can click the pencil icon to update the app.

Removing apps

Consumers can remove an app they installed at any time. To do so, they click Apps in the Power BI left navigation bar. In the Apps page, they hover on the app and then click the Trash button to delete the app. An app might also reach the end of its lifecycle and it's no longer needed. Then, a workplace member with edit permissions can remove it. Deleting an app removes the installed app from all consumers. Suppose that the Sales app is outdated, and Elena needs to remove it.

1. In the navigation bar, Elena clicks Workspaces and then she selects the Sales workspace.
2. In the workspace content page, Elena expands the ellipsis (…) menu in the top-right corner and clicks Unpublish App.
3. When Maya clicks Apps in the navigation bar, she notices that the app is gone.

12.3.2 Comparing Sharing Options

To recap, Power BI supports three ways of sharing BI content: simple dashboard sharing, workspaces, and organizational apps. Because having that many options could be confusing, **Table 12.4**Table 12. summarizes their key characteristics. Below the table, you'll find some high-level best practices for content sharing.

Table 12.4 This table compares the sharing options supported by Power BI.

	Dashboard Sharing	Workspaces	Organizational Apps
Purpose	Ad hoc dashboard sharing	Team collaboration	Broader content delivery
Discovery	Invitation email or direct sharing to another user's workspace	Workspace content	AppSource (My Organization tab)
Target audience	Selected individuals (like your boss)	Groups (your team)	Anyone who might be interested
Content permissions	Read-only dashboards and underlying content	Read/edit to all workspace content	Read-only dashboards and reports

	Dashboard Sharing	**Workspaces**	**Organizational Apps**
Memberships	Individuals, O365 distribution lists, security groups	Individuals and groups	Individuals, O365 distribution lists, and security groups
Content isolation	No	No	Yes
Collaboration features	No	Files (v1), calendar (v1), conversations	No
License	Power BI Pro Power BI Free with Power BI Premium	Power BI Pro	Power BI Pro Power BI Free with Power BI Premium

Dashboard sharing

The primary purpose of dashboard sharing is the ad hoc sharing of dashboards and underlying reports by sending an email to selected individuals or direct sharing to their workspace. For example, you might want to share your dashboard with your boss or a teammate. Consumers can't edit the shared dashboards (not even to rearrange tiles).

When the user clicks a tile, they see the underlying content, which could be a Power BI report (if the tile was pinned from a report visual), Excel report (if the tile was pinned from an Excel report), a Reporting Services report (if the tile was pinned from SSRS), Q&A page (if the tile was pinned from Q&A), or a Quick Insight report (if the tile was pinned from Quick Insights). Dashboard sharing allows you to distribute dashboards to Power BI Free users from a Power BI Premium workspace.

Workspaces

Workspaces foster team collaboration and communication. They're best suited for departments or project teams. V2 workspaces support roles for permissions to content. Workspaces are the only option that supports collaboration features, including OneDrive for Business file sharing, a shared calendar, and conversations. They are also the only option that allows members to edit shared content.

Organizational apps

Organizational apps are designed for delivery of specific workspace content, such as across groups or even across the entire organization. Consumers discover apps in Power BI AppSource. Consumers get read-only access to the published content. Like dashboard/report sharing, apps allow you to distribute content to Power BI Free users from Power BI Premium workspaces.

Best practices

I'd like to provide some best practices around sharing that I harvested from my consulting practice:

- Create workspaces to reflect your organization structure, such Sales, Finance, Customer Care. Allow members to collaborate on self-service BI content in their respective workspace.
- Establish a data governance committee that meets regularly (for example, monthly) to oversee self-service BI and review content submitted for broader sharing. To avoid wrong decision making, discourage users from distributing content on their own.
- Consider creating a Certified workspace for approved reports and dashboards. You don't have to clone datasets to this workspace. Remember that Power BI Desktop includes a Power BI Service data source that allows you to create reports from published datasets. So, you can leave datasets in the original workspaces and create or deploy reports connected to these datasets to the Certified workspace. Share content out of this workspace using apps or specific dashboards.
- Constantly monitor what data your users are importing and what business metrics they are producing. Consider including useful and common entities into an organizational semantic model.

- Encourage self-service BI for what's suited best: agile BI, such as to mash up data from multiple data sources. For most users, the best self-service BI would be an organizational semantic model that delivers a single version of the truth. I discuss pros and cons of self-service BI in Chapter 2.

12.3.3 Working with Organizational Apps

Several departments at Adventure Works have expressed interest in some content that the Sales Department has produced, so that they can have up-to-date information about the company's sales performance. Elena decides to create an organizational app to publish these artifacts to a broader audience.

Creating an organizational app

As a prerequisite, Elena needs to discover if there are any existing Office 365 or security groups that include the authorized consumers. This is an important step from a security and maintenance standpoint. Elena doesn't want the app to reach unauthorized users. She also doesn't want to create a new group if she can reuse what's already in place. Elena needs to be an admin or a member of the Sales Department workspace so that she has access to this workspace.

1. Elena discusses this requirement with the Adventure Works system administrator, and she discovers that there's already a security group for the Finance Department. Since the rest of the users come from other departments, the system administrator recommends Elena creates a security group (or O365 distribution list) for them.
2. If Adventure Works is not on Power BI Premium, Elena ensures that all members have Power BI Pro licenses. This restriction doesn't apply to Power BI Premium, but then Elena needs to ensure that the workspace is in a premium capacity to share with Power BI Free users.
3. In Power BI Service, she clicks Workspaces and then she selects the Sales Department workspace. She does this so that, when she creates an app, the app includes the content from this workspace.
4. In the workspace content page, Elena clicks "Publish app".
5. In the "Publish app" page (see **Figure 12.12** again), Elena enters a description. She switches to the Access tab and enters the authorized groups. She clicks Publish.

At this point, the Adventure Works Sales app is published and ready for authorized consumers.

Consuming an organizational app

Maya learns about the availability of the Sales app, and she wants to use it. Maya belongs to one of the groups that's authorized to use the app. If Elena has checked the "Installed app automatically" when she published the app, Maya will see the app when she clicks the Apps menu in the navigation bar, and she can start using it. Otherwise, Maya will need to install the app by following these steps:

1. Maya logs in to Power BI and clicks Apps ⇨ Get Apps.
2. If there are many apps available, Maya uses the search box to search for "sales".
3. Maya discovers the Sales app. She clicks "Get it now". Power BI installs the app. Maya can now gain insights from the prepackaged content.
4. (Optional) Review and practice the different steps of the app lifecycle, such as to make changes to the workspace content and republish the app.

12.3.4 Sharing with External Users

Many organizations share reports with external users for Business to Business (B2B) or Business to Consumer (B2C) scenarios. Consider Power BI Embedded (discussed in Chapter 16), if these reports need to be embedded in an Internet-facing web portal so that they appear as a part of an integrated offering for your external customers. However, Power BI Embedded requires coding effort to extend your app with the Power BI REST APIs and many organizations do not have the time or resources to create a custom app just to distribute Power BI content to their external partners. If all you need is granting some external users access to content inside Power BI Service, you can do so by just sharing it out using dashboard/report sharing or apps, as you do with internal users. But there are some special considerations though so read on.

Understanding Azure Active Directory
Like using Power BI for internal use, external users need to be authenticated by a trusted authority. To authenticate external users, Power BI relies on Azure Active Directory (AAD). Therefore, the external user needs an AAD account. If the user doesn't have an AAD account, the user will be prompted to create one. **Figure 12.14** shows the high-level flow.

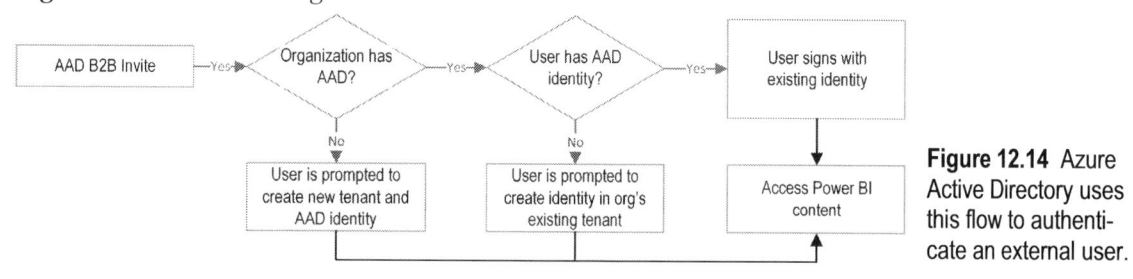

Figure 12.14 Azure Active Directory uses this flow to authenticate an external user.

Let's say Elena from Adventure Works wants to grant Matthew from Prologika access to some Power BI content. Elena creates a workspace to host the external content and then she invites Matthew using one of these options:

- Planned invite – She can go to Azure portal and create a new guest user (Azure Active Directory ⇨ Users and groups ⇨ All users ⇨ New guest user). Elena can also use the Azure Portal to set up policies that control external sharing, such as to turn off invitations and specify which users and groups can invite external users.
- Ad-hoc invite – She can simply share a dashboard or create an app, and then add Matthew's email as a recipient. Elena can use the Tenant Settings in Power BI Admin Portal to control which users and groups can share with external users.

In both cases, Matthew receives an invitation email with a link to the shared dashboard/report or app. Because the link contains some important information, Matthew must save that link somewhere, such as by adding it to its browser's favorites. Matthew clicks the link to access the content. Azure AAD checks if Prologika has an AAD tenant. If not, Matthew will be asked to create a new tenant. If a Prologika tenant exists, AAD checks if Matthew has an account in that tenant. If not, he'll be asked to create an account and specify credentials. This is no different than internal users signing up for Power BI. Then, AAD will ask Matthew to sign in with his AAD credentials and grant him access to the shared Power BI content.

> **NOTE** What about the B2C scenario where external users sign in with their personal emails? This should work too because Power BI supports personal emails for sharing, such as Gmail or Outlook accounts. However, this doesn't mean that users will be able to sign up for Power BI with their personal emails. Personal emails are supported only to access Power BI content shared with users by other organizations.

Understanding licensing
Power BI licensing for external users is not much different from licensing internal users. In a nutshell, the external user must have a Power BI Pro license to access Power BI content in the sharing tenant. This license can be acquired in one of three ways:

1. The sharing organization is on Power BI Premium – If Adventure Works is on Power BI Premium and the sharing workspace is in a premium capacity, Elena can share content to external users, just like she can share content with internal Power BI Free users.
2. The sharing organization assigns Power BI Pro licenses – Elena can assign one of her organization's Power BI Pro licenses to Matthew.
3. The external organization assigns Power BI Pro licenses – In this case, Matthew has a Power BI Pro license from the Prologika's Power BI tenant. Matthew can bring in his license to all organizations that share content with Prologika.

Understanding data security

Like internal users, external users access content under their identity. If you need to restrict access to data with row-level security (RLS), you have the following options:

- RLS for Power BI models and Azure Analysis Services -- The external user email can be added to the appropriate role to grant the user restricted access to data. Or, the model can obtain the user identity, such as by using the USERPRINCIPALNAME function (see Chapter 9).
- RLS for on-premises SSAS models –Things can get more complicated here because the AAD accounts are not available to the on-premises Active Directory. However, the Power BI data gateway supports a CustomData option that lets you pass the user identity to the model.

For more information about external sharing, read the "Distribute Power BI content to external guest users using Azure Active Directory B2B" whitepaper by Microsoft at https://aka.ms/powerbi-b2b-whitepaper.

12.4 Centralizing Data Management

Because it's a cloud platform, Power BI requires special connectivity software to access on-premises data. You saw in the "Working with Workspaces" section how the data gateway (personal mode) allows end users to refresh datasets connected to on-premises data sources, such as relational databases and files. However, this connectivity mechanism doesn't give IT the ability to centralize and sanction data access. Moreover, in personal mode the gateway is limited to refreshing datasets with imported data, and it doesn't support DirectQuery to on-premises databases. The on-premises data gateway fills in these gaps.

12.4.1 Understanding the On-premises Data Gateway

The On-premises Data Gateway supports the following features:

- Serving many users – Unlike the personal gateway, which is for individuals, the administrator can configure one or more on-premises gateways for entire teams and even the organization.
- Centralizing management of data sources, credentials, and access control – The administrator can use one gateway to delegate access to multiple databases and can authorize individual users or groups to access these databases.
- Providing DirectQuery access from Power BI Service to on-premises data sources – Once Martin creates a model that connects directly to a SQL Server database, Martin can publish the model to Power BI Service and its reports will just work.
- Cross-application support – Besides Power BI, the On-premises Data Gateway can be used by other applications, including PowerApps, Flow, and Azure Logic Apps.

Comparing gateways

Thanks to Microsoft unifying the gateways, deciding which gateway to use is much simpler. In a nutshell, the personal gateway is meant for a business user who wants to set up automated data refresh without bothering IT by installing the gateway on his computer. By contrast, the On-premises Data Gateway will be used by IT for centralizing data access to both refreshable and DirectQuery data sources. **Table 12.5** compares the two gateways.

Table 12.5 This table compares the two gateways.

	On-premises Data Gateway	On-premises Data Gateway (personal mode)
Purpose	Centralized data management	Isolated access to data by individuals
Audience	IT	Business users
DirectQuery/Live connection	Yes	No
Data refresh	Yes	Yes
User access	Users and groups managed by IT	Individual user
Data sources	Multiple data sources (DirectQuery and refreshable)	All refreshable data sources
Data source registration	Must register data sources	Registration is not required
Installation	Installs as a Windows service	Installs as a Windows app
High availability	Yes	No

12.4.2 Getting Started with the On-Premises Data Gateway

Next, I'll show you how to install and use the On-Premises Data Gateway. While you can install the gateway on any machine, you should install it on a dedicated server within your corporate network. You can install multiple gateways if needed, such as to assign department-level admin access.

Installing the on-premises data gateway

For your convenience, Microsoft has packaged both gateways in a single installation package. Follow these steps to download the gateway:

1. Remote in to the server where you want to install the gateway. This server should have a fast connection to the on-premises databases that the gateway will access. Verify that you can connect to the target databases.
2. Open the web browser and log in to Power BI Service.
3. In the Application Toolbar located in the upper-right corner of the Power BI portal, click the Download menu, and then click "Data Gateway". You can also access the download page directly at https://powerbi.microsoft.com/gateway/.
4. In the next page, click "Download gateway".
5. Once you download the setup executable, run it. On the "Choose the type of the gateway you need", leave the default option of "On-premises data gateway" selected.
6. Select the installation folder, read and accept the agreement, and then click Install. The gateway installs and runs as a Windows service called "On-premises data gateway service" (PBIEgwService) and its default location is the "C:\Program Files\On-premises data gateway" folder. The setup program configures the service to run under a low-privileged NT SERVICE\PBIEgwService Windows account.

What's interesting about the gateway is that it doesn't require any inbound ports to be open in your corporate firewall. Data transfer between the Power BI service and the gateway is secured through Azure Service

Bus (relay communication). The gateway communicates on outbound ports 443 (HTTPS), 5671, 5672, 9350 thru 9354. By default, the gateway uses port 443, which is used for all secure socket layer (SSL) connections (every time users request HTTPS pages). If this port is congested, consider allowing outbound connections through the other outbound ports (my experience has been that port 443 is enough). What all this means is that in most cases the gateway should just work with no additional configuration.

> **REAL LIFE** I helped a large organization to implement a Power BI hybrid architecture to keep their data on premises. In this case, the gateway failed to register after installation. The reason was that this organization used a web proxy server. Had the proxy supported Windows Authentication, we could have solved the issue by just changing the gateway service account to an account that had rights to the proxy. However, their proxy server was configured for Basic Authentication, so we had to pass the account password to the proxy. We had to change the gateway configuration file to specify the account credentials. For more technical details, read my "Power BI Hybrid Architecture" blog at http://prologika.com/power-bi-hybrid-architecture.

Configuring the on-premises data gateway

Next, you need to configure the gateway:

1. Once the setup program installs the gateway, it'll ask you to sign in to Power BI.
2. In the next step, leave the default option of "Register a new gateway on this computer". Notice that the second option is to migrate, restore, or take over an existing gateway.
3. Specify the gateway name and a recovery key (see **Figure 12.15**). Save the recovery key in a safe place. Someone might need it to restore the gateway if admin access is lost or the gateway needs to be moved to another server.
4. Click Configure. This registers the gateway with Power BI. You should see a message that the gateway is connected.

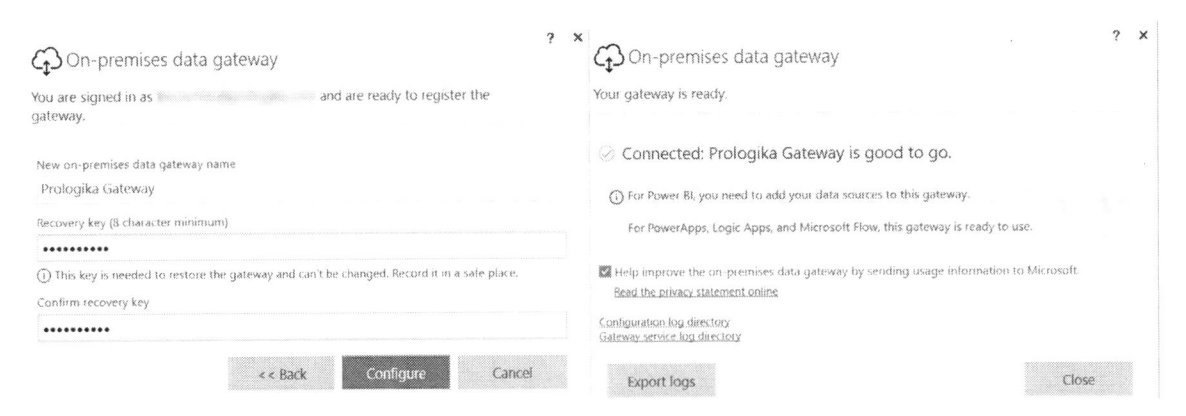

Figure 12.15 When you configure the on-premises gateway, you need to give it a name and provide a recovery key.

Registering data sources

Now that the gateway is connected, it's time to add one or more data sources to the gateway. Note that unlike the Personal Gateway which doesn't require data source registration, the On-premises Data Gateway requires you to register all data sources that the gateway serves. This needs to be done in Power BI Service, as follows:

1. Log in to Power BI Service. Click the Settings menu in the Application Toolbar in the upper-right corner, and then click "Manage gateways".
2. In the Gateways page, select your gateway and notice that you can enter additional gateway settings, such as the department and description. Moreover, you can specify additional administrators who can manage the gateway (the person who installs the gateway becomes the first administrator).

3. Next, add one or more data sources that the gateway will delegate access to. Suppose you want to set up DirectQuery to the AdventureWorksDW2012 database (I'll show how to connect to SSAS in Chapter 14).

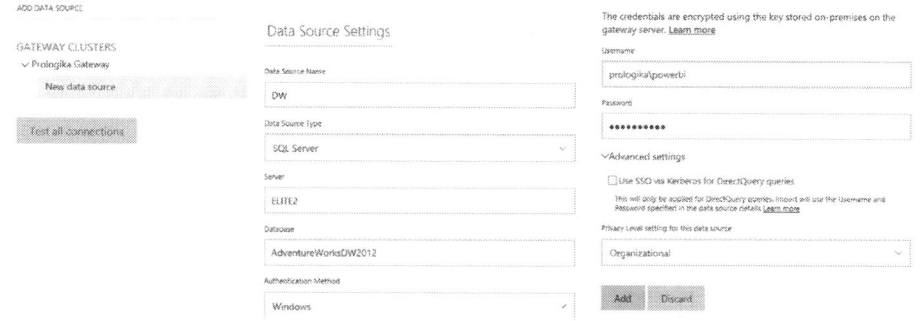

Figure 12.16 The On-Premises Data Gateway can provide access to many data sources.

4. In the Gateways page, click "Add Data Source" (see **Figure 12.16**).
5. Fill in the data source settings to reflect your database setup.
6. The Authentication method allows you to specify the credentials of a trusted Windows account or a standard SQL Server login that has access to the database. Remember to grant this account at least read credentials to the database, such by assigning it to the SQL Server db_reader role. Note that all queries from all users will use these credentials to connect to the database, so grant the account only the minimum set of permissions it needs to the SQL Server database. This might result in different data permissions than the permissions a data analyst had when he used Power BI Desktop to connect to SQL Server under *his* credentials.

> **NOTE** Currently, the only data source that supports passing the user identity via Windows security is Analysis Services. Microsoft is working on enabling this scenario for SQL Server as well. If you are concerned about compromising the communication from Power BI to the gateway, the gateway uses asymmetric encryption to encrypt the credentials so that they cannot be decrypted in the cloud. Power BI sends the credentials to the gateway server, which decrypts the credentials when the data sources are accessed.

7. (Important!) Once you add a data source and click the data source in the Gateways page, you'll see a new Users tab. For an added level of security, all users who will be publishing reports that will connect to this data source, must be added to the Users tab. Note that you need to add *only* the publishers and not the rest of the users who will be just viewing reports.

> **TIP** If you have issues with the On-premises Data Gateway setup or data source access, you can configure it for troubleshooting. You can find the troubleshooting steps in the "Troubleshooting the On-Premises Data Gateway" article by Adam Saxton at https://docs.microsoft.com/en-us/power-bi/service-gateway-onprem-tshoot.

That's almost all you need to know about the gateway. There are special considerations that apply when connecting to Analysis Services, but I'll discuss them in the next chapter. Let's now put our business user's hat on and see how you can create reports that connect to on-premises data via the gateway.

12.4.3 Using the On-Premises Data Gateway

Once the On-premises Data Gateway is set up and functional, you can use it for setting up automated data refresh and for reports that connect directly to on-premises data sources. In Chapter 2, I showed you how a business user can connect to an on-premises Analysis Services model via the gateway. Next, I'll show you how to use the gateway to connect directly to an on-premises SQL Server database. Except for Analysis

Services, setting up DirectQuery connections to on-premises databases are currently only available in Power BI Desktop, so you must create a data model.

> **NOTE** The gateway is completely transparent to Power BI Desktop. You never specify a gateway when you connect to a data source in Power BI Desktop. Instead, you connect as usual by entering the server name and database. Only after you publish the Power BI Desktop file, Power BI Service examines the connections and determines which gateway services the data source(s). So, gateways are only for Power BI Service and don't apply to Power BI Desktop.

Connecting directly to SQL Server

Follow these steps to create a simple data model that you can use to test the gateway:

1. Open a new instance of Power BI Desktop and expand the Get Data button in the ribbon's Home tab. Select SQL Server.
2. In the SQL Server Database prompt, specify the name of the SQL Server instance. Choose the DirectQuery data connectivity mode, and then click OK.
3. In the Navigator Window, expand the desired database, select one or more tables, and then click Load.
4. (Optional) Create a report that shows some data.
5. Publish the model to Power BI Service by clicking the Publish button in the ribbon's Home page.

Testing connectivity

Next, test that you can create reports from Power BI Service:

1. Log in to Power BI. In the navigation bar, select the workspace where you publish the model, and then click the dataset to explore it. Note that it's not enough to see the model metadata showing in the Fields pane because the list comes from the Tabular backend database in the Microsoft data center where the model is hosted. You need to visualize the data to verify that the gateway is indeed functional.
2. In the Fields pane, check a field to create a visualization. If you see results on the report, then the gateway works as expected. You can also use the SQL Server Profiler to verify that the report queries are sent to the SQL Server database.

12.5 Summary

Power BI has comprehensive features for establishing a trustworthy environment. As an administrator, you can use the Office 365 Admin Center to manage users and grant them access to Power BI. You can use the Power BI Admin Portal to monitor utilization and configure tenant-wide settings.

Power BI allows teams to collaborate and share BI artifacts via dashboard/report sharing, workspaces, and organizational apps. Workspaces allow a team to collaborate on shared Power BI content. The new workspace experience removes the dependency to Office 365 groups and adds roles for content security. Organizational apps are designed to complement workspaces by letting you share specific content (dashboards, reports, and workbooks) with other teams and even with the entire organization. Authorized users can discover apps in Power BI AppSource. When consumers install an app, they can view all the published content, but they can't edit the content and they are isolated from changes to the content. As the content changes, Power BI Pro users can update the app to propagate the changes.

This chapter compared the three sharing and collaboration options and recommended usage scenarios. It also walked you through a few exercises to help you practice the new concepts. Finally, I showed you how the On-premises Data Gateway is positioned to centralize access to on-premises data.

Remember that if your organization is on Power BI Premium, you can distribute content to internal or external viewers for free by sharing specific dashboards or using organizational apps. But Power BI Premium has much more to offer and it's the subject of the next chapter.

Chapter 13

Power BI Premium

13.1 Understanding Power BI Premium 351
13.2 Managing Power BI Premium 355
13.3 Understanding Power BI Report Server 359
13.4 Summary 367

As you've seen, Power BI Service is packed with features for both free and paid users. Power BI Pro is a good choice for most smaller to midsize organizations. Larger organizations, however, gravitate towards Power BI Premium for cloud deployments and I'll show you why in this chapter. Not interested in the cloud yet? If your organization is looking for an on-premises report portal for hosting different types of reports, including Power BI reports, Power BI Report Server should warrant your serious interest.

This chapter starts by introducing you to Power BI Premium. I'll discuss its features and I'll compare it with Power BI Service. You'll understand how to save licensing cost when distributing content to users who only need to view it, and how to manage Power BI Premium. Although Power BI Report Server has no dependencies on Power BI Premium, it can be licensed under Power BI Premium, so I included essential coverage of this product.

13.1 Understanding Power BI Premium

Think of Power BI Premium as an add-on to Power BI Pro. It's for organizations requiring predictable performance and scalability, and the ability to distribute content to many "viewers" without requiring per-user licensing. As its name suggests, Power BI Premium is the Power BI most advanced edition for cloud deployments. To recap from Chapter 1 where I compared features and editions side by side, the Power BI Service portfolio includes the following editions:

- Power BI Free – Power BI Free is for personal use. Once Maya signs up for Power BI Free, she can enjoy most of Power BI Service features for free, but she can't share content with other users.
- Power BI Pro – A step above Power BI Free, this edition includes sharing and collaboration and it carries a $9.99 price tag per user, per month. When she upgrades to Power BI Pro, Maya can now share content with other colleagues using any of the three supported options (dashboard sharing, workspaces, and organizational apps). She can also subscribe to reports and create reports from published datasets in Excel or Power BI Desktop.
- Power BI Premium – This edition offers greater scale and performance, flexibility to license by capacity, embedded analytics, and extends Power BI to on-premises so that you can license Power BI Report Server under Power BI Premium.

Let's dive in the Power BI Premium features to understand what they really mean for you.

13.1.1 Understanding Premium Performance

When you use Power BI Free or Power BI Pro, your organization is effectively sharing resources with other organizations. In other words, all your BI content is in shared capacity. Datasets in a shared capacity workspace can be randomly distributed to different shared capacities and get moved around depending on the current workload. This isn't any different than other Software as a Service (SaaS) offerings, such as Salesforce, Amazon Web Services, or other Microsoft Azure services. Microsoft has done its job to scale out report loads across clusters of servers and to enforce restrictions that ensure that hyper active users can't monopolize the shared environment. Examples include restricting the maximum dataset size to 1 GB, limiting the number of dataset refreshes to eight per day, and capping the number of rows when users export or drill through reports. However, the performance of your reports might still be impacted in a shared environment.

Understanding dedicated (premium) capacity

When you purchase Power BI Premium, Microsoft allocates a dedicated capacity (hardware) to your organization. Although some of the cluster resources are dedicated, they are still integrated with Power BI Service, meaning that Power BI Premium doesn't lag in features. To the contrary, since this hardware is yours, Microsoft can safely remove some of the shared limitations and add more features. For example, Power BI Premium ups the number of refreshes to 48 per day and increases the dataset size to up to 10 GB and more restrictions will probably go away. Moreover, as you've learned in Chapter 1 (see Table 1.2), Power BI Premium adds new features, such as incremental refreshes (discussed in Chapter 8) and computed dataflow entities (discussed in Chapter 7), and more premium features are planned.

Dedicated capacity is completely transparent to end users. They continue to log in to the Power BI Portal as usual. Power BI administrators control which workspaces are in a shared or dedicated capacity. With a mouse click, a workspace can be moved in and out of a dedicated capacity, and this all happens in the background.

Understanding capacity nodes

When you sign up for Power BI Premium (you can start the process from the "Capacity settings" tab in the Admin Portal), you need to decide how much capacity you need, expressed as capacity nodes (or plans), which are listed in **Table 13.1**.

> **NOTE** Although not listed in the table, there are two larger P4 (64 v-cores and 200 GB RAM) and P5 (128 v-cores and 400 GB RAM) Power BI Premium nodes but Microsoft hasn't rolled them out globally yet because organizations prefer distributing their models across multiple smaller (P1-P3) nodes. However, when Microsoft increases the model size limits in future, P4 and P5 could become more appealing for hosting extremely large models.

Table 13.1 Power BI provides several capacity nodes.

Node	Total V-cores	Backend Cores	Frontend Cores	Max Page Renders per hour	Max Dataset Size (GB)	DirectQuery max connections per second	Price per month
P1	8	4 (25 GB RAM)	4	1201-2400	3	30	$4,995
P2	16	8 (50 GB RAM)	8	2401-4800	6	60	$9,995
P3	32	16 (100 GB RAM)	16	4801-9600	10	120	$19,995
EM1 (EA only)	1	5 (3 GB RAM)	5	1-300	1	5	$625
EM2 (EA only)	2	1 (5 GB RAM)	1	301-600	1	10	$1,245
EM3	4	2 (10 GB RAM)	2	601-1200	1	15	$2,495

Like a virtual machine (VM), a capacity node includes a predefined number of virtual frontend and backend cores (v-cores). The frontend cores are responsible for the user experience (web service, dashboard and report document management, access rights management, scheduling, APIs, uploads and downloads). The backend cores do the heavy lifting (query processing, caching, data refresh, rendering of reports). Each capacity node also reserves a specific amount of memory for the backend cores.

> **NOTE** What's a page render? A page render happens when a report page needs to be refreshed. A page render occurs when the page is initially shown and every time the page is updated because of some user activity, such as applying filters or changing the visual configuration. Typically, multiple queries processed by the backend cores are involved in a page render because every visual sends a query.

Microsoft provides an interactive calculator (https://powerbi.microsoft.com/en-us/calculator/) to help you calculate how much capacity you need. Most organizations start with the P1 capacity node. The embedded (EM) plans are for embedding Power BI content in custom apps (the EM1 and EM2 plans can be acquired only through Enterprise Agreement with Microsoft). You can also acquire Power BI Embedded via the Azure Power BI Embedded (A*) plans (https://azure.microsoft.com/pricing/details/power-bi-embedded/), as I'll discuss in more detail in Chapter 16.

Understanding capacity features

Why do we need so many different capacities? The short answer is to give you the most licensing flexibility to distribute Power BI content to different audiences. **Table 13.2** shows how capacity SKUs differ in terms of content accessibility for different types of users. For example, the P capacities allow all user types to access any Power BI content (in Power BI Portal and embedded in custom apps). By contrast, an EM capacity allows only Power BI Pro users to view reports in Power BI Portal because EM capacities are mostly for embedding reports for third party.

Table 13.2 Understanding capacity features for content distribution.

Capacity	Audience	Power BI Portal	Custom app with embedded content
P capacity	Power BI Pro users	Yes	Yes
	Power BI Free users	Yes	Yes
	External users	Yes	Yes
EM capacity	Power BI Pro users	Yes	Yes
	Power BI Free users	No	Yes
	External users	No	Yes
A capacity	Power BI Pro users	Yes	Yes
	Power BI Free users	No	No
	External users	No	Yes

When you work the calculator, you'll notice that you can purchase more nodes to scale out. When would you scale out by adding more nodes versus scaling up to a higher node? As I mentioned, each node has a specific amount of memory associated with the backend cores. One consideration is the maximum dataset size supported in Power BI Premium compared to the available memory of the smallest node. Currently, all P plans have more memory than the maximum dataset size Power BI Premium supports (up to 10 GB with P1). But in the future, Microsoft might be increasing the maximum dataset size to the point where some datasets may be too large to fit in a smaller node's memory, but if you had purchased a larger node size, they would have fit in the available memory. Conversely, there are reasons why you may want to have multiple smaller capacities rather than one large one, such as to provide isolation between workloads and delegate management to different groups of people.

13.1.2 Understanding Premium Workspaces

Allocating Power BI content to a dedicated (premium) capacity happens at the workspace level. For example, realizing the importance of the Sales workspace, Elena might decide to move to a premium capacity so that it can benefit from Power BI Premium features. If she changes her mind later, she can move it back to a shared capacity.

How workspaces relate to nodes
Figure 13.1 shows a few possible options for assigning workspaces to capacity nodes. In this case, Adventure Works has scaled out Power BI Premium to two P1 nodes and one P2 node. The administrator has allocated some workspaces across the premium nodes, but other workspaces are left in a shared capacity.

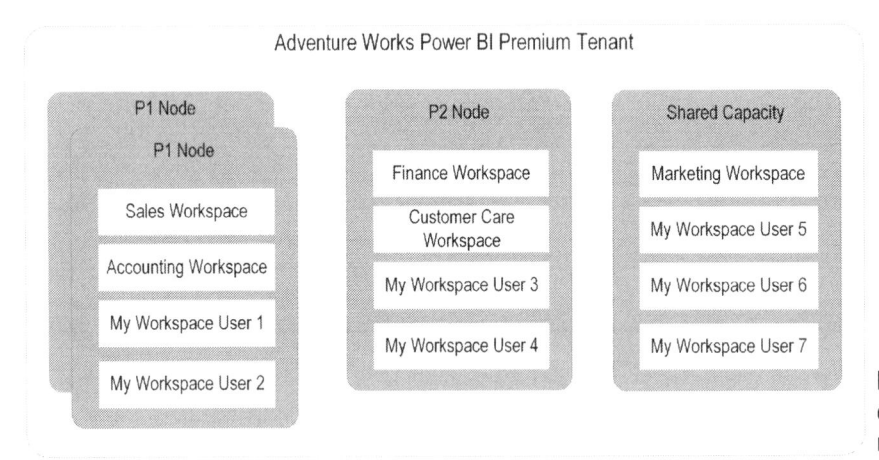

Figure 13.1 The administrator can assign workspaces to premium and shared capacities.

Therefore, the workspaces in a premium capacity would benefit from consistent performance and Power BI Premium features, while non-significant workspaces can remain in a shared capacity. Notice also that personal "My Workspace" workspaces can be in a premium capacity as well.

Sharing content to Power BI free users
A workspace in a shared capacity requires Power BI Pro licenses for any form of sharing (dashboard sharing, workspace membership, or apps). But one of the Power BI Premium benefits is that a premium workspace can share out content to Power BI Free users. There are two options to distribute content to viewers without requiring Power BI Pro licenses:

- Dashboard/report sharing – Any Power BI Pro member of a premium workspace can share dashboards and reports. Consider this option when you need to share out only specific dashboards and reports.
- Organizational apps – Any Power BI Pro member of a premium workspace can create an app to distribute all the workspace content to other users, including Power BI Free users.

Power BI Free users can only view shared content. Users contributing content to an app workspace (examples include creating or editing reports and dashboards) still require Power BI Pro licenses.

> **NOTE** From a costing perspective alone, the break-even point between Power BI Pro and Power BI Premium is 500 users, if all users would need access to shared content. That's because licensing 500 users with Power BI Pro costs $5,000 per month, which is the monthly cost of the lowest Premium (P1) plan for one node. Of course, there are other compelling reasons to consider Power BI Premium and there will be even more over time as Microsoft adds more premium features.

13.2 Managing Power BI Premium

Power BI Premium adds security and administration features to let you manage premium workspaces and capacities. The first time you land at the Power BI Admin Portal under "Capacity settings", you will find a "Buy" button, which will redirect you to the Office 365 Admin Portal. There you can purchase a subscription to Power BI Premium and capacity nodes. For more information, read "How to purchase Power BI Premium" at https://docs.microsoft.com/en-us/power-bi/service-admin-premium-purchase.

Note that you must be an Office 365 global admin to buy a capacity. Besides purchasing Power BI Premium, no further management is required in the Office 365 portal. All Power BI Premium management features are accessible from the "Capacity settings" tab in Power BI Admin Portal.

13.2.1 Managing Security

To delegate rights to specific users for managing premium features, Power BI Premium introduces two new security roles (Capacity Admins and Capacity Assignment), as shown in **Table 13.3**.

Table 13.3 Power BI Premium adds two security roles.

Capacity Admin	Capacity Assignment
Add capacity	Assign workspaces to capacity
Assign admins	Grant other Pro users access to their capacity workspace
Granting workspace permissions	
Bulk assign workspaces to capacity	
Remove workspaces from capacity	
Monitor capacity usage	

Understanding Capacity Admin role
Each capacity has its own admins. Capacity administrators can add capacity, assign admins, and assign and remove workspaces. Capacity admins can also grant permissions to a workspace, increase capacity, and monitor logging and auditing. All Office 365 Global admins and Power BI admins are automatically capacity admins of both Power BI Premium capacity and Power BI Embedded capacity. They can grant this right to other people and for *specific* capacities. Assigning a capacity admin to a capacity does not grant him Power BI Admin rights. For example, a capacity administrator can't control tenant settings or access usage metrics. Only Global admins or Power BI admins have access to those items.

Understanding Capacity Assignment role
While Capacity Admin is restricted to a specific capacity, the Capacity Assignment role is even more restricted. It grants Power BI Pro users rights to assign workspaces to a specific capacity. This means members of the Capacity Assignment role can move workspaces from a shared capacity to a dedicated capacity and can also grant other Pro users access to that capacity workspace.

So, if I'm a Pro user and I have assignment permissions, I can create a workspace, give other Pro users access to that workspace, so everyone can collaborate on its content. However, unlike a regular workspace admin, I can move the workspace in and out of a premium capacity at any time. For example, to address peak demand, such to scale with seasonal increases in business, I can move the workspace to a premium capacity, but when the demand drops, I can move it to a shared capacity to free up resources.

13.2.2 Managing Capacities

After you've purchased capacity nodes in Office 365, you can go to the Power BI Admin Portal to set up a new capacity. In the process, you need to specify a capacity size, such as P1, and capacity admins.

Setting up a new capacity
You set up a new capacity in the "Capacity settings" tab of the Power BI Admin Portal (see **Figure 13.2**). The Power BI Premium tab (available if your organization is on Power BI Premium) is for creating and managing Power BI Premium capacities.

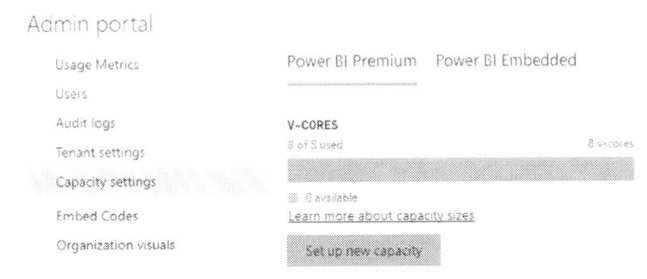

Figure 13.2 Click "Set up new capacity" to create a new capacity.

The Power BI Embedded tab is for managing embedded capacities (they need to be created in the Azure Portal). For example, your organization might not be on Power BI Premium, but it might need to embed reports for third party. After purchasing a Power BI Embedded plan in the Azure Portal, the administrator can manage the embedded capacity under the Power BI Embedded tab, while the Power BI Premium tab will be empty. On the next page, you give the capacity a name, specify its size, and assign capacity administrators. Now Office 365 global administrators, Power BI administrators, and the capacity administrators can see the new capacity in the "Capacity settings" tab, as shown in **Figure 13.3**.

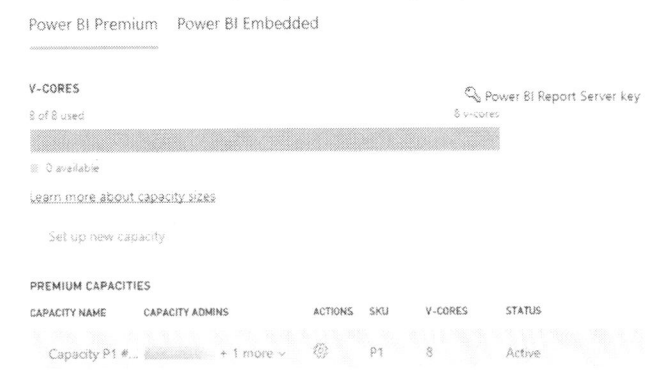

Figure 13.3 The "Capacity settings" tab shows available capacities.

Once the capacity is added, you can access its settings by clicking the Actions (gear) icon next to the capacity name. In the Settings page, you can change the capacity name, see its admins, or delete the capacity.

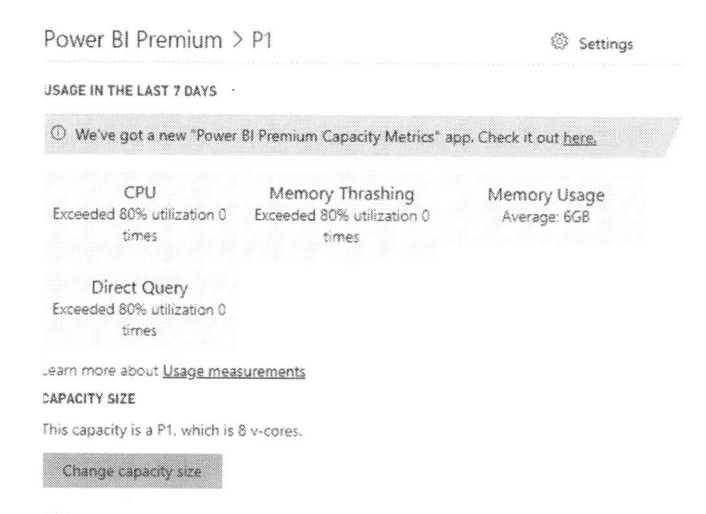

Figure 13.4 You can monitor the capacity utilization and upgrade the capacity.

Managing capacity settings

Going back to the "Capacity settings" page, you can click the capacity name in the Premium Capacities section. This brings you to the page shown in **Figure 13.4**. For each capacity, you can monitor the following indicators:

- CPU – Shows how many times the CPU usage of the capacity cores exceeded 80%.
- Memory Thrashing – Shows how many times the memory consumption exceeded 80%.
- Memory Usage – Shows the average memory usage.
- Direct Query – Shows how many times the number of live connections per second exceeded 80% of the capacity limit (refer to **Table 13.1** to see the limits per capacity).

You should monitor these metrics and consider upgrading the capacity if you constantly see that it's overutilized. You can click each indicator to get more detailed statistics. Power BI admins and Office 365 global admins can also use this page to change the capacity size, such as by downgrading or upgrading the capacity depending on the available resources. They can also add or remove users from the Capacity Admin and Capacity Assignment roles.

> **TIP** As the note above states, Microsoft published a "Power BI Premium Capacity Metrics" app. I recommend the app, because it provides much more detail. To learn more about the app, read the article "Monitor Power BI Premium and Power BI Embedded capacities" at https://docs.microsoft.com/power-bi/service-admin-premium-monitor-capacity/.

Managing workloads

The Capacity Settings page has a Workloads section (under More Options) that deserves more attention (see **Figure 13.5**). By default, a premium capacity can only run workloads associated with Power BI datasets and reports (hosting datasets with imported data, running reports and dashboards, subscriptions, alerts, and others). You must turn on Dataflow and Paginated Reports workloads if you want to enable them for that premium capacity. In addition, you can allocate how much memory the premium capacity can allocate to these services, as follows:

- Dataflow workloads – Specifies the maximum memory dataflows can consume in this capacity. Dataflows request memory as needed. The default setting of 20% tells Power BI that dataflows running in all premium workspaces in this capacity can consume up to 20% of the available memory. However, keep in mind that a dataflow requires a minimum of 700 MB to run.

- Paginated Reports workloads – If you plan to deploy SSRS paginated (RDL) reports, you can specify the maximum memory allocated for running these reports. However, unlike dataflows, Power BI will allocate that memory irrespective if users run paginated reports or not. So, be on the conservative side here.

Figure 13.5 Use the Workloads section to configure the memory available to dataflows and paginated reports.

13.2.3 Assigning Workspaces to Capacities

A workspace can use the Power BI Premium features only if it's assigned to a premium capacity. Power BI Premium supports two ways to do this: bulk assignments and individual assignments.

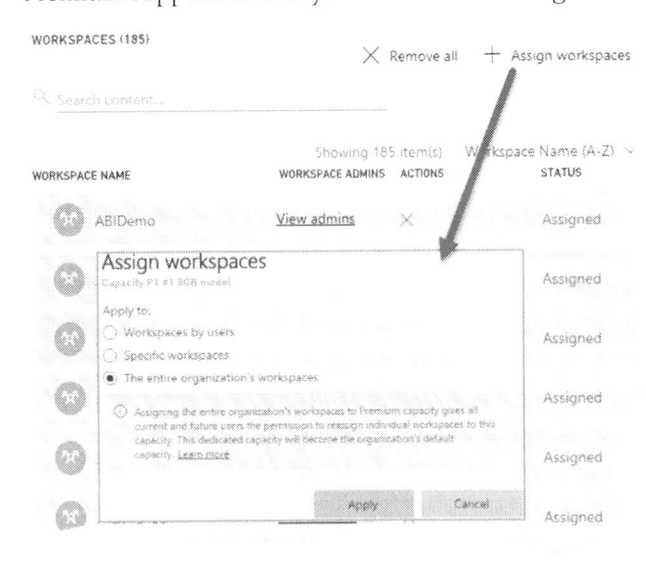

Figure 13.6 Use the "Assign workspaces" page to bulk assign workspaces.

Understanding bulk assignments

Capacity admins, along with Power BI admins and Office 365 admins, can bulk assign workspaces to a capacity. The bottom half of the "Capacity settings" page shows the available workspaces, including personal workspaces (My Workspace) for every user in the organization. You can use this page to see the workspace admins assigned to each workspace. You can click the "Assign workspaces" button to open the "Assign workspaces" page (see **Figure 13.6**), which gives you three choices for bulk assignment:

- Workspaces by users – Allows you to enter one or more email addresses of specific users and assign their workspaces to a premium capacity.
- Specific workspaces – Allows you to search and assign specific workspaces.
- The entire organization's workspaces – Assigns all app workspaces and personal workspaces (My Workspace) to this capacity. Moreover, future workspaces will be assigned to this capacity because it's now the default capacity.

Understanding individual assignments

If you're a workspace admin and you have Capacity Assignments rights to the workspace, you can assign that workspace to a premium capacity. To do this, go to the workspace settings and expand the Advanced section (see **Figure 13.7**). Then move the Premium slider to On and choose one of the existing capacities to which you have Capacity Assignments rights, and then click Save.

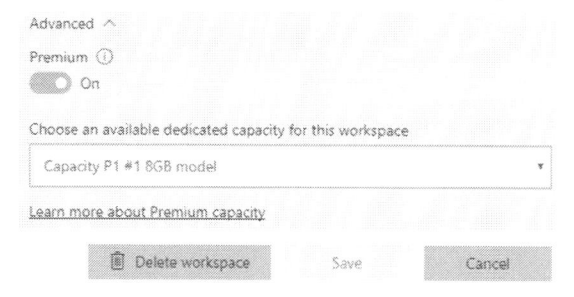

Figure 13.7 Workspace admins with Capacity Assignment can assign a workspace to an existing capacity.

The workspace is now in a premium capacity. You can easily tell which ones of the workspaces you have access to are in a premium capacity because they have a diamond icon, as shown in **Figure 13.8**.

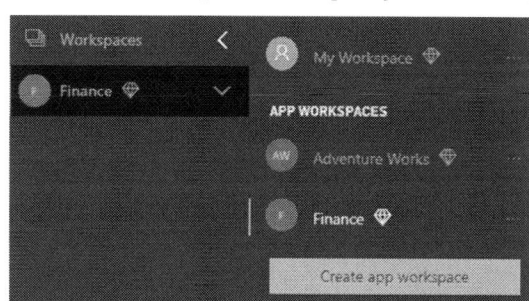

Figure 13.8 Workspaces in a premium capacity have a diamond icon next to their name in the navigation bar.

13.3 Understanding Power BI Report Server

As a cloud SaaS service, Power BI accelerates data analytics, so you can derive insights from your data faster. There isn't much for you and your users to install besides Power BI Desktop and Power BI Mobile apps. But there are cases, such as compliance and security requirements, where on-premises hosting is preferred. Enters Power BI Report Server.

> **NOTE** I've been privileged to contribute to and witness the evolution and success of Microsoft SQL Server Reporting Services since its debut in 2004. SSRS is Microsoft's most mature and extensible reporting platform and I can't cover its breath of features in one section. Instead, I'll focus on its integration with Power BI reports. Although written a decade ago, my book "Applied Microsoft SQL Server 2008 Reporting Services" should help you learn SSRS. To learn how to integrate Power BI Report Server with Office Online Server to render Excel reports online, read the "Configure your report server to host Excel workbooks using Office Online Server" at https://docs.microsoft.com/en-us/power-bi/report-server/excel-oos.

13.3.1 Understanding Reporting Roadmap

Think of Power BI Report Server as an add-on to Microsoft SQL Server Reporting Services (SSRS). It extends SSRS with Power BI interactive reports and Excel reports. It allows you to set up an on-premises report portal for hosting all popular Microsoft report types: traditional (RDL) reports, mobile reports, Power BI reports, and Excel reports. As far as the reason for the name change, the Power BI name has a strong recognition for modern BI while SSRS has been associated with paginated reports.

Understanding deployment options

With Power BI Report Server, Microsoft delivers on their promise for a unified reporting platform on cloud and premises. For more information about their vision, read the blog "Microsoft Business Intelligence – our reporting roadmap" at https://blogs.technet.microsoft.com/dataplatforminsider/2015/10/29/microsoft-business-intelligence-our-reporting-roadmap. **Figure 13.9** shows how Power BI Report Server fits into the reporting roadmap.

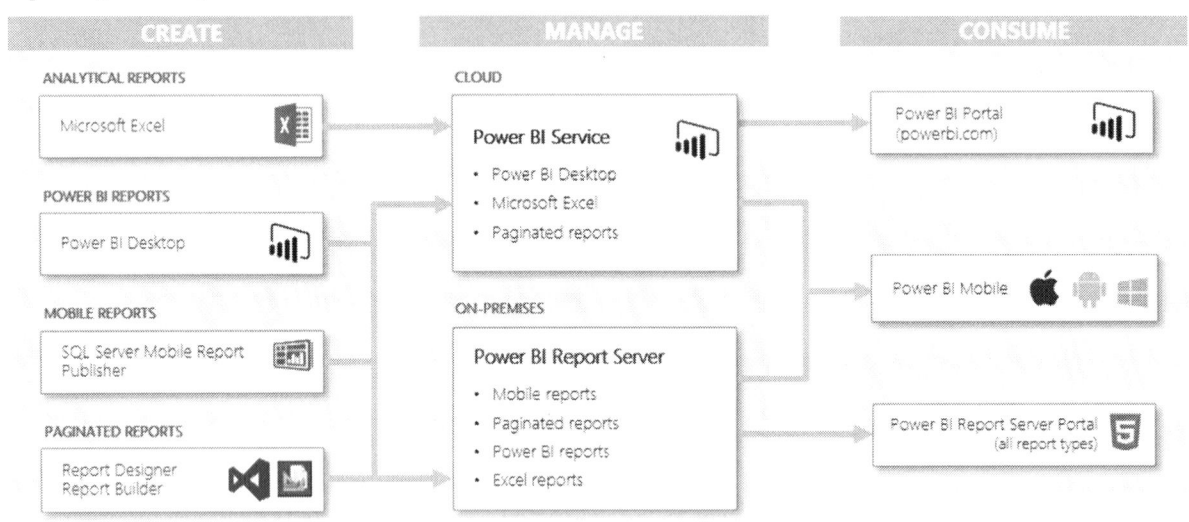

Figure 13.9 The Microsoft roadmap envisions a unified reporting platform delivered in cloud and on premises.

Microsoft BI has four popular report types: analytical Excel reports, Power BI reports, mobile reports (introduced in SSRS 2016), and paginated (RDL) reports. **Table 13.4** shows how these report types can be deployed to the cloud and on premises, and the main limitations.

Table 13.4 How the four main report types integrate with Power BI Service and Power BI Report Server.

Report Types	Power BI Service	Power BI Report Server
Excel reports	Pros: Can connect to Excel files. Cons: Excel reports can't have external connections, such as to connect live to Analysis Services or Power BI datasets	Pros: Can render Excel reports (including external connections) Cons: You need to install Office Online Server. For live connections, Kerberos authentication might be required
Power BI reports	Pros: Natively supported Cons: Power BI Service lacks modeling features	Pros: You can deploy Power BI reports to the report server Cons: Lagging in features compared to Power BI Service
SSRS mobile reports	Pros: Power BI Mobile can display on-premises mobile reports Cons: Can't deploy these reports to Power BI Service	Pros: Natively supported Cons: Difficult to find a good fit for these reports as they as not as interactive as Power BI reports

Report Types	Power BI Service	Power BI Report Server
SSRS Paginated reports	Pros: Can pin report items from on-premises report server to Power BI dashboards, can deploy them to Power BI Premium Cons: Publishing reports to the cloud requires Power BI Premium, limited features are supported	Pros: Natively supported, most extensible report type Cons: Power BI Mobile can't display them, pinned report items are exported as images and lose interactivity

Comparing reporting options

If you have used SSRS in the past, you might wonder how Power BI Report Server compares to it and to Power BI Service. **Table 13.5** compares these three products side by side.

Table 13.5 Feature comparison between SSRS, Power BI Report Server, and Power BI Service.

	SQL Server Reporting Services	Power BI Report Server	Power BI Service Power BI Premium
Deployment	On-premises	On-premises	Cloud
Excel reports	No	Yes	Yes (external connections are not supported)
Power BI reports	No	Yes (restricted features)	Yes
SSRS mobile reports	Yes	Yes	No
Paginated (RDL) reports	Yes	Yes	Yes (Power BI Premium) (can also pin report items to dashboards)
Max imported dataset size	N/A	2 GB	1 GB (Power BI Pro), up to 10 GB (Premium)
Apps	No	No	Yes
Q&A	No	No	Yes
Quick Insights	No	No	Yes
Embedding Power BI reports for third party	No	Planned	Yes
Subscriptions	Paginated reports only	Paginated reports only	Page-level subscriptions for Power BI reports
Data alerts	No	No	Yes (dashboard tiles)
Power BI Mobile support	No	Yes (mobile and Power BI reports)	Yes

To summarize, based on my experience, most organizations gravitate toward cloud deployments, so Power BI Service would be their natural choice. Some organizations prefer on-premises report portals. If you're looking for a report portal that can host all the four main report types in Microsoft BI, then Power BI Report Server is the way to go. One caveat that you need to be aware of if you plan to embed reports for external customers is that the ASP.NET Report Viewer control, which you probably use to embed paginated reports, doesn't support Power BI reports. While waiting for Microsoft to enable the Power BI Embedded APIs in Power BI Report Server, consider configuring the report server for custom security.

> **NOTE** To give Microsoft credit, embedding Power BI reports in internal web apps is easy and it can be done with iframe, such as <iframe src="https://server/reports/powerbi/ReportName?rs:Embed=true" width="800px" height="600px"></iframe>. However, this approach probably won't work for external users where Windows security is not an option.

13.3.2 Getting Started with Power BI Report Server

Now that you understand how Power BI Report Server fit into the Microsoft reporting roadmap, let's cover some important considerations of how to acquire and install it. Starting with SQL Server 2017, Microsoft has removed SSRS from the SQL Server setup program so that it can be enhanced more frequently. Similarly, Power BI Report Server is not included in the SQL Server setup.

How to acquire Power BI Report Server
Power BI Report Server can be acquired in one of two ways:

- Power BI Premium – If your organization has Power BI Premium, Microsoft gives you rights to concurrently deploy Power BI Report Server to the same number of on-premises cores. Let's say you purchased one Power BI Premium P1 node. It gives you eight v-cores. You get also eight on-premises cores to run Power BI Premium Server! If you decide to acquire Power BI Report Server this way, you can obtain the Power BI Report Server product key from the "Capacity settings" page in the Power BI Admin Portal.
- SQL Server Enterprise license with Software Assurance – If you don't use Power BI Premium or you need more cores, you can license Power BI Report Server under the SQL Server Enterprise Edition license just like you license SSRS. However, your organization needs a Software Assurance (SA) agreement with Microsoft. With this option, you can obtain the product key from the Volume Licensing Service Center at https://www.microsoft.com/Licensing/servicecenter/.

Like SQL Server Developer Edition, Power BI Report Server doesn't require a license for development and testing (during the setup, simply select the Developer edition which doesn't require a product key). It's important to understand that like Power BI Service, every user who deploys reports to the report server must be covered by a separate Power BI Pro license. This is an honor-based system as Power BI Report Server has no checks to enforce this requirement.

Installing Power BI Report Server
Microsoft is actively working on enhancing Power BI Report Server and have committed to three releases per year starting in 2019 (January, May, and September). To achieve this goal, Power BI Report Server is available as a standalone product that can be downloaded from the Microsoft Download Center at https://aka.ms/pbireportserver. There isn't much to install and configure. Once you acquire the product key (assuming production use), you only need to decide where to install the server and the Report Server Database.

Like SSRS, Power BI Report Server stores report definitions and management settings in a SQL Server database (its default name is ReportServer), and temporary data in another SQL Server database (its default name is ReportServerTempDB). You can install the SQL Server Database Engine on the same machine where the report server is installed. In this case, both products could be covered by the same license. Or, you might decide to host the databases on a separate SQL Server instance (SQL Server 2008 is the minimum lowest version supported). Keep in mind that not all editions of SQL Server can be used to host the database. For example, you can't install Power BI Report Server for production use and have the report database on SQL Server Developer Edition.

Installing Power BI Desktop
Here is something unfortunate for those of us who plan to deploy Power BI reports to both Power BI Service (powerbi.com) and Power BI Report Server. Because Power BI is evolving faster (new features are released every month), Power BI Report Server is lagging Power BI. So, there are two Power BI Desktop versions:

- Untethered version – Adds features at a monthly cadence and can be downloaded from the Power BI Desktop download page or from Microsoft Store.

- Power BI Report Server version – This version is locked to Power BI Report Server and updated when a new report server release is available. You can download it from the Power BI Report Server download page. The unfortunate side effect is that if you want to publish to both Power BI Service and Power BI Report Server, you need to install and keep both versions.

You can install both versions side by side because the Power BI Report Server version installs in a separate folder (\Program Files\Microsoft Power BI Desktop RS). Only the Power BI Report Server version has an option to deploy the file to Power BI Report Server (Save as ⇨ Power BI Report Server).

> **NOTE** Why couldn't the Power BI Report Server just ignore Power BI features it doesn't recognize, so we can have just one Power BI Desktop app? Unfortunately, the PBIX file format doesn't yet have the infrastructure to consistently and reliably do so because it was developed for Power BI Service. Therefore, Microsoft had to resort to Power BI Desktop builds optimized for specific Power BI Report Server.

13.3.3 Understanding Integration with Power BI

In Chapter 4, I showed you how you can pin report items from paginated reports to Power BI dashboards. And in Chapter 5, I showed you how to view Power BI and mobile reports deployed to a report server in Power BI Mobile. You have also the option to deploy Power BI Desktop files to Power BI Reports Server. Let's provide some additional guidance about these three options from a management perspective.

Pinning report items

Your users can pin image-generating report items, such as charts, gauges, maps, and images, to a Power BI dashboard. When the user clicks a dashboard tile that is pinned from a report item, the user is navigated by default to the underlying report (you can change the URL in the tile properties to navigate the user elsewhere). Consequently, the user must be on the corporate network to navigate to the report (the user doesn't have to be on the corporate network to view the tile). However, you can set up a web application proxy to view SSRS reports outside the corporate network. The Chris Finlan's "Leveraging Web Application Proxy in Windows Server 2016 to provide secure access to your SQL Server Reporting Services environment" blog has the details at bit.ly/ssrsproxy.

Pinning report items requires specific configuration steps that are well documented by Microsoft in the "Power BI Report Server Integration (Configuration Manager)" article at bit.ly/2g0vHW0. Microsoft has also done a good job documenting limitations, but I'd like to add a few comments for you to consider before you enable this feature. First, the source reports must use stored credentials. This is because the underlying mechanism for refreshing pinned items rely on individual subscriptions that are scheduled and run unattended with SQL Server Agent. What this limitation means is that when configuring the report data source, you must specify user name and password of a login that has read rights to the data source.

This limitation has been a personal frustration of mine since the early days of SSRS because it's impractical when connecting to data sources that require Windows authentication, such as Analysis Services. For example, it's a common requirement to implement dynamic security in SSAS models to restrict data depending on the user identity. But now you have a predicament because you must store the user credentials and the data security won't work.

> **REAL LIFE** Power BI Report Server uses individual subscriptions to refresh the Power BI tiles. Because individual subscriptions are associated with the user who pinned the item, Microsoft could have implemented a mechanism to pass the user identity without requiring the password, like how Power BI uses EffectiveUserName.

Continuing the list of limitations, you can't pin tables and matrices, which happen to be the most popular report items. Another thing to watch for is that deleting a dashboard tile with a pinned report item doesn't remove the individual subscriptions. So, if 10 users pin a report item and all users decide that they don't need that tile anymore and delete it from their dashboards, you still have 10 scheduled subscriptions that will continue running on report-specific schedules! Since currently the report server doesn't give the administrator an easy way to view what individual subscriptions exist, it might not be long before your report server starts experiencing performance issues.

Viewing reports in Power BI Mobile
Users can use the Power BI Mobile apps to view Power BI reports and SSRS mobile reports. SSRS mobile reports (not to be confused with Power BI Mobile) were introduced in SSRS 2016. A BI developer creates them using Microsoft SQL Server Mobile Report Publisher. As I explain in my blog "Choosing a reporting tool" at http://prologika.com/choosing-a-reporting-tool, I have reservations about this report type.

In my opinion, besides Power BI reports, it would have been much more useful to support traditional (now referred to as paginated) reports, which is the most popular report type. The good news is that if you deploy paginated reports to Power BI Premium, you can view them in Power BI Mobile.

Deploying Power BI reports to report server
Only Power BI Report Server supports rendering Power BI reports online. While you can deploy Power BI Desktop files to SQL Server Reporting Services (you can upload any file to the report catalog), when the end user clicks the report, the Power BI Desktop file is downloaded locally. Consequently, the user needs to have Power BI Desktop installed to view reports. So, you need Power BI Report Server for a better user experience. Next, let's review essential considerations for deploying and managing Power BI reports.

13.3.4 Managing Power BI Reports

As I mentioned, Microsoft has committed to frequent releases of Power BI Report Server. As of this time, the latest release is the August 2018 release. You can learn about what's new in the current release and change log in the Power BI Report Server documentation at https://docs.microsoft.com/power-bi/report-server/whats-new.

Managing Power BI settings
The administrator can control some settings specific to Power BI by following these steps:

1. Open SQL Server Management Studio. In Object Explorer, expand the Connect drop-down and choose Reporting Services.
2. Enter either the report server machine name or URL address, such as http://<ServerName>/reportserver.
3. Right-click the report server in Object Explorer and click Properties.
4. In the Server Properties window, select the Advanced tab. **Table 13.6** shows the properties specific to Power BI Report Server.

Table 13.6 Power BI specific settings in Power BI Report Server.

Report Types	Default Setting	Purpose
EnableCustomVisuals	True	Enables rendering custom visuals in reports.
EnablePowerBIReportEmbeddedModels	True	Enables reports with imported data
EnablePowerBIReportExportData	True	Allows exporting data from Power BI reports
MaxFileSizeMb	1 GB	Maximum file size for uploaded reports. Default is 1000 MB (1 GB). Maximum is 2 GB.
ModelCleanupCycleMinutes	15 minutes	Defines how often the model is checked to evict it from memory.
ModelExpirationMinutes	60 minutes	Defines how long until the model expires based on the last time used and is evicted
ScheduleRefreshTimeoutMinutes	120 minutes	Defines how long the data refresh can take for a model before connection expires

These settings allow you to govern certain aspects of Power BI reports. For example, if you don't want to support custom visuals, you can turn off the EnableCustomVisuals setting, or if you want to support 2 GB datasets, you can increase the MaxFileSizeDb setting.

Deploying reports

Remember that you need the Power BI Report Server version of Power BI Desktop to deploy pbix files. This version is available on the Power BI Report Server download page. To deploy a Power BI Desktop file to the report catalog:

1. Open the file in Power BI Desktop. Click Save As ⇨ Power BI Report Server.
2. If this if the first time you connect to the report server, enter the Web Portal address of the report server, such as http://ServerName/reports. Once the address is validated, it will be added to "Recent report servers", so you don't have to type it in every time. If you're unsure about the address, open the Report Server Configuration Manager (not the SSRS Reporting Services Configuration Manager), connect to the server, and check the address in the Web Portal URL tab.
3. Select a folder in the report catalog where you want to publish the file to and click OK. Another way to upload your file is to navigate to the Power BI Report Server portal and upload it manually.

> **NOTE** If you try using the latest untethered version of Power BI Desktop to upload the *.pbix file manually to the report catalog, you'd probably be greeted with the "Can't upload this report" error. As the error explains, the reason is that either the file is a newer version or has component parts that are not supported. Instead of starting from scratch, try opening the file in the Power BI Report Server version to ignore the features it doesn't recognize, and then upload the file to the report catalog.

Back to Power BI Desktop, if you want to open a published Power BI Desktop (*.pbix) file, use the Open ⇨ Power BI Report Server menu.

Figure 13.10 Power BI reports render online in the Power BI Report Server portal and preserve their interactive features.

Viewing reports

The whole reason why you'd want to have Power BI Report Server is to view Power BI reports online. "Online" means that reports are rendered in the browser, instead of prompting the user to download the file and open it in Power BI Desktop. End users must have permissions to view reports and Power BI reports share the same security model as other report types. For example, you can add AD groups and individual users to the predefined Browser role to let them view reports in a folder and its subfolders.

Figure 13.10 shows the Adventure Works report (discussed in the previous chapter) rendered inside the Power BI Report Server portal. The report preserves its interactivity, but some Power BI Desktop features, such as Explain Increase/Decrease, are not available. Like conversations in Power BI Service, you can click the Comments menu to start a discussion thread regarding the report data.

Managing data sources

As an IT Pro, you need to manage different aspects of deployed Power BI reports. And one of the most common tasks is managing the report data sources.

1. Hover on any Power BI report and click the ellipsis (…) menu. Click Manage.
2. In the Manage Report page, click Data Sources.
3. Notice that the Data Sources page lists all the data sources in the *.pbix file. However, you can only change the authentication type (not the connection string), as shown in **Figure 13.11**.

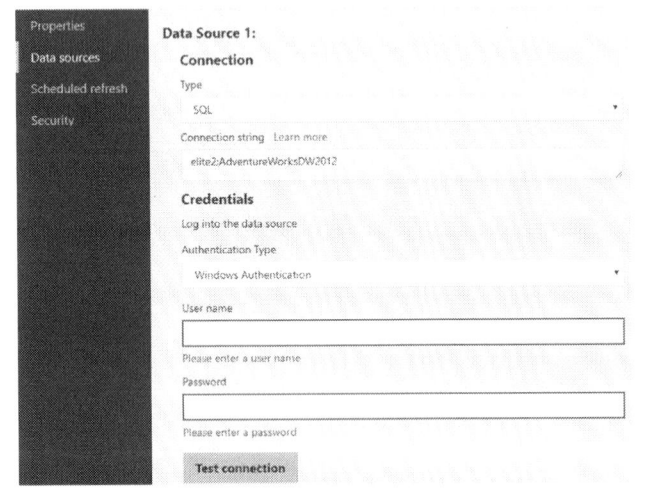

Figure 13.11 You can only change the data source authentication type for published Power BI reports.

If you plan to schedule a model with imported data for automated refresh, you must specify stored credentials in the data sources. That's because the report server will start the refresh operation on its own and there won't be an interactive user to authenticate. You can use either Windows Authentication or Basic Authentication. With the former, you must specify a Windows account that has read rights to the data source. The latter is only available for relational databases, such as SQL Server, and lets you specify the credentials of a login that has read rights to the data.

> **TIP** If your model imports data from files, the connection string needs to reference network shares. If you import local files, open the file in Power BI Desktop, expand the Edit Queries button (Home ribbon) and click "Data source settings". Select the file data source and click Change Source. Then, change the file path to be a UNC file path. For example, instead of referencing C:\PowerBI\Resellers.xlsx, enter \\YourComputerName>\C$\PowerBI\Resellers.xlsx, and upload the file to Power BI Report Server.

Managing scheduled refresh

Like deploying datasets with imported data to Power BI Service, you'd probably want to schedule them for automatic refresh to keep them synchronized with changes to the data sources. Two conditions need to be met before you can schedule automatic refresh:

- You must change all data sources to use stored credentials before you can schedule a report for automated refresh.
- The SQL Server Agent service needs to be running on the SQL Server hosting the report database.

Setting up automated refresh requires a refresh plan. Think of a refresh plan as a set of refresh properties related to a specific Power BI report, including a description and schedule. A report can have multiple refresh plans, such as to refresh multiple times per day Monday to Friday, and once per day on weekends.

1. In the Manage Report page, click the "Schedule refresh" tab.
2. Click "New scheduled refresh plan". In the next page, choose between an existing shared schedule or create a report-specific schedule. This works the same way as when you schedule SSRS subscriptions.
3. Click "Create scheduled refresh plan" to create the plan. Going back to the "Scheduled refresh" page, you should now see the refresh plan (see **Figure 13.12**).

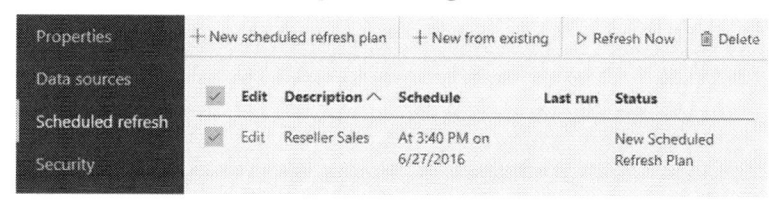

Figure 13.12 A refresh plan specifies how often the report will be refreshed.

4. Check the checkbox preceding the plan name. Notice that you can create a new plan from the one you selected. You can also click "Refresh now" to trigger manual refresh, such as to test the plan.
5. Observe that the Status column says "Started data refresh". After some time, click F5 to refresh the page. If the refresh is still running, the status should read "Refreshing". If all is well, the status should say "Completed Data Refresh". If something goes wrong, it should read "Several errors occurred during data refresh…". You can click the icon next to the status to see the error.

TIP Currently, the report server doesn't have a user interface to show the refresh history. However, the status messages are logged in the SubscriptionHistory table in the ReportServer database. Report refreshes are logged in the ExecutionLog table with RequestType=DataRefresh. You can use the ExecutionLog3 view to monitor the overall status, frequency, and outcome of refreshes for all reports.

13.4 Summary

This chapter focused on two important products in the Power BI portfolio: Power BI Premium and Power BI Report Server. Larger organizations will benefit from the Power BI Premium dedicated capacity that ensures consistent performance and protection from activities of other tenants in Power BI Service. Such organizations can also reduce licensing cost by sharing content of premium workspaces to Power BI Free users by either dashboard sharing or apps. Power BI Premium adds important features, including incremental data refresh, advanced dataflows, and paginated reports.

Power BI Report Server allows you to implement an on-premises report portal to centralize BI assets and manage them in one place. An add-on to SSRS, Power BI Report Server can accommodate the four most popular report types in Microsoft BI: Excel analytical reports, Power BI reports, SSRS mobile reports, and traditional paginated (RDL) reports. Power BI Report Server can be acquired by a Power BI Premium plan or under a SQL Server Enterprise Edition with Software Assurance license. Microsoft has committed to enhancing Power BI Report Server bi-monthly and keeping it up to date with Power BI Service.

Power BI is a part of a much broader Microsoft Data Platform. You've seen how Power BI can integrate with popular cloud services and on-premises report servers. The next chapter will show you how you can create BI Pro solutions that integrate with Power BI!

Chapter 14

Organizational BI

14.1 Implementing Classic BI Solutions 369
14.2 Integrating Paginated Reports 377
14.3 Implementing Real-time BI Solutions 380
14.4 Summary 387

So far, the focus of this book has been the self-service and team aspects of Power BI, which empower business users and data analysts to gain insights from data and to share these insights with other users. Now it's time to turn our attention to BI pros who implement organizational BI solutions. Back in Chapter 2, I compared self-service and organizational BI at a high level. I defined organizational BI as a set of technologies and processes for implementing an end-to-end BI solution where the implementation effort is shifted to BI professionals.

This chapter shows BI pros how to build common organizational BI solutions around Power BI. You'll understand the importance of having an organizational semantic layer, and you'll learn how to integrate it with Power BI. You'll also learn how to deploy SSRS paginated (RDL) reports to Power BI Premium. Implementing real-time BI solutions is one of the fastest growing BI trends. I'll show you how this can be done using the Power BI real-time API and Azure Stream Analytics Service, while you use Power BI for real-time dashboards.

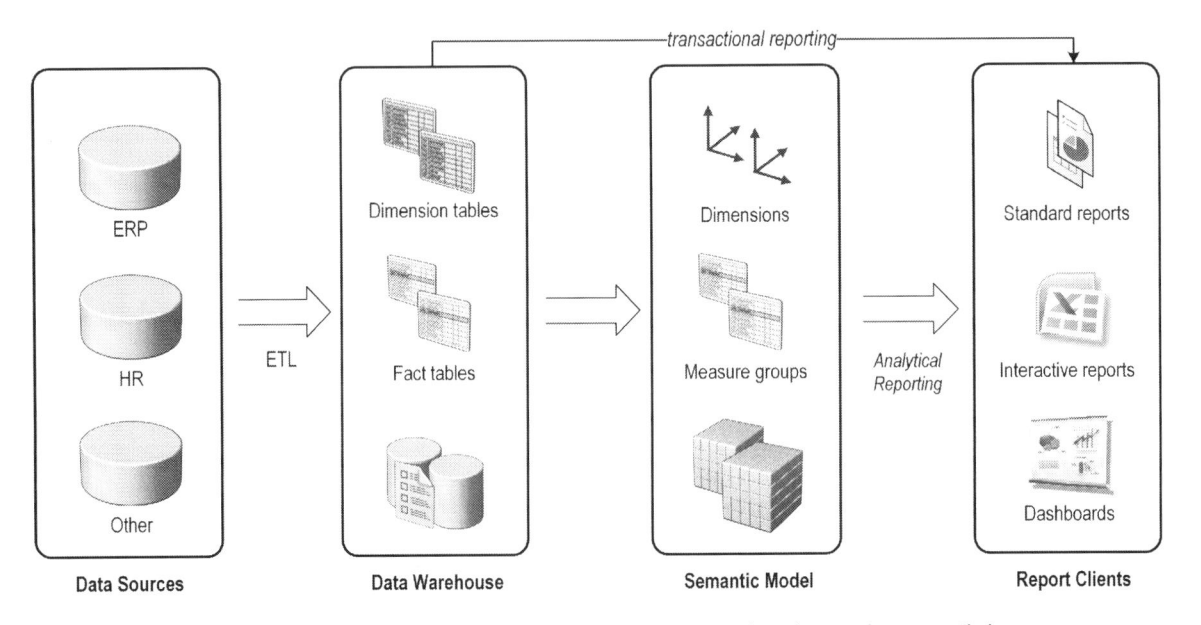

Figure 14.1 Organizational BI typically includes ETL processes, data warehousing, and a semantic layer.

14.1 Implementing Classic BI Solutions

In Chapter 2, I introduced you at a high level to what I refer to as a classic BI solution (see **Figure 14.1**). This diagram should be familiar to you. Almost every organization nowadays has a centralized data repository, typically called a data warehouse or a data mart, which consolidates cleaned and trusted data from operational systems.

> **REAL LIFE** Data warehousing might mean different things to different people. In my consulting practice, I've seen data warehouse "flavors" ranging from normalized operational data stores (ODS) to hub-and-spoke architectures. If they work for you then that's all that matters. I personally recommend and implement a consolidated data repository designed in accordance with Ralph Kimball's dimensional modeling (star schema), consisting of fact and dimension tables. For more information about dimensional modeling, I recommend the book "The Data Warehouse Toolkit" by Ralph Kimball and Margy Ross.

You might not have an organizational semantic layer that sits between the data warehouse and users, and you might not know what it is. In general, semantics relates to discovering the meaning of the message behind the words. In the context of data and BI, semantics represents the user's perspective of data: how the end user views the data to derive knowledge from it. As a BI pro, your job is to translate machine-friendly database structures and terminology into a user-friendly semantic layer that describes the business problems to be solved. In Microsoft BI, the role of this layer is fulfilled by Microsoft BI Semantic Model (BISM).

14.1.1 Understanding Microsoft BISM

Microsoft BISM is a unifying name for several Microsoft technologies for implementing semantic models, including self-service models implemented with Excel Power Pivot or Power BI Desktop, and organizational Microsoft Analysis Services models. From an organizational BI standpoint, BI pros are most interested in Microsoft Analysis Services modeling capabilities.

> **NOTE** Besides the necessary fundamentals, this chapter doesn't attempt to teach you Multidimensional or Tabular. To learn more about Analysis Services, I covered implementing Analysis Services Multidimensional models in my book "Applied Microsoft Analysis Services 2005" and Tabular models in "Applied Microsoft SQL Server 2012 Analysis Services: Tabular Modeling".

Introducing Multidimensional and Tabular
Since its first release in 1998, Analysis Services has provided Online Analytical Processing (OLAP) capabilities so that IT professionals can implement Multidimensional OLAP cubes for descriptive analytics. The OLAP side of Analysis Services is referred to as *Multidimensional*. Multidimensional is a mature model that can scale to large data volumes. For example, Elena can build a Multidimensional cube on top of a large data warehouse with billions of rows, while still providing an excellent response time where most queries finish within a second!

Starting with SQL Server 2012, Microsoft expanded the Analysis Services capabilities by adding a new path for implementing semantic models, where entities are represented as relational-like constructs, such as two-dimensional tables, columns, and relationships. Referred to as *Tabular*, this technology uses the same xVelocity engine that powers Power BI Desktop, Excel Power Pivot, Power BI, and SQL Server columnstore indexes. Although not as scalable as Multidimensional, Tabular gains in simplicity and flexibility. And because Tabular uses the same storage engine, if you know how to create self-service data models in Power BI Desktop or Excel, you already know 90% of Tabular! That's right, while you were learning how to build self-service data models with Power BI Desktop you were also learning how to implement Tabular models.

Understanding implementation paths
Microsoft organizational BISM can be visualized as a three-tier model that consists of data access, business logic, and data model layers (see **Figure 14.2**). The data model layer is exposed to external clients. Clients

can query BISM by sending Multidimensional Expressions (MDX) or Data Analysis Expressions (DAX) queries. For example, Excel can connect to both Multidimensional and Tabular and send MDX queries, while Power BI and Power View send DAX queries.

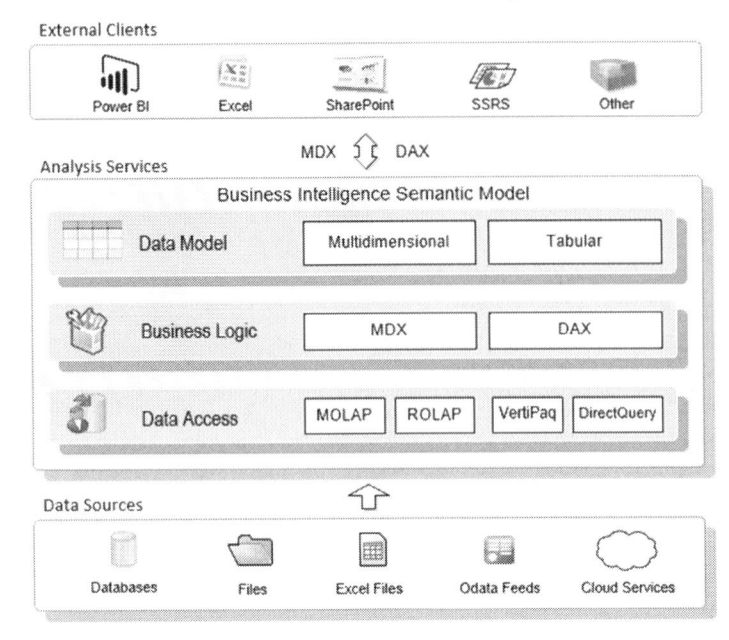

Figure 14.2 BISM has two organizational BI implementation paths: Multidimensional and Tabular.

The business logic layer allows the modeler to define business metrics, such as variances, time calculations, and key performance indicators (KPIs). In Multidimensional, you can implement this layer using Multidimensional Expressions (MDX) constructs, such as calculated members, named sets, and scope assignments. Tabular embraces the same Data Analysis Expressions (DAX) that you've learned about in Chapter 9 when you added business calculations to the Adventure Works model.

The data access layer interfaces with external data sources. By default, both Multidimensional and Tabular import data from the data sources and cache the dataset on the server for best performance. The default multidimensional storage option is Multidimensional OLAP (MOLAP), where data is stored in a compressed disk-based format. The default Tabular storage option is xVelocity, where data is initially saved to disk but later loaded in memory when users query the model.

Both Multidimensional and Tabular support real-time data access by providing a Relational OLAP (ROLAP) storage mode for Multidimensional and a DirectQuery storage mode for Tabular. When a Multidimensional cube is configured for ROLAP, Analysis Services doesn't process and cache the data on the server. Instead, it auto-generates and sends native queries to the database. Similarly, when a Tabular model is configured for DirectQuery, Analysis Services doesn't keep data in xVelocity; it sends native queries directly to the data source. As I mentioned in Chapter 6, the DirectQuery mode of Tabular enables DirectQuery connections in Power BI Desktop.

Understanding the BISM advantages
Having a semantic model is very valuable for organizational BI for the following main reasons:
- Larger data volumes – Remember that Power BI Service currently limits imported files to 250 MB each, including Power BI Desktop models. This size limit won't be adequate for organizational solutions that are typically built on top of corporate data warehouses. By contrast, BISM can scale to billions of rows and terabytes of data!

- Great performance – BISM is optimized to aggregate data very fast. Queries involving regular measures and simple calculations should be answered within seconds even, when aggregating millions of rows!
- Single version of the truth – Business logic and metrics can be centralized in the semantic model instead of being defined and redefined in the database or in reports.

REAL WORLD The BI department of a retail company included some 20 report developers on staff whose sole responsibility was creating operational reports from stored procedures. Over time, stored procedures have grown in complexity, and developers have defined important business metrics differently. Needless to say, operational reports didn't tally. Although the term "a single version of the truth" is somewhat overloaded, a centralized semantic model can get you very close to it.

- Data security – Like row-level security (RLS) in Power BI Desktop, BISM models can apply data security based on the user's identity, such as to allow Maya to only see the data for the customers she's authorized to access.
- Implicit relationships – In the process of designing the semantic layer, the modeler defines relationships between entities, just like a data analyst does when creating a self-service model. As a result, end users don't need to join tables explicitly because the relationships have already been established at design time. For example, you don't have to know how to join the Product table to the Sales table. You simply add the fields you need on the report, and then the model knows how to relate them!
- Interactive data analysis – From an end-user perspective, data analysis is a matter of dragging and dropping attributes on the report to slice and dice data. A "smart" client, such as Power BI, auto-generates report queries, and the server takes care of aggregating data, such as to summarize sales at the year level.
- Good client support – There are many reporting tools, including Power BI, Excel, Reporting Services, and third-party tools, that support BISM and address various reporting needs, including standard reports, interactive reports, and dashboards.

When should you upgrade to organizational BI?

You might have started your BI journey with a self-service model in Excel or Power BI Desktop. Why can't this be your semantic model given that it could be as feature-rich as a Tabular model. At what point should you consider switching to an organizational solution? What would you gain?

REAL WORLD Everyone wants quick and easy BI solutions, ideally with a click of a button. But the reality is much more difficult. I often find that companies have attempted to implement organizational BI solutions with self-service tools, like Power BI Desktop, Excel, or some other third-party tools. The primary reasons are cutting cost and misinformation (that's why it's important to know who you listen to). The result is always the same – sooner or later the company finds that it's time to "graduate" to organizational BI. Don't get me wrong, though. Self-service BI has its important place, as I explain in Chapter 2. But having trusted organizational-level solutions will require the right architecture, toolset, and investment.

You should consider moving to an organizational solution when the following happens:

- Data integration – The requirements call for extracting data from several systems and consolidating data instead of implementing isolated self-service data models.
- Data complexity – You realize that the data complexity exceeds the capabilities of the Power BI Desktop queries. For example, the integration effort required to clean and transform corporate data typically exceeds the simple transformation capabilities of self-service models.
- Data security – Security requirements might dictate leaving data on premises without compromising report performance. This excludes deploying data extracts to the cloud.

- Enterprise scalability – Power BI Desktop and Excel models import data in files. Once you get beyond a few million rows, you'll find that you stretch the limits of these tools. For example, it'll take a while to save and load the file. It'll take even longer to upload the file to Power BI. By contrast, organizational models must be capable of handling larger data volumes. Just by deploying the model to an Analysis Services instance, you gain better scalability that's boosted by the hardware resources of a dedicated server.
- Faster data refresh – Unlike the Power BI Desktop sequential data refresh, organizational models support processing tables and partitioned tables in parallel, to better utilize the resources of a dedicated server. Also, to reduce the data load window and to process data incrementally, you can divide large tables in partitions.
- Richer model – Tabular supports additional features that might be appealing to you, including international translations, drillthrough actions, display folders, and programmatically generating the model schema. Because you'll be using Visual Studio to design your BISM, you can enjoy all the Visual Studio IDE features, including source control integration.

NOTE What if you have started with Power BI Desktop but want to upgrade to Tabular? Currently, only Azure Analysis Services officially supports upgrading from Power BI Desktop (although new desktop features may prevent upgrading). There's no officially supported upgrade path from Power BI Desktop models to SSAS. That's because Microsoft updates Power BI Desktop monthly, and it can get ahead of Tabular, which is included in the SQL Server box product and only releases a new version every few years. However, I outlined an unsupported way in my blog "Upgrading Power BI Desktop Models to Tabular" at http://prologika.com/upgrading-power-bi-desktop-models-to-tabular. Use it at your own risk!

Comparing self-service and organizational models
Since you're reading this book, the logical transition path is from Power BI Desktop (or Excel) to Tabular. Then you'll discover that you can seamlessly transition your knowledge to organizational projects. Indeed, an organizational Tabular model has the same foundation as Power Pivot or Power BI Desktop, but it adds enterprise-oriented and advanced features, such as options for configuring security, scalability, and low latency. **Table 14.1** provides a side-by-side comparison between self-service and organizational features.

Table 14.1 This table highlights the differences between self-service and organizational semantic models.

Feature	Self-service Models	Organizational Models
Target users	Business users	Professionals
Environment	Power BI Desktop or Excel	Visual Studio (SSDT)
xVelocity Engine	Out of process (local in-memory engine)	Out of process (dedicated Analysis Services instance)
Size	One file (dataset size limits apply)	Large data volumes, table partitions
Refreshing data	Sequential table refresh	Parallel table refresh, incremental processing (parallel partition refresh starting with SQL Server 2016)
Data transformation	Power Query in Excel, queries in PBI Desktop	Not available (typically ETL processes are in place)
Development	Ad-hoc development	Project (business case, plan, dates, hardware, source control)
Lifespan	Weeks or months	Years

How Power BI Service connects to on-premises Analysis Services
Now that you understand the benefits of an organizational semantic model, let's see how Power BI integrates with Analysis Services. One implementation path leads to hosting your semantic model in the cloud using Azure Analysis Services. In this case, no gateways are needed because Power BI can connect directly

to cloud data sources. If operational or other requirements dictate on-premises deployment, Power BI can access on-premises Analysis Services models with the Power BI On-premises Data Gateway.

> **NOTE** Currently, the gateway doesn't support connecting to Tabular in SharePoint integration mode (Power Pivot for SharePoint uses this mode). I hope this limitation is lifted soon so that you can connect Power BI to cubes and to Power Pivot models deployed to SharePoint if you have invested in Power Pivot. Unfortunately, Power BI doesn't support HTTP access to Analysis Services using a special component called data pump (HTTP access to SSAS is discussed in the "Configure HTTP Access to Analysis Services on Internet Information Services (IIS) 8.0" article at https://msdn.microsoft.com/library/gg492140.aspx). So, you can't avoid using a gateway to access on-premises SSAS models.

From the Power BI standpoint, the BISM integration scenario that will inspire the most interest is the hybrid architecture shown in **Figure 14.3**. This architecture will be also appealing for companies that prefer to keep data on premises but want to host only report and dashboard definitions to Power BI. Elena has implemented an Analysis Services Tabular model layered on top of the Adventure Works data warehouse, and she deployed it to an on-premises server. "On premises" could mean any model that is not hosted in Azure Analysis Services, such as a server hosted in the company's data center or on an Azure virtual machine. So that Power BI can connect to the model, Elena installs the On-premises Data Gateway on a machine that can connect to the Analysis Services instance. Elena has granted Maya access to the model.

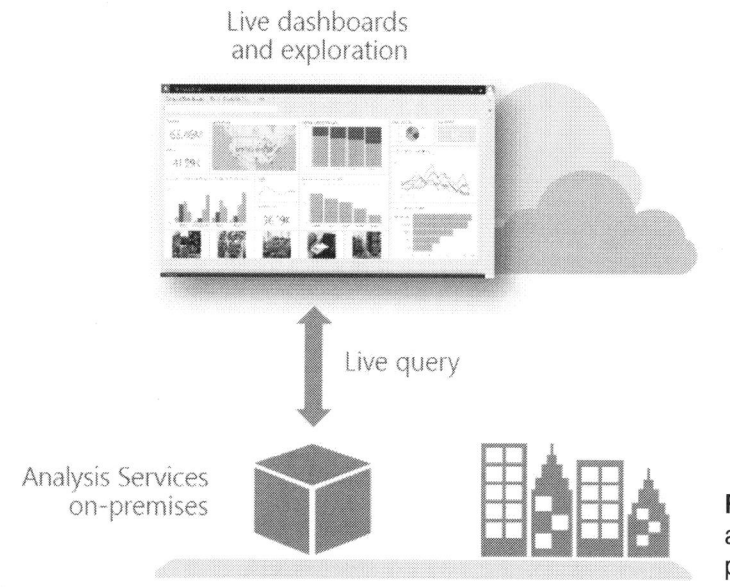

Figure 14.3 You can implement a hybrid architecture by connecting Power BI to on-premises Analysis Services models.

Maya logs in to Power BI and uses Get Data to connect to Analysis Services. Maya selects the Adventure Works model. Power BI establishes a live connection. Now Maya can create reports and dashboards, as I demonstrated in Chapter 2. If the model is configured for data security, Maya can only see the data that the model security authorizes her to access. When she explores the data, Power BI auto-generates DAX queries and sends them to the Adventure Works model. The model sends results back. No data is hosted on Power BI!

14.1.2 Understanding Setup Requirements

Because Power BI needs to connect to the on-premises model and pass the user identity, IT needs to take care of certain prerequisites for both on premises and in the cloud. The exact setup steps depend on how your company is set up for Microsoft Azure.

Understanding domain considerations

The following special considerations apply when setting up a gateway data source that connects to SSAS.

1. Analysis Services must be installed on a domain-joined machine. That's because Analysis Services supports only Windows security.
2. The Windows account that you specify in the data source properties of the On-premises Data Gateway, must have admin rights to the Analysis Services instance. That's because behind the scenes the gateway passes the user identity by appending an EffectiveUserName setting to the connection string. This connectivity mechanism requires admin rights.

> **NOTE** Behind the scenes, the gateway appends a special EffectiveUserName connection setting when it connects to an on-premises SSAS. If Maya connects to the Analysis Services server, then EffectiveUserName will pass Maya's email, such as EffectiveUserName=maya@adventureworks.com. To verify or grant the account admin rights to SSAS, open SQL Server Management Studio (SSMS) and connect to your SSAS instance. Right-click on the instance, and then click Properties. In the Security tab of the Analysis Services Properties page, add the account to the server administrators list.

3. Without special mapping (see next section), the end user and Analysis Services must be on the same domain or trusted domains. For example, if I log in to Power BI as teo@adventureworks.com, Analysis Services must be on the adventureworks.com domain, or on a domain that has a trust relationship.

Checking access

Follow these steps to verify whether the On-premises Data Gateway can delegate the user identity:

1. Make sure that you have administrator access to the Analysis Services instance.
2. Open SQL Server Management Studio (SSMS). In Object Explorer, expand the Connect drop-down, and then click Connect ⇨ Analysis Services.
3. In the "Connect to Server", enter your Analysis Services instance name. Don't click Connect yet.
4. Click Options. In the Additional Connection Parameters tab, enter EffectiveUserName, followed by the Universal Principal Name (UPN) of the user who you want to test (see **Figure 14.4**). Typically, UPN is the same as the user's email address. If you're not sure, ask the user to open the command prompt and enter the following command: whoami /upn.

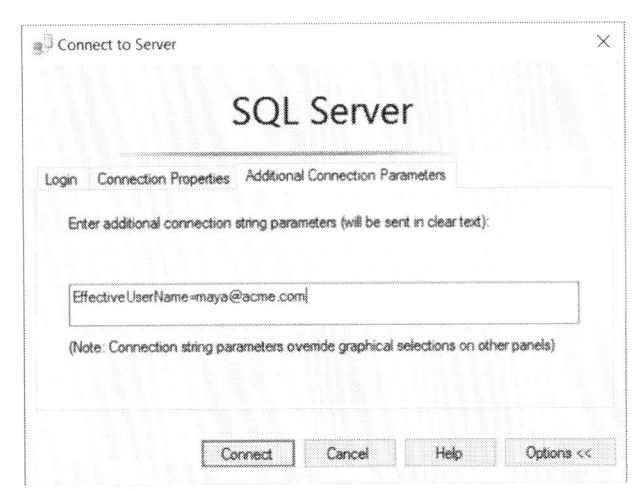

Figure 14.4 Use SSMS to verify if the interactive user will gain access to Analysis Services by passing the EffectiveUserName setting.

5. Click Connect. If you can connect successfully, the gateway should be able to delegate the user identity. If you get an error, see the next section.

Mapping user names

If you get an error, more than likely there isn't a trust relationship between the two domains. For example, Adventure Works might have acquired Acme and the Acme employees might still be on the acme.com domain. This will cause an issue when these employees attempt to connect to Analysis Services and the connection will fail. If you follow the steps to test EffectiveUserName and open SQL Server Profiler to monitor connections to Analysis Services, you'll see the error "The following system error occurred: The user name or password is incorrect."

Fortunately, Power BI has a simple solution. When setting up a data source to Analysis Services in the On-premises Data Gateway, the Users tab has a "Map user names" button, which brings you to the "Map user names" window (see **Figure 14.5**).

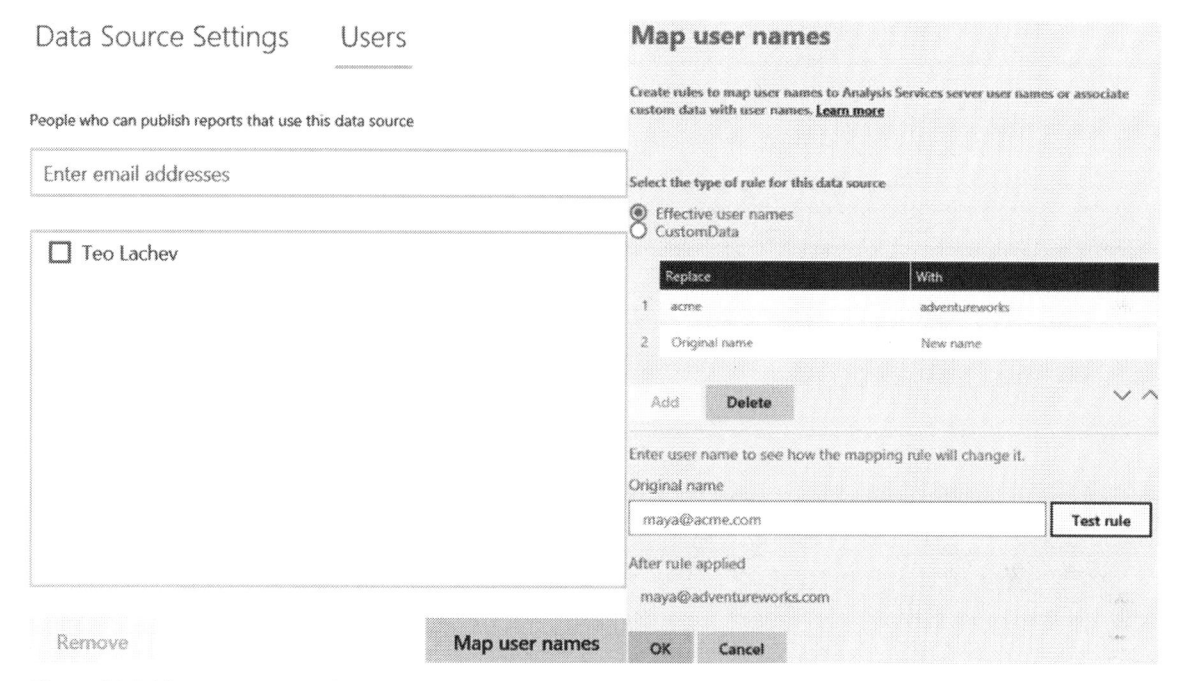

Figure 14.5 Map user names when users and Analysis Services are on different domains.

You can set up a simple mapping rule to replace some text in the user's email, such as to replace "acme" with "adventureworks" if Analysis Services is installed on somedomain.com domain. Make sure to click the Add button to add the rule to the grid. Use "Test rule" to test it by providing a sample email address.

> **TIP** What is the CustomData setting? When USERNAME isn't enough, another option that's less frequently used for dynamic data security is to use the CustomData setting. This option could be useful when you share reports and dashboards with external users. In this case, you can't use EffectiveUserName because there is no Active Directory account for the external user. However, the user identity can be passed under the CustomData option. Then, a row filter can use the CUSTOMDATA DAX function to obtain the identifier. For example, the expression IF(CUSTOMDATA()="<UserIdentity>", TRUE, FALSE) allows the user to see all rows associated with that external user.

ORGANIZATIONAL BI

14.1.3 Using Analysis Services in Power BI Service

Once you register Analysis Services with the On-Premises Data Gateway, users can go to Power BI and connect live to Analysis Services. However, users still might not be able to connect if they don't have rights to access the Analysis Services models. As you can see, there are multiple levels of security so be patient.

Granting user access

By default, users don't have access to Analysis Services models. To grant users access, you need an Analysis Services database role. For the purposes of this exercise, you'll use SQL Server Management Studio (SSMS) to add users to a role. Let's grant user access to the Adventure Works Tabular model:

> **TIP** As a best practice, the BI developer should use SQL Server Data Tools (SSDT) to define role membership in the Analysis Services project, instead of using SSMS. This way the role membership becomes a part of the project and can be deployed together with the project. But we're using SSMS here for the sake of simplicity.

1. Open SQL Server Management Studio (SSMS) and connect to the Analysis Services instance.
2. In the Object Explorer in the left pane, expand the Analysis Services instance, and then expand the Databases node.
3. Expand the "AdventureWorks Tabular Model SQL 2012" database, and then expand the Roles folder.
4. The Adventure Works SSAS database includes an Analysts role that grants access to the model. For the purposes of this exercise, you'll use this role. Double-click the Analysts role.
5. In the Role Properties window (see **Figure 14.6**), select the Membership tab and add the users.

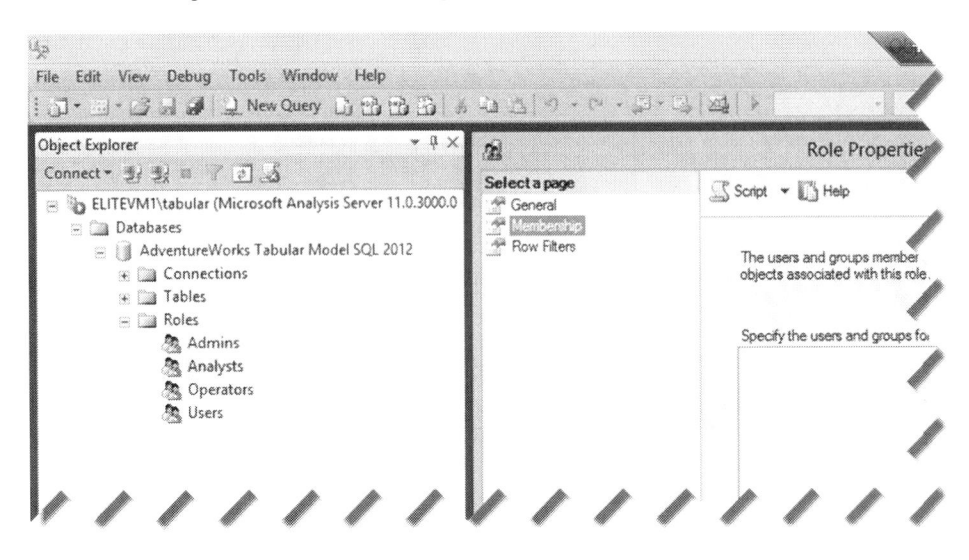

Figure 14.6 You must grant users access to the SSAS model by assigning users to a database role.

Verifying user connectivity

Once you grant the users access to the model, they should be able to run reports in Power BI Service that connect to SSAS. I showed you how they do this back in Chapter 2. From an administrator standpoint, you need to know how to troubleshoot connectivity issues.

Ask the user to go to Power BI Service and connect to SSAS (Get Data ➪ Databases ➪ SQL Server Analysis Services). The user will see all the registered gateways (see **Figure 14.7**), even though he might not have rights to access any of the databases. Power BI Service will make the actual connection only when the user selects a gateway and clicks Connect. At this point, the user will only see the SSAS databases they can access on that instance.

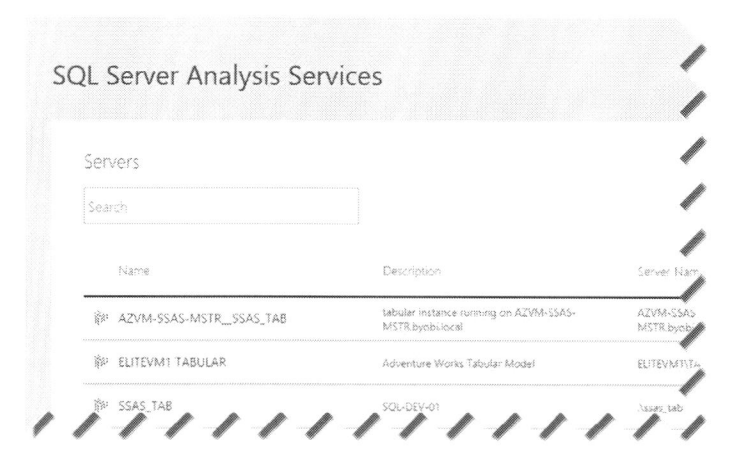

Figure 14.7 Power BI lists all the registered gateways, regardless if the user has permissions to any of the databases hosted on that SSAS instance.

If the connection fails, the best way to verify what identity the user connects under is to use the SQL Server Profiler connected to the SSAS instance. Many events, such as Discover Begin or Query Begin, have a PropertyList element that includes the EffectiveUserName property (see **Figure 14.8**).

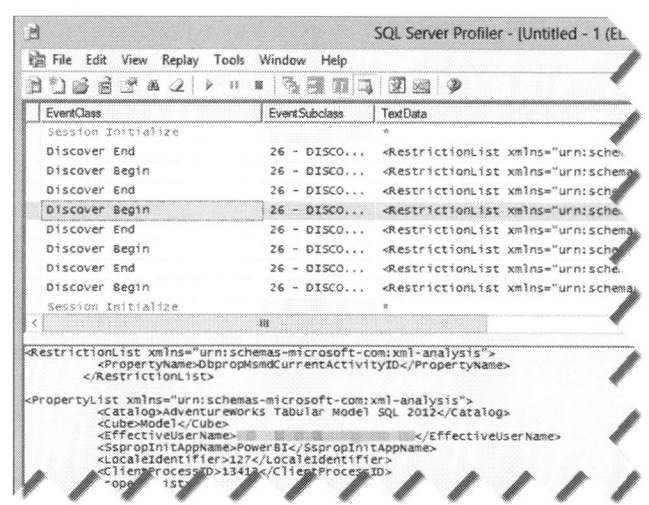

Figure 14.8 The EffectiveUserName property includes the identity of the interactive user.

The EffectiveUserName should match the work email that the user typed to log in to Power BI, such as maya@adventureworks.com. If you need data security, you can set up row filters in your Tabular model to filter the SSAS model data, based on the user identity, just like you can set up roles in Power BI Desktop.

14.2 Integrating Paginated Reports

You saw in the "Understanding Reporting Roadmap" section in the previous chapter that you can deploy SSRS paginated (RDL) reports to a Power BI Premium capacity. To recap, Power BI gives you a deployment choice:

- On-premises deployments – Use Power BI Report Server to host Power BI reports, paginated reports, SSRS mobile reports, and Excel reports so that all report types stay in your data center.

ORGANIZATIONAL BI   377

- Cloud deployment – Deploy Power BI reports, paginated reports, and Excel reports to Power BI Service if you want Power BI to become your one-stop platform for BI in the cloud.

> **NOTE** Because paginated reports can run custom .NET code, they could compromise security in a shared environment. Therefore, currently they require Power BI Premium to isolate them in an environment dedicated to your organization.

14.2.1 Understanding Paginated Reports

SQL Server Reporting Services (SSRS) has preceded Power BI for more than a decade (Microsoft introduced SSRS in 2004). Many organizations have invested in SSRS reports so they're not going away. And nowadays many organizations are moving their workloads to the cloud. Naturally, such organizations would be interested in migrating their SSRS reports to Power BI.

> **NOTE** As I write this, Power BI paginated reports are in preview and they have many limitations that more than likely will preclude migrating your reports to the cloud. However, Microsoft seems to be committed to bring a feature parity by the time this integration scenario becomes generally available, so don't rule it out. From a migration standpoint, one prominent difference is that connecting to an on-premises data source requires a Power BI gateway. This is no different than Power BI reports.

When to use paginated reports?

Besides migrating legacy reports, why should you consider paginated reports? Paginated reports are the most customizable and extensible report type in the Microsoft Data Platform. You'll be hard pressed to face a reporting requirement that you can't meet with a paginated report. Almost all report properties can be expression-based (the default expression language is VB.NET but you can use custom code written in any .NET language), which brings a lot of flexibility. For example, depending on the parameter value selected by the user (or some other condition), you can change how the report groups data or how data is formatted. You can also extend your reports with external custom code, such as to integrate it with a .NET assembly that implements special security or formatting rules, or to protect your intellectual property.

Another reason to favor paginated reports is that they are designed to be exported or printed. Most organizations require a set of standard (pixel-perfect) reports that managers can easily access and distribute. Compared to the other report types, only SSRS reports expand their report items to multiple pages to accommodate all the data when they are viewed, printed or exported (the other report types force you to scroll when the visual data exceeds the visual dimensions).

While paginated reports gain in extensibility and customization, they fall behind in interactivity. Their layout is fixed at design time and interactive features are limited to dynamic sorting, expanding and collapsing sections (hidden visibility), and hyperlinks. If you're after the "wow" effect, you should stay with Power BI reports. Continuing the list of limitations, drilling through data entails creating additional paginated reports. Lastly, authoring paginated reports requires specific knowledge of designing the report layout and working with database queries, such as SQL. Therefore, paginated reports are typically produced and maintained by BI developers.

How to create paginated reports?

There are two common ways to create paginated reports:
- SQL Server Data Tools (SSDT) – BI pros typically favor the SSDT Report Designer because they can benefit from professional Visual Studio features, such as solutions and projects, source control and integrated deployment.
- Report Builder – Microsoft positioned Report Builder as a tool for creating paginated reports by business users. Distributed as a Windows desktop app, Report Builder resembles the Power BI Desktop user interface and it's designed for creating one report at the time.

I provided a sample paginated report (Parameterized Sales Report) for this practice in the \Source\ch14 folder. If you want to get a taste of what the report authoring experience is like, you can follow the steps in the "Add a Parameter to Your Report (Report Builder)" tutorial at http://bit.ly/reportbuilderdemo to create this report in Report Builder.

> **TIP** The report uses a SQL statement that returns static data (hardcoded in the statement) but it still requires a connection to a SQL Server database. To avoid gateways whatsoever, consider connecting to an Azure SQL Database. The database itself doesn't matter. When creating the data source, just choose any Azure SQL Database you have at least read permissions to.

14.2.2 Working with Paginated Reports

As I mentioned, as a prerequisite for using paginated reports, make sure to enable the Paginated Reports workflow in the capacity settings page. In addition, make sure that you deploy the reports to an app workspace in a premium capacity (the workspace has a diamond icon next to it in the navigation pane). Lastly, Power BI will reject the report if it has any unsupported features. For example, preview limitations preclude shared data sources and datasets, subreports, and drillthrough reports.

Managing paginated reports

Currently, the SSRS toolset (SSDT and Report Builder) doesn't support publishing to Power BI so you must upload the report manually by following these steps:

1. Sign in to Power BI Service (powebi.com) and navigate to an app workspace in a premium capacity.
2. Click Get Data. In the Get Data page, click the Files tile and choose Local File.
3. Navigate to the folder where the report file (*.rdl) is saved and double-click the file to upload it.
4. In the Power BI navigation bar, click the workspace to go to the workspace content page and then click the Reports tab (see **Figure 14.9**).

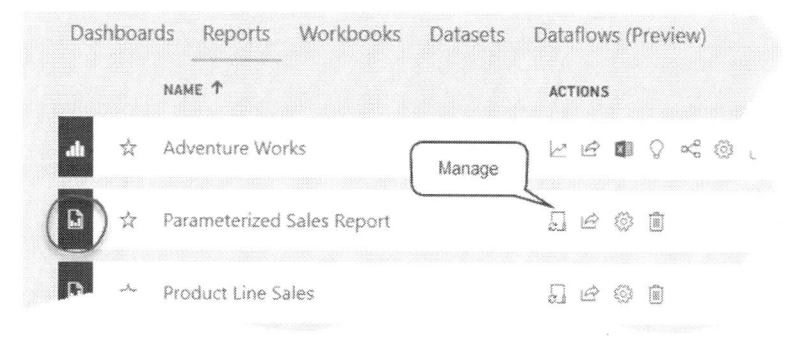

Figure 14.9 You can manage and share paginated reports in the Power BI Portal.

Notice that paginated reports have a special icon and have associated actions. The Manage action lets you manage the report settings (a preview limitation is that you can manage only the data source settings). Click Share to share the report with other users just like you can share a Power BI report. The Settings action lets you change the report name and the Delete action removes the report.

5. Click Manage. Click the AdventureWorks data source link. Verify the authentication method and make changes if needed.

Viewing paginated reports

Now that the report is published and configured, you can view it.

1. In the Reports tab, click the Parameterized Sales Report to run it.

Figure 14.10 You can view and interact with published paginated reports.

Power BI renders the report online (see **Figure 14.10**). Power BI generates a helpful report toolbar.

2. Expand the File menu and notice that you can print the report and download the report file.
3. Expand the Export menu and notice that you can export the report in any of the SSRS supported export formats, such as Excel and PDF.
4. Change the Store Identifier report parameter and click View Report to regenerate the report.
5. (Optional) Open the Power BI app on your mobile device and view the paginated report. Unlike on-premises paginated reports, which are not supported in Power BI Mobile, paginated reports published to Power BI are supported.

14.3 Implementing Real-time BI Solutions

The growing volume of real-time data and the reduced time for decision making are driving companies to implement real-time operational intelligence systems. You might have heard the term "Internet of Things" (IoT), which refers to sensors, devices, and systems that constantly generate data. Unlike the classic descriptive BI architecture (which is all about analyzing the past), real-time data analytics is concerned about what happens now. For example, Adventure Works might be interested in sentiment analysis, based on customer feedback that was shared on popular social networks, such as Twitter. A descriptive approach would require you to import customer data, transform it, and then analyze it.

But what if you're interested in what customers are saying *now*? Your implementation approach might depend on your definition of "now", and what data latency is acceptable. Perhaps, you can run ETL more often and still address your requirements with the classic BI architecture? However, if you need to analyze data as it streams, then you'll need a different approach. Fortunately, Power BI supports streaming API, that makes it easy to push data to Power BI and show the data in a dashboard that changes as the new data streams in. You can meet more advanced requirements with complex event processing (CEP) solutions. Microsoft StreamInsight, which ships with SQL Server, allows you to implement on-premises real-time BI solutions. And Microsoft Azure Stream Analytics is its cloud-based counterpart.

14.3.1 Using the Streaming API

The simplest way to stream data in Power BI is to use its real-time API – a lightweight, simple way to get real-time data onto a Power BI dashboard. It only takes a few lines of code to write a custom app that programmatically accesses the data as it streams in and then pushes the data to Power BI! For example, you might have a requirement to show call center statistics real-time as calls are handled. The phone system might provide a TCP socket, which your application can connect to and get the data stream. Then your app can push some statistics, such as the count of handled calls, to a Power BI dashboard. Let's cover quickly the implementation steps.

> **REAL LIFE** Before streaming datasets, a developer had to programmatically create a dataset using the Power BI API (discussed in the next chapter), define a table, and then call the "Add Rows to Table" API to populate the dataset. This approach doesn't require much code and it's still supported but Power BI has subsequently made data streaming even easier with streaming datasets and streaming tiles.

To help you get started with the real-time streaming API, Microsoft has provided a sample C# console app PBIRealTimeStreaming. For your convenience, I included the source code in the \Source\ch14\Real-time folder. The app pushes the current date and a random integer to the Power BI REST API every second. As a first step to implementing a real-time dashboard, you need to create a streaming dataset.

Implementing a streaming dataset

A streaming dataset is a special dataset that has a push URL attached to it. Your app calls this URL using HTTP POST to push the data. Follow these steps to create a streaming dataset:

1. Log in to Power BI Service. If you want to create the dataset in an app workspace so it can be shared with other people, navigate to that workspace. Otherwise, click My Workspace to go to the workspace content page.
2. In the upper-right corner, expand the Create menu and then click "Streaming dataset".

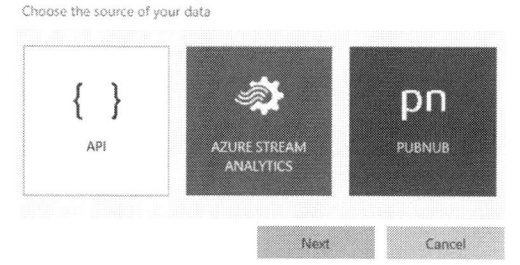

Figure 14.11 Power BI supports API, Azure Streaming Analytics, and PubNub as sources for pushing data into a streaming dataset.

3. On the "Choose the source of your data" page (see **Figure 14.11**), you choose where the streaming data will come from. Currently, Power BI supports the streaming API, Azure Stream Analytics, and PubNub as streaming sources (see **Figure 14.11**). Leave API selected and click Next.

> **NOTE** What's PubNub? PubNub (https://www.pubnub.com) is a cloud service that allows developers to build real-time web, mobile, and IoT apps. With Power BI's PubNub integration, you can connect your PubNub data streams to Power BI in seconds, to create low latency visualizations on top of streaming data.

4. In the dataset properties page (**Figure 14.12**), enter *Real-time API* as the dataset name. Our dataset will have only two fields: *ts* (DateTime data type) and *value* (Text data type).

The "Historic data analysis" slide corresponds to the dataset's defaultRetentionPolicy setting. The dataset will store up to 200,000 rows. After that, as new rows come in, old rows will be removed from the dataset. If you turn the slider on, the dataset won't remove old rows and it will grow until its maximum allowed size allowed by Power BI Service.

5. Click Create. The Real-time API dataset is added to the workspace.

The next page (API info on Real-time API) shows the Push URL and different ways to load the dataset (Raw, cURL, and PowerShell). For example, your app can submit the following raw payload to insert the value 98.6 for a specific date in the dataset.

[{"ts" :"2016-12-04T18:17:01.020Z", "value" :98.6}]

6. Copy the Push URL and click Done. You can also get the Push URL later from the dataset properties.
7. Locate the dataset in the Datasets tab and notice that its API Access property shows Streaming.

Figure 14.12 Specify the dataset name, fields, and retention policy.

Implementing a real-time tile

Now that we have a place to store the streamed data, let's visualize it in a real dashboard.

1. Back to the workspace content page, expand the Create menu again and create a new dashboard. Type in *Real-time API* as the dashboard name, and then click Create.
2. In the Real-time API dashboard, click "+Add tile" in the dashboard menu.
3. In the Add Tile page, select the "Custom Streaming Data" source under Real-time Data, and click Next.
4. In the "Add a custom streaming data tile" page, select the Real-time API dataset and click Next. Notice if you don't have a streaming dataset, you can use this page to create one by clicking the "+Add streaming dataset" button.

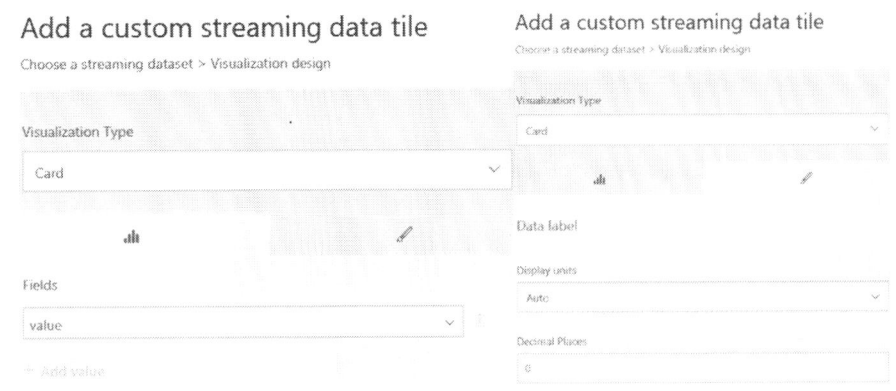

Figure 14.13 When configuring the real-time tile, specify the visualization type and fields to show.

5. In the "Visualization design" page (**Figure 14.13**), leave the Card visualization preselected. Click "Add value", then expand the Fields drop-down and select the *value* field. You can also show data as various charts or a gauge. Each visualization type requires different fields. For example, if you want to show the

streaming data as a line chart, you can bind the timestamp (ts) field to the Axis area and the value field to the Values area. By contrast, the Card visualization can show a single field.

6. Click the Format tab (the one with the pencil icon). Notice that you can specify basic format settings, including display units and the number of the decimal places. Click Next.
7. In the Tile Details page, enter *Real-time API* as the tile name. Notice that you can specify additional tile properties, such as a Subtitle and URL to navigate the user to a report when he clicks the tile. Click Apply to add the tile to the dashboard. A confirmation message will pop up and will give you an option to create a Phone view for the dashboard, which you can ignore.

Streaming data

The last piece left is to stream the actual data. This is where the PBIRealTimeStreaming sample comes in.

1. Open the PBIRealTimeStreaming.sln solution file in Visual Studio. If you don't have Visual Studio, install the free Visual Studio Community Edition from https://www.visualstudio.com/vs/community.
2. In the Solution Explorer, double-click the Program.cs file.
3. Locate the realTimePushURL variable and replace its value with the Push URL of your dataset.
4. Press Ctrl+F5 to run the application. Switch to Power BI Service and notice that the Real-time API tile updates every second with new data.

Behind the scenes, the sample uses the .NET WebRequest class to create a new POST request for each new row. The sample then sends the request to the dataset Push URL. You now have a real-time dashboard!

14.3.2 Using Azure Stream Analytics

As you've seen, it's easy to meet basic real-time BI needs with the Power BI streaming API. But what if your solution needs to ingest thousands of events per second and scale on demand. Or, what if you need to aggregate data as it streams in, such as to calculate the average count of calls for a given duration. Such requirements call for a complex event processing (CEP) solution, which you can implement with Azure Stream Analytics.

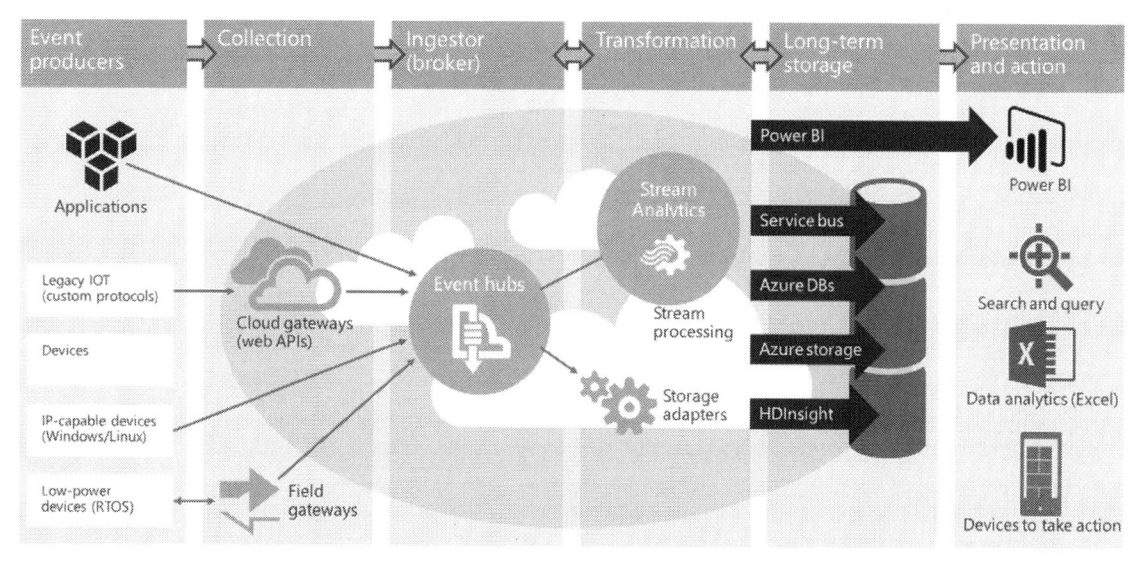

Figure 14.14 Stream Analytics is a cloud-based service and it's capable of processing millions of events per second.

Understanding Microsoft Azure Stream Analytics

Traditionally, implementing a complex event processing (CEP) solution has been difficult because…well, it's complex, and it requires a lot of custom code. Microsoft sought to change this by introducing Azure Stream Analytics as a fully managed stream-processing service in the cloud. Azure Stream Analytics provides low latency and real-time processing of millions of events per second in a highly resilient service (see its architecture in **Figure 14.14**).

Common real-time BI scenarios that will benefit from Stream Analytics include fraud detection, identity protection, real-time financial portfolio analysis, click-stream analysis, energy smart grid utilization, and Internet of Things (IoT) projects. Stream Analytics integrates with Azure Event Hubs, which is a highly scalable service for ingesting data streams. It enables the collection of event streams at high throughput from a diverse set of devices and services.

For example, Event Hubs is capable of processing millions of events per second via HTTP(S) or Advanced Message Queuing Protocol (AMQP) protocols. Once data is brought into Event Hubs, you can then use Stream Analytics to apply a standing SQL-like query for analyzing the data as it streams through, such as to detect anomalies or outliers. The query results can also be saved into long-term storage destinations, such as Azure SQL Database, HDInsight, or Azure Storage, and then you can analyze that data. Like the Power BI streaming API, Stream Analytics can output query results directly to Power BI streaming datasets, which in turn can update dashboard streaming tiles! This allows you to implement a real-time dashboard that updates itself constantly when Stream Analytics sends new results.

Now that you've learned about real-time BI, let me walk you through a sample solution that demonstrates how Azure Stream Analytics and Power BI can help you implement CEP solutions. Suppose that Adventure Works is interested in analyzing customer sentiment from messages that are posted on Twitter. This is immediate feedback from its customer base, which can help the company improve its products and services. Adventure Works wants to monitor the average customer sentiment about specific topics in real time. **Figure 14.15** shows you the process flow diagram.

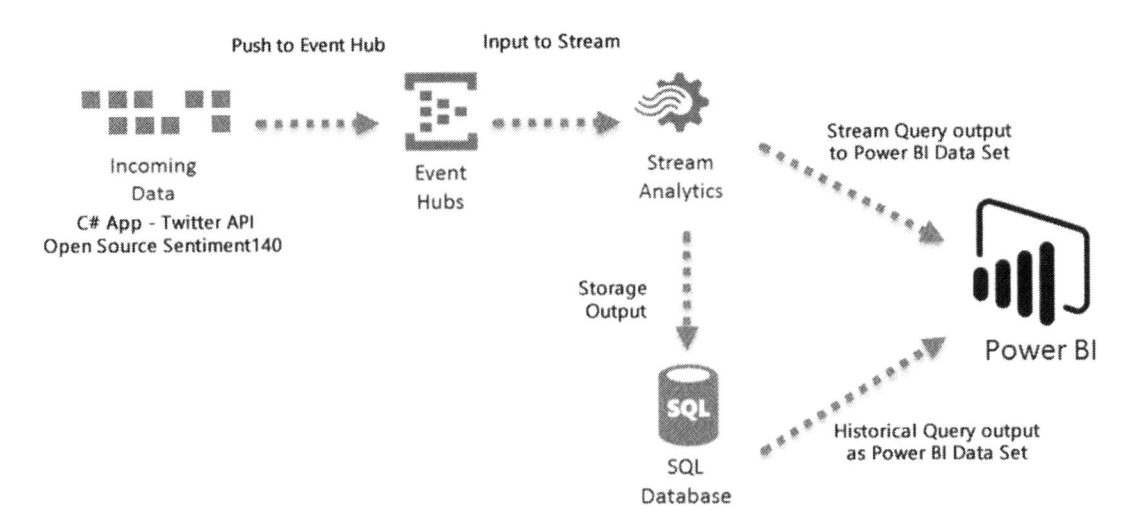

Figure 14.15 This solution demonstrates how you can integrate Stream Analytics with Power BI.

Instead of building the entire solution from scratch, I decided to use the Real-time Twitter sentiment analysis sample by Microsoft. You can download the code from GitHub (https://github.com/Azure/azure-stream-analytics/tree/master/DataGenerators/TwitterClient) and read the documentation from https://github.com/Azure/azure-content/blob/master/articles/stream-analytics/stream-analytics-twitter-sentiment-analysis-trends.md or online at https://azure.microsoft.com/en-us/documentation/articles/stream-analytics-twitter-sentiment-analysis-trends.

> **NOTE** This sample demonstrates how remarkably simple it is to implement CEP cloud solutions with Stream Analytics. You only need to write custom code to send events to Events Hub. By contrast, a similar StreamInsight-based application would require much more coding on your part, as the Big Data Twitter Demo (http://twitterbigdata.codeplex.com) demonstrates. That's because you'd need to write the plumbing code for observers, adapters, sinks, and more.

Understanding the client application

Designed as a C# console application, the client app uses the Twitter APIs to filter tweets for specific keywords that you specify in the app.config file. To personalize the demo for our fictitious bike manufacturer, (Adventure Works), I used the keywords "Bike" and "Adventure". In the same file, you must specify the Twitter OAuth settings that you obtain when you register a custom application with Twitter. For more information about registering an application with Twitter and about obtaining the security settings, read the "Tokens from dev.twitter.com" topic at https://dev.twitter.com/oauth/overview/application-owner-access-tokens.

Note that the client app (as coded by Microsoft) doesn't have any error handling. If you don't configure it correctly, it won't show any output and won't give you any indication of what's wrong. To avoid this and to get the actual error, I recommend that you re-throw errors in every catch block in the EventHubObserver.cs file.

```
catch (Exception ex)
{
   throw ex;
}
```

The application integrates with an open source tool (Sentiment140) to assign a sentiment value to each tweet (0: negative, 2: neutral, 4: positive). Then the tweet events are sent to the Azure Event Hubs. Therefore, to test the application successfully, you must first set up an event hub and configure Stream Analytics. If all is well, the application shows the stream of tweets in the console window as they're sent to the event hub.

Configuring Stream Analytics

The documentation that accompanies the sample provides step-by-step instructions to configure the Azure part of the solution. You can perform the steps using the old Azure portal (https://manage.windowsazure.com) or the new Azure portal (http://portal.azure.com). Instead of reiterating the steps, I'll just emphasize a few points that might not be immediately clear:

1. Before setting up a new Stream Analytics job, you must create an event hub that ingests that data stream.
2. After you create the hub, you need to copy the connection information from the hub registration page and paste it in the EventHubConnectionString setting in the client application app.config file. This is how the client application connects to the event hub.
3. When you set up the Stream Analytics job, you can use sample data to test the standing query. You must have run the client application before this step so that the event hub has some data in it. In addition, make sure that the date range you specify for sampling returns tweet events.
4. This is the standing query that I used for the Power BI dashboard:

```
SELECT System.Timestamp as Time, Topic, COUNT(*), AVG(SentimentScore), MIN(SentimentScore),
Max(SentimentScore), STDEV(SentimentScore)
FROM TwitterStream TIMESTAMP BY CreatedAt
GROUP BY TUMBLINGWINDOW(s, 5), Topic
```

This query divides the time in intervals of five seconds. A tumbling window is one of the window types that's supported by both Stream Analytics and SQL Server StreamInsight (read about windowing at https://msdn.microsoft.com/en-us/library/azure/dn835055.aspx). Within each interval, the query groups the incoming events by topic and calculates the event count, minimum, maximum, average sentiment score, and the standard deviation. Because stream analytics queries are described in a SQL-like grammar, you can leverage your SQL query skills.

> **NOTE** Unlike SQL SELECT queries, which execute once, Stream Analytics queries are standing. To understanding this, imagine that the stream of events passes through the query. As long as the Stream Analytics job is active, the query is active and it's always working. In this case, the query divides the stream in five-second intervals and calculates the aggregates on the fly.

Outputting data to Power BI

A Stream Analytics job can have multiple outputs, such as to save the query results to a durable storage for offline analysis and to display them on a real-time dashboard. **Figure 14.16** shows that I selected Power BI as an output (other input types include SQL Database, Blob Storage, Cosmos DB, Azure Data Lake, and more). Follow these steps to configure Stream Analytics to send the output to Power BI.

> **NOTE** If Power BI has a dataset and table that have the same names as the ones that you specify in the Stream Analytics job, the existing ones are overwritten. Although you can create a Stream Analytics dataset beforehand, you should let Stream Analytics create it. The dataset will be automatically created when you start your Stream Analytics job and the job starts pumping output into Power BI. If your job query doesn't return any results, the dataset won't be created.

1. In the "Add an output to your job" step, select Power BI. Click the Authorize button to sign in to Power BI.
2. In "Output details" (see again **Figure 14.16**), enter the name of the Power BI dataset and table names. You can send results from different queries to separate tables within the same dataset. If the table with the same name exists, it'll be overwritten.

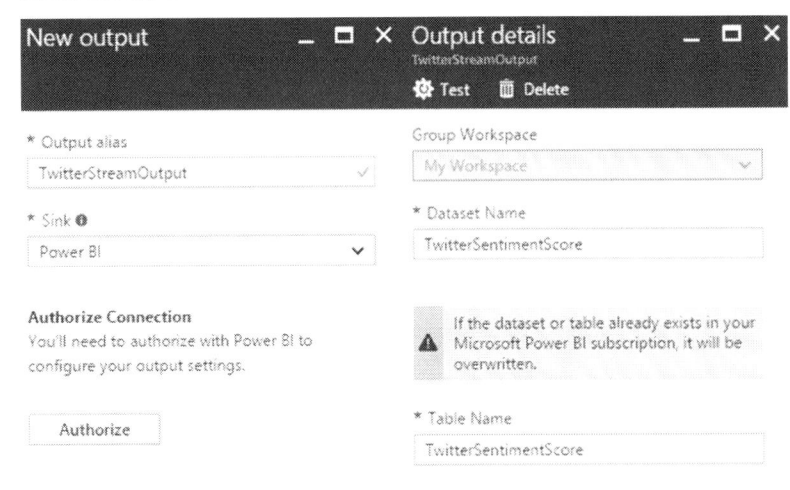

Figure 14.16 Specify Power BI as a sink and then the names of the dataset and table where the results will be loaded.

Creating a real-time dashboard

Now that all the setup steps are behind us, we're ready to have fun with the data:

1. Run the Stream Analytics job. It might take a while for the job to initiate, so monitor its progress on the Stream Analytics dashboard page.
2. Once the job is started, it'll send the query results to Power BI, assuming there are incoming events that match the query criteria. Power BI will create a dataset with the name you specified.

> **TIP** You can create a streaming tile using the Azure Streaming Analytics dataset type, like what you did in the previous example. This allows you to implement the two most common real-time requirements: 1) showing the latest value and 2) showing values on a line chart over a time window. However, if you want to use another Power BI visual, you can just explore the dataset.

3. Now you log in to Power BI Service and explore the dataset.
4. To show the data in real time, you need to create a dashboard by pinning the report visualization. The dashboard tile in **Figure 14.17** is based on a report visualization that uses a Combo Chart. It shows the count of events as columns and the average sentiment score as a line over time.

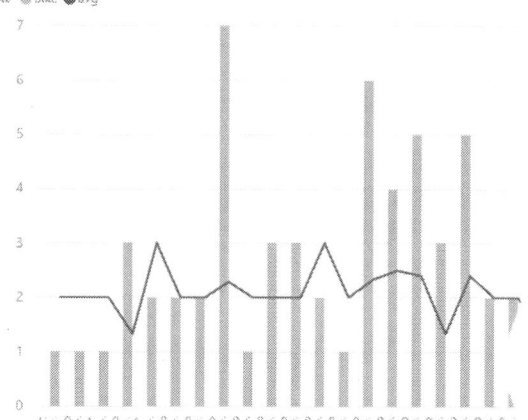

Figure 14.17 Power BI updates a real-time dashboard as Stream Analytics streams the events.

5. Watch the dashboard update itself as new data is coming in, and you gain real-time insights from your CEP solution!

14.4 Summary

As a BI pro, you can meet more demanding business requirements and implement versatile solutions with Power BI and Azure cloud services. You can preserve the investments you've made in classic BI by integrating Power BI with Analysis Services. This allows you to implement a hybrid scenario, where data remains on premises, and Power BI reports and dashboards connect live to Analysis Services.

Many organizations have made significant investments in SQL Server Reporting Services (SSRS). SSRS paginated (RDL) reports are the most customizable and extensible report type in the Microsoft BI ecosystem. You can publish and integrate these reports with Power BI so that you have a one-stop cloud BI platform for Power BI reports, Excel reports, and paginated reports.

If you need to implement real-time solutions that analyze data streams, you'll save significant effort by using the Power BI Streaming API. And, when requirements call for complex event processing (CEP) solutions, Azure Stream Analytics Service will make your task much easier. It's capable of ingesting millions of events per second. You can create a standing query to analyze the data stream and send the results to a real-time Power BI dashboard.

Thanks to its open architecture, Power BI supports other integration scenarios that application developers will find very appealing, as you'll see in the next part of this book.

PART

Power BI for Developers

One of Power BI's most prominent strengths is its open APIs, which will be very appealing to developers. When Microsoft architected the Power BI APIs, they decided to embrace popular industry standards and formats, such as REST, JSON, and OAuth2. This allows any application on any platform to integrate with the Power BI APIs. This part of the book shows developers how they can extend Power BI and implement custom solutions that integrate with Power BI.

I'll start by laying out the necessary programming fundamentals for programming with Power BI. I'll explain how Power BI security works. Then I'll walk you through a sample application that uses the REST APIs to programmatically retrieve Power BI content and to load datasets with application data. If you're a PowerShell fan, I'll show you how you can automate similar tasks with PowerShell scripts.

Chances are that your organization is looking for ways to embed insightful BI content on internal and external applications. Thanks to the embedded APIs, Power BI supports this scenario, and I'll walk you through the implementation details of embedding dashboards and reports. Then you'll see how Power BI Embedded makes report embedding even easier.

As you've likely seen, Power BI has an open visualization framework. Web developers can implement custom visuals and publish them to Microsoft Store. If you're a web developer, you'll see how you can leverage your experience with popular JavaScript-visualization frameworks, such as D3, WebGL, Canvas, or SVG, to create custom visuals that meet specific presentation requirements, and if you wish, you can contribute your custom visualizations to the community!

Chapter 15

Programming Fundamentals

15.1 Understanding Power BI APIs 389
15.2 Understanding OAuth Authentication 394
15.3 Working with Power BI APIs 402

15.4 Working with PowerShell 405
15.5 Summary 407

Developers can build innovative solutions around Power BI. In the previous chapters, I've showed examples of descriptive, predictive, and real-time BI solutions that use existing Microsoft products and services. Sometimes, however, developers are tasked to extend custom applications with data analytics features, such as to implement real-time dashboards for operational analytics. Because of the open Power BI APIs, you can integrate any modern application on any platform with Power BI!

If you're new to Power BI development, this chapter is for you. I'll start by introducing you to the Power BI APIs. You'll find how to register your custom applications so that they can access the Power BI APIs. I'll demystify one of the most complex programming topics surrounding Power BI programming: OAuth authentication. I'll walk you through some sample code that demonstrates how a custom app can integrate with the Power BI APIs. Lastly, I'll show you how you can use PowerShell to automate Power BI tasks if you prefer scripts.

15.1 Understanding Power BI APIs

When Microsoft worked on the Power BI APIs, they adopted the following design principles:

- Embrace industry standards – Instead of implementing proprietary interfaces, the team looked at other popular cloud and social platforms, and decided to adopt already popular open standards, such as Representational State Transfer (REST) programming (https://en.wikipedia.org/wiki/Representational_state_transfer), OAuth authorization (https://en.wikipedia.org/wiki/OAuth), and JavaScript Object Notation (JSON) for describing object schemas and data (https://en.wikipedia.org/wiki/JSON).

- Make it cross platform – Because of the decision to use open standards, the Power BI APIs are cross platform. Any modern native or web app on any platform can integrate with Power BI.

- Make it consistent – If you have experience with the above-mentioned industry specifications, you can seamlessly transfer your knowledge to Power BI programming. Consistency also applies within Power BI so that the APIs reflect the same objects as the ones the user interacts with in the Power BI portal.

- Easy to get started – Nobody wants to read tons of documentation before writing a single line of code. To help you get up to speed, the Power BI team created a Power BI Developer Center site where you can try the APIs as you read about them!

TIP Are you a PowerShell fan? Besides the APIs, Microsoft has provided PowerShell cmdlets for automating tasks. I'll provide comprehensive coverage of PowerShell for Power BI in the last section of this chapter.

15.1.1 Understanding Object Definitions

As I've just mentioned, one of the design goals was consistency within Power BI. To understand this better, let's revisit the three main Power BI objects: *datasets*, *reports*, and *dashboards*. Please refer to the diagram shown in **Figure 15.1**, which shows their relationships.

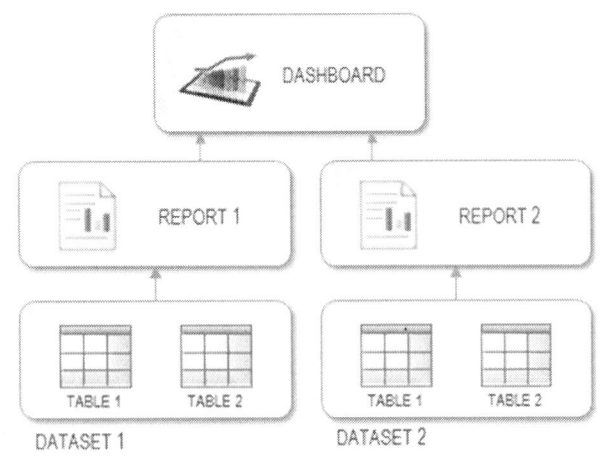

Figure 15.1 The main Power BI objects are datasets, reports, and dashboards.

Understanding dataset definitions

As you might know by now, the dataset object is the representation of your data in Power BI. A dataset connects to the data, and the other two main objects (reports and dashboards) show data from datasets. Specifically, a report can reference a single dataset. A dashboard can include visualizations from multiple reports, and thus display data from multiple datasets. From a developer standpoint, the dataset object has this JSON definition:

```
{
    "id": "<dataset guid>",
    "name": "<dataset name>",
    "addRowsAPIEnabled": <True, if the dataset allows adding new rows>,
    "configuredBy": "<dataset author's email>",
    "isRefreshable": <True, if the dataset can be refreshed>,
    "isEffectiveIdentityRequired":  <True, if the dataset is configured for row-level security or connects live to AS>,
    "isEffectiveIdentityRolesRequired": <True, if the dataset has security roles>,
    "isOnPremGatewayRequired": <True, if the dataset users on-premises data sources>
}
```

As you can see, a dataset has a unique identifier of a GUID data type and a name. The JSON name property returns the dataset name you see in the Power BI portal's navigation bar.

> **NOTE** If the dataset is created programmatically (using the Datasets Post Dataset API), its definition includes additional items, such as tables[], relationships[], and measures[] collections. This allows you to programmatically create datasets that have the same parity as datasets created in Power BI Desktop and load their tables with data.

Understanding report definitions

A report has the following JSON definition:

```
{
    "datasetId": "<dataset guid>",
    "id": "<report guid>",
    "name": "<report name>",
    "webUrl": "<the report web Url>",
    "embedUrl": "<the report embed Url"
}
```

This definition specifies the identifier of the dataset the report is bound to (recall that a report can connect to only one dataset), report identifier, report name, the report Url (as shown in the browser address bar), and embedUrl (required for Power BI Embedded).

Understanding dashboard definitions
A dashboard has the following definition:

```
{
  "id": "<dashboard guid>",
  "displayName": "<dashboard name>",
  "embedUrl": "<the dashboard embed Url>",
  "isReadOnly": <True, if the dashboard is cannot be changed, such as when distributed by an app>
}
```

This definition specifies the dashboard identifier, dashboard name, the embedUrl (required for Power BI Embedded), and if the dashboard is read-only in the workspace.

15.1.2 Understanding Operations

Some of the tasks you can perform in the Power BI Portal are exposed as Power BI APIs to let developers automate them. Because of the importance of datasets, the initial set of APIs was centered around dataset manipulation. Later, the team added APIs to list and manage groups, dashboards, reports, push datasets, gateways, and more. In this section, you'll learn about the capabilities of the existing operations. These operations are fully described in the "Power BI REST API reference" documentation at bit.ly/powerbiapi.

> **NOTE** The Power BI documentation has previously integrated with Apiary to let you test and learn the APIs interactively. This integration was discontinued in 2018 but the team has plans to provide a similar feature in near future.

Understanding verbs
As I mentioned, the Power BI REST APIs are based on a programming specification for method invocation over HTTP, called Representational State Transfer (or REST for short). Because the same API can serve different purposes, REST supports a set of HTTP verbs to indicate the purpose of the operation. For example, to get the list of existing datasets, you'll use the GET verb. Power BI supports the most common HTTP verbs, as shown in **Table 15.1**.

Table 15.1 Power BI supports four HTTP verbs.

Verb	Operation	Success Response Codes	Error Response Codes
GET	Read	200 (OK)	404 (Not Found) or 400 (Bad Request).
POST	Create	201 (Created)	404 (Not Found), 409 (Conflict) if resource already exists
PUT	Update	200 (OK) (or 204 if not returning any content in response body)	404 (Not Found) if ID is not found
DELETE	Delete	200 (OK)	404 (Not Found) if ID is not found

The HTTP GET operation is used to retrieve a representation of a resource, such as a dataset collection using the Get Datasets operation. When executed successfully, GET returns the JSON representation in the response body. POST is used to create a new resource, such as a new dataset. Upon successful completion, it returns the HTTP status 201 and a Location header with a link to the newly created resource.

You typically use the PUT verb to update an existing resource by using the unique identifier of the resource, such as to create a push dataset using the PostDataset operation. Upon a successful update, you'll get a response code of 200 (or 204 if the API doesn't return any content in the response body). Finally, given an identifier, DELETE removes the specified resource, such as a given row in a dataset table using the DeleteRows operation.

Let's explain the purpose of the most significant operations.

Understanding the Admin operations

This group of operations is for automating administrative tasks, such as to get a list of all published dashboards in the entire tenant or dashboards in a specific workspace. We further organize the admin operations into these groups:

- Dashboard operations – Get dashboards in tenant or workspace, get dashboard tiles.
- Datasets operations – Get datasets in tenant or workspace, get data sources in a dataset.
- Workspace operations – Get workspaces, grant user rights to a workspace, delete workspace members, restore deleted workspaces. Some operations, such as a restoring a deleted workspace, require the new workspace experience.
- Imports – Get a list of datasets that are programmatically imported from Power BI Desktop, Excel, or text files.
- Reports – Get a list of reports in tenant or workspace.

Understanding the Capacity operations

These operations are automating Power BI Premium capacities. They allow you to enumerate provisioned capacities and assign workspaces to capacities. For example, you can call GetGroupsAsAdmin to enumerate all app workspaces in the tenant, check the isOnDedicatedCapacity property of each workspace and move in or out of the capacity.

Understanding the Dashboard operations

The dashboard operations allow you to work with dashboards and tiles. This is useful if you need to embed dashboards and tiles in a custom app, as I'll cover in the next chapter. We can organize the dashboard operations into these groups:

- Dashboard operations – Create an empty dashboard in My Workpace or an app workspace, enumerate dashboards in a workspace, get the dashboard definition.
- Tile operations – Clone tiles, get the definition of a tile, enumerate tiles in a dashboard.

For example, the "Get Dashboards" operation returns a list of dashboards in My Workspace. Every dashboard element in the response body has a GUID identifier, name, and an *isReadOnly* property that indicates whether the dashboard is read-only, such as when it's shared with you by someone else or when you're a member with read-only permissions of a workspace. The "Get Tiles" operation takes the dashboard identifier and returns a collection of the dashboard tiles. Here's a sample JSON format that describes the "This Year's Sales" tile of the Retail Analysis Sample dashboard:

{
    "id": "b2e4ef32-79f5-49b3-94bc-2d228cb97703",
    "title": "This Year's Sales",
    "subTitle": "by Chain",
    "embedUrl": https://app.powerbi.com/embed?dashboardId=<dashboard id>&tileId=b2e4ef32-79f5-49b3-94bc-2d228cb97703,

```
    "rowSpan": 0,
    "colSpan": 0,
    "reportId": "{report_id}",
    "datasetId": "{dataset_id}"
}
```

From a content embedding standpoint, the most important element is *embedUrl*, because your application needs it to reference a tile.

Understanding the Dataset operations
The dataset-related operations are centered around the manipulation of datasets and automating refresh.

- Dataset operations – Enumerate and delete datasets, get the dataset definition.
- Gateway operations – Discover gateways used by a dataset, bind a dataset to a gateway.
- Data source operations – Discover data sources in a dataset, set connection strings.
- Refresh operations – Refresh a dataset.
- Parameter operations -- Get and set the Power Query parameters for a dataset.

Understanding the Embed Token operations
Power BI Embedded uses embed tokens to authorize access to content. The Embed Token operations are for generating tokens to access dashboards, reports, and datasets for the purpose of embedding them in custom apps.

Understanding the Gateways operations
You can use the Gateway operations to manipulate gateways configured in standard mode and registered in your tenant. Besides enumerating gateways and data sources, there are operations to create, delete, and update data sources for a specific gateway.

Understanding the Group operations
Instead of referring to "groups", these are workspace-related operations (recall that the old-style workspaces are backed by Office 365 groups). Recall that besides My Workspace, users can access other workspaces that they are members of. Therefore, to present the user with all the objects he has access to, a custom app must enumerate not only the user's My Workspace but also all other app workspaces he's a member of.

The operations let you enumerate, create and delete workspaces, as well as manipulate the workspace membership, such as to add or delete a workspace member. What if you want to retrieve objects from another workspace that you're a part of through your group membership, such as to list the datasets from the Finance workspace, or to create a new dataset that's shared by all the members of a group? Fortunately, the dataset, dashboard, and report operations support specifying a group. For example, to list all the datasets for a specific group, you can invoke https://api.PowerBI.com/v1.0/myorg/**groups/{group_id}**/datasets, where group_id is the unique group identifier that you can obtain by calling the "List all groups" operation. As it stands, the developer's console doesn't allow you to change the operation signature, so you can't use the group syntax when testing the APIs, but you can use it in your applications.

Understanding the Import operations
The import APIs let you programmatically upload a Power BI Desktop file (*.pbix) or an Excel file to a workspace. This could be useful if you want to automate the deployment process of uploading datasets and reports but remember that organizational apps might be an easier and a more flexible option to distribute content to many users.

For example, the "Get Imports" operation lists all files that were imported in "My Workspace". For each file, the operation returns when the file was imported and updated, and the datasets and reports that were included in the file. The "Create Import" operation is for automating the task for importing a file. To call this operation, you must create a "POST" request whose body includes a filePath parameter that points to the file to be uploaded. The actual import operation executes asynchronously.

Understanding the Push Datasets operations

You can programmatically create datasets just like you can do this in Power BI Desktop. Datasets that are created programmatically are called "push" datasets. These operations are for manipulating the dataset definition, such as enumerating and creating tables. For example, the PostDataset and PostDatasetInGroup operations are for creating push datasets in MyWorkspace or an app workspace.

> **NOTE** Besides tables, the "Create a dataset" operation also supports specifying relationships programmatically, DAX calculations, and additional modeling properties. This allows you to create datasets programmatically with the same features as in Power BI Desktop. For more information about these features, refer to the "New features for the Power BI Dataset API" blog by Josh Caplan at https://powerbi.microsoft.com/blog/newdatasets.

You can specify an optional *defaultRetentionPolicy* parameter of the push dataset. It controls the store capacity of the dataset. The retention policy becomes important when you start adding rows to the dataset, such as to supply data to a real-time dashboard. By default, the dataset will accumulate all the rows. However, if you specify defaultRetentionPolicy=basicFIFO, the dataset will store up to 200,000 rows. Once this limit is reached, Power BI will start purging old data as new data comes in (see **Figure 15.2**).

Figure 15.2 The basic FIFO dataset policy stores up to 200,000 rows and removes old data as new data flows in.

Once the dataset is created, you can load its tables with data using the Datasets PostRows operation or remove rows with Datasets DeleteRows.

Understanding the Report operations

Lastly, the report operations allow you to retrieve, clone, and export reports. There are also Rebind operations to rebind a report to another dataset in My Workspace or an app workspace. The Update Report Content operations are for updating the report definition (currently, you can only update the report definition from another report).

15.2 Understanding OAuth Authentication

Apiary makes it easy to understand and test the Power BI REST APIs. However, it hides an important and somewhat complex part of Power BI programming, which is security. You can't get much further beyond the console if you don't have a good grasp of how Power BI authentication and authorization works. And security is never easy. In fact, sometimes implementing security can be more complicated than the application itself. The good news is that Power BI embraces another open security standard, OAuth2, which greatly reduces the plumbing effort to authenticate users with Power BI! As you'll see in this chapter and the next one, OAuth2 is a flexible standard that supports various security scenarios.

> **REAL LIFE** Security can get complicated. I once architected a classic BI solution consisting of a data warehouse, cube, and reports for a card processing company. After a successful internal adoption, their management decided to allow external partners to view their own data. One of the security requirements was federating account setup and maintenance to the external partners. This involved setting up an Active Directory subdomain, a web application layer, and countless meetings. At the end, the security plumbing took more effort than the actual BI system!

15.2.1 Understanding Authentication Flows

OAuth2 allows a custom application to access Power BI Service on the user's behalf, after the user consents that this is acceptable. Next, the application gets the authorization code from Azure AD, and then exchanges it for an access token that provides access to Power BI.

Understanding the OAuth parties
There are three parties that are involved in the default three-leg authentication flow:
- User – This is the Power BI user.
- Application – This is a custom native client application or a web application that needs to access Power BI content on behalf of the user.
- Resource – In the case of Power BI, the resource is some content, such as a dataset or a report.

With the three-leg flow, the custom application never has the user's credentials because the entire authentication process is completely transparent to the application. However, OAuth opens a sign-in window so that the user can log in to Power BI. Microsoft refers to the three-leg flow as "user owns the data". In the case when the application knows the user credentials, OAuth2 supports a two-leg flow where the application directly authenticates the user to the resource. The two-leg flow bypasses the sign-in window, and the user isn't involved in the authentication flow. Microsoft refers to the two-leg flow as "application owns the data". I'll demonstrate the two-leg scenario in the next chapter.

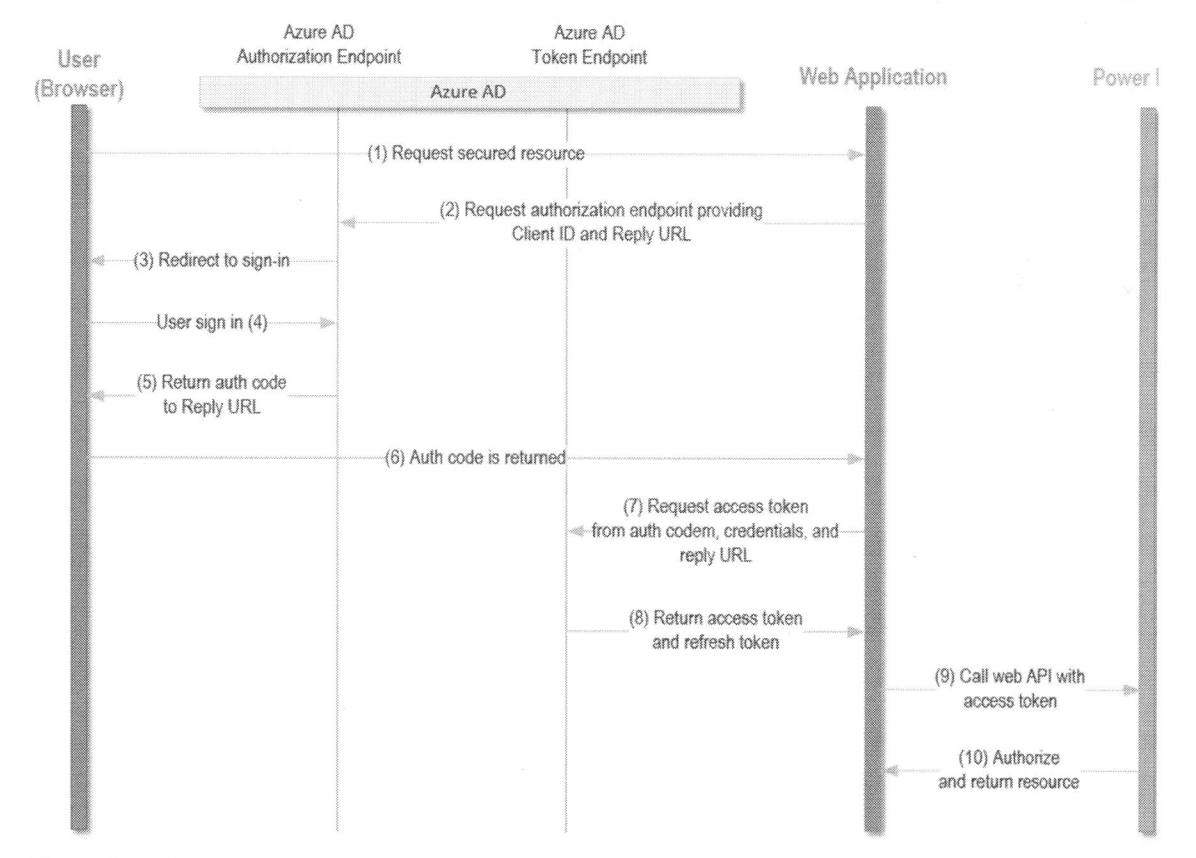

Figure 15.3 This sequence diagram shows the OAuth2 flow for web applications.

PROGRAMMING FUNDAMENTALS

Understanding the web application flow

Figure 15.3 shows the OAuth flow for web applications. By "web application", I mean any browser-based application, such as a custom ASP.NET application.

The typical authentication flow involves the following steps:

1. The user opens the Web browser and navigates to the custom application to request a Power BI resource, such as to view a report.
2. The web application calls to and passes the application client ID and Reply URL (AD). Azure Active Directory uses the client ID to identify the custom application. You obtain the client ID when you register your application with Azure AD. The Reply URL is typically a page within your application where Azure AD will redirect the user after the user signs in to Power BI.
3. Azure AD opens the Power BI sign-in page.
4. The user signs in using valid Power BI credentials. Note that the actual authentication is completely transparent to the application. The user might sign in using his Power BI credentials or, if the organization policy requires it, the user might use a smart card to authenticate. Azure AD determines the authentication mechanism depending on the AD corporate policy.

   NOTE The first time the user signs in, he will be asked to authorize the custom app for all the permissions you granted the app when you register it in the Azure AD. To see the authorized custom apps, the user can open the Power BI portal, and then click the Office 365 Application Launcher button (at the top-left corner of the portal) ⇨ "View all my apps". The user can use this menu to remove authorized custom applications at any point, and then see the granted permissions.

5. The Azure AD Authorization Endpoint service redirects the user to the page that's specified by the Reply URL, and it sends an authorization code as a request parameter.
6. The web application collects the authorization code from the request.
7. The web application calls down to the Azure AD Token Endpoint service to exchange the authorization code with an access token. In doing so, the application presents credentials consisting of the client id and client secret (also called a key). You can specify one or more keys when you register the application with Azure AD. The access token is the holy grail of OAuth because this is what your application needs to access the Power BI resources.
8. The Azure AD Token Endpoint returns an access token and a refresh token. Because the access token is short-lived, the application can use the refresh token to request additional access tokens instead of going again through the entire authentication flow.
9. Once the application has the access token, it can start making API calls on behalf of the user.
10. When you register the application, you specify an allowed set of Power BI permissions, such as "View all datasets". Power BI will evaluate these permissions when authorizing the call. If the user has the required permission, Power BI executes the API and returns the results.

Understanding the native client flow

A native client is any installed application that doesn't require the user to use the Web browser. A native client could be a console application, desktop application, or an application installed on a mobile device. **Figure 15.4** shows the OAuth sequence flow for native clients. As you can see, the authentication flow for native clients is somewhat simpler than the flow for web apps.

1. Before making a Power BI API call, the native client app calls to the Azure AD Authorization Endpoint and presents the client id. A native client application probably won't have a redirect page. However, because Azure AD requires a Redirect URI, a native client app can use any URI, if it matches the one you specified when you register the app with Azure AD. Or, if you're running out of ideas of what this artificial URI might be, you can use the Microsoft suggested URI for native clients, which is https://login.live.com/oauth20_desktop.srf.

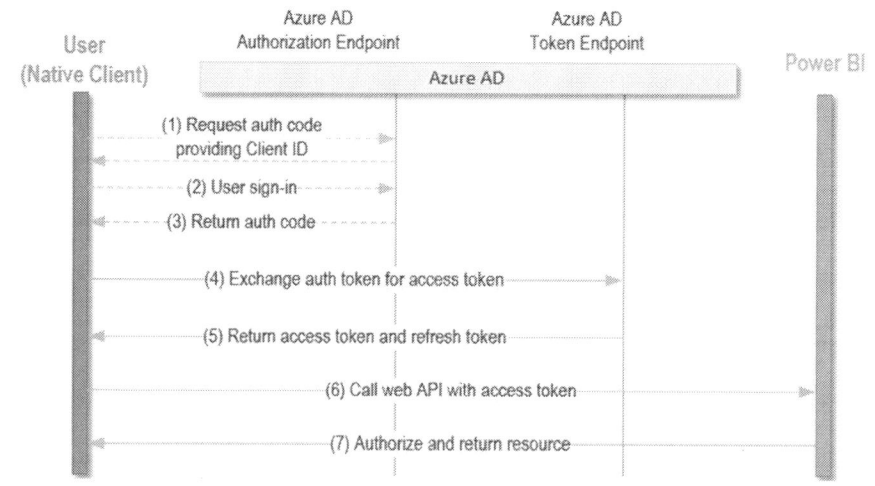

Figure 15.4 This sequence diagram shows the OAuth2 flow for native clients.

2. As with the web application flow, Azure AD will open the Web browser so that the user can sign in to Power BI. Again, the sign-in experience depends on how the organization is set up with Azure AD, but typically the user is asked to enter credentials in the Power BI sign-in page.

3. The Azure AD Authorization Endpoint returns an authorization code. The dotted lines in **Figure 15.4** represent that this handshake happens within a single call. All a .NET application needs to do is call the *AcquireToken* method of the *AuthenticationContext* class to get the user to sign in, and then acquire the authorization code. In fact, the *AquireToken* method also performs the next step (step 4) on the same call.

4. A handshake takes place between the native client and the Azure AD Token Endpoint to exchange the authorization code for an access token.

5. The Azure AD Token Endpoint returns an access token and a refresh token.

6. The client calls the Power BI resource passing the access token.

7. Power BI authorizes the user and executes the call if the user has the required permissions.

15.2.2 Understanding Application Registration

As a prerequisite of integrating custom applications with Power BI REST APIs, you must register the app with Azure AD. In the process of registering the application, you specify the OAuth2 details, including the type of the application (web or native client), keys, Redirect URL, and permissions. The easiest way to register a custom application is to use the Power BI registration page. You can also use the Azure Management Portal to register your application, but the process is more involved.

Note that although you can use the Power BI registration page for the initial registration process, you still need to use the Azure Management Portal to make subsequent changes, such as to change the Redirect URL. Next, I'll walk you through the steps to register web and native client applications using the Power BI registration page and Azure Management Portal.

Getting started with registration
The application registration page helps you create a new application in Azure AD that has all the information required to connect to Power BI. Anyone can register a custom application. You can find the Power BI registration page in the Power BI Developer Center, as follows:

1. Open your Web browser and navigate to the Power BI App Registration Tool at https://dev.powerbi.com/apps.
2. Sign in to Power BI with your existing account

Registering your application using the Power BI registration page
Figure 15.5 shows the app registration page (to preserve space, steps 3 and 4 are shown on the right).

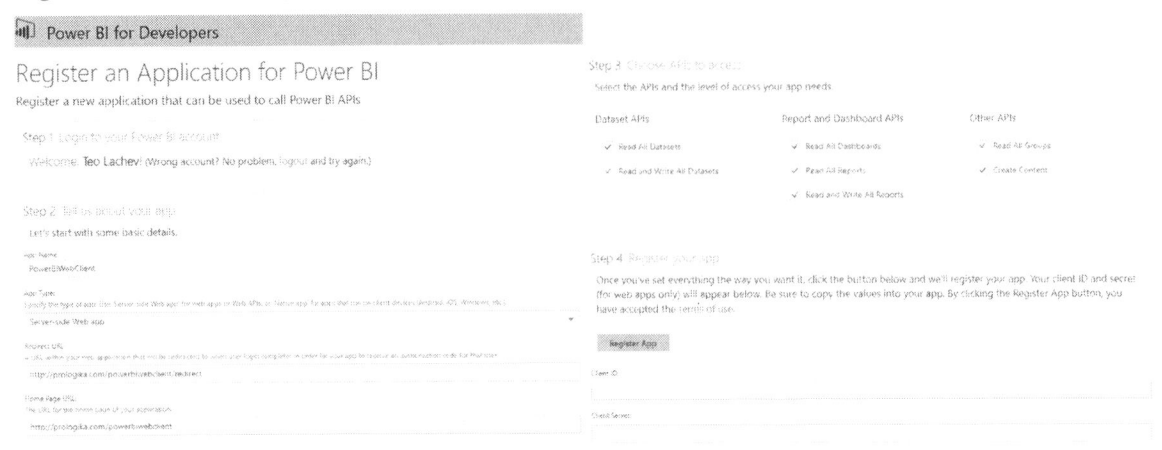

Figure 15.5 Register your custom app in four steps, using the Power BI registration page.

Registering a custom application takes four simple steps:

1. Sign in to Power BI. Specify the app details (see **Table 15.2**).

Table 15.2 This table describes the application registration details.

Setting	Explanation	Example
App Type	Choose "Server-side Web app" for browser-based web apps, and choose "Native app" for an installed application, such a console app	
Redirect URL	The web page where Azure AD will redirect the user after the Power BI sign-in completes	http://localhost:999/powerbiwebclient/redirect (for web apps) https://login.live.com/oauth20_desktop.srf (for native apps)
Home Page URL (web apps only)	The URL for the home page of your application (used by Azure AD to uniquely identify your application)	http://prologika.com/powerbiwebclient

2. Specify which Power BI REST APIs your app needs permissions to call. For example, if the custom app needs to push data to a dataset table, you'll have to check the "Read and Write All Dataset permissions". As a best practice, grant the app the minimum set of permissions it needs. You can always change this later if you need to.
3. Click the Register App button to register your app. If all is well, you'll get back the client ID. For web apps, you'll also get a client secret (also called a key). As I mentioned, your custom web app needs the client secret to exchange the authorization code for an access token.

Because managing registered applications can't be done in Power BI, next I'll show you how you can use the Azure Management Portal to view, register, and manage custom apps. You must have Azure AD admin rights to your organization's Active Directory to register an application. In addition, although the basic features of Azure Active Directory are free, you need an Azure subscription to use the portal and this subscription must be associated with your organizational account.

> **TIP** Because Power BI currently doesn't let you update the registration details (you need to use the Azure Management Portal for this), if you develop a web app I recommend you put some thought in the Redirect URL. Chances are that during development, you would use the Visual Studio Development Server or IIS Express. The Redirect URL needs to match your development setup, such as to include localhost. Once the application is tested, your Azure administrator can use the Azure Management Portal to change your web app and to add a production Redirect URL, such as http://prologika.com/powerbiwebclient/redirect.

Registering web applications using Azure Management Portal

Follow these steps to register a custom web application in the Azure Management Portal:

1. Navigate to the Azure Management Portal (at https://portal.azure.com) and sign in with your organizational account. Again, the account you use must be associated with an Azure subscription.
2. In the navigation bar on the left, select Azure Active Directory. In the next page, click "App registrations" to view the registered applications (see **Figure 15.6**).

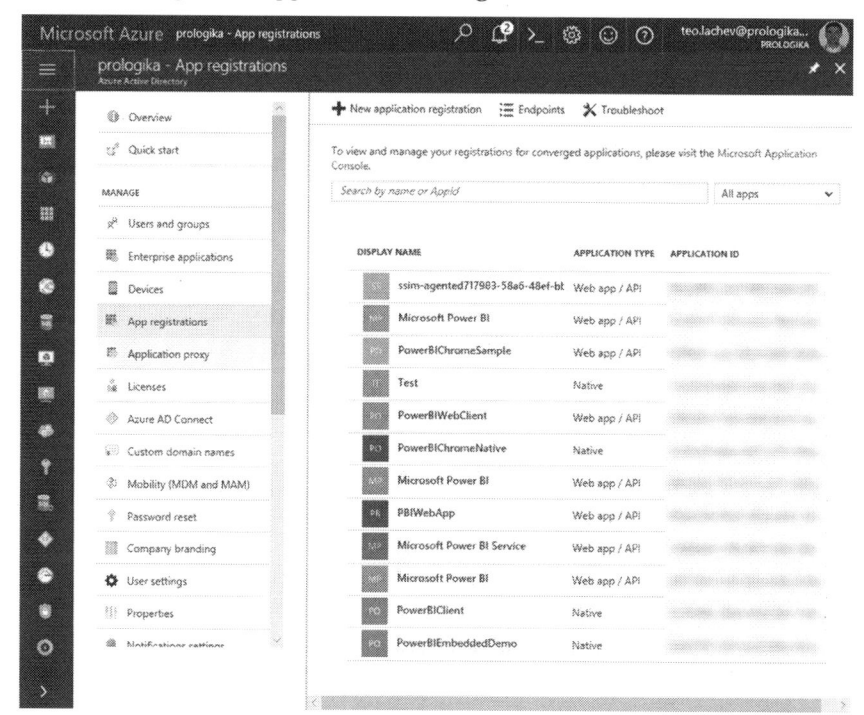

Figure 15.6 Select the "App registrations" tab to view and register custom applications.

3. On the top of the page, click "New application registration" to register a new app.
4. In the Create blade, enter the name of your application, such as *PowerBIWebClient* (see **Figure 15.7**). The name must be unique across the registered application within your organization. Because this is a web application, leave the default type of "Web app / API" selected. Enter the application Sign-on URL (same as "Home Page URL" in the Power BI registration page). This is the address of a web page where users can sign in to use your app, such as http://prologika.com/powerbiwebclient. Azure AD doesn't validate this URL, but it's required. Click Create to create the application. Once Azure creates the app, it adds it to the list of the registered apps.

PROGRAMMING FUNDAMENTALS

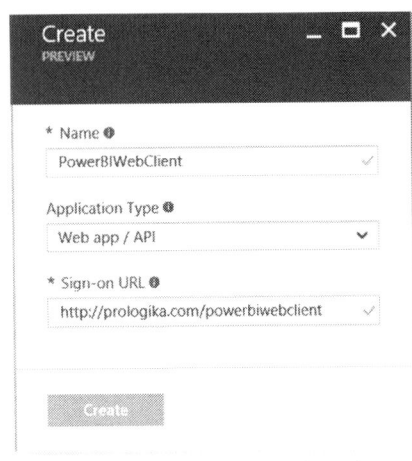

Figure 15.7 Specify the application name, application type (web or native), and sign-on URL.

5. In the app registrations, select the app you just registered to show its settings. The Settings blade is where you can configure the rest of the application registration details. It has Properties, Reply URLs, Owners, "Required permissions", and Keys tabs (see **Figure 15.8**).

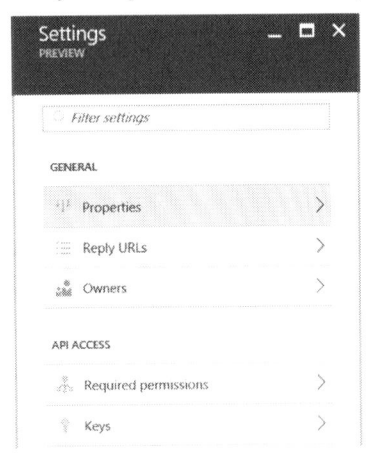

Figure 15.8 Use the Settings blade to configure the rest of the application registration details.

For example, in the Properties tab you can configure if the app has a multi-tenant scope. By default, the application isn't multi-tenant, meaning that only users on your domain can access the app. The "Reply URLs" tab allows you to specify one or more reply URLs (fulfill the same role as the redirect URL in the Power BI registration page) where Azure AD will redirect the user after the user signs in to Power BI. Enter a valid URL, such as http://prologika.com/powerbiwebclient/redirect. The Owners tab lets you register additional owners who can change the app settings.

6. So that Power BI can authorize your application, use the "Required permissions" tab to grant your app permissions to Power BI. To do this, select the "Power BI Service (Microsoft.Azure.AnalysisServices)" API. If you don't see "Power BI Service" in the list of applications, make sure that at least one user has signed up for and accessed Power BI. **Figure 15.9** shows you the permissions that Power BI currently supports or that are currently in preview.

Some of these permissions correspond to the available REST APIs that you see in the Power BI registration page. For example, if the application wants to get a list of the datasets available for the signed user, it needs to have the "View all Datasets" permission. As a best practice, grant the application the minimum permissions it needs.

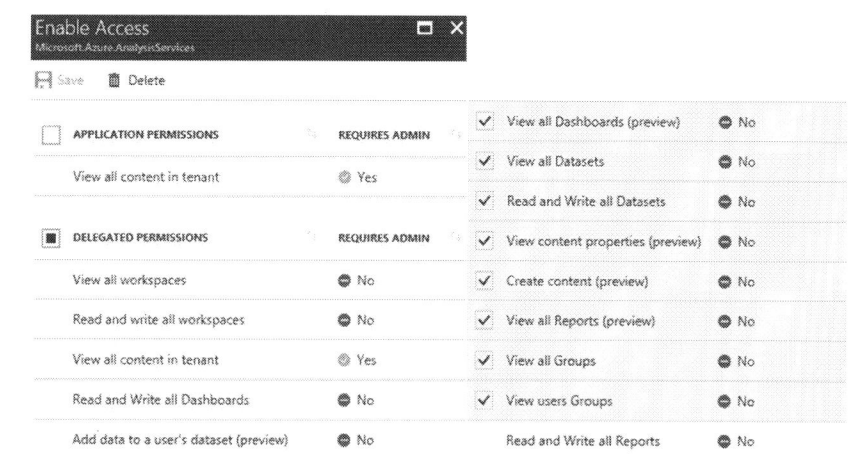

Figure 15.9 You must grant your application permissions to Power BI.

7. Use the Keys tab (see **Figure 15.10**) to create a key(s) (same as the client secret in the Power BI registration page) that you can use as a password when the application exchanges the authorization code for an access token. Currently, the maximum duration for the key validity is two years.

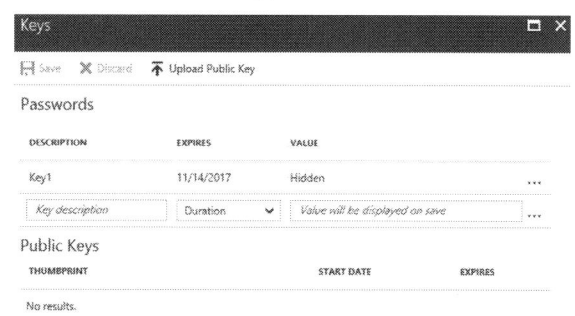

Figure 15.10 Create one or more client keys that your app will use to authenticate with Power BI.

Registering native clients
The native client registration is much simpler. The only required properties are the application name and Redirect URI. As I mentioned, you can use https://login.live.com/oauth20_desktop.srf as a Redirect URI. **Figure 15.11** shows a sample configuration for a native client application. As with registering a web app, you need to grant the native app permissions to Power BI (not shown in **Figure 15.11**).

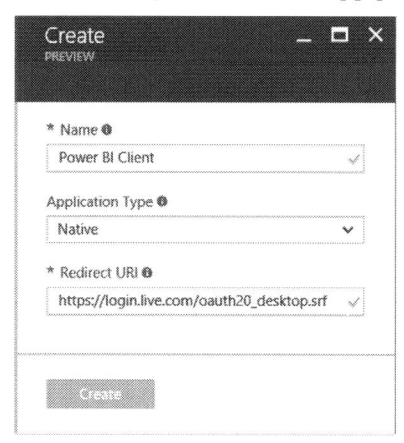

Figure 15.11 Registering a native client application requires a name and Redirect URI.

PROGRAMMING FUNDAMENTALS

15.3 Working with Power BI APIs

Now that you know about the Power BI REST APIS and how to configure custom applications for OAuth, let's practice what you've learned. Next, I'll walk you through a sample application that will help you get started with Power BI programming. While I was considering writing a sample from scratch, as it turned out Microsoft has already provided a sample app.

Implemented as a .NET console application, the PBIGettingStarted application demonstrates how a native client can authenticate and integrate with Power BI. I included the sample in the \Source\ch15 folder. You'll need Visual Studio 2015 or a higher version and valid Power BI credentials.

15.3.1 Implementing Authentication

Let's start with understanding how the application uses OAuth2 to authenticate the user before she makes calls to Power BI. As a prerequisite, you'll need to register a native client application in Azure AD.

Configuring the application

Before running the application, you need to change a few class-level variables to reflect your setup.

1. Open the PBIGettingStarted application in Visual Studio.
2. In Solution Explorer, double click Program.cs to open it.
3. Change the following variables:

```
private static string clientID = "<client_id>";
private static string redirectUri = "https://login.live.com/oauth20_desktop.srf";
private static string datasetName = "SalesMarketing";
private static string groupName = "Finance";
```

Replace the *clientID* variable with the Client ID of your application when you register it using either the Power BI registration method or from Azure AD (see **Figure 15.10** again). Replace the redirectUri variable with the Redirect URI of your application or leave it set to https://login.live.com/oauth20_desktop.srf if this is the Redirect URI that you register. One of the tasks that the application demonstrates is programmatically creating a new "SalesMarketing" dataset. If the dataset name isn't what you want, change it accordingly. The application demonstrates working with groups. To try this feature, use Power BI Service to create a workspace group, such as "Finance". Then, change the groupName variable to the name of the group. If you use Power BI Free, which doesn't support groups, you can just skip this part of the application.

Implementing OAuth

Every API invocation calls the *AccessToken* method, which performs the actual authentication. **Figure 15.12** shows the *DatasetRequest* method that is used by all dataset-related examples, such as when the application lists datasets (the *GetDatasets* method). The *DatasetRequest* method creates a web request object as required by the Power BI API specification. It adds an Authorization header with a Bearer property that specifies the access token. In case you're wondering, the access token is a base64-encoded hash that looks like this: "eyJ0eXAiOiJKV1QiLCJhbGciOiJSUzI1N…".

Remember that you need the access token to authenticate successfully with OAuth. The application obtains the token by calling the *AccessToken* method. Line 551 constructs a .NET *AuthenticationContext* class, passing the URL of the Azure AD Token Endpoint and an instance of a *TokenCache* class. I separated the original code to call *AcquireToken* into two lines to illustrate better what happens next. Line 553 calls *AcquireToken*. It passes the URL of the resource that needs to be authorized. In your case, the resource is Power BI and its resource URI is https://analysis.windows.net/powerbi/api. The code also passes the Client ID and the redirect URI.

```
543         static string AccessToken()
544         {
545             if (token == String.Empty)
546             {
547                 //Get Azure access token
548                 // Create an instance of TokenCache to cache the access token
549                 TokenCache TC = new TokenCache();
550                 // Create an instance of AuthenticationContext to acquire an Azure access token
551                 authContext = new AuthenticationContext(authority, TC);
552                 // Call AcquireToken to get an Azure token from Azure Active Directory token issuance endpoint
553                 AuthenticationResult result = authContext.AcquireToken(resourceUri, clientID, new Uri(redirectUri), PromptBehavior.RefreshSessic
554                 token = result.AccessToken;
555             }
556             else
557             {
558                 // Get the token in the cache
559                 token = authContext.AcquireTokenSilent(resourceUri, clientID).AccessToken;
560             }
561 
562             return token;
563         }
593         private static HttpWebRequest DatasetRequest(string datasetsUri, string method, string accessToken)
594         {
595             HttpWebRequest request = System.Net.WebRequest.Create(datasetsUri) as System.Net.HttpWebRequest;
596             request.KeepAlive = true;
597             request.Method = method;
598             request.ContentLength = 0;
599             request.ContentType = "application/json";
600             request.Headers.Add("Authorization", String.Format( "Bearer {0}", accessToken));
601 
602             return request;
603         }
604     }
605 }
```

Figure 15.12 The AccessToken method performs the OAuth authentication flow.

When the application calls *AcquireToken*, you'll be required to sign in to Power BI. Once you type in your credentials and Power BI authenticates you successfully, you'll get back an instance of the Authentication-Result class. AuthenticationResult encapsulates important details, including the access token, its expiration date, and refresh token. On line 554, the application stores the access token so that it can pass it with subsequent API calls without going through the authentication flow again. As it stands, the application doesn't use the refresh token flow, but you can enhance it to do so. For example, you can check if the access token is about to expire and then call the authContext.AquireAccessTokenByRefreshToken method.

15.3.2 Invoking the Power BI APIs

Once the application authenticates the interactive user, it's ready to call the Power BI APIs. The next sample demonstrates calling various APIs to create a dataset, adding and deleting rows to and from a dataset table, changing the dataset table schema, and getting the groups that the user belongs to. I'll walk you through the PBIGettingStarted code for creating datasets and loading a dataset table with data.

Creating datasets

A custom application can create a Power BI dataset to store data from scratch. The sample application demonstrates this with the *CreateDataset* method (see **Figure 15.13**). Line 213 constructs the API method signature for creating datasets by using the POST verb. Line 216 calls the *GetDatasets* method (not shown in **Figure 15.13**), which in turns calls the "List all datasets" Power BI API.

Line 221 passes an instance of the Product object, and it serializes the object to the JSON format. As a result, the request body contains the JSON representation of a dataset that has a single table called Product with five columns (ProductName, Name, Category, IsComplete, and ManufacturedOn). Once the call completes, you should see the SalesMarketing dataset in the Power BI Service navigation bar.

At this point, the dataset Product table contains no data. However, I recommend you take a moment now to create a table report for it, and then pin a visualization from the report to a dashboard. This will allow you to see in real time the effect of loading the dataset with data. Next, the code loads some data.

```csharp
static void CreateDataset()
{
    //In a production application, use more specific exception handling.
    try
    {
        //Create a POST web request to list all datasets
        HttpWebRequest request = DatasetRequest(String.Format("{0}/datasets", datasetsUri), "POST", AccessToken());

        //Get a list of datasets
        dataset ds = GetDatasets().value.GetDataset(datasetName);

        if (ds == null)
        {
            //POST request using the json schema from Product
            Console.WriteLine(PostRequest(request, new Product().ToDatasetJson(datasetName)));
        }
        else
        {
            Console.WriteLine("Dataset exists");
        }
    }
    catch (Exception ex)
    {
        Console.WriteLine(ex.Message);
    }
}
```

Figure 15.13 The CreateDataset method demonstrates how to programmatically create a dataset.

Loading data

The custom application can programmatically push rows to a dataset table. This scenario is very useful because it allows you to implement real-time dashboards, like the one we've implemented with Azure Stream Analytics Service in the previous chapter. The difference is that in this case, it's your application that pushes the data and you have full control over the entire process, including how the data is shaped and how often it pushes data to Power BI. The *AddRows* method demonstrates this (see **Figure 15.14**).

```csharp
static void AddRows(string datasetId, string tableName)
{
    //In a production application, use more specific exception handling.
    try
    {
        HttpWebRequest request = DatasetRequest(String.Format("{0}/datasets/{1}/tables/{2}/rows", datasetsUri, datasetId, tableName), "POST", AccessToken());

        //Create a list of Product
        List<Product> products = new List<Product>
        {
            new Product{ProductID = 1, Name="Adjustable Race", Category="Components", IsCompete = true, ManufacturedOn = new DateTime(2014, 7, 30)},
            new Product{ProductID = 2, Name="LL Crankarm", Category="Components", IsCompete = true, ManufacturedOn = new DateTime(2014, 7, 30)},
            new Product{ProductID = 3, Name="HL Mountain Frame - Silver", Category="Bikes", IsCompete = true, ManufacturedOn = new DateTime(2014, 7, 30)},
        };

        //POST request using the json from a list of Product
        //NOTE: Posting rows to a model that is not created through the Power BI API is not currently supported.
        //      Please create a dataset by posting it through the API following the instructions on http://dev.powerbi.com.
        Console.WriteLine(PostRequest(request, products.ToJson(JavaScriptConverter<Product>.GetSerializer())));
    }
    catch (Exception ex)
    {
        Console.WriteLine(ex.Message);
    }
}
```

Figure 15.14 The AddRows method demonstrates how your custom app can load a dataset table.

On line 380, the code creates the API method signature for creating rows using the POST verb. Then the code creates a list collection with three products. This collection will be used to add three rows to the dataset. On line 393, the code calls the *PostRequest* method and passes the collection (serialized as JSON). This JSON output will be included in the request body. Once this method completes, three rows will be added to the Product table in the *SalesMarketing* dataset. If you watch the Power BI dashboard, you should see its tile data updating in real time. Now you have a real-time BI solution!

15.4 Working with PowerShell

Many administrators use PowerShell to automate tasks. PowerShell is an automation framework from Microsoft, consisting of a command-line shell and associated scripting language. Administrators favor PowerShell because they don't have to learn a programming language. An additional benefit for using PowerShell specific to Power BI is that it doesn't require an app registration.

15.4.1 Understanding Power BI Cmdlets

PowerShell includes modules written in .NET called *cmdlets* (pronounced command-lets), which are designed to perform a specific operation. Microsoft has provided PowerShell for Power BI cmdlets in the Microsoft GitHub repo at https://github.com/Microsoft/powerbi-powershell.

Understanding modules
The Power BI cmdlets are organized in modules. Let's take a moment to familiarize ourselves with these modules, which are listed in **Table 15.3**.

Table 15.3 This table lists the PowerShell modules for automating Power BI tasks.

Module	Description	Purpose
MicrosoftPowerBIMgmt.Data	Data module for Power BI cmdlets	Work with datasets
MicrosoftPowerBIMgmt.Profile	Profile module for Power BI Cmdlets	Log in to Power BI and invoke Power BI REST API
MicrosoftPowerBIMgmt.Reports	Reports module for Power BI	Work with reports, dashboards, and tiles
MicrosoftPowerBIMgmt.Workspaces	Workspaces module for Power BI	Work with workspaces

All modules are rolled up in the MicrosoftPowerBIMgmt module, so you need to install only this module to gain access to all cmdlets. Most of the cmdlets included in each module are just wrappers on top of the corresponding REST API. When there isn't a cmdlet, you can call any Power BI REST API by using the Invoke-PowerBIRestMethod cmdlet in the MicrosoftPowerBIMgmt.Profile module.

Why use PowerShell?
Just like using the Power BI REST APIs, you can use PowerShell to automate various tasks, including:
- Content management – Enumerate all workspaces, dashboards, tiles, reports, datasets, data sources, and imports in a Power BI tenant.
- Export reports – You can back up all reports created in Power BI Desktop by exporting them to *.pbix files.
- Workspace management – For example, if someone accidentally deletes a v2 workspace, you can restore it. You can also rename a workspace and add or remove members.

15.4.2 Automating Tasks with PowerShell

Now that you know about PowerShell for Power BI, let me show you how to use it. You'll find the demo script (PowerShell Demo.ps1) in the \Source\ch15 folder. I'll use the Windows PowerShell Integrated Scripting Environment (ISE) for the demo but if you're an experienced PowerShell user you can use the PowerShell command line.

Getting started with PowerShell scripting

As a first step, install the PowerShell for Power BI cmdlets.

1. In Windows Search, type *powershell* and right-click Windows PowerShell ISE and click Run as Administrator because you need to run PowerShell ISE in elevated permissions to install the cmdlets.
2. In the PowerShell console, type the following command and press Enter:

PS C:\Users\<login> Install-Module -Name MicrosoftPowerBIMgmt

This command will install all the PowerShell for Power BI modules.

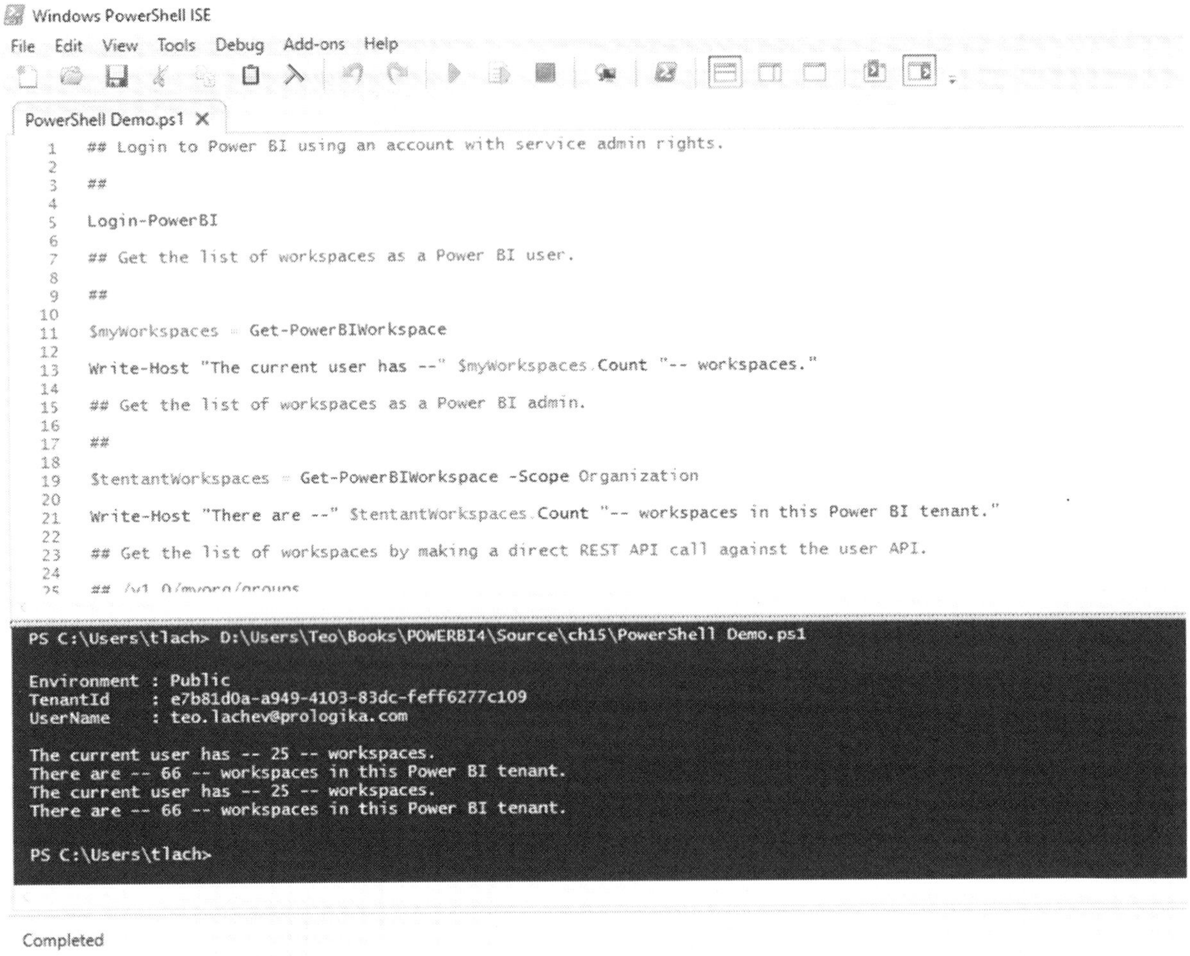

Figure 15.15 This PowerShell script enumerates the workspaces for the current user and across the entire tenant.

Understanding the demo script

Once the modules are installed, open and run the demo script.

1. Click File ⇨ Open and open the PowerShell Demo.ps1 file.
2. Click the Run button (F5) to run the script. If all is well, you'll see the output shown in **Figure 15.15**.

The script starts by calling the Login-PowerBI cmdlet. You'll see a prompt to log in to Power BI. The script then calls the Get-PowerBIWorkspace cmdlet to obtain the list of workspaces that you're a member of and shows the count of these workspaces. Next, the script calls the same cmdlet but passes *-Scope Organization* as a parameter. This is the equivalent of calling the Groups GetGroupsAsAdmin API.

Almost all management cmdlets have an optional parameter called -Scope. This parameter can take one of two values: Individual and Organization. The default is Individual, which only returns those items that you can access as a regular Power BI user. If you have Power BI Admin rights, you can specify Organization to enumerate content in the entire Power BI tenant. What happens if you don't have Power BI admin rights, but you use the Organization scope? You'll get an error. You can use the *Resolve-PowerBIError - Last* cmdlet to get more detail about the error.

Next, the script does the same task but this time uses the Invoke-PowerBIRestMethod to demontrate how you can call any Power BI REST API. Specifically, it first calls the Groups - Get Groups API.

$myRestResult = Invoke-PowerBIRestMethod -Url 'Groups' -Method Get | ConvertFrom-Json

> **TIP** To understand the URL parameter in Invoke-PowerBIRestMethod, examine the signature of the Power BI REST API. The "Groups - Get Groups" API has the following signature: https://api.powerbi.com/v1.0/myorg/**groups**. So, to invoke a Power BI REST API, you only need to specify the last part after *myorg* in the PowerBIRestMethod argument.

This API returns the workspaces for the current user. Next, the script calls the "Groups GetGroupsAsAdmin" API whose URL is *admin/groups*. This returns again all workspaces in the tenant.

15.5 Summary

The Power BI APIs are based on open industry standards, such as REST, JSON, and OAuth. These APIs allow you to automate content management and data manipulation tasks, including creating and deleting datasets, loading dataset tables with data, changing the dataset schema, and determining the user's group membership. You can use the Power BI Developer Center to learn and try the APIs.

As a trustworthy environment, Power BI must authenticate users before authorizing them to access the content. The cornerstone of the Power BI authentication is the OAuth2 protocol. By default, it uses a three-leg authentication flow (user owns the data) that asks the user to sign in to Power BI. As a prerequisite to integrating a custom app with Power BI, you must register the custom app with Azure AD.

The PBIGettingStarted sample app demonstrates how a Windows native client app can authenticate and call the Power BI REST APIs. I walked you through the code that creates a new dataset and loads it with data. This allows you to implement real-time dashboards that display data as the app pushes the data. I also showed you how you can use the PowerShell cmdlets for Power BI to create scripts for automating tasks without registering an app.

Another very popular integration scenario that the Power BI APIs enable is embedding reports in custom applications. This is the subject of the next chapter.

Chapter 16

Power BI Embedded

16.1 Understanding Power BI Embedded 408
16.2 Understanding Embedded Features 412
16.3 Report-enabling Intranet Applications 423
16.4 Report-enabling Internet Applications 428
16.5 Summary 432

Because Power BI generates HTML5, users can enjoy insightful reports on any platform and on any device. Wouldn't it be nice to bring this experience to your custom apps? Collectively known as Power BI Embedded, Power BI includes REST APIs that allow you to embed reports and dashboards in any modern web app. This avoids navigating users out of your app and into powerbi.com. Embedded reports preserve their interactive features and offer the same engaging experience as viewing them in Power BI Service. Users can even edit existing reports or create their own reports if you let them do it! Tasked to embed reports in a web portal for external customers? It gets even better thanks to the Power BI Embedded special licensing that lets you embed content for third party without requiring a per-user license!

As with the previous chapter, this is a code-intensive chapter, so be prepared to wear your developer's hat. I'll start by introducing you to the Power BI REST APIs that let you embed dashboards and reports. I'll walk you through some sample code that demonstrates how your intranet and Internet apps can use these features. You can find the sample web applications in the \Source\ch16 folder.

16.1 Understanding Power BI Embedded

Embedded reporting is a common requirement for both internal and external (customer-facing) applications. The subset of the Power BI REST APIs that let developers embed content is known as Power BI Embedded. Because Power BI Embedded has its own licensing model, it's listed as a separate product in the Power BI product portfolio.

16.1.1 Getting Started with Power BI Embedded

The first thing you need to understand about Power BI Embedded is how to acquire it. As a developer, if you have a Power BI Pro license, you can start using the Power BI Embedded APIs right away. If all your users have Power BI Pro subscriptions, they can view the embedded content and you're all set. But from a pure licensing standpoint, things get more complicated when your app services many users, especially Power BI Free internal users or external users. At that point, licensing by user, by month is not practical. So, you need to consider purchasing an embedded capacity to support many users in a cost-efficient way.

Understanding Power BI Embedded capacities
There are two ways to acquire an embedded capacity. If your organization is on a Power BI Premium P plan, you already have everything you need to embed content for both internal and external users. Power BI Premium EM plans are more restrictive. Refer to section 13.1.1 to understand how P, EM, and A plans compare as far as targeting internal and external users.

Another way to obtain an embedded capacity is to purchase an Azure plan. Most smaller companies and Independent Software Vendors (ISV) looking for embedding content to only external users would gravitate toward the Azure Power BI Embedded plans. The Azure plans can also result in significant cost savings because they allow you to quickly scale up and down, and even pause the capacity, as I'll explain when I walk you through the steps to acquire an Azure embedded capacity! For example, if the most report activity happens within normal working hours, you can scale it down to a lower capacity out-side the peak period.

REAL LIFE I've helped a few ISVs integrate their apps with Power BI Embedded (see one related Microsoft study at https://powerbi.microsoft.com/blog/zynbit-empowers-sales-with-microsoft-power-bi-embedded/). All of them have considered other vendors and third-party libraries for embedding content but were attracted to Power BI Embedded because of its rich code-free visualizations and very cost-effective licensing model.

Understanding Azure capacity nodes

Like Power BI Premium, an Azure plan represents a capacity node and its associated hardware. Currently, there are size Azure capacity nodes, which are shown in **Table 16.1**.

Table 16.1 Power BI Embedded has six Azure capacity nodes.

Node	Capacity Type	Total V-cores	Memory	Max Page Renders (per hour)	Direct Query connection limits (per sec)	Estimated Price (per month)
A1	Shared	1	3 GB	300	5	$750
A2	Shared	2	5 GB	600	10	$1,500
A3	Dedicated	4	10 GB	1,200	15	$3,000
A4	Dedicated	8	25 GB	2,400	30	$6,000
A5	Dedicated	16	50 GB	4,800	60	$12,000
A6	Dedicated	32	100 GB	9,600	120	$24,000

Estimating how much capacity your app would need isn't an exact science, but the most important factor (especially if your reports will connect live to an external data source) is the hourly distribution of page renders. Like Power BI Premium, a page render happens every time a report page is refreshed. So, if a report has two pages, and the user visits the first page and then the second page, and changes a filter on the second page, there will be three page renders. Exceeding the maximum page renders per capacity won't result in Power BI refusing to render reports, but it will likely degrade the report performance because Power BI will start queuing the report requests.

TIP You can pause or scale down your Power BI Embedded capacity in the Azure portal to reduce your cost. For example, if the most report activity happens within normal working hours, you can scale it down to a lower capacity outside the peak period.

Purchasing an Azure embedded capacity

To reduce cost during app development and testing, developers can use any Power BI workspace and the workspace doesn't have to be in an embedded capacity. The only requirement is that each developer must be covered with a Power BI Pro license. However, deploying the app to production requires the workspace from which the content is embedded to be in either a Power BI Premium or Power BI Embedded capacity. If you prefer to acquire Power BI Embedded via an Azure pricing plan, follow these steps to purchase an embedded capacity:

1. Go to https://azure.portal.com and sign in with your work account (needs to be on the same tenant as Power BI). As a prerequisite, you must have previously signed in to Power BI and you must have a subscription associated with that tenant.
2. Click New and search for "Power BI", as shown in **Figure 16.1**. In the search results, select "Power BI Embedded". Don't select "Power BI Workspace Collection" because this is the old Power BI Embedded (Microsoft will support it until July 2018). In the information page, click Create.

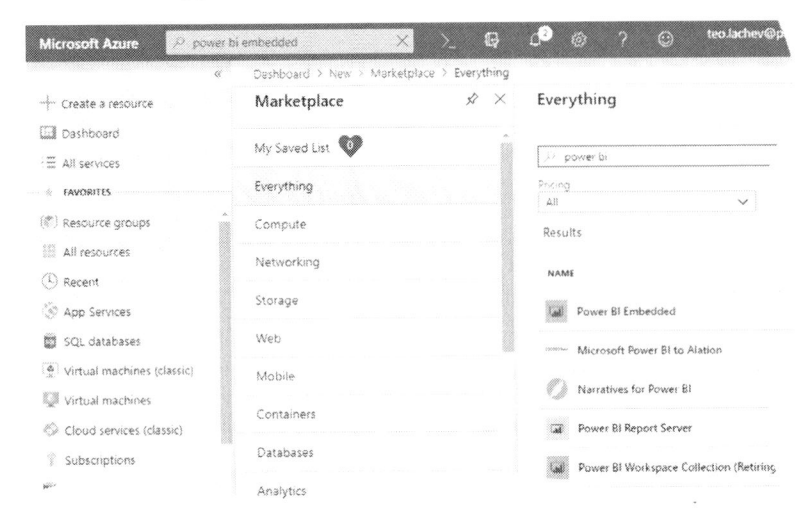

Figure 16.1 Choose Power BI Embedded to purchase an embedded capacity.

3. In the Power BI Embedded page (see **Figure 16.2**), specify the capacity details.

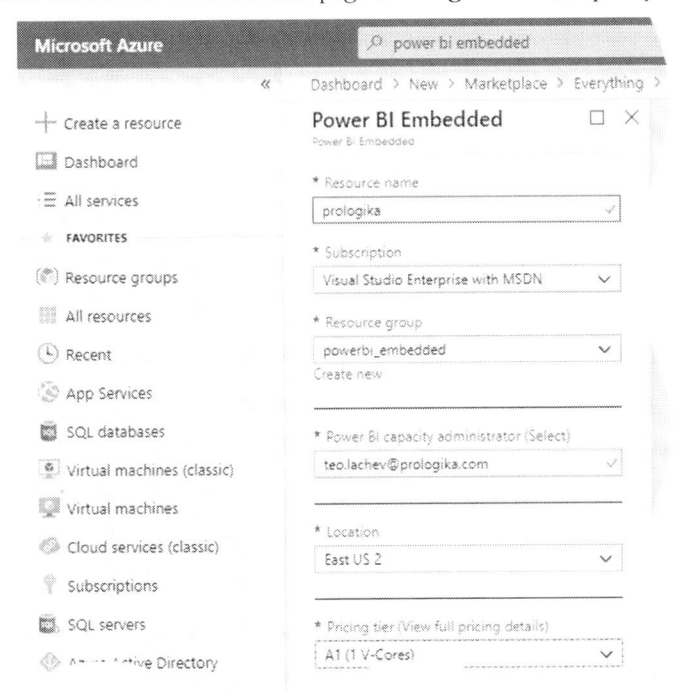

Figure 16.2 Specify the embedded capacity details, including the resource group, administrator, and pricing tier.

Let's explain these settings in more detail:

410 CHAPTER 16

- Resource name – Give the capacity a name. This is the name that you'll see in Power BI when you assign a workspace to an embedded capacity so choose a descriptive name.
- Subscription – Chose the subscription that will be billed.
- Resource group – Choose an existing resource group (an Azure resource group represent a logical container for managing related resources).
- Power BI capacity administrator – Specify a default capacity administrator. Later, you can add other capacity admins in the "Capacity settings" page for the embedded capacity in Power BI Admin Portal.
- Location – Associate the data center where the capacity will reside in. The only choice would be the data region where your Power BI tenant resides in.
- Pricing tier – Select one of the six Azure capacity nodes.

4. Click Create to let Azure create the embedded capacity.
5. Now that the capacity is created, go to its properties and notice that you can pause the capacity. You can also scale up and down the capacity from the Scale tab.

Understanding high-level flow for embedding content
Once you have the embedded capacity, you can start writing code to integrate your app with the embedded APIs. In a nutshell, these are the high-level steps to embed Power BI content into your app:

1. Register your app – I've shown you how to register web and native apps in the preceding chapter.
2. Authenticate – You can't go far with anything Power BI unless you take care of security first. You need to call the Power BI REST APIs to obtain an access token that determines the end-user permissions. Let's skip this step for now. We will revisit it later in this chapter in the content of internal and external apps.
3. Embed Power BI content – Once you have an access token, you can embed specific tiles, reports, or dashboards.

The content that you want to embed in your app needs to reside in a Power BI workspace within your Power BI tenant. Next, I'll provide some considerations that you need to keep in mind when planning your content.

16.1.2 Configuring Workspaces

As with sharing content via the powerbi.com portal, you use Power BI Desktop to create datasets and reports that you plan to embed. Once you are done with the reports, you upload the Power BI Desktop file to an app workspace in your Power BI tenant.

Planning content storage
How many workspaces do you need? Consider a custom app that connects to a multi-tenant database and uses Power BI row-level security (RLS) to isolate data among customers. You can provision just one workspace that will host a single Power BI Desktop file.

What if you want to physically separate data by providing each customer with a data extract as a separate (*.pbix) file? Or, to provide customer-specific reports. Then, you might create a workspace per customer and deploy each file to a separate workspace. You'll end up having as many workspaces as customers that you want to support (with all the maintenance headaches to support that many files). It's up to you how you want to organize the content across workspaces. Since you're not charged per workspace, you can have as many as you want.

Assigning a workspace to an embedded capacity

Remember that you must assign a workspace to either a premium or embedded capacity before you go live. The workspace must have a diamond icon next to its name in the Power BI navigation pane. Recall from Chapter 13 that you can use the Advanced section in the workspace properties to assign the workspace to a premium or embedded capacity. Alternatively, you can use the Capacity settings in the Admin Portal (see **Figure 16.3**).

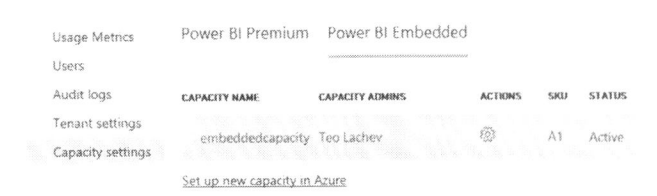

Figure 16.3 The Power BI Embedded tab in the Admin Portal shows workspaces in embedded capacities.

Now that you've learned about Power BI Embedded, let's see what features it supports for embedding content in your custom apps.

16.2 Understanding Embedded Features

Typically, the application presents a list of reports or dashboards to the user, so the user can pick which one to view. Then the application embeds the content in the presentation layer, so that reports and dashboards appear to be a part of the application itself (as opposed to redirecting the user to Power BI). When you embed Power BI content in a web app, it's important to understand where you need to write code: server or client.

- Server – You typically call the Power BI REST APIs on the server to handle user authentication and content management, such as enumerating reports. As discussed in the previous chapter, Microsoft has provided Power BI REST and OAuth APIs that you can call on the server.

- Client – Microsoft has also provided a Power BI JavaScript library (https://microsoft.github.io/PowerBI-JavaScript/) to reduce the JavaScript code you need to write to embed content on the client. You call the JavaScript APIs to embed content and manipulate objects, such as to navigate report pages or do something when the interactive user clicks a visual.

NOTE Although the Power BI documentation is very good in general, Microsoft hasn't documented the JavaScript objects well. If you want to find what properties, methods, and events are exposed by the embedded objects (reports, dashboards, tiles) in JavaScript, you can browse their somewhat cryptic definitions at https://microsoft.github.io/PowerBI-JavaScript/globals.html.

Microsoft has also provided an online Microsoft Power BI Embedded Playground (https://microsoft.github.io/PowerBI-JavaScript/demo) that demoes the embedded features and the client-side code that you need to write to embed reports, dashboards, and tiles, and to add Q&A features in your apps. I'll use this app to demonstrate the capabilities of the embedded APIs and explain what you need to do on the client to embed content.

NOTE It's important to understand that because JavaScript code is not secure, you can't use the JavaScript APIs to overwrite Power BI security. The actual permissions are controlled by an access token that reflects Power BI security (in User Owns Data scenario) or by permissions granted in the embed token (in the App Owns Data scenario). For example, you can't switch a report from Reading View to Editing View if the user doesn't have permissions to edit reports.

0.1.1 Embedding Tiles

Power BI includes dashboard APIs that let you embed specific dashboard tiles in your apps. One benefit of tile embedding is to let the user select which tiles they want to see on a consolidated dashboard provided by your application. This way your app can mimic the dashboard features of Power BI Service. It can allow the user to compile its own dashboards from Power BI dashboard tiles, and even from tiles in different Power BI dashboards!

Understanding implementation steps
At a high level, the embedding tile workflow consists of the following steps (excluding authentication):

- Obtain the tile identifier – You need to gain access programmatically to a dashboard before you get to a tile. So, you'd need to find the dashboards available for the user, and then enumerate the dashboard tiles. Once the user chooses a tile, then you work with the tile identifier. Typically, the code to authenticate the user and enumerate content will be executed on the server.
- Embed a tile – Embed the tile in your application. This code takes place on the client.
- (Optional) Handle tile interaction – For example, you might want to open the underlying report when the user clicks a tile. This is client-side code.

Select the "Sample tool" ⇨ "Sample Tile" option and click Run to execute the code that embeds a tile on a web page (see **Figure 16.4**).

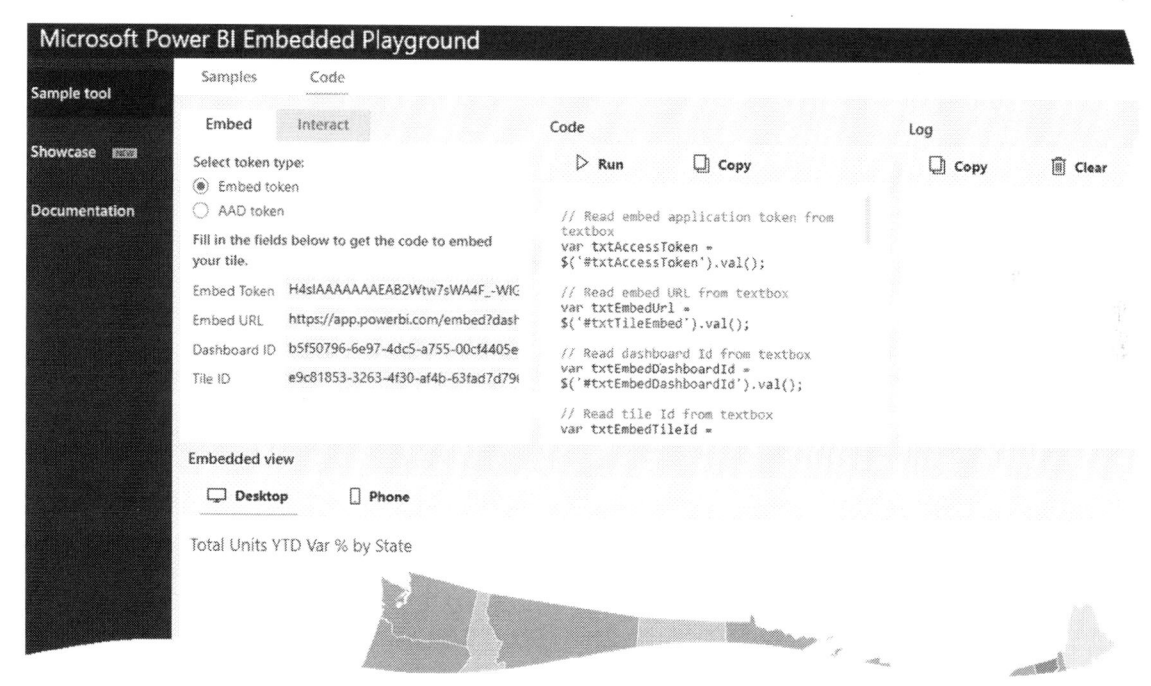

Figure 16.4 You can use the embedded APIs to embed specific dashboard tiles.

Enumerating dashboards
I mentioned in the previous chapter that Power BI includes REST APIs for enumerating dashboards and tiles. Your application can call these APIs to present the users with a list of tiles that they might want to see in your application. For example, the "Get Dashboards" operation returns the dashboards available in the user's My Workspace. This method has the following signature:

```
https://api.powerbi.com/v1.0/myorg/dashboards
```

And the "Get Dashboards In Group" method enumerate dashboards in an app workspace by passing the workplace identifier. You can get the workspace identifier by clicking the workspace in the Power BI portal and copying the GUID portion from the URL in the browser address bar. For example, if the workspace identifier of the Finance workspace is e6e4e5ab-2644-4115-96e0-51baa89df249 (you can also obtain a list of workspaces that the user belongs to by calling the "Get Groups" operation), you can get a list of dashboards available in the Finance workspace by using this signature:

```
https://api.powerbi.com/v1.0/myorg/groups/e6e4e5ab-2644-4115-96e0-51baa89df249/dashboards
```

Enumerating tiles

Once you retrieve the list of dashboards, you can present the user with a list of tiles from a specific dashboard by calling the "Get Tiles" operation. This operation takes an *id* parameter that corresponds to the dashboard identifier, which you obtain from the "Get Dashboards" operation, or by copying the GUID portion from the URL in the browser address bar after you click the dashboard to view it. Here is a sample "Get Tiles" method invocation:

```
https://api.powerbi.com/v1.0/myorg/dashboards/<dashboard_id>/tiles
```

The result of this method is a JSON collection of all the tiles hosted in that dashboard. The following snippet shows the definition of the "This Year's Sales" tile from the Retail Analysis Sample dashboard:

```
{
"id": "a2e8ee89-d321-4932-b26b-840c770d488d",
"title": "This Year's Sales",
"subTitle": "New & Existing Stores",
"embedUrl": "https://app.powerbi.com/embed?dashboardId=9a9a94b8-07a1-4e70-b29e-9f16dea08afc&tileId=a2e8ee89-d321-4932-b26b-840c770d488d",
"rowSpan": 0,
"colSpan": 0,
"datasetId": "f183dd3c-4474-46c5-9850-88781e02d816"
}
```

The *embedUrl* element is what you need to embed the tile in your app.

Embedding a tile

Once you have the embed URL, the next step it to embed the tile on a web page. In the most common scenario, you'd probably embed content in a web app. You don't have to write much client-side code if you use the Power BI JavaScript library. Start by creating the embed configuration.

```
// Read embed application token from textbox
var txtAccessToken = $('#txtAccessToken').val();
// Read embed URL from textbox
var txtEmbedUrl = $('#txtTileEmbed').val();
// Read dashboard Id from textbox
var txtEmbedDashboardId = $('#txtEmbedDashboardId').val();
// Read tile Id from textbox
var txtEmbedTileId = $('#txtEmbedTileId').val();
// Read embed type from radio
var tokenType = $('input:radio[name=tokenType]:checked').val();
// Get models. models contains enums that can be used.
var models = window['powerbi-client'].models;
// Embed configuration used to describe the what and how to embed.
// This object is used when calling powerbi.embed.
// You can find more information at https://github.com/Microsoft/PowerBI-JavaScript/wiki/Embed-Configuration-Details.
var config= {
```

```
  type: 'tile',
  tokenType: tokenType == '0' ? models.TokenType.Aad : models.TokenType.Embed,
  accessToken: txtAccessToken,
  embedUrl: txtEmbedUrl,
  id: txtEmbedTileId,
  dashboardId: txtEmbedDashboardId
};
// Get a reference to the embedded tile HTML element
var tileContainer = $('#tileContainer')[0];

// Embed the tile and display it within the div container.
var tile = powerbi.embed(tileContainer, config);
```

The code obtains the OAuth access token from the user interface but in real life, it could obtain it from the Model controller (assuming an ASP.NET MVC application). Next, it obtains the tile embed URL, title identifier, and dashboard identifier. It creates an embedded configuration (var config) from these properties. Then, the code gets a reference to an HTML DIV element (#tileContainer) where the tile will be rendered. The actual embedding magic happens with a single (last) line of code. Don't you appreciate how simple this is?

Handling user interaction

Table 16.2 shows the interactive features that JavaScript library supports on the client. One difference between Power BI Service dashboards and embedding tiles in your app is that, by default, clicking a tile doesn't do anything. You need to write code for something to happen, such as to navigate the user to the underlying report (from which the visualization was pinned). On the upside, your custom code has more control over what happens when the end user clicks a tile.

Table 16.2 Embedded tiles support these interactive features.

Interaction	Name	Purpose
Events	tileLoaded	Fires when the tile is fully loaded
	tileClicked	Fires when the tile is clicked

Remember that when the user clicks a tile in Power BI Service it's navigated to the underlying report from which the tile was pinned. You can add a similar feature to your app. Tiles support two events: tileLoaded and tileClicked, that you can handle in JavaScript.

```
// Get a reference to the embedded tile HTML element
var tileContainer = $('#tileContainer')[0];
// Embed the tile and display it within the div container.
var tile = powerbi.embed(tileContainer, config);
// Tile.off removes a given event handler if it exists.
tile.off("tileLoaded");
// Tile.on will add an event handler which prints to Log window.
tile.on("tileLoaded", function(event) {
    Log.logText("Tile loaded event");
});
// Tile.off removes a given event handler if it exists.
tile.off("tileClicked");
// Tile.on will add an event handler which prints to Log window.
tile.on("tileClicked", function(event) {
    Log.logText("Tile clicked event");
    Log.log(event.detail);
});
```

It's up to you what you want to do when your code intercepts the event. For example, you can show the report from which the tile was pinned.

Filtering tile content

You can pass optional filters in the embed configuration object to filter the tile content. The syntax is the same as the filters you use on reports. There are two types of filters:

- Basic filters – They have a single operation with one or more values, such as Country In ("USA", "Canada").
- Advanced filters – They can have multiple AND and OR conditions, just like when you use advanced filters and configure multiple conditions in the Filters area of the Visualizations pane.

For more information about how to construct filters, refer to the Filters topic at https://github.com/Microsoft/PowerBI-JavaScript/wiki/Filters.

16.2.2 Embedding Dashboards

Besides individual tiles, you can embed entire dashboards deployed to Power BI Service. The sample app demonstrates this feature when you select the "Sample Dashboards" option.

Embedding a dashboard

I've already explained that the "Get Dashboards" API can be used to enumerate dashboards. Once you obtain the dashboard identifier and embedUrl, you can embed the dashboard on the client side using embedded configuration. You need to pass the dashboard embed URL and the dashboard identifier.

```
var config = {
   type: 'dashboard',
   tokenType: models.TokenType.Embed,
   accessToken: txtAccessToken,
   embedUrl: txtEmbedUrl,
   id: txtEmbedDashboardId
};
```

Understanding dashboard interaction

Table 16.3 shows the most significant interactive features that are available for dashboards.

Table 16.3 Embedded dashboards support these interactive features.

Interaction	Name	Purpose
Methods	getId	Returns the dashboard identifier
	fullscreen	Opens the dashboard in full screen mode
	exitfullscreen	Exists full screen
Events	tileClicked	Fires when a tile is clicked
	Loaded	Fires when the dashboard is fully loaded
	error	Fires when an error occurs during dashboard loading

Your JavaScript code can call the fullscreen method to show the dashboard in full screen. The following code does this:

```
// Get a reference to the embedded dashboard HTML element
var dashboardContainer = $('#dashboardContainer')[0];
// Get a reference to the embedded dashboard.
dashboard = powerbi.get(dashboardContainer);
// Displays the dashboard in full screen mode.
dashboard.fullscreen();
```

As with tiles, the most interesting event is tileClicked, which is fired when the user clicks a tile. The event argument includes the report URL for embedding (reportEmbedUrl), if the tile was added by pinning a report visual. You need this URL to embed the report.

16.2.3 Embedding Q&A

Recall that users can use natural questions to get insights from data. Wouldn't be nice to add Q&A features to your apps? Of course, it would! The embedded APIs allow developers to add such capabilities in several configurations:

- Show Q&A only – Shows the Q&A box without a predefined question.
- Show Q&A with a predefined question -- Shows a predefined question and the resulting visual.
- Show answer only – This could be useful if your app collects the question from the user and only wants to show a visual that best answers the question.

Embedding Q&A

As a prerequisite, you need to obtain the identifiers of the datasets that you'd want Q&A to use. You can use the "Get Datasets in Group" REST operation. For example, this method returns all datasets within the specified app workspace whose identifier is e6e4e5ab-2644-4115-96e0-51baa89df249.

https://api.powerbi.com/v1.0/myorg/groups/e6e4e5ab-2644-4115-96e0-51baa89df249/datasets

This code shows the embedded configuration for embedding Q&A with a predefined question.

```
var config= {
  type: 'qna',
  tokenType: models.TokenType.Embed,
  accessToken: txtAccessToken,
  embedUrl: txtEmbedUrl,
  datasetIds: [txtDatasetId],
  viewMode: models.QnaMode[qnaMode],
  question: txtQuestion
};
```

The configuration type is set to 'qna'. The embedUrl has the format https://app.powerbi.com/qnaEmbed?groupId=<groupId>, where groupId is the workspace identifier. Unlike Power BI Service, where Q&A is a dashboard-level feature, embedding Q&A doesn't require a dashboard. Instead, you need to pass the identifiers of one or more datasets in the datasetIds property. Finally, you can use the question property to pass a predefined question, such as "Sales by country for year 2017".

Understanding Q&A interaction

Table 16.4 shows the most interesting interactive features for embedded Q&A.

Table 16.4 Embedded Q&A supports these interactive features.

Interaction	Name	Purpose
Methods	setQuestion	Passes a question to Q&A, such as "This year sales"
Events	Loaded	Fires when the Q&A is loaded
	questionChanged	Fires when the question has changed

For example, to change the question, you can call the setQuestion method.

```
// Get a reference to the embedded Q&A HTML element
var qnaContainer = $('#qnaContainer')[0];
// Get a reference to the embedded Q&A.
qna = powerbi.get(qnaContainer);
qna.setQuestion("This year sales")
```

16.2.4 Embedding Reports

For years, Microsoft hasn't had a good story about embedded interactive reporting. If developers wanted to distribute interactive reports with their applications, they had to use third-party components. The good news is that Power BI supports this scenario and even allows users to edit reports! This means that users can enjoy report interactive features, such as filtering and highlighting, and they can change the report layout if your app lets them, such as to reconfigure the visuals. In other words, the embedded APIs have similar feature parity as viewing and editing reports in Power BI Service, although some features that depend on Power BI Service are missing, such as pinning tiles and report pages, and subscribing to report pages.

Enumerating reports

As a first step, you'd probably want to present the user with a list of reports. Your application can call the "Get Reports" operation to show a list of reports in the user's My Workspace.

https://api.powerbi.com/v1.0/myorg/reports

The resulting JSON response is a collection of report elements. Each report element has *id* (report identifier), name, webUrl, embedUrl, and datasetId properties. Here's the definition of the Internet Sales Analysis report:

```
{
    "id":"b605950b-4f18-4eba-9292-82720f215693",
    "name":"Internet Sales Analysis",
    "webUrl":"https://app.powerbi.com/reports/b605950b-4f18-4eba-9292-82720f215693",
    "embedUrl":https://app.powerbi.com/reportEmbed?reportId=b605950b-4f18-4eba-9292-82720f215693,
    "datasetId": "cf6ea374-1d1e-4288-bc41-5e25ccbe4967"}
```

Chances are that your users will share their content. The "Get Reports in Group" operation enumerates reports in an app workspace by passing the workspace identifier. For example, if the identifier of the Finance workspace is e6e4e5ab-2644-4115-96e0-51baa89df249, you can get a list of the reports available in the Finance workspace by using this signature:

https://api.powerbi.com/v1.0/myorg/**groups/e6e4e5ab-2644-4115-96e0-51baa89df249**/reports

> **TIP** To show all the reports that the user can access, you need to enumerate the reports in the user's My Workspace and the reports from all the groups (workspaces) that the user belongs to.

Understanding embedded features for reports

When you select the "Sample Report" option in the Microsoft Power BI Embedded Playground, you get a sample report embedded in a web page (see **Figure 16.5**). Note that the report supports the same features as when you open the report in Reading View in Power BI Service. For example, you can hover a visual and use the icons in the visual header to drill down, drill through, sort and export the data. The Filters pane is also available. If the report has multiple pages, users navigate through the report pages. Users can also pop out visuals to examine them in more detail and access more tasks from the ellipsis (…) menu.

Viewing reports

When the user picks a report, client-side JavaScript embeds the report. This is very similar to embedding dashboards and tiles. However, your embedded configuration can specify the default mode (view or edit the report). You can also let the user create a report from scratch.

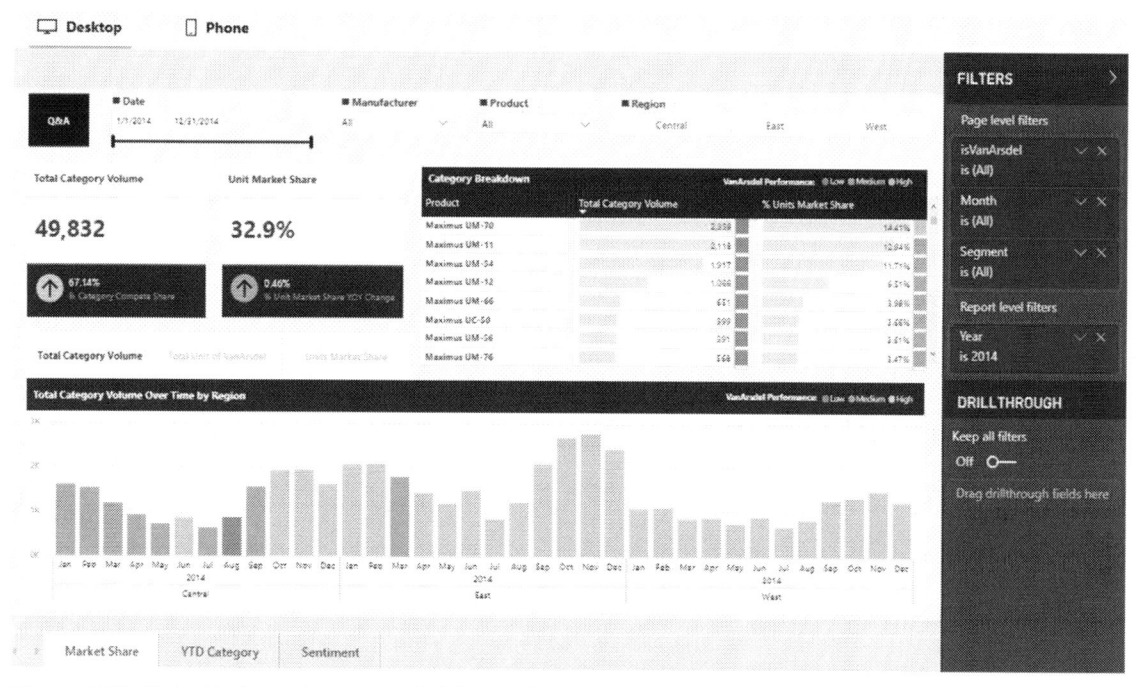

Figure 16.5 Embedded reports preserve their interactive features.

Here is the embedded configuration for real-only reports (like Reading View in Power BI Service).

```
var config= {
  type: 'report',
  tokenType: tokenType == '0' ? models.TokenType.Aad : models.TokenType.Embed,
  accessToken: txtAccessToken,
  embedUrl: txtEmbedUrl,
  id: txtEmbedReportId,
  permissions: permissions,
  settings: {
    filterPaneEnabled: true,
    navContentPaneEnabled: true
  }};
var embedContainer = $('#embedContainer')[0];
var report = powerbi.embed(embedContainer, config);
```

POWER BI EMBEDDED

The embedUrl property has the report embedUrl. You also need to set the id property to the report identifier. The settings collection lets you specify if you want the report to include the Microsoft-provided filter pane (filterPaneEnabled setting) and page navigation (setting navContentPaneEnabled to false will hide the page navigation pane).

Editing reports

If the user is authorized to edit the report, the client-side code can alternate between Reading View and Editing View. For example, you can switch to Editing View by only appending the viewMode.Edit setting in the embedded configuration:

```
var config = {
   ...
   viewMode: models.ViewMode.Edit,
   settings: ...
```

As a result, the report now shows the Visualization and Fields panes. The user can make layout changes and save the report if the user has permissions to change the report (the access token controls the user permissions). The Editing View also shows File and View menus. The user can save the layout changes by overwriting the report or save the report as new.

Creating reports

If the user has permissions to create reports, the client-side code can call the createReport method to navigate the user to a blank report connected to a given dataset.

```
var embedCreateConfiguration = {
   tokenType: tokenType == '0' ? models.TokenType.Aad : models.TokenType.Embed,
   accessToken: txtAccessToken,
   embedUrl: txtEmbedUrl,
   datasetId: txtEmbedDatasetId,
};
var report = powerbi.createReport(embedContainer, embedCreateConfiguration);
```

In this case the configuration specifies the identifier of the dataset. Power BI responds with a blank report connected to that dataset, just like when you explore the dataset in Power BI Service. The user can save the report in the workspace.

Understanding report interaction

Because reports inspire the most interest, the JavaScript library includes many methods and events to handle user interaction. **Table 16.5** shows the most interesting interactive features for embedded reports.

Table 16.5 Embedded reports support these interactive features.

Interaction	Name	Purpose
Properties	BookmarkManager	For performing various bookmark tasks, such as applying bookmarks
Methods	getId	Get the report identifier
	getPages, setPage (report or page)	Enumerate or set the active report page
	setFilters, getFilters, removeFilters	Set, get, or remove basic or advanced visual-level, page-level, report-level filters
	setSlicerState, getSlicerState	Set or get the slicer filters
	Print	Prints the report
	updateSettings	Updates the report settings, such as layout, filters, bookmarks, and menu extensions

Interaction	Name	Purpose
	reload, refresh	Reloads (call it after creating a new report to show the new report) or refreshes a report
	fullscreen, exitFullscreen	Display report in full screen mode
	switchMode	Switches between Reading View and Editing View
	save, saveAs	Saves the report
	exportData	Exports the visual data (summarized and underlying)
Events	pageChanged	Fires when the user navigates to a new page
	dataSelected	Fires when the user selects a visual element, such as clicking a data point
	saveAsTriggered	Fires when the user clicks the Save As menu
	bookmarkApplied	Fires when the user applies a bookmark

Filtering the report data

One interactive feature that you might need is implementing application-level filtering instead of using the Microsoft-provided Filter pane. The following code demonstrates how your app can pass filters.

```
// Instead of a constant, your app would gather the filters
const filter = {
 $schema: "http://powerbi.com/product/schema#basic",
 target: {
  table: "Store",
  column: "Chain"
 },
 operator: "In",
 values: ["Lindseys"]
};
// Get a reference to the embedded report HTML element
var embedContainer = $('#embedContainer')[0];
// Get a reference to the embedded report.
report = powerbi.get(embedContainer);
// Set the filter for the report (you can also filter at page level)
// Pay attention that setFilters receives an array.
report.setFilters([filter])
// Remove the Filter pane but leave page navigation enabled
const newSettings = {
 navContentPaneEnabled: true,
 filterPaneEnabled: false
};
report.updateSettings(newSettings);
```

Like tiles, reports support filtering capabilities. This could be useful when you want to further filter the report content based on some user-specified filter, after the report filters are applied. You can filter on any field in the underlying model, even though the field might not be used in the report itself.

Extending menus

Another interesting option is the ability to extend the following visual menus (see **Figure 16.6**):

- The visual options menu that appears when you hover on the visual and click the ellipsis (…) button in the top-right corner.
- The visual context menu that appears when you right-click a data point, such as a slice in a pie chart.

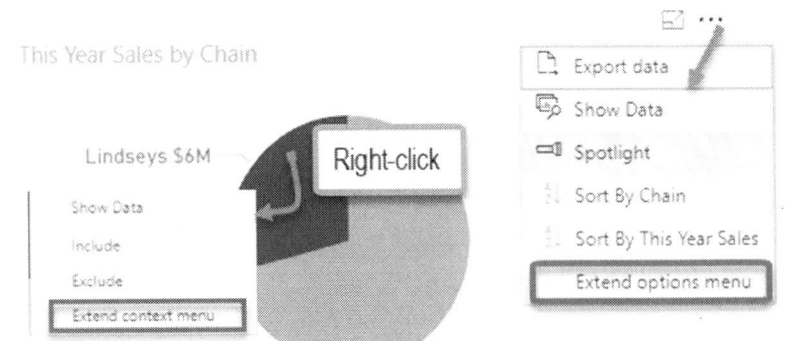

Figure 16.6 You can add your own menu options to the visual options and context menus.

For example, this code adds a "Extend context menu" submenu to the visual context menu.

```
// The new settings that you want to apply to the report.
const newSettings = {
 extensions: [ {
   command: {
    name: "extension command",
    title: "Extend command",
    extend: {
     // Define visualContextMenu to extend context menu.
     visualContextMenu: {
      // Define title to override default title.
      //You can override default icon as well.
      title: "Extend context menu", } } } } ]};

// Get a reference to the embedded report HTML element
var embedContainer = $('#embedContainer')[0];
// Get a reference to the embedded report.
report = powerbi.get(embedContainer);
// Update the settings by passing in the new settings you have configured.
report.updateSettings(newSettings)
   .then(function (result) {
     $("#result").html(result);
   })
   .catch(function (error) {
     $("#result").html(error);
   });
// Report.on will add an event handler to commandTriggered event which prints to console window.
report.on("commandTriggered", function(event) {
   var commandDetails = event.detail;
   // Do something with the data point
});
```

When the user clicks the menu, the commandTriggered event fires and the JavaScript library passes the data point details, including the data point identity and value. For example, if the user right-clicks the Lindseys slice in the pie chart, the event argument will include "Lindseys" as a data point identity and "$6,393,844" as a data point value. This feature allows you to extend embedded visuals in interesting ways, such as by navigating the user to another system and passing the context of the user action.

16.3 Report-enabling Intranet Applications

Now that you've learned about the Power BI embedding capabilities, let me walk through sample code to help you report-enable your intranet applications. You can use this code to embed Power BI reports in internal applications when your end users already have Power BI licenses. For example, you can use this approach to embed Power BI reports in report portals or Line of Business (LOB) systems, such as SharePoint or Dynamics. If you plan to embed reports in apps for external customers, skip to the next section where I discuss Power BI Embedded. The sample demonstrates the following features:

- Authenticating users – The sample code shows both a three-leg authentication flow (a Power BI sign-on page opens). Microsoft refers to this authentication type as "user owns data" because the user authenticates with Power BI and content embedding happens under the user identity.
- Embedding reports – The application shows a list of reports to the end user. Once the user picks a report, the JavaScript code embeds the report on a web page.

16.3.1 Understanding the Sample Application

The book source code includes a sample PBIWebApp ASP.NET application in the \Source\ch16\User Owns Data\ folder. The code is from the Microsoft's pbi-saas-embed-report sample (https://github.com/Microsoft/PowerBI-Developer-Samples), The Microsoft code also includes samples to show how to embed dashboards and tiles.

Registering the application

I mentioned in the previous chapter that any custom application that integrates with Power BI must be registered in Azure Active Directory. While you can follow the steps in the last chapter to register your app, Microsoft has provided a Power BI Embedded onboarding page to help you set up your environment:

1. Go to https://app.powerbi.com/embedsetup.
2. Choose Embed for Your Organization and follow the steps. **Table 16.6** lists the important app registration settings for a demo app called PBIWebApp.

Table 16.6 The registration settings for the PBIWebApp sample.

Setting	Value	Notes
Name*	PBIWebApp	Defines the name of the application
Type	Web app/API	Defines the app type
Home page	http://localhost:13526/	The URL of the home page
Application is multi-tenant	No	The application won't need access to data owned by other organizations
Keys	Auto-generated	Create a key because this is a web app.
Reply URL*	http://localhost:13526/	The redirect page for three-leg authentication (make sure that the port number matches your development setup)
Permissions*	Power BI Service (all permissions)	Grant all Power BI Service permissions

For the sake of completeness, the table lists all settings that you need if you register the application using the Azure Management Portal (the settings you need for the Power BI registration page are suffixed with an asterisk).

Configuring the application

Before you run the application, you need to change a few configuration settings to match your setup.

1. Open the PBIWebApp project file in Visual Studio (version 2015 or higher) from the \User Owns Data\integrate-report-web-app\PBIWebApp folder. If you don't have Visual Studio, you can download and install the free Visual Studio 2017 Community Edition.
2. In Solution Explorer, right-click the project, and then click Properties ⇨ Settings (see **Figure 16.7**).

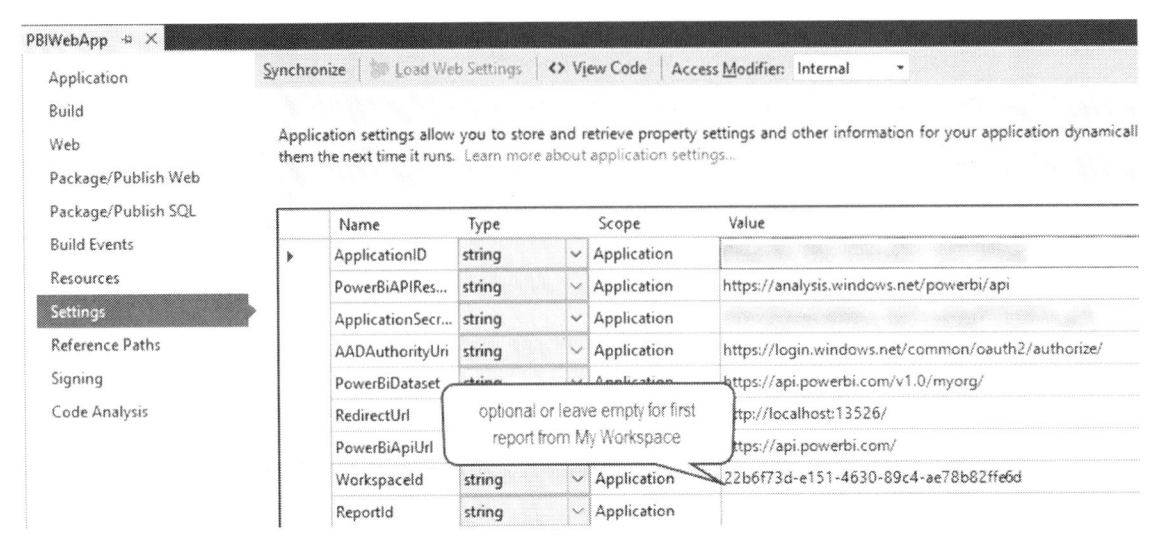

Figure 16.7 Update the PBIWebApp settings to match your setup before you run the application.

3. Change the *ApplicationID* setting to match the client ID of your app (you get it after you register the app).
4. Change the *ApplicationSecret* setting to match one of the app keys.
5. If you leave WorkspaceId empty, the app will embed the first report from My Workspace. If you want to embed reports from a specific app workspace, change the *WorkspaceId* setting accordingly. Recall that you can get the workspace id from the browser address bar once you navigate to that workspace in powerbi.com.
6. Change the *ReportID* setting to match one of the report identifiers in the workspace (or leave empty for the first report listed alphabetically in that workspace).

16.3.2 Authenticating Users

Intranet applications would typically authenticate users with Windows integrated security. However, Power BI is a cloud application that requires the user to sign in. In the three-leg flow (user owns data) the app navigates the user to the Power BI sign-in page. I explained this flow in detail in the previous chapter.

Implementing the three-leg flow

When the app starts, the default page shows a Get Report button. When you click it, the page calls the server-side GetAuthorizationCode method, which is shown in **Figure 16.8**. The application creates a query string that includes the client id, the Power BI API authorization URL, and the Redirect URI that you specified when you registered the application. Line 146 sends the request to the authorization endpoint, which redirects the user to the Power BI sign-on page. Once the user authenticates with Power BI, the user is redirected back to the Default.aspx page (the app Redirect URL is set to the web root URL).

```
110  public void GetAuthorizationCode()
111  {
112      //NOTE: Values are hard-coded for sample purposes.
113      //Create a query string
114      //Create a sign-in NameValueCollection for query string
115      var @params = new NameValueCollection
116      {
117          //Azure AD will return an authorization code.
118          {"response_type", "code"},
119
120          //Client ID is used by the application to identify themselves to the users that they are requesting permissions from.
121          //You get the client id when you register your Azure app.
122          {"client_id", Settings.Default.ApplicationID},
123
124          //Resource uri to the Power BI resource to be authorized
125          //The resource uri is hard-coded for sample purposes
126          {"resource", Settings.Default.PowerBiAPIResource},
127
128          //After app authenticates, Azure AD will redirect back to the web app. In this sample, Azure AD redirects back
129          //to Default page (Default.aspx).
130          { "redirect_uri", Settings.Default.RedirectUrl}
131      };
132
133      //Create sign-in query string
134      var queryString = HttpUtility.ParseQueryString(string.Empty);
135      queryString.Add(@params);
136
137      //Redirect to Azure AD Authority
138      // Authority Uri is an Azure resource that takes a application id and application secret to get an Access token
139      // QueryString contains
140      //      response_type of "code"
141      //      client_id that identifies your app in Azure AD
142      //      resource which is the Power BI API resource to be authorized
143      //      redirect_uri which is the uri that Azure AD will redirect back to after it authenticates
144
145      //Redirect to Azure AD to get an authorization code
146      Response.Redirect(String.Format(Settings.Default.AADAuthorityUri + "?{0}", queryString));
147  }
```

Figure 16.8 The three-leg flow redirects the user to the Power BI sign-on page.

Obtaining the access token
The access token is the cornerstone of every OAuth security flow. Upon successful authentication, the authority passes the authorization code to the redirect Uri you specified. Because in this case, we don't have a redirect page, the Page_Load event in the Default.aspx page is executed. It calls the GetAccessToken method (see **Figure 16.9**).

This method gets the authorization code (passed as a first argument) and creates an AuthenticationContext object. Then it calls AuthenticationContext.AcquireTokenByAuthorizationCode to obtain an AuthenticationResult object, which has the access token, refresh token, and other details, such as the token expiration date. Then the app extracts the access token from AuthenticationResult, and passes it back to the Page_Load event. The Page_Load event caches the token into a session variable to avoid reauthenticating for subsequent page reposts.

Remember that for additional security, the access token has a limited lifespan, and your code needs to catch errors that are caused by expired tokens. This is explained in more detail in the "Configurable token lifetimes in Azure Active Directory" article at https://docs.microsoft.com/azure/active-directory/active-directory-configurable-token-lifetimes. Although PBIWebApp doesn't demonstrate this flow, your code can use the refresh token in the AuthenticationResult object to extend the user session when the access token expires. By default, the access token expires in one hour and the refresh token expires in 14 days. Instead of caching just the access token, consider caching the entire AuthenticationResult object in a session variable and calling AC.AcquireTokenByRefreshTokenAsync to renew the access token from the refresh token.

```csharp
149  public string GetAccessToken(string authorizationCode, string applicationID, string applicationSecret, string redirectUri)
150  {
151      //Redirect uri must match the redirect_uri used when requesting Authorization code.
152      //Note: If you use a redirect back to Default, as in this sample, you need to add a forward slash
153      //such as http://localhost:13526/
154
155      // Get auth token from auth code
156      TokenCache TC = new TokenCache();
157
158      //Values are hard-coded for sample purposes
159      string authority = Settings.Default.AADAuthorityUri;
160      AuthenticationContext AC = new AuthenticationContext(authority, TC);
161      ClientCredential cc = new ClientCredential(applicationID, applicationSecret);
162
163      //Set token from authentication result
164      return AC.AcquireTokenByAuthorizationCode(
165          authorizationCode,
166          new Uri(redirectUri), cc).AccessToken;
167  }
```

Figure 16.9 The GetAccessToken method extracts the access token from the authorization code.

Power BI Embed Report

Basic Sample
First make sure you register your app. After registration, copy Application ID and Application Secret to web.config file.
The application will embed the first report from your Power BI account. If you wish to embed a specific report, please copy

Select "**Get Report**" to embed the report.

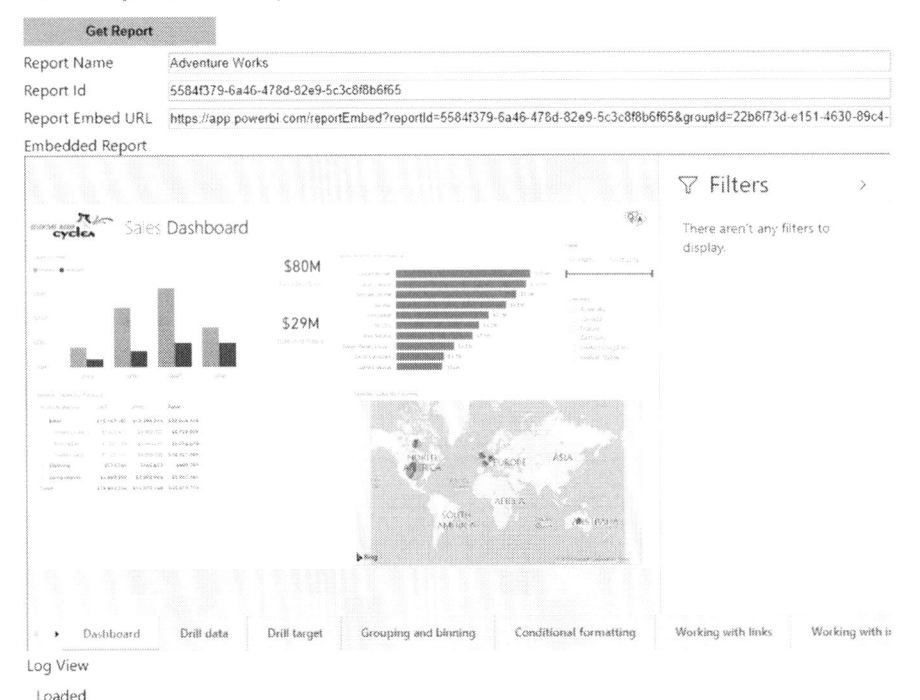

Get Report	
Report Name	Adventure Works
Report Id	5584f379-6a46-478d-82e9-5c3c8f8b6f65
Report Embed URL	https://app.powerbi.com/reportEmbed?reportId=5584f379-6a46-478d-82e9-5c3c8f8b6f65&groupId=22b6f73d-e151-4630-89c4-

Embedded Report

Log View
Loaded
Rendered

Figure 16.10 PBI-WebApp shows the embedded Internet Sales Analysis report.

16.3.3 Embedding Reports

Once the app obtains the access token, it can embed Power BI content that the user has permissions to access in Power BI Service. The PBIWebApp demonstrates the minimum code you need to write to embed reports in your apps. **Figure 16.10** shows the Internet Sales Analysis report embedded on a web page.

Getting reports

The Default.aspx page demonstrates how a custom app can embed a report. As a first step, the app would probably present the user with a list of reports to choose from. But to make things simpler, the sample skips this step and shows the report you specified in the configuration settings. As I mentioned, the ReportId app setting controls which report the app would show and the WorkspaceId setting specifies the workspace where the report is located. The GetReportFromWorkspace method (see **Figure 16.11**) demonstrates the server-side code you need to write to obtain the report details required for embedding.

Line 173 calls the Get Groups REST API to retrieve a list of workspaces the user has access to. If the specified workspace identifier is not in the list, the app returns an error message. If the ReportId is not specified, the app calls the "Get Reports In Group" API (line 187) to retrieve all the reports in that workspace and defaults to the first one.

Once the calling method (GetReport) gets the report object, it populates the textboxes on the GetReport page wit the report embedUrl, report id, and report name.

```
169  // Gets the report with the specified ID from the workspace. If report ID is emty it will retrieve the first report from the workspace.
170  private Report GetReportFromWorkspace(PowerBIClient client, string WorkspaceId, string reportId)
171  {
172      // Gets the workspace by WorkspaceId.
173      var workspaces = client.Groups.GetGroups();
174      var sourceWorkspace = workspaces.Value.FirstOrDefault(g => g.Id == WorkspaceId);
175
176      // No workspace with the workspace ID was found.
177      if (sourceWorkspace == null)
178      {
179          errorLabel.Text = string.Format("Workspace with id: '{0}' not found. Please validate the provided workspace ID.", WorkspaceId);
180          return null;
181      }
182
183      Report report = null;
184      if (string.IsNullOrEmpty(reportId))
185      {
186          // Get the first report in the workspace.
187          report = client.Reports.GetReportsInGroup(sourceWorkspace.Id).Value.FirstOrDefault();
188          AppendErrorIfReportNull(report, "Workspace doesn't contain any reports.");
189      }
190
191      else
192      {
193          try
194          {
195              // retrieve a report by the workspace ID and report ID.
196              report = client.Reports.GetReportInGroup(WorkspaceId, reportId);
197          }
198
199          catch(HttpOperationException)
200          {
201              errorLabel.Text = string.Format("Report with ID: '{0}' not found in the workspace with ID: '{1}', Please check the report ID."
202
203          }
204      }
205
206      return report;
207  }
```

Figure 16.11 This code demonstrates how to enumerate reports in a workspace.

Embedding the report

Next, you'd need to write client-side JavaScript code that does the actual report embedding by calling the Power BI JavaScript library. Open the markup code of the Default.aspx page (shown in **Figure 16.12**) to

```
1   <%@ Page Title="Home Page" Language="C#" MasterPageFile="~/Site.Master" AutoEventWireup="true" CodeBehind="Default.aspx.cs" Inheri
2   <asp:Content ID="BodyContent" ContentPlaceHolderID="MainContent" runat="server">
3       <script type="text/javascript" src="scripts/powerbi.js"></script>
4       <script type="text/javascript">
5
6           //This code is for sample purposes only.
7           //Configure IFrame for the Report after you have an Access Token. See Default.aspx.cs to learn how to get an Access Token
8           window.onload = function () {
9               var accessToken = document.getElementById('MainContent_accessToken').value;
10              if (!accessToken || accessToken == "")
11              {
12                  return;
13              }
14              var embedUrl = document.getElementById('MainContent_txtEmbedUrl').value;
15              var reportId = document.getElementById('MainContent_txtReportId').value;
16
17              // Embed configuration used to describe the what and how to embed.
18              // This object is used when calling powerbi.embed.
19              // This also includes settings and options such as filters.
20              // You can find more information at https://github.com/Microsoft/PowerBI-JavaScript/wiki/Embed-Configuration-Details.
21              var config= {
22                  type: 'report',
23                  accessToken: accessToken,
24                  embedUrl: embedUrl,
25                  id: reportId,
26                  settings: {
27                      filterPaneEnabled: true,
28                      navContentPaneEnabled: true
29                  }
30              };
31              // Grab the reference to the div HTML element that will host the report.
32              var reportContainer = document.getElementById('reportContainer');
33              // Embed the report and display it within the div container.
34              var report = powerbi.embed(reportContainer, config);
```

Figure 16.12 The client-side JavaScript code that embeds the report.

see how this works. Line 3 references the Power BI JavaScript library. Line 8 defines an event for window.onload that obtains the previously-generated access token. For demonstration and testing purposes, the app shows the access token on the web page although this presents a security vulnerability. In real life, the client code would obtain the server-generated token and the report details to construct the embedded configuration.

> **NOTE** The transfer of the access token from the server to the client must happen over the HTTPS protocol to prevent a hacker from intercepting the token. It's true that JavaScript code is not secure, but before getting to the access token, the hacker must gain access to the user machine to open the page client-side code. If this happens, you have a much bigger security issue. Recall that all web apps that require authentication must somehow pass the user identity between the client and the server, so OAuth is no less secure than any other LOB web-based app, including Salesforce, Dynamics Online, and internal apps. Moreover, if the hacker obtains the token, he might not be able to do much with it as the token expires in a few minutes.

Line 21 shows the embedded configuration. At minimum, you need to include the access token, report embedUrl, and report identifier. The actual embedding happens with just one line of code (line 34)! This line calls the embed method and passes as arguments the html element where the report will be rendered and the embed configuration.

16.4 Report-enabling Internet Applications

Many organizations provide reports to their external customers to support both (Business-to-Business) B2B and (Business-to-Consumer) B2C scenarios. In Chapter 12, I explained that you can use dashboard/report sharing and apps to share content out to external users. But this approach has some important drawbacks:

- Dependency on Azure Active Directory (AAD) – Although Power BI will handle this on its own, every user must have an AAD external account added to your tenant. This might present maintenance and security issues.
- Per-user license – Despite that Power BI offers three licensing options for external users, every user must be covered by a Power BI Pro license.
- Read-only reports – Users are limited to read-only reports. They can't change existing reports or create new reports.

These limitations present challenges for external reporting. An Internet-facing app typically authenticates users with Forms Authentication, by showing a login form to let the users enter application credentials. Then the application verifies the credentials against a profile store, such as a table in a SQL Server database. If you plan many external users, you'd want to avoid registering your users twice: with your application and with Power BI (Azure Active Directory). Power BI Embedded lets you address these challenges in a cost-effective way.

16.4.1 Understanding the Sample Application

To help you get started with Power BI Embedded, Microsoft included another sample "App Owns Data" in the same location (https://github.com/Microsoft/PowerBI-Developer-Samples). However, this app is designed as an ASP.NET MVC app and it might be difficult to configure and understand it. So, for your convenience, I converted the User Owns Data app and provided the source code in the \Source\ch16\App Owns Data\ folder.

Configuring the app
I recommend you use the Power BI Embedded onboarding experience to create a new app registration.
1. Go to https://app.powerbi.com/embedsetup.
2. Choose Embed for Your Customers and follow the steps to create a new *native* app. If you need more guidance about registration, the "Tutorial: Embed a Power BI report, dashboard, or tile into an application for your customers" article at https://docs.microsoft.com/power-bi/developer/embed-sample-for-customers provides the necessary steps to register the native app.
3. Open the solution file from the \ch16\App Owns Data folder in Visual Studio. Open the project properties and change the project settings listed in **Table 16.7**.

Table 16.7 The configuration settings for the PBIWebApp sample.

Setting	Notes
ApplicationID	The Client ID of the app from the registration (in Azure Portal, this is Application ID)
WorkspaceId	The identifier of the workspace where the Power B content is located (get it from the browser address bar after you navigate to the workspace content page in Power BI)
ReportId	The identifier of the report to embed (get it from the browser address bar after you open the report)
pbiUsername	The email address of a Power BI user who is added as an admin to the workspace
pbiPassword	The password of the that user that the user uses to log in to Power BI

It's important to understand that the app will authenticate to Power BI using the credentials of a "trusted" Power BI account on your tenant and then embed the content on behalf of the user. By default, all users would see the same data unless the report is set up for row-level security (RLS) and the app handles RLS.

> **NOTE** The app stores the password of the admin user in clear text in web.config for the sake of simplicity. This is not a best practice. For your real-life apps, consider storing the password encrypted or retrieve it from Microsoft Key Vault.

4. Deploy a Power BI Desktop file with a report to the workspace. If you want to test dashboard embedding, create a dashboard in Power BI Service. By default, the app shows the first dashboard in the workspace.
5. Recall that when your real-life app is ready to be used by other users, you need to assign the workspace to a premium or embedded capacity.

That's all that's needed to configure the app. Remember that while embedding has a dependency on the Power BI service, there is not a dependency on Power BI for your customers. They do not need to sign up for Power BI to view the embedded content in your app.

Running the app
Let's now take the app for a ride.

1. Open the app in Visual Studio.
2. Right-click the project in Solution Explorer and then click Build. The app should build successfully. If it doesn't, you're probably missing some dependencies. To fix this, right-click the app, click "Manage NuGet Packages", and then install all dependencies the app requires.
3. Press Ctrl-F5 to run the app. On the startup screen, click "Get Report". You should see the Adventure Works report embedded (see again **Figure 16.10**). Take some time to test interactive features to make sure they work.

16.4.2 Authenticating Users

Next, let me walk you through the code changes to help you understand how the app differs from the intranet app.

Obtaining access token
The main difference from the intranet app is authentication. **Figure 16.13** shows how the GetReport method handles authentication. Your real-life app should refactor the authentication code in one place.

```
52  protected async Task<AuthenticationResult> GetReport()
53  {
54      // Create a user password cradentials.
55      var credential = new UserPasswordCredential(Username, Password);
56      // Authenticate using created credentials
57      var authenticationContext = new AuthenticationContext(AuthorityUrl);
58      var authenticationResult = await authenticationContext.AcquireTokenAsync(ResourceUrl,
59          ApplicationId, credential).ConfigureAwait(false);
60
61      if (authenticationResult == null)
62      {
63          errorLabel.Text = "Authentication Failed.";
64      }
65
```

Figure 16.13 The server-side code that handles authentication.

Line 55 creates a credential object from the credentials of the admin user that you specified in the project settings. Line 58 calls AcquireTokenAsync to authenticate the user. Again, the app authenticates directly with Power BI and uses a trusted account on your domain that has admin access to the workspace. The user is not asked to authenticate with Power BI and there is no redirection to a login form.

> **NOTE** Because the app is designed as a regular ASP.NET app, I used ConfigureWait(false) method of AcquireTokenAsync to avoid deadlocking the main application thread. This is not required for MVC-style apps.

Then the code is the same as in the User Owns data scenario. The app discovers what reports are available for the user and retrieves the report you specified in web.config.

Obtaining embed token

As you've seen, the intranet sample demonstrates the "User Owns Data" scenario. Once the user authenticates with Power BI, embedding happens under his identity and the access token controls what he can do, such as only view reports or edit and create reports. However, external users are authenticated and authorized by your application, and your application uses a trusted account that has admin access to the workspace. This presents a security issue because you don't want external users to gain more permissions they need and to access content under the admin account.

To further restrict the permissions of the interactive user, your app needs to issue a less-permissive type of token, called an *embed token*. Here is the relevant code:

```
// Generate Embed Token for reports without effective identities.
GenerateTokenRequest generateTokenRequestParameters = new GenerateTokenRequest(accessLevel: "view");
var tokenResponse = await client.Reports.GenerateTokenInGroupAsync(WorkspaceId, report.Id, generateTokenRequestParameters).ConfigureAwait(false);
```

The *accessLevel* parameter of the GenerateTokenRequest method specifies a view permission to the report. This method takes another *allowSaveAs* argument, which when set to true, allows the user to change the report and save it as another report. The documentation for the GenerateTokenRequest method specifies how to invoke the method for other operations, such as creating reports, Q&A, viewing dashboards, and tiles. The embed token (not the access token) is what your app needs to pass to client-side code to embed content. For example, the client-side code in the default.aspx page uses the embed token to embed the report. The rest of the client-side embedded APIs should be familiar to you by now.

16.4.3 Implementing Data Security

If all users will see the same data on the report, there is no need to propagate the user identity to the data source. However, the chances are that your app would need to restrict access to data for different users. In Chapter 9, I showed you how to implement data security in Power BI Desktop models. Another popular scenario for using an effective user identity is when the report connects to an Analysis Services model.

Checking if RLS is configured

Data security is also known as row-level security (RLS). Here is the code you need to write to handle RLS.

```
var datasets = await client.Datasets.GetDatasetByIdInGroupAsync(WorkspaceId, report.DatasetId)
var IsEffectiveIdentityRequired = datasets.IsEffectiveIdentityRequired;
var IsEffectiveIdentityRolesRequired = datasets.IsEffectiveIdentityRolesRequired;
GenerateTokenRequest generateTokenRequestParameters;
// This is how you create embed token with effective identities
if (!string.IsNullOrWhiteSpace(username))
{
  var rls = new EffectiveIdentity(username, new List<string> { report.DatasetId });
  if (!string.IsNullOrWhiteSpace(roles))
  {
    var rolesList = new List<string>();
    rolesList.AddRange(roles.Split(','));
    rls.Roles = rolesList;
```

POWER BI EMBEDDED

431

    }
    // Generate Embed Token with effective identities.
    generateTokenRequestParameters = new GenerateTokenRequest(accessLevel: "view", identities: new List<EffectiveIdentity> { rls });
};
```

First the code obtains a reference to the dataset that the report uses. Then the code checks if the dataset requires an effective identity. This will be the case when the Power BI Desktop model has security roles or when you connect live to Analysis Services. Then the code checks if the dataset requires roles. If RLS is defined in Power BI Desktop, you must pass one or more roles that match the ones in the file. Using roles is optional when you connect live to Analysis Services.

### Using effective identity and roles

If RLS uses dynamic security, USERNAME() and USERPRINCIPALNAME() will return whatever username your app passes as an effective identity. Typically, this will be the login name that the user enters to authenticate with your app, but it can be whatever is required for dynamic security to work (recall that external users don't sign to Power BI Service, so the username can be anything).

The roles that you pass to the method must exist in the Power BI Desktop file or the Analysis Services semantic model. If the app passes multiple roles, the user will get the superset of all the role permissions. The code creates an effective identity from the user name and the dataset identifier. If you specify roles, they are added to the effective identity. The last line obtains an embed token from the effective identity.

## 16.5 Summary

Developers can enrich custom applications with embedded BI content. Thanks to the Power BI open architecture, you can report-enable any web-enabled application on any platform! Collectively known as Power BI Embedded, the Power BI embed API are for embedding tiles, dashboard, reports, and Q&A in your apps.  You can acquire Power BI Embedded with Power BI Premium or by purchasing an embedded capacity. Embedded reports preserve their interactive features, such as filtering, highlighting, and sorting. Because the Power BI embedded APIs have the same feature parity as Power BI Service, users can view, edit, and create reports. Microsoft has provided JavaScript APIs and a report object model to help you extend your apps with interactive features, such as to handle events resulting from user actions or to extend the Microsoft-provided menus.

One of the most challenging aspects of report-enabling custom applications is security. If you're tasked to report-enable internal business apps and your users have Power BI licenses, your app can pass the user identity to Power BI with OAuth and then call the Power BI embedded APIs. As you saw, OAuth is a flexible security framework that supports different authentication flows. The default three-leg (User Owns Data) flow navigates the user to a sign-on page, so the user owns the data.

External (Internet-facing) apps can avoid registering users twice and benefit from the per-render licensing model of Power BI Embedded. Most apps will use the two-leg authentication (Apps Owns Data) flow, where the app uses a trusted account to authenticate with Power BI but issues a restricted embed token to avoid granting the user admin rights to the workspace.

Besides report-enabling custom applications, the Power BI APIs allow web developers to extend Power BI's visualization capabilities. You can read about custom visuals in the next chapter!
```

Chapter 17

Creating Custom Visuals

17.1 Understanding Custom Visuals 433
17.2 Custom Visual Programming 435
17.3 Implementing Custom Visuals 443

17.4 Deploying Custom Visuals 449
17.5 Summary 451

The Power BI visuals can take you far when it comes to presenting data in a visually compelling and engaging way, but there is still room for the occasional requirement that simply cannot be met with the built-in visuals. For example, suppose you want to convey information graphically using a graph that Power BI does not support. Or, you might need a feature that Microsoft currently doesn't have, such as a 3D chart. Fortunately, web developers can extend the Power BI data visualization capabilities by implementing custom visuals. They can do this with open source JavaScript-based visualization frameworks, such as D3.js, WebGL, Canvas, or SVG.

In this chapter, I'll introduce you to this exciting extensibility area of Power BI. I'll start by explaining what a custom visual is and the developer toolset that Microsoft provides for implementing visuals. Then, I'll walk you through the steps of implementing a sparkline visual for showing data trends. Finally, I'll show you how to deploy the custom visual and use it in Power BI. This chapter targets web developers experienced in TypeScript and JavaScript, D3.js and Node.js.

17.1 Understanding Custom Visuals

In Chapter 3, I introduced you to custom visuals from an end user standpoint. You saw that you can click the ellipsis (...) button in the Visualizations pane (both in Power BI Service and Power BI Desktop) and import a custom visual from Microsoft AppSource (https://appsource.microsoft.com). Now let's dig deeper and understand the anatomy of a custom visual before you learn how to implement your own.

17.1.1 What is a Custom Visual?

A custom visual is a JavaScript plug-in that extends the Power BI visualization capabilities. Because the custom visual is dynamically rendered in the Web browser, it's not limited to static content and images. Instead, a custom visual can do anything that client-side JavaScript code and JavaScript-based presentation frameworks can do. As you can imagine, custom visuals open a new world of possibilities for presenting data and new visuals are posted to AppSource every week!

> **NOTE** BI developers might remember that SSRS has been supporting .NET-based custom report items. They might also recall that SSRS custom report items render on the server as static images with limited interactivity. By contrast, Power BI runs the custom visual JavaScript code on the client side. Because of this, custom visuals can be more interactive. To emphasize this, the sparkline visual (whose implantation I discuss in this chapter) demonstrates animated features, although this might not necessarily be a good visualization practice.

Understanding the custom visual framework

To allow developers to implement and distribute custom visuals, Microsoft provides the following toolset:

1. Support of custom visuals in Power BI reports – Users can create reports with custom visuals in Power BI Service and Power BI Desktop. Reports with custom visuals can also render in Power BI Report Server.
2. Microsoft AppSource – A community site (https://appsource.microsoft.com) that allows developers to upload new Power BI visuals and users to discover and download these visuals. Both Microsoft and the community have donated custom visuals to AppSource.
3. Power BI custom visual developer tools – Custom Visual Developer Tools (https://github.com/Microsoft/PowerBI-Visuals/) that integrate with Power BI to assist developers in debugging and testing the visual code.

Understanding host integration

Power BI has different hosting environments where visuals can be used, including dashboards, reports, Q&A, native mobile applications, and Power BI Desktop. From an end user standpoint, once the user imports a custom visual, the user can use it on a report just like the visualizations that ship with Power BI. In **Figure 17.1**, the last icon in the Visualizations pane shows that I've imported the Sparkline visual and then added it to the report.

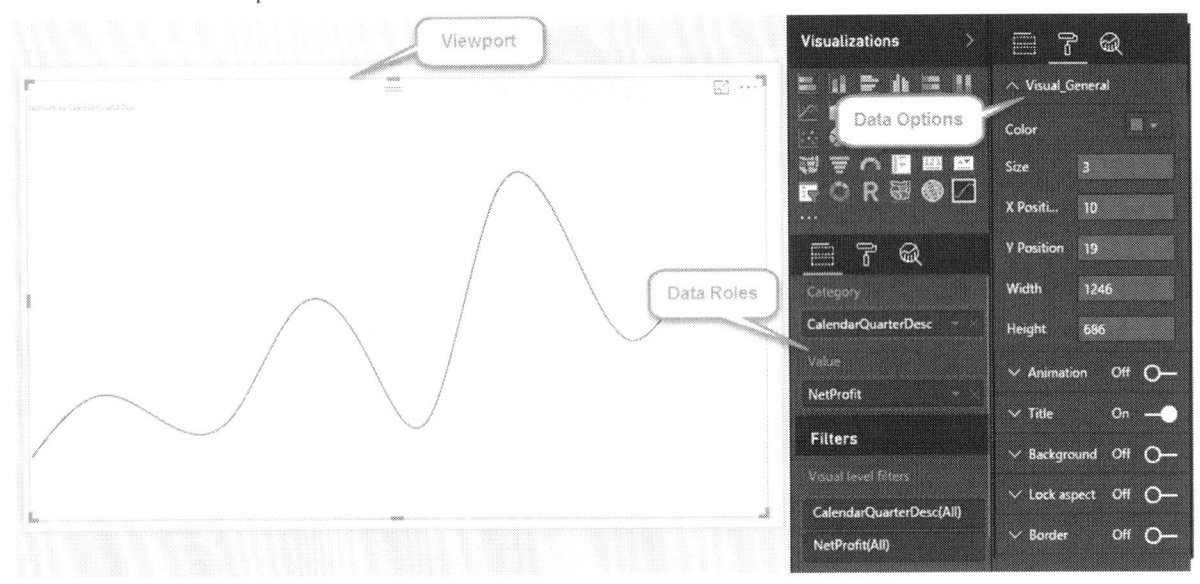

Figure 17.1 The host takes care of the plumbing work required to configure the visual.

When a custom visual is added to a report, the user can specify the size of the visual by dragging its resize handles. The resulting area determines the boundaries of the canvas (also called a viewport) that is available to the visual to draw whatever visualization it creates. When you create a visual, you need to adhere to a specification that determines how the visual interacts with the host environment.

The hosting environment takes care of most of the plumbing work required for configuring the visual. It is the host that takes care of configuring the Fields and Format tabs of the Visualizations pane. The visual simply advertises what capabilities it supports. For example, the Sparkline visual tells the host that it supports one category field and one value field. Once the host discovers this information, it configures the Fields tab of the Visualizations pane accordingly.

The Format tab (shown expanded on the right of the Fields tab in **Figure 17.1**) works in the same way. The visual advertises the formatting options it supports and how they should be presented. However, it is the host that configures the UI (the Format tab). For example, the Sparkline visual tells the host that it supports two properties for formatting the graph: Color (for the line color) and Size (for the line width). It also supports an optional animation feature under the Animation section that controls the delay of each redraw and the duration of how fast the graph is drawn. Given this information, the host configures the Format pane accordingly so that the user can configure these settings.

The host integration adds a slew of additional features that don't require any coding on your part. The host gets the data based on how the Fields tab is configured, and passes the data to the visual. Interactive highlighting, that cross filters the rest of visualizations on the page (when the user selects an element in one visual), also works without any coding. The host also takes care of report-level, page-level and visual-level filters, and adds common settings, such as Tile and Background, in the Format pane.

17.1.2 Understanding the IVisual Interface

As I noted, a custom visual must adhere to a design specification. This specification defines an IVisual interface, which every custom visual must implement. The specification is documented and available at https://github.com/Microsoft/PowerBI-visuals/blob/master/Visual/IVisualApi.md. The IVisual interface defines four key methods, as follows:

- *constructor (options: VisualConstructorOptions)* – when you place a visual on a report, the host calls the *constructor()* method to give the visual a chance to perform some initialization tasks. The host passes an options argument, which among other things includes the viewport height and width. Microsoft recommends that you don't draw the visual in the *constructor* method. Instead, use this method to execute one-time code for initializing the visual, such as to class and style the visual div container.
- *update (options: VisualUpdateOptions): void* – This is the workhorse of the visual. The *update()* method is responsible for drawing the visual presentation. Every time the host determines that the visual needs to be refreshed, such as a result of configuration changes or resizing, the host will call the *update()* method. Similar to the *constructor()* method, the host passes an options parameter.
- *enumerateObjectInstances (options: EnumerateVisualObjectInstancesOptions): VisualObjectInstancesEnumeration* – As I mentioned, the visual is responsible for advertising its capabilities. You can use the
enumerateObjectInstances() method to return objects that the host discovers to populate the Fields and Formats pane. This method is called for each object defined in the visual capabilities. The host won't display the property if it's not enumerated.
- *destroy(): void* – The host calls this method when the visual is about to be disposed. This typically happens when the visual is removed from the report or the report is closed. The code in *destroy()* should release any resources that might result in memory leaks, such as unsubscribing event handlers.

I'll walk you through implementing IVisual when I discuss the implementation of the Sparkline visual. For now, let's understand what skillset is required to code custom visuals.

17.2 Custom Visual Programming

How do you implement custom visuals and what development tools are available to code and test custom visuals? Microsoft provided a comprehensive toolset to assist web developers to implement custom visuals. In addition, Microsoft published sample visuals, so there is plenty of reference material to get you started.

Creating custom visuals is not that difficult but as with any coding effort, it requires a specific skillset. First, you need to know TypeScript and JavaScript to code custom visuals. To save you coding effort (drawing graphics elements in plain JavaScript is hard), you should also have experience in a JavaScript-based visualization framework, such as Data-Driven Documents (D3.js). However, you can also use other JavaScript-based frameworks if you prefer something else than D3.js, such as SVG or WebGL. Finally, you need to have web developer experience, including experience with HTML, browser Document Object Model (DOM), and Cascading Style Sheets (CSS). You can use an integrated development environment (IDE) of your choice for coding custom visuals, such as Microsoft Visual Studio Code.

To get you started with custom visual programming, let me introduce you to TypeScript – the programming language for coding custom visuals.

17.2.1 Introducing TypeScript

So that they work across platforms and devices, custom visuals are compiled and distributed in JavaScript. But writing and testing lots of code straight in JavaScript is difficult. Instead, for the convenience of the developer, custom visuals are implemented in TypeScript.

What is TypeScript?
When you implement custom visuals, you use TypeScript to define the visual logic and interaction with the host. TypeScript is a free and open source (http://www.typescriptlang.org) programming language, developed and maintained by Microsoft for coding client-side and server-side (Node.js) applications. Its specification (http://www.typescriptlang.org/docs/) describes TypeScript as "a syntactic sugar for JavaSript". Because TypeScript is a typed superset of JavaScript, when you compile TypeScript code you get plain JavaScript. So, why not write directly in JavaScript? Here are the most compelling reasons that favor TypeScript:

- Static typing – TypeScript extends tools, such as Visual Studio, to provide a richer environment for helping you code and spotting common errors as you type. For example, when you use Visual Studio and Power BI Developer Tools you get IntelliSense as you type. And when you build the code, you get compile errors if there are any syntax issues.
- Object-oriented – TypeScript is not only data-typed but it's also object-oriented. As such, it supports classes, interfaces, and inheritance.

Comparing TypeScript and JavaScript
To compare TypeScript and JavaScript, here's a short sample from the Typescript Playground site (http://www.typescriptlang.org/Playground), which is shown in **Figure 17.2**.

The TypeScript code on the left defines a Greeter class that has a member variable, a constructor, and a *greet*() method. Notice that the TypeScript window supports IntelliSense. This is possible because TypeScript defines the type of member variables and method parameters. These types are removed when the code is compiled to JavaScript, but can be used by the IDE and the compiler to spot errors and help you code. TypeScript is also capable of inferring types that aren't explicitly declared. For example, it would determine that the *greet*() method returns a string, so you can write code like this:

someMethodThatTakesString(greeter.greet());

To learn more about what led to TypeScript and its benefits, watch the video "Introducing TypeScript" by Anders Hejlsberg at https://channel9.msdn.com/posts/Anders-Hejlsberg-Introducing-TypeScript. Although he doesn't need an introduction, Anders Hejlsberg is a Microsoft Technical Fellow, the lead architect of C#, and creator of Delphi and Turbo Pascal. Anders has worked on the development of TypeScript.

Figure 17.2 The TypeScript Playground allows you to compare TypeScript and JavaScript side by side.

17.2.2 Introducing D3.js

Coding the application flow in TypeScript is one thing but visualizing the data is quite another. Again, using plain JavaScript and CSS to draw graphs would be a daunting experience. Fortunately, there are open-source visualization frameworks that are layered on top of JavaScript. Microsoft decided to adopt the Data-driven Documents (D3.js) framework to implement all the Power BI visualizations, but you are not limited to it if you prefer other JavaScript-based visualization frameworks.

What is D3.js?
As you know, JavaScript is the de facto standard language as a client-side browser language. But JavaScript was originally designed for limited interactivity, such as clicking a button or handling some input validation. As Internet evolved, developers were looking for tools that would enable them to visually present data within Web pages without requiring reposting the page and generating visuals on the server side. There were multiple projects sharing this goal but the one that gained the most acceptance is D3.js.

According to its site (http://d3js.org), "D3.js is a JavaScript library for manipulating documents based on data". Documents in this context refer to the Document Object Model (DOM) that all Web browsers use to manipulate client-side HTML in an object-oriented way. D3 uses other web standards, such as HTML, CSS, and Scalable Vector Graphics (SVG) to bind data to DOM, and then to apply data-driven transformations to visualize the data. The D3.js source code and a gallery with sample visualizations are available on GitHub (https://github.com/mbostock/d3).

Automating visualization tasks with D3.js
To give you an idea about the value that D3.js brings to client-side visualization, consider the bar chart shown in **Figure 17.3**.

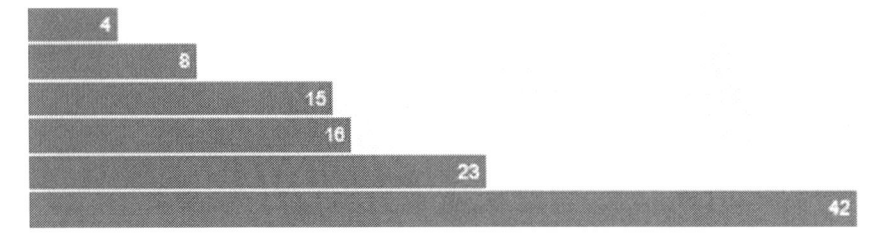

Figure 17.3 Although simple, this bar chart is not easy to update in plain JavaScript and CSS.

The left section in **Figure 17.4** shows how a web developer would implement the same chart using HTML and CSS. The code has one div element for a container, and one child div for each bar. The child DIV elements have a blue background color and a white foreground color.

```
.chart div {
  font: 10px sans-serif;
  background-color: steelblue;
  text-align: right;
  padding: 3px;
  margin: 1px;
  color: white;
}

</style>
<div class="chart">
  <div style="width: 40px;">4</div>
  <div style="width: 80px;">8</div>            d3.select(".chart")
  <div style="width: 150px;">15</div>            .selectAll("div")
  <div style="width: 160px;">16</div>            .data(data)
  <div style="width: 230px;">23</div>          .enter().append("div")
  <div style="width: 420px;">42</div>            .style("width", function(d) { return d * 10 + "px"; })
</div>                                           .text(function(d) { return d; });
```

Figure 17.4 The left section shows the chart definition in HTML/CSS while the right section shows the D3 code.

So far so good. But what if you want to bind this chart dynamically to data, such as when the report is refreshed, or new fields are added? This would require JavaScript code that manipulates DOM to put the right values in the right div element. By contrast, the right section shows how you can do this in D3.js. Let's break it down one line at a time.

First, the code selects the chart element using its class selector (.chart). The second line creates a data join by defining the selection to which you'll join data. The third line binds the data to the selection. The actual data could be supplied by the application as a JavaScript array, which may look like this:

var data = [4, 8, 15, 16, 23, 42];

The fourth line outputs a div element for each data point. The fifth line sets the width of each div according to the data point value. The last line uses a function to set the bar label. Note that you'd still need the CSS styles (shown on the left code section) so that the chart has the same appearance. If you have experience with data-driven programming, such as using ADO.NET, you might find that D3.js is conceptually similar, but it binds data to DOM and runs in the Web browser on the client side. It greatly simplifies visualizing client-side data with JavaScript!

17.2.3 Understanding Developer Tools

Microsoft has provided the Custom Visual Developer Tools (https://github.com/Microsoft/PowerBI-visuals) to help developers implement custom visuals. The toolset includes documentation, tools for testing and packaging your visual, and sample visuals that demonstrate implementation details.

> **NOTE** This section is intended to get you introduced and get started with Custom Visual Developer Tools. For more in-depth information, see the reference documentation within the Power BI Visuals repo at https://github.com/Microsoft/PowerBI-visuals. While you're there, look at the tool roadmap at https://github.com/Microsoft/PowerBI-visuals/tree/master/Roadmap.

Getting started with Developer Tools

The Developer Tools consists of a command-line tool (pbiviz) and integration hooks to Power BI Service. The toolset brings the following benefits to developers interested in implementing Power BI visuals:

- Ability to use external libraries – Because the Developer Tools use the standard typescript compiler, you can bring any external library and use it within your visual. Moreover, a custom visual runs in a sandboxed iframe. This allows you to use specific versions of libraries and global styles, without worrying that you'll break other visuals.
- Your choice of IDE – The Developer Tools doesn't force you into a coding environment. It's implemented as a command-line tool that works across platforms with any IDE of your choice, including Visual Studio, Visual Studio Code, CATS, Eclipse, and so on.
- Integration with Power BI Service – You can add your visual on a report to test and debug it as you code and see how it'll work when a Power BI user decides to use it. You can also turn on a special live preview mode where the visual automatically updates when you make changes to the source.

Configuring the Developer Tools involves the following high-level steps:

1. Follow the installation steps at https://github.com/Microsoft/PowerBI-visuals/tree/master/tools to install NodeJS, the command-line tool (pbiviz), and server certificate. The server certificate is needed to enable the live preview mode for testing the visual in Power BI Service. In this mode, the visual code runs in a trusted https server, so you need to install an SSL certificate (included with the tool) to allow the visual to load in your browser.

2. To view and test your visual, you need to enable this feature in Power BI Service. To do so, log in to powerbi.com, then click the Settings menu in the top-right corner. In the Developer section (General tab), check "Enable developer visual for testing" (see **Figure 17.5**). When checked, this setting adds a special Developer Tools icon to the Visualizations pane.

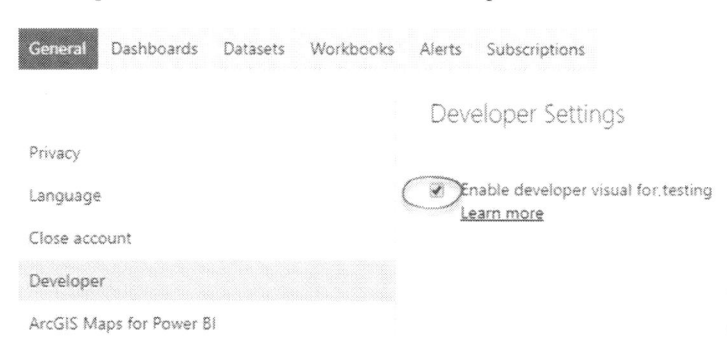

Figure 17.5 Check the "Enable developer visual for testing" checkbox to view and test custom visuals in Power BI Service.

> **TIP** If you find that the "Enable developer visual for testing" setting doesn't stay enabled after you check it, make sure to follow the installation steps for installing the server certificate.

Creating a new visual

The Developer Tools can generate the folder structure and required dependencies for new visuals. You can create a new project by opening the command prompt, navigating to the folder where you want the project to be created, and typing the following command (replace VisualName with the name of your visual):

pbiviz new VisualName

This command will create a new project folder with the same name as the VisualName you provided and will then add some files organized in subfolders. **Table 17.1** shows the structure of the project folder and describes the purpose of the most important folders and files.

Table 17.1 This table shows the structure of the project folder.

Item	Purpose	Item	Purpose
.api/	Power BI libraries and interfaces	.gitignore	Lists files to ignore when check in source in GitHub
.vscode/	Settings for launching and debugging custom visuals	capabilities.json	Defines the Data and Format settings of your visual
assets/	Stores additional information to distribute, such as icon, image, screenshot	package.json	Used by package manager for JavaScript (npm) to manage modules
dist/	Outputs the *.pbiviz file when you package your visual	package-lock.json	Describers the dependency tree and dependencies
node_modules/	Created after you run "npm I", it contains the Node.js libraries	pbiviz.json	Main configuration file
src/	The TypeScript code of your visual goes here	tsconfig.json	Specifies compiler options (see bit.ly/2gdIbuv)
style/	CSS styles	tslint.json	Specifies coding rules when compiling source

Once the project is created, the next step is to open the src/visual.ts file in your favorite editor and start coding your visual.

Configuring D3.js types

Recall that Power BI custom visuals are coded in TypeScript - a typed superset of JavaScript. But where do you get the actual type definitions (known as *typings*) from? Instead of installing files containing the typings, the current recommendation is to use *npm @types*. For example, if you target D3.js and you want to install version 3.5.5 (Power BI does not yet support D3 v4) along with its types, you can use the following syntax (see npmjs.com/package/@types/d3).

npm install d3@3.5.5 @types/d3@3.5.36 --save

Installing dependencies

To test the visual with Power BI Service, you need to install the required dependencies. These dependencies are distributed as Node.js modules. Node.js modules are JavaScript libraries that you can reference in your code. Follow these steps to install the dependencies:

1. Open the Windows Command Prompt as Administrator.
2. Navigate to the folder that has your visual source.
3. Run the following command:

npm install

> **TIP** Installing the dependencies results in a node_modules folder whose size exceeds 80 MB! To avoid including the dependencies when you check in your visual to GitHub, add the node_modules folder to the .gitignore file. When sending the code to someone else, don't include the node_modules folder. Other developers can restore node_modules by executing "npm install".

Testing custom visuals

To test the visual, you need to build it and then add it to a report in Power BI Service. Use the pbiviz command-line to build the visual (open the command prompt, navigate to the project folder, then type the command and press Enter).

```
pbiviz start
```

First, the command-line tool builds the visual and notifies you of any errors. If all is well, it packages the visual for testing. Next, it launches an https server that will serve your visual for testing. If there are no errors, the command window should show the following output:

```
info  Building visual...
done  build complete
info  Starting server...
info  Server listening on port 8080.
```

Next, go to powerbi.com. Find a test dataset that will supply the data to the visual and click it to create a new report. Notice that a Developer Tools icon is added to the Visualizations Pane (see **Figure 17.6**).

Figure 17.6 Use the Developer Tools icon to test your custom visual in Power BI Service.

When you click this icon, Power BI Service will add a frame to the report canvas and connect it to the visual you're testing (make sure to execute "pbiviz start" before you click the Developer Tools icon. A toolbar appears on top of the frame. **Table 17.2** describes the toolbar buttons.

Table 17.2 This table describes the toolbar buttons for testing custom visuals in Power BI Service starting from left.

Button	Purpose
Reload Visual Code	Manually refresh the visual if auto reload is disabled.
Toggle Auto Reload	When turned on, the visual will automatically update every time you make changes and save the visual file.
Show Dataview	Shows the dataview (actual data) that is passed to the visual's update method.
Export Dataview	Exports the dataview to a JSON format if you want to inspect it further or send it to someone else.
Get Help	Navigates to the tool documentation on GitHub.
Send Feedback	Navigates to GitHub where you can leave feedback.

Debugging custom visuals

You can use the browser debugging capabilities to step through the visual code in Power BI Service. However, you can put breakpoints because the visuals script is entirely reloaded every time the visual is updated and all breakpoints are lost. Instead, use the JavaScript debugger statement.

1. Put a debugger statement somewhere in the visual code that you want the script execution to stop.
2. Start your visual test session as explained before in the "Testing custom visuals" section.

CREATING CUSTOM VISUALS

3. Assuming you use Chrome, press F12 to open its developer environment.
4. Perform the task on the report that triggers that code. For example, if you put a breakpoint in the update method, simply resize the visual on the report (this will invoke the update method). If your code is reachable, the execution should stop at the debugger statement (see **Figure 17.7**).
5. Step through the code and examine it. For example, in Chrome you can press F10 to step over to the next line and hover over a variable to examine its value. You can also use the Console tab to test variables, or you can add a variable to the Watch window.

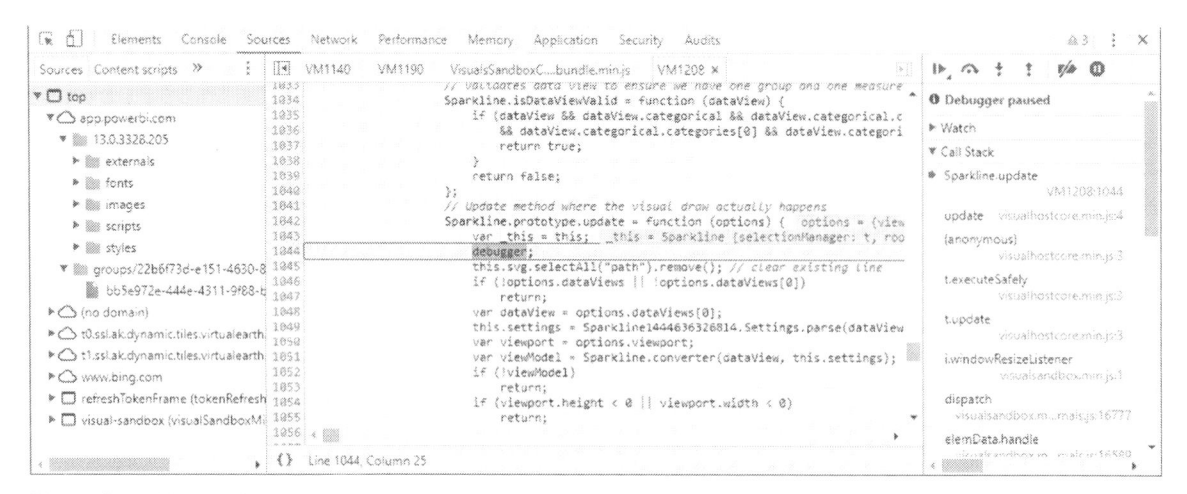

Figure 17.7 Use the browser debugging capabilities to step through your visual code in Developer Tools.

Although you can change variable values while debugging your code, you won't be able to make changes to the visual source in the browser. You need to do so in the IDE you use to code the visual. However, if Auto Reload is turned on, the visual will update in Power BI Service automatically when you save the source file. For more debugging tips, refer to the "PowerBI Visual Tools (pbiviz) – Debugging" article at https://github.com/Microsoft/PowerBI-visuals/blob/master/tools/debugging.md.

Upgrading the Developer Tools
Overtime, Microsoft will upgrade both the Developer Tools and scripts. The roadmap (https://github.com/Microsoft/PowerBI-visuals/blob/master/Roadmap) informs you when a new version is available. You can upgrade your visual by executing these commands:

```
#Update the command-line tool (pbiviz)
npm install -g powerbi-visuals-tools
```

```
#run update from the root of your visual project, where pbiviz.json is located
pbiviz update
```

The first command will download the latest command-line tool from npm, including the updated type definitions and schemas. The second command will overwrite the apiVersion property in your pbiviz.json.

Now that you've learned about programming and testing custom visuals, let me walk you through the implementation steps of the Sparkline visual.

17.3 Implementing Custom Visuals

A sparkline is a miniature graph, typically drawn without axes or coordinates. The term sparkline was introduced by Edward Tufte for "small, high resolution graphics embedded in a context of words, numbers, images". Tufte describes sparklines as "data-intense, design-simple, word-sized graphics". Sparklines are typically used to visualize trends over time, such as to show profit over the past several years. Although other Microsoft reporting tools, such as Excel and Reporting Services include sparkline elements, Power BI doesn't have a sparkline visual. Yet, sparklines are commonly used on dashboards so I hope you'll find my sparkline implementation useful not only for learning custom visuals but also for your real life projects.

17.3.1 Understanding the Sparkline Visual

Sparklines come in different shapes and forms. To keep things simple, I decided to implement a "classic" smooth line sparkline that is shown in **Figure 17.8**.

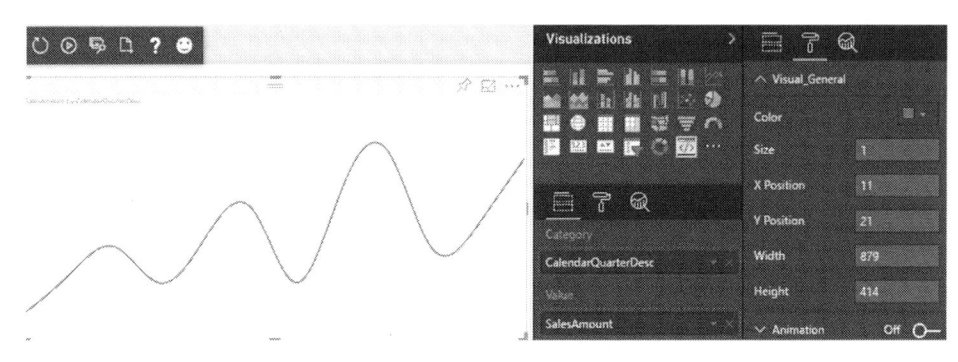

Figure 17.8 You can configure the sparkline using the Data and Format tabs.

Understanding capabilities
Once you import and add the sparkline to a report, you bind the sparkline to data using the Data tab of the Visualization pane. **Figure 17.8** shows that I'm aggregating a SalesAmount field added to the Value area by the CalendarQuarterDesc field, which is added to the Category area. The resulting graph shows how sales fluctuate over quarters. You can use any field to group the data, not just a field from the Date table. The sparkline supports several formatting options to customize its appearance. The General section lets you change the line color and width. The default properties are "steelblue" as a color and one pixel for the line width.

The Animation section lets you turn on an animation effect that draws the line gradually from left to right. Although in general I advise against animations and other visual distractors in real-life reports, I wanted to emphasize the fact that Power BI visuals can support anything clients-side JavaScript can do. If you expand the Animation section, you'll see that you can specify two settings: Duration and Delay. The Duration setting controls how fast the line draws (the default setting is 1,000 milliseconds) and the Delay setting controls the interval between redraws (the default is 3,000 milliseconds).

Understanding limitations
The main limitation of the current implementation is that the sparkline doesn't render multiple times in the same visualization, such as for each product category. This limitation also applies to Microsoft-provided visuals, such as the Gauge visual. Preferably, at some point Power BI would support a repeater visual, like the SSRS Tablix region. This would allow nesting the sparkline into other visualizations, such as a table, that could repeat the sparkline for each row. As Power BI stands now, the only way to implement this feature is to draw the visual for each category value. Although the sparkline doesn't repeat, it could be

used to display multiple measures arranged either horizontally or vertically by adding it multiple times on the report.

Another limitation related to the one I've just discussed is that the sparkline supports only a single field in the Category area and a single field in the Value area. In other words, the sparkline is limited to one measure and one group.

17.3.2 Implementing the IVisual Interface

I coded the sparkline using Microsoft Visual Studio Code. Visual Studio Code (https://code.visualstudio.com) is a free source code editor developed by Microsoft for Windows, Linux, and macOS. Think of Visual Studio Code as a light-weight version of Visual Studio, which is specifically useful if you spend most of your time writing client-side JavaScript code. Visual Studio Code includes support for debugging, embedded Git control, syntax highlighting, intelligent code completion, snippets, and code refactoring.

Let's start its implementation with the IVisual interface. Remember that IVisual has four key methods: *constructor()*, *update()*, *enumerateObjectInstances()* and *destroy()*. You can find the project code in the /Source/Ch16/sparkline folder. The sparkline visual code is in the src/sparkline.ts file.

Implementing the constructor() method
Power BI calls the *constructor()* method to give a chance to the visual to initialize itself. Figure 17.9 shows its implementation.

```
112 public constructor(options: VisualConstructorOptions) {
113     this.selectionManager = options.host.createSelectionManager();
114     this.root = d3.select(options.element);
115     this.tooltipServiceWrapper = createTooltipServiceWrapper(options.host.tooltipService,
116                             options.element);
117
118     this.svg = this.root
119         .append('svg')
120         .classed('sparkline', true)
121         .attr('height', options.element.clientHeight)
122         .attr('width', options.element.clientWidth);
123 }
```

Figure 17.9 The constructor() method initializes the visual.

First, the code creates an instance of the SelectionManager, which the host uses to communicate to the visual user interactions, such as clicking the graph. The sparkline doesn't handle user selection events but it's possible to extend it, such as to navigate to another page or highlight a line segment. Line 114 initializes the D3.js framework with the DOM element that the visual owns, which is passed to the *constructor()* method as a property of the VisualConstructorOptions parameter.

Line 115 is for the tooltip support which I'll explain in section 17.3.3. Line 118 creates a *svg* HTML element and classes it as "sparkline". It's a good practice to create another element instead of using the root in case you need to draw more elements in the future. The code also sizes the *svg* element so that it occupies the entire viewport.

Implementing the update() method
The *update()* method is where the actual work of drawing the graph happens (see **Figure 17.10**). Line 127 removes the existing graph so that redrawing the sparkline doesn't overlay what's already plotted on the canvas and to avoid drawing new lines when the visual is resized.

When the host calls the *update()* method, it passes the data as a dataView object. For example, if you add the CalendarQuarter field to the Category area and SalesAmount field to the Value area, the host will aggregate SalesAmount by quarter and pass the corresponding data representation and the metadata describing the columns under the *options.DataView* object.

The definition of the *DataView* object is documented at https://github.com/Microsoft/PowerBI-visuals/blob/master/Capabilities/DataViewMappings.md. When binding the visual to the CalendarYear and

SalesAmount fields, the DataView object might look like the example shown in **Figure 17.11**. Since the sparkline visual supports only one field in the Category area, there is only one element in the *DataView.categorical.categories* array. The values property returns the actual category values, such as Q1 2015. The *identity* property returns system-generated unique identifiers for each category value. The *DataView.categorical.values* property contains the values of the field added to the Value area. Because the sparkline visual supports only one field in the Value area, the values array has only one element.

```
126 public update(options: VisualUpdateOptions) {
127     this.svg.selectAll("path").remove(); // clear existing line
128     if (!options.dataViews || !options.dataViews[0]) return;
129     const dataView: DataView = options.dataViews[0];
130     this.settings = Settings.parse(dataView) as Settings;
131     var viewport = options.viewport;
132     var viewModel: SparklineModel = Sparkline.converter(dataView, this.settings);
133
134     if (!viewModel) return;
135     if (viewport.height < 0 || viewport.width < 0) return;
136     var graph = this.svg;
137
138     // stop animation if graph is animating for update changes to take effect
139     this.stopAnimation();
140     // resize draw area to fit visualization frame
141     this.svg.attr({
142         'height': viewport.height,
143         'width': viewport.width
144     });
145
146     var data = viewModel.data;
147     // X scale fits values for all data elements; domain property will scale the graph width
148     var x = d3.scale.linear().domain([0, data.length - 1]).range([0, viewport.width]);
149     // Y scale will fit values from min to max calibrated to the graph higth
150     var y = d3.scale.linear().domain([Math.min.apply(Math, data), Math.max.apply(Math, data)]).range([0, viewport.height]);
151     // create a line
152     var line = d3.svg.line<number>()
153         .interpolate("basis") // smooth line
154         // assign the X function to plot on X axis
155         .x(function (d, i) {
156             // enable the next line when debugging to output X coordinate
157             // console.log('Plotting X value for data point: ' + d + ' using index: ' + i + ' to be at: ' + x(i) + ' using xScale.');
158             return x(i);
159         })
160         .y(function (d) {
161             // enable the next line when debugging to output X coordinate
162             // console.log('Plotting Y value for data point: ' + d + ' to be at: ' + y(d) + " using yScale.");
163             return viewport.height - y(d); // values are plotted from the top so reverse the scale
164         })
165
166     // display the line by appending an svg:path element with the data line we created above
167     var path = this.svg.append("svg:path")
168         .attr("d", line(data))
169         .attr('stroke-width', function (d) { return viewModel.size })
170         .attr('stroke', function (d) { return viewModel.color });
```

Figure 17.10 The update() method draws the graph.

Working directly with the DataView object is impractical. Therefore, line 132 calls the converter method, which converts the DataView object into a custom object for working with the data in a more suitable format. Using a converter is a recommended pattern since it allows you to organize the data just as you are to draw it, which makes your code focused on the task at hand and not on manipulating the data. For example, in our case the *data* property on line 146 returns the data points as a JavaScript array.

CREATING CUSTOM VISUALS

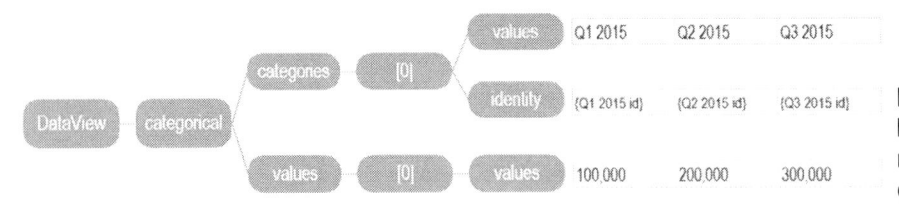

Figure 17.11 When the host calls the update() method it passes a DataView object with the actual data.

The D3.js code starts at line 148. First, the code calibrates the X axis to plot the number of data points. Conveniently, D3.js supports quantitative scaling and the *d3.scale.linear.domain* property scales the X axis to fit the data points. Next, the code calibrates the Y axis to fit the values given the minimum and maximum data point values. Lines 152-164 plot the line. One cautionary note here is that the zero coordinate of the Y axis starts at the top of the viewport. Therefore, line 163 inverts the data point Y coordinate. Line 167 draws the line using the user-specified line width and color.

Animating the graph
If the user turns on the Animate setting, the line constantly redraws itself using a configurable delay and redrawing speed. The code that animates the graph is shown in **Figure 17.12**. Line 186 checks if the animation effect is turned on. If so, it uses the JavaScript *setInterval()* function to call periodically the *redrawWithAnimation()* function.

```
173 function redrawWithAnimation() {
174     var totalLength = (<SVGPathElement>path.node()).getTotalLength();
175     graph.selectAll("path")
176         .data([data]) // set the new data
177         .attr("d", line)
178         .attr("stroke-dasharray", totalLength + " " + totalLength)
179         .attr("stroke-dashoffset", totalLength)
180         .transition()
181         .duration(viewModel.duration)
182         .ease("linear")
183         .attr("stroke-dashoffset", 0);
184 }
185
186 if (viewModel.animate) {
187     this.timer = setInterval(function () {
188         redrawWithAnimation();
189     }, viewModel.delay);
190 }
```

Figure 17.12 The graph supports animated line redrawing by calling repeatedly the redrawWithAnimation function.

D3.js and SVG make the task of animating the graph easy. Line 174 calls the SVG *getTotalLength()* function to calculate the length of the graph. The stroke-dasharray attribute lets you specify the length of the rendered part of the line. The stroke-dashoffset attribute lets you change where the dasharray behavior starts. Then the SVG transition() function is used to animate the path.

Implementing the destroy() method
Remember that the host calls the *destroy()* method to give the visual a chance to release any resources that might result in memory leaks. Our implementation releases the D3.js graph elements. It also releases the timer variable that holds a reference to the timer identifier when the animation effect is used.

```
public destroy(): void {
  this.svg = null;
  this.root = null;
  this.timer = nulll;}
```

17.3.3 Implementing Capabilities

Power BI hosts enumerate the visual's capabilities to provide various extensions. For example, the report host uses this information to populate the Field and Format tabs in the Visualizations pane. For this to work, the custom visual needs to tell Power BI what data and formatting capabilities it supports.

Advertising data capabilities

Figure 17.13 shows how the Sparkline visual advertises its data capabilities. This code is located in the capabilities.json file. The *dataRoles* property informs the host about the field areas the visual is expecting, while the *dataViewMappings* property describes how these fields relate to one another, and informs Power BI how it should construct the Fields tab areas. It can also inform the host about special conditions, such as that only one category value is supported.

```
1  {
2    "dataRoles": [
3      {
4        "name": "Category",
5        "kind": 0,
6        "displayName": "Category"
7      },
8      {
9        "name": "Value",
10       "kind": 1,
11       "displayName": "Value"
12     }
13   ],
14   "dataViewMappings": [
15     {
16       "conditions": [
17         {
18           "Category": { "max": 1 },
19           "Value": { "max": 1 }
20         }
21       ],
22       "categorical": {
23         "categories": {
24           "for": { "in": "Category" },
25           "dataReductionAlgorithm": { "bottom": { "count": 100 } }
26         },
27         "values": {
28           "group": {
29             "by": "Series",
30             "select": [ { "bind": { "to": "Value" } } ]
31           }
32         }
33       }

36   "objects": {
37     "general": {
38       "displayName": "Visual_General",
39       "properties": {
40         "fill": {
41           "type": { "fill": { "solid": { "color": true } } },
42           "displayName": "Color"
43         },
44         "size": {
45           "type": { "numeric": true },
46           "displayName": "Size"
47         }
48       }
49     },
50     "labels": {
51       "displayName": "Animation",
52       "properties": {
53         "show": {
54           "type": { "bool": true },
55           "displayName": "Visual_Show"
56         },
57         "delay": {
58           "type": { "numeric": true },
59           "displayName": "Delay"
60         },
61         "duration": {
62           "type": { "numeric": true },
63           "displayName": "Duration"
64         }
65       }
66     }
67   }
68 }
```

Figure 17.13 The visual describes its data capabilities in the capabilities.jscon file.

On line 2, the Sparkline custom visual uses *dataRoles* to tell Power BI that it needs a Category area for grouping the data and a Value area for the measure. When the host interrogates the visual capabilities, it'll add these two areas to the Fields tab of the Visualizations pane. On line 14, the custom visual uses dataViewMappings to instruct the host that the Category and Value areas can have only one field. To avoid performance degradation caused by plotting too many data points, line 25 specifies a bottom 100 data reduction condition to plot only the last 100 categorical values. So, if the user adds the Date field from the Date table, only the last 100 dates will be displayed.

Advertising formatting capabilities

Custom visuals are not responsible for implementing any user interface for formatting the visual. Instead, they declare the formatting options they support, and the host creates the UI for them. As it stands, Power BI supports three types of objects:

- Statically bound – These are formatting options that don't depend on the actual data, such as the line color.

- Data bound – These objects are bound to the number of data points. For example, the funnel chart allows you to specify the color of the individual data points.
- Metadata bound – These objects are bound to actual data fields, such as if you want to color all the bars in a series of a bar chart in a given color.

The Sparkline supports additional settings that allow the user to customize its appearance and animation behavior (shown in the right pane in **Figure 17.13**). All the sparkline formatting settings are static. They are grouped in two sections: General and Animation (it might be beneficial to refer to **Figure 17.1** again). The fill property (line 40) allows the user to specify the line color. The type of this property is color. This will cause the host to show a color picker. The *displayName* property defines the name the user will see ("Color" in this case). The Size property is for the line width and has a numeric data type.

The labels section defines the animation settings. The *show* property (line 53) is a special Boolean property that allows the user to turn on or off the entire section. The *delay* property controls how often the line is redrawn, while the *duration* property controls the speed of redrawing the line.

Providing default values

When the host discovers the visual capabilities, it calls the *IVisual.enumerateObjectInstances()* method to obtain the default values for each setting. And when the user changes a setting, the host calls this method again to push the new property values. This is all handled by the framework. Besides declaring the visual capabilities, you only need to provide default settings. As a best practice, the setting default values are stored in another src\settings.ts file (see **Figure 17.14**).

```
27 module powerbi.extensibility.visual {
28      "use strict";
29
30      import DataViewObjectsParser = powerbi.extensibility.utils.dataview.DataViewObjectsParser;
31
32      export class Settings extends DataViewObjectsParser {
33          public general: GeneralSettings = new GeneralSettings();
34          public labels: LabelsSettings = new LabelsSettings();
35      }
36
37      export class GeneralSettings {
38          public fill: string = "#4682b4";
39          public size: number = 1;
40      }
41
42      export class LabelsSettings {
43          public show: boolean = false;
44          public delay: number = 3000;
45          public duration: number = 1000;
46      }
47 }
```

Figure 17.14 The host calls enumerateObjectInstances to get and set the visual capabilities.

The *fill* general setting in the GeneralSettings class defaults the line stroke to SteelBlue color (#4682b4) and the *size* setting specifies 1pt for the line width. The LabelsSetting section defaults the *show* parameter to false (animation is off by default), and specifies default settings for line redraw delay and duration when the user turns animation on.

Handling tooltips

Tooltips allow users to see the values behind a data point. Follow these to support tooltips:

1. Add tooltipInterfaces.ts, tooltipeService.ts, and tooltipTouch.ts fields from the framework code (https://github.com/Microsoft/powerbi-visuals-utils-tooltiputils) to the src folder.
2. Reference these files in tsconfig.json.
3. In the visual *constructor* method, initiate the tooltipServiceWrapper object (see again Figure 17.9).
4. In the visual *update* method, call addTooltip.

```
this.tooltipServiceWrapper.addTooltip(this.svg.selectAll("path"),
  (tooltipEvent: TooltipEventArgs<number>) => this.getTooltipData(tooltipEvent, dataView, viewport),
  (tooltipEvent: TooltipEventArgs<number>) => null);
```

This method calls your implementation of what the tooltip shows. The sparkline implementation calls a helper function getTooltipeData and passes the tooltipEvent object, the visual dataView and viewport. **Figure 17.15** shows the implementation of the getTooltipData method.

```
213 private getTooltipData(value: any, dataView:DataView, viewport:IViewport): VisualTooltipDataItem[] {
214     var model = Sparkline.converter(dataView, this.settings);
215     var tooltip = <TooltipEventArgs<number>> value;
216     var x = tooltip.coordinates[0];
217     var width = viewport.width;
218     var i = Math.floor((x/width) * model.data.length); // find the closest data point from coordinates
219     var d = model.data[i];
220
221     return [{
222         displayName: dataView.categorical.categories[0].values[i].toString(),
223         value: d.toString()
224     }];
225 }
```

Figure 17.15 The getTooltip method returns what the tooltip should show when the user hovers on the line.

Line 214 obtains the Sparkline model from dataView. Line 216 obtains the coordinates of the hover event. Because the sparkline draws a line, it needs to approximate the nearest data point from the coordinates. This is done in line 218 which divides the x coordinate by the viewport width and multiplies the result by the number of data points. Line 219 retrieves the data point. Line 221 returns a tooltip object with a display name set to the data point category and actual value.

17.4 Deploying Custom Visuals

Once you test the custom visual, it's time to package it, so that your users can start using it to visualize data in new ways. If you want to make the visual publicly available, consider also submitting it to Microsoft AppSource.

17.4.1 Packaging Custom Visuals

Sot that end users can import your custom visual in Power BI Service and Power BI Desktop, you need to package the visual as a *.pbiviz file.

Understanding visual packages

A pbiviz file is a standard zip archive. If you rename the file to have a zip extension and double-click it, you'll see the structure shown in **Figure 17.16**.

resources — File folder
package.json — JSON File

Figure 17.16 A *.pbiviz file is a zip archive file that packages the visual code and resources.

The package.json file is the visual manifest which indicates which files are included and what properties you specified when you exported the visual. The resources folder includes another JSON file. This file bundles the visual code and all additional resources, such as the visual icon from the \assets folder.

Packaging custom visuals
The Custom Visual Developer Tools make it easy to export and package the visual.

1. In Visual Studio Code, open the pbiviz.json file.
2. Fill in the visual properties. **Figure 17.17** shows the settings that I specified for the Sparkline visual.

3. (Optional) Create a visual icon (20x20 pixels) and save it as an icon.png file under the assets/ folder. This is the icon the users see in the Visualizations pane after they import the visual.

```
1 {
2   "visual": {
3     "name": "Sparkline",
4     "displayName": "Sparkline",
5     "guid": "Sparkline1444636326814",
6     "visualClassName": "Sparkline",
7     "version": "1.2.0",
8     "description": "",
9     "supportUrl": "",
10    "gitHubUrl": ""
11  },
12  "apiVersion": "1.9.0",
13  "author": {
14    "name": "",
15    "email": ""
16  },
17  "assets": {
18    "icon": "assets/icon.png"
19  },
20  "externalJS": [
21    "node_modules/d3/d3.min.js",
22    "node_modules/powerbi-visuals-utils-dataviewutils/lib/index.js"
23  ],
24  "style": "style/visual.less",
25  "capabilities": "capabilities.json",
26  "dependencies": "dependencies.json",
27  "stringResources": []
28 }
```

Figure 17.17 Enter information that you want to distribute with the visual in the pbiviz.json file.

4. Open the Command Prompt, navigate to your project and execute the *pbiviz package* command. The last four lines represent the output the command generates.

pbiviz package

info   Building visual...
done   build complete
info   Building visual...
done   packaging complete

This command-line tool packages the visual and saves the pbiviz file under the dist/ folder. If only users within your organization will use the visual, you are done! You just need to distribute the *.pbiviz file to your users so they can import it in Power BI Desktop or Power BI Service.

Publishing to Microsoft AppSource

If you would like to make your visual publicly available, consider submitting it to Microsoft AppSource. To learn more about how to do so:

1. Open your web browser and navigate to Microsoft AppSource (https://appsource.microsoft.com).
2. If you haven't done so already, create an individual or corporate developer account.
3. Click the "List on AppSource" menu.
4. On the next page, scroll all the way down and then click the "Submit Your App" button. This will bring you to a page that will ask you to describe your app.

NOTE Is your organization concerned about quality and security of visuals published to AppSource? From a personal experience I can tell you that Microsoft follows a strict process to validate submissions. They'll check the custom visual thoroughly for bugs and best practices. Be patient because it will probably take a few cycles for your visual to appear in the gallery.

17.4.2 Using Custom Visuals

Once downloaded, custom visuals can be added to a report in Power BI Service or Power BI Desktop. Your users can add your custom visual to a report by clicking the ellipsis (...) button in the Visualizations pane. They will see options to import a custom visual from a file or from AppSource.

Understanding import limitations

As it stands, Power BI imports the custom visual code into the report. Therefore, the visual exists only within the hosting report that imports the visual. If you create a new report, you'll find that the Visualizations pane doesn't show custom visuals. You must re-import the custom visuals that the new report needs.

> **NOTE** As a best practice, you should test a custom visual for privacy and security vulnerabilities by using the Microsoft recommendations at https://powerbi.microsoft.com/en-us/documentation/powerbi-custom-visuals-review-for-security-and-privacy. I recommend you compare the TypeScript and JavaScript files to make sure they have the same code and test the JavaScript code with an anti-virus software.

Removing custom visuals

As you can see, users can easily add custom visuals to reports. Fortunately, Power BI makes it easy to remove visuals from a report if you no longer need them. To do so, edit the report, right-click the visual in the Visualizations pane (works in both Power BI Service and Power BI Desktop) and then click "Delete custom visual" (see **Figure 17.18**).

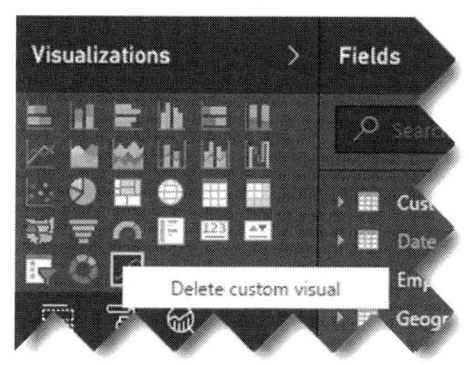

Figure 17.18 Right-click the custom visual to remove it if you no longer need it on the report.

17.5 Summary

The Microsoft presentation framework is open source to let web developers extend the Power BI visualization capabilities and to create their own visuals. Consider implementing a custom visual when your presentation requirements go beyond the capabilities of the Microsoft-provided visuals or the visuals contributed by the community. Custom visuals help you convey information as graphics and images. Any data insights that can be coded and rendered with JavaScript and client-side presentation frameworks, such as D3.js and SVG, can be implemented as a custom visual and used on Power BI reports.

You create custom visuals by writing TypeScript code that implements the Power BI IVisual interface. You can code a custom visual in your IDE of choice. Once the visual is ready and tested, you can export it to a *.pbiviz file, and then import it in Power BI Service or Power BI Desktop. You can also share your custom visuals with the community by submitting them to Microsoft AppSource.

With this chapter, we've reached the last stop of our Power BI journey. I sincerely hope that this book has helped you understand how Power BI can be a powerful platform for delivering pervasive data analytics. As you've seen, Power BI has plenty to offer to all types of users who are interested in BI:

- Information worker – You can use content packs and the Power BI Service Get Data feature to gain immediate insights without modeling.
- Data analyst – You can build sophisticated BI models for self-service data exploration with Power BI Desktop or Excel. And then you can share these models with your coworkers by publishing these models to Power BI or Power BI Report Server.
- BI or IT pro – You can establish a trustworthy environment that promotes team collaboration. And you can implement versatile solutions that integrate with Power BI, such as solutions for descriptive, predictive and real-time BI.
- Developer – Thanks to the Power BI open architecture, you can extend the Power BI visualization capabilities with custom visuals and integrate your apps with Power BI.

Of course, that's not all! Remember that Power BI is a part of a holistic vision that Microsoft has for delivering cloud and on-premises data analytics. When planning your on-premises BI solutions, consider the Microsoft public reporting roadmap at http://bit.ly/msreportingroadmap. Keep in mind that you can use both Power BI (cloud-based data analytics) and the SQL Server box product on-premises to implement synergetic solutions that bring your data to life!

Don't forget to download the source code from http://bit.ly/powerbibook and stay in touch with me on the book discussion list. Happy data analyzing with Power BI!

Appendix A

Glossary of Terms

The following table lists the most common BI-related terms and acronyms used in this book.

Term	Acronym	Description
Analysis Services Tabular		An instance of SQL Server Analysis Services that's configured in Tabular mode and is capable of hosting tabular models for organizational use.
App		A mechanism for packaging and distributing Power BI content.
AppSource		An area in Power BI Service where users can discover apps
Application Programming Interface	API	Connectivity mechanism for programmatically accessing application features
Azure Marketplace		The Windows Azure Marketplace is an online market buying and selling finished software as a Service (SaaS) applications and premium datasets.
Azure Machine Learning	AzureML	An Azure cloud service to creating predictive experiments
Business Intelligence Semantic Model	BISM	A unifying name that includes both Multidimensional (OLAP) and Tabular (relational) features of Microsoft SQL Server Analysis Services.
Capacity		A set of hardware resources dedicated to Power BI.
Content pack (superseded by apps)		A packaged set of dashboards, reports, and datasets from popular cloud services or from Power BI content (see organizational content pack)
Custom visual		A visualization that a web developer can create to plug in to Power BI or Power BI Desktop
Composite model		A data model with hybrid (import and DirectQuery) storage
Corporate BI		Same as Organizational BI.
Cube		An OLAP structure organized in a way that facilitates data aggregation, such as to answer queries for historical and trend analysis.
D3.js		A JavaScript-based visualization framework
Dataflow		A collection of Power Query queries that are scheduled and executed together for data staging and preparation outside a data model.
Dashboard		A Power BI page that can combine visualizations from multiple reports to provide a summary (preferably one-page) view of important business metrics.
Data Analysis Expressions	DAX	An Excel-like formula language for defining custom calculations and for querying tabular models.
Data model		A BI model designed with Power BI Desktop or Analysis Services.
Dataset		The definition of the data that you connect to in Power BI, such as a dataset that represents the data you import from an Excel file.

Term	Abbr	Definition
Descriptive analytics		A type of analytics that is concerned about analyzing history.
DirectQuery		A data connectivity configuration that allows Power BI to generate and send queries to the data source without importing the data.
Dimension (lookup) table		A table that represents a business subject area and provides contextual information to each row in a fact table, such as Product, Customer, and Date.
Extraction, transformation, loading	ETL	Processes extract from data sources, clean the data, and load the data into a target database, such as data warehouse.
Fact table		A table that keeps a historical record of numeric measurements (facts), such as the ResellerSales in the Adventure Works model.
Group		A Power BI group is a security mechanism to simplify access to content.
HTML5		A markup language used for structuring and presenting content on the World Wide Web.
Key Performance Indicator	KPI	A key performance indicator (KPI) is a quantifiable measure that is used to measure the company performance, such as Profit or Return on Investment (ROI).
Measure		A business calculation that is typically used to aggregate data, such as SalesAmount, Tax, OrderQuantity.
Microsoft AppSource		A site where developers can share apps.
Multidimensional		The OLAP path of BISM that allows BI professionals to implement multidimensional cubes.
Multidimensional Expressions	MDX	A query language for Multidimensional for defining custom calculations and querying OLAP cubes.
Office 365		A cloud-hosted platform of Microsoft services and products, such as SharePoint Online and Exchange Online.
OneDrive and OneDrive for Business		Cloud storage for individuals or businesses to uploading, organizing, and storing files.
Online Analytical Processing	OLAP	A system that is designed to quickly answer multidimensional analytical queries to facilitate data exploration and data mining.
On-premises Data Gateway		Connectivity software that allows Power BI to refresh and query directly on-premises data.
OAuthentication	OAuth	Security protocol for authentication users on the Internet
Paginated report		A standard, paper-oriented report that is one of the report types supported by SSRS
Personal BI		Targets business users and provides tools for implementing BI solutions for personal use, such as PowerPivot models, by importing and analyzing data without requiring specialized skills.
Personal Gateway		Connectivity software that allows business users to automate refresh data from on-premises data sources by installing it on their computers.
Power BI		A data analytics platform for self-service, team, and organizational BI that consists of Power BI Service, Power BI Desktop, Power BI Premium, Power BI Mobile, Power BI Embedded, and Power BI Report Server products.
Power BI Desktop		A free desktop tool for creating Power BI reports and self-service data models.
Power BI Embedded		Power BI APIs for embedding Power BI content in apps for internal and external customers.
Power BI Mobile		Native mobile applications for viewing and annotating Power BI content on mobile devices.
Power BI Portal		The user interface of Power BI Service that you see when you go to powerbi.com.
Power BI Premium		A Power BI Service add-on that allows organizations to purchase a dedicated environment.
Power BI Report Server		An extended edition of SSRS that supports Power BI reports and Excel reports.

Power BI Service		The cloud-based service of Power BI (powerbi.com). The terms Power BI and Power BI Service are used interchangeably.
Power Map		An Excel add-in for 3D geospatial reporting.
Power View		A SharePoint-based reporting tool that allows business users to author interactive reports from PowerPivot models and from organizational tabular models.
Power Pivot for Excel		A free add-in that extends the Excel capabilities to allow business users to implement personal BI models.
Power Pivot for SharePoint		Included in SQL Server 2012, PowerPivot for SharePoint extends the SharePoint capabilities to support PowerPivot models.
Power Query		An Excel add-in for transforming and shaping data.
Predictive analytics		Type of analytics that is concerned with discovering patterns that aren't easily discernible
Questions & Answers	Q&A	A Power BI feature that allows users to type natural questions to get data insights.
Representational State Transfer	REST	Web service communication standard
Row-level Security	RLS	A security mechanism for ensuring restricted access to data.
Self-service BI		Same as Personal BI.
Semantic model		Layered between the data and users, the semantic model translates database structures into a user-friendly model that centralizes business calculations and security.
SharePoint Products and Technologies	SharePoint	A server-based platform for document management and collaboration that includes BI capabilities, such as hosting and managing PowerPivot models, reports, and dashboards.
SQL Server Analysis Services	SSAS	A SQL Server add-on, Analysis Services provides analytical and data mining services. The Business Intelligence Semantic Model represents the analytical services.
SQL Server Integration Services	SSIS	A SQL Server add-on, Integration Services is a platform for implementing extraction, transformation, and loading (ETL) processes.
SQL Server Management Studio	SSMS	A management tool that's bundled with SQL Server that allows administrators to manage Database Engine, Analysis Services, Reporting Services and Integration Services instances.
SQL Server Reporting Services	SSRS	A SQL Server add-on, Reporting Services is a server-based reporting platform for the creation, management, and delivery of standard and ad hoc reports.
Snowflake schema		Unlike a star schema, a snowflake schema has some dimension tables that relate to other dimension tables and not directly to the fact table.
Star schema		A model schema where a fact table is surrounded by dimension tables and these dimension tables reference directly the fact table.
StreamInsight		An Azure cloud service for streaming
Tabular		Tabular is the relational side of BISM that allows business users and BI professionals to implement relational-like (tabular) models.
Team BI		Provides tools to allow business users to share BI solutions that they create with co-workers.
Tile		A dashboard section that can be pinned from an existing report or produced with Q&A.
TypeScript		A typed superset of JavaScript
Visualization		A visual representation of data on a Power BI report, such as a chart or map.
Workspace		A Power BI content area that is allocated for either an individual (My Workspace) or a team
xVelocity		xVelocity is a columnar data engine that compresses and stores data in memory.

index

A

AAD *See* Azure Active Directory
access token 425
ACE OLE DB provider 208
AcquireTokenAsync 430
Active Directory 149
active relationships 221
Admin Portal 65, 326
aggregation hits 167
aggregation table 167
aggregations 165
alerts 20, 97, 99, 116
    in Power BI Mobile 120
ALL function 244, 256
ALLEXCEPT function 244
ALLNOBLANKROW function 244
Analysis Services
    connecting to 61, 137
    importing data from 158
    integrating with Power BI 373
analytical features 232
Analytics tab 71
Analyze in Excel 49, 93, 330
    for drilling through 280
Android native app 116
animation 446
annotations 24, 126
appFigures 149
application registration 397
apps 23, 46
AppSource 35, 37, 57, 71, 341
ArcGIS 78, 330
Area Chart 74
auditing 331
AuthenticationContext class 402
AuthenticationResult 425
AutoComplete 243
AVERAGEX function 244
Azure Active Directory 27, 44
    external users 345
Azure Analysis Services 51, 372
Azure Data Catalog 11
Azure Data Factory 11
Azure Event Hubs 384
Azure Machine Learning 7, 11, 36, 312
    creating models 313
    integrating with Power BI 316
Azure Management Portal 399

Azure Marketplace 149
Azure Search Service 330
Azure SQL Data Warehouse 29, 51
Azure SQL Database 51
Azure Stream Analytics 11, 384, 385
Azure Table Storage 11
Azure Traffic Manager 27

B

B2B 344
B2C 344
background image 272
Bar Chart 74, 85
bar chart visualization 273
Basic Map 77
BI pro 34
Big Data 12
Binary data type 207
binning 284
BISM 369
bitness considerations 139
bookmarks 66, 295
Bookmarks Pane 143, 295
Bullet Chart 81
business intelligence 1
business user 30

C

CALCULATE function 244, 245, 256
calculated columns
    and row context 238
    implementing 248
    introducing 238
    storage 238
    when to use 239
calculated tables 247
CALCULATETABLE function 244
calendars 333
Canvas 37
Canvas apps 298
Capacity Admins 355
Capacity Assignment 355
capacity nodes 352
Capacity settings 356
capacity workloads 357
chromeless mode 49
cloud services 18, 50
Clustered Bar Chart 74

Clustered Column Chart 74
clustering 305
collaborative features 333
Column Chart 74, 85, 86
column from examples 173, 180
columns
    hiding 209
    referencing in DAX 242
    removing 209
    renaming 209
    resizing 209
    sorting 210
columnstore index 6
Combination Chart 74
Combo Chart 85
comments 98
    in Power BI Mobile 124
Common Data Model 192, 298
Common Data Service for Apps 193
composite model
    introduced 33
composite models 162
computed entity 195
conditional access 323
conditional formatting 76, 285
Content Delivery Network 28
content packs 49
conversation *See* comments
correlations 88
Cortana 12, 291, 330
Cortana Analytics Suite 3, 11, 313
Cortana answer cards 293
Cosmos DB 11, 149
COUNT function 244
COUNTA function 244
COUNTAX function 244
COUNTBLANK function 244
COUNTROWS function 244
COUNTX function 244
Create Relationship window 225
credit risk management 12
cross filtering 134, 222
cross highlighting 19
cross-sell 11
crosstab report 274
CSS 437
CSV files 157
Currency data type 207
custom apps

permissions 398
registering in Azure 398
registering in Power BI 423
custom columns
　adding in query 180
　in Query Editor 172
custom page sizes 65
custom sorting 205, 210
custom visuals 34, 37
　capabilities 447
　debugging 441
　host integration 434
　importing 70, 451
　packaging 449
　publishing 450
　understanding 80, 433
CUSTOMDATA function 375
customer acquisition 11

D

D3.js 37, 437
dashboard actions 101
dashboards
　actions 56
　API 392
　defined 55
　distributing 56
　duplicating 102
　in Power BI portal 48
　mobile viewing 119
　options for creating 56, 105
　printing 102
　sharing in Power BI Mobile 125
　sharing options 102
　understanding 96
　working with 111
Data Analysis Expressions 370
　functions 243
　operators 242
　understanding 237
data analyst 32
data bars 285
data categories 234
data classification 330
data collation 205
data connectors 37
data entry form 300
data frames 309
data import API 393
Data Lake 12, 149, 196
data mart 369
Data Mining add-in 7
data models
　publishing 146
　understanding 129
data refresh

　scheduling 337
data security 262
　and embedding 431
　and workspaces 336
　testing 265
Data Source Settings 147
data sources
　in Power BI Desktop 33
　managing 366
　types of access 51
data storytelling 289
data types 206
　reason for changing 207
Data View 140
data warehouse 369
data warehousing 35, 40
Data-driven Documents See D3.js
dataflow entities 195
dataflows
　connecting to 200
　exporting 199
　introduced 22
　settings 329
　storage 196
　when to use 194
dataRoles 447
datasets
　actions 52
　creating programmatically 403
　definitions 390
　deleting 53
　understanding 50
dataView object 444
dataViewMappings 447
Datazen 11
Date data type 207
date table 235
date tables
　creating with Power Query 188
　importing 155
　understanding 132
DATEADD function 247
DATESBETWEEN function 247
DATESINPERIOD function 247
DATESMTD function 247
DATESQTD function 247
DATESYTD function 247
DAX 237, See Data Analysis Expressions
DAX Studio 255
DAXMD 137
Decimal Number data type 206
Decision Tree 314
defaultRetentionPolicy 394
denormalization 131
descriptive analytics 3
dimensions 40, 131

DirectQuery 82, 136, 370
　limitations 164
DirSync 321
display folders 235
DISTINCT function 244, 245
DISTINCTCOUNT function 244
distribution lists 325
DNS Service 27
Doughnut Chart 75
Drill tab 145
drilling across 279
drilling down 66, 145, 273, 278
drilling through 56, 97, 113, 120, 280
drillthrough filters 281
drillthrough pages 280
dual storage 163
duplicating pages 70
Duration data type 207
dynamic data security 266
Dynamic Management Views 255
Dynamics CRM 18, 31

E

EARLIER function 244
EARLIEST function 244
Edit Interactions 144, 274
Edit Queries 140
Editing View 69
effective identity 432
EffectiveUserName 363, 374
embed codes 65, 328
embed configuration 414
embed token 431
embedded capacity 408
embedding reports 37
encrypted connections 147, 151
Enter Data 161
enumerateObjectInstances 448
error handling 182
Esri 78
ETL 40, 41, 169
Excel
　connecting to 91
Excel AzureML Add-in 315
Excel files
　importing 59, 156
　reporting options 94
Excel Online 123
Excel reports 63, 82
　in Power BI Mobile 123
Explain Increase/Decrease 303
explicit measures
　implementing 255
　introducing 240
exporting data 67, 329
external sharing 104, 329, 345

INDEX   457

F

Facebook 149
fact tables 40, 130
favorites 24, 101
Field Properties Pane 143
fields
　adding to reports 73
　and icons 73
Fields pane 72
Filled Map 77
FILTER function 244, 245
filter types 71
filtering data 178
filters
　compared to slicers 277
　locking and hiding 278
Filters pane 66, 278
fixed-length files 158
Flow 13, 37
focus mode 98
forecasting 71, 304
foreign key 133
Format Painter 141
formatting columns 208
Forms Authentication 429
formula bar
　in Data View 242
　in Query Editor 175
fraud detection 12
fully-additive measures 261
Funnel Chart 75

G

gateway 35, 50
　defined 52
Gateway Role 28
Gauge 78
GDPR 44
GenerateTokenRequest 431
geo fields 73
Geoflow 7
Geography data type 207
GeoJSON 77
Get Datasets API 417
Get Groups API 414
Get Reports API 418
Get Tiles API 414
GetAccessToken 425
GetAuthorizationCode 424
ggplot2 307
GitHub 149
GlobeMap 8, 17
Google Analytics 18, 31, 51, 57, 149
gridlines 69, 142
grouping data 143, 283

H

Hadoop 149
HDInsight 11, 51
hierarchies 232, 233
Home page 47
HTML5 23
HTTP verbs 391
hybrid BI solutions 35

I

IBM DB2 149
image areas 289
images 288
implicit measures 239
　implementing 252
implicit relationships 371
importing data 51, 135
　filtering 154
　from relational databases 152
　from text files 157
　from Web 160
inactive relationships 222, 228
incremental refresh 216
individual subscriptions 110, 364
in-focus mode 67
in-line date hierarchies 232
Inner Join 184
interactive data analysis 371
interactive features 19, 66, 68
　in native apps 122
interactive highlighting 67
Internet of Things 36, 380
iOS 23
iOS native app 114
IoT *See* Internet of Things
iPad 114
iPhone 115
IVisual interface 435

J

JavaScript Object Notation *See* JSON
JSON 142, 149, 192, 196, 199

K

key columns 133
KPI 79, 158

L

LASTNONBLANK function 262
Left Outer Join 184
licenses 323
Line Chart 74
line chart visualization 275
linked entity 196
links 287
live connections 18, 29, 46, 51, 82, 136
　and Power BI 61
logo 272
lookup tables 131
LOOKUPVALUE function 244, 245, 260, 268

M

M language 37, 171
MailChimp 149
mail-enabled groups 325
many-to-many relationships
　implementing 261
Map Shaper 78
Map visual 275
maps 77
Marketo 18
Master Data Services 11
Matrix visual 76, 85, 274
MAX function 244
MAXX function 244
MDX 159, 370
measures
　implicit vs. explicit 240
　introducing 239
　vs. calculated columns 240
　when to use? 240
Microsoft Data Platform 10
Microsoft Surface 117
MIN function 244
MINX function 244
mobile reports 123
Model-driven apps 298
MOLAP *See* Multidimensional OLAP
Multi Row Card 79
Multidimensional 369
multidimensional cubes 40
Multidimensional Expressions 370
Multidimensional OLAP 370
multifactor authentication 323
My Workspace 47, 332
MySQL 149

N

naming conventions 203
narratives 294
natural questions 107
navigation links 234
Navigator window 151
NodeJS 439
NoSQL 11

O

OAuth

for native clients 396
for web apps 396
implementing 402
parties 395
three-leg flow 395
understanding 394
OAuth2 36
OData feeds 149
ODBC 149
Office 365 8, 44
Office 365 Application Launcher 48
Office 365 groups 325
On premises Gateway 61, 137
and SSAS 373
configuring 348
installing 347
mapping users 375
using 349
vs Personal Gateway 346
OneDrive 61, 91
one-to-many cardinality 133
one-to-one cardinality 133
operators 242
Oracle 149
organization visuals 329
organizational apps 20
rights 341
understanding 340
organizational BI 2
challenges 40
classic solution 39, 368
vs. personal BI 372
organizational content packs
viewing 49
outliers 88

P

page render 353, 409
page-level filter 73, 86
paginated reports 377
PARALLELPERIOD function 247
parent-child relationships 259
PATH function 260
PATHCONTAINS function 268
PATHITEM function 260
pbiviz file 80, 439
pbix files 18
Performance inspector 102
persistent filters 54
personal gateway
confguring 338
Phone View 101, 142
phone-optimized view 121
Pie chart 275
Pie Chart 75, 121
pinning live pages 66

pinning report items 363
pinning reports 106
pinning visualizations 105
PostgreSQL 149
Power BI
browser support 114
data security 29
design tenets 9
editions 13
problems it solves 8
product line 4
role in Microsoft BI 13
signing up 43
Power BI Admin 326
Power BI Desktop
availability 139
compared with Excel 17
defined 16
downloading 49
features 16
for Power BI Report Server 362
importing from Excel 18
introduced 4
updating 147
Power BI Developer Center 37
Power BI editions 49
Power BI Embedded
capacities 356
features 25
getting started 408
introduced 4
introduced 4
licensing 26
Power BI for Office 365 8
Power BI Free 14
sharing content 354
Power BI Mobile 32
defined 23
downloading 49
features 23
introduced 4
Power BI portal 45
Power BI Premium
calculator 14
introduced 4
managing 355
understanding 22
Power BI publisher for Excel 49
Power BI Publisher for Excel 93
Power BI Report Server 63
in Power BI Mobile 117
introduced 4
licensing 362
pinning items 109
understanding 26, 359
Power BI Service
architecture 27

defined 4
Power BI visuals gallery 450
Power Map 7
Power Pivot 5, 16
Power Platform 12
Power Query 7, 16, 169
Power View 6, 16
PowerApps 37
integrating with Power BI 299
introduced 12
understanding 298
PowerPoint 65
PowerShell 405
predictive analytics 303
defined 3
predictive experiment 3, 315
predictive features 3
predictive solutions 36
premium capacity 22
understanding 352
premium workspaces 354
prescriptive analytics 3
primary key 133, 220
publish to web 65, 329
publishing content 339
PubNub 381
Python 310
Python 7

Q

Q&A 19, 49, 290
disabling 102
embedding 417
for creating dashboards 56, 107
in Power BI Desktop 141
limitations 20
tuning 108
working with 113
Q&A Explorer 290
QR Code
Quick Response Code 99
quantitative scaling 446
queries
appending 185
defined 135
disabling load 171
disabling refresh 171
merging 183
understanding 174
Query Editor 152, 153
understanding 169
query folding 176, 218
query functions
creating 185
for AzureML 317
query parameters 171, 216

creating 190
Quick Insights 53
    adding to dashboard 108
    in Power BI Desktop 303
    working with 88
Quick Response Code 99
quick styles 76
Quickbooks Online 149

R

R 7, 306, 330
    data shaping with 172
ranking functions 247
RANKX function 251
Reading View 54, 64
real-time BI 36, 380
real-time dashboards 386
real-time tile 382
recent sources 214
refresh plan 367
refresh policy 218
refreshing
    data 51
    reports 66
refreshing data 52
RELATED function 244, 251
related insights 99
RELATEDTABLE function 244, 251
Relational OLAP 370
relationship cardinality 225
relationships
    auto-detecting 223, 224
    auto-discovering 177
    cardinality 133
    changing to inactive 228
    creating in Data View 225
    creating in Relationships View 229
    introduced 132
    limitations 221
    managing 226, 228
    redundant paths 133
    rules 220
    strong and weak 164
    understanding 219
Relationships View 140
    understanding 227
reply URL 396
Report Builder 11
report pages 65
Report View 141
Report Viewer control 361
reporting roadmap 360
Reporting Services reports 63
report-level filter 71
reports
    actions 53

API 394
    defined 53
    distributing 55
    filtering by URL 421
    importing 55
    options for creating 55
    types of 63
    working with 83
ReportServer database 362
ReportServerTempDB database 362
Representational State Transfer 389
resharing dashboards 103
REST APIs 36, 37
Revolution Analytics 307
Ribbon Chart 74
ROLAP *See* Relational OLAP
role membership 264
role-playing relationships 221, 228
    implementing 258
roles
    creating 265
    defined 263
    testing 268
root cause analysis 87
row context 238
row-level security 143, 262, 336
    adding members 266
RScript 149
RStudio 308

S

Salesforce 18, 31, 149
SAMEPERIODLASTYEAR 247
samples 46
SAP Hana 149
scalability 372
Scanner 118
Scatter Chart 75, 120
seasonality 88, 304
security groups 325
security policies 268
See Data 145
See Records 66, 145, 280
segmentation 305
Selection Pane 66, 142, 297
self-service BI 1
    benefits 41
    cautions 42
    understanding 39
    vs. organizational BI 372
self-service data models 33
semantic model 369
semi-additive measures 261
sentiment analysis 384
service apps 57
Shape charts 75

Shape Map 77
shapes 69
shared capacity 22, 352
SharePoint lists 149
SharePoint Online 61, 91
SharePoint Server 7
sharing
    comparing options 342
    dashboards 14, 23, 32
    options 20
    with Power BI Mobile 24
Single Card 79, 273
Sketch Tool 117
Slicer 79, 106
slicers
    synchronizing 276
    with dates 275
snapping to grid 69
snowflake schema 131
solution templates 144
sorting 76, 273
Spark 29, 51, 149
sparkline 443
Spotlight 297
spreadmarts 42
SQL Data Warehouse 12, 149
SQL Server Mobile Report Publisher 364
SQL Server Profiler 377
SQL Server Reporting Services *See* SSRS
SQL Server StreamInsight 11
SSRS
    importing from reports 160
    KPIs 123
    limitations for Power BI 363
Stacked Bar Chart 74
Stacked Column Chart 74
star schema 130
STDEV.P function 244
STDEV.S function 244
STDEVX.P function 244
STDEVX.S function 244
steady share 88
stepped layout 279
storage limits 49
stored credentials 366
stored procedures 150
streaming API 380
streaming datasets 53, 381
subscriptions 21, 66
    creating 81
    limitations 83
SUM function 244, 262
SUMX function 244, 251
supply chain 12
SVG 37

Sybase 149
synonyms 108, 229
Synoptic Panel 289

T

table columns 203
table filters 263
Table Storage 149
Table visual 76, 274
tables
    importing 214
    renaming 211
    understanding 203
Tabular 369
    role in Power BI 29
Tabular models 40
team BI 2, 35
templates 146, 330
tenant 45
Teradata 149
text boxes 69
Text data type 206
tile flow 56, 96
tiles
    embedding 413
    refreshing 102
    understanding 96
    working with 111, 112
Time data type 207
time intelligence functions 246
time series forecasting 304, 308
time series insights 88
tooltip pages 282
tooltips 281
top N filtering 72
TopoJSON 77
TOTALYTD function 257

transactional reports 40
transforming data 178
Treemap 76, 87
TRUE/FALSE data type 207
trusted account 431
Twillio 149
Twitter 384
type definitions 440
TypeScript 37, 436

U

Universal Principal Name 374
unknown member 226
unmanaged tenant 321
unpivoting columns 179
Usage metrics 327
USERELATIONSHIP function 244, 259
USERNAME function 267, 432
USERPRINCIPALNAME function 267, 432

V

VALUES function 244
VAR.P function 244
VAR.S function 244
VARX.P function 244
VARX.S function 244
v-cores 353
Visio diagrams 289
visual header 54
visual Interactions 70
VisualInitOptions 444
visualizations
    best practices 74
    formatting 71
    types of 73

Visualizations pane 70
visual-level filter 73, 87

W

web application proxy 363
Web URL category 287
Web view 101
WebGL 37
whoami 374
Whole Number data type 207
Windows credentials 150
Windows native app 116
Windows Store 139
workspaces
    and Power BI Embedded 411
    bulk assignments 358
    comparing v1 and v2 334
    for Power BI Embedded 411
    individual assignments 359
    introduced 20
    limitations 334
    list of 329
    moving to capacity 358
    understanding 332
writeback 299

X

xVelocity 6, 135, 369

Y

YTD calculations 257

Z

Zendesk 18, 149

Increase your BI IQ!

Prologika offer consulting, implementation and training services that deliver immediate results and great ROI. Check our services, case studies, and training catalog at https://prologika.com and contact us today to improve and modernize your data analytics at info@prologika.com.

Currentlly, we offer these training courses:

Applied Power BI

Power BI is a cloud-based business analytics service that gives you a single view of your most critical business data. Monitor the health of your business using a live dashboard...

Learn More >>

Applied DAX with Power BI

Power BI promotes rapid personal BI for essential data exploration and analysis. Chances are, however, that in real life you might need to go beyond just simple aggregations...

Learn More >>

Applied BI Semantic Model (Tabular and Multidimensional)

Targeting BI developers, this intensive 5-day class is designed to help you become proficient with Analysis Services Tabular and Multidimensional...

Learn More >>

Applied Microsoft Visualization Tools

Reporting is an essential feature of every business intelligence solution. One way to extract and disseminate the wealth of information is to author Reporting Services standard reports...

Learn More >>

Applied SQL Server Fundamentals

This 2-day instructor led course provides you with the necessary skills to query Microsoft SQL Server databases with Transact-SQL. It teaches novice users how to query data stored in SQL Server data structures.

Learn More >>

Applied MS BI End-to-End

This four-day class is designed to help you become proficient with the Microsoft BI toolset and acquire skills to implement an end-to-end organizational BI solution, including data warehouse, ETL processes, and a semantic model.

Learn More >>

Applied SQL Server Reporting Services

This intensive 4-day class is designed to help you become proficient with Microsoft SQL Server Reporting Services and acquire the necessary skills to author, manage, and deliver reports.

Learn More >>

Applied Master Data Management and Data Quality

Organizations that invest in master data management and improving the quality of their informational assets will be best positioned to reap...

Learn More >>

Applied SQL Server Analysis Services (Multidimensional)

This intensive 4-day class is designed to help you become proficient with Analysis Services (Multidimensional) and acquire the necessary skills to implement OLAP and data mining solutions.

Learn More >>

Applied Excel and Analysis Services

This 1-day class is designed to help business users become proficient with using the Excel BI features to analyze corporate data in Analysis Services Multidimensional cubes or Tabular models.

Learn More >>

Applied Power BI with Excel

Power BI is a suite of products for personal business intelligence (BI). It brings the power of Microsoft's Business Intelligence platform to business users. At the same time, Power BI lets IT monitor and manage published...

Learn More >>

Customized Classes

Printed in Poland
by Amazon Fulfillment
Poland Sp. z o.o., Wrocław